MEASURING
EMPOWERMENT

MEASURING
EMPOWERMENT

Cross-Disciplinary Perspectives

Edited by
Deepa Narayan

THE WORLD BANK
Washington, DC

Contents

Foreword

Poor people are the most important resource in the fight against poverty. They have imagination, guts, knowledge, experience, and deep motivation to move out of poverty. As our Voices of the Poor study showed, poor people are no different from those of moderate or substantial means in their desire to live in a safe and secure world and to have access to income so they can educate, clothe, and house their children with dignity. They long to belong and participate in their communities on an equal footing with others. Most of all, they do not want charity. They want opportunity—economic opportunity that gives them fair returns for their labor.

When poor people are able to connect to basic services provided by government, they have consistently demonstrated their intelligence and competence in using public funds effectively. They have managed construction of rural roads and water systems and have monitored government employees, including health providers and schoolteachers, to improve their performance. When poor men and women gain access to banks, they have shown that even in a national financial crisis—as in Indonesia, for example—they can be trusted to repay their loans. When poor women come together in credit groups to build their confidence and their understanding of how financial systems work, they can outperform all other customers in profitability. And they have proved willing to reinvest in their communities to strengthen the collective welfare.

Yet most decision makers still resist trusting poor people to make rational decisions and to take care of public or private investments. We hope that this book, with its focus on measuring empowerment, will help spread approaches to poverty reduction that empower poor people. Unless poor people are at the center of poverty reduction, policy making and program design will not benefit them.

Poor people the world over have shown that they work hard to reduce poverty. It is now time for the private sector to establish innovative partnerships with the millions of poor entrepreneurs, including vendors, shopkeepers, and craftspeople, in developing countries. It is time for governments to make policies that create space for poor people to participate in society and in the governance of their countries. And it is time for civil society to listen to poor people's voices and to help amplify them so that they are heard, and acted upon, by decision makers at the local, national, and global levels.

James D. Wolfensohn
President
The World Bank

Preface

This book is dedicated to those who work on making human rights a reality for all. The human rights framework is universal, but its form must be local. The cover photo illustrates the complexities in taking universal principles and translating and applying them correctly in different cultural, political, and economic contexts.

The woman in the burqa appeared on the front page of the *Times of India,* a leading Indian newspaper, on October 14, 2004, following elections in the state of Maharashtra. Circulating the photograph to friends and colleagues as the choice for the cover of this book drew mixed reactions. A woman in burqa to some was *not* a message of women's empowerment, but one of oppression. Others said that the picture represented the woman's strength and freedom. Many Islamic scholars and women in burqa themselves have stated that the burqa for them is a symbol of freedom. It means freedom of movement, and freedom from unwanted male attention or harassment in public spaces. The woman's raised finger also served as a Rorschach test, being variously interpreted depending upon the viewer's cultural frame of reference. In the Indian context, however, the symbolism is clear. The black indelible ink on the woman's finger shows she has exercised her right to vote and thus to influence the election of leaders of her state. While we know little about her level of oppression or freedom in other aspects of her life, in the domain of electoral politics she is free, and choosing to make her voice heard.

The picture of the woman in the burqa thus reflects the complexities in measuring empowerment and in moving from universal concepts to context-specific measures. However complex and difficult, this is a problem that must be tackled. Poverty reduction on a large scale depends on empowering the central actors, those who are most motivated to move out of poverty—poor people themselves. But if empowerment cannot be measured, it will not be taken seriously in development policy making and programming.

This book brings together perspectives of economists, anthropologists, sociologists, psychologists, demographers, and political scientists who are grappling with the challenge of measuring empowerment. It is intended for planners, practitioners, evaluators, and students—indeed for all who are interested in an approach to poverty reduction that deals with the inequitable power relations that keep poor people trapped in poverty despite their back-breaking toil.

The book is based on proceedings of an international, interdisciplinary workshop on measuring empowerment organized by the World Bank's Poverty Reduction and Economic Management network in 2003. The workshop followed publication of *Empowerment and Poverty Reduction: A Sourcebook* (Narayan 2002) and sought to respond to questions about how to monitor and evaluate empowerment in large programs and make it central in policy making. I am grateful to John Page, then director of the Poverty Reduction Group, for his early and strong support of the empowerment agenda. The workshop and publication of the current volume were made possible by grants from the U.K. Department for International Development (DFID), the Swedish International Development Cooperation Authority (Sida), and the World Bank.

Our deepest thanks go to the authors of the 18 chapters, all of whom are well known in their fields: Robert Biswas-Diener, Steven Brown, Joy Deshmukh-Ranadive, Larry Diamond, Ed Diener, Carol Graham, Christiaan Grootaert, Volkhart Finn Heinrich, Asim Ijaz Khwaja, Stephen Knack, Michael Lokshin, Carmen Malena, Anju Malhotra, Karen Oppenheim Mason, Caroline Moser, Gerardo Munck, Patti Petesch, Stefano Pettinato, Vijayendra Rao, Martin Ravallion, Sidney Ruth Schuler, Catalina Smulovitz, Norman Uphoff, Ashutosh Varshney, Michael Walton, and Michael Woolcock. I am grateful to them for contributing to this conversation and for staying engaged with the issue.

Soumya Kapoor, Bryan Kurey, and Sibel Selcuk provided invaluable coordination and support during different phases of the creation of this book. The chapters benefited from detailed comments by an external reviewer, and Soumya Kapoor also provided useful comments on several chapters. Kaushik Barua and Talat Shah provided expert research assistance. I thank Patricia Katayama for her support at a critical juncture when I was ready to give up. All of us benefited from Cathy Sunshine's sharp editorial eye, warmth, and tenacity through successive drafts.

Deepa Narayan
Senior Adviser
The World Bank

Contributors

Robert Biswas-Diener is an adjunct faculty member at Portland State University in Oregon. His research interests include culture, income and subjective well-being, and empathy. He has worked with various groups around the world, including sex workers in Calcutta, seal hunters in Greenland, homeless people in California, Israeli peace protesters, Maasai in Kenya, and Amish in the United States.

Steven R. Brown is professor of political science at Kent State University. His research has revolved around a central interest in subjectivity, as described in his book *Political Subjectivity* (Yale University Press, 1980). He was a founder of the International Society for the Scientific Study of Subjectivity, the International Society of Political Psychology, and the Society for the Policy Sciences, and has served as editor of two scholarly journals as well as editorial board member of several others. He is currently at work on projects on value clarification, quantum foundations of subjectivity, and decision making, among other topics.

Joy Deshmukh-Ranadive is senior fellow at the Centre for Women's Development Studies, an independent research institute in New Delhi supported by the Indian Council of Social Science Research. She has focused her research on the concept of power, particularly intra-household power dynamics. Her other areas of interest include economic, social, and cultural human rights; structural adjustment; globalization; and the impact of microcredit and self-help groups on women's empowerment in India. She is the author of *Space for Power: Women's Work and Family Strategies in South and South-East Asia* (Rainbow Publishers, 2002).

Larry Diamond is senior fellow at the Hoover Institution, Stanford University, and founding co-editor of the *Journal of Democracy*. He is also co-director of the International Forum for Democratic Studies of the National Endowment for Democracy. At Stanford, he is professor by courtesy of political science and sociology and coordinates the democracy program of the Center on Democracy, Development, and the Rule of Law. His research focuses on the relationship between democracy, governance, and development in poor countries. He is the author of *Developing Democracy* (Johns Hopkins University Press, 1999) and *Promoting Democracy in the 1990s* (Carnegie Corporation of New York, 1999).

Ed Diener is Alumni Professor of Psychology at the University of Illinois, Champaign. His research focuses on theories and measurement of subjective well-being and on temperamental, demographic, and cultural influences on well-being. He is the editor of *Perspectives on Psychological Science* and the *Journal of Happiness Studies*. His recent books include *Advances in Quality of Life Theory and Research* (with D. Rahtz, Kluwer, 2000); *Culture and Subjective Well-being* (with E. Suh, MIT Press, 2000); and *Well-being: The Foundations of Hedonic Psychology* (with D. Kahneman and N. Schwarz, Russell Sage Foundation, 1999). He heads a project on national accounts of well-being for the Positive Psychology Network.

Carol Graham is senior fellow in the Economic Studies Program at the Brookings Institution. She is also co-director of the Brookings Center on Social and Economic Dynamics and visiting professor of economics at Johns Hopkins University. She has served as a consultant to various international organizations, helping to design safety net and social insurance programs in Latin America, Africa, and Eastern Europe. Her recent books include *Happiness & Hardship: Opportunity and Insecurity in New Market Economies* (with S. Pettinato, Brookings Institution Press, 2002) and *Private Markets for Public Goods: Raising the Stakes in Economic Reform* (Brookings Institution Press, 1998).

Christiaan Grootaert recently retired after 23 years at the World Bank and is an international development consultant. At the Bank, he was lead economist in the Social Development Department and manager of the Social Capital Initiative, and he co-authored *World Development Report 2000/2001: Attacking Poverty*. His research focuses on measurement and analysis of poverty, risk and vulnerability, education and labor markets, child labor, and the role of institutions and social capital in development. Recent books include *The Role of Social Capital in Development* (with T. van Bastelaer, Cambridge University Press, 2002) and *Understanding and Measuring Social Capital* (with T. van Bastelaer, World Bank, 2002).

Volkhart Finn Heinrich is project manager of the civil society index program coordinated by CIVICUS: World Alliance for Citizen Participation, which is currently implemented in more than 50 countries around the world. Before joining the Johannesburg-based CIVICUS in 2000, he worked with organizations, particularly youth groups, in Germany and South Africa on advocacy, capacity building, and intercultural exchange issues. His interests focus on comparative social research on issues such as civil society, governance, and democratization.

Asim Ijaz Khwaja is assistant professor of public policy at the John F. Kennedy School of Government, Harvard University. His research interests include economic development, contract theory, industrial organization, mechanism design, and computational economics. Combining fieldwork, micro-level empirical analysis, and theory, his recent projects involve comparing factors that determine a group's collective success, understanding the private provision of public services, and examining firms, business groups, and financial markets in low-income countries.

Stephen Knack is a senior economist in the Development Research Group and Public Sector Governance Group of the World Bank. His current research focuses on the social and institutional determinants of effective government and the impact of aid on democratization, policy reform, and the quality of governance. He is editor of *Democracy, Governance and Growth* (University of Michigan Press, 2002). Before joining the World Bank in 1999, he was a research associate at the University of Maryland's Center for Institutional Reform and the Informal Sector and assistant professor in the School of Public Affairs at American University.

Michael Lokshin is a senior economist in the Development Research Group (Poverty Team) of the World Bank. His research focuses on poverty and inequality measurement, labor economics, and applied econometrics. Recently he has been involved in the World Bank's efforts to develop a methodology for evaluating the effects of crisis and public policies on households in developing countries.

Carmen Malena is an independent social development specialist based in Quebec City, Canada. Focusing on issues related to civil society, participation, governance, gender, and community development, she has served as a development practitioner, trainer, researcher, and analyst in more than 20 countries across the developing world. She has worked with many civil society organizations and with bilateral and multilateral development institutions including the World Bank, the United Nations Development Programme, and the African Development Bank.

Anju Malhotra is group director for Social and Economic Development at the International Center for Research on Women. She leads the center's research and work on social, economic, and demographic issues, particularly in the areas of women's empowerment, adolescence, reproductive health and rights, migration, and program evaluation. Before joining ICRW, she was assistant professor at the University of Maryland and a National Institutes of Health fellow at the University of North Carolina.

Karen Oppenheim Mason was director for gender and development at the World Bank from 1999 to 2004. She previously held research posts at the University of Wisconsin, Research Triangle Institute, University of Michigan, and East-West Center in Honolulu. Her research interests include gender and development, gender and population change, and gender and family change, particularly in Asia. Recent books include *The Changing Family in Comparative Perspective: Asia and the United States* (with N. Tsuya and M. Choe, East-West Center, 1998) and *Gender and Family Change in Industrialized Countries* (with A. Jensen, Oxford University Press, 1995).

Caroline Moser is a visiting fellow in the Economic Studies Program at the Brookings Institution and senior research associate at the Overseas Development Institute. Her recent research includes participatory appraisals of urban violence in Colombia, Guatemala, and Jamaica, and research on urban poverty in the context of adjustment in Ecuador, Zambia, the Philippines, and Hungary. She was previously lead specialist on social development in the World Bank's Latin America and Caribbean Region and a lecturer at the London School of Economics. Recent books include *Encounters with Violence in Latin America* (with C. McIlwaine, Routledge, 2004) and *Victims, Perpetrators, or Actors?* (with F. Clark, Zed, 2001).

Gerardo L. Munck teaches in the School of International Relations at the University of Southern California. He is currently editing a two-volume work on regimes and democracy in Latin America, and is completing (with Richard Snyder) a book of interviews with leading scholars in comparative politics. He is the author of *Theorizing Action: Game Theory and Comparative Politics* (Cambridge University Press, forthcoming) and *Authoritarianism and Democratization: Soldiers and Workers in Argentina, 1976–83* (Pennsylvania State University Press, 1998). He was chief technical adviser for *Democracy in Latin America,* a report of the United Nations Development Programme.

Deepa Narayan is senior adviser in the Poverty Reduction and Economic Management Network of the World Bank, where she works on issues of empowerment as they relate to poverty reduction. Her current interests focus on how to make capitalism and democracy work for the poor. She was team leader for Voices of the Poor, a multicountry research initiative to understand poverty from the perspective of poor people, undertaken to inform the Bank's activities and *World Development Report 2000/2001.* She is lead author of the three-volume series *Voices of the Poor* (Oxford University Press, 2000–02) and editor of *Empowerment and Poverty Reduction: A Sourcebook* (World Bank, 2002). She is currently leading a 15-country study aimed at understanding how people create wealth to move out of poverty.

Patti Petesch is a consultant to the World Bank and other international development organizations. She has managed studies, evaluations, and training programs on poverty, civil society participation, the environment, aid effectiveness and coordination, and campaigns to reform the international financial institutions. She co-edited two volumes in the *Voices of the Poor* series (Oxford University Press, 2000–02) and is the author of *Sustaining the Earth: The Role of Multilateral Development Institutions* (with M. Williams, Overseas Development Council, 1993) and *North-South Environmental Strategies, Costs, and Bargains* (Overseas Development Council, 1992).

Stefano Pettinato is program manager at the United Nations Development Programme (UNDP). He is a co-author of the 2003 and 2004 editions of UNDP's *Human Development Report*. He was senior research analyst at the Brookings Institution from 1999 to 2002, and he previously worked at the Carnegie Endowment for International Peace and at the United Nations Economic Commission for Latin America and the Caribbean. His research interests include inequality, poverty, and subjective well-being. He is co-author of *Happiness & Hardship: Opportunity and Insecurity in New Market Economies* (with C. Graham, Brookings Institution Press, 2002).

Vijayendra Rao is a lead economist in the Development Research Group of the World Bank. He uses economic and ethnographic methods to study the social and cultural dimensions of poverty, an approach he calls "participatory econometrics." His publications include studies of dowries, domestic violence, sex worker behavior, festivals, and the political economy of village democracy. He is co-editor of *Culture and Public Action* (with M. Walton, Stanford University Press, 2004). He serves on the editorial boards of *Economic Development and Cultural Change* and the *Journal of Development Studies*.

Martin Ravallion is research manager in the Development Research Group of the World Bank. He has advised numerous governments and international agencies on poverty reduction and has written extensively on this and other subjects in economics, including two books and more than 150 papers in scholarly journals and edited volumes. He serves on the editorial boards of 10 economics journals and is a senior fellow of the Bureau for Research in Economic Analysis of Development. He has taught economics at the London School of Economics, Oxford University, Australian National University, and Princeton University.

Sidney Ruth Schuler directs the Empowerment of Women Research Program at the Academy for Educational Development's Center for Applied Behavioral and Evaluation Research. A social anthropologist, she does international research on issues of gender, women's empowerment, health, and development, and has undertaken studies with colleagues in Bangladesh, Nepal, India, and Bolivia. She uses anthropological approaches to convey client and community perspectives to policy makers in health and development and has worked to develop indicators for assessing women's empowerment. Her current research focuses on early marriage and childbearing and on violence against women.

Catalina Smulovitz is director of the Department of Political Science and International Relations at the Universidad Torcuato Di Tella and a researcher at the Consejo Nacional de Investigaciones Científicas y Técnicas, both in Buenos Aires. Her research interests include accountability and citizen security in Latin America, as well as human rights and access to justice. She is co-editor of *Descentralización, Políticas Sociales y Participación Democrática en Argentina* (with A. Clemente, IIED-AL, 2004). She is an editorial board member of the *International Political Science Review* and a number of Spanish-language policy journals.

Norman Uphoff is professor of government and international agriculture at Cornell University and directs the Cornell International Institute for Food, Agriculture and Development. He has worked with the World Bank's program on social capital, measuring the productivity of social capital in watershed management in the Indian state of Rajasthan. His current research focuses on agroecological innovations, in particular the system of rice intensification. His recent books include *Reasons for Success: Learning from Instructive Experiences in Rural Development* (with M. Esman and A. Krishna, Kumarian Press, 1998) and *Learning from Gal Oya* (Intermediate Technology Publications, 1996).

Ashutosh Varshney is professor of political science at the University of Michigan, Ann Arbor. His book *Ethnic Conflict and Civic Life: Hindus and Muslims in India* (Yale University Press, 2002) won the Luebbert award of the American Political Science Association for best book in comparative politics in 2002. His other recent books are *India and the Politics of Developing Countries* (Sage, 2004); *India in the Era of Economic Reforms* (with J. Sachs and N. Bajpai, Oxford University Press, 1999); and *Democracy, Development and the Countryside* (Cambridge University Press, 1995), which won the Daniel Lerner prize. He serves on the United Nations task force on the Millennium Development Goals.

Michael Walton is a lecturer in international development at the John F. Kennedy School of Government, Harvard University. He is on leave from the World Bank, where he has over 20 years of experience as an economist and practitioner focusing on poverty, inequality, and the role of culture in development. As director for poverty reduction from 1997 to 2000, he was part of the management group for *World Development Report 2000/2001: Attacking Poverty*, and he is currently co-leader of *World Development Report 2006: Equity and Development*. His recent books include *Culture and Public Action* (with V. Rao, Stanford University Press, 2004) and *Inequality in Latin America and the Caribbean* (with D. de Ferranti and others, World Bank, 2003).

Michael Woolcock is a senior social scientist with the Development Research Group of the World Bank and a lecturer in public policy at the John F. Kennedy School of Government, Harvard University. His research focuses on the role of social and political institutions in poor communities and has been published widely. He is co-chair of the World Bank's Social Capital Thematic Group and contributed to *World Development Report 2000/2001: Attacking Poverty*. He is a team member of *World Development Report 2006: Equity and Development*. Before joining the World Bank in 1998 he taught at Brown University and at the University of Queensland in Australia.

Abbreviations

ACIN	Asociación de Cabildos Indígenas del Norte del Cauca (Colombia)
BSP	Bahujan Samaj Party (India)
BEEPS	Business Environment and Enterprise Performance Surveys
CDD	community-driven development
CPI	Corruption Perceptions Index (of Transparency International)
CSI	CIVICUS Civil Society Index project
CSO	civil society organization
ECA	Eastern Europe and Central Asia
ELN	Ejército de Liberación Nacional de Colombia
ELQ	Economic Ladder Question
FARC	Fuerzas Armadas Revolucionarios de Colombia
FFS	Farmer Field Schools (Peru)
GDI	Gender-related Development Index
GEM	Gender Empowerment Measure
ICRG	International Country Risk Guide
IDB	Inter-American Development Bank
IGO	intergovernmental organization
ILO	International Labour Organisation
INML	Instituto Nacional Mejoramiento Lechero (Uruguay)
JSIF	Jamaica Social Investment Fund
KDP	Kecamatan Development Program (Indonesia)
MAD	mobility assessment discrepancy
MLE	maximum likelihood estimation
NGO	nongovernmental organizations
OECD	Organisation for Economic Co-operation and Development
OLS	ordinary least squares
PG	perceptions gap
PHC	primary health care
PLQ	Power Ladder Question

POUM	prospects of upward mobility
PPA	participatory poverty assessment
PPM	perceived past mobility
PRA	participatory rural appraisal
PRSP	Poverty Reduction Strategy Paper
PT	Partido dos Trabalhadores (Brazil)
RLMS	Russia Longitudinal Monitoring Survey
RNME	Red Nacional de Mujeres Ex-combatientes (Colombia)
RRA	rapid rural appraisal
Rs	rupees
Sida	Swedish International Development Cooperation Agency
SEWA	Self-Employed Women's Association (India)
SWB	subjective well-being
UNDP	United Nations Development Programme
UPP2	Urban Poverty Project 2 (Indonesia)
WBES	World Business Environment Survey
WDR	*World Development Report*
WLQ	Welfare Ladder Question

SECTION ONE

Frameworks, Concepts, and Methods

Chapter 1

Conceptual Framework and Methodological Challenges

Deepa Narayan

> *Only the well-off can believe in tomorrow.*
>
> —Poor people, Azerbaijan[1]

Empowerment is not a new concept. Every society has local terms for autonomy, self-direction, self-confidence, self-worth. What is new is the attempt to measure empowerment in a systematic way.

The Voices of the Poor study conducted in 60 countries showed that voicelessness and powerlessness are pervasive among the poor, affecting every aspect of their lives.[2] Trapped in poverty and barred from opportunity, poor people live with little expectation that tomorrow will bring anything good, despite their arduous work. In recognition of these realities, the World Bank has identified a two-pronged strategy to reduce poverty on a large scale. The strategy focuses on improving the overall investment climate in developing countries and on empowering poor people by investing in their assets.[3]

An empowering approach to poverty reduction is grounded in the conviction that poor people themselves are invaluable partners for development, since they are the most motivated to move out of poverty. Nobody has more at stake in reducing poverty than poor people themselves. A growing body of evidence points to linkages between empowerment and development effectiveness at both the society-wide level and the grassroots level (Narayan 2002). Empowerment approaches can strengthen good governance, which in turn enhances growth prospects. When citizens are engaged, exercise voice, and demand accountability, government performance improves and corruption is harder to sustain. Citizen participation can also build consensus in support of difficult reforms needed to create a positive investment climate and induce growth. In addition, the empowerment agenda supports development effectiveness by promoting growth patterns that are pro-poor. This involves reducing inequalities by investing in poor people's capabilities through education and access to basic health care, as well as by increasing their access to land, financial capital, and markets.

Experience also demonstrates that empowerment can improve development effectiveness and pro-poor impact at the individual project level. Under certain conditions, grassroots community involvement is a powerful tool for the production, monitoring, and maintenance of local public goods such as water supply, sanitation, schools, health clinics, roads, and forests, which in turn increases the development effectiveness of investments. Empowerment strategies at the project level are supported by civil liberties in society. Evidence shows that projects in countries with strong civil liberties—particularly citizen voice, participation, and accountability—significantly outperform projects in countries with weak civil liberties.[4]

However, despite this widespread interest in and support for empowerment, work has only recently begun on construction of an analytical framework on empowerment that can be used to guide state reform and action. The World Bank's *Empowerment and Poverty: A Sourcebook* provides an outline of such a framework (Narayan 2002). It views empowerment broadly as increasing poor people's freedom of choice and action to shape their own lives. It identifies four key elements that can change power relations between poor people and powerful actors: access to information, inclusion and participation, social accountability, and local organizational capacity. What is possible in a particular context depends on the nature of social and political structures, on poor people's individual and collective assets and capabilities, and on the complex interaction between these factors.

Building on this framework, the present volume focuses on the challenge of evaluating empowerment and its contribution to development effectiveness. It represents a first attempt to launch a dialogue on empowerment and the measurement of empowerment across disciplines, including economics, anthropology, sociology, psychology, and political science. This overview chapter first presents an analytical framework for empowerment based on the structure set forth in the empowerment sourcebook, with some refinements. It goes on to briefly discuss key challenges in the effort to measure empowerment. The final section highlights issues explored in greater detail by the authors of the 18 chapters that follow.

The Empowerment Framework

In order to measure and monitor empowerment, it is important to have a clear definition of the concept and to specify a framework that both links empowerment to improved development outcomes and identifies determinants of empowerment itself.

Empowerment refers broadly to the expansion of freedom of choice and action to shape one's life. It implies control over resources and decisions. For poor people, that freedom is severely curtailed by their powerlessness in relation to a range of institutions, both formal and informal. Since powerlessness is embedded in a culture of unequal institutional relations, an institutional definition of empowerment has been adopted:

> *Empowerment is the expansion of assets and capabilities of poor people to participate in, negotiate with, influence, control, and hold accountable institutions that affect their lives.*[5]

This definition can be applied to understand and track changes in the unequal relationships between poor people and the state, markets, or civil society, as well as gender inequalities, even within the household.

Moving from this broad definition, with its emphasis on institutions and interaction between poor people and more powerful actors, figure 1.1 outlines a conceptual framework that is helpful in understanding the key factors that facilitate or constrain poor people's efforts to improve their own well-being and also affect broader development outcomes.

The conceptual framework contains four building blocks:

- Institutional climate
- Social and political structures
- Poor people's individual assets and capabilities
- Poor people's collective assets and capabilities

The concepts of opportunity structure and agency developed by Patti Petesch, Catalina Smulovitz, and Michael Walton are superimposed on these

Figure 1.1 Overview of the Conceptual Framework

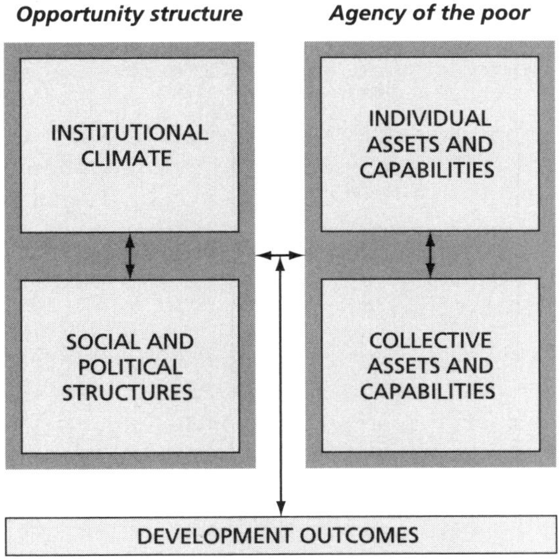

four building blocks.[6] The first two building blocks constitute the opportunity structure that poor people face, while the second two make up the capacity for agency of poor people themselves. The opportunity structure of a society is defined by the broader institutional, social, and political context of formal and informal rules and norms within which actors pursue their interests. Agency is defined by the capacity of actors to take purposeful action, a function of both individual and collective assets and capabilities.[7] All four components influence each other, and together they have effects on development outcomes. Empowerment of poor, excluded, or subordinate groups is a product of the interaction between the agency of these individuals and groups and the opportunity structure in which this agency is potentially exercised, as discussed in chapter 2.

Four aspects of this conceptual framework are worth highlighting. First, empowerment is fundamentally a relational concept, emerging out of the interaction between poor people and their environment. This takes place through the rights, rules, resources, and incentives as well as the norms, behaviors, and processes governing the interactions between poor people and more powerful actors. The relationship plays out at multiple levels, from the global down to the state, community, and household levels, and in different arenas (state, civil society, and market).

Second, poor people's assets and capabilities are usually conceptualized as individual attributes. However, poor people's collective capabilities and organizations are often critical in helping them break through constraints of powerlessness and voicelessness.

Third, empowerment of poor people on a large scale requires both top-down changes in institutions and organizational processes and bottom-up changes in poor people's organizations and networks and in their individual assets.

Fourth, the intervention or entry points vary depending on the nature of the constraints and barriers, on what is feasible, and on the development outcomes desired. The appropriate intervention points will also change over time.

To extend our understanding of this conceptual framework, it is helpful to examine the building blocks in greater detail. Figure 1.2 shows the individual elements that make up each of the building blocks, as well as aspects of the interaction between them.

The Opportunity Structure

Investment in poor people's assets and capabilities on a large scale requires changes in the opportunity structure within which poor people pursue their interests. This involves the removal of formal and informal institutional barriers that prevent the poor from taking effective action to improve their well-being—individually or collectively—and that limit their choices. It also implies the need for changes in social and political structures that perpetuate unequal power relations.

Figure 1.2   Detailed Overview of the Conceptual Framework

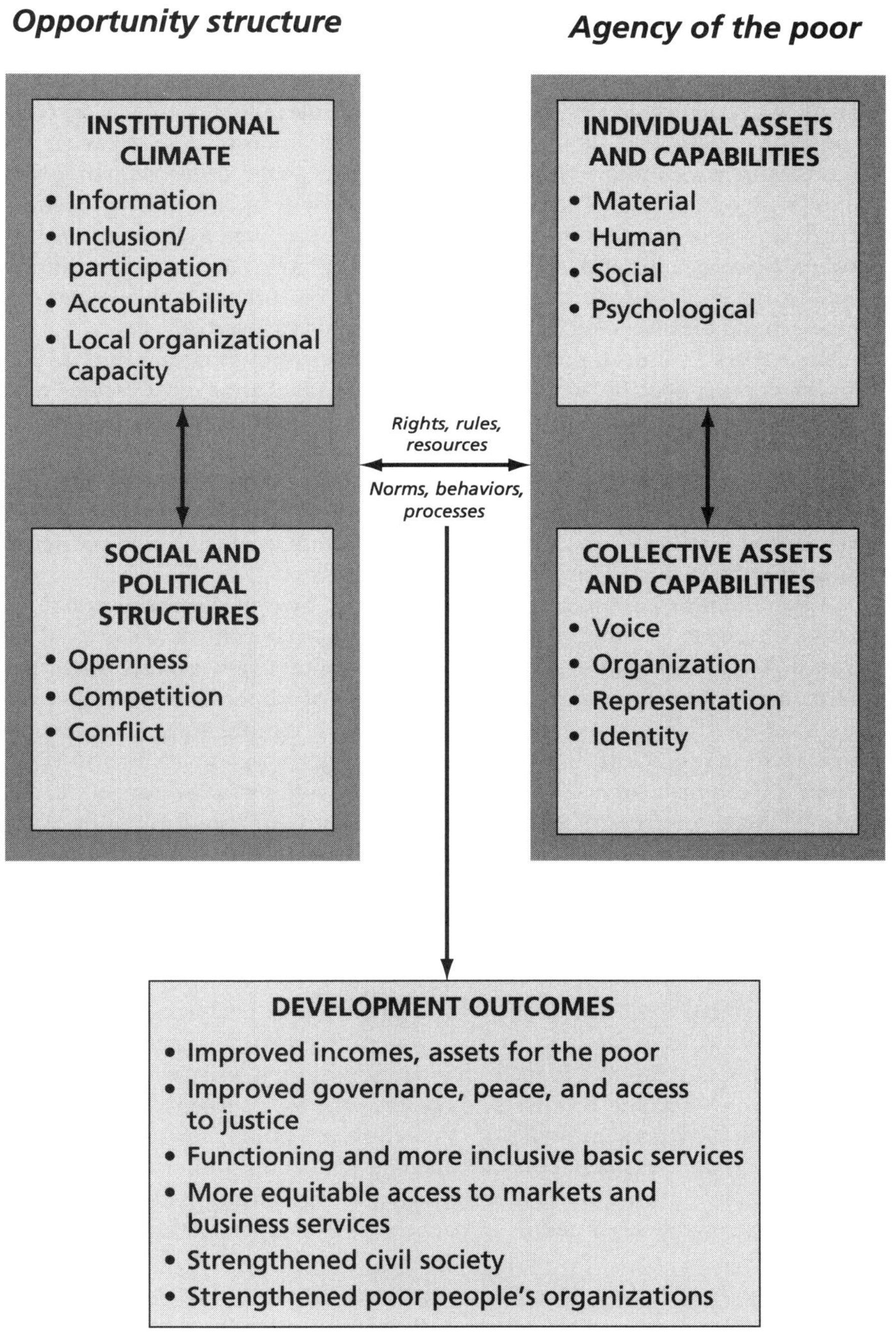

Opportunity structure   *Agency of the poor*

INSTITUTIONAL CLIMATE

- Information
- Inclusion/ participation
- Accountability
- Local organizational capacity

INDIVIDUAL ASSETS AND CAPABILITIES

- Material
- Human
- Social
- Psychological

Rights, rules, resources

Norms, behaviors, processes

SOCIAL AND POLITICAL STRUCTURES

- Openness
- Competition
- Conflict

COLLECTIVE ASSETS AND CAPABILITIES

- Voice
- Organization
- Representation
- Identity

DEVELOPMENT OUTCOMES

- Improved incomes, assets for the poor
- Improved governance, peace, and access to justice
- Functioning and more inclusive basic services
- More equitable access to markets and business services
- Strengthened civil society
- Strengthened poor people's organizations

Institutional climate

The institutional climate creates incentives for action or inaction. Key formal institutions include the laws, rules, regulations, and implementation processes upheld by states, markets, civil society, and international agencies. Informal institutions include norms of social solidarity, superiority, social exclusion, helplessness, and corruption that can subvert formal rules. Because the rules, regulations, processes, and actions of states are so important in creating the conditions in which poor people and other actors make decisions, empowerment efforts often focus on changing the unequal power relationship between the state and poor people. The same analysis can be applied to the relationships between poor people and private businesses or civil society organizations. In reality, the impetus for changes in state regulations often emerges because of on-the-ground experiences of civil society or the private sector.

Since social, cultural, political, and economic conditions vary and institutions are context-specific, strategies for institutional change must vary as well. Although there is no single institutional model for empowerment of poor people, experience shows that four key elements are almost always present when such efforts are successful. These elements act in synergy and strengthen the demand side of governance. The four elements of empowerment that must underlie institutional reform are access to information, inclusion and participation, accountability, and local organizational capacity.[8]

Access to information: Information is power. Two-way information flows from government to citizens and from citizens to government are critical for responsible citizenship and responsive and accountable governance. Informed citizens are better equipped to take advantage of opportunities, access services, exercise their rights, negotiate effectively, and hold state and nonstate actors accountable. Critical areas include information about rules and rights to basic government services, about state and private sector performance, and about financial services, markets, and prices. Information and communication technologies often play a pivotal role in broadening access to information.

Inclusion and participation: An empowering approach to participation treats poor people as co-producers, with authority and control over decisions and resources devolved to the lowest appropriate level. Inclusion of poor people and other traditionally excluded groups in priority setting and decision making is critical to ensure that use of limited public resources reflects local knowledge and priorities, and to build commitment to change. However, in order to sustain inclusion and informed participation, it is usually necessary to change rules, rights, and processes to create space for people to debate issues, participate in local and national priority setting and budget formation, and access basic and financial services. Customizing financial products such as loans and insurance and modifying distribution and purchasing networks are actions that can enable poor people to participate in markets on less exploitative terms.

Accountability: State officials, public employees, private providers, employers, and politicians must be held to account, making them answerable for their policies and actions that affect the well-being of citizens. There are three main types of accountability mechanisms. *Political* accountability of political parties and representatives takes place increasingly through elections. *Administrative* accountability of government agencies is enforced through internal accountability mechanisms, both horizontal and vertical, within and between agencies. *Social* or *public* accountability mechanisms hold agencies accountable to citizens and can reinforce both political and administrative accountability.

Local organizational capacity: This refers to the ability of people to work together, organize themselves, and mobilize resources to solve problems of common interest. Organized communities are more likely to have their voices heard and their demands met than communities with little organization. When membership-based groups federate at higher levels, they can gain voice and representation in policy dialogues and decisions that affect their well-being. Government rules, procedures, and resources that support civil liberties—for example, by guaranteeing the right to form independent associations and unions—provide an institutional climate in which such organizations can flourish.

Social and political structures

Since societies are always stratified to a greater or lesser degree, empowerment outcomes are also mediated by the nature of social and political structures— the extent to which they are open or closed, inclusive or exclusionary, cooperative or conflictual. When social structures and social cleavages are deep and systemic, opportunities and access to services are determined less by individual characteristics than by a culture of inequality that discriminates against and excludes entire social groups (Tilly 1999). The more powerful groups control the entry and exit options of the less powerful and prevent or limit their participation and voice in economic, political, and social life, often along ethnic lines. While those who "belong" benefit, the unequal access to power based on ethnicity can generate conflict (Bates 1999; Varshney 2003a; Weiner 2001).

Over time, however, change may occur, partly as a result of feedback loops. For example, when poor people organize themselves and demand information about the disappearance of government funds meant to assist them, the process not only changes them but also can help to reform the government. The government may pass a freedom of information act, making access to information a right.[9] This success empowers the group further and encourages other citizen groups to organize. As poor people increasingly demand information, governments gradually improve access to information through Internet kiosks, public information booths, and so on. Over time, the behavior of government officials changes from resisting public demands for information to expecting to inform the public. As norms in this sphere slowly change, they feed back into social structures and relations between the more powerful and less powerful, spilling over into other domains.

Political scientists emphasize the importance of politics, political regimes, political competition, and the strength of civil society.[10] At the broadest level,

democracies by definition are about inclusion, civil liberties, free flows of information, accountable governments, and political competition. Democracies
are better at managing conflict (Rodrik 2000). However, democracies are far
from perfect, and their functioning reflects existing social structures. Thus the
functioning of democracies may be distorted by pervasive patron-client
relations, by purchase of votes, and by purchase of influence by big business.[11]
At the national and local levels, regulations regarding political competition and
the extent of public information available to citizens affect the responsiveness
of political actors and the ability of voters, including poor people, to make informed electoral choices. Within democracies, the rule of law and accessible
and functioning enforcement mechanisms are critical in generating optimism
about the future, creating a positive investment climate, and managing conflict
(Keefer and Knack 1995; Rigobon and Rodrik 2004; Besley and Burgess 2002).

The importance of conflict resolution mechanisms for peace and economic prosperity has been underestimated. Democracies generally are better
able to manage conflict (UNDP 2002b). Of the 47 most heavily indebted poor
countries, nearly half are conflict-affected. Conflict can take place between
nation-states, areas within a country, communities, social groups, or households, and even between members of a household, as evidenced by widespread
domestic violence.[12]

Poor People's Agency

Poor women and men have limited ability to act to further their own interests.
This "inequality of agency" plays a central role in perpetuating inequality and
poverty (Rao and Walton 2004). Embedded in a culture of inequality, poor
people need a range of assets and capabilities to influence, negotiate, control,
and hold accountable other actors in order to increase their own well-being.
These assets and capabilities can be *individual* or *collective*. Because poverty
is multidimensional, so are these assets and capabilities.

Individual assets and capabilities

"Assets" refers to material assets, both physical and financial. Such assets—
including land, housing, livestock, savings, and jewelry—enable people to
withstand shocks and expand their horizon of choices. The extreme limitation
of poor people's physical and financial assets severely constrains their capacity to negotiate fair deals for themselves and increases their vulnerability.

Capabilities are inherent in individuals and enable them to use their assets
in different ways to increase their well-being. Human capabilities include
good health, education, and productive or other life-enhancing skills. Social
capabilities include social belonging, leadership, relations of trust, a sense of
identity, values that give meaning to life, and the capacity to organize.
Psychological capabilities include self-esteem, self-confidence, and an ability
to imagine and aspire to a better future. The psychological aspect has been
generally overlooked and is discussed in the next section. Political capabilities
include the capacity to represent oneself or others, access information, form
associations, and participate in the political life of a community or country.

Collective assets and capabilities

The importance of poor people's collective organizations in poverty reduction is only gradually being recognized. Given their lack of voice and power, and given the deeply entrenched social barriers that exist even in many formal democracies, poor people are often unable to take advantage of opportunities to effectively utilize or expand their assets or to exercise their individual rights.

To overcome problems of marginalization in society, poor people critically depend on their *collective* capability to organize and mobilize so as to be recognized on their own terms, to be represented, and to make their voices heard. These aspects of voice, representation, collective identity, solidarity, and terms of recognition help overcome the deep external social and psychological barriers that are usually internalized by poor people. Women who are abused, for example, often justify as appropriate violence against them by domestic partners. It is usually when they join women's solidarity groups that they begin to question whether the violence against them is justified.

Social capital, the norms and networks that enable collective action, allows poor people to increase their access to resources and economic opportunities. Poor people are often high in "bonding" social capital—close ties and high levels of trust with others like themselves. Given limited resources, these ties help them cope with their poverty (Narayan 1999; Woolcock and Narayan 2000; Grootaert and van Bastelaer 2002). There are important gender differences in social capital (Narayan and Shah 2000).

Bonding social capital is not enough, however; it must be accompanied by "bridging" social capital in order to generate social movements that can bring about structural change. This can happen when small groups of poor people federate, gaining strength in numbers, or when their leaders take advantage of political opportunities to form alliances with powerful actors (Tarrow 1994). When poor people's groups establish ties with other groups unlike themselves, bridging social capital enables them to access new resources managed by other groups. Bridging can be established with organizations of the state, civil society, or the private sector.

Working through representative organizations that have legitimacy, poor people can express their preferences, exercise voice, and hold governments and state service providers accountable for providing quality services in education, health, water, sanitation, agriculture, and other areas. Collective action through poor people's membership-based organizations can also improve access to business development and financial services and to new markets where people can buy needed items and sell their produce. As previously excluded groups organize, this organizing may serve to change political structures through the creation of new political parties whose presence and interests are felt at the national level, as has happened in Bolivia, Peru, and India. Leaders often engage in deeply symbolic behaviors that coalesce around issues of identity, often oppositional identity, to energize mass movements. Gandhi's peaceful salt march in defiance of the British, which mobilized an entire nation, is one powerful example.[13]

There is a reciprocal relationship between individual assets and capabilities and the capability to act collectively. This two-way relationship holds true for all groups in society, although the focus here is on poor people. Poor people who are healthy, educated, and secure can contribute more effectively to collective action; at the same time, collective action can improve poor people's access to quality schools or health clinics.

Improving Development Outcomes

An empowering approach to state reform can be viewed as strengthening the *demand side of governance*. A demand-side approach focuses on creating laws, rules, and procedures that enable citizens and poor people's organizations to interact effectively with their governments. Such an approach invests in educating and informing citizens, in creating institutional mechanisms for their sustained inclusion and participation, and in enabling the emergence of strong poor people's organizations and other citizens' groups. The form that an empowering approach takes and the elements needed to support it vary by context and over time.

An empowering approach is not the most appropriate for achieving every development outcome. For example, certain macroeconomic functions such as regulation of the money flow would not benefit from this approach. An empowering approach is often useful in the following five areas:

- Provision of basic services
- Pro-poor market development
- Improved local governance
- Improved national governance
- Access to justice and legal aid

Provision of basic services

This refers to improving poor people's access to and effective use of basic services, including health care, education, water, and roads. The World Bank supports government efforts to get resources down to the community level through a variety of institutional models. Implementation can be carried out through private or public actors; through central agencies, sectoral agencies, or decentralized authorities of local government; through stand-alone sector projects; or through multisectoral community-driven development projects.

An empowering approach to the provision of basic services focuses on a variety of co-production strategies. The first concentrates on putting information about government performance in the public domain. The second makes use of mechanisms for inclusion and participation, including service delivery schemes that poor people can afford or demand-side financing strategies. The third focuses on promoting social accountability and local organizational capacity by giving community groups authority and control over key decisions and financial resources in community-driven development projects.[14]

Pro-poor market development

Poverty and vulnerability will not be reduced without broad-based economic growth fueled by markets that poor people can access at fair terms. Economic growth cannot be sustained if poor people are excluded from optimal engagement in productive activities. While an overall investment climate that fosters entrepreneurship, job creation, competition, and security of property or benefit rights is important, it is not enough. Micro and small enterprises face constraints and exclusion that are not automatically corrected by improvements in the macro investment climate. Poor people are often excluded from equal access to economic opportunity because of regulations and because they lack information, connections, skills, credit, and organization. Elements of empowering approaches can help to overcome many of these barriers that prevent poor people's entry into markets or limit their returns. Changes in regulations can encourage private sector actors to innovate and develop new products that can potentially reach large numbers of poor people with financial and insurance products to manage their vulnerability. Because poor people are both producers and consumers, connecting small rural producers to markets can be profitable to private companies, as illustrated by the case of India's e-choupals (box 1.1).[15]

Improved local governance

Improved local governance is critical to better service delivery and greater responsiveness to poor people's priority problems. Decentralization and local government reform have so far focused primarily on the supply side of formal systems and not on strengthening the demand side through actions that enable citizens to effectively use the space created by new rules and regulations. Empowered local governments (with authority *and* resources) need to empower local communities through mechanisms that increase citizen access to information, promote inclusion and participation, increase accountability of governments to citizens, and invest in local organizational capacity. In general, there has been insufficient attention to the relationship between citizens and local governments, and there are very few cases of investment in strengthening poor people's organizations or other local civil society intermediaries so they can effectively play the new roles assigned to them.

Improved national governance

Macroeconomic policy and choices are areas that are just beginning to open to societal engagement. Since national processes and policies determine poor people's access to resources and opportunities, it is critical that these processes incorporate the four empowerment elements. Actions that can be taken to keep national governments responsive and accountable include linking information from poor people to the process of national budget and policy formulation, as well as enabling civil society groups to become involved in expenditure tracking, citizen feedback, or social accountability mechanisms. This will require strengthening the capacity of poor people's organizations and other civil society groups to perform these new functions.

Participatory processes are increasingly being incorporated in some policy-based lending, in programmatic loans, and in the formation of national poverty reduction strategies. Mechanisms are now needed to institutionalize participatory strategies and increase their effectiveness by incorporating the other three elements of the empowerment framework—access to information, social accountability, and local organizational capacity.

Box 1.1   A Case Study: E-choupals

In India, more than 2 million farmers are now connecting to markets through village-based computer stations called e-choupals. This experience shows how strategic changes in the institutional climate—that is, in the rules, resources, norms, behaviors, processes, and trust that govern the relationships between farmers and private companies—can quickly create incentives that lead to greater empowerment and increased incomes. These benefits can be achieved without changes in government rules and regulations, without direct intervention in longer-term processes of changing social and political structures, and without first increasing the collective and individual assets of poor people.

This innovation came from an Indian private sector company, ITC, which has annual revenues of $2.6 billion and a large, diversified, and growing involvement in agribusiness trade. The e-choupal scheme was developed by S. Shivakumar, CEO of ITC's agribusiness section, who was trained at IRMA, India's premier institute of management in rural development.

Choupal is the Hindi word for the village square, a place where elders meet. E-choupals use information technology to bring about virtual meetings between farmers, buyers, and suppliers. ITC installs each Internet access kiosk, powered by solar-charged batteries, in the house of a farmer who is trained to operate it. Local farmers use the computer to access information free of charge. After checking prices, they can choose to buy or sell through ITC or go to local markets instead. ITC pays the operator, known as a *sanchalak*, 5 rupees on each transaction completed, whether purchase of inputs or sale of produce. Efficiency improvements in buying and selling have led to increased revenues for farmers and for ITC.

At the heart of the e-choupal system's success is a social, cultural, and technical design that provides incentives for farmers to participate because it increases their profits. At the same time, it makes money for ITC; hence it is in their mutual interest to make the system work. Even when ITC's prices for inputs are higher, farmers sometimes choose them because of greater reliability.

Access to justice and legal aid

The rule of law and a functioning judicial system are important not only for the investment climate, but also for protecting poor people and their livelihoods. New thinking about making judicial and legal systems work for the poor is leading to greater use of modern and traditional mediation, conflict resolution, and enforcement mechanisms. These include (a) improving administrative justice and making administrative decisions accountable and affordable to ordinary citizens; (b) promoting judicial independence and accountability; (c) improving legal education; (d) expanding poor people's cultural, physical, and financial access to justice; and (e) strengthening public outreach and education.[16]

Use of inputs such as improved seeds and fertilizers has gone up because ITC provides quality assurance. Moreover, the *sanchalak*, as a local resident and a farmer, knows the community. With the operator's revenue depending on repeated transactions, there is a built-in incentive to satisfy the farmers and build trust. Operators take a public oath to serve all members of their communities without discrimination, and to spend part of their earnings on village welfare.

Farmers in India, as in many other parts of the world, are isolated from urban markets and dependent on middlemen, who monopolize information, sale of inputs, and crop purchasing. By providing easy access to information and hence transparency, e-choupals have helped to change the relationship between farmers and their buyers and suppliers from one of exploitation and dependence to one of respect, trust, fairness, and equity. No attempt is made to directly address issues of caste, class, or untouchability, or to create formal farmers' groups. The computer becomes the aggregator of thousands of farmers. Nevertheless, the e-choupal system brings people together across social barriers for business, newspaper reading, or watching movies on farming techniques.

Within four years, the e-choupal network has spread to 30,000 villages and has 37 active partners, including companies, nongovernmental organizations, universities, and state governments. By 2004 ITC was adding 30 new villages a day. All this has been achieved without any change in government policy and or any attempt to create new farmers' organizations. Additional partnerships include one ITC has established with SEWA, the Self-Employed Women's Association, a trade union of poor women in India's informal economy. In 2003, the initial year of that agreement, SEWA farmers sold 250 tonnes of sesame seed through ITC, at Rs 29 per kilogram as compared to Rs 18 per kilogram the previous year.

Sources: Presentations by Mr. Shivakumar at the World Bank workshops in Bangalore in February 2004 and Shanghai in June 2004, and personal communication with Mr. R. Kidwai, CEO of the Grassroots Trading Network, in 2004.

Issues in Measuring Empowerment

One of the biggest challenges in measuring empowerment is that empowerment is a latent phenomenon. Its presence can only be deduced through its action or its results. Hence, most observed behaviors are proxies for the underlying phenomenon.

While empowerment of the poor and other excluded groups has become part of the development agenda, attempts to systematically monitor and evaluate programs that use empowerment approaches for poverty reduction lag behind.[17] This section highlights 10 challenges in measuring empowerment and assessing its contribution to improving development outcomes.

Intrinsic or Instrumental

If you wear a suit, you are treated as "Sir," but if you are wearing sandals they send you away.

—Poor men and women in Vila Junqueira, Brazil

Empowerment has intrinsic value. It is an end in itself. Feeling self-confident, walking with dignity, feeling respected, living without fear, is of value in itself. Empowerment is also important as a means of achieving specific development outcomes, ranging from improved attendance of teachers at schools to increased incomes for poor people. For the purposes of constructing a specific evaluation, therefore, it is important to specify whether empowerment is conceptualized as a means or an end or both.

For instance, participation in decision making can be viewed as a measure of empowerment. When such participation is seen as having intrinsic value, then the number of meetings held or attendance at meetings can be an appropriate measure. However, if participation is considered important because it leads to decision making that reflects the priorities of the poor, then participation is a means, and the evaluation framework has to compare the decisions made when poor people attended meetings with those made when they did not. In fact, research indicates that in some contexts, poor people's attendance at meetings may be a poor indicator of their influence on decisions and hence outcomes.[18] When attendance at village meetings is compulsory, as was true in Indonesia under Suharto, attendance is not a discriminating measure of influence.

Asim Ijaz Khwaja expands this argument (chapter 12) and shows how the distinction between empowerment as an end in itself and as a means to an end affects the entire evaluation framework, including specification of causality mechanisms.

Universal or Context-Specific

He scolded her and physically assaulted her for not preparing his meal.

—A poor woman, Bangladesh

Empowerment as a value and phenomenon is clearly universal. People all over the world, including poor people, want to feel efficacious, to exert control over their lives, and to have some freedom of choice among options. While there can be a common conceptual framework across cultures, the context needs to be taken into account both at the analytical level (what matters) and in choice of measures (how it matters or manifests itself). The cultural context is important because culture consists of a relational system of norms, values, and beliefs on which there is simultaneously consensus and dissensus, and that are permeable and subject to change (Appadurai 2004).[19]

The community and household, with all their heterogeneity, cleavages, and bonds, are important sites of cultural learning within which empowerment strategies are located. Yet few studies of empowerment have taken community cultural context into account. The five-country study done by Karen Oppenheim Mason and her colleagues on women's empowerment and demographic change is a notable exception (chapter 4). Their theoretical assumption is that women's empowerment in the domestic sphere is mainly a property of social and cultural systems rather than of individual traits and preferences. In other words, the shared norms, values, and beliefs that characterize a group are key determinants. For instance, in certain communities the shared belief that men have more rights than women to determine family size may have more influence over women's fertility levels than do the traits of individual men and women, although there will still be some individual differences. In their survey, Mason and her colleagues do find that country and community of residence predict women's domestic empowerment better than their personal socioeconomic and demographic traits do. They also demonstrate that the primary variation across communities is explained by variation in community values and norms about gender roles.

The second way in which context needs to be taken into account is in the measures or indicators of empowerment. There may be some universal measures, such as freedom from domestic abuse. But many other measures will be culturally specific. In a Muslim society such as Bangladesh, for instance, a woman's movement beyond her home may be an indicator of increasing freedom, whereas in Jamaica, where women's movements are not culturally restricted, it has little relevance. Even when culture is taken into account, certain indicators may be ambiguous. The veil is perhaps the most controversial symbol, interpreted either as restricting and oppressing women or as providing them safety and freedom to move about without male harassment.

Individual or Collective

Only if we go together to the politicians, are we powerful. If we were to go alone, nothing would have happened. Our collective strength is our power.

—A poor woman, Tigri slum, New Delhi, India

Most social science research on poverty is concerned with individuals, even though the concept of social groups and group identity has a long tradition in sociology. The unit of analysis in most poverty research is the individual. Yet we know from the vast literature on social exclusion that opportunities are not equally distributed but are stratified by social group. In attempting to measure the empowerment of those previously excluded, it is essential to locate individuals within the historical, social, and political context of their social groups in order to correctly interpret the impact of development interventions.

Unequal access is remarkably resistant to change, as evidenced by persistent and growing income inequality reflected in Gini coefficients. The Minorities at Risk data set estimates that almost 900 million people worldwide belong to groups that are discriminated against or disadvantaged because of their identity and face cultural, economic, or political exclusion (UNDP 2004). In Latin America, to cite just one example, the gap between indigenous and mestizo populations on almost any development indicator—income, infant mortality, access to electricity, education—is deep and persistent (Glewwe and Hall 1998; Psacharopoulos and Patrinos 1994).

In this context of group-based poverty and exclusion, individual efforts at empowerment may be costly or futile. Responding to this reality, many poverty interventions focus on collective action through organizations of the poor, such as farmers', indigenous, women's self-help, credit, and water users' groups. Collective action, using processes and rituals that have cultural resonance, is often critical in building confidence and new identity. In poor villages in Andhra Pradesh, India, poor *dalit* women, as their first collective act, chose to walk through the high-caste areas of the village with their shoes on (rather than taking them off in deference) and with their heads held high.[20] Their success in doing so without retribution from the high-caste villagers electrified the *dalit* women's movement, which then went on to address livelihood issues.

Level of Application

> *There has never been anyone who represented us in any of the different governments.*
>
> —A woman, Thompson Pen, Jamaica

The concept of empowerment and the conditions that enable empowerment of poor men and women can be considered at the individual household, group, community, local government, or national government level or, indeed, at the global level. The primary focus of empowerment strategies has been at the individual and community levels. However, for large-scale poverty reduction, the rules, regulations, organizations, norms, and values that operate at other levels become important and influence what is possible at the community level. India's 73rd constitutional amendment, which requires that one-third of *panchayat* leaders be women, has led to the election of a million women as heads of these local government bodies—and this in a cultural context where women not only lack many rights but also have lower survival rates, leading to a national demographic profile increasingly skewed in favor of men.

More than 120 countries worldwide have decentralized at least expenditures to local governments, with the expectation that bringing these functions closer to the affected citizens will generate greater accountability and responsiveness to local needs. In this context of decentralization, local government rules and regulations, including formulas for allocation of resources, have an impact on empowerment of poor people. So do local social and political structures, including norms of political competition and openness that govern public resource allocation within and between communities. All these are therefore important to measure (Bardhan 2004; Besley, Pande, and Rao 2004; Foster and Rosenzweig 2003).

The ethnic composition of a local government relative to the ethnicity of the local population can also influence local government investment decisions and performance (Grootaert and Narayan 2004; Schady 2000). A recent study in Pakistan documents how, since decentralization and elections at the union level, the distribution of public goods reflects biases in favor of the villages of elected union leaders and those who belong to a *dhara* (faction of influential villagers) (Cheema and Mohmand 2004).

Although district-level analyses are relatively rare, a recent study in Indonesia shows the tremendous variation in frequency of conflict across districts. It found that 15 districts, inhabited by only 6.5 percent of the country's population, accounted for 85 percent of all deaths in reported conflicts (Varshney, Panggabean, and Tadjoeddin 2004). This statistic, showing that violent conflict is largely limited to certain areas within the country, has important implications for policy.

At the countrywide level, state and national policies that enable or hinder the sharing of control and authority with local people are critical. Uphoff (1996) explains how farmer involvement in a large, broken-down irrigation system in Sri Lanka led not only to the rehabilitation and more efficient functioning of the system but also to revisions of national policy. Today more than 500,000 farmers are members of participatory irrigation management systems throughout Sri Lanka.

Given the importance of state-society relations and the relative weakness of research linking local actions to the national political and social climate, it is important to consider indicators at the national level that govern state-society interactions. These include measures of state efficacy, the nature of political regimes, and the strength of civil society.

While the emphasis varies from author to author, there is agreement that a subset of governance indicators are important in enabling the empowerment of poor people and citizens. Christiaan Grootaert (chapter 14) focuses on assessing state responsiveness, social barriers, social institutions, and social capital. Gerardo Munck (chapter 19) suggests indicators to measure the nature of political regimes, governance, and rule of law. Stephen Knack (chapter 16) focuses on economic rights measured by property rights and on political rights measured by accountability and the extent of clientelistic relationships between citizens and public officials. Larry Diamond (chapter 18) examines the extent of free and fair elections, the presence of democratic political parties, and the nature of democracy as reflected in civil liberties and government responsiveness.

The nature of social capital, the extent of trust embedded in public institutions, and the nature of civil society are critical aspects of state-society relations. At the national level, the "national barometer" studies inspired by the World Values Survey provide indicators of trust and social capital that are representative at the national level. The Social Capital group at the World Bank has developed a social capital questionnaire that has been tested in several developing countries (Grootaert et al. 2004).

There is no globally agreed measure of the strength of civil society. Civil society is sometimes defined as the space in society where collective citizen action takes place (Knight, Chigudu, and Tandon 2002). Others define it more broadly as the space between the household and the state (Varshney 2003a). The CIVICUS Civil Society Index is the first attempt to develop an index at the national level that can be compared across countries (see Carmen Malena and Volkhart Finn Heinrich, chapter 15).

Dimensions of Empowerment: Neglect of the Psychological

Before I joined SEWA, I was treated like an animal—by my employer,
by my husband, by my village. Now I am treated like a human . . . I am
not afraid anymore.

—A tobacco worker, Gujarat, India

Empowerment is not a unitary concept. It has many dimensions, and these dimensions do not necessarily move together at the same pace, or even in the same direction. Two studies can look at the same phenomenon yet come up with different conclusions depending on the dimensions of empowerment they measure.

To a large extent, the availability of data has dictated how empowerment is measured. The most commonly studied dimension of empowerment is the economic dimension. This includes objective indicators such as income and expenditure profiles, ownership of assets, and subjective measures of control and authority over decision making. The latter are closer to direct measures of empowerment, whereas the former may be enablers or outcomes, depending on the conceptual framework. The economic dimension can be studied at different levels. For example, women's control over income can be studied within the household. At the community level, women's access to employment, common property, membership in trade associations, and access to markets may be key. At the national level, women's representation in jobs, the inclusion of women's economic interests in federal budgets, and laws guaranteeing equal pay for equal work may be important. These variables are discussed by Anju Malhotra and Sidney Ruth Schuler in chapter 3.

Less attention has been paid to the social and political dimensions of empowerment. Least studied of all is the psychological dimension. Nonetheless, the fact that individuals with similar abilities and resources exhibit different propensities to act on their own behalf has led to a growing interest among researchers in the psychological dimensions of empowerment. Self-confidence and a sense of self-efficacy are important precursors to action. The process of taking action and reaping the rewards further reinforces these feelings, creating virtuous cycles of reflection and action.

Albert Bandura (1995), a psychologist, has demonstrated experimentally that when beliefs about self-efficacy are manipulated independent of performance and external conditions, it affects future performance. Thus a person's internal sense of efficacy plays an independent causal role. Reviewing the psychological literature, Bandura (1998) concludes: "People's beliefs that they can produce desired effects by their actions influence the choices they make, their aspirations, level of effort and perseverance, resilience to adversity, and vulnerability to stress and depression.[21]

Arjun Appadurai (2004) uses two phrases, "terms of recognition" and "capacity to aspire," to capture the collective aspects of psychological empowerment among impoverished groups. Both are characteristics embedded in social groups and determined by their collective cultural experience. Poor and excluded groups are defined by more powerful social groups and held in place by social norms and expectations of behavior, often reified in public debate and even interpretation of scriptures. Unless poor people fight to change their terms of recognition as a group, opportunities will bypass them. Thus the Indian *dalit* women, walking together through the high-caste village, defied higher-caste norms of what is appropriate behavior for the lowest caste and in so doing sought to change the terms of their recognition by the higher-caste group. Capacity to aspire is defined as the forward-looking capacity of individuals and groups to envision alternatives and to aspire to different and better futures. If a person cannot conceive of better times, he or she is unlikely to take action toward that end. Generating the capacity to envision a different future is therefore an important part of interventions and solidarity movements. Martha Nussbaum's (2000) term "adaptive preference" captures a similar phenomenon, one in which marginalized groups internalize low possibilities for themselves because of their life experiences.[22]

Ed Diener and Robert Biswas-Diener argue that while certain external conditions are necessary for empowerment, they are not sufficient without internal feelings of competence, energy, and the desire to act (chapter 6). These authors focus on subjective well-being, which they define as people's positive evaluations of their lives, including pleasant emotions, fulfillment, and life satisfaction. Psychological empowerment, or belief in one's own efficacy, is one important aspect of subjective well-being. At the same time, subjective well-being—positive emotions such as joy, happiness, and love—heightens people's feelings of empowerment and, thus, the probability of their taking action. Diener and Biswas-Diener contend that the most important aspect of empowerment is not objective power but feelings of power, and that just because people have objective power does not mean that they will feel empowered or will act. Diener and Fujita (1995) found that self-confidence was the resource that most strongly predicted life satisfaction, more than material resources or social resources.

Joy Deshmukh-Ranadive (chapter 5) looks at the psychological aspect with respect to empowerment of women, using the concept of mental space. Mental space, according to this author, is the sense of freedom from restrictions and constraints; it refers to self-esteem or *power within*. Focusing on marginalized women in South and Southeast Asia, Deshmukh-Ranadive contends that collective action and information play important roles in expanding women's mental space. Without such expansion, they are unlikely to feel empowered, even when physical or economic conditions of their lives improve.

The extreme opposite of empowerment is fear. Fear freezes action; since time immemorial, it has been used by the powerful to subjugate and control the less powerful. Fear is probably the single most debilitating, disempowering, and dehumanizing experience. It keeps women trapped in homes that are physically or mentally abusive. It keeps landless laborers working for less than minimum wage and silent even when they have not been paid for months. In countries where access to even basic services is contingent on patronage, fear of violent retribution keeps citizens and poor people quiet about corruption and prevents action against corrupt officials.

Caroline Moser (chapter 11) argues that peace and security are part of empowerment because violence and crime result in fear, insecurity, and a decline in socioeconomic well-being. In Colombia, participants in a community-led peace-building process highlighted the importance of psychological dimensions in measuring their own empowerment. In one project, participants focused on the term *convivencia,* which means to live together in harmony, with tolerance, respect for difference, and peaceful resolution of conflicts. In the second project, participants identified individual self-esteem as particularly important. Indicators included increased ability to speak in public, letting go of past trauma, overcoming the sense of being a victim, and recognizing one's own agency. The affirmation *sí puedo* (yes I can) came up repeatedly in all groups.

Hence, subjective and psychological well-being—one's self-judgment as a happy, well-functioning, competent, self-confident human being—is a critical asset that men and women across cultures, particularly poor men and women, must have to improve their lives. The behavioral manifestations of this sense of self-efficacy will of course vary across cultures, and may be situation- or domain-specific. They will also be influenced by an iterative process in which the poor engage with their environment, accomplish tasks, are surprised at their success, gain more confidence, and take on expanding roles and challenges.

The relationships between income, power, and subjective well-being are complex, and the quantitative exploration of these relationships has intensified in recent years.[23] One of the most common assumptions in development has been that if a woman earns an income, it empowers her. Studies have shown, however, that women may become income earners but still not increase their power in decision making, in social relations, or in freedom of movement.

There are a range of qualitative and quantitative techniques for measuring psychological characteristics, mostly based on self-assessment. They include life stories, scales of subjective well-being, batteries of psychometric tests, and event or mood sampling, as well as measurement of brain impulses, changes in body temperature, and so on.

Origins and Change

If a woman works hard and saves enough to buy a cow, she feels more competent and has more assets; she is empowered. If she inherits a cow or receives a gift of a cow because of her social relationships, she may be wealthier, but is she empowered? One group might say yes, but those who focus on agency and the importance of going through a learning process in bringing about change would say no. Malhotra and Schuler (chapter 3) are strong proponents of the view that the origins of empowerment are important and that the process of learning is the critical ingredient. That is, empowerment is said to have occurred if it results from the agency of the person who feels empowered.

However, it may also happen that a woman acquires a cow through her own hard work and still feels no different about herself; that is, she does not gain self-confidence or feel that she has more choice or freedom. Hence, the extent of change in empowerment remains an empirical issue.

Also implicit in the focus on process is progression; that is, empowerment entails change from a previous state to a new state of greater freedom or choice. This idea is captured in Naila Kabeer's (2001) definition of empowerment as "the expansion in people's ability to make strategic life choices in a context where this ability was previously denied to them." Indicators of disempowerment or empowerment will vary depending upon the specific context and time. For example, when all women acquire certain rights previously denied to them—such as freedom of movement or the right to open a bank account without a male signature—then these rights become norms and are no longer valid indicators of empowerment.

A third aspect of the process is that it is relative. Empowerment does not happen in a vacuum. A woman is empowered, or not, relative to her previous status and relative to others in her reference group. However, conditions that enable empowerment can be absolute or relative. Women's right to vote is an absolute measure: women either have this right or they do not. The institutional climate may make it easier or more difficult to vote. Whether women choose to exercise their right without coercion is an indicator of their empowerment in practice. Women's participation in electoral politics compared with men's is a relative concept. For an individual woman, self-empowerment can never be an absolute concept because no person is ever totally empowered; empowerment is always defined in relation to prior status or to others in one's reference group.

Establishing Causality

> When the village council calls a meeting, all the decisions about a
> project have already been made, that it should be this way and that way.
> The poor only remain silent and listen.
>
> —Poor men, Indonesia

Measuring empowerment is most useful if it is done in a framework that defines the role of empowerment in achieving positive development outcomes and defines the pathways of causation, depending on the type of intervention and the constraint being addressed. Different disciplines have different research paradigms. Psychology and medical sciences have traditionally placed greater reliance on experimental designs with randomization, whereas economics, sociology, and demography have traditionally used large surveys to statistically manipulate data to establish causality.[24] Anthropology has traditionally relied on ethnographies, life histories, and event and process tracing to establish causality in small samples. Participatory practitioners rely on a learning-by-doing approach to understand causality. These more subjective approaches can be supplemented by more objective external evaluations using any of the research designs mentioned above.

Establishing causality requires three steps: (1) specifying the conceptual framework, (2) specifying the sampling frame, and (3) specifying data collection methods and tools and analytical techniques. Issues of causality are discussed by Petesch, Smulovitz, and Walton in chapter 2 and by Khwaja in chapter 12. Lokshin and Ravallion (chapter 8) and Graham and Pettinato (chapter 7) focus on large-sample surveys and use of statistical techniques to trace causality. Moser (chapter 11) focuses on learning by doing, participatory research, and process mapping. Uphoff (chapter 10) and Mason (chapter 4) advocate participatory research techniques while also emphasizing the benefits of drawing on results of evaluations performed by outsiders.[25]

What Is Measured: Clear Concepts, Linked Measures

What is measured has to be linked to a theoretical causal framework that specifies a limited set of clear concepts. Since empowerment is multidimensional, and many enabling factors such as the political regime are also multidimensional, one must start by specifying the relevant concepts. Measures must then be chosen that have a close link to these concepts and the pathway specified. Scales should be designed to capture variation in the measure. Munck (chapter 19) discusses the challenges in developing appropriate measures for democratic governance, and Uphoff (chapter 10) emphasizes the importance of linking the concepts of power resources and power results to a set of indicators.

Since empowerment is difficult to observe except in action, most measures are either proxies or factors that enable empowerment or its proximate determinants. Having a clearly specified causal framework helps in sorting out potential variables.

Who Measures: Self or Others

For some I am poor, for others not, but compared to my own former situation, I am a beggar.

—A poor man, Armenia

A fundamental principle of evaluation is objectivity and dispassion in measurement. To achieve objectivity, it is generally assumed that the subject should not be the person doing the measuring and that the measures themselves should be objective as far as possible. However, even so-called objective measures such as income or land holdings are not free from reporting bias. For example, land holdings may be self-reported, based on actual measurement of field sizes, or based on land records, all of which are subject to error.

Participatory research evolved out of the need to understand complex realities from the perspectives of the people whose behavior external agents were trying to change—farmers, laborers, mothers with young children, and so on. It emerged in part as a reaction to research methods that kept subjects at a distance by generating data through household surveys that were processed, managed, used, and publicized far away from those most affected. The information produced by these surveys often was not sufficiently nuanced to provide a good picture of local realities; thus, the studies did not lead to behavioral change. Two principles underlying the participatory research approach distinguish it from other types of research. First, it seeks to close the distance between the researcher and the respondent by making the respondent also the researcher. The respondents own and carry out the entire research process. Second, participatory research assumes that this process of active engagement will empower the respondents to take follow-up action. The data collection methods can be open-ended or closed-ended, qualitative or quantitative.

While there is a history of mistrust of self-assessment techniques, these measures are increasingly used in poverty assessments, for several reasons. Not all variance in incomes can be explained by objective conditions in the external environment. Researchers need to understand complex social and psychological realities and processes in order to correctly interpret behavior and explain why certain individuals take advantage of economic opportunities while others with the same demographic profile do not. Q-sort methodology, which uses factor analysis to sort individuals into groups based on shared attitudes, is one way of tapping into these underlying attributes of individuals and groups (see Brown, chapter 9).

People's assessments of their own well-being tend to be only modestly correlated with their life circumstances as reflected in more objective welfare measures. Rather than dismissing self-assessments as "faulty measures," however, recent studies show that subjective measures may be more important than objective ones in predicting people's probability of taking action. A major conclusion from these studies is that beyond a minimum threshold level, relative income matters more than absolute income (Graham and Pettinato 2002).

How to Measure: Quantitative or Qualitative

There has been a fierce debate across disciplines on the value of different data collection methods. Three overall conclusions have emerged. First, no one method is always superior; methods must be matched to the questions of interest and must be credible to the end users, often policy makers. Second, it is important to distinguish between methods and tools for data collection. Third, in most situations a mix of data collection tools provides a more reliable and complete picture of the phenomenon under study, as the tools balance out each other's weaknesses.

For example, conflict and its impact on livelihoods can be studied in different ways. If national policy makers are mainly interested in the incidence of conflict across a country, a four-community study that describes conflict in those four communities in detail is unlikely to provide the answers they are looking for. If, however, they are interested in the roots of conflict, then they may find useful a four-community study in which the four communities are randomly selected after a stratification process to represent different types of conflicts or types of communities. A detailed ethnographic investigation using process tracing, complemented by household surveys to provide numbers on conflict incidence over the past 20 years, may yield answers that are of interest to policy makers.

Hentschel (1999) makes a distinction between quantitative data collection methods such as large representative surveys, and qualitative methods such as interviews or observation. But the data collected using any of these methods can be either qualitative or quantitative. Thus a large household survey can include subjective data or self-assessments of well-being, power, or wealth, while an interview process can include open-ended questions or life histories as well as short questionnaires. The life histories can be analyzed qualitatively or they can be quantified after setting up coding categories. The coding can be done manually or facilitated by content analysis software (Narayan, Chambers, et al. 2000).

To take optimal advantage of different methods, Rao and Woolcock (chapter 13) identify three different ways of integrating qualitative and quantitative methods: parallel, sequential, and iterative. When the research enterprise is large and complex and time is short—as in some national poverty assessments—survey research and in-depth case studies of communities may be done by different teams simultaneously. Integration takes place at the time of writing. Hence, qualitative data do not inform the design of the survey questionnaire, but they add richness when findings are integrated. A sequential approach often starts with in-depth qualitative work using a range of open-ended methods that provide insight into a complex process and thus help to define the hypotheses of interest and appropriate quantitative questions. An iterative approach is similar but involves return visits to the field to successively understand anomalies in data or to probe new issues revealed by the data.

Guide to Chapters

Section 1 of this book focuses on key concepts and methodological issues in measuring empowerment. Following this overview chapter, chapter 2 presents a framework for evaluating empowerment, offering important conceptual advances in this area. Patti Petesch, Catalina Smulovitz, and Michael Walton view empowerment of poor, excluded, or subordinate groups as a product of interaction between the agency of these groups and the opportunity structure in which this agency is potentially exercised. They identify three influences on agency: economic and human capital, capacity to aspire, and organizational capacity. The opportunity structure within which actors pursue their interests is also seen as a product of three influences: the openness or permeability of the state, the extent of elite fragmentation, and the state's implementation capacity. The authors argue that a framework for evaluating empowerment must include two explicit causal frameworks, one specifying how empowerment influences development outcomes, the other specifying the determinants of empowerment itself. This framework is applied to several Latin American development interventions in education and participatory budgeting.

Section 2 of the volume focuses on household and gender issues and sets forth three main points. First, the household is not simply a neutral consumer, producer, and distributor of tangible and intangible resources. It is also a site of unequal formal and informal rules and social norms that result in unequal power relations within domestic units. These inequalities are deeply embedded and resistant to change. Second, the sociocultural context matters and may be more important than individual traits in determining women's empowerment. Third, psychological or mental space plays a key role at both the community or social group level and the individual level. These points lead to these authors' the common emphasis on women's empowerment through collective action.

Anju Malhotra and Sidney Ruth Schuler (chapter 3) provide a useful comprehensive review of the literature on women's empowerment in development, focusing on measurement challenges. Comparing empowerment to related concepts such as women's autonomy and gender equality, the authors find two distinguishing features in women's empowerment: process and agency. Process implies change, that is, progression from one state to another. Agency implies that women themselves must be significant actors in the change process being described or measured. The term "agency" is also used to distinguish this process from top-down approaches. Thus, a hypothetical improvement in gender equality would not be considered empowerment unless the intervening process involved women as agents of change.

Citing a review of 45 empirical studies, Malhotra and Schuler conclude that most empirical work is focused on the micro level, with some attempts at the macro level and a missing middle (or meso) level. Despite the vast literature and extensive community-based work on women's empowerment, they conclude that the evidence is weak both on the contribution of empowerment to development outcomes and on determinants of empowerment. The authors focus on three methodological issues: multidimensionality, aggregation levels, and context-specificity of indicators. The chapter concludes with a list of possible indicators of different dimensions of empowerment at various levels.

In chapter 4, Karen Oppenheim Mason discusses the definition and determinants of women's empowerment in the domestic sphere. Drawing from a five-country comparative study of women's empowerment and demographic change, Mason suggests that women's empowerment is multidimensional, with only weak correlations between the dimensions. It is also relational: women are not empowered or disempowered in a vacuum, but always in relation to others with whom they interact. And empowerment is cultural, rooted in the community and its shared beliefs, values, and norms. Women's empowerment is therefore determined not only by individualistic traits such as earnings and education but also by a shared cultural consensus about who has the right to power and resources. Given the strong impact of community culture on women's domestic empowerment, Mason argues for the strategic importance of collective action by women themselves. She notes that measuring women's domestic empowerment is difficult and probably best approached through multiple methods, each of which has specific advantages and drawbacks.

Joy Deshmukh-Ranadive (chapter 5) introduces the concept of spaces, including mental space, as a device for understanding women's empowerment in the domestic unit. A woman's placement in the family hierarchy determines her access to spaces, which in turn influences her capacity to act and her behavior. Empowerment comes through an expansion of spaces, allowing her greater freedom to move, maneuver, and negotiate to achieve what she wants. Spaces can be economic, sociocultural, political, cultural, or mental. Mental space in particular allows a person the freedom to think and act. Expansion of mental space is an essential condition for empowerment, since without it a person will be unable to take advantage of opportunities that emerge from the environment.

Section 3, including contributions from both psychologists and economists, further highlights the importance of the subjective psychological aspects of empowerment. The chapters in this section make the case for including subjective well-being as an aspect of empowerment and discuss methods for measuring such psychological aspects.

Ed Diener and Robert Biswas-Diener (chapter 6) summarize the extensive literature on subjective well-being, defined as people's life satisfaction, sense of fulfillment, and experiences of pleasant emotions. Psychological empowerment, linked to subjective well-being, occurs when people gain confidence that they have the resources, energy, and competence to achieve important goals. The authors argue that external conditions are necessary but not sufficient for empowerment; psychological feelings of competence, energy, and the desire to act are also required. Thus, empowerment includes both the objective ability to control one's environment and the subjective conviction that one can do so. The authors also consider causes of subjective well-being and highlight differences across countries. They find that increases in income make more difference to subjective well-being at poverty levels than they do at higher income levels.

In chapter 7, Carol Graham and Stefano Pettinato provide empirical evidence on the relationships between subjective well-being and income mobility in Peru and Russia. They conclude that relative income within a society matters more to happiness than absolute income does. They found that people with the greatest absolute gains were the most critical of their own mobility, becoming "frustrated achievers." In Peru, 44 percent of the high performers in terms of income gains said they were worse off, while in Russia 72 percent had that pessimistic assessment. The authors suggest that two factors explain the negative ratings. With global integration, people's comparison point is no longer only their local community but also a national or global community against which they do not measure up. Second, given macroeconomic volatility and unemployment, middle-class households feel more insecure than before about their capacity to hang onto their rank on the mobility ladder. Because sustaining market reforms depends on the support of the middle class, the authors note that in globalized economies perceptions of mobility may be as important politically as the actual economic circumstances.

Michael Lokshin and Martin Ravallion (chapter 8) examine relationships among subjective well-being, subjective power, and household incomes, using a panel data set of 3,800 households in Russia surveyed in 1998 and 2000. Their findings challenge somewhat the case for the independent importance of empowerment, as they note that higher individual and household incomes raise both perceived power and perceived welfare. Although the relationship is not perfect, with many in the highest welfare rung not perceiving themselves as having comparable power, the two subjective measures are highly correlated. The authors also find that the same set of variables matter for improving subjective well-being and power. Examining changes over time, they find that the number of people moving up the power ladder exceeded the number of people falling down, an indicator that power should not be considered a zero-sum game.

In chapter 9, Steven Brown presents the Q sort, a methodology for clustering attitudinal statements through factor analyses. This results in the identification of groups that are distinguished from each other by their attitudes and perceptions regarding particular issues rather than by a priori categories such as age, education, or gender. This clustering of people with shared attitudes permits the development of interventions that are tailored to fit them. If the statements and participants chosen to develop the factors are diverse, then the clusters that emerge can be applied more widely even though the initial sample may be small. Brown illustrates the use of the methodology with reference to interventions in schools for farmers in Peru, dairy herd improvement in Uruguay, and health care in Serbia.

Section 4 focuses on the community and local governance levels. Two chapters discuss conceptual issues at the community level, including issues of power, community structures, organization, solidarity, and peace. Two other chapters focus more specifically on methodological issues in measuring empowerment at the community and local levels, including causal models and the use of qualitative and quantitative methods.

In chapter 10, Norman Uphoff begins with Weber's (1947) classic definition of power as the probability that someone in a social relationship will be able to achieve his or her will despite resistance and regardless of the bases upon which the probability rests. He then distinguishes six types of power based on kinds of resources (economic, social, political, informational, moral, and physical) that influence the probability of achieving desired results. Uphoff develops an analytical framework including direct focus on assets and capabilities, power processes, and the broader social, political, and cultural context, all of which either constrain or enable achievement of what is desired. Drawing from his extensive experience with rural organizations, particularly in irrigation, he highlights challenges faced at different local levels, including the levels of group, community, and locality.

Caroline Moser (chapter 11) makes the case for including peace as a critical condition for empowerment and development effectiveness. Civil war and conflict affect 35 of the poorest countries, with devastating economic effects at both the macro and micro levels. Crime, violence, fear, and insecurity all affect assets, capabilities, and institutions at the individual, household, and community levels. Drawing on her long involvement in Colombia, Moser argues that participation in the peace process itself can be empowering. She describes participatory evaluations of two local peace-building projects in which participants themselves identified changes in their capacity to participate in the peace process. The research indicates the importance of developing context-specific indicators, as what was perceived to be important varied from community to community.

For Asim Ijaz Khwaja (chapter 12), the starting point for measuring empowerment should be clarity on the underlying theory of empowerment, paying particular attention to whether empowerment is conceptualized as a means or an end. Theory, he argues, is needed to guide development of relevant context-specific indicators. If empowerment is viewed as a means to an end, the causal relationship showing how empowerment leads to desired outcomes needs to be specified. This allows explicit consideration of the possibilities of reverse causality or of omitted variables that might affect both empowerment and the desired outcome. Khwaja illustrates this use of theory in developing measurement methodology by focusing on two potential dimensions of empowerment: information and influence. He draws from his research on a rural development program in Baltistan, Pakistan, with data from 100 communities.

Vijayendra Rao and Michael Woolcock (chapter 13) provide an overview of the advantages and disadvantages of quantitative and qualitative methods in assessing the impact of development programs and policies on poor people's empowerment. They argue for a mixed-methods approach to overcome the disadvantages that each approach has when used in isolation. Quantitative methods are more suited for allowing generalization to wider populations, enabling researchers to validate findings by repeating analyses and providing greater objectivity by maintaining distance from the subjects. The methods are not as useful, however, in understanding context and processes, or in integrating hypotheses generated by participants themselves or minority opinions. While qualitative methods do not have these drawbacks, they have their own limitations. With small sample sizes, generalizations are difficult. It is harder to protect against researcher bias and more difficult to replicate results. The authors highlight three ways to combine the different approaches to take advantage of their complementary strengths.

Finally, section 5 consists of six chapters focusing on policies and structures at the national level. These have dramatic effects on both agency and opportunity structure and thus strongly influence what is possible at the local level. These chapters focus on two sets of issues. The first is conceptual, that is, determining what should be measured at the national level and how these measures are linked to empowerment of poor people. This discussion relates empowerment to concepts of governance, social capital, civil society, and democracy. Second, the chapters address methodological issues specifically related to measurement, with some attempts to develop indicators at the national level.

Christiaan Grootaert (chapter 14), building on *World Development Report 2000/2001,* first identifies conceptual dimensions that facilitate empowerment and then suggests indicators at the national level for measuring state responsiveness, removing social barriers, and building social institutions and social capital. Starting with 50 potential empowerment indicators from databases on countries in the Eastern Europe and Central Asia regions, Grootaert develops an aggregate empowerment score at the national level using 10 of these indicators. These include measures of government effectiveness, corruption, illicit payments, rule of law, regulatory quality, voice and accountability, women in political office, and income inequality. Two important dimensions that could not be included because of lack of data were social capital and decentralization.

In chapter 15, Carmen Malena and Volkhart Finn Heinrich describe a unique three-year participatory process that is being used to develop an index to measure the strength of civil society. Rather than starting with existing databases, the nongovernmental coalition CIVICUS has led efforts in 60 countries and territories to build local ownership and consensus on dimensions and indicators to assess civil society. The project emphasizes the role of marginalized groups within civil society and the extent to which civil society serves the interests of these groups. The index measures four dimensions: the structure of civil society, the external environment within which civil society functions, the values held by civil society, and the impact of civil society activities. The 74 indicators are scored by stakeholders and then aggregated, after which a national workshop is held to discuss the results and develop a national action plan.

Stephen Knack (chapter 16) argues for understanding empowerment of the poor within a positive-sum framework. Rather than focusing on power, an approach that, he argues, tends to lead to zero-sum perspectives, he presents empowerment within a framework of "potential Pareto efficiency." That is, a policy change is considered efficient if it adds more value to society than it subtracts. Given that policy making is a political process that requires the support of the elite and the middle class, Knack argues that it is important to identify policies that will make the poor better off without making others worse off. He identifies two types of economic and political reforms that benefit the poor as well as other groups, namely, improving the security of property rights and changing the nature of political participation by citizens to focus on the public interest rather than on individual benefits.

The final three chapters focus on the concept of democracy and its relationship to empowerment, addressing both conceptual and methodological issues. Ashutosh Varshney (chapter 17), reviewing the relationship between democracy and poverty, concludes that "democracies tend to fall almost exclusively in the unspectacular but undisastrous middle," while dictatorships have extremely varied records. He offers two responses to the question of why the poor in democracies have not had more effect on the adoption of policies leading to rapid poverty reduction. First, policy makers feel compelled to adopt politically popular direct methods rather than less popular indirect methods that may be more effective in producing inclusive economic growth. Second, the power of numbers of the poor gets diffused across ethnic groups, since it is easier to mobilize poor people along ethnic lines than as an economic class. Varshney argues that when ethnicity and class intersect and the ethnic group is numerically large, poor people's voices are more likely to bring an effective policy response, as in Malaysia and in Kerala, India.

Larry Diamond (chapter 18) characterizes the problem of poverty as essentially political in nature. That is, the issue is not lack of resources but lack of political power and voice among the poor at all levels. This denies poor people the ability to articulate and defend their interests. Democracies, Diamond argues, should provide a corrective to poor people's powerlessness. Free and fair elections provide strong incentives to political leaders to listen and respond. In addition, civil society can articulate and represent the interests of the poor, and civil society and elected representatives can monitor the conduct of public officials and seek redress in courts and in administrative forums. According to Diamond, democracies have not been more successful in reducing poverty because such democratic practices are not, in fact, fully implemented in many nominally democratic countries. He identifies three dimensions for characterizing democracies: free and fair elections, civil liberties, and responsible and accountable governance.

In the final chapter, Gerardo Munck discusses the challenge of coming up with good measures for concepts that are essentially political, including both empowerment and democracy. The spread of democracy around the world has led to a proliferation of data sets that include a variety of indicators of governance and politics in a country. Munck cautions against easy assumptions that any given measure is valid and reliable. He explores four aspects of the development of indicators and related measures of democracy: definition of concepts, identification of indicators to measure the concepts, construction of scales to measure variation, and aggregation rules for developing indexes that combine several measures. Munck concludes by cautioning against "overcomplicating" the concepts being measured.

The chapters in this volume highlight the many different approaches that can be taken to measuring and evaluating empowerment. Irrespective of the approach, good research must be logical and rigorous, yet presented in a way that is simple. It must be easy to interpret and understand, and this includes being understood by poor people themselves. If we return to villages and slums and find that people comprehend neither our measuring instruments nor our results, the research will lead to erudite discussions among specialists but will not bring about change in the real world. Nor will opaque or overly complex findings command the attention of time-pressed politicians, public officials, civil society activists, or CEOs in the private sector. Without their support, large-scale programs and policies that empower poor men and women will not be implemented.

The challenge of measuring, monitoring, and evaluating empowerment taken up in this book is only worth pursuing because of its central importance in poverty reduction. Our task is complex, but in the end we have to be simple.

Notes

1. Epigraphs in this chapter are drawn from the World Bank's Voices of the Poor study, from field notes by Soumya Kapoor for the World Bank pilot study on Moving Out of Poverty, and from a group meeting attended by Deepa Narayan in Anand, Gujarat, India.

2. The *Voices of the Poor* series includes three volumes: *Can Anyone Hear Us?* (Narayan, Patel, et al. 2000); *Crying Out for Change* (Narayan, Chambers, et al. 2000); and *From Many Lands* (Narayan and Petesch 2002).

3. This strategy draws on *World Development Report 2000/2001: Attacking Poverty,* which highlights three concepts: opportunity, empowerment, and security (World Bank 2000).

4. Isham, Kaufmann, and Pritchett (1997) studied the rates of return on World Bank projects across developing countries and found that each 1-point improvement in the Gastil scale measuring civil liberties increased the project rate of return by more than 1 percent. Isham, Narayan, and Pritchett (1995), in a study of 121 rural water supply projects, found that participation by the intended beneficiaries improved project performance.

5. For a more detailed discussion see the empowerment sourcebook (Narayan 2002, chap. 2).

6. The "opportunity structure and agency framework" developed by these authors was presented at the World Bank workshop on measuring empowerment in February 2003 and refined over the next year. It is discussed in detail in chapter 2 of this volume. Several efforts are under way to apply the framework to the evaluation of development programs (Alsop and Heinsohn 2005).

7. Sen (1985, 1999) has been the earliest and clearest proponent of the notion of poor people's agency, arguing that poor people often lack the capability to articulate and pursue their interests fully as they are "unfree."

8. For a detailed review of evidence and program experience that led to the selection of these four empowerment elements, see the empowerment sourcebook (Narayan 2002).

9. This in fact has happened in India. The Mazdoor Kisan Shakti Sangathan (MKSS), an organization created by poor farmers and workers in the state of Rajasthan, started by fighting for workers' rights and transparency of information on government programs meant to help poor people. Based on this work, MKSS advocated a freedom of information law to promote transparency more widely in state institutions. In 2000 the Rajasthan state legislature passed the Right to Information Act, and a similar bill was introduced in the Indian Parliament in 2004. Freedom of information laws now exist in more than 50 countries (see http://www.freedominfo.org).

10. Section 5 of this book focuses on issues of democracy and how they function. It includes important reviews by Ashutosh Varshney, Larry Diamond, and Stephen Knack.

11. For a good review of democracy and poverty reduction, see Przeworski et al. (2000). On capture of the state in many former Soviet Union countries, see Jones, Hellman, and Kaufmann (2000). On the functioning of democracy in Latin America, see UNDP (2002a).

12. See Collier et al. (2003) for a history and analysis of civil conflict; Bates (1999) and Varshney (2003b) on ethnic conflict; and Barron, Kaiser, and Pradhan (2004) on conflict at the community level.

13. The term "oppositional identity" is used by Akerlof and Kranton (2000). They argue that a person's sense of self, or identity, should be incorporated in economic

models because it affects individual interactions and outcomes. Excluded groups that can never fully integrate with dominant groups often adopt oppositional identities.

14. Differential access and the difficulties faced by the poor in accessing basic services are the subject of *World Development Report 2004* (World Bank 2003). The authors highlight the importance of accountability and voice. For an analysis of how basic services fail the poor, concentrating on problems of incomplete information, insincere political promises, and social polarization, see Keefer and Khemani (2004).

15. Prahalad (2004) presents case studies from across the developing world in which companies are successfully providing products and services that improve the living conditions of the poorest of the poor.

16. The Open Society Justice Initiative (http://www.justiceinitiative.org/) promotes and tracks legal reform activities around the world that are grounded in the protection of human rights.

17. For a useful overview and case studies of applications by nongovernmental organizations, see Oakley (2001).

18. See Alsop, Krishna, and Sjoblom (2001). In contrast, a more recent study by Besley, Pande, and Rao (2004) across 522 villages in India found that people from socially and economically disadvantaged groups were more likely to attend *gram sabha* meetings (called by local government) and to be chosen as beneficiaries in villages that held such meetings.

19. For an analysis of the role of culture in poverty and inequality, see Rao and Walton (2004).

20. *Dalits,* or untouchables, face many forms of exclusion, including the social norm that they must walk barefoot through the streets of higher-caste areas.

21. See chapter 6 of this volume by Diener and Biswas-Diener.

22. In cases of adaptive preference, individuals in deprived circumstances are forced to develop preferences that reflect their restricted options. A woman's perception of her self and her world may be so skewed by her circumstances and cultural upbringing that she may say and believe that she genuinely prefers certain things that she would not prefer if she were aware of other possibilities.

23. Ed Diener has been engaged in research on happiness and its determinants throughout his career. After examining data on happiness and income across countries and across time, Diener has concluded that there is no strong relationship between happiness and income above a certain income threshold.

24. The Poverty Action Lab at the Massachusetts Institute of Technology (http://www.povertyactionlab.org/) has launched several evaluation and research projects based on random assignment of intervention to treatment and control groups. See also Duflo and Kremer (2003).

25. For an account of the evolution of a successful participatory development experience in irrigation management, see Uphoff (1996).

References

Akerlof, George A., and Rachel E. Kranton. 2000. "Economics and Identity." *Quarterly Journal of Economics* 115 (3): 715–53.

Alsop, Ruth, and Nina Heinsohn. 2005. "Measuring Empowerment in Practice: Structuring Analysis and Framing Indicators." Policy Research Working Paper 3510, World Bank, Washington, DC.

Alsop, Ruth, Anirudh Krishna, and Disa Sjoblom. 2001. "Inclusion and Local Elected Governments: The Panchayat Raj System in India." Social Development Paper 37, South Asia Region, Social Development Unit, World Bank, Washington, DC.

Appadurai, Arjun. 2004. "The Capacity to Aspire: Culture and the Terms of Recognition." In *Culture and Public Action,* ed. Vijayendra Rao and Michael Walton, 59–84. Stanford, CA: Stanford University Press.

Bandura, Albert. 1995. "Comments on the Crusade against the Causal Efficacy of Human Thought." *Journal of Behavior Therapy and Experimental Psychiatry* 26: 179–90.

———. 1998. "Personal and Collective Efficacy in Human Adaptation and Change." In *Advances in Psychological Science,* vol. 1, *Social, Personal, and Cultural Aspects,* ed. J. G. Adair, D. Belanger, and K. L. Dion, 51–71. Hove, UK: Psychology Press.

Bardhan, Pranab. 2004. "Governance Issues in Delivery of Public Services." *Journal of African Economies* 13, Supplement 1: i167–i182.

Barron, Patrick, Kai Kaiser, and Menno Pradhan. 2004. "Local Conflict in Indonesia: Measuring Incidence and Identifying Patterns." World Bank Working Paper 3384, World Bank, Washington, DC.

Bates, Robert H. 1999. "Ethnicity, Capital Formation, and Conflict." CID Working Paper 27, Center for International Development, Harvard University, Cambridge, MA.

Besley, Timothy, and Robin Burgess. 2002. "The Political Economy of Government Responsiveness: Theory and Evidence from India." *Quarterly Journal of Economics* 117 (4): 1415–52.

Besley, Timothy, Rohini Pande, and Vijayendra Rao. 2004. "Politics as Usual? Local Democracy and Public Resource Allocation in South India." Paper presented at the Comparative Politics Workshop, Department of Political Science, Yale University, October 5.

Cheema, Ali, and Shandana Khan Mohmand. 2004. "The Political Economy of Devolved Provision: Equity-based Targeting for Elite Capture—Case Evidence from Two Pakistani Unions." Paper presented at the World Bank workshop on Equity and Development in South Asia, New Delhi, December 7–8. Also available from Center for Management and Economic Research, Lahore University of Management Sciences, Lahore, Pakistan. http://ravi.lums.edu.pk/cmer/detail_wpapers.php3?id=62.

Collier, Paul, Lani Elliot, Havard Hegre, Anke Hoeffler, Marta Reynal-Querol, and Nicholas Sambanis. 2003. *Breaking the Conflict Trap: Civil War and Development Policy.* Washington, DC: World Bank; New York: Oxford University Press.

Diener, Ed, and Frank Fujita. 1995. "Resources, Personal Strivings, and Subjective Well-Being: A Nomothetic and Idiographic Approach." *Journal of Personality and Social Psychology* 68 (5): 926–35.

Duflo, Esther, and Michael Kremer. 2003. "Use of Randomization in the Evaluation of Development Effectiveness." Paper prepared for the Fifth Biennial World Bank Conference on Evaluation and Development, Washington, DC, July 15–16.

Foster, Andrew D., and Mark R. Rosenzweig. 2003. "Democratization, Decentralization and the Distribution of Local Public Goods in a Poor Rural Economy." BREAD Working Paper 010, Bureau for Research in Economic Analysis of Development. http://www.cid.harvard.edu/bread.

Glewwe, Paul, and Gillette Hall. 1998. "Are Some Groups More Vulnerable to Macroeconomic Shocks than Others? Hypothesis Tests Using Panel Data from Peru." *Journal of Development Economics* 56 (1): 181–206.

Graham, Carol, and Stefano Pettinato. 2002. "Frustrated Achievers: Winners, Losers, and Subjective Well-Being in New Market Economies." *Journal of Development Studies* 38 (4): 100–40.

Grootaert, Christiaan, and Deepa Narayan. 2004. "Local Institutions, Poverty, and Household Welfare in Bolivia." *World Development* 32 (7): 1179–98.

Grootaert, Christiaan, Deepa Narayan, Veronica Nyhan Jones, and Michael Woolcock. 2004. *Measuring Social Capital: An Integrated Questionnaire.* World Bank Working Paper 18, World Bank, Washington, DC. http://poverty.worldbank.org/library/view/11998.

Grootaert, Christiaan, and Thierry van Bastelaer, eds. 2002. *The Role of Social Capital in Development: An Empirical Assessment.* Cambridge: Cambridge University Press.

Hentschel, Jesko. 1999. "Contextuality and Data Collection Methods: A Framework and Application to Health Service Utilization." *Journal of Development Studies* 35 (4): 64–94.

Isham, Jonathan, Daniel Kaufmann, and Lant Pritchett. 1997. "Civil Liberties, Democracy and the Performance of Government Projects." *World Bank Economic Review* 11 (2): 219–42.

Isham, Jonathan, Deepa Narayan, and Lant Pritchett. 1995. "Does Participation Improve Performance? Establishing Causality with Subjective Data." *World Bank Economic Review* 9 (2): 175–200.

Jones, Geraint, Joel S. Hellman, and Daniel Kaufmann. 2000. "Seize the State, Seize the Day: State Capture, Corruption and Influence in Transition." Policy Research Working Paper 2444, World Bank, Washington, DC.

Kabeer, Naila. 2001. "Reflections on the Measurement of Women's Empowerment." In *Discussing Women's Empowerment: Theory and Practice.* Sida Studies 3. Stockholm: Swedish International Development Cooperation Agency.

Keefer, Philip, and Stuti Khemani. 2004. "Why Do the Poor Receive Poor Services?" *Economic and Political Weekly,* February 28.

Keefer, Philip, and Stephen Knack. 1995. "Institutions and Economic Performance: Cross-Country Tests Using Alternative Institutional Measures." *Economics and Politics* 7 (November): 207–27.

Knight, Barry, Hope Chigudu, and Rajesh Tandon. 2002. *Reviving Democracy: Citizens at the Heart of Governance.* London: Earthscan.

Narayan, Deepa. 1999. "Bonds and Bridges: Social Capital and Poverty." Poverty Reduction and Economic Management Network, World Bank, Washington, DC.

Narayan, Deepa, ed. 2002. *Empowerment and Poverty Reduction: A Sourcebook.* Washington, DC: World Bank.

Narayan, Deepa, Robert Chambers, Meera K. Shah, and Patti Petesch. 2000. *Voices of the Poor: Crying Out for Change.* New York: Oxford University Press for the World Bank.

Narayan, Deepa, with Raj Patel, Kai Schafft, Anne Rademacher, and Sarah Koch-Schulte. 2000. *Voices of the Poor: Can Anyone Hear Us?* New York: Oxford University Press for the World Bank.

Narayan, Deepa, and Patti Petesch, eds. 2002. *Voices of the Poor: From Many Lands.* New York: Oxford University Press for the World Bank.

Narayan, Deepa, and Talat Shah. 2000. "Gender Inequity, Poverty and Social Capital." Poverty Reduction and Economic Management Network, World Bank, Washington, DC.

Nussbaum, Martha. 2000. *Women and Development: The Capabilities Approach.* Cambridge: Cambridge University Press.

Oakley, Peter, ed. 2001. "Evaluating Empowerment: Reviewing the Concept and Practice." NGO Management and Policy Series 13, International NGO Training and Research Centre (INTRAC), Oxford, UK.

Prahalad, C. K. 2004. *The Fortune at the Bottom of the Pyramid: Eradicating Poverty through Profits.* Upper Saddle River, NJ: Wharton School Publishing.

Przeworski, Adam, Michael E. Alvarez, Jose Antonio Cheibub, and Fernando Limongi. 2000. *Democracy and Development: Political Institutions and Well-Being in the World, 1950–90.* Cambridge: Cambridge University Press.

Psacharopoulos, George, and Harry Patrinos, eds. 1994. *Indigenous People and Poverty in Latin America: An Empirical Analysis.* Washington, DC: World Bank.

Rao, Vijayendra, and Michael Walton. 2004. "Culture and Public Action: Relationality, Equality of Agency, and Development." In *Culture and Public Action,* ed. Vijayendra Rao and Michael Walton, 3–36. Stanford, CA: Stanford University Press.

Rigobon, Roberto, and Dani Rodrik. 2004. "Rule of Law, Democracy, Openness, and Income: Estimating the Interrelationships." NBER Working Paper w10750, National Bureau of Economic Research, Cambridge, MA.

Rodrik, Dani. 2000. "Participatory Politics, Social Cooperation and Economic Stability." Paper presented at the American Economic Association Meeting, Boston, January 7–9.

Schady, Norbert. 2000. "Political Economy of Expenditures by the Peruvian Social Fund (FONCODES), 1991–95." *American Political Science Review* 94 (2): 289–304.

Sen, Amartya. 1985. "Well-Being, Agency and Freedom: The Dewey Lectures." *Journal of Philosophy* 82 (4): 169–221.

———. 1999. *Development as Freedom.* New York: Knopf.

Tarrow, Sidney. 1994. *Power in Movement: Social Movements, Collective Action and Politics.* Cambridge: Cambridge University Press.

Tilly, Charles. 1999. *Durable Inequality*. Berkeley: University of California Press.

UNDP (United Nations Development Programme). 2002a. *Democracy in Latin America: Towards a Citizen's Democracy*. New York: UNDP.

———. 2002b. *Human Development Report 2002: Deepening Democracy in a Fragmented World*. New York: Oxford University Press.

———. 2004. *Human Development Report 2004: Cultural Liberty in Today's Diverse World*. New York: Oxford University Press.

Uphoff, Norman. 1996. *Learning from Gal Oya: Possibilities for Participatory Development and Post-Newtonian Social Science*. London: Intermediate Technology Publications.

Varshney, Ashutosh. 2003a. *Ethnic Conflict and Civic Life: Hindus and Muslims in India*. New Haven: Yale University Press.

———. 2003b. "Nationalism, Ethnic Conflict and Rationality." *Perspectives on Politics* 1 (1): 85–99.

Varshney, Ashutosh, Rizal Panggabean, and Mohammad Tadjoeddin. 2004. "Patterns of Collective Violence in Indonesia (1990–2003)." Working Paper 04/03, United Nations Support Facility for Indonesian Recovery (UNSFIR), Jakarta.

Weber, Max. 1947. *The Theory of Social and Economic Organization*. New York: Oxford University Press.

Weiner, Myron. 2001. "The Struggle for Equality: Caste in Indian Politics." In *The Success of India's Democracy*, ed. Atul Kohli, 193–225. Cambridge: Cambridge University Press.

Woolcock, Michael, and Deepa Narayan. 2000. "Social Capital: Implications for Development Theory, Research and Policy." *World Bank Research Observer* 15 (2): 225–49.

World Bank. 2000. *World Development Report 2000/2001: Attacking Poverty*. New York: Oxford University Press.

———. 2003. *World Development Report 2004: Making Services Work for Poor People*. New York: Oxford University Press.

Chapter 2

Evaluating Empowerment: A Framework with Cases from Latin America

Patti Petesch, Catalina Smulovitz, and Michael Walton

There is a growing literature on how to evaluate the role and importance of empowerment in poverty reduction and development. The interest in evaluation has emerged with the rising recognition of empowerment as a promising source of more effective, and more inclusive, development. It is seen particularly as a means of increasing the capacity of poor people and subordinate groups to influence development processes. Empowerment was highlighted as one of the primary forces for poverty reduction by the World Bank in its millennium *World Development Report 2000/2001: Attacking Poverty,* and in subsequent strategy statements. The World Bank's empowerment sourcebook states that "A growing body of evidence points to the linkages between empowerment and development effectiveness both at the society-wide level and at the grassroots level" (Narayan 2002).

There has been considerable study of the role of empowerment-related factors in poverty reduction and overall development. Yet there are few, if any, rigorous evaluations that allow the contribution of empowerment to be measured and compared with other influences on developmental outcomes, whether at the local or society-wide level. There is also a paucity of empirical analysis of the causal influences on empowerment itself. Yet this type of information is crucial to assessing the potential for public action to foster empowerment and for according it priority relative to other pressing concerns of policy makers and other development actors. Since the early 1990s, a growing number of development projects and activities (including those supported by the World Bank) have featured components that seek to directly empower poorer groups. These activities have worked, for instance, to combat corruption and improve the functioning of public services, or to foster more open and inclusive governing structures. The specific empowerment interventions encompass a diverse set of actions to promote participation, increase transparency, build capacity among poor groups, and strengthen accountability mechanisms in development processes (Narayan 2002).

This chapter sets forth a framework for analyzing how empowerment influences the development process, and for analyzing the causal forces on empowerment. It is intended to help guide applications to case studies (to be undertaken by the World Bank and others) that will pilot, test, and undoubtedly modify the approach.

The litmus test for empowerment is whether poor and subordinate groups have *effectively* advanced their particular interests through their own choice and action. Such processes are a product of complex forces, and a two-part framework is presented here for analyzing these multiple forces and their development effects. The first part of the framework examines causal forces on empowerment in terms of interactions between the *agency* of poor citizens and the *opportunity structure* of a society. The second part considers how to assess the contribution of empowerment to development *outcomes*, recognizing explicitly that empowerment is only one of many influences. The final sections of the chapter discuss methodological issues in undertaking an evaluation within this framework and look briefly at three cases from Latin America that illustrate key evaluation challenges.

What Is Empowerment and Why Does It Matter?

By empowerment we mean increasing both the capacity of individuals or groups to make purposeful choices and their capacity to transform these choices into desired actions and outcomes. This can apply to any social group, but the framework developed here is particularly concerned with the empowerment of poorer, excluded, or subordinate groups. Of particular relevance for empowerment are inequalities that are produced by the *relations* between different groups, through unequal social interactions and associated processes of socialization. Poorer and subordinate groups experience inequalities not only with respect to economic resources (including "human capital"), but also with respect to social, cultural, and political factors. Such *relational* and *categorical* (or group-based) inequalities serve to disempower the poor, reducing their capacity to influence the world to further their interests.[1]

Empowerment can have value for both intrinsic and instrumental reasons. Having more power over one's life is valued for its own sake in almost all societies, and it is important to recognize this intrinsic value. But empowerment is also potentially of importance for its direct and indirect impacts on other aspects of development.[2]

The terms most often included in technical definitions of empowerment are options, choice, control, and power. Naila Kabeer, for example, asserts that empowerment is "the expansion in people's ability to make strategic life choices in a context where this ability was previously denied to them" (1999, 437). This definition highlights both the actor's ability to make choices and the process of change in the achievement of this ability. In interpreting the process of empowerment, Kabeer emphasizes the need to examine a poor group's resources, agency, and achievements. According to the World Bank's empowerment sourcebook, "empowerment is the expansion of assets and capabilities of poor people to participate in, negotiate with, influence, control, and hold accountable institutions that affect their lives" (Narayan 2002, 14). Like Kabeer's, this definition refers to actors' abilities to make purposeful choices, but it also emphasizes the role of institutions within which individuals and groups interact, which form part of the "context" in Kabeer's definition. This should be interpreted as referring to both formal and informal institutions.

The evaluation framework presented here follows these approaches in seeing empowerment as a product of the *interaction* between, on one hand, the capacities of people and groups to make purposeful choices (that is, to be agents), and on the other hand, the social and institutional context in which actors live, which affects the likelihood that their agency will achieve favorable outcomes. We can conclude that empowerment has occurred when poor individuals and groups exercise agency with a reasonable prospect of having an influence on development processes and outcomes.

A Causal Framework for Empowerment

A simple framework for analyzing processes of empowerment is presented in figure 2.1. Empowerment of poor individuals or groups is influenced by (a) a change in the capacity of these actors to take purposeful actions, that is, to exercise *agency*, and (b) a change in the social, political, and institutional context that defines the broader *opportunity structure* in which these actors pursue their interests. There are multiple interactions between agency and opportunity structure, indicated by the double-headed arrow in the center of the figure. In sum, *empowerment of poor, excluded, or subordinate groups is a product of the interaction between the agency of these groups and the opportunity structure in which this agency is potentially exercised.*

An example can be found in Porto Alegre, Brazil, where the municipal government of the newly elected Partido dos Trabalhadores (Workers' Party) introduced participatory budgeting in the late 1980s. The reforms allowed for direct citizen involvement in identifying municipal spending priorities and neighborhood public works, and channeled funds based on population and need. The changes associated with participatory budgeting involved both popular mobilization, on one side, and an opening of public institutions, on the other. Writing about empowerment of local groups in Mexico, Jonathan Fox (1992) has characterized such two-sided change as a "sandwich" approach.

Influences on agency included possession of human and economic capital, the "capacity to aspire," and organizational capacity. Influences on the

Figure 2.1   A Causal Framework for Empowerment in State-Society Contexts

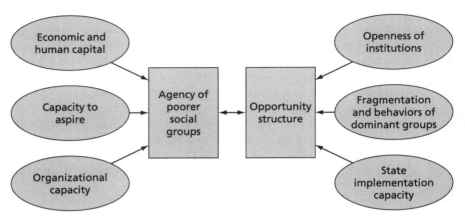

opportunity structure include the openness of institutions, the extent of elite fragmentation, and government capacity. These six factors are discussed below.

Agency

Individuals behave as *agents* when they can pursue purposeful courses of action that further their goals. The goals may relate to their individual well-being but can also relate to the range of other objectives that an individual or group may deem desirable. The capacity to act as an agent implies that the actor is able to envision alternative paths of action, decide among them, and take action to advance the chosen path as an individual or collectively with others.

Economic and human capital

A key factor in agency is possession of economic resources, skills, and good health, known as economic and human capital. This concept can also be extended to include the strength of safety nets in hard times. Possessing more of such capital helps limit poor people's dependence on others and increases their capacity to make choices. As one example, Amartya Sen has in much of his work emphasized that educating girls provides the basis for enhancing women's agency (1999). These questions of economic and human capital represent familiar territory in the development literature and are not further elaborated here.

The capacity to aspire

"The capacity to aspire" refers to the culturally formed capacity of poor groups to envision alternatives and aspire to different futures. This concept, developed by Arjun Appadurai, is a cultural feature of groups in the sense that it is a product of the relations between groups, including the fundamentally unequal relations typical of almost all societies. In contrast to common treatments of culture that focus on the past (heritage, tradition, inherited norms), aspiration is fundamentally about the future. Appadurai (2004) refers to it as a "navigational" capacity, which includes the capacity to express voice. The capacity to aspire to a better life implies not only dissatisfaction with the present situation but also a nonfatalistic perception about the possibilities for social change. The capacity to aspire is typically unequally distributed. But it can also be influenced or produced by group-based interactions, mobilizations, and alliance building.

The capacity to aspire is probably best interpreted through careful documentation of processes at the individual and group levels on the ground, using ethnographic or other qualitative techniques. Ethnographic work in Porto Alegre, Brazil, while not using the language of capacity to aspire, documents transformations in group and individual attitudes, behaviors, and self-esteem as a result of participatory budgeting (see, for example, Abers 2000). On the other hand, ethnographic work by Scheper-Hughes (1992) in northeastern Brazil illustrates the weakness of aspirations for change among poor women who suffer extreme economic vulnerability and dependence as a consequence of the structures of domination, patron-client relationships, and unequal racial relations that shape their lives.

Organizational capacity

Participation in formal or informal organizations enlarges poor people's access to ideas, information, and camaraderie; strengthens their capacities for planning, decision making, problem solving, collective action, and conflict negotiation; and expands their ties to other networks and resources. Organizational capacity has both sociocultural and technical dimensions, and numerous obstacles must be overcome for poor people's collective action to have force. Communities are heterogeneous, often with divided local power structures and with norms and practices that reinforce the privileges of local elites. These divisions typically mirror economic and social divisions in the larger society (by gender, class, caste, race, ethnicity, religion), and impede organization, consensus, and action on priorities.

The literature on collective action draws attention to problems of managing public goods (such as water for irrigation) because of the difficulty of enforcing rules (such as restrictions on water use) across a large number of beneficiaries. Individual action to "free ride" on the efforts of the collective or disregard the rules can undercut collective efforts (Olsen 1973; Hardin 1968). However, the literature also shows that communities can develop systems with functioning rules, incentives, and punishments—in short, strong organizational capacities (see Ostrom 1990; Wade 1987; Uphoff 1986). Among others, Hirschman (1982) challenges perceptions that unduly stress the negative costs of participation.

Yet even when poor groups have extensive ties among themselves, they are typically weakly connected to, or excluded from, the more extensive networks of powerful actors. In the language of social capital, even when "bonding" ties within poor communities are strong, ties that link communities to governments or elites may be weak, or deeply embedded in unequal social re-lations.[3] Thus, to transform aspirations into actions, poor and disadvantaged groups need to devise strategies for penetrating the networks of more power-ful actors. Often these strategies involve taking advantage of divisions among elite groups (see Lichbach 1998) or forming alliances with middle groups.

More generally, "social capital" is not inherent in preexisting social struc-tures but is a product of dynamic processes of mobilization or division. Indi-cators of an organization's capacity could include the scope of membership, geographic coverage, breadth of participation in decision making, means of mobilizing resources, ties to other organizations, internal processes of ac-countability and problem solving, and so forth.[4]

Understanding the dynamics of agency

Among the issues to be considered in relation to this portion of the evaluation framework are interactions among the various influences on agency, and dif-ferences between "objective" and contextual assessment.

Analysis of agency conditions and trends requires consideration of how the influences interact with each other, and how they affect and are affected by wider forces. There are significant complementarities, with all influencing the potential for exercise of agency. Possession of economic and human capital can powerfully shape the potential for influence, but it is not always a neces-sary condition. Poor, unskilled actors can be active agents where aspirations are high and the organizational basis for collective action exists. Conversely, the exercise of agency is unlikely without aspirations and organizational ca-pacities, which are intimately linked.

Some of the influences on agency can be measured in terms of "objective" attributes (such as levels of schooling, number of organizations, and size of their memberships).[5] However, it is almost always necessary to interpret the capacities in terms of the sociocultural history and context in which individu-als and groups are acting. This is not only because capacities to aspire and organize are in part the product of cultural conditions, but also because interpretation of an action has to take into account what it means in a partic-ular context.

As one example, questions of agency will frequently have important gen-der dimensions. Drawing on Gita Sen, Naila Kabeer cites reproductive choice as an area where interpretations of an action can only be understood within its cultural context. In societies that link a woman's status to her fertility, "bearing the approved number of children will grant a woman the rights and privileges accorded to a fertile woman, but does not necessarily give her greater autonomy in decision making" (Kabeer 1999, 458). In this context, how should we evaluate the decision to bear many children? Is it evidence of a woman's inability to exercise choice in critical areas of her life, or a sign of the strategic use of choice to achieve rights and privileges in other social are-nas where she participates?[6] The interpretation of actions needs to consider the specific cultural meaning of each choice. Although this may complicate comparisons in evaluations, it cannot be avoided, since the exercise of choice can only be evaluated in relation to the alternatives that are perceived to be available to those who must choose.

Finally, it is important to note that the *capacity* to act as an agent is not the same as *achievement* of the desired results (Sen 1985b, 1992). The exercise of agency has an indispensable causal influence on results, but this influence will be mediated by many other factors, including the broader opportunity structure and other factors that have nothing to do with empowerment.

The Opportunity Structure

Poor actors do not operate in a vacuum. Both their own aspirational and organizational capacities and the probability of effecting change through their actions are fundamentally products of relations within the broader social and political system. The empowerment framework seeks to organize assessment of this social and political context, building on what the social movement literature characterizes as the political opportunity structure.[7] The opportunity structure can be seen as the product of three main influences: the openness, or permeability, of institutions; the unity and behavior of powerful groups; and the state's implementation capacity. Together these provide the contextual conditions and opportunities that shape the ability of individuals and organizations to participate, negotiate, influence, and hold institutions accountable. Although this section concentrates on the role of the opportunity structure within a society, the effect of international forces and the way in which they interact with empowerment in the domestic sphere is also relevant.[8]

The "openness" of formal and informal institutions

Institutions and the dynamics of political competition have a significant influence on whether poor people (including those with significant agency capacities) are able to influence government policy in their favor. Institutions are understood as the "rules of the game" for social interaction. These rules can be formal, in the sense of being explicitly defined and written and "enforced by an actor or set of actors *formally recognized as possessing such power*" (Levi 1988, 405). They can also be informal, in the form of social norms, habits, and routines. In informal contexts, rules can be imprecise, and no actor is *legally* entitled to enforce them. "Although formal rules may change overnight as a result of political or judicial decisions," notes Douglass North, "informal constraints . . . are much more impervious to deliberate policies" (1990, 6).

Historically, formal and informal institutional structures in Latin America and the Caribbean (as in many other parts of the developing world) have evolved in ways that reduce the prospects of influence by poor and subordinate groups. A variety of mechanisms and structures at the macro-institutional level as well as sociocultural interactions at the micro level foster the lack of voice. These include clientelistic political structures, deeply entrenched patterns of unequal gender and social relations (notably with respect to indigenous and Afro-Latino groups), top-down corporatist forms of inclusion, and, in extreme cases, the capture of the state by powerful private interests.[9] These mechanisms have persisted despite the broadening of the franchise in the post-independence era and the recent formal democratization of most states in the region. They limit the potential for the poor to exert influence in the full array of a society's organizations—from individual households to local government offices, private firms, civic organizations and networks, and national elected bodies.

Once institutions are formed, note Patrick Heller and James Mahoney, "they are not neutral instruments, but mechanisms through which durable patterns of inequality are produced and reproduced" (2003, 29). Recent work on Bolivia, for instance, discusses the dissonance between generally sound civil service policies and the potent history of informal norms, for example in the clientelistic granting of jobs to political supporters of those in power (World Bank 2000b). Analysis of Peru's social fund in the early 1990s found that it was well targeted to the poor, but also well targeted to constituencies whose vote was important to the party in power (Schady 2000). Moreover, formal rules that restrict access to information, or that impose patrimonial restrictions on the organization of civil society actors, can also undermine the ability of the less powerful to question privileges of elite groups in the region. In assessing the rules of the game in a particular context, it is always important to analyze how these rules *really* work, or how informal and formal structures interact and whose interests are being served.

The many norms that sustain inequalities are both enforced by formal authority structures and self-enforced by the internalized dispositions of groups. Often culturally formed dispositions reflect and reinforce differences of power and wealth, simultaneously reducing the agency of subordinate groups, as noted earlier, and increasing the discriminatory or exclusionary beliefs and behaviors of dominant groups.[10]

It can be useful to characterize institutions in terms of the formal or informal rules that affect their openness or "permeability" to the influence of poor and subordinate groups. These rules include the following:

- *Competition rules,* determining how to win
- *Inclusion rules,* defining who can engage in what and
- *Accountability rules,* establishing a system for policy implementation, monitoring, and sanctioning policy makers when necessary

Competition rules affect the openness of institutions because they determine what resources are needed to win a given contest. This can be illustrated by comparing formal rules for gaining a seat in national legislatures, but elections are not the only field. Where election for national legislatures is based on majoritarian or winner-take-all electoral rules, for example, weak minority actors find it more difficult to advance their interests, since this requires greater effort to build alliances with other more powerful actors. For these reasons, majoritarian rules are often associated with a relatively closed environment, at least for minorities.[11] By contrast, proportional electoral rules may offer advantages because this kind of competition is less demanding of organizational capacity. Proportional representation, however, may bring other drawbacks for disadvantaged groups, including less decisive government, more fragmented opposition, or a greater voice for extremist positions. Similar considerations may apply at local as well as national levels.

Inclusion rules determine who can participate and in which issue areas. The rules can be used to exclude or favor disadvantaged groups by establishing formal employment, income, gender, geographic, racial, or religious requirements for specific entitlements. The most general example is the gradual extension of the electoral franchise. More targeted examples include workplace policies on affirmative action and the application of poverty-based geographic or income criteria for allocating public investments. Inclusion rules also define the policy areas where actors are entitled to participate; new advocacy work often begins with demanding legitimacy for broader civic engagement in a particular arena of decision making. Informal factors also play significant roles. A formal right to participation for poor and subordinate groups may in fact get little recognition. Cumbersome processes can make participation costly or easily manipulated (for example, long waits, documentation requirements, or bribes for access to public services).

Finally, *accountability rules* define who has authority, as well as responsibilities and processes for oversight. Strong accountability mechanisms allow actors to ensure that their representatives, service providers, or other leaders are answerable for their actions. This implies that constituents are informed about decisions, and that, where necessary, sanctions can be administered for wrongdoing (Schedler 1999).[12] In the Voices of the Poor study, poor people repeatedly described a lack of accountability on the part of elected officials. They also cited employers who refuse to pay them for work, police who harass them, doctors who charge side payments, teachers who don't show up, and so on (Narayan et al. 2000).

Accountability mechanisms can be vertical, involving mechanisms that hold state agencies accountable to citizens: these range from the periodic, indirect mechanism of elections to direct accountabilities of school administrations to parent boards. They can also be horizontal, involving mechanisms of reporting within the state. These are highly complementary processes, not alternative routes to accountability (see O'Donnell 1999; Fox 2000; Ackerman 2004).

To hold public agents accountable, actors need information. Without information citizens cannot monitor public decisions, budget allocations, or private company behavior. They cannot determine who is responsible for public acts, or who is not complying with past promises. If access to public information is restricted, or if media property is highly concentrated, the likelihood of poor people influencing decisions decreases.

The unity, strength, and ideology of dominant groups

A second factor to consider in the opportunity structure is the power, unity, and behavior of elites and other important nonpoor social actors. Indicators of fragmentation among elites can include the emergence of new political parties, social cleavages, or interest groups. Divisions may also be signaled by sudden changes or instability in the composition of electoral coalitions, in policies and policy decisions, or in senior appointments for government offices. These all reveal an inability among elites to produce clear and uncontested winners or sufficient consensus to advance a policy agenda.

A fragmented elite can facilitate the exercise of agency by subordinate groups because fragmentation weakens the elite's ability to oppose, repress, or neutralize the claims of challengers. Divisions can also encourage disgruntled elite factions to look for new sources of support, which may make them more receptive to the claims of weak actors. From the challengers' point of view, a divided elite thus expands the number of potential allies. The literature on Latin America points up tensions between, on one hand, central or state authorities seeking to expand agricultural production, reduce food prices, raise export earnings, and increase regional security and, on the other hand, entrenched landholders with little stake in improving opportunities for the rural poor.

In addition to elites, other important groups in a society may also oppose or support increased empowerment of poor or subordinate groups. In many developing countries, formal sector workers (notably in the public sector) and the middle class play an important role, although with less influence than in the industrial societies. Often they benefit from existing patterns of service provision, social security, or jobs, and so may oppose changes that threaten these relative advantages. One of the major issues for the success in empowerment of poorer groups is whether these middle groups opt to ally with the elites or with the poor.

At the local level, evidence from evaluations of community-driven development projects suggests that elite capture is an important problem, particularly in more heterogeneous communities (Mansuri and Rao 2004). Nevertheless, the literature also finds that local leadership can be an important asset if divisions are not too large and some processes exist for checks and balances. Many of these projects incorporate external facilitators and rules requiring more inclusive and transparent procedures precisely in order to support more equal and accountable relations between local elites and poor people.

State implementation capacity

The state's implementation capacity, the third dimension of the opportunity structure, refers to the effectiveness with which government authorities carry out policies that have been adopted. This can encompass the state's basic bureaucratic capabilities such as technical and managerial skills, the adequacy of administrative and financial resources for delivering services, and the actual reach of state agencies. While the first two aspects relate to the qualifications of the bureaucratic personnel and the existence of administrative infrastructure and procedures, the third refers to the ability of the state to penetrate and rule different geographic areas and arenas of social life. The ability to administer public resources effectively, to control corruption, to guarantee rule of law, to ensure citizen security, and to protect civil and political rights—all public goods that greatly affect the empowerment of poor and subordinate groups—requires strong state implementation capacities.

As Peter Evans has noted, "bureaucracy is not enough" (1995, 249). State implementation capacities are also determined by the specific ties that social groups establish with the state. As discussed below, implementation capacities can be very uneven across different functions, levels, and "localities" of the state, and strong capacities along some of these dimensions are *not* necessarily features of empowering opportunity structures. Certain capacities require a state that enjoys some autonomy from powerful groups in order to formulate and advance coherent goals that advance wider interests (Evans 1995).

Understanding the dynamics of the opportunity structure

As with the analysis of agency, inquiry into the opportunity structure requires exploring how the three influences—openness of institutions, unity and behaviors of dominant groups, and state implementation capacity—interact with each other to support or hinder the agency of weak actors. Poor and disadvantaged groups have the greatest chance of obtaining favorable outcomes when they operate in an open institutional context, where nonpoor social actors are fragmented or allied with the poor, and where state implementation capacity is strong. This ideal might be best typified by Scandinavian societies and states.

By contrast, empowerment is least likely when the context is closed, there is a strong and unified political and social elite, and there is strong implementation capacity. In this case, formal and informal institutions work in ways that prevent poor people's claims from being heard, and this is reinforced by a powerful and united elite that has strong bureaucratic means to effectively enforce its interests. Chile under authoritarian auspices may be the best Latin American example. Significant poverty reduction certainly can occur in such contexts, but the underlying processes will not be shaped by specific pressures for reform or proactive concerns about future elections. For some measures that require a long-term vision and do not offer short-term payoffs (for example, finding the budget for quality health care or for teachers in remote areas that have little electoral clout), this isolation from politics *can* bring benefits, but only if elites have some other interest in effecting pro-poor changes.[13]

It is also important to stress that the state is not monolithic. Elected bodies, the civil service, and the judiciary—and different levels within these organizations—often work at loggerheads. This unevenness can be very important for empowerment and development outcomes. Central, state, and local governments, the different branches and agencies, and their rules, leadership, political loyalties, and bureaucratic effectiveness will often need to be unpacked for sound analysis of the opportunity structure. For example, decentralization may increase local responsiveness and flexibility. But it also implies the incorporation of new actors into decision making and implementation, which may weaken the national state's ability to ensure the implementation of decisions. This is especially the case where local elite influences are strong and the state's technical capacities are weak.

Other combinations of the three variables would be expected to result in incomplete forms of empowerment in terms of the opportunity structure. Some degree of institutional permeability and elite fragmentation is indispensable for empowerment, with the former being of overriding importance. Aspirations cannot be voiced and heard in completely closed systems, unless elites are divided and a powerful policy champion can somehow be found. Even then, the reforms will also require a very strong state apparatus to counter the inevitable resistance.

Furthermore, there can be large gaps between formal and informal rules, as between formal democratic practices such as voter registration and genuine citizenship, or between participation in projects and the actual engagement and influence of weaker groups. The real rules of the games are products of the histories of power structures and the associated sociocultural processes, and understanding the opportunity structure will often require analyzing informal rules jointly with the behaviors and interests of elite groups.

In cases where there is an open context and strong state implementation capacities, but opposition is entrenched, poor people's claims can be voiced and heard. But whether they are converted into outcomes depends on how effective the elite or other powerful groups are in preventing implementation. This set of conditions is also likely to produce uneven results at best. Examples can be found in many arenas of public action in Brazil. Since the transition to democracy, Brazil has had a lively and open democratic process at both the national and local levels. The state also has a reasonably effective implementation capacity. Yet in many policy areas, entrenched opposition—by local elites in patron-client relationships, or by middle-class interests opposed to reform of an inequitable social security system—has effectively barred redistributive change. In such contexts, the informal influence of powerful, united actors often determines outcomes.

In many instances in Brazil, however, divisions exist between local, state, and national elites, and reforms are possible. This was the case with the participatory budgeting in Porto Alegre, as well as with a health workers' initiative in the very poor and highly unequal state of Ceará in the late 1980s and 1990s (Tendler 1997). Elite divisions have also opened the door to policy initiatives at the national level in both the Cardoso and Lula administrations.

Of the three influences on the opportunity structure, state implementation capacity is perhaps the least clear in its impact; moreover, in the long run it is largely a product of the openness and fragmentation of the political system. Indeed, implementation capacities can either help or hinder poorer groups, depending on the particular context. From the perspective of empowering weak actors, a second-best opportunity structure might be one where the context is open and poorer groups have ties to influential modernizing elites, but the state's implementation capacities are weak. Openness and elite fragmentation create opportunities for poor actors, but weak state capacity reduces the probability that their agency will be translated into outcomes. In certain localities, poor groups may attain some of their goals. The influence of local political conditions will make a large difference here, as in the other intermediate scenarios. In the case of a closed system and united elite, by contrast, weak capacities may prevent the state from enforcing unfavorable policies, or they may provide openings for disadvantaged groups to influence their local authorities. Thus, while implementation capacity is not a sufficient condition to explain outcomes that empower disadvantaged groups, the way state capacities vary across functions and levels of government and interact with the other two dimensions is nevertheless important for understanding the overall opportunity structure.

The possibilities for change diminish when poorer groups face combinations of disadvantages in the opportunity structure. The experience across municipalities in Bolivia is of interest here, given their relatively weak state capabilities and embedded patronage politics (World Bank 2000b). A policy known as Participación Popular (popular participation) was introduced by the national government in 1994 and extended in 2000. It involved a decentralization of decision making over budgetary transfers to elected local governments, along with the introduction of mechanisms to increase local accountability. The reform also legalized local-level civil society groups, of which campesino syndicates were the most important in many parts of the country. While the changes brought benefits on average (Faguet 2002), the dynamics depended on the local institutional context. In some parts of the country, notably the Cochabamba valley, elite domination was relatively limited and poorer groups were highly organized, increasing their capacity for agency. There the legal changes appear to be bringing about better public action. In the city of Sucre in Potosí, by contrast, which has traditionally had a more closed political culture and a stronger elite, the decentralizing reforms may have increased the power of local elites and thus worked to further disempower the poor (Gray-Molina 2002; Calderón and Szmukler 2004; Blackburn 2001).

Interactions between Agency and Opportunity Structure

As noted above, there is a powerful two-way influence between the structure of political opportunities and the agency of poorer groups. Any analysis must therefore include an assessment of how these forces interact to contribute to (or block) empowerment and improved development outcomes. As Joel Migdal (2001) argues, state and society embody a melange of institutions and multiple sets of rules that are in continuous competition for predominance. Openings can occur in this complex playing field when the status quo can be successfully challenged, and in such situations tangible benefits for the poor may result. The EDUCO program in El Salvador is a case in point.

In the early 1990s a new administration in El Salvador needed to establish legitimacy after a horrific civil war. This opened the door for sweeping pro-poor changes in education policies. Among other goals, the government sought to rapidly expand the number of schools by tapping into the desires, energies, and inventiveness of parents in very poor rural areas. Parents were encouraged to form voluntary associations to oversee schools. Community associations received legal authority, funds, and training to manage school budgets, rebuild and equip schools, and hire and fire teachers.

Between 1991 and 1999, enrollment in EDUCO schools expanded from 8,400 children to 237,000. Student performance was comparable to that of students in conventional schools, including those in better-off areas of the country. The program's achievements reflected both a favorable opportunity structure and effective agency on the part of poor rural Salvadorans.

The opportunity structure within which the program was launched featured a new and relatively open institutional system without entrenched rules of the game. An essential ingredient in the program's success was the high level of state implementation capacity under Minister of Education Cecilia Gallardo de Cano, a well-connected and technically strong policy champion. The minister enjoyed close ties to President Alfredo Cristiani and the legislative assembly, and secured sustainable state financing for the program. The ministry overcame numerous barriers to administering the new decentralized program in very poor areas of the country by constantly adapting program rules, resources, and staffing. Strong backing from the World Bank and other donors facilitated the program's learning-by-doing, and civic and private providers helped to fill gaps.

The pilot also benefited from lack of concerted opposition from nonpoor groups. The country's elite was fragmented in the wake of the war. The relatively small and weak union movement displayed little interest in the impoverished rural areas where the program began. Over time, as EDUCO expanded, the ministry faced street protests from teachers over perceived threats to their tenure and career paths. But negotiations with the union resulted in an agreement not to extend parental authority in urban areas to the hiring and firing of teachers.

On the agency side, the program quickly strengthened the capacities of an ever-growing network of parent associations. These formed federations at the departmental level and even established a presence in the capital, changing the pattern of education policy making and implementation throughout the country. EDUCO built in many design elements from other successful community-driven development models. It disseminated public information about the reforms, required a demonstration of community commitment, and matched new local responsibilities with training and resources. It also actively supported the creation of institutional mechanisms that would foster transparency and accountability to those with the biggest stake in the program's success—the parents of schoolchildren. Together these activities facilitated the transfer of decisions and resources to the local level and supported the development of institutions that helped poor people to mobilize and assert their interests.

The experience suggests that well-designed and well-delivered programs that enjoy strategic support at the national level and resonate closely with local priorities can overcome seemingly weak institutions and political opposition, as well as severe poverty and a society torn apart by war and intense mistrust of government. From this perspective, reformist state coalitions that can work in partnership with society's most disadvantaged groups can be a force for striking institutional transformations.

Empowerment and Development Outcomes

We turn now to the second part of the framework for evaluating empowerment: assessing the impact on development outcomes. The hypothesis is that increased empowerment, in the sense outlined in the preceding section, has a causative influence on factors such as incomes, health status, security, education, and self-esteem of the poor. However, a wide range of factors are germane to the realization of development outcomes. Development actions may include public spending on roads, schools, health centers, and safety nets; private investment in machines and skills; pricing polices; and financial flows, to cite just a few examples. The research design must therefore address the fundamental question of *how much* of a given outcome can be attributed to empowerment rather than to the many other influences on the development process being analyzed. Figure 2.2 illustrates this evaluation challenge in its simplest form, analogous to a "reduced form" account in a simple model of determination of outcomes. This illustrates the view that empowerment-related factors are omitted variables in traditional accounts.

However, this is problematic even as a starting point for an evaluation. In particular, it fails to take account of the interactions between empowerment processes and other factors affecting development outcomes (and runs the risk of treating empowerment and other factors as exogenous). For example, if public spending on social services goes up under participatory budgeting in a Brazilian municipality, is that a product of the empowerment implicit in the institutional reform, or simply a change in policy for other reasons?

A slightly more complicated schema is presented in figure 2.3, which builds in two extensions to the simple hypothesis of figure 2.2. First, poorer groups can potentially influence *policy making* (how much is spent on roads

Figure 2.2   The Simple Hypothesis: Empowerment Affects Outcomes

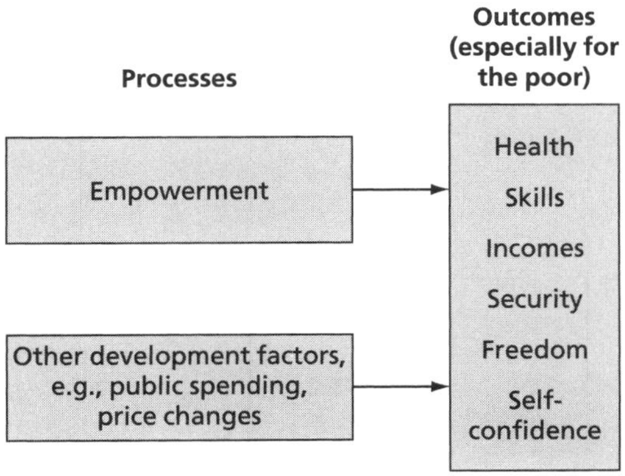

Figure 2.3   Some Interactions between Empowerment, Policy, and Conditions

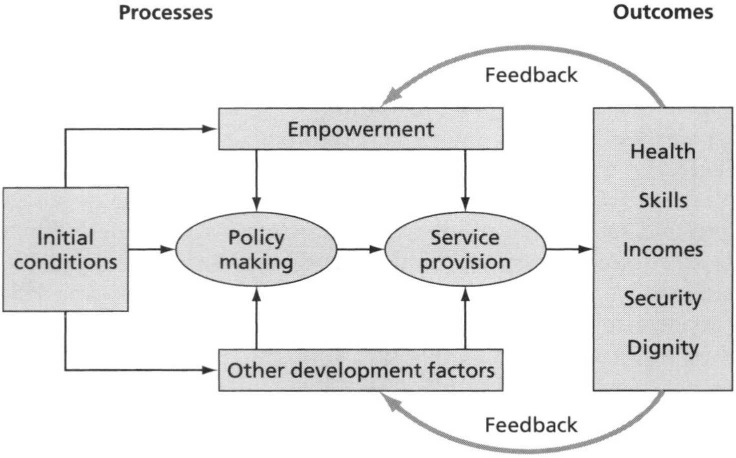

or schools, what are the design features of policies or programs?) by exercising political voice. They can also influence *service provision* (do teachers turn up to teach, are roads maintained, do police treat poor groups fairly?) by exercising client power. Both clearly matter for development effectiveness.

Second, there are potentially significant feedback loops on both empowerment and other development factors. These may be positive, as when economic and other outcomes for the poor feed back into their capacity to make choices or hold authorities accountable. They can also be negative, however, and trigger resistance from other groups, heightened conflict, or decreased economic opportunities.

This flow chart, although still simplified, has significant implications for evaluation of empowerment, and especially for the types of information required. Independent sources of information on the following will be needed:

- Initial (or baseline) conditions regarding influences both on empowerment and on wider development forces of importance to the outcomes under study
- Explicit treatment of the social, cultural, and political *context* within which actions take place
- Intermediate processes and final development outcomes, with particular attention to capturing the impacts that resulted from a change in one or two of the causal influence(s) on empowerment
- Other important influences on the processes and outcomes under study

Although we have said that assessing the impact on outcomes must be the second part of any approach to evaluating empowerment, this step is deliberately left general or, more accurately, underspecified. This is because most domains of public action come with well-developed sectoral frameworks for the flows of causal influence between policy, implementation, and outcomes. The causal framework for getting better schooling is quite different from that for getting better roads, even if underlying principles are similar. As figure 2.3 shows, incorporating empowerment is not just a matter of adding another variable, but entails applying hypotheses of how empowerment processes should modify or be integrated within these established frameworks. For example, in the realm of education, the literature typically argues that outcomes are influenced by teacher presence (not always guaranteed), the quality and motivation of teachers, and complementary teaching materials. The empowerment processes discussed in the preceding section need to be incorporated within sector-specific frameworks, for example, via the effects of empowerment on the behavior of teachers or health providers.

Some Methodological Issues in Evaluating Empowerment and Its Effects

Empowerment-related factors are typically missing from both the design and interpretation of current studies of development processes. But taking account of empowerment can increase our understanding of what does and does not work, over and above the "traditional" influences on development. This in turn can inform the design of public actions that will achieve better results, from school attendance to health status to incomes of the poor.

As noted in the chapter introduction, despite growing interest in the role of empowerment in development, there have been few structured impact evaluations that systematically take account of both empowerment-related and other influences. Such evaluations would allow the contribution of empowerment to be measured and compared with other influences on developmental outcomes, whether at the household, local, or society-wide level. This is essential to assessing *how much* difference empowerment can make to development effectiveness, which in turn provides guidance on how much effort should be made to foster greater empowerment. Empirical analysis of the causal influences on empowerment itself can help shape the design of effective public action to empower poorer groups in diverse social and institutional contexts.

Sound approaches to evaluating empowerment can draw on general experience in evaluating the impact of development change on outcomes. However, the nature of empowerment raises special challenges in interpretation. For this reason the use of mixed methods—combining quantitative and qualitative techniques—is an intrinsic feature of a sound evaluation. This chapter does not deal with technical questions of how to undertake an evaluation.[14] Rather, we outline some important issues that have to be addressed in any evaluation, and that evaluators, advocates, and policy makers need to take into account.

Key Evaluation Challenges

The structure of the processes described above suggests that there will generally be three principal challenges in evaluating empowerment, all common to many other evaluation studies.

The first is *identification*, that is, distinguishing the influence of empowerment from other possible simultaneous influences. This classic evaluation problem is typically tackled by attempting to quantify the impact of an intervention and comparing it with the counterfactual of a case in which everything else was the same *except* the intervention—the "treatment" group and the "control" group, respectively.

Identification is ideally achieved with a controlled experiment, with random assignment of participants to treatment and control groups. These remain rare in the development field, unfortunately. Alternative approaches make use of natural experiments or apply a variety of econometric techniques that seek to statistically identify the effects of some variables while controlling for others. To get statistically robust results, such techniques need large numbers of observations ("large N") of households or communities, even when the relevant experiment includes only a small number of independent effects, such as the implementation or nonimplementation of land titling over a set of geographical areas.

The second challenge, interlinked with identification, is to understand *interactions with context*. The ways in which empowerment-related action works typically depend on the sociopolitical context. Even if an average effect of an intervention (such as participatory budgeting or greater community influence on schooling) can be identified and calculated, the variation across distinct contexts may be of equal or greater importance. Such variation can involve differences in the nature of an intervention; for example, participatory budgeting may mean something quite different from one municipality to another, implying differences in "treatments." There can also be variation in how the intervention responds to different sociopolitical contexts (heterogeneity of treatment effects, in the language of evaluation).

Interpretation of process is the third problem. In the case of empowerment, it is important to consider the process as well as to measure effects. This implies use of a range of ethnographic and other sociological techniques that support such an interpretive approach. Examples include semi-structured interviews with participants, structured participation (as in rapid rural appraisal), participant observation, and in-depth interviews with key informants. These are best combined with in-depth descriptive accounts of the historical and contemporary processes of change. As Rao and Woolcock (2003) argue, these are powerful complements to statistical large-N approaches. Best results are obtained through the interaction between statistical and qualitative approaches, in which each can influence the design of the other.

In cases where interventions are taking place in specific parts of a society—in certain schools, health centers, municipalities, or geographic areas, for example, and not others—it is possible to take advantage of the observed variation to deal with issues of identification, context, and process. This chapter has focused on cases for which there is such within-society variation, since these offer the greatest potential for the application of the extended version of classic evaluation techniques.

Even more difficult issues arise, however, in the case of society-wide changes, such as the introduction of a participatory approach to the design of a poverty reduction strategy. This too is a classic evaluation problem, dealt with in economics, for example, by modeling macro or economy-wide processes. It is probably fair to say that there are no economy-wide models that incorporate empowerment. However, there is still scope for systematically framing hypotheses of how empowerment may influence economy-wide processes, using a mixture of interpretation of process, comparative case study across countries, and before-and-after examinations.

Designing an Inquiry with Multiple Methods

Taking into account these issues, an inquiry into empowerment requires two specific kinds of hypotheses. First, there are hypotheses about the processes affecting empowerment, which include influences on agency and on opportunity structure. Second, there are hypotheses about the influence of empowerment on other development outcomes, preferably nested within frameworks that specify "traditional" influences on outcomes for schooling, road maintenance, management of risks, and so on. A serious evaluation effort requires the use of both sets of hypotheses as well as the evaluation techniques sketched above.

The preferred approach in any evaluation will combine statistically robust large-N analysis with in-depth case studies. However, it is often the case that resources are not available for such a large-scale evaluation exercise. Another alternative is to draw on the rich tradition of comparative small-N studies of policy or institutional changes across subnational units or regions within countries. This can look at provinces, cities, legal or geographic regions, economic sectors and so forth within the same country, or it can analyze similar units across countries. As Richard Snyder points out, "within nation comparisons do not *necessarily* improve our ability to hold constant cultural, historical, economic and socioeconomic conditions: there may be as much, if not more, variation within countries as between them" (2001, 96). Alternatively, one can control better for these explanatory factors by looking at contiguous units with otherwise similar characteristics across national borders or subnational boundaries. A case study framework that combines within- and between-nation cases, suggests Snyder, can provide a way forward.

Jonathan Fox also proposes the use of a comparative case study approach to uncover the conditions under which promising policies for increasing empowerment have their intended effects. His proposed matrix, shown in table 2.1, provides cells that can be filled in with field research. If a national policy reform produces significant subnational results in the lower left cell (good results in an area with low agency), further in-depth research will be

Table 2.1 A Comparative Case Study Approach to Evaluating Empowerment

Opportunity context and degree of implementation of enabling reforms	*Agency*	
	Low	*High*
Low	Cases here have starting points that are difficult for empowerment processes, but needs are high.	Cases here have high levels of potential agency or social mobilization but weak initial contexts for the exercise of agency.
High	Cases here have favorable opportunity contexts for empowerment, but low levels of initial agency, with uncertain outcomes.	Cases here have high potential for empowerment through advantageous initial conditions in terms of both agency and opportunity context.

Source: Adapted from an unpublished memorandum by Jonathan Fox.

Note: Both opportunity context and agency are continuums, with many cases falling in between the low and high ends of the scales.

valuable for understanding how reform could be effective even when groups were initially unempowered.[15]

Such case study approaches do not provide statistically robust results, but they can lead to valuable insights. They can also, of course, be applied in concert with large-N results, when the data allow, for a preferred mix of techniques.

A valuable means to ensure that the results from evaluations will be used to inform future policy actions, although this is rarely easy to implement, is to engage directly in the research program those actors who are important for effective follow-up. Participatory evaluation designs entail an inclusive learning and action process whereby the relevant stakeholders can negotiate study goals and indicators; engage jointly in the design, collection, analysis, and quality control of data; and collaborate in dissemination and follow-up of results. As empowerment of poor and excluded groups is a clear objective of this work, these groups need to be given a central role so they can influence and benefit from the study agenda and process. There are now well-established planning, management, and research tools for making this happen.

Illustrating Evaluation Challenges

While space does not allow a full account of an evaluation in this paper, we conclude by briefly mentioning some of the issues with respect to several cases under implementation at the time of writing. These include evaluations of participatory budgeting in Brazil, of a natural experiment in land titling in the province of Buenos Aires, Argentina, and of school decentralization in Central America.

Participatory Budgeting in Brazil

In the case of participatory budgeting in Brazil, there have been extensive, in-depth ethnographic or sociological studies, especially of Porto Alegre, along with some essentially qualitative comparisons between cities.[16] Such studies have been rich in descriptions of processes, with documentation of transitions in the aspirations, behaviors, and mobilization of subordinate groups and their interactions with a shifting opportunity structure at the municipality level (for example, see Abers 2000; Baiocchi 2002, 2003). What has been lacking is an analysis that integrates such in-depth accounts of process with consideration of how the role of participatory budgeting may vary in the diverse sociopolitical and economic contexts across Brazil. While the Porto Alegre experience is widely known, participatory budgeting has in fact been introduced in approximately 100 Brazilian municipalities spanning a wide range of types. There is also a much larger number of municipalities in the country where it has not been introduced. This opens the door for a large-N approach.

The challenge for such an approach is that participatory budgeting has not been introduced in a random fashion. While it is possible to control for certain variables (for example, location and wealth of the municipality), it would be expected that unobservables, such as factors related to social and political mobilization, would have important effects. Such factors might affect the "selection" of the treatment group—that is, choices by localities to adopt participatory budgeting—and the consequences of interactions with local conditions. One method being used to address this challenge in current research is a technique known as regression discontinuity.[17]

The assumption is that where there is a discontinuity in some process affecting a treatment, cases that are otherwise similar, including with respect to unobservable constant factors, will experience different treatments. In the case of participatory budgeting, the discontinuity being investigated stems from election outcomes and government formation in closely contested elections. Local governments formed by the Partido dos Trabalhadores (PT) had a higher probability of adopting participatory budgeting. Comparing cases with broadly similar voting patterns but different governments due to close contests—and so different probability of adopting participatory budgeting—has the potential for separating the effects of the intervention from the effects of more constant background factors.[18] This approach will also potentially allow for estimation of any differences in the varying contexts of Brazil with respect to geography, wealth, human capital, and so on.

Use of this statistical technique is being combined with in-depth comparisons of matched pairs of municipalities, with and without participatory budgeting, to provide a richer understanding of the processes at work. Final results were not available at the time of writing, but preliminary results suggest that the adoption of participatory budgeting does indeed make a statistically significant difference to some behaviors of municipalities. At least in some cases, the evidence suggests that what makes the difference is the institutional change itself rather than the distinct histories of the different cities or towns.

Land Titling in Argentina

The case of land titling provides an example of a different approach to the evaluation challenge. It is hypothesized that granting of land titles may increase the "capacity to aspire" and thus increase the organizational capacity of poor families, and that local governments and utilities may be more responsive to citizens with legal status as property holders. In the Argentine case it is possible to make use of a natural experiment (see Galiani, Kessler, and Schargrodsky 2004).

In 1981 some 2,000 poor families carried out a large land "invasion" in an urban area in the province of Buenos Aires. Three years later the provincial government sought to transfer title to the squatters, with compensation to the original owners. Some of the former owners accepted, while others did not; as a result, some but not all of the squatter families received land titles. There was no reason to assume any relationship between whether a former landowner accepted the offer and the characteristics of the poor family occupying the land. This, then, was a potentially "clean" natural experiment in which otherwise similar families with and without titles could be compared.

The evaluation combined in-depth qualitative investigation (involving interviews with a small number of households and key informants) with a statistical comparison between the two groups that considered variables such as participation in associational activity and access to services. In this case, the qualitative and statistical analyses yielded different preliminary results. The qualitative analysis suggested that titling indeed had an impact on families through empowerment-related processes, in terms of their reported attitudes and behaviors as well as the perceived response from the government and private utilities. However, with only minor exceptions, this same effect did not show up in statistically significant differences. As a "result" this may be disappointing. It is unclear whether the qualitative approach is capturing processes that are not representative, or whether these effects are swamped by other factors, most likely the highly turbulent national economic context in Argentina during this period. Nevertheless, the case is still interesting as an example of a natural experiment and as a case showing the importance of triangulation between different methodological approaches.

School Decentralization in Central America

Finally, there has been significant econometric investigation of greater school autonomy in Central America (for example, Jimenez, King, and Tan 2003). In the case of El Salvador this research found significant effects, with greater enrollment of poorer groups in EDUCO schools and test scores equivalent to other schools, despite lower socioeconomic status in EDUCO schools. What has been missing from these studies is an integrated approach that documents differences in both outcomes and processes across different contexts. New research is exploring two types of context. First, there is a comparative case study at the country level examining autonomous schooling reforms in El Salvador, Guatemala, Honduras, and Nicaragua. Second, within-country variation across schools is being examined in the case of Honduras, using both large-N analysis and in-depth school and community studies to document the effects of school reforms and associated processes. Since the reforms were not introduced randomly in any of the countries, important challenges remain in identifying effects of the reform. But the combination of systematic comparative case study, at the country and school-community levels, and statistical analysis promises a richer account than we have now on the nature of these processes.

While final results were not available from these cases at the time of writing, they do serve to illustrate some of the issues in evaluation methodology that have been introduced here. We can look forward to a rich range of results from these and other structured evaluations of the process of empowerment and its effect on development outcomes.

Conclusion

The concept of empowerment is relatively new. Different disciplinary perspectives are involved, and the contexts in which evaluation is of interest vary considerably. The framework for evaluating empowerment presented here is intended as part of an ongoing process. It is hoped that this collective work will provide both meat for understanding the role of empowerment and ideas for modification of the analytical approach suggested here.

Many development practitioners and observers, activists, and poor people believe that empowerment lies at the core of effective development—and especially sustainable poverty reduction, in all its dimensions. We are sympathetic to this view. However, to genuinely push the debate forward, it is critical that assessment of empowerment be integrated within systematic approaches to evaluation, with respect to both the forces affecting empowerment and the possible impacts of empowerment on development outcomes. Development is a complex business, and there is a wide array of competing demands on the resources, effort, and political capital of different groups in a society. Only when it can be systematically evaluated will empowerment be accorded its appropriate place in the diagnosis and practice of development.

Notes

Valuable comments were received on earlier versions of this chapter from Ruth Alsop, Kathy Bain, Lynn Bennett, Peter Evans, Jonathan Fox, Peter Hakim, Patrick Heller, Phil Keefer, Yasuhiko Matsuda, Ernesto May, Deepa Narayan, Guillermo Perry, Lant Pritchett, Ray Rist, Judith Tendler, Warren van Wicklin, and Michael Woolcock.

1.   For sociological approaches that develop such relational and categorical accounts of inequality see the work of Bourdieu (for example, 1990) and Tilly (1999).

2.   For discussion of intrinsic and instrumental effects of the related concepts of agency, freedom, and capabilities, see Sen (1985a, 1985b, 1992).

3.   There is a large literature on social capital that cannot be summarized here. See Woolcock (1998) and Woolcock and Narayan (2000) for useful review of key concepts and recent literature, and Fox (1996) for an application relevant to the approach here.

4.   For a useful list of indicators for measuring local organizational capacities, see Uphoff (1997).

5.   Work on cross-country indicators of empowerment is part of a global empowerment study under way at the World Bank in 2004, though we would emphasize the risks of relying on either country or local indicators that are not interpreted in terms of local context.

6.   Scott (1985) shows that to understand how subordinate groups achieve goals and rebel, one must consider the way in which these groups use and interact with the specific system of values in which they operate. Forms of resistance that work within the system can be a practical choice that does not imply acceptance of the system's values.

7.   Tarrow (1996, 54) defines the political opportunity structure as the "consistent— but not necessarily formal, permanent or national—signals to social or political actors which either encourage or discourage them to use their internal resources to form social movements." Although Tarrow focuses on the role of the political opportunity structure in the emergence of social movements, other authors have also related its features to the success or failure of such movements. See also Tarrow (1998) and Kitschelt (1986).

8.   The international relations literature has developed different models and typologies to address these transnational interactions (Evans, Jacobson, and Putnam 1993; Risse-Kappen 1995; Keck and Sikkink 1998). While some approaches concentrate on the impact of international variables on domestic factors, others emphasize how domestic factors operate within given international constraints. Recent work has extended the political opportunity structure framework to the international arena (Khagram, Riker, and Sikkink 2002). Specifically, these studies show how actors use opportunities found in one of these arenas to achieve results in the other (Sikkink 2003). The "boomerang" model (Keck and Sikkink 1998) and the "spiral" model (Risse, Ropp, and Sikkink 1999) have been used to explain possible patterns of actions developed under those circumstances. However, actors also face situations in which closed international opportunities hinder gains achieved in the domestic environment, or in which both national and international opportunity structures are closed. The international relations literature has also emphasized that these patterns vary. For example, international institutions dealing with human rights have been more open to transnational activists than those dealing with trade, and regional institutions in Europe have been more open than those in Asia.

9.   Peter Siavelis (2002) argues that informal institutions can also bring important benefits. He shows how informal coordination mechanisms were used to enhance the democratic transition and governability in Chile in the face of difficult formal institutional arrangements (a very strong presidency and majoritarian representation in the legislature).

10. See Rao and Walton (2004) for discussion of the dynamic influence of cultural factors on such inequalities. This approach draws on the work of Bourdieu and Tilly, among others.

11. An exception to the difficult context of majoritarian systems would be the U.S. context, where a consolidated two-party system leads candidates to focus on swing districts—which may or may not contain poorer groups seeking influence. In more typical cases around the world where there are more than two parties, or where the political parties are not the same from one election to the next, winner-take-all approaches can make it difficult for poorer sectors to gain national influence.

12. It should be noted that elections, while important, often provide insufficient means of holding public authorities accountable. First, most bureaucrats are not selected through elections, and competition rules do not allow citizens to sanction their performance (Manin, Przeworski, and Stokes 1999, 21). Second, a large literature on representation and accountability has questioned the efficacy of competition and elections as a privileged mechanism of political accountability. Manin, Przeworski, and Stokes (1999), for example, argue that an intrinsic limitation of electoral competition is that it grants citizens only "one shot" to punish or reward numerous governmental decisions. They also argue that there is no way to tell whether a particular electoral result was guided by prospective or retrospective concerns. Finally, they note that information deficits on the part of most citizens make it difficult for them to adequately evaluate government performance and decisions.

13. Drèze and Sen (1989) argue that part of the progress in human development indicators for the poor in Chile under Pinochet was due to the political need to show progress to poorer groups, in light of both external pressure and internal potential threat. There was, nevertheless, a more concerted move to improve social conditions after the democratic transition.

14. For accessible discussions see Ravallion (2001) for an introduction, Baker (2000) for a survey of techniques and examples of applications, and Rao and Woolcock (2003) for a discussion of mixed methods in evaluation.

15. This section and the matrix draw on a helpful memorandum by Jonathan Fox, reviewing an earlier draft of this paper.

16. Baiocchi et al. (2004) provide a brief account of the approach and initial results.

17. See Baiocchi and others (2004) for a discussion of the technique in the case of the Brazil evaluation, and Angrist and Lavy (1999) for an example of its application.

18. The issues are more complex than this, especially with respect to separating the influence of a PT government from adoption of participatory budgeting. The purpose here is to illustrate the kinds of issues to be considered in evaluations.

References

Abers, Rebecca Neaera. 2000. *Inventing Local Democracy: Grassroots Politics in Brazil*. Boulder, CO: Lynne Rienner.

Ackerman, John. 2004. "State-Society Synergy for Accountability: Lessons for the World Bank." World Bank Working Paper 30, World Bank, Washington, DC.

Angrist, Joshua, and Victor Lavy. 1999. "New Evidence on Classroom Computers and Pupil Learning." NBER Working Paper 7424, National Bureau of Economic Research, Cambridge, MA.

Appadurai, Arjun. 2004. "The Capacity to Aspire: Culture and the Terms of Recognition." In *Culture and Public Action*, ed. Vijayendra Rao and Michael Walton, 59–84. Stanford, CA: Stanford University Press.

Baiocchi, Gianpaolo. 2002. "Synergizing Civil Society: State-Civil Society Regimes in Porto Alegre, Brazil." *Political Power and Social Theory* 15: 3–86.

———. 2003. "Participation, Activism and Politics: The Porto Alegre Experiment in Participatory Governance." In *Deepening Democracy: Institutional Innovations in Empowered Participatory Governance*, ed. Archon Fung and Erik Olin Wright. Real Utopias Project, vol. 4. New York: Verso.

Baiocchi, Gianpaolo, Shubham Chaudhuri, Patrick Heller, and Marcelo Kunrath Silva. 2004. "The Evaluation of Participatory Budgeting in Brazilian Municipalities: An Interim Report." World Bank, Washington, DC.

Baker, Judy L. 2000. *Evaluating the Impact of Development Projects on Poverty: A Handbook for Practitioners*. Washington, DC: World Bank.

Blackburn, James. 2001. "Popular Participation in a Prebendal Society: An Actor-Oriented Analysis of Participatory Municipal Planning in Sucre, Bolivia." PhD diss., Institute of Development Studies, University of Sussex, Brighton, UK.

Bourdieu, Pierre. 1990. *The Logic of Practice*. Stanford, CA: Stanford University Press.

Calderón, Fernando, and Alicia Szmukler. 2004. "Political Culture and Development." In *Culture and Public Action*, ed. Vijayendra Rao and Michael Walton. Stanford, CA: Stanford University Press.

Drèze, Jean, and Amartya Sen. 1989. *Hunger and Public Action*. New York: Oxford University Press.

Evans, Peter. 1995. *Embedded Autonomy: States and Industrial Transformation*. Princeton, NJ: Princeton University Press.

Evans, Peter, Harold Jacobson, and Robert Putnam, eds. 1993. *Double-Edged Diplomacy: International Bargaining and Domestic Politics*. Studies in International Political Economy 25. Berkeley: University of California Press.

Faguet, Jean-Paul. 2002. "Does Decentralization Increase Government Responsiveness to Local Needs? Evidence from Bolivia." Policy Research Working Paper 2516, World Bank, Washington, DC.

Fox, Jonathan. 1992. *The Politics of Food in Mexico: State Power and Social Mobilization*. Ithaca, NY: Cornell University Press.

———. 1996. "How Does Civil Society Thicken? The Political Construction of Social Capital in Rural Mexico." *World Development* 24 (6): 1089–1103.

———. 2000. "Civil Society and Political Accountability: Propositions for Discussion." Paper presented at conference on Institutions, Accountability and Democratic Governance in Latin America, Helen Kellogg Institute for International Studies, University of Notre Dame, Notre Dame, IN, May 8.

Galiani, Sebastián, Gabriel Kessler, and Ernesto Schargrodsky. 2004. "Land for the Poor: Evaluating the Effects of Property Rights on Empowerment." Universidad San Andres, Universidad Nacional de General Sarmiento, and Universidad Torcuato di Tella, Argentina.

Gray-Molina, George. 2002. "The Offspring of 1952: Poverty, Exclusion and the Promise of Popular Participation." Paper presented at conference on The Bolivian

Revolution at 50: Comparative Views on Social, Economic and Political Change, Harvard University, Cambridge, MA, May 2–3.

Hardin, Garrett. 1968. "The Tragedy of the Commons." *Science* 162: 1243–48.

Heller, Patrick, and James Mahoney. 2003. "The Resilience and Transformability of Social Inequality in Latin America." Background paper for *Inequality in Latin America and the Caribbean: Breaking with History?* Latin America and Caribbean Region, World Bank, Washington, DC.

Hirschman, Albert O. 1982. *Shifting Involvements: Private Interest and Public Action.* Princeton, NJ: Princeton University Press.

Jimenez, Emmanuel, Elizabeth M. King, and Jee-Peng Tan. 2003. "Economic Analysis of Education Investments." In *Measuring Government Performance in the Delivery of Public Services.* Vol. 2 of *Handbook on Public Sector Performance Reviews,* ed. Anwar Shah. Washington, DC: World Bank.

Kabeer, Naila. 1999. "Resources, Agency, Achievements: Reflections on the Measurement of Women's Empowerment." *Development and Change* 30: 435–64.

Keck, Margaret, and Kathryn Sikkink. 1998. *Activists beyond Borders: Advocacy Networks in International Politics.* Ithaca, NY: Cornell University Press.

Khagram, Sanjeev, James Riker, and Kathryn Sikkink. 2002. *Restructuring World Politics: Transnational Social Movements, Networks and Norms.* Minneapolis: University of Minnesota Press.

Kitschelt, Herbert. 1986. "Political Opportunity Structures and Political Protest: Anti-Nuclear Movements in Four Democracies." *British Journal of Political Science* 16 (1): 57–85.

Levi, Margaret. 1988. *Of Rule and Revenue.* Berkeley: University of California Press.

Lichbach, Mark I. 1998. *The Rebel's Dilemma.* Ann Arbor: University of Michigan Press.

Manin, Bernard, Adam Przeworski, and Susan Stokes. 1999. "Elections and Representation." In *Democracy, Accountability and Representation,* ed. Adam Przeworski, Bernard Manin, and Susan Stokes. Cambridge: Cambridge University Press.

Mansuri, Ghazala, and Vijayendra Rao. 2004. "Community-Based (and Driven) Development: A Critical Review." *World Bank Research Observer* 19 (1): 1–39.

Migdal, Joel S. 2001. *State in Society: Studying How States and Societies Transform and Constitute One Another.* Cambridge: Cambridge University Press.

Narayan, Deepa, ed. 2002. *Empowerment and Poverty Reduction: A Sourcebook.* Washington, DC: World Bank.

Narayan, Deepa, with Raj Patel, Kai Schafft, Anne Rademacher, and Sarah Koch-Schulte. 2000. *Voices of the Poor: Can Anyone Hear Us?* New York: Oxford University Press for the World Bank.

North, Douglass C. 1990. *Institutions, Institutional Change and Economic Performance.* Cambridge: Cambridge University Press.

O'Donnell, Guillermo. 1999. "Horizontal Accountability in New Democracies." In *The Self-Restraining State: Power and Accountability in New Democracies*, ed. Andreas Schedler, Larry Diamond, and Marc F. Plattner, 29–52. Boulder, CO: Lynne Rienner.

Olsen, Mancur. 1973. *The Logic of Collective Action: Public Goods and the Theory of Groups*. Cambridge, MA: Harvard University Press.

Ostrom, Elinor. 1990. *Governing the Commons: The Evolution of Institutions for Collective Action*. Cambridge: Cambridge University Press.

Rao, Vijayendra, and Michael Walton. 2004. "Culture and Public Action: Relationality, Equality of Agency, and Development." In *Culture and Public Action*, ed. Vijayendra Rao and Michael Walton, 3–36. Stanford, CA: Stanford University Press.

Rao, Vijayendra, and Michael Woolcock. 2003. "Integrating Qualitative and Quantitative Approaches in Program Evaluation." In *Tool Kit for Evaluating the Poverty and Distributional Impact of Economic Policies*, ed. François Bourguignon and Luiz Pereira da Silva. New York: Oxford University Press for the World Bank.

Ravallion, Martin. 2001. "The Mystery of the Vanishing Benefits: An Introduction to Impact Evaluation." *World Bank Economic Review* 15 (1): 115–40.

Risse, Thomas, Stephen Ropp, and Kathryn Sikkink, eds. 1999. *The Power of Human Rights: International Norms and Domestic Change*. Cambridge: Cambridge University Press.

Risse-Kappen, Thomas, ed. 1995. *Bringing Transnational Relations Back In: Non-State Actors, Domestic Structures and International Institutions*. Cambridge: Cambridge University Press.

Schady, Norbert. 2000. "Political Economy of Expenditures by the Peruvian Social Fund (FONCODES), 1991–95." *American Political Science Review* 94 (2): 289–304.

Schedler, Andreas. 1999. "Conceptualizing Accountability." In *The Self-Restraining State: Power and Accountability in New Democracies*, ed. Andreas Schedler, Larry Diamond, and Marc F. Plattner, 13–28. Boulder, CO: Lynne Rienner.

Scheper-Hughes, Nancy. 1992. *Death Without Weeping: The Violence of Everyday Life in Brazil*. Berkeley: University of California Press.

Scott, James. 1985. *Weapons of the Weak: Everyday Forms of Peasant Resistance*. New Haven, CT: Yale University Press.

Sen, Amartya. 1985a. *Commodities and Capabilities*. Amsterdam: Elsevier.

———. 1985b. "Well-Being, Agency and Freedom: The Dewey Lectures." *Journal of Philosophy* 82 (4): 169–221.

———. 1992. *Inequality Reexamined*. Cambridge, MA: Harvard University Press.

———. 1999. *Development as Freedom*. New York: Knopf.

Siavelis, Peter. 2002. "Informal Institutions and Democratization: Theoretical Lessons from Chile." Paper presented at conference on Informal Institutions and Politics in the Developing World, Weatherhead Center for International Affairs, Harvard University, Cambridge, MA, April 5–6.

Sikkink, Kathryn. 2003. "Beyond the Boomerang: Transnational Networks and the Dynamic Interaction of Domestic and International Opportunity Structures." Paper presented at workshop on Patterns of Dynamic Multilevel Governance, Bellagio, Italy, July 22–26.

Snyder, Richard. 2001. "Scaling Down: The Subnational Comparative Method." *Studies in Comparative International Development* 36 (1): 93–110.

Tarrow, Sidney. 1996. "States and Opportunities: The Political Structuring of Social Movements." In *Comparative Perspectives on Social Movements: Political Opportunities, Mobilizing Structures, and Cultural Framings*, ed. Doug McAdam, John McCarthy, and Mayer Zald. Cambridge: Cambridge University Press.

———. 1998. *Power in Movement: Social Movements and Contentious Politics*. Cambridge: Cambridge University Press.

Tendler, Judith. 1997. *Good Government in the Tropics*. Baltimore: Johns Hopkins University Press.

Tilly, Charles. 1999. *Durable Inequality*. Berkeley: University of California Press.

Uphoff, Norman. 1986. *Local Institutional Development: An Analytical Sourcebook with Cases*. West Hartford, CT: Kumarian Press.

———. 1997. "Indicators and Methods to Measure Participation, Demand Orientation, and Local Organizational Capacity in Community-Driven Projects." Workshop presentation, World Bank, Washington, DC, January 29–31.

Wade, Robert. 1987. "Common Property Resource Management in South Indian Villages." In *Proceedings of the Conference on Common Property Resource Management*, ed. National Research Council. Washington, DC: National Academy Press.

Woolcock, Michael. 1998. "Social Capital and Economic Development: Toward a Theoretical Synthesis and Policy Framework." *Theory and Society* 27 (2): 151–208.

Woolcock, Michael, and Deepa Narayan. 2000. "Social Capital: Implications for Development Theory, Research and Policy." *World Bank Research Observer* 15 (2): 225–49.

World Bank. 2000a. *World Development Report 2000/2001: Attacking Poverty*. New York: Oxford University Press.

———. 2000b. *Bolivia: From Patronage to a Professional State: Bolivia Institutional and Governance Review*. Report 20115-BO, World Bank, Washington, DC.

SECTION TWO

Gender and Household

Chapter 3

Women's Empowerment as a Variable in International Development

Anju Malhotra and Sidney Ruth Schuler

The empowerment of women has been widely acknowledged as an important goal in international development. But the meanings and terminologies associated with this concept vary, and methods for systematically measuring and tracking changes in levels of empowerment are not well established. A diverse body of literature has emerged regarding the conceptualization and measurement of women's empowerment and its relationships with other variables of interest in international development. Drawing from a review of theoretical, methodological, and empirical literature on empowerment from the fields of demography, sociology, anthropology, and economics, this chapter attempts to clarify basic definitional and conceptual issues and identifies common threads in the various definitions used. It then discusses some of the key issues to be addressed in measuring women's empowerment empirically, highlighting points on which important progress has been made as well as challenges that remain.

The World Bank's *Empowerment and Poverty Reduction: A Sourcebook* defines empowerment in its broadest sense as the "expansion of freedom of choice and action" (Narayan 2002, xviii). Although this applies to women as well as to other disadvantaged or socially excluded groups, it is important to acknowledge that *women's* empowerment encompasses some unique additional elements. First, women are not just one group among various disempowered subsets of society (the poor, ethnic minorities, and so on); they are a cross-cutting category of individuals that overlaps with all these other groups. Second, household and interfamilial relations are a central locus of women's disempowerment in a way that is not true for other disadvantaged groups.

This means that efforts at empowering women must be especially cognizant of the household-level implications of broader policy action. Third, it can be argued that while empowerment in general requires institutional transformation, women's empowerment requires systemic transformation not just of any institutions, but specifically of those supporting patriarchal structures.

Conceptualization: Emphasis on Process and Agency

The literature reflects considerable diversity in the emphases, agendas, and terminology used to discuss women's empowerment. For example, it is not always clear whether authors who use terms such as "women's empowerment," "gender equality," "female autonomy," or "women's status" are referring to similar or different concepts. Nonetheless, the concept of women's empowerment can be distinguished from others by two defining features. The first is *process* (Kabeer 2001; Oxaal and Baden 1997; Rowlands 1995). None of the other concepts explicitly focuses on processes of change—toward greater equality, or greater freedom of choice and action. The second is *agency:* in other words, women themselves must be significant actors in the process of change that is being described or measured. Thus, hypothetically there could be an improvement in gender equality by various measures, but unless the intervening processes involved women as agents of that change rather than merely as its beneficiaries, we would not consider it empowerment. However desirable, it would merely be an improvement in outcomes from one point in time to another.

A definition proposed by Kabeer serves as a good reference point for conceptualizing and measuring women's empowerment. It contains both the process and agency elements, and also implicitly distinguishes "empowerment" from the general concept of "power" as exercised by dominant individuals or groups. Kabeer (2001) defines empowerment as "the expansion in people's ability to make strategic life choices in a context where this ability was previously denied to them." This fits well within the broad definition of empowerment as "the expansion of freedom of choice and action to shape one's life" in the World Bank's empowerment sourcebook (Narayan 2002).

Much of the literature also emphasizes the importance of resources. We see resources, however, not as a feature of empowerment per se but as catalysts for empowerment, as "enabling factors" that can foster an empowerment process. This distinction may be useful in the context of policy and evaluation. In particular, many of the variables that have traditionally been used as proxies for empowerment, such as education and employment, might be better described as enabling factors, resources, or sources of empowerment (Kishor 2000a).

The second component noted above, agency, is at the heart of many conceptualizations of empowerment. Among the various concepts and terms we encountered in the literature on empowerment, "agency" probably comes closest to capturing what the majority of writers see as the essence of empowerment. It encompasses the ability to formulate strategic choices and to control resources and decisions that affect important life outcomes.

The importance of agency in the discourse on empowerment emerges from the rejection of "top-down" approaches to development. At the institutional and aggregate levels, this concept emphasizes popular participation and social inclusion. At the micro level, it is embodied in the idea of self-efficacy and the significance given to the individual woman's realization that she can be an agent of change in her own life. In many ways, the emphasis on agency in the literature on women's empowerment is comparable to the emphasis in the overall empowerment literature on generating demand for information and accountability and on facilitating inclusion, participation, and mobilization of those who are in disadvantaged positions.

Agency as the essence of women's empowerment does not imply that all improvements in the position of women must be brought about through the actions of women alone, or that it is the responsibility of individual women to empower themselves. There is ample justification for governments and multilateral organizations to promote policies that strengthen gender equality through various means, including legal and political reform, and to mount interventions that give women (and other socially excluded groups) greater access to resources. The question is whether it is useful to describe all actions taken toward that end as "empowerment." We would suggest that it is not. There are many examples in the literature showing that women's access to resources does not necessarily lead to their greater control over resources, that changes in legal statutes often have little influence on practice, and that female political leaders do not always work to promote women's interests. Thus while resources—economic, social, and political—are often critical in ensuring that women are empowered, they are not by themselves sufficient. Without women's individual or collective ability to recognize and utilize resources in their own interests, resources cannot bring about empowerment.

Measurement Issues

As we move from a discussion of conceptualizing empowerment to measuring it, it is important to note that measures of empowerment must involve standards that lie outside localized gender systems. This entails a recognition of universal elements of gender subordination (Sen and Grown 1987; Bisnath and Elson 1999; Nussbaum 2000). It is clear from the literature on gender and empowerment that the role of gender in development cannot be understood without understanding the sociocultural (as well as political and economic) contexts in which development takes place. The concept of empowerment only has meaning within these specific contexts. At the same time, operational definitions (such as definitions embodied in indicators to be applied in the context of development assistance policies, programs, and projects) should be consistent with the spirit of international conventions to which countries providing development assistance are signatories. The approach based on universal human rights offers the best operational framework for this task.

Key measurement issues to be addressed include the multidimensional character of empowerment, the need to operationalize the concept at various levels of aggregation and across different contexts, the infrequency of "strategic life choices" that figure in the basic definition of empowerment, and the difficulties inherent in measuring a process.

Multidimensionality

As early as 1981, Acharya and Bennett noted that status is a function of the power attached to a given role, and because women fill a number of roles, it may be misleading to speak of "*the* status of women." Another early writer on the topic, Mason (1986), pointed out that the phenomenon of gender inequality is inherently complex and spread across different dimensions, including the social, economic, political, and psychological, among others. She contends that men and women are typically unequal in various ways, and that the nature or extent of their inequality can vary across these different dimensions (as well by social setting and stage in the life cycle). Since that time, a number of studies have shown that women may be empowered in one area of life while not in others (Malhotra and Mather 1997; Kishor 1995, 2000b; Hashemi, Schuler, and Riley 1996; Beegle, Frankenberg, and Thomas 1998). Thus it should not be assumed that if a development intervention promotes women's empowerment along a particular dimension, empowerment in other dimensions will necessarily follow. It may or may not.

Several efforts have been made in recent years to develop comprehensive frameworks delineating the various dimensions along which women can be empowered (for example, see CIDA 1996; Jejeebhoy 1995; Kishor 2000a; Schuler and Hashemi 1993; Stromquist 1995; A. Sen 1999). When sorted by sphere or level of aggregation (which we discuss more fully below), frameworks delineating dimensions of women's empowerment offer potential roadmaps for operationalizing and measuring women's empowerment. These frameworks have been important in highlighting the potential independence of the various areas within which women can be empowered—for example, women can be empowered in the familial sphere without making similar gains in the political sphere. In terms of practical measurement, however, it is difficult to neatly separate the dimensions. For one thing, many aspects of economic or social empowerment overlap considerably with empowerment in the familial dimension, as when a woman achieves greater control over domestic spending or savings, or reduces limitations on her mobility or social activities.

Because empowerment is multidimensional, researchers must use care in constructing index or scale variables relating to empowerment. Such variables may mask differential effects of interventions on distinct aspects of empowerment. Inappropriate combining of items relating to gender and empowerment may also mask differential effects of the component variables on outcomes of interest. Ghuman, for example, critiques a logit regression analysis by Durrant and Sathar (2000) that found that mothers' decision-making autonomy on child-related issues demonstrated a weak, statistically insignificant effect on child survival. Ghuman points out that this finding was based on a summative scale of items related to mothers' decision making about child-related issues such as schooling, care of illness, and punishment for misbehavior, but that these items varied greatly with respect to their individual associations with child survival. Although Durrant and Sathar found a weak aggregate effect, one item on the scale had an important negative association with child mortality—a relationship that was effectively hidden (Ghuman 2002, 99–100).

While combining multiple indicators can obscure the relationships of interest, it is also true that a single indicator is usually insufficient to measure even a specific dimension of empowerment (Kishor 2000b; Estudillo, Quisumbing, and Otsuka 2001). Additional information is usually needed to interpret data on any given indicator—that is, to judge whether the indicator in fact reflects women's empowerment.

Levels of Aggregation

Many writers have noted that because power relations operate at different levels, so does empowerment (Mayoux 2000; Bisnath and Elson 1999). However, there is considerable variation in exactly how these levels are defined. For example, when economists differentiate between the macro and micro levels, the macro level is generally meant to include market and political systems, while the micro level often comprehends not only individuals and households but also communities and institutions (Pitt and Khandker 1998; Rao 1998; Tzannatos 1999; Winter 1994; Narayan, Patel, et al. 2000; Narayan, Chambers, et al. 2000). In contrast, when sociologists and demographers refer to the micro level, they usually mean the individual or the household, while the macro level may include anything from the community to the polity (Gage 1995; Jejeebhoy and Sathar 2001; Kritz, Makinwa-Adebusoye, and Gurak 2000; Malhotra, Vanneman, and Kishor 1995).

Thus, while there is clarity at the highest and lowest levels of aggregation, this is less the case with the intermediate (or "meso") levels. This also means that in operationalizing empowerment, there is theoretical interest but less empirical attention to aggregations that fall in the middle, especially at the community level, where institutional and normative structures such as family systems, infrastructure, gender ideologies, regional or local market processes, and so on are most likely to affect women's empowerment. It is often precisely at these intermediate levels that normative changes occur, and programmatic or policy interventions operate.

Theoretically, the frameworks that delineate dimensions of empowerment can be operationalized at any level of aggregation. For example, the legal dimension can be measured in terms of individual women's knowledge and exercise of their legal rights, or in terms of women's interests and concerns in local, regional, or national laws. Our review suggests, however, that in the studies to date, the political and legal dimensions tend to be operationalized at fairly high levels of aggregation (regional or national), while the familial, social, and economic dimensions are generally operationalized at the individual or household levels, with some limited efforts to consider these at the level of the community or institution. The psychological dimension of empowerment is rarely operationalized in empirical research at any level.

The most cutting-edge empirical research makes efforts to measure empowerment at multiple levels. Anthropological and qualitative studies are particularly adept at blending individual or household situations with institutional structures and normative conditions at the meso level (Kabeer 1997; Mayoux 2001; Hashemi, Schuler, and Riley 1996). Quantitative studies that have attempted multilevel analyses of empowerment have used both aggregations of individual and household data and direct measures of community-level characteristics (Kritz, Makinwa-Adebusoye, and Gurak 2000; Mason and Smith 2000; Jejeebhoy and Sathar 2001). Generally these studies find that both individual and community-level effects are important in determining empowerment or related outcomes. At the same time, aggregate-level, contextual factors may be considerably more important in defining certain aspects of women's empowerment than women's individual characteristics or circumstances (Mason and Smith 2000; Jejeebhoy 2000; Kritz, Makinwa-Adebusoye, and Gurak 2000; Malhotra and Mather 1997).

Research that blends theory with empirical work tends to focus on women's empowerment in their relationships within the household and local community. Much of this literature focuses on individual rather than collective empowerment, and examines conjugal relationships and sometimes women's relationships with others in the household as well. The discourse on collective forms of empowerment emerges largely from the activist literature (G. Sen 1994). Oxaal and Baden (1997) argue that to the extent that mainstream development discourse views empowerment as an individual rather than collective process, it emphasizes entrepreneurship and self-reliance rather than cooperation to challenge power structures. The discourse on social inclusion also sees the potential for empowerment in a collective form, whether through political, economic, or social mobilization of groups. Narayan and colleagues find that poor people's organizations often lack transformational power, but that with capacity building, access to information, and increased accountability in both state and civil society institutions, both groups and individuals can become empowered (Narayan, Patel, et al. 2000; Narayan, Chambers, et al. 2000).

The Importance of Context

One of the major difficulties in measuring empowerment is that the behaviors and attributes that signify empowerment in one context often have different meanings elsewhere. For example, a woman being able to visit a health center without getting permission from a male household member may be a sign of empowerment in rural Bangladesh but not in, for example, urban Peru, where women routinely move about in public on their own. Context can also be important in determining the extent to which empowerment at the household or individual level helps drive development outcomes. It could be argued, for example, that where investments in public health systems are weak, empowering women to manage their children's health through better education or more decision-making power in the household will be more important than it would be in a setting where the public health system is strong.

Context varies not only across sociocultural settings but also within settings over time, as the behavioral and normative frontiers that give meaning to particular behaviors evolve. Within a particular sociocultural context, the relevance of a particular behavior as an empowerment indicator that can be used to predict other outcomes of interest is likely to change over time—and it may change very rapidly. For example, data from the early 1990s suggested that in rural Bangladesh, empowered women were more likely than others to use contraception (Schuler, Hashemi, and Riley 1997). Now contraceptive use is the norm—over half of all married women of reproductive age currently use it and more than three-quarters have used it at one time or another. Once a behavior becomes the accepted norm there is little reason to expect that it would be influenced by an individual actor's level of empowerment.

The variation in the nature and importance of empowerment, both across and within contexts, poses a challenge in terms of both consistency and comparability in measurement schemes. How important is context in defining empowerment in different settings? Does the context-specific nature of empowerment mean that we must constantly reinvent indicators to suit socioeconomic, cultural, and political conditions? What is the role of context in determining the relationship between women's empowerment and development outcomes? How dependent is this statistical relationship on the choice of indicators and on whether they are appropriate to the setting in question?

In the past decade there have been a few pioneering efforts at sorting out some of these issues through empirical research (Mason and Smith 2000; Jejeebhoy 2000; Kritz, Makinwa-Adebusoye, and Gurak 2000; Schuler, Jenkins, and Townsend 1995; Hashemi, Schuler, and Riley 1996). The body of work emerging from this research unequivocally confirms the importance of context in both defining and measuring the impact of women's empowerment on development outcomes. A series of studies on the status of women and fertility conducted by Mason and her colleagues aimed for comparability in measuring women's empowerment and its impact on reproductive behavior across five countries in Asia: India, Malaysia, Pakistan, the Philippines, and Thailand (Mason and Smith 2000; Jejeebhoy and Sathar 2001). Although there were small variations in wording to make each question appropriate to the country setting, there was an effort to employ similar indicators across countries and within 59 communities in the five countries. In her 1998 analysis, for example, Mason is able to compare "economic decision-making power in the family" based on a scale constructed from six indicators that were collected relatively consistently across the five countries.

In this approach, contextual factors are brought in as important determinants at the analytical rather than the measurement stage. Thus, analyses from this set of studies include community-level measures of family systems, marriage systems, religion and ethnicity, female participation in the work-force, rates of child mortality, and so forth. Kritz, Makinwa-Adebusoye, and Gurak (2000) employ a similar approach by developing an index of the gen-der contexts in four communities using eight indicators, such as mean spousal age difference, percentage of wives in modern work, mean score on wives' physical mobility, and percentage of wives who control the use of income. A consistent finding from this approach is that the contextual factors are often more important than factors at the individual level in determining women's empowerment and its outcomes. At the same time, there is inconsistency in the studies' findings on which particular contextual conditions are most empow-ering to women. Mason (1998, 130) summarizes: "While our analysis sug-gests that the community context is very important for the empowerment of individual women, it also makes clear that the community conditions which empower women tend to be idiosyncratic rather than universal."

Studies that apply indicators across cultures can be useful for making in-ternational or interregional comparisons with reference to an external yard-stick of power, women's status, or gender equity, but they raise the issue of how appropriate similar indicators are in measuring empowerment across settings. A possible alternative approach to addressing the challenges of context is to rely on a consistent conceptual framework for measuring empowerment and its effects, but to allow flexibility in the specific indicators used to define the key components of that framework across different settings. Any given context at any given point in time can be seen as having behavioral and normative "frontiers," which need to be crossed for women to be empowered along a spe-cific dimension and within a specific arena. Specifying these frontiers helps de-fine the indicators of relevance to that particular context at that particular time.

This is the approach that Schuler and colleagues advocate (Schuler, Hashemi, and Pandit 1995; Schuler, Jenkins, and Townsend 1995). In their work on Bangladesh, India, and Bolivia, they relied on a common conceptual framework in which they specified the dimensions along which women's em-powerment or its effects could vary. In measuring the dimensions, however, they used indicators relevant to each particular country and community setting. Their analysis also allowed for greater or lesser weight on certain dimensions as opposed to others across contexts. Hashemi, Schuler, and Riley (1996) argue that laying initial groundwork through qualitative and exploratory methods, conceptual analysis, and stakeholder consensus achieved through participatory processes is essential to establishing parameters that define empowerment in specific country and development project contexts.

The Infrequency of Strategic Life Choices

In our basic definition of empowerment drawn from Kabeer (2001), "strategic life choices" refers to decisions that influence a person's life trajectory and sub-sequent ability to exercise autonomy and make choices. Examples include deci-sions related to marriage, education, employment, and childbearing. As such de-cision points are likely to come up relatively infrequently in a person's life, it is often difficult to link those decisions with policy and program interventions unless the time frame of the research is very long. Given the measurement constraints imposed by the infrequency of such strategic life choices, it almost becomes necessary to consider "small" actions and choices if one is to measure empowerment in the short term. Indeed, given their scope, most household-level studies that have included indicators of women's empowerment have focused not on strategic life choices but rather on what might be termed "empowerment in small things."

An operating assumption (albeit not always directly stated) in most household-level studies is that a person's ability to make strategic life choices is linked with her access to, and control over, economic and other resources and her ability to make smaller, quotidian decisions. There is some published evidence from empirical studies that this assumption is valid, but results from other studies suggest that this is not always the case. And it is not clear from the existing body of research to what extent the negative results reflect an actual disjuncture between women's abilities to make small versus large choices; in some cases they may reflect methodological limitations of the studies, such as relying on cross-sectional data rather than measuring indicators at multiple points in time.

Difficulties in Measuring a Process

Many writers describe empowerment as a "process," as opposed to a condition or state of being, a distinction that we have emphasized as a key defining feature of empowerment. However, as moving targets, processes are difficult to measure, especially with the standard empirical tools available to social scientists. The major methodological challenges in measuring the process of women's empowerment include the use of direct measures rather than proxy indicators, the lack of availability and use of data across time, the subjectivity inherent in assessing processes, and the shifts in relevance of indicators over time.

Some authors who have made efforts to empirically measure empowerment have argued that as a process it cannot be measured directly, but only through proxies such as health, education level, and knowledge (Ackerly 1995). For example, Kishor (2000a) contends that while the end product of empowerment can be measured through direct indicators, the process can only be measured through proxies such as education and employment. Several large studies of relationships between gender and economic or demographic change have used proxy variables. However, an increasing body of research indicates that commonly used proxy variables such as education or employment are conceptually distant from the dimensions of gender stratification that are hypothesized to affect the outcomes of interest in these studies; thus, such variables may be irrelevant or misleading (Mason 1995, 8–11; Govindasamy and Malhotra 1996). Studies have found that how closely a proxy measure relates to more direct measures of women's empowerment may depend on the geographic region (Jejeebhoy 2000), the outcome being examined (Kishor 2000a), or the dimension of empowerment that is of interest (Malhotra and Mather 1997).

In response, there have been increasing efforts to capture the process through direct measures of decision making, control, and choice. Many authors see such measures as the most effective representations of the process of empowerment since they are closest to measuring agency. In addition, they have what might be termed "face validity"; that is, they refer to very specific, concrete actions whose links with empowerment are relatively easy to see in a particular sociocultural context (Hashemi, Schuler, and Riley 1996; Mason 1998; Mason and Smith 2000; Malhotra and Mather 1997).

Ideally, the best hope of capturing a process is to follow it across at least two points in time. Moreover, the elapsed time required to measure the process may depend on the nature and extent of change in empowerment. Depending on the dimension of empowerment, the context, and the type of social, economic, or policy catalyst, women may become empowered in some aspects of their lives in a relatively short period of time (say one to three years), while other changes may evolve over decades. For policy and programmatic action, defining success or failure depends upon specifying the aspects of women's empowerment that are expected to change, as well as the time period required for change to occur at a level that can be measured. As conceptual frameworks and indicators of empowerment become more sophisticated, however, there is an enormous problem with regard to the availability of adequate data across time. For example, while there is increasing agreement that measures with face validity are preferable to proxy indicators, survey data that include face validity measures are often one-of-a-kind attempts and are not systematically or routinely collected across more than one point in time.

Qualitative studies of empowerment make an effort to capture the process through in-depth interviews and case studies that follow life changes for specific women (and men) through retrospective narratives. G. Sen (1994) has suggested that the process of empowerment is essentially qualitative in nature. Even indicators such as women's participation in the political system or other power structures are often inadequate as a means to capture this process; without a qualitative sense of what that participation is like or what it means, we cannot tell whether empowerment is occurring (Oxaal and Baden 1997). Kabeer's work suggests that the assessment of the process is not only qualitative but subjective as well. According to Kabeer (1997, 1998), the subjectivity of the process should extend to measuring empowerment in terms of women's own interpretations. This means that program evaluators, rather than relying on their own judgments as to what is of value, should judge the process of empowerment as having occurred if it is self-assessed and validated by women themselves.

Empirical Research: A Brief Review

Studies from a range of disciplines—anthropology, sociology, demography, and economics—have attempted to empirically measure various aspects of women's empowerment, either as the outcome of interest or as the intermediary factor affecting other development outcomes. Efforts at data collection and analysis, especially at the household and individual levels, have become more common and sophisticated in recent years, and although they continue to have limitations, they provide important guidance for future efforts at measuring women's empowerment.

We reviewed approximately 45 empirical studies that used quantitative and/or qualitative data to assess some aspect or variation of women's empowerment, in an effort to understand how existing research has handled the challenges and promises of measuring empowerment and related outcomes (Malhotra, Schuler, and Boender 2002). We found that although a majority of studies use quantitative methodologies, a significant proportion—especially those focusing on empowerment as a dependent rather than intermediary variable—incorporate a combination of quantitative and qualitative techniques and attempt triangulation in their analyses. However, only three of the studies in our review use data from more than one point in time to assess empowerment.

We also found that the range of development outcomes examined in research that focuses on women's empowerment as an intermediary factor is limited. The heaviest concentration is on outcomes related to fertility and contraceptive use (12 studies) or child health and welfare (8), with just a handful of studies focusing on broader issues of household well-being (5), women's health (3), or development processes (1). Similarly, the examination of the impact of policy and program initiatives does not seem to be a high priority in empirical research. There is extensive research on the impact of microcredit programs on women's empowerment (mostly for Bangladesh), but few other initiatives are included.

Our review indicates that empirical analyses of women's empowerment are heavily concentrated at the individual and household levels. Given the centrality of the household to gender relations, it is not surprising that the greatest strides in the measurement of empowerment have been made at this level of aggregation. It may also be true that the feasibility of operationalizing both the agency and process components of women's empowerment in a concrete manner is more readily apparent at the household level than at larger levels of aggregation.

Conceptual frameworks of how women's empowerment should be operationalized at the macro level are less well developed, and the indicators utilized in empirical studies are less sophisticated, with continued reliance on proxy measures such as education, employment, and political representation. The review suggests that single indicators or even composite indexes such as the Gender Empowerment Measure (GEM) are inadequate to the task of measuring women's empowerment at the aggregate level. An important finding is that the lack of studies addressing levels of aggregation in between the levels of individual/household and district/state/nation is one of the most significant gaps in efforts to empirically measure women's empowerment.

We conclude that the vast majority of these studies do not measure empowerment effectively enough to provide conclusive evidence regarding the factors that empower women, or to answer the question of whether or not the empowerment of women results in positive development outcomes. Most studies capture only a slice of empowerment—they do not even come close to measuring all potentially relevant dimensions. Within this limited range, the evidence from the empirical literature seems to be heavily weighted toward positive relationships. Most studies conclude that enabling factors such as education, employment, positive marriage or kinship conditions, or programmatic interventions such as microcredit lead to women having more choice, options, control, or power over their life conditions. Similarly, studies examining the intermediary role of empowerment also conclude that women's control of assets, income, household decision making, and so forth leads to better outcomes for their families, improved child well-being, and reduced fertility rates.

At the same time, the review notes that the results are not unequivocally positive, and that in fact, considerable subjective judgment is involved in the types of analyses conducted and the results that are highlighted. For example, in considering the one programmatic intervention that is most studied in the literature, microcredit, we find conflicting results depending on the studies' orientation and emphasis. For example, some studies conclude that microcredit participation is empowering for women in Bangladesh (Hashemi, Schuler, and Riley 1996; Kabeer 1998), while others conclude that it is not (Goetz and Gupta 1996; Ackerly 1995). The empirical research also indicates contextual differences in the impact of microcredit programs. Studies in certain settings find a substantial positive impact on outcomes such as household expenditures or contraceptive use (on Bangladesh, see Khandker 1998; Pitt and Khandker 1998; Schuler and Hashemi 1994; Schuler, Hashemi, and Riley 1997). But those in some other settings do not find such effects (Schuler, Hashemi, and Pandit 1995 for India; Schuler, Jenkins, and Townsend 1995 for Bolivia; Mayoux 2001 for Cameroon).

The review also found that most empirical studies use a limited and narrow range of indicators and analyses of empowerment that do not effectively operationalize the consensus-based definition and conceptualization of empowerment outlined earlier. In particular, the vast majority of empirical studies do not measure the process element of empowerment. Additionally, macro-level studies are especially weak on measuring agency and often do not employ a relevant conceptual framework. Household-level studies have made significant progress in conceptualizing broader, context-specific frameworks and in specifying indicators that can be said to capture aspects of agency, but considerably more work is required in this area. The lack of empirical research at meso levels presents an important gap, as does the relative lack of rigorous research on policy and programmatic efforts. Data limitations have also presented an important constraint in efforts to measure women's empowerment. Macro-level studies are especially limited by the lack of gender-disaggregated data from developing countries on a vast majority of relevant indicators.

Toward a Framework for Developing Empowerment Indicators

The natural next step for building on the strengths of the existing literature would be to develop a comprehensive framework of domains or dimensions of women's empowerment that can be applied across settings and contexts, and used as a reference point in developing context-specific indicators. In table 3.1, we make a first attempt at this by drawing on the frameworks

Table 3.1 Proposed Framework of Dimensions and Indicators of Women's Empowerment in the Household, Community, and Broader Arenas

Dimension	Household	Community	Broader arenas
Economic	Control over income; ownership of assets and land; relative contribution to family support; access to and control of family resources	Access to employment; access to credit; involvement and representation in local trade associations; access to markets	Representation in high-paying jobs; number of women CEOs; representation of women's economic interests in macroeconomic policies and state and federal budgets
Social and cultural	Freedom of movement; lack of discrimination against daughters; education of daughters/commitment to educating daughters; participation in domestic decision making; control over sexual relations; ability to make child-bearing decisions, use contraception, obtain abortion; control over spouse selection and marriage timing; freedom from violence	Access to and visibility in social spaces; access to modern transportation; existence and strength of extrafamilial groups and social networks; shift in patriarchal norms (such as son preference); representation of the female in myth and ritual; shifts in marriage and kinship systems indicating greater value and autonomy for women (e.g., later marriages, self-selection of spouses, reduction in practice of dowry, acceptability of divorce); local campaigns against domestic violence	Literacy and access to a broad range of educational options; positive media images of women and their roles and contributions; regional/national trends favoring women in timing of marriage, options for divorce; political, legal, religious support for (or lack of active opposition to) such shifts; health systems providing easy access to contraception, safe abortion, reproductive health services
Legal	Knowledge of legal rights and mechanisms; familial support for exercising rights	Community mobilization for rights; campaigns for rights awareness; access to legal mechanisms; effective local enforcement of legal rights	Laws supporting women's rights, access to resources, and options; advocacy for rights and legislation; use of judicial system to redress rights violations
Political	Knowledge of political system and means of access to it; familial support for political engagement; ability to exercise right to vote	Involvement or mobilization in local political system/campaigns; support for specific candidates or legislation; representation in local government	Representation in regional and national government; strength as a voting bloc; representation of women's interests in effective lobbies and interest groups
Psychological	Self-esteem; self-efficacy; psychological well-being	Collective awareness of injustice, potential of mobilization	Collective expressions of inclusion and entitlement; systemic acceptance of women's entitlement and inclusion

developed by various authors in order to propose potential indicators within each dimension and at different levels of aggregation.

Conclusions

Women's empowerment has been identified as an essential commitment in the development goals of national governments and international agencies. It is important, therefore, to establish a consensus regarding what this concept means. If governments and agencies are to be held accountable for achieving this goal, then clear, systematic frameworks and indicators for measuring changes in women's empowerment are needed to assess the effectiveness of policy and programmatic efforts.

Our review indicates that there is in fact broad consensus regarding the definition of women's empowerment. The majority of writers characterize it as the enhancement of women's ability to make strategic life choices. While employing a multiplicity of terms, the literature focuses on two essential elements, process and agency, which we suggest should be treated as defining features that distinguish empowerment from related concepts such as gender equality.

Significant progress has been made in developing operational measures of the concept, providing useful guidance to those who want to track changes in women's empowerment as a critical component in the achievement of poverty reduction, human rights, and the Millennium Development Goals. Arguments based on human rights considerations have been important in establishing that women's empowerment must be considered from a universalist perspective; thus, measures of empowerment must involve standards that lie outside localized gender systems. Empirical research has established that women's empowerment has multiple dimensions, which do not necessarily evolve simultaneously. Measurement schemes must therefore extend beyond single indicators or indexes. Empowerment also operates at multiple levels of aggregation, and analyses at the micro, meso, and macro levels are needed to assess the impact of program and policy efforts. Furthermore, the path to empowerment for women may be through individual behavior, normative change, or collective action.

The development field still faces substantial methodological challenges in moving from the conceptualization of women's empowerment to its measurement. Empowerment is a process that is poorly captured by proxy measures, yet due to a lack of adequate longitudinal data, it is only infrequently tracked across time with measures that have face validity. Because of the relative infrequency of strategic choices in a person's life, data collection efforts often focus on women's decision making in quotidian matters; often there is little objective basis for evaluating the relative significance of such decisions. The context-specific nature of women's empowerment poses a challenge in terms of consistency and comparability in the indicators used to measure empowerment across social settings. There is also a need to reconcile universal perspectives with the realities and values of those whose empowerment is at issue, and to take into account the evolving meanings and correlates of empowerment in specific contexts.

While the concept of women's empowerment is inherently complex and poses substantial measurement challenges, the same is true of other concepts used in the development field, such as demand, poverty reduction, health, well-being, and social inclusion. As has been the case with these other concepts, sustained efforts at analysis and refinement are necessary for moving the measurement agenda forward.

References

Acharya, Meena, and Lynn Bennett. 1981. "Rural Women of Nepal: An Aggregate Analysis and Summary of 8 Village Studies." In *The Status of Women in Nepal*, vol. 2, *Field Studies*, part 9. Kathmandu: Centre for Economic Development and Administration, Tribhuvan University.

Ackerly, Brooke A. 1995. "Testing the Tools of Development: Credit Programmes, Loan Involvement, and Women's Empowerment." *IDS Bulletin* 26 (3): 56–68.

Beegle, Kathleen, Elizabeth Frankenberg, and Duncan Thomas. 1998. "Bargaining Power within Couples and Use of Prenatal and Delivery Care in Indonesia." *Studies in Family Planning* 32 (2): 130–46.

Bisnath, Savitri, and Diane Elson. 1999. "Women's Empowerment Revisited." Background paper for *Progress of the World's Women 2000*. United Nations Development Fund for Women, New York.

CIDA (Canadian International Development Agency). 1996. *Guide to Gender-Sensitive Indicators*. Gatineau, Quebec: CIDA.

Durrant, V. L., and Z. A. Sathar. 2000. "Greater Investments in Children through Women's Empowerment: A Key to Demographic Change in Pakistan." Paper presented at annual meeting of the Population Association of America, Los Angeles, March 23–25.

Estudillo, Jonna P., Agnes R. Quisumbing, and Keijiro Otsuka. 2001. "Gender Differences in Land Inheritance, Schooling and Lifetime Income: Evidence from the Rural Philippines." *Journal of Development Studies* 37 (4): 23–48.

Gage, Anastasia J. 1995. "Women's Socioeconomic Position and Contraceptive Behavior in Togo." *Studies in Family Planning* 26 (5): 264–77.

Ghuman, Sharon J. 2002. "Women's Autonomy and Child Survival in Five Asian Countries." PhD diss., University of Pennsylvania, Population Studies Center.

Goetz, Anne Marie, and Rina Sen Gupta. 1996. "Who Takes the Credit? Gender, Power, and Control over Loan Use in Rural Credit Programs in Bangladesh." *World Development* 24 (1): 45–63.

Govindasamy, Pavalavalli, and Anju Malhotra. 1996. "Women's Position and Family Planning in Egypt." *Studies in Family Planning* 27 (6): 328–40.

Hashemi, Syed M., Sidney Ruth Schuler, and Ann P. Riley. 1996. "Rural Credit Programs and Women's Empowerment in Bangladesh." *World Development* 24 (4): 635–53.

Jejeebhoy, Shireen J. 1995. *Women's Education, Autonomy, and Reproductive Behaviour: Experience from Developing Countries*. International Studies in Demography. Oxford: Clarendon Press.

———. 2000. "Women's Autonomy in Rural India: Its Dimensions, Determinants, and the Influence of Context." In *Women's Empowerment and Demographic Processes: Moving Beyond Cairo*, ed. Harriet Presser and Gita Sen, 204–38. New York: Oxford University Press.

Jejeebhoy, Shireen J., and Zeba A. Sathar. 2001. "Women's Autonomy in India and Pakistan: The Influence of Religion and Region." *Population and Development Review* 27 (4): 687–712.

Kabeer, Naila. 1997. "Women, Wages and Intra-household Power Relations in Urban Bangladesh." *Development and Change* 28: 261–302.

———. 1998. "'Money Can't Buy Me Love'? Re-evaluating Gender, Credit and Empowerment in Rural Bangladesh." Discussion Paper 363, Institute of Development Studies, University of Sussex, Brighton, UK.

———. 2001. "Reflections on the Measurement of Women's Empowerment." In *Discussing Women's Empowerment: Theory and Practice*. Sida Studies 3. Stockholm: Swedish International Development Cooperation Agency.

Khandker, Shahidur R. 1998. *Fighting Poverty with Microcredit: Experience in Bangladesh*. Washington, DC: World Bank.

Kishor, Sunita. 1995. *Autonomy and Egyptian Women: Findings from the 1988 Egypt Demographic and Health Survey*. Occasional Papers 2. Calverton, MD: Macro International.

———. 2000a. "Empowerment of Women in Egypt and Links to the Survival and Health of Their Infants." In *Women's Empowerment and Demographic Processes: Moving Beyond Cairo*, ed. Harriet Presser and Gita Sen. New York: Oxford University Press.

———. 2000b. "Women's Contraceptive Use in Egypt: What Do Direct Measures of Empowerment Tell Us?" Paper presented at annual meeting of the Population Association of America, Los Angeles, March 23–25.

Kritz, Mary M., Paulina Makinwa-Adebusoye, and Douglas T. Gurak. 2000. "The Role of Gender Context in Shaping Reproductive Behaviour in Nigeria." In *Women's Empowerment and Demographic Processes: Moving Beyond Cairo*, ed. Harriet Presser and Gita Sen. New York: Oxford University Press.

Malhotra, Anju, and Mark Mather. 1997. "Do Schooling and Work Empower Women in Developing Countries? Gender and Domestic Decisions in Sri Lanka." *Sociological Forum* 12 (4): 599–630.

Malhotra, Anju, Sidney Ruth Schuler, and Carol Boender. 2002. "Measuring Women's Empowerment as a Variable in International Development." Background paper prepared for the World Bank Workshop on Poverty and Gender: New Perspectives. Gender and Development Group, World Bank, Washington, DC.

Malhotra, Anju, Reeve Vanneman, and Sunita Kishor. 1995. "Fertility, Dimensions of Patriarchy, and Development in India." *Population and Development Review* 21 (2): 281–305.

Mason, Karen Oppenheim. 1986. "The Status of Women: Conceptual and Methodological Issues in Demographic Studies." *Sociological Forum* 1 (2): 284–300.

———. 1995. *Gender and Demographic Change: What Do We Know?* IUSSP Occasional Paper. Paris: International Union for the Scientific Study of Population.

———. 1998. "Wives' Economic Decision-making Power in the Family: Five Asian Countries." In *The Changing Family in Comparative Perspective: Asia and the United States*, ed. Karen Oppenheim Mason, 105–33. Honolulu: East-West Center.

Mason, Karen Oppenheim, and Herbert L. Smith. 2000. "Husbands' versus Wives' Fertility Goals and Use of Contraception: The Influence of Gender Context in Five Asian Countries." *Demography* 37 (3): 299–311.

Mayoux, Linda. 2000. "Micro-finance and the Empowerment of Women: A Review of the Key Issues." International Labor Organization, Geneva. http://www.ilo.org/public/english/employment/finance/download/wpap23.pdf

———. 2001. "Tackling the Down Side: Social Capital, Women's Empowerment and Micro-finance in Cameroon." *Development and Change* 32: 435–64.

Narayan, Deepa, ed. 2002. *Empowerment and Poverty Reduction: A Sourcebook.* Washington, DC: World Bank.

Narayan, Deepa, Robert Chambers, Meera K. Shah, and Patti Petesch. 2000. *Voices of the Poor: Crying Out for Change.* New York: Oxford University Press for the World Bank.

Narayan, Deepa, with Raj Patel, Kai Schafft, Anne Rademacher, and Sarah Koch-Schulte. 2000. *Voices of the Poor: Can Anyone Hear Us?* New York: Oxford University Press for the World Bank.

Nussbaum, Martha C. 2000. *Women and Human Development: The Capabilities Approach.* Cambridge: Cambridge University Press.

Oxaal, Zoë, with Sally Baden. 1997. "Gender and Empowerment: Definitions, Approaches and Implications for Policy." Bridge Report 40. Briefing prepared for the Swedish International Development Cooperation Agency (Sida), revised edition. Institute of Development Studies, University of Sussex, Brighton, UK.

Pitt, Mark M., and Shahidur R. Khandker. 1998. "The Impact of Group-based Credit Programs on Poor Households in Bangladesh: Does the Gender of Participants Matter?" *Journal of Political Economy* 106: 958–96.

Rao, Vijayendra. 1998. "Wife-Abuse, Its Causes and Its Impact on Intra-household Resource Allocation in Rural Karnataka: A 'Participatory' Econometric Analysis." In *Gender, Population and Development*, ed. Maithreyi Krishnaraj, Ratna M. Sudarshan, and Abusaleh Shariff, 94–121. New York: Oxford University Press.

Rowlands, Jo. 1995. "Empowerment Examined." *Development in Practice* 5 (2): 101–7.

Schuler, Sidney Ruth, and Syed M. Hashemi. 1993. "Defining and Studying Empowerment of Women: A Research Note from Bangladesh." JSI Working Paper 3, JSI Research and Training Institute, Boston.

————. 1994. "Credit Programs, Women's Empowerment, and Contraceptive Use in Rural Bangladesh." *Studies in Family Planning* 25 (2): 65–76.

Schuler, Sidney Ruth, Syed M. Hashemi, and Harshida Pandit. 1995. "Beyond Credit: SEWA's Approach to Women's Empowerment and Influence on Women's Reproductive Lives in Urban India." JSI Research and Training Institute, Boston.

Schuler, Sidney Ruth, Syed M. Hashemi, and Ann P. Riley. 1997. "The Influence of Changing Roles and Status in Bangladesh's Fertility Transition: Evidence from a Study of Credit Programs and Contraceptive Use." *World Development* 25 (4): 563–75.

Schuler, Sidney Ruth, Ann Hendrix Jenkins, and John W. Townsend. 1995. "Credit, Women's Status and Fertility Regulation in Urban Market Centers of Bolivia." JSI Working Paper 8, John Snow, Inc., Washington, DC.

Sen, Amartya. 1999. *Development as Freedom*. New York: Knopf.

Sen, Gita. 1994. "Women's Empowerment and Human Rights: The Challenge to Policy." In *Population, the Complex Reality: A Report of the Population Summit of the World's Scientific Academies*, ed. Francis Graham-Smith. Golden, CO: Fulcrum.

Sen, Gita, and Caren Grown. 1987. *Development, Crises, and Alternative Visions: Third World Women's Perspectives*. New York: Monthly Review.

Stromquist, Nelly P. 1995. "The Theoretical and Practical Bases for Empowerment." In *Women, Education and Empowerment: Pathways towards Autonomy*, ed. Carolyn Medel-Añonuevo. Report of the International Seminar held at UNESCO Institute for Education, Hamburg, January 27–February 2, 1993. Paris: UNESCO.

Tzannatos, Zafiris. 1999. "Women and Labor Market Changes in the Global Economy: Growth Helps, Inequalities Hurt and Public Policy Matters." *World Development* 27 (3): 551–69.

Winter, Carolyn. 1994. "Working Women in Latin America: Participation, Pay, and Public Policy." Latin America and Caribbean Region, World Bank, Washington, DC.

Chapter 4

Measuring Women's Empowerment: Learning from Cross-National Research

Karen Oppenheim Mason

This chapter discusses three questions: What is empowerment, particularly as this concept applies to women in the context of their families and households? What determines or influences the extent of women's domestic empowerment? And what is the best way to measure and analyze the effectiveness of interventions to empower poor women in developing countries?

The material and ideas presented here derive in part from the author's decade-long experience working on a collaborative, survey-based study of women's empowerment and demographic change in five Asian countries (India, Malaysia, Pakistan, the Philippines, and Thailand). The study surveyed rural and peri-urban married women ages 20–39 and a subset of their husbands (interviewed separately) in the winter of 1993–94. Either all eligible women or a probability sample of them were interviewed in approximately 55 purposively selected communities.[1] The questions used to measure empowerment focused on women's reported participation in household decisions, their ability to make certain types of purchases without permission from husbands or other family members, their reported freedom of movement in and beyond the community, and their reports of domestic violence and intimidation. (Question wording is given in the appendix.) Information on education, employment, and demographic history was also collected. Although analysis of the data from this study provides some valuable insights into the problems of measuring women's empowerment, the study does not pretend to provide the final word on either the determinants of women's domestic empowerment or the best way to measure and analyze it.

What Is Empowerment?

Empowerment refers to power. It is about the extent to which some categories of people are able to control their own destinies, even when the people with whom they interact oppose their interests. In the approach to empowerment that my colleagues and I have taken, the *relational* nature of empowerment is critical. People are not empowered or disempowered in a vacuum. Rather, they are empowered or disempowered relative to other people or groups whose lives intersect with theirs and whose interests differ from theirs, at least in part.

The theoretical framework that my collaborators and I have used to study women's empowerment in the domestic sphere (the focus of our research) makes two key assumptions. The first is that empowerment is basically a property of social or cultural systems rather than of individual experiences and traits (Smith 1989). This means that a group's shared values, norms, beliefs, traditions, and practices give some members a greater *right* to exercise power than other members or better access to the *means* to exercise power. Individuals with certain traits (for example, those who are male) will be more empowered than other members of the group, but the point is that this is precisely because there is some degree of consensus within the group that they have the *right* to greater power or the *right* to control resources and activities that are power-bearing—not because individuals who have particular traits or experiences thereby gain power automatically. Thus, women's empowerment is likely to involve not only their gaining new individual capabilities, but also the emergence of new beliefs about their *right* to exercise these capabilities and take advantage of opportunities in their community.

To be sure, in addition to the variation in power that can be predicted from a group's culture and practice, there is always unexplained variation among individuals in the exercise of power that reflects personality and other personal characteristics and experiences. We are all familiar with the brash wife who wears the pants in the family or the ruthless individual who claws his way up the social hierarchy. At heart, though, the extent to which men control women, the rich control the poor, or the elderly control the young—either directly or indirectly through agents—is a matter of group culture and practice. From a development perspective, then, what is critical in conceptualizing and measuring empowerment is a focus on groups or categories of persons and the cultural precepts under which they operate. Individual experiences and traits may provide insights into the *outcomes* associated with empowerment, but they are not the ultimate determinant of the extent to which women are or are not empowered in a given social context.

An additional assumption that my colleagues and I have made is that empowerment is multidimensional, with imperfect associations among its different dimensions. This is particularly clear in the case of gender relations, which span the private and public spheres and the social, economic, political, and psychological sectors. Levels of women's empowerment in the private and public spheres are often dissimilar: there are many cultures that give women domestic power of certain types but deny them power in the public sphere. Moreover, the extent of women's (or men's) power is not necessarily the same in the social, economic, and political spheres. For instance, Akan women in the city of Kumasi in northern Ghana are powerful economically—they work as traders, control a large market, and hire men to do their bookkeeping and hauling—but they are sexually and socially submissive to their husbands in the domestic arena and peripheral to the political process (Milne 1982). Likewise, Thai wives typically engage in income-earning activities, but, although they are independent in the arena of birth control, they are sexually submissive to their husbands and largely excluded from politics (Knodel, Chamratrithirong, and Debavalya 1987; Mueke 1992).[2]

Of course, in many societies the different dimensions of gender inequality are correlated and mutually reinforcing. Women's relative lack of education often results in their having fewer job opportunities and lower incomes than men enjoy; this in turn perpetuates their dependency on men's earnings and a consequent need to be submissive to men's decisions and desires. But, conceptually, the different dimensions of inequality between women and men are indeed different—and are by no means perfectly correlated with each other. This insight suggests the need to identify *types* of empowerment if the impact of public policy or development interventions on women's empowerment is to be fully understood.

Although the theoretical assumptions described here are difficult to prove or disprove, the findings from the five-country study of women's empowerment and demographic change are largely consistent with them (Mason and Smith 2003). We have found, for example, that country and community of residence predict women's reported domestic empowerment better than their personal socioeconomic and demographic traits do (table 4.1). When data from all five countries are combined, a dummy variable classification representing all of the communities in the sample accounts for about three times as much variation in women's empowerment as do women's personal traits, on average. Thus, unmeasured differences among communities—including differences in norms about male-female relations—predict women's levels of empowerment more strongly than do their own characteristics.

Further evidence that women's empowerment reflects community norms rather than women's individual traits is the finding that a substantial portion of the inter-community variation in women's reported domestic empowerment (40–80 percent) can be explained statistically by aggregations of responses to normative questions about the roles of women and men (data not shown). This result is consistent with the hypothesis that an important source of inter-community variation in women's empowerment is community values and norms about gender roles (Mason and Smith 2003). We also have found that different aspects of women's reported empowerment—for example, their say in important economic decisions within the household versus their freedom to move around outside the household—tend to be poorly correlated. Correlations rarely exceed an absolute value of 0.3 (data not shown) and are correlated differently in different communities (Mason and Smith 2003).

Table 4.1 Coefficients of Determination, or Approximations Thereof, for Regression and Logit Models of Women's Empowerment (Five Countries Combined)

Empowerment measure	Community only	Individual variables	Full model	N
Economic decision-making scale	0.45**	0.34**	0.50**	7,287
Family size decision making	0.22**	0.12**	0.22**	7,298
Freedom of movement scale[a]	0.40**	0.17**	0.42**	4,895
Freedom of movement item	0.22**	0.03**	0.22**	7,302
Afraid to disagree with husband	0.12**	0.03**	0.13**	7,291
Husband beats or hits wife[b]	0.08**	0.07**	0.12**	6,013

Note: The first three empowerment measures were modeled using ordinary least squares (OLS) regressions; the last three were modeled using maximum likelihood estimation (MLE) logits. The first column shows the R-squareds or pseudo-R-squareds for models that predict the dependent variable from the dummy variables representing community. The second column shows R-squareds for models that predict the dependent variable from age, age at first union, education, husband's education, household possessions, income, whether the wife owns land, whether she worked for pay in the past year, whether she is the wife of the household head, and whether she is related to her husband. The third column shows R-squareds from models that include both sets of predictors.

a. Thailand sample points are omitted from these equations.
b. Malaysia sample points are omitted from these equations.
** Significant at 0.01 level.

Taken together, these results are consistent with the assumptions that empowerment is a group-based process and that it is multidimensional.

What Determines Empowerment?

Individualistic theoretical models typically assume that an individual's control of economic resources—human capital, earned income, or liquid assets—will determine his or her power. For example, wives who are employed in income-earning activities are assumed to be more empowered than wives who engage exclusively in unpaid work. This assumption is often correct. For example, studies of recipients of microcredit in Bangladesh find that borrowing tends to enhance women's incomes *and* their empowerment as measured through survey questions about decision-making autonomy and freedom of movement (Hashemi, Schuler, and Riley 1996; Kabeer 1998). Obviously, *control* of assets or income normally is power-bearing, so if earning an income means controlling it, then paid employment is likely to be empowering.

Community traditions, taxation policies, employer practices, and many other factors can, however, weaken or remove the link between earning an income and controlling its use. For example, a study of Indians living and working on a Malaysian rubber plantation in the first half of the twentieth century reported that plantation managers paid wives' wages to their husbands, not to the wives, even though the wives were employed in different tasks than were the husbands (Jain 1970).

The empirical evidence that my colleagues and I have collected also shows a variable relationship between women's paid employment and different aspects of their empowerment. For example, although paid work is positively associated with having a greater say in the household's economic decisions in all five countries, the strength of this relationship varies, being relatively weak in Pakistan and strongest in Thailand (table 4.2). In addition, in at least three of the five countries, women's paid employment is unrelated to having a say in decisions about family size, to enjoying freedom of movement, and to being unafraid to disagree with the husband (the three countries are different in each case). A woman's paid work is also unrelated to whether her husband beats or hits her in two of the four countries that asked about domestic violence

Table 4.2   Regression or Logit Coefficients Predicting Empowerment Measures from Whether the Woman Had Paid Work in the Previous Year, by Country

Empowerment measure	Pakistan	India	Malaysia[a]	Thailand	Philippines
Economic decision-making scale	0.293**	0.600**	0.812**	0.969**	0.469**
Family size decision-making scale	0.089+	0.059	0.113*	0.085+	0.085*
Freedom of movement scale or item (Thailand)	0.353**	0.472**	0.228+	0.275+	−0.067
Afraid to disagree with husband? (yes = 1, no = 0)	−0.051	0.089	−0.265*	−0.106	0.186
Husband beats or hits wife? (yes = 1, no = 0)	0.734**	0.572**	—	−0.090	−0.261

Note: Each coefficient is from a separate OLS regression equation (first three empowerment measures except freedom of movement in Thailand) or MLE logit equation (last two measures plus freedom of movement in Thailand) in which the empowerment measure is predicted from a measure of whether the woman herself worked for pay during the past year, controlling for the proportion of all women in the community who worked for pay in the past year. The results shown thus are intended to illustrate the impact of women's own employment on their empowerment while controlling for community levels of women's employment. The empowerment measures are described in the appendix.

a. Information on domestic violence not available for Malaysia.

+ Significant at 0.10 level.

* Significant at 0.05 level.

** Significant at 0.01 level.

— Not available.

(the Philippines and Thailand), and is *positively* related to being beaten or hit in the remaining two (India and Pakistan).

This last result may indicate that paid work does indeed empower women. As has been observed in Bangladeshi microcredit programs, husbands may resort to violence when wives borrow and set up independent economic enterprises, perhaps because these enterprises allow wives to become more independent from and less submissive to the husband (Rahman 1999, although for contradictory results see Kabeer 1998). Consistent with this hypothesis is the existence of a positive relationship between women's paid work and violence only in the two most conservative countries in the study. In Thailand and the Philippines, where women typically enjoy more rights and freedom than they do in India and Pakistan, their gainful employment does not increase domestic violence.

Nonetheless, the results reviewed here suggest that engaging in remunerative work is no guarantee of having a say in important household decisions or being able to pursue one's interests if community norms and the actions of the powerful determine otherwise. Individual traits and experiences such as education, health, or paid employment may influence women's empowerment, but they do not automatically determine it (Kabeer 1998; Malhotra, Pande, and Grown 2003). Rather, the impact of individual capabilities and assets is mediated by community norms and ideologies that define the rights of women and men.

If human capital and paid employment are not sufficient to empower women, then what can development practitioners do to help empower women, especially poor women in developing countries? The work done by my colleagues and me suggests that sustainable empowerment will only be achieved by changing the cultures that give males and females distinct rights—and that result in inequalities between them. This answer is not very helpful, however, because our understanding of how to change cultures is fairly rudimentary (Rao and Walton 2004). One important way in which poor women can be helped to empower themselves is through collective action, the effectiveness of which is suggested by World Bank experience (Narayan 2002) as well as the extensive literature on collective movements and revolutions.

For example, the government of Andhra Pradesh, India, has instituted the Velugu program (the term means "light" in the Telugu language). The program assists poor women in forming self-help groups, then helps these groups create collective economic enterprises and social action committees. My own observations of Velugu and more formal evaluations (World Bank 2004) suggest that this program has done a remarkable job helping very poor women and men to empower themselves economically, socially, and psychologically by promoting a variety of forms of collective action. These actions include collective economic activity, which helps the poor multiply the effects of their meager resources and gain a better position in the marketplace as producers; collective consumption schemes, which help the poor gain a better market position as consumers; and collective social action to end practices that disempower women such as child marriage, abandonment by husbands, and domestic violence. The success of Velugu and of similar programs elsewhere suggests that, in addition to ensuring that individual women's capacities are enhanced, development practitioners can help empower poor women by assisting them in forming collectivities that in turn act as economic, social, or political corporations.

Alternative Measurement Approaches

Measuring the impact of attempts to empower poor women is obviously very difficult. If we want to be serious about this, then we need to design randomized experiments or at least compare cases that received the "treatment" with those that did not (while attempting to equalize them, statistically, in terms of possible confounding factors). For example, for a program like Velugu, which was initially established in six of Andhra Pradesh's 22 districts, we should, at a minimum, be measuring levels of empowerment among poor women both in the Velugu districts and in a sample of similar non-Velugu districts.[3] Better still would be baseline measures in both Velugu and control districts prior to the start of the project, so that *change* in women's empowerment could be compared in the treatment and control areas. Alternatively, households involved in the program could be compared with other households in the same village, although such comparisons often founder on problems of selectivity bias (Hashemi, Schuler, and Riley 1996). Such quasi-experimental approaches are conceptually fairly straightforward, but their success hinges on solving a number of often difficult problems, including the measurement of empowerment.

Power relations are notoriously difficult to measure. This is partly because the flow of power is less observable than the flow of, say, money or goods, and partly because, in institutionalized systems of inequality, there often are ideologies that hide the realities of power from sight. (These include ideologies to which the disempowered as well as the powerful subscribe—for example, the belief in Western democracies in the mid-twentieth century that women were "uninterested" in high-level positions in the economic or political sphere, or worked only for "pin money," not as family breadwinners.) The difficulties of observing the flow of power are compounded when we want to employ quantitative techniques.

Basically, we have four choices regarding the measurement of empowerment, none of which is wholly satisfactory. The first is to measure the factors that we hypothesize empower women, such as paid employment.[4] The evidence presented earlier that supposed drivers of empowerment do not, in fact, always empower suggests the drawback of this approach.

The second possible approach is to measure the outcomes that empowerment is supposed to achieve. Thus, in the Velugu program, we could ask whether, in treatment as compared to control districts, the incomes of the very poor and the age at marriage of girls have risen, abandonment of wives by husbands has declined, and so forth.[5] The advantage of this approach is that we have neatly avoided all the complexities of measuring a hidden-from-view, ideologically freighted, multidimensional concept. But there are disadvantages as well. First, measuring outcomes such as higher incomes and less abandonment of wives can itself be difficult, especially when we try to tap into outcomes that are not commonly measured in surveys or censuses, such as the increased voice of women in local governance or a reduced level of domestic violence against women.

Second, some would argue that the "outcomes" are less important than is empowerment itself, indeed, that empowerment is the "master outcome" from which all other desirable outcomes flow. For example, studies of community water and sanitation projects have found that when women have a strong say in project design and implementation, projects are more effective and sustainable than when women's participation is minimal (Gross, van Wijk, and Mukherjee 2001). For understanding the role of empowerment, measuring women's participation would therefore be preferable to measuring the sustainability of rural water projects.

Finally, such outcomes as rising income or falling levels of domestic violence can be produced by factors other than women's empowerment, and any analysis would therefore have to ensure that it is indeed empowerment, rather than other unmeasured factors, that explains the relative outcomes in treatment and nontreatment villages or districts. This task can itself be challenging.

The third approach to measuring empowerment is through observational studies. Some students of empowerment believe that this is the best way to assess the extent to which women enjoy freedom of movement, their ability to prevail in household decision making, their autonomy to realize the ends they desire, and other aspects of their empowerment (Touliatos et al. 2000). The reason is that the observer can judge the actual outcomes of conflict—that is, whose interests prevailed—without the distortions often associated with reports to outsiders by the parties to the relationship.[6] The obvious drawback of this approach is the difficulty of covering enough households and communities to be able to aggregate data to a group level and perform quantitative analysis. Gathering information on the different dimensions of empowerment also tends to be time-consuming because the observer has to wait until conflicts concerning a particular dimension arise. And where women's empowerment is very low, few such conflicts may occur, precisely because women are afraid to openly dissent from their husbands' decisions.[7]

The final approach to measuring empowerment is through sample survey questions that ask respondents to report on different aspects of their empowerment. This is the approach that my colleagues and I used in our study of five Asian countries and that has been used in many other studies (for example, Balk 1994; Basu 1992; Hashemi, Schuler, and Riley 1996). Surveys allow one to ask large samples of individuals spread across many households and communities about a variety of aspects of empowerment. They thus lend themselves to aggregation to the group level and to quantitative analysis.[8] Drawbacks, however, include the reporting distortions mentioned earlier, the difficulties of framing questions in a way that will provide a commonly understood stimulus to most respondents (an especially acute problem if the study involves different language or cultural groups), the difficulties of validating what is measured, plus all of the usual problems of measurement in sample surveys, including the difficulty of conducting interviews privately, interviewer effects, respondent inattention that gives rise to random measurement error, and so on.

A closer examination of some of the most commonly used survey questions designed to elicit information about women's empowerment makes clear why survey measurement in this area is problematic. For example, questions about who makes particular household decisions (such as those used in the five-country study, which are shown in the appendix) cannot possibly cover all instances of decision making in a household. For this reason, respondents must either choose among instances, create some sort of average across all such instances, or report on the instance that is most memorable to them. Because different respondents are likely to use different approaches—and because there is likely to be more than one instance per household of most types of decision making—it is little wonder that husbands and wives frequently give contradictory reports about the wife's decision-making power. The emotional and normative freight that surrounds some aspects of empowerment (for example, domestic violence and other forms of interpersonal intimidation or coercion) also is likely to lead to biased or inconsistent responses. While aggregating over large numbers of respondents may compensate for a high level of random error in individual responses, it will not solve the problem of biased responses.

What to do? Use of multiple methods is probably the best approach, albeit an expensive one (see Hashemi, Schuler, and Riley 1996 for an example). In other words, use sample surveys to directly measure empowerment, its desired outcomes, *and* its possible causes, and do partial validation in selected settings through observational studies. One promising approach is to use subjective questions on how empowered individuals feel in relation to particular actors or settings. An example: "On the whole, how much do you think you control the decisions that are made within your household: very much, somewhat, very little, or not at all?" Similarly worded questions have been shown to produce valid and reliable information on such dimensions as happiness, health, and empowerment vis-à-vis the state (Bradburn 1969; Cantril 1965; Case and Deaton 2003; Lokshin and Ravallion 2002). I do not know of any studies that have attempted to use this approach to measuring women's perceived empowerment vis-à-vis household members, but in principle there is no reason why it shouldn't work. A multimethod study that includes such subjective ratings of empowerment as part of the survey—and collects observational data capable of providing validation—would be highly worthwhile.

Conclusion

Women's domestic empowerment is conceptually complex and methodologically challenging to measure and analyze. This is particularly the case when the effectiveness of particular interventions is the issue at hand. Because the links between the supposed causes of women's empowerment and particular aspects of that empowerment often are weak, resorting to easier-to-measure proxies for women's empowerment, such as education or employment, does not provide a satisfactory answer. And because empowerment is multidimensional, particular interventions may help to empower women in some respects but not in others.

Two recommendations flow from the evidence reviewed here. The first is substantive: it is that collective action can be used to empower poor women. Because empowerment is strongly influenced by shared values, norms, beliefs, and traditions, that is, by culture, enhancing the capabilities and opportunities of individual women, although a step in the right direction, may fail to empower them if the surrounding culture remains unchallenged. Collective action is powerful in part because it involves changing ideas about the social order. And some of the interventions that have been designed to increase opportunities or capabilities of individual women may have succeeded precisely because they involved organizing women into groups (for example, the Grameen Bank in Bangladesh).

The second recommendation is methodological. It is to combine qualitative and survey-based approaches to measuring and analyzing women's empowerment in an attempt to overcome some of the shortcomings of each approach (difficulties of quantification and generalization versus measurement problems). A particular approach to measurement that, to my knowledge, has not been tried and that would be worthy of testing is to employ subjective self-ratings of empowerment vis-à-vis different actors or groups (my family, my community, etc.). It may be easier for women—and men—to give interviewers an overall rating of how empowered or disempowered they feel than to report on such potentially sensitive or complex issues as whether they are excluded from important household decisions or subjected to beatings and intimidation by their husbands.

Appendix: Empowerment Measures

Economic Decision Making

1. Please tell me who in your family decides the following: whether to purchase major goods for the household, such as a TV/refrigerator/etc.? (wife participates = 1, does not = 0; note that the major goods mentioned as examples varied from country to country)
2. Please tell me who in your family decides the following: whether you should work outside the home? (wife participates = 1, does not = 0)
3. Who of these people usually has the greatest say in this decision: major purchases? (wife = 1, others = 0)
4. Who of these people usually has the greatest say in this decision: whether you should work outside the home? (wife = 1, others = 0)
5. If you wanted to buy yourself a dress/sari, would you feel free to do it without consulting your husband (or a senior member of your family)? (yes = 1, no or undecided = 0)

6. If you wanted to buy yourself a small item of jewelry, such as a bangle/beads/etc., would you feel free to do it without consulting your husband (or a senior member of your family)? (yes = 1, no or undecided = 0; note that specific item of jewelry mentioned varied from country to country)

The scale was created by summing the six items. Range: 0–6.

Family Size Decision Making

1. Please tell me who in your family decides the following: how many children to have? (wife participates = 1, does not = 0)
2. Who of these people usually has the greatest say in this decision: how many children to have? (wife = 1, others = 0)

The scale was formed by summing these two items. Range: 0–2.

Freedom of Movement

Do you have to ask your husband or a senior family member for permission to go to:

1. The local market? (no = 0, yes = 1)
2. The local health center? (no = 0, yes = 1)
3. Fields outside the village? (no = 0, yes = 1)
4. A community center, park, or plaza in the village? (no = 0, yes = 1)
5. The home of relatives or friends in the village? (no = 0, yes = 1)

The scale was formed by summing these five items. Range: 0–5.

Interpersonal Coercive Control Items

1. Are you afraid to disagree with your husband for fear he may become angry with you? (yes = 1, no = 0)
2. Does your husband ever hit or beat you? (yes = 1, no = 0)

Notes

The opinions expressed in this paper are those of the author and do not reflect the opinions of her research collaborators, the World Bank, its Board of Executive Directors, or its member countries. The author thanks her primary collaborators on the study reported herein: Professor Herbert L. Smith, University of Pennsylvania; Dr. Napaporn Chayovan, Chulalongkorn University, Bangkok; Dr. Shireen J. Jejeebhoy, Population Council, New Delhi; Professor Shyamala Nagaraj, University of Malaysia, Kuala Lumpur (who replaced Dr. Lin Lean Lim, International Labour Organisation, Bangkok, when Dr. Lim joined the ILO); Dr. Corazon M. Raymundo, University of the Philippines, Manila; and Dr. Zeba A. Sathar, Population Council, Islamabad. Data collection and analysis were supported by the Andrew W. Mellon

Foundation, the Rockefeller Foundation, and the National Institute of Child Health and Human Development of the National Institutes of Health.

1.   The exception was the Thai survey, which used a probability sample frame developed for the 1987 Thai Demographic and Health Survey. In India, Muslim and Hindu communities of high and low socioeconomic status were selected from districts in Uttar Pradesh and Tamil Nadu. In Malaysia, predominantly Malay, Chinese, and Indian rural and urban communities were purposively chosen. In Pakistan, communities representing different agro-economic zones in rural and peri-urban Punjab were selected. In the Philippines, predominantly Christian and Muslim rural and metro-Manila communities with different economic bases were selected. All five countries used comparable questionnaires. A total of approximately 7,400 women were interviewed, with a minimum of 1,000 in each country. Further information on the Survey on the Status of Women and Fertility is available from the Population Studies Center at the University of Pennsylvania (http://www.pop.upenn.edu/swaf).

2.   This finding also reflects unpublished data from the Asian Marriage Survey conducted by the East-West Center, Honolulu, Hawaii, in the 1980s.

3.   This strategy is no longer possible, as Velugu has now expanded to all 22 districts in the state.

4.   Examples of this approach abound. See, for example, Cain (1993), who uses the age difference between husband and wife as a proxy for women's empowerment; Mauldin, Berelson, and Sykes (1978), who use the proportion of 20- to 24-year-old women who have never been married as a proxy for their empowerment; and any number of demographic studies that use women's education or employment as the proxy for their empowerment (Mason 1986).

5.   An example of this approach can be found in Dev and Rao (2002).

6.   Evidence consistent with such distortions was found in our five-country study, in an analysis that compared responses by husbands and wives to a series of questions about the wife's autonomy and decision-making power. (Husbands and wives were interviewed separately to avoid cross-contamination of their responses.) Husbands and wives tended to give different reports about the wife's autonomy in a large proportion of the couples who were interviewed. See Ghuman, Lee, and Smith (2004).

7.   A skilled observer may be able to pick up on this and thus judge the extent of women's empowerment. But quantifying the extent of women's empowerment would be difficult.

8.   Malhotra, Schuler, and Boender (2002) detail the most common approaches to measuring women's empowerment, not only in the domestic sphere, but at the community and national levels as well.

References

Balk, Deborah. 1994. "Individual and Community Aspects of Women's Status and Fertility in Rural Bangladesh." *Population Studies* 48 (1): 21–45.

Basu, Alaka M. 1992. *Culture, the Status of Women and Demographic Behaviour: Illustrated with the Case of India.* Oxford: Clarendon Press.

Bradburn, Norman, with the assistance of C. Edward Noll. 1969. *The Structure of Psychological Well-Being.* Chicago: Aldine.

Cain, Mead T. 1993. "Patriarchal Structure and Demographic Change." In *Women's Position and Demographic Change,* ed. Nora Federici, Karen Oppenheim Mason, and Solvi Sogner, 43–60. Oxford: Clarendon Press.

Cantril, Hadley. 1965. *The Pattern of Human Concerns*. New Brunswick, NJ: Rutgers University Press.

Case, Anne, and Angus Deaton. 2003. "Consumption, Health, Gender and Poverty." Policy Research Working Paper 3020, World Bank, Washington, DC. http://econ.worldbank.org/view.php?type=5&id=25577.

Dev, S. Mahendra, and P. Padmanabha Rao. 2002. *Poverty Alleviation Programmes in Andhra Pradesh—An Assessment*. Hyderabad, India: Centre for Economic and Social Studies.

Ghuman, Sharon J., Helen J. Lee, and Herbert L. Smith. 2004. "Measurement of Women's Autonomy According to Women and Their Husbands: Results from Five Asian Countries." PSC Research Report 04-556, Population Studies Center, University of Michigan, Ann Arbor. http://www.pop.upenn.edu/swaf/publicationspage.html.

Gross, Bruce, Christine van Wijk, and Nilanjana Mukherjee. 2001. *Linking Sustainability with Demand, Gender and Poverty: A Study of Community-Managed Water Supply Projects in 15 Countries*. Washington, DC: International Water and Sanitation Centre and World Bank Water and Sanitation Program.

Hashemi, Syed M., Sidney Ruth Schuler, and Ann P. Riley. 1996. "Rural Credit Programs and Women's Empowerment in Bangladesh." *World Development* 24 (4): 635–53.

Jain, Ravindra. 1970. *South Indians on the Plantation Frontier in Malaya*. New Haven, CT: Yale University Press.

Kabeer, Naila. 1998. "'Money Can't Buy Me Love?' Re-evaluating Gender, Credit and Empowerment in Rural Bangladesh." Discussion Paper 363, Institute of Development Studies, University of Sussex, Brighton, UK.

Knodel, John, Aphichat Chamratrithirong, and Nibhon Debavalya. 1987. *Thailand's Reproductive Revolution: Rapid Fertility Decline in a Third-World Setting*. Madison: University of Wisconsin Press.

Lokshin, Michael, and Martin Ravallion. 2002. "Rich *and* Powerful? Subjective Power and Welfare in Russia." Policy Research Working Paper 2854, World Bank, Washington, DC.

Malhotra, Anju, Rohini Pande, and Caren Grown. 2003. "Impact of Investments in Female Education on Gender Quality." Gender and Development Group, World Bank, Washington, DC.

Malhotra, Anju, Sidney Ruth Schuler, and Carol Boender. 2002. "Measuring Women's Empowerment as a Variable in International Development." Background paper prepared for the World Bank Workshop on Poverty and Gender: New Perspectives. Gender and Development Group, World Bank, Washington, DC.

Mason, Karen Oppenheim. 1986. "The Status of Women: Conceptual and Methodological Issues in Demographic Studies." *Sociological Forum* 1 (2): 284–300.

Mason, Karen Oppenheim, and Herbert L. Smith. 2003. "Women's Empowerment and Social Context: Results from Five Asian Countries." Gender and Development Group, World Bank, Washington, DC.

Mauldin, W. Parker, Bernard Berelson, and Zenas Sykes. 1978. "Conditions of Fertility Decline in Developing Countries, 1965–75." *Studies in Family Planning* 9 (5): 89–147.

Milne, Claudia. 1982. *Asanti Market Women.* Video recording, Granada Television International. http://www.therai.org.uk/film/catalogue_2/11_ashante.html.

Mueke, Marjorie A. 1992. "Mother Sold Food, Daughter Sells Her Body: The Cultural Continuity of Prostitution." *Social Science and Medicine* 35 (7): 891–901.

Narayan, Deepa, ed. 2002. *Empowerment and Poverty Reduction: A Sourcebook.* Washington, DC: World Bank.

Rahman, Aminur. 1999. "Micro-credit Initiatives for Equitable and Sustainable Development: Who Pays?" *World Development* 27 (1): 67–82.

Rao, Vijayendra, and Michael Walton, eds. 2004. *Culture and Public Action.* Stanford, CA: Stanford University Press.

Smith, Herbert L. 1989. "Integrating Theory and Research on the Institutional Determinants of Fertility." *Demography* 26 (2): 171–84.

Touliatos, John, Barry F. Perlmutter, Murray A. Strauss, and George W. Holden. 2000. *Handbook of Family Measurement Techniques.* 3 vols. Thousand Oaks, CA: Sage.

World Bank. 2004. "Collective Enterprise and Action as a Path to Empowering Poor Rural Women: The Andhra Pradesh Experience." Promising Approaches to Engendering Development Series. World Bank, Washington, DC. http://www.worldbank.org/gender/promising/index.htm.

Chapter 5

Gender, Power, and Empowerment: An Analysis of Household and Family Dynamics

Joy Deshmukh-Ranadive

The dynamics of empowerment are complex and multifaceted. Power and the potential for empowerment are linked to all levels of society, including its macro, meso, and micro dimensions. For understanding the gender dimensions of empowerment, however, the position of the individual within the domestic arena is of particular importance. It is within the supposedly "private" domain of the domestic unit that multiple hierarchies of power between men and women intersect, affecting their opportunities and capacity for empowerment.

This chapter explores the concept of "spaces" as a tool for measurement of both power and empowerment, focusing on the hierarchical positions of men and women within domestic units. This framework and associated measures lend themselves both to analysis of existing power relationships and to investigation of potential processes of empowerment.

Household, Family, and Domestic Unit

In order to understand the gender dimensions of power and empowerment, it is necessary to open the "Pandora's box" of the household and family.[1] It is here that the main roots of gender discrimination are located.

The terms "household" and "family" are often used interchangeably in development research. Both terms refer to a domestic unit, and in some contexts they may be taken as equivalent. In empowerment research, however, it is important to distinguish them conceptually. Making this distinction provides a more adequate framework for grasping the complex power dynamics within domestic arenas.

Both terms are culturally defined, and their meanings therefore vary both between and within societies. Conceptually, however, the household is usually visualized as a task-oriented unit with common residence. The family is a broader kinship-based unit that is not necessarily localized in one place. Each concept can be specified by its basic characteristic, its formal definition, and its functional definition.

The basic characteristic of the *household* is that its members co-reside under one roof. The formal definition (which varies from household to household) lists these members and specifies how they are connected—by blood, marriage, adoption, employment (for example, a servant), social ties (such as friends living together), or mere acquaintance (such as fellow residents of a lodging house). The functional definition consists of specifying the functions that a household performs, that is, consumption, production, and distribution.

The basic characteristic of the *family* is that members are tied to one another by kinship relations of birth, marriage, or adoption, governed largely by a set of culturally determined rules. The ideology that governs a certain kinship system in turn determines the placement of individuals within the institution of the family. The formal definition of the family specifies the kinds of relationships that exist between family members and varies depending on the type of family, which may be nuclear, extended, single-parent, same-sex-parented, etc. The functional definition spells out the functions performed by a family, that is, reproduction, nurturing, and socializing of members, so that children grow up to be functioning members of society. Family relationships in part define how people are recruited into the material relations of the household.[2]

The concept of the *domestic unit* juxtaposes the concepts of household and family by combining the functional definition of the household with the formal definition of the family.[3] Thus the common functions carried out by a household can be used to analyze similarities between household members as well as similarities between households, while the diverse formal definitions of family can be used to analyze differences between family members as well as differences between families. The intersection of both concepts in a domestic unit provides a rich but still manageable framework for description and analysis of power dynamics.

What determines power dynamics within a domestic unit? Households, across classes, countries, and time, perform three basic functions: they consume (goods and services); they produce (goods, services, and human beings); and they distribute (resources and time, that is, work and leisure, among members). These functions are similar across households and have to be performed if the household is to survive, sustain its standard of living, reproduce itself over time, and in the process develop.

It is the third function of distribution that is the key determinant of intra-household power dynamics. All members of the household have similar intent—to survive, sustain, reproduce, and develop over time—and similar needs for nutrition, shelter, education, health care, and so forth, to make this possible. In a domestic group, however, each individual member has a place within the domestic hierarchy that entails specific endowments, rights, and responsibilities. These in turn are determined by familial rules of distribution and by norms based on ideology, kinship patterns, religious and cultural factors, the household's present stage in its life cycle, and its position in class, caste, and racial terms within society and the economy. If a member, for example, a servant, is *not* kin, then her or his placement is determined by the rules that define norms for "insiders" versus those for "outsiders." In light of the similar needs and intent of household members, their differential placement in the hierarchy and the associated differential distribution of resources cause friction.

Within the domestic unit, therefore, it is suggested that the "household" be analyzed in terms of its functions that reveal similarity, while the "family" be the focus for analysis of differences that determine unequal access to power.[4] Such an approach provides a way to take into account the differences in familial structures around the world. In unilateral societies such as India, Sri Lanka, Bangladesh, and Pakistan, for example, there do exist nuclear families consisting of a couple and their children living by themselves, but more commonly the couple and their children reside with the marital family of the woman (that is, the husband's natal family). It is specifically this extended family that constitutes the household. The picture is different in bilineal societies such as the Philippines. There, the residence of a married couple is flexible and can fluctuate between the woman's natal and marital families. Hence, even though households are functionally similar, there are differences in form among families.

Besides unilateral and bilineal kinship patterns, sociocultural and religious codes also may lead to different family patterns. For example, in Karnataka, India, different behavior and kinship rules apply when a girl is dedicated to the temple god or goddess and becomes a *basavi* (*devdasi*) woman. The girl achieves the status of being a married woman forever. She is considered auspicious because she can never be a widow. The girl is expected to have multiple sexual relations with different men, all of whom have to be of the same or higher caste, although often *basavis* prefer to have a continuous relationship with one man. Her children are accepted by society, and the concept of fatherhood is absent from her family. She can inherit property from her natal family as if she were a son. She can also perform the obsequies of her parents. All the rights otherwise denied to girls in Hindu society are bestowed upon *basavi* girls. Her household consists of her parents' side of the family and her children; her visiting mate has no rights and no obligations.

The differences among family members lie in their individual endowments, rights, and responsibilities within the domestic unit. Likewise, within the wider society, each domestic unit has a similar intent and requirement to survive, sustain, reproduce, and develop. The differences between domestic units lie in their relative positions within society and the economy, as determined by class, caste, race, and other factors.

Power Dynamics within Domestic Units

Allocation of resources within a domestic unit is embedded within the allocation of rights, needs, and duties. Rights and needs are intimately related. Women and girls may have rights to pooled resources within the household, but their ability to exercise those rights is likely to be determined by various cultural and contextual evaluations of need. For instance, among extended families in South Asia, especially in rural areas, women are in charge of family stocks of grain, but the allocation of food among children is influenced by cultural assumptions that boys need more and better food than girls.

Equally important is the allocation of duties and responsibilities. It is the social identity of the person that ascribes roles, and roles in turn entail duties according to sociocultural norms. The duties of caring and rearing are ascribed to women, while men are supposed to provide resources and income. In reality, however, men do not always fulfill their duties as providers, while women do not always get their rights as wives, daughters, daughters-in-law, and mothers.

Within domestic units in South Asia, the pattern is that for men rights are actual but duties nominal, while for women rights are nominal but duties actual. Moreover, the accepted rights and duties for men and for women are in themselves gender-biased and unjust. The family ethos is one of sharing and sacrifice, but socialization of gender means that much of the onus falls upon women. Given limited collective resources and limited time available for work, sharing becomes in practice a zero-sum exercise of determining relative shares for women and men. Gender discrimination results in women getting smaller shares of resources and larger shares of work.

The microdynamics of power within the domestic unit are structured by hierarchies (rankings or placements) that integrate gender differences with other factors differentiating individuals within the unit. Margolis (1989) shows such hierarchies arranged into three major tiers. At the top is a set of higher ranks for certain adults. In the middle are the intermediate ranks, which consist of training positions and service positions. The training positions prepare individuals for promotion to the highest ranks. The service positions are designed for household maintenance and for service to the higher and lower ranks; adults in these positions are barred from the top ranks by definition. The lowest ranks contain the immature and the incapacitated, including children and ill family members.

Persons in the highest ranks generally control decision making, distribution of material resources, and admission to all positions in the hierarchy. They may be obliged to protect everyone in the unit. They issue commands to those in the lower ranks and in return get deference and service. Margolis suggests that the extent and limit of an individual's power are defined by his or her position within the hierarchy.

Figure 5.1 draws on Margolis's formulation, with some modifications, to show the placement of individuals within a domestic unit based on a stereotypical male-headed nuclear family. The arrows in the figure indicate what one

FIGURE 5.1   Hierarchical Placement within a Nuclear Family

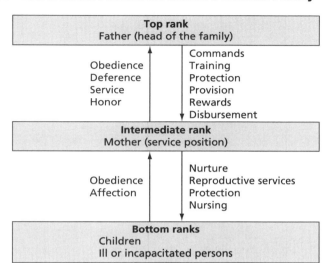

person gives or owes to another. Occupying the top rank is the father, who controls decision making, issues commands, and trains subordinates. The father is also supposed to protect and provide for others and disburse resources; in return he receives obedience, deference, and service. The intermediate rank consists of the service position, occupied by the mother. She is an economic dependent who has to serve the father. She also bears, nurtures, and protects children, who in turn obey her and give her affection. Children and ill or incapacitated members are in the bottom ranks. Adult children are not placed in the structure since, given the definition of a nuclear family, they will move on to form separate domestic units.

To capture the reality of South Asian society, one also has to look at extended families. Figure 5.2 illustrates a typical South Asian extended family that is unilateral, kinship-based, and patrilineal. As in the case of the nuclear family, the hierarchy has three major tiers, with the father or senior male occupying the top rank. Unlike the nuclear family, however, the extended family generally has several adult men and women at various intermediate ranks, because adult sons with their wives and children remain part of the household. Another difference is that within the extended family there is the possibility of promotion from one rank to another within the hierarchy. No promotion ladder exists within the nuclear family, where sons and daughters leave the household when they marry.

The intermediate ranks in the extended family consist of training, training-cum-service, and service positions. Someone in a training position has a better chance to eventually move up in the hierarchy than someone in a service

FIGURE 5.2   Hierarchical Placement within an Extended Family

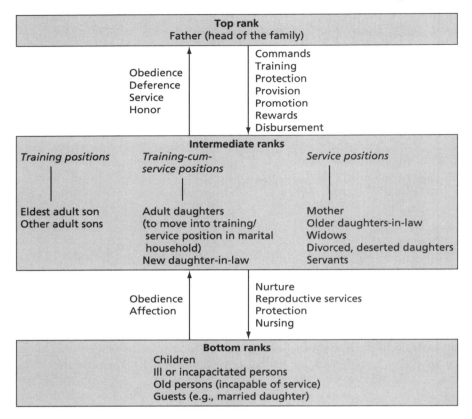

position. The main training position is occupied by the eldest adult son, who has the possibility of promotion to the top rank if his father dies or becomes too old or ill to function. The younger adult sons do not have that opportunity if they continue to live within the same extended family. However, when the eldest brother becomes head, they can move up in the hierarchy *within* the training positions.

The training-cum-service positions contain adult daughters, who serve their natal families while being trained to move into new positions in their marital households. A new daughter-in-law also finds herself in a training-cum-service position, since while serving her marital family she is also being trained in the ways of that family. Occupying service positions are the mother, older daughters-in-law, widows (such as the father's sister or aunt), divorced or deserted daughters, and servants. There is a further subranking within the intermediate ranks, where women with children are placed higher than childless women, and women with sons are placed higher than those with only daughters.

As in the nuclear family, children and ill persons occupy the bottom ranks. Boys will move up to training positions and girls to training-cum-service positions as they mature, while adults who are ill or incapacitated will move back to their former places after recovery. In an extended family, the bottom ranks also include old people incapable of service, as well as guests, such as married daughters visiting their natal families.

In South Asian extended families, the world of women functions essentially separately from that of men. Within a domestic unit, therefore, a separate hierarchy simultaneously exists *among women*. The highest rank in this women-only hierarchy is usually occupied by the wife of the senior male (although her top rank among women is equivalent only to an intermediate rank in the overall domestic hierarchy). Intermediate women's ranks are filled mainly by daughters and daughters-in-law of the senior woman. These intermediate ranks include service and training-cum-service positions, and distinguish between service positions with and without authority. As in the overall extended-family hierarchy, the bottom ranks are occupied by children, the ill, the very old, and married daughters visiting their natal families.

The existence of a women-only hierarchy has implications for empowerment. A woman may achieve a measure of power in relation to other women in the domestic unit while remaining relatively powerless in relation to men and the larger society. The eldest daughter-in-law can move from a training position to a service position with authority, and may even rise to the top (women's) rank after the death, illness, or widowhood of her mother-in-law. Hence, in the world of men and women, women always remain in the intermediate ranks, but among women considered separately, there is a chance of moving from intermediate to top rank.

Spaces, Power, and Empowerment

In order to understand how constraints to equality can be reduced, we have to consider the concept of "spaces."[5] Every person has an allotment of spaces—physical, economic, sociocultural, and political—at a given moment in time.[6] This allotment is determined by the domestic and larger environment within which the person lives. In the context of the domestic unit, a person's position within the hierarchy largely determines his or her access to, and control over, spaces within the domestic arena. When a person's position in the hierarchy changes (as through marriage, birth of a child, illness, or death of another family member), his or her access to spaces may increase or decrease accordingly. At the same time, the relationship also works in the other direction: the expansion and contraction of spaces may influence the relative positions and movement of household members in the domestic hierarchy.

Spaces influence a person's capacity to act and his or her behavior both within the household and outside it. The stimulus for an individual's empowerment comes when something changes in that person's life in a way that expands spaces, allowing the person the place, freedom, or margin to do what she or he intends to do.[7] Conversely, a constriction of space takes away capacity to act and narrows the number of alternatives for behavioral decisions. Finally, spaces are also an end for which negotiations take place. Each of the four main types of external spaces affects the empowerment of women in particular ways.

Physical Space

An important aspect of physical space is a woman's access to, ownership of, and control of her natal and marital houses, including spaces within these houses. Also included is her access to, ownership of, and control of space and immovable property outside the home: land, commercial premises (such as a shop), school, or place of work. Finally, physical space includes a woman's personal mobility and control over her own body and its reproductive, productive, and consumptive functions.[8]

By controlling and sometimes denying women's access to the natal and marital homes, unilateral patrilineal kinship systems such as those in South Asia perpetuate women's disempowerment. In these kinship systems, a woman has little claim over her natal house. Sociocultural norms determine her to be a guest in her father's house once she marries. Because of social conditioning, a woman typically believes that her father's property will automatically become her brothers' and that as a woman she should not try to claim it. Even when she holds a stake in the natal property, a woman often gives it up so as to maintain good relations with her brothers (in part so she can count on their support in the event of a breakdown of her marriage or other friction in her marital home).

At the same time, women in these kinship systems are considered to be outsiders in the marital house. It may take them years to carve a niche for themselves in the husband's family. The right of women to the marital house is only usufructuary and hence unstable and insecure, since in the face of marital strife she can be divested of her access to it. A case study from Uttar Pradesh, India, is illustrative.[9] As a new bride, Gondi was ill-treated by her mother-in-law. Her husband was having an affair with his sister-in-law (his brother's wife). When Gondi's first-born son was seven months old, she was beaten and turned out of the house. Her son was kept behind by her mother-in-law and given to her husband's childless sister. Gondi had no option but to return to her parents' house.[10]

Also important is a woman's access to physical space *within* the house, in terms of the areas she is expected or allowed to be in. Most often, the spaces that women inhabit are related to the domestic work they do, so the kitchen is considered to be their primary space. In many households of the extended type, women are barred from certain areas of the house. These restrictions on where a woman's body may move are often accompanied by restrictions on her control of and access to her body. A case study from Nepal shows these types of control.[11] The daughter of a wealthy *pradhan panch,* or village leader, faced strictures in her marital home despite her father's status and her own education. She was not permitted to leave the domestic compound. Before cooking she had to bathe behind the house even though other family members could use the central tap. Inside the house she was expected to be submissive and to observe *purdah* by wearing a veil to hide her face from the elders.

When women are restricted to a physical domain within the house, the hierarchies between them become more overtly visible. A case study from Bengal describes how the *anthapur*—the inner chambers of the house inhabited exclusively by women—housed a web of power dynamics that operated among women ranked hierarchically according to kin status.[12] The study focused on the impact of formal education on the lives of middle-class Bengali women in the nineteenth century. According to the author, changes were introduced into the lives of these women without an adequate understanding of the organizational principles, hierarchy, and internal rules that characterized the separate world of women. Education was meant to provide an emergent Bengali middle class with women steeped in Victorian values, and also to bring women within the ambit of the male world. But with the advent of women's education, the restrictive *anthapur* was dismantled. Women could not, even with education, measure up to men as equals in the household. As a result, women's power within the geographically defined space of their chambers was replaced with relative powerlessness in the context of wider physical space occupied by women and men.

Economic Space

The second type of space that affects women's empowerment is economic space, determined by ownership of immovable and movable property, access to assets both tangible and intangible, and income, which allows control of goods and services and can thereby enhance a woman's economic independence. However, the mere presence of assets or income does not signify an expansion of economic space unless there is accompanying control. For instance, in South Asian societies a daughter is often given dowry instead of property rights. The bride thus becomes a vehicle for the transfer of valuables from her own kin to her husband's kin. This transfer begins with the dowry but does not end there. The woman is supposed to receive gifts from the natal family on festive occasions, on the birth of children, and on visiting the natal home; gifts are also given to the parents-in-law. However, the goods transferred via dowry and gifts cannot be said to enhance the woman's economic space as she does not usually have control over them. Articles and clothing are mostly controlled by the mother-in-law, and cash by the father-in-law. Even if the couple live on their own, their control (even jointly) over the dowry is questionable.

Sociocultural Space

The third kind of space that affects women's power is sociocultural space. This space widens when a person's position within kin-based hierarchies is higher than that of others. The ranking of members within families is an essential aspect of the milieu the family is based in, determined in part by the type of family (nuclear or extended) and the kinship structure (unilateral or bilineal). As seen earlier, in comparison to the nuclear family with its simple three-tiered structure, the extended family is more complex. Age is a major factor in determining status in extended families: the parents-in-law usually are the most important members, with the sons and daughters-in-law ranked by age. Marital status is also an important determinant, as widows have lower status than married women. The woman's childbearing capacity also affects her status. A woman who has no children is labeled "barren" and faces tremendous discrimination. In societies where son preference is prevalent, a woman who has borne no sons is also scorned.

Caste, class, religion, and ethnic origins are important determinants of socioeconomic status and access to or control of sociocultural space, both within society and within a domestic unit. A case study from Pakistan reports that girls from low-class "sweeper" families were not taught by teachers in schools, but instead were made to sweep the school.[13] In conservative, rural, patrilineal societies it is unlikely that the caste barrier will be crossed through marriage.

Political Space

Finally, women's political space can be perceived at two levels: private political space and public political space. The first relates to the political situation within the domestic unit. This space differs in concept from sociocultural space, since the latter determines individual placements in the hierarchy, whereas political space deals with the *working* of those placements. Political space hence correlates to hierarchical allocations of authority and responsibility that are sanctioned by sociocultural spaces.

The second level, public political space, has to do with women's access to and control of public office and their participation in the administration and governance of society and institutions locally, regionally, and nationally. Access to this public space is in part a function of personality traits such as courage, determination, and qualities of leadership. But it depends even more on structural factors. The divide between the private and the public is very significant in the lives of women: public political space exists on the public side of the divide, while women are largely confined to the private side, and few bridges exist to assist the crossing. As a result, women's access to and control of public political space is severely restricted.

Spaces and Movement within Hierarchies: The Importance of Mental Space

Women's ownership of, access to, and control of spaces facilitates their movement from lower to higher positions within hierarchies. Usually promotion within the domestic hierarchy is based upon age, but catalysts that contribute toward an expansion of spaces can hasten promotions. Hence, at one level, a ranking accords spaces to the woman within which she can bargain for more spaces. At another level, the macro environment can accord the woman greater or lesser access to spaces, thereby altering her position within hierar-chical structures. Hence, with time and with the evolution of the life cycle of the domestic unit, members change ranks and positions. It is within and with these spaces that women have to negotiate for larger spaces in an attempt at empowerment.

The interface between the macro environment and the microdynamics at the domestic level lies in the increase and decrease of spaces accorded to dif-ferent members of the domestic unit. Sometimes changes in the macro envi-ronment alter opportunity structures so that positions of household members change. For example, a policy change that allows women access to livelihood generation activities may assist women in circumventing prescribed directions of movement within domestic hierarchies. Women also sometimes undertake covert individual strategies with the veiled intent of circumventing given hier-archies or increasing or acquiring superiority within the household's organi-zational structure.

Expansion of spaces does not always result in empowerment, however. For example, it often happens that interventions that expand a woman's economic space with increased income do not empower her, because she has no control over that income. On the contrary, the increased income may even lead to an increase in domestic violence, as has been found in studies of microcredit in Bangladesh (Goetz and Sen Gupta 1996). This happens because the interven-tion has not altered the woman's socioeconomic space. When an intervention does nothing to change the socioeconomic environment of the household, an expansion of economic space alone will not bring about empowerment.

However, if the intervention increases a woman's levels of confidence and self-esteem, then a process of empowerment has begun. Sometimes even be-fore an action is taken, the decision to act instills a feeling of confidence and well-being. This points to the importance of a fifth type of space—mental space. Mental space consists of the feeling of freedom that allows a person to think and act. An expansion of this space implies a change in perceptions, leading to a feeling of strength. Mentally there is a movement away from restriction and constraints, which facilitates action in a positive direction. Mental space facilitates "power within." *The most important condition for empowerment to take place is an expansion of the person's mental space.*

There is, however, no linear relationship between the expansion of physi-cal, economic, sociocultural, or political spaces and the expansion of mental space. What, then, actually leads to an expansion of mental space? The first factor is bringing women together in new settings, such as collectives orga-nized around livelihood issues or other issues of concern to them. Experience in India and elsewhere suggests that when women operate through collectives they gain confidence, leading to empowerment on both an individual and group level.[14] This is because it is not enough to expand the mental space of individual women within the setting of the traditional community. Traditional communities stubbornly restrict sociocultural spaces, and their members, ac-cordingly, have restricted mental space. Rather, women must be mobilized into new communities, such as women's solidarity groups, where they can collectively express injustices and address common problems. In such settings, expansion of mental space can take place on a collective basis.

However, since women's lives are intimately related to the domestic unit, an expansion of mental space within *this* collective is also needed to carry forward the process of empowerment. This is precisely the reason that attempts at empowerment based on forming collectives such as self-help groups and on encouraging leadership in women often end up accentuating discrimination and violence within households. Research that delves into power relationships must take into account the three-sided relationship between individuals, the domestic collective, and other collectives.

The second factor that leads to an expansion of mental space is information. Information is a very important source of power as well as an instrument of empowerment. Women who are illiterate and do not have access to knowledge are easily oppressed. It has been found, however, that formal education is not a necessary precondition for empowerment to take place. In the first place, the information that is most critical to unleash a process of empowerment is knowledge of the power structures within which individuals' lives are embedded. Such knowledge changes self-perception and brings about an awareness of the nature of oppression. Equally vital is information about people's rights and duties both as citizens of civic society and as members of families. This includes knowledge about legal processes and about human rights and entitlements.

Information also helps to make social mobilization possible. Groups formed around social, environmental, and economic issues gain strength and solidarity when members share their experiences. Apart from these kinds of information, knowledge about matters related to livelihoods, finances, political processes, and so forth also equips women to take action to change the situation they find themselves in.

Linking and Evaluating Spaces

Studies that investigate intra-domestic dynamics in the context of individual or domestic strategies can use the concept of "spaces" to explain consequences of gender discrimination.[15] While it is important to investigate all five kinds of spaces, a first step can be made by translating economic, sociocultural, and political space into physical space, which is often more easily measured. For example, when a woman is permitted to work for income outside the home, this increases her economic space. But her ability to go outside the home to a place of work also amounts to an increase in her physical space, which can be documented. This would also be true when a girl is permitted to pursue high school studies that require her to attend school in another village. A woman who stands for election to the village *panchayat* gains access to public political space; by attending meetings outside the home and seeing to official matters in adjoining villages, she also widens her access to physical space. A woman who owns land at her natal home and does not till it, but receives income in cash or in kind from it, has ownership of that physical space even without traversing it. On the other hand, a woman who has to cover her face and not be seen in the "public" courtyard has less access to physical space. Whatever the method of inquiry, whether survey, life history, or case study, an investigation into women's ownership of, access to, and control of *physical* space can throw light upon gender inequities in power within domestic groups.

A mere recording of increased physical space, however, does not necessarily indicate a positive change in a woman's life. Physical spaces have to be evaluated for the *meaning* they have to the lives of the women concerned. It is this subjective meaning that determines empowerment (or the lack of it). Empowerment is as much a matter of emotion as of practical access to and control of spaces. If a woman does not feel that increased access to physical space has empowered her—allowed her, for example, a role in decision making, or given her the ability to take action along with responsibility for that action—then the expansion of space has to be seen in a different light.

This brings us to mental space, which allows for freedom of thought and hence of action. It may seem as if in the Asian context, where a large number of women come from poor families, mental space would be meaningless. This is not true. The mode of articulation may be different, but the need for mental space and the advantages that accrue from access to it are universal across classes. There is a close connection between perceiving physical space as positive and enjoying the mental space that it accords. Hence, the researcher cannot study physical spaces without taking into consideration the perceptions of the person in question. For instance, impact evaluation studies on self-help groups in India considered women who, because of participation in microcredit and livelihood generation activities, had widened their physical space by going into banks to transact business. These women, who earlier would look with downcast eyes while speaking with a man, were able to speak with male bank officers while looking them in the eye, increasing their self-confidence tremendously. Greater physical space was thus accompanied by an increase in mental space—an indicator of empowerment.[16]

Measuring Empowerment: Linking Macro, Meso, and Micro Environments

Just as the individual is placed within a domestic environment and has to negotiate spaces within it, the domestic unit is placed within a larger macro environment, which also has physical, economic, sociocultural, and political components. Macro factors operate at the level of the global system, nation, region, or state. The macro physical environment is shaped by physical characteristics related to geographic location, soil, climate, landscape, and so on. The macro economic environment is shaped by economic opportunities that depend in turn on forms of production, institutions, level of industrialization, state of the rural economy, and related factors. The macro sociocultural environment depends upon the structures of caste, class, race, religion, and intergroup as well as intragroup relations within each category. This environment also is shaped by kinship patterns and gender norms. The macro political environment is determined by the level, quality, and transparency of public office, the quality of governance, and the nature and extent of citizen participation in public life.

Macro-level changes, in the form of political and economic interventions by both state and nonstate actors, have a direct impact on the micro (domestic) level by changing opportunities for domestic units and individuals. Macro-level factors, together with social structures at the community level, also act upon the meso environment, which consists of villages and neighborhoods. Changes in the meso environment in turn alter the domestic environment, which alters spaces for the individual. These linkages are shown in figure 5.3.

Interventions may succeed in having an impact upon the macro environment. However, of all the components of the macro environment, the sociocultural environment is the most stubborn and difficult to alter, and as a consequence, sociocultural space is difficult to negotiate. An individual woman who achieves an expansion in this space often does so at the cost of her own isolation. Thus, collectives and collective action are a more effective vehicle to set in motion a process of empowerment.[17]

The connection from macro to meso to micro has to be made to ascertain the empowerment effects of development interventions. Gender discrimination affects individuals most intimately at the level of the domestic unit, but at this level it is particularly difficult for the researcher to carry out detached observation (as the proverbial "fly on the wall"). A woman may not report discrimination even when asked directly, since the victim herself may be unaware of any injustice being done. Because of social norms, many injustices are understood and accepted as part of "being a woman." Female self-sacrifice and self-denial are expected for the "good of the family." Conceptualizing behaviors and processes through the prism of spaces helps to bypass this problem. The four dimensions—physical, economic, sociocultural, and political spaces—can be linked vertically to the similar dimensions of the various environments.

When this framework is applied in research, physical, political, and policy changes will be reflected in shifts in macro environments. Meso environments will capture anthropological profiles of the areas under consideration. Domestic environments will be context- and place-specific, reflecting cultural realities. When linkages between these are found through research investigations, changes in mental space will have to be gauged in connection with the shifts in nonmental spaces.

It is not possible to devise a general list of indicators that will be relevant to all kinds of societies. However, keeping in mind that universal principles of humanity and democracy are conducive to human well-being, it is possible to come up with a tentative list of positive indicators for mental space. As noted, mental space expands when collectives impart solidarity and information converts into knowledge. In addition, mental space is enhanced when public and private political spaces become more democratic; when there is social, economic, and political inclusion; and when there is mutual accountability between institutions.

FIGURE 5.3   Empowerment Linkages

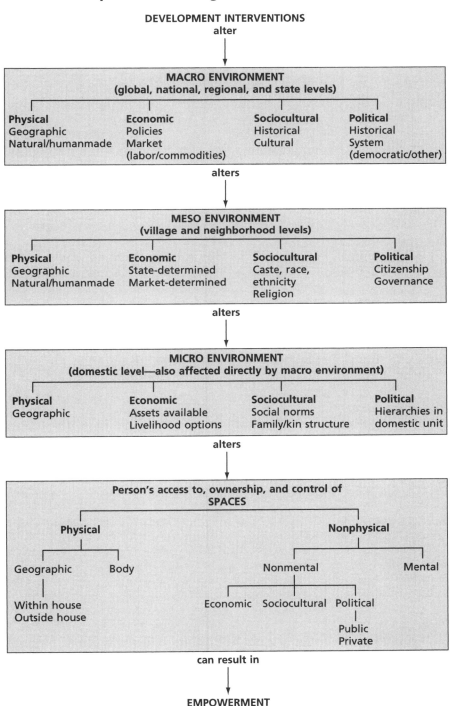

Conclusions

In order to measure and promote empowerment it is necessary first to arrive at a realistic understanding of power dynamics. What happens in the family and household is central to gender-based discrimination and to the goal of women's empowerment, making it imperative to include the domestic unit with all its hierarchies in the analysis.

One way of looking at intra-domestic power dynamics is through the concept of individuals' access to and control of different "spaces." These configurations are not static, however. Shifts in spaces across the domestic unit are closely connected to changes in the micro, meso, and macro environments in both forward and backward linkages. Catalysts that initiate such changes can work from the outside as well as from within the domestic unit. In particular, democratizing the form of the family and the functions of the household are critical to widen women's access to spaces and generate processes of empowerment. Conversely, failure to take into account intra-domestic dynamics can thwart the empowerment efforts of development interventions.

Mental space is the most critical of all spaces. Its relationship to nonmental spaces is complex. Understanding the links between them helps us understand why some development interventions seem to reach dead ends in empowering people in spite of increases in their physical, economic, and political spaces. The framework suggested in this chapter can help to illuminate the complicated institutional and human dynamics of the family and household, a step toward the measurement and ultimate enhancement of empowerment for women.

Notes

1.   Feminist researchers have discussed the dimensions of empowerment from the perspective of women. See, for example, Agarwal (1995), Batliwala (1994), Elson (1995), Kabeer (2000), and Oxaal and Baden (1997).
2.   According to Moore (1994), the analysis of the household and the conceptual and empirical difficulties inherent in defining the relationship between the family and the household are areas of concern in all the social sciences. She draws attention to the shift in the last 15 years from the analysis of the household as a bounded unit toward a view that stresses its permeability.
3.   This framework was first conceptualized in terms of the functions of the household in the context of structural adjustment policies in India; see Ranadive (1994). Also see Deshmukh-Ranadive (2001, 2002) for subsequent formulations.
4.   The differences that are established by norms also determine who constitutes the co-residential unit. For example, unilateral kinship rules result in norms that do not allow a married woman to reside with her natal family; instead, the couple moves in with her husband's natal family, which becomes her marital family. Hence, the formal definition of the household is given shape by the formal definition of the family. Furthermore, the act of reproduction takes place within the precincts of familial codes of conduct, but the maintenance of children takes place in the household through the functions of consumption and production. Again, through the function of distribution

within the household, differential allocation of endowments, rights, and responsibilities automatically translates into socialization.

5. For a detailed discussion of the use of "spaces" as a concept to capture power and empowerment, see Deshmukh-Ranadive (2002).

6. These four dimensions are not necessarily exclusive of each other. The purpose of demarcating different kinds of spaces is to facilitate analysis and to devise reasonably differentiated categories that can be operationalized in research.

7. Space is different from capability. The term "capability" as used by Amartya Sen (1982) and developed by Martha Nussbaum (1995) signifies characteristics within human beings that are necessary for a human or a humane existence. Space, on the other hand, allows a person to move, maneuver, and negotiate to develop capabilities.

8. Physical space has been a focus of analysis within feminist geography, which recognizes behavior and space as mutually dependent. One method used is time geography, in which women's everyday routines are traced to ascertain the spaces they occupy. The divide between "male" public space and "female" private space is seen as one of the most oppressive aspects of women's lives. See Women and Geography Study Group (1984) and Rose (1993).

9. Illustrations in this chapter are taken from reports of a project titled Women's Work and Family Strategies in South and South-East Asia, conducted by the Centre for Women's Development Studies, New Delhi, under the sponsorship of the United Nations University. The project included 30 interregional collaborative studies conducted during the mid-1980s in India, Pakistan, Sri Lanka, Bangladesh, Nepal, the Philippines, and Malaysia. For abstracts of these studies and an analysis based on them, see Deshmukh-Ranadive (2002). Some of the studies have also been revised and published individually.

10. Surinder Jetley, "Women's Work and Family Strategies: Meerut District, Western Uttar Pradesh, India." This 1987 study was conducted for the project Women's Work and Family Strategies in South and South-East Asia (see note 9). For further information see Deshmukh-Ranadive (2002).

11. Centre for Women and Development, "Women's Work and Family Strategies under Conditions of Agricultural Modernization and Resettlement: Case of the Cotton Programme in Nepal." This 1989 study was conducted for the project Women's Work and Family Strategies in South and South-East Asia (see note 9). For further information see Deshmukh-Ranadive (2002).

12. Malavika Karlekar, "Changing Family Strategies and Educated Women: A Case Study from Bengal." This 1987 study was conducted for the project Women's Work and Family Strategies in South and South-East Asia (see note 9). For further information see Deshmukh-Ranadive (2002).

13. Nigar Ahmed, "Women's Work and Family Strategies." This study of five villages in Pakistan was conducted for the project Women's Work and Family Strategies in South and South-East Asia (see note 9). For further information see Deshmukh-Ranadive (2002).

14. Formation of women's development collectives in India has often been facilitated by nongovernmental organizations. For example, in 1981 the Centre for Women's Development Studies in New Delhi began an action research project in the rural areas of West Bengal in Bankura, mobilizing and organizing women around livelihood issues. More information is available on the center's Web site at http://www.cwds.org.

15. A "domestic strategy" refers to decisions made by a domestic unit in relation to the marriage, work, migration, education, and so on of its members, supposedly to enhance the good of the unit as a whole. Such strategies may seem consensual but need not be so.

16. Dr. V. Puhazendi of National Bank for Agriculture and Rural Development, Mumbai, personal communication with author, 2001.

17. It may seem as if conceptualizing power and empowerment in terms of spaces results in a static understanding of empowerment that does not reflect its dynamic nature as a process. However, the act of negotiating for more space is the central dynamic in the struggle toward empowerment.

References

Agarwal, Bina. 1995. "Gender, Property, and Land Rights: Bridging a Critical Gap in Economic Analysis and Policy." In *Out of the Margin: Feminist Perspectives on Economics,* ed. Edith Kuiper and Jolande Sap with Susan Feiner, Notburga Ott and Zafiris Tzannatos, 264–94. New York: Routledge.

Batliwala, Srilatha. 1994. "The Meaning of Women's Empowerment: New Concepts from Action." In *Population Policies Reconsidered: Health, Empowerment and Rights,* ed. Gita Sen, Adrienne Germain, and Lincoln C. Chen. Cambridge, MA: Harvard University Press.

Deshmukh-Ranadive, Joy. 2001. "Placing the Household in Perspective: A Framework for Research and Policy." *Asian Journal of Women's Studies* 7 (1): 40–79.

———. 2002. *Space for Power: Women's Work and Family Strategies in South and South-East Asia.* Published in collaboration with the Centre for Women's Development Studies. New Delhi: Rainbow Publishers.

Elson, Diane. 1995. "The Empowerment of Women: Comments on Chapters by Trzcinski, Hopkins and Agarwal." In *Out of the Margin: Feminist Perspectives on Economics,* ed. Edith Kuiper and Jolande Sap with Susan Feiner, Notburga Ott and Zafiris Tzannatos, 295–99. New York: Routledge.

Goetz, Anne Marie, and Rina Sen Gupta. 1996. "Who Takes the Credit? Gender, Power, and Control over Loan Use in Rural Credit Programs in Bangladesh." *World Development* 24 (1): 45–63.

Kabeer, Naila. 2000. "Resources, Agency, Achievements: Reflections on the Measurement of Women's Empowerment." In *Gendered Poverty and Well-Being,* ed. Shahra Razavi, 27–56. Oxford: Blackwell.

Margolis, Diane Rothbard. 1989. "Considering Women's Experience: A Reformation of Power Theory." *Theory and Society* 18: 387–416.

Moore, Henrietta L. 1994. *A Passion for Difference: Essays in Anthropology and Gender.* Cambridge: Polity Press.

Nussbaum, Martha C. 1995. "Human Capabilities, Female Human Beings." In *Women, Culture, and Development: A Study of Human Capabilities,* ed. Martha C. Nussbaum and Jonathan Glover. Oxford: Clarendon Press.

Oxaal, Zoë, with Sally Baden. 1997. "Gender and Empowerment: Definitions, Approaches and Implications for Policy." Bridge Report 40. Briefing prepared for the Swedish International Development Cooperation Agency (Sida), revised edition. Institute of Development Studies, University of Sussex, Brighton, UK.

Ranadive, Joy. 1994. "Gender Implications of the Adjustment Policy Programme in India: Significance of the Household." *Economic and Political Weekly* (Mumbai), April 30, WS-12.

Rose, Gillian. 1993. *Feminism and Geography: The Limits of Geographical Knowledge.* Cambridge: Polity Press.

Sen, Amartya. 1982. *Choice, Welfare and Measurement.* Cambridge, MA: MIT Press.

Women and Geography Study Group of the IBG. 1984. *Geography and Gender: An Introduction to Feminist Geography.* London and Dover, NH: Hutchinson, in association with the Explorations in Feminism Collective.

Subjective Well-Being and Power

Chapter 6

Psychological Empowerment and Subjective Well-Being

Ed Diener and Robert Biswas-Diener

In this chapter we describe and relate two psychological concepts: subjective well-being (SWB) and psychological empowerment. Subjective well-being is defined as people's positive evaluations of their lives, including pleasant emotions, fulfillment, and life satisfaction (for general background on SWB, see Diener 1984 and Kahneman, Diener, and Schwarz 1999). Psychological empowerment represents one facet of SWB—people's belief that they have the resources, energy, and competence to accomplish important goals. Subjective well-being is one important variable by which the quality of life in societies can be measured—the fact that people in the society find their lives to be fulfilling and happy. We review some of the causes of facets of subjective well-being, as well as their consequences, including feelings of empowerment. We also describe some cultural variations in SWB and differences between societies in what causes SWB.

Psychological empowerment often accompanies and follows from certain other facets of SWB such as positive affect (pleasant moods and emotions). Such positive emotions, when induced in laboratory experimental studies, have been found to have certain predictable consequences, including sociability, self-confidence, leadership and dominance, flexible thinking, altruism, active engagement with the environment, and self-regulatory ability. In other words, positive moods produce a state that appears to be similar to psychological empowerment. Success can lead to psychological empowerment when it heightens positive emotions, and psychological empowerment in turn can lead to further success if external conditions allow it.

We argue that although external conditions are necessary for empowerment, they are not sufficient for it without psychological feelings of competence, energy, and the desire to act. Thus, empowerment consists of both the actual ability to control one's environment (external empowerment) and the feeling that one can do so (internal empowerment), which is influenced by additional variables such as positive emotions. We reject the behavioristic and mechanistic position that empowerment resides only outside of people in the material world, and we instead argue for the view that empowerment must include the causal force of people's beliefs about their efficacy.

The study of subjective well-being (for example, happiness and life satisfaction) sheds considerable light on psychological empowerment. First, internal empowerment is one facet of subjective well-being, because people's feelings of well-being are inherently tied to their beliefs about whether they can achieve their goals. Second, certain types of SWB, such as positive emotions (for example, joy and love), heighten people's feelings of empowerment. Finally, concepts related to subjective well-being and its measurement give us insights into defining and measuring empowerment.

The Importance of Subjective Well-Being

Subjective well-being is necessary for quality of life, but is not sufficient for it. It is difficult to imagine a life, no matter how positive in objective respects, that we would label as ideal if the individual living that life were dissatisfied and depressed. Therefore, SWB is necessary for us to consider a life an ideal one. SWB, however, is not sufficient for a full life because we would consider a happy person's life incomplete if he or she were not free, or were missing other basic qualities that we consider necessary for dignity. Robert Nozick's (1974) example of a hypothetical "experience machine" that can make people happy, even though they are only imagining happy experiences, is instructive here. The fact that most people do not want to be happy based on artificial experiences indicates clearly that most people do not simply want SWB—they want happiness coming from valuable experiences.

However, just as SWB is not sufficient by itself for a good life, neither are economic or social indicators by themselves sufficient to indicate the well-being of a society. We want people to feel happy and fulfilled, not just live in a benign environment. If people consistently felt depressed in a healthy and wealthy society, it would not be a desirable place. Thus, SWB is a complement to objective indicators in assessing the quality of life in a society. In addition, knowledge of SWB is important to economists and policy makers because people's choices are dependent on their feelings of well-being and their predictions about what will enhance their SWB.

Research suggests that the experience of positive emotions leads to a syndrome of related behavioral characteristics: sociability, feelings of self-confidence and energy, engaged activity, altruism, creativity, and perhaps better immune functioning and cardiovascular fitness. Because there are longitudinal and formal experimental studies on the effects of positive emotions, we know that these emotions often cause the listed attributes and are not simply a result of them. It should be noted that several of the characteristics associated with positive emotions sound similar to empowerment in that the happy individual is self-confident and likely to pursue goals in an active way.

Chronically happy people exhibit the above characteristics, and individuals who are in a temporary positive mood also exhibit the characteristics listed above. It is not surprising, then, that happy people are more successful in a number of life domains: they have more friends, are more likely to get married and stay happily married, make more money on average, are more likely to receive superior ratings from their supervisors at work, are more likely to be involved in community and volunteer activities, and are more likely to fill leadership roles. They also may live longer. It should be mentioned, however, that virtually all of the research findings are from Western nations, especially the United States, and therefore we do not know the degree to which happy people are more successful in other cultures. Furthermore, it might be that mildly dysphoric individuals are better at certain types of jobs, for example, those requiring constant vigilance. Thus, it appears that happy people are in many ways more successful than unhappy people, but we do not know the limiting conditions on this conclusion. A caveat is that most of the research on the benefits of SWB has been conducted in Westernized and industrial nations.

Measuring Subjective Well-Being

Over the past decade substantial advances have been made in measuring SWB. Simple self-report survey instruments have been the mainstay of the field since its inception. Respondents are asked questions such as "How happy are you?" "How frequently do you feel happy?" and "How satisfied are you with your life?" Respondents typically provide their responses in terms of a numerical scale value. The survey items are moderately valid and correlate acceptably with other measures, such as the reports of family and friends about the target's happiness. Nevertheless, research artifacts or biases can influence these self-report scales, such as different self-presentational styles among respondents and memory biases for one's experiences.

Because of the limitations of global self-report measures, a battery of measures can be employed for assessing SWB (see Sandvik, Diener, and Seidlitz 1993). These might include experience sampling (random sampling of moods and thoughts over time with a palm computer), informant reports from family and friends, biological measures (such as prefrontal brain asymmetry, the eye blink startle response, and cortisol levels, all of which are correlated with emotional experience), interviews, reaction time computer measures, and ratings of smiling. Taken together, these measures provide a more accurate assessment of SWB.

Many behavioral scientists, including demographers and economists, who have been trained in the behaviorist tradition have a distrust of self-report measures such as those used in SWB surveys. This is reasonable because there are cases in which self-report measures have yielded manifestly incorrect data. Psychologists know that memory problems can plague self-report measures, as can biases due to impression management. For this reason results on SWB should not be considered definitive until conclusions drawn from self-report studies are confirmed with other types of measures, such as experience sampling, informant reports, and biological measures. The concerns apply to self-report measures of empowerment as well as to self-report measures of SWB, and therefore multiple methods of measurement should be used, when possible, in both cases.

At the same time, skepticism of self-report measures should not be taken to extremes. After all, no type of data, including demographic or economic measures, is free from error. Self-report measures have shown considerable convergence with other types of SWB measures, and the measures predict hard objective outcomes such as suicide and job turnover. Mood and emotion reports predict behavior in laboratory settings where the behavior is measured by external observers, and self-reports of happiness correlate with activation in certain brain regions. Thus, complete distrust of self-report SWB and empowerment data is unwarranted and unwise, although a cautious stance is warranted, as it is with other types of data.

Our theoretical model indicates that there are four stages in well-being: (a) environmental circumstances and events to which the person reacts; (b) the person's immediate reactions to these events, such as feelings of joy or sadness; (c) a person's recall of her or his reactions; and (d) a person's global constructed judgments of his or her life, such as life satisfaction. Each of these stages differs from the one before, and is translated from the stage before it through processes that are increasingly understood. Because of the intervening psychological processes occurring between stages, people's circumstances and their life satisfaction are only modestly correlated.

In the transition from life circumstances to people's immediate reactions to these circumstances, appraisals, goals, temperament, and attention all moderate the influence of circumstances on a person's reactions. For example, a person with a phlegmatic temperament who has few materialistic goals is less likely to be upset by a personal loss in the stock market than a person with a reactive temperament who believes that money is the key to happiness.

Moving from ongoing reactions to people's memories of them, we also have a set of factors that can moderate the relation by changing people's recall. For example, people tend to recall feelings that are in line with expectations and situational norms, and they tend to forget feelings that are incongruent with self-beliefs. Finally, when people make global constructions of their well-being (for example, being satisfied with life), there are discrepancies with the recall of emotions because people use different standards in computing their satisfaction and base their global judgments of well-being on information in addition to the recall of their emotional reactions.

It is important to keep the above steps in mind later when we discuss empowerment. Feelings of empowerment can be measured "online" (over time at random moments in everyday life) in reference to specific goals, or they can be measured in a global way. Like SWB, power starts at the level of objective, external events. However, people's reactions to these events—whether they believe they have power, and act on that belief—are not the same as having external power. Similarly, the later reconstructive stages (recall and global beliefs) will be moderated by factors that can alter the relation between immediate feelings of empowerment and global judgments about the person's abilities and power. Thus, measures of empowerment at each of these stages are likely to show only modest correlations with one another. An important point for those working in the area of societal development is that conditions themselves are not identical to people's beliefs about those conditions. A series of factors such as temperament and culture influence whether conditions of empowerment are translated into psychological empowerment.

Causes of Subjective Well-Being

We know through studies of the SWB of twins, and other methodologies, that about half of the variance in SWB is due to genes, to a person's inheritance. Identical (monozygotic) twins who are reared apart are more similar to each other in SWB than are fraternal (dizygotic) twins who are reared together. This indicates that there are genetic influences on how happy people are. However, we also know that conditions can, and do, influence SWB. For example, wives typically show dramatic drops in life satisfaction when their husbands die, and only very slowly, over a period of five years on average, do they climb back toward their former baselines of life satisfaction. Similarly, most people show a dramatic drop in SWB when they lose their jobs, and they do not completely return to their former levels of SWB even after they obtain new jobs, results that hold after controlling for income. When people partially lose control of their lives, as in widowhood or unemployment, it is likely that their feelings of empowerment also will drop.

Two personality traits in particular have been implicated in happiness. On the positive side, extraverts tend to show more upbeat emotions. They are happier on average even when they are alone, and across all of the days of the week. Extraverts seem to have a predisposition to experience more pleasant emotions, although the specific reason for this is not fully understood. In contrast, neurotic individuals are prone to worry, sadness, and anger. The neurotic individual seems to be more reactive to negative events. Extraversion and neuroticism are two separate traits, and therefore there are extraverted neurotics (high levels of both positive and negative emotions), introverted neurotics (low pleasant emotions and high negative emotions), introverted nonneurotics (low on both types of affect), and extraverted nonneurotics (high pleasant emotions and low negative emotions). Individuals with these different types of temperaments are likely to exhibit different behaviors, including in the workplace, and different feelings of empowerment as well.

Research findings suggest that social relationships are important to happiness, probably even necessary for it. In a group of very happy people we studied, every single individual had high-quality social relationships. This does not mean that all of their social relationships were of high quality, of course. In this case, the very happy people experienced high-quality social relationships in at least two out of three areas—friends, family, and romantic partner. On the other hand, some unhappy individuals also had good social relationships. Thus, relationships are necessary for happiness, but not sufficient by themselves.

Another cause of high SWB is making progress toward one's personal goals. People have different values and goals, so the type of success that makes them happy can be idiosyncratic, dependent on their aims. When we studied the types of resources that are most related to SWB, we found that personal attributes such as self-confidence were very important. Perhaps self-confidence was a good prediction of life satisfaction because it is a helpful resource for such a wide variety of goals. It appears that individuals who feel self-confident, and are thus "psychologically empowered," are more likely to make progress toward their personal goals and are more likely to be happy. In order to be empowered, people need to possess the resources to reach their goals, and they also need to have the psychological mind-set that they can and will reach the goals. Thus, objective resources, feelings of self-efficacy, and positive emotions all work together to create empowerment.

The effects of income on happiness have been studied in some detail (see Diener and Biswas-Diener 2002 for a review). In wealthy nations there are small, but positive, correlations between income and reports of happiness. For instance, more poor people than wealthy people report dissatisfaction with life. These findings have been replicated hundreds of times. We found that among respondents drawn from *Forbes* magazine's list of the richest Americans, life satisfaction scores were modestly higher than the average found in national surveys. However, the correlations between income and happiness are often larger in poorer nations. This finding is usually interpreted to mean that increases in income make more difference to SWB at poverty levels than they do in higher income strata. Diener and Biswas-Diener (2002) and Frey and Stutzer (2002) provide a full discussion of the relation between money and SWB.

When we examine the mean levels of happiness of different nations and plot these figures against per capita income, there is often a curvilinear relation such that the rise in SWB is steep in the lower income ranges and becomes very gradual in the higher income ranges. Wealthy nations show higher SWB on average than do poorer ones, but wealthy nations are more likely to have more equality, greater longevity, and other desirable characteristics beyond material abundance.

When one analyzes changes in SWB over the decades, there is often little movement in wealthy nations such as the United States or Japan. This is often interpreted to mean that income makes little impact on SWB once basic needs are met. However, one finds that material desires have increased at about the same rate as has real income in the United States. Therefore, the absence of increases in SWB might be due to the fact that people's rising incomes do not enable them to satisfy a larger proportion of their material desires. There are other plausible explanations for why SWB often has not increased over time as developed nations have become wealthier. For example, increases in wealth might be accompanied by mobility or higher divorce rates, which counterbalance the positive effects of material wealth, although these explanations have not been rigorously tested against one another.

One explanation for the pattern of SWB findings across nations is that income matters only at those levels where increases make a difference in whether people can meet basic needs such as food, shelter, and health. An alternative explanation for the fact that poor nations show low average levels of SWB is that people in poor nations have a large number of desires that they cannot fulfill, especially because they see the goods and services that people consume in wealthy nations. An explanation that brings together the idea of basic needs with the concept of unfulfilled desires is that needs drive desires and do so in a compelling way for most people, but other factors such as social comparison can also influence desires. It is the extent to which people can meet their desires, in turn, that directly influences SWB. Thus, needs might have strong influences on SWB because evolution has built humans so that biological needs affect their desires.

We have studied people who live materially simple lives—the Amish in the United States, the slum dwellers of Calcutta, the East African Maasai, the Inughuit of Northern Greenland, and homeless individuals in Calcutta and California. The Maasai (who rarely have electricity, indoor plumbing, or quality health care) show surprisingly high SWB, while the homeless in California show low SWB (despite income superior to that of the Maasai). Recall that social relationships are very important to SWB, and in this domain of life, the Maasai are better off than the California homeless. The lifestyle of the Maasai allows them to fulfill many of their desires, whereas the California homeless experience lives that are deficient in certain basic needs such as security and respect. Clearly there are psychological influences on SWB beyond objective material circumstances.

Table 6.1 shows the life satisfaction scores of selected groups of respondents. It is interesting to note that the *Forbes* group of richest Americans are the highest in life satisfaction, but just a little above other groups who have considerably less money. At the same time, dire poverty in the context of homelessness or prostitution does seem to substantially lower people's life satisfaction. Thus, people's expectations and the respect they receive from society seem to moderate the effects of income on life satisfaction. However, it should be noted that the homeless and sex workers sometimes also suffer from mental illness or drug addiction, which might contribute to their lower SWB.

Cultural Influences on Subjective Well-Being

Latin Americans on average report higher levels of SWB than do East Asians (Diener, Oishi, and Lucas 2003). It appears that Latin Americans are more "approach oriented," focusing on desirable goals, whereas East Asians are more "avoidance oriented," focusing on preventing bad outcomes. In addition, Latin Americans believe that positive emotions are very desirable, whereas East Asians believe that positive emotions and negative emotions are almost equally appropriate. Thus, Latin American countries often score

Table 6.1   Life Satisfaction of Selected Groups

Group	Score
Forbes richest Americans	5.8
Maasai (Kenya)	5.4
Amish (Pennsylvania)	5.1
Inughuit (Northern Greenland)	5.1
Cloistered nuns (United States)	4.8
Illinois nurses	4.8
Illinois college students	4.7
Calcutta slum dwellers	4.4
NEUTRAL	4.0
Calcutta sex workers	3.6
Uganda college students	3.2
Calcutta homeless	3.2
California homeless	2.8
New prisoners (Illinois)	2.4
Mental inpatients	2.4
Detroit sex workers	2.1

Response scale: 7 = extremely satisfied; 4 = neutral; 1 = extremely dissatisfied.
Note: Scores are based on averages from the five items of the Satisfaction with Life Scale and from a one-item satisfaction scale for the *Forbes* group.

higher than expected on SWB surveys, relative to the incomes in these nations, and East Asian nations such as Japan and the Republic of Korea often score lower than expected. It should be remembered, however, that culture is dynamic and that these trends therefore might be changing over time.

Cultures can be arrayed on a continuum ranging from individualistic (individual well-being and choice are granted high importance) to collectivistic (the group is seen as more important than the individual). It appears that both cultural orientations have their costs and benefits in terms of SWB. Individualistic societies offer people greater personal freedom, and on average people in these societies report high SWB. However, these cultures also have higher levels of problems such as divorce and suicide. They have high marital satisfaction rates and, paradoxically, high divorce rates. They experience high average SWB, and yet on average also have higher levels of suicide. One explanation is that in individualistic societies people receive credit for their successes but also feel the sting of failure more strongly. It might also be that the extended families of collectivistic cultures impair people's freedom, but also provide a safeguard against loneliness and the acting out of aberrant behaviors. Finally, because the achievement of happiness is a goal in individualistic nations, it might be seen as a personal shortcoming if a person is unhappy.

Empowerment as a Facet of Subjective Well-Being

Box 6.1 lists the component parts of subjective well-being. It can be seen that empowerment is included as one facet of SWB, because the experience of well-being includes the feeling and belief that one can accomplish one's goals. Several different concepts in turn are listed as facets of empowerment. Although psychologists draw distinctions among these concepts (see Pearlin and Pioli 2003), they all include the overarching idea that the person is confident of his or her ability to accomplish goals. Communal efficacy is the idea that a person can with his or her group accomplish group goals. Whereas personal efficacy is often emphasized in Western nations, communal efficacy is often the focus in more traditional cultures. Various facets of SWB, such as positive affect, can influence psychological empowerment and in turn can be influenced by it.

We distinguish two types of empowerment. First, there is external or situational empowerment—the external conditions that allow efficacious action. People have this type of empowerment to the extent that their environment allows successful action, and they have the personal and material resources to effectively take such action. Second, there is psychological empowerment—a

---

Box 6.1   Facets of Subjective Well-Being

Life satisfaction
Satisfaction in specific domains, such as marriage, work, and health
Low levels of unpleasant affect ("negative" emotions and moods, such as
    depression and anger)
High levels of pleasant affect ("positive" emotions and moods, such as
    affection and joy)
Meaning and purpose
Engagement (interest in one's activities)
Empowerment
        Self-efficacy
        Self-confidence
        Mastery
        Communal efficacy (can with others accomplish group goals)

Figure 6.1 Two Types of Empowerment Are Necessary for Deliberate Action

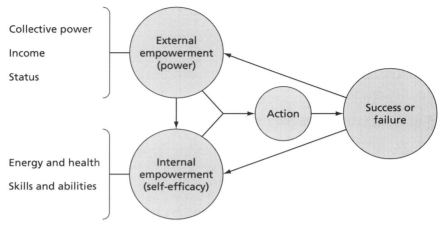

person's belief that action can be effective along with the energy and desire to carry out such action. If the environment allows effective action but the person's cultural or personal beliefs indicate that the action will be ineffective, the person is not truly empowered. Conversely, if a person feels psychologically empowered but external conditions do not in fact allow for effective action, the person is not truly empowered. Both external and psychological empowerment are necessary for efficacy, and neither is sufficient in itself. Whether a particular environment is empowering can only be assessed in reference to specific goals. Every environment will be empowering for certain goals, and frequently only for individuals who possess specific resources and fill particular roles. Thus, external empowerment can be broad or narrow and is meaningful only in reference to specified goals and actions.

In figure 6.1 we present the hypothesized relations between action, external empowerment, and internal empowerment. Notice that both external and internal empowerment are necessary for action, and work together. Although external conditions in many instances influence whether people believe they are efficacious, other factors can influence internal empowerment as well. Furthermore, even if the conditions of external empowerment occur, people may fail to discover that they have power because of the persistence of belief systems that were shaped by conditions in the past. Therefore, external empowerment does not inevitably lead to psychological empowerment. Notice too that other variables such as positive emotions and social support also influence internal empowerment.

Concepts related to psychological empowerment have a rich history in the discipline of psychology. Albert Bandura (1997) has extensively studied the effects of self-efficacy, the belief that one can accomplish specific goals. Julian Rotter (1992) and Martin E. P. Seligman (1991) have both written about an internal locus of control, that is, attributing outcomes to one's own actions.

Optimistic outcome expectancies have been studied by Charles Carver and Michael Scheier (1990), and Seligman, among others. Finally, feelings of autonomy and competence have been explored by Ed Deci and Richard Ryan (1980) and their colleagues. An idea that underlies each of these approaches is that an optimistic expectancy that actions will be successful is essential for people to take action in seeking their goals. Without feelings of competence, self-efficacy, autonomy, and optimism, people are unlikely to pursue goals. Furthermore, low self-perceived competence leads to negative feelings.

We can use the model of subjective well-being to design measures of psychological empowerment. For example, we can assess psychological empowerment with simple self-report instruments and obtain moderately valid scores from respondents. More accurate assessment, however, requires a battery of assessment devices, including self-reports, experience sampling, an assessment of environmental conditions, informant reports, behavioral observations, and assessment by trained experts. A complete assessment should include not only general self-efficacy, but also psychological empowerment within specific domains of life and for specific aspirations, because general self-efficacy does not guarantee feelings of efficacy in a specific domain. Success at measuring empowerment across cultures is especially likely to come from a battery of measures, because there are substantial challenges in comparing simple self-report scores across cultural groups. Ultimately, understanding will come from determining how the various measures relate to one another. Like subjective well-being, psychological empowerment is likely to be multidimensional, including cognitive, affective, and behavioral components.

Psychological empowerment is likely to result from high SWB, especially from positive emotions. People who are chronically happy are likely to feel more empowered than unhappy individuals. Research shows that self-confidence, sociability, activity, and energy follow from positive emotions (for example, see Lyubomirsky, King, and Diener 2004) and studies also reveal that external power leads to positive emotions (Keltner, Gruenfeld, and Anderson 2003). Because positive emotions are likely to arise from goal success, people are more likely to feel empowered and to pursue new goals when they have been successful in the past and when they perceive that they have the resources to meet their goals. That is, empowered feelings and successful action can form a self-reinforcing loop, but repeated failures and the resulting negative emotions can stop the cycle of psychological empowerment and result in depression, resignation, or learned helplessness.

Thus, empowered feelings are likely to arise from good events occurring in a person's life because such events create positive emotions, which in turn lead to self-confidence and other feelings that create psychological empowerment. However, external efficacy and empowerment for specific goals and tasks also depend on a person's skills and resources in that specific area, as well as on external circumstances, which together allow successful actions. Thus, empowerment is a multifaceted concept.

Our argument is that psychological empowerment arises in part from the experience of success. When a person succeeds in obtaining a goal, he or she then feels self-confident and energized to pursue additional goals. In contrast, when a person experiences repeated failures, sadness and feelings of helplessness arise, which lead to inaction. These cycles of mood and action make evolutionary sense. A person whose actions are successful is rewarded, and also has the feelings that lead to further action. In contrast, when actions are not effective, the person has feelings that lead to withdrawal and the conservation of energy.

Although empowerment and positive emotions form a cycle, they are not the same thing, and it is useful to consider them separately. For one thing, positive emotions can arise from success in one important area of life but lead to self-confident feelings that carry over to action in other areas of life. For another thing, factors in addition to successful goal pursuit can influence the level of positive emotions a person feels—for example, temperament and mental outlook. Thus, having success does not create the same level of positive feelings in all cases, and the resultant feelings of empowerment can also vary. In other words, in some cases a person might be successful but not have pleasant emotions and feelings of empowerment. For example, severe depression can interfere with positive feelings even when one experiences success. For this reason, having an environment that allows successful action is helpful to psychological empowerment, but not necessarily sufficient for it to occur.

Some believe that if people have power, they are empowered. However, people need to know they have power, they need to experience the positive emotions and self-confidence that produce feelings of empowerment, and they need to have goals that they believe are worth pursuing in the domain in question. Just because people objectively have power does not mean that they will feel empowered or that they will act. An optimistic sense of personal competence, that is, psychological empowerment, can be influenced by factors in addition to objective power. Factors that predispose people to positive emotions, such as the temperament characteristic of extraversion, will also dispose them to psychological empowerment.

In some cases interventions are needed to help powerless people by giving them more external power—for example, by giving them voting rights or a greater voice in their work. However, such interventions can prove ineffective if people continue to feel powerless, and in this case psychological interventions might be needed to produce empowerment. People might need education, positive mood inductions, or role models to gain psychological empowerment. In some cases individuals might believe so strongly that events are outside of their control, and have a cultural ideology that supports such beliefs, that obtaining objective power will not in itself change their behavior. A difficult challenge is that cultural beliefs and practices arise as adaptations to certain conditions, such as the lack of efficacy and power, but can persist even when those conditions no longer exist. Because cultural beliefs are usually built on a network of assumptions and values, they may be relatively resistant to change, and concerted efforts will be required to produce psychological empowerment.

It is noteworthy that Diener and Fujita (1995) found that self-confidence was the resource that most strongly predicted life satisfaction, more than material resources or social resources. This might be because those with high self-confidence have a feeling of empowerment—they believe they have efficacy regarding their important pursuits, and therefore are optimistic that they can make progress toward a wide variety of goals.

Is Empowerment a Good Thing?

We have assumed throughout this discussion that empowerment is desirable, but several cautions are warranted. First, people can use power and empowerment for goals that society considers to be bad. They do not necessarily use power to obtain goals that benefit others or the world. From society's point of view, empowerment is good only when it is combined with values that benefit societies and the world. Another caveat is that there is both personal and collective power. Exercising personal power in a collectivistic society can potentially disrupt longstanding cultural structures. Although Westerners might think of power in a personal, individualistic sense, some groups might find collective power to be more consistent with the structure of their culture. Thus, it is important not only to consider self-empowerment from an individualistic and Western point of view, but also to recognize that communal or collective power is likely to be a major source of empowerment in many cultures. Of course, in all cultures both types of empowerment are important, but the relative weighting is likely to vary from society to society. For a discussion of communal mastery in contrast to personal mastery, see Hobfoll et al. (2002).

A more subtle limitation of empowerment is that it induces an implemental mind-set and suppresses a deliberative one (Keltner, Gruenfeld, and Anderson 2003). In deliberation people think about what they should or should not do, and why. That is, they are analytical and examine various possible courses of action. In an implemental mind-set, people are prepared to move forward, and they look for the means to action. Feelings of power tend to lead to action. Although this is often desirable, in some cases it is not. Keltner and his colleagues showed that people with power sometimes act when they should desist, become more self-focused, and lack complexity of thought. Because power implies action psychologically, a person with an implemental mind-set might focus on actions rather than on deep analyses of problems. Thus, feelings of power have clear benefits, but some potential drawbacks as well. After all, not everyone who gains power thereafter acts in rational and compassionate ways. Thus, psychological empowerment must also be accompanied by rational analysis and compassion for others in order for it to be desirable for societies.

One objection that might be raised about psychological empowerment is that it is not necessary for action because only external empowerment matters. A behavioristic view of human action might suggest that only external power matters, and that concepts such as internal empowerment are merely epiphenomenal. Refuting this view, Bandura (1995) points out that when beliefs about self-efficacy are experimentally manipulated independently of performance and external conditions (and in some cases, even contrary to performance), this leads to changes in future performance. This finding indicates that internal self-efficacy does play a causal role. Similarly, training in general self-efficacy can boost performance (Eden and Aviram 1993). Another relevant study found that children's feelings of efficacy were a better predictor of their preferred occupation than was their academic achievement (Bandura et al. 2001). Furthermore, social factors other than competency, such as falling in love (Aron, Paris, and Aron 1995) and emotional social support (McAvay, Seeman, and Rodin 1996), can boost people's feelings of empowerment, leading in turn to motivation and performance enhancements (Bandura and Locke 2003). Thus, the case that psychological empowerment plays a causal role in action, and is not simply an epiphenomenal result of externally empowering conditions, is strong. In the words of Bandura, "People's beliefs that they can produce desired effects by their actions influence the choices they make, their aspirations, level of effort and perseverance, resilience to adversity, and vulnerability to stress and depression" (1998, 51).

Conclusions

When we induce external empowerment for a group of people, we might be surprised if they do not avail themselves of the new opportunities. Resignation or passivity sometimes prevail, despite the fact that the new opportunities for effective action are real. What is lacking in these cases is psychological empowerment. Because feelings of agency and psychological empowerment are often highly intertwined with cultural belief systems, feelings of psychological disempowerment may persist long after external conditions have changed. In these cases, educational and behavioral interventions are needed to enhance psychological empowerment. Efforts to empower people will succeed only when external conditions allowing efficacious action are present, when people have the skills and abilities to act effectively, and when they feel and believe that they are empowered.

What does the concept of internal empowerment offer in understanding societal development? It suggests that giving power to people without power might not in all cases lead them to take effective action that promotes development. In addition to favorable external conditions, they will need psychological or internal empowerment, and factors such as education, social support, beliefs about fate, and positive emotions will all influence the potential for effective action. People working in the development area need to assess forms of subjective well-being such as positive emotions that can influence empowerment, as well as internal empowerment itself (such as feelings of self-efficacy and the belief that one's actions can be effective). Unless a broad view of empowerment is adopted that recognizes the importance of psychological variables, development efforts can fail even though adequate material resources have been provided. Longitudinal research is needed to trace the cycle of influence between internal and external empowerment and action, but it is unlikely that action will occur unless people believe it will be effective and have adequate energy and motivation to act. One priority for future research is to discover when external empowerment does and does not lead to internal empowerment.

Planners should seriously consider the possibility that levels of SWB—for example, the level of positive emotions people experience—can influence people's psychological empowerment and are therefore also precursors of development. When people experience substantial amounts of depression and stress, they are not likely to actively work toward development. Ultimately, of course, the goal of empowerment and development is to enhance people's subjective well-being, and thus psychological empowerment and SWB are interlocking goals toward which all development practitioners should strive. Diener and Seligman (2004) recommend that societies track the SWB of their citizens over time, and a system of national accounts for tracking subjective well-being and psychological empowerment is particularly useful in the context of developing nations. Because of material scarcities, economic development is an important goal for poor nations. However, we must not lose sight of the fact that well-being is the ultimate goal of economic development, and possibly a cause of it as well.

References

Aron, A., M. Paris, and E. N. Aron. 1995. "Falling in Love: Prospective Studies of Self-Concept Change." *Journal of Personality and Social Psychology* 69: 1102–12.

Bandura, A. 1995. "Comments on the Crusade against the Causal Efficacy of Human Thought." *Journal of Behavior Therapy and Experimental Psychiatry* 26: 179–90.

———. 1997. *Self-Efficacy: The Exercise of Control.* New York: Freeman.

———. 1998. "Personal and Collective Efficacy in Human Adaptation and Change." In *Advances in Psychological Science,* vol. 1, *Social, Personal, and Cultural Aspects,* ed. J. G. Adair, D. Belanger, and K. L. Dion, 51–71. Hove, UK: Psychology Press.

Bandura, A., C. Barbaranelli, G. V. Caprara, and C. Pastorelli. 2001. "Self-Efficacy Beliefs as Shapers of Children's Aspirations and Career Trajectories." *Child Development* 72 (1): 187–206.

Bandura, A., and E. A. Locke. 2003. "Negative Self-Efficacy and Goal Effects Revisited." *Journal of Applied Psychology* 88 (1): 87–99.

Carver, C. S., and M. F. Scheier. 1990. "Origins and Functions of Positive and Negative Affect: A Control-Process View." *Psychological Review* 97 (1): 19–35.

Deci, E. L., and R. M. Ryan. 1980. "Self-Determination Theory: When Mind Mediates Behavior." *Journal of Mind and Behavior* 1: 33–43.

Diener, E. 1984. "Subjective Well-Being." *Psychological Bulletin* 95 (3): 542–75.

Diener, E., and R. Biswas-Diener. 2002. "Will Money Increase Subjective Well-Being? A Literature Review and Guide to Needed Research." *Social Indicators Research* 57: 119–69.

Diener, E., and F. Fujita. 1995. "Resources, Personal Strivings, and Subjective Well-Being: A Nomothetic and Idiographic Approach." *Journal of Personality and Social Psychology* 68 (5): 926–35.

Diener, E., S. Oishi, and R. E. Lucas. 2003. "Personality, Culture, and Subjective Well-Being: Emotional and Cognitive Evaluations of Life." *Annual Review of Psychology* 54: 403–25.

Diener, E., and M. E. P. Seligman. 2004. "Beyond Money: Toward an Economy of Well-Being." *Psychological Science in the Public Interest* 5 (1): 1–31.

Eden, D., and A. Aviram. 1993. "Self-Efficacy Training to Speed Reemployment: Helping People to Help Themselves." *Journal of Applied Psychology* 78 (3): 352–60.

Frey, B. S., and A. Stutzer. 2002. *Happiness and Economics.* Princeton, NJ: Princeton University Press.

Hobfoll, S. E., A. Jackson, I. Hobfoll, C. A. Pierce, and S. Young. 2002. "The Impact of Communal-Mastery versus Self-Mastery on Emotional Outcomes during Stressful Conditions: A Prospective Study of Native American Women." *American Journal of Community Psychology* 30: 853–72.

Kahneman, D., E. Diener, and N. Schwarz, eds. 1999. *Well-Being: The Foundations of Hedonic Psychology.* New York: Russell Sage Foundation.

Keltner, D., D. H. Gruenfeld, and C. Anderson. 2003. "Power, Approach, and Inhibition." *Psychological Review* 110: 265–84.

Lyubomirsky, S., L. King, and E. Diener. 2004. "Happiness Is a Good Thing: A Theory of the Benefits of Positive Affect." University of California, Riverside.

McAvay, G., T. E. Seeman, and J. Rodin. 1996. "A Longitudinal Study of Change in Domain-Specific Self-Efficacy among Older Adults." *Journals of Gerontology Series B: Psychological Sciences and Social Sciences* 51 (5): P243–53.

Nozick, Robert. 1974. *Anarchy, State, and Utopia.* New York: Basic Books.

Pearlin, L. I., and M. F. Pioli. 2003. "Personal Control: Some Conceptual Turf and Future Directions." In *Personal Control in Social and Life Course Contexts: Societal Impact on Aging,* ed. S. H. Zarit, L. I. Pearlin, and K. W. Schaie, 1–21. New York: Springer.

Rotter, J. 1992. "Cognates of Personal Control: Locus of Control, Self-Efficacy, and Explanatory Style." *Applied and Preventive Psychology* 1: 127–29.

Sandvik, E., E. Diener, and L. Seidlitz. 1993. "Subjective Well-Being: The Convergence and Stability of Self-Report and Non-Self-Report Measures." *Journal of Personality* 61: 317–42.

Seligman, M. E. P. 1991. *Learned Optimism.* New York: Knopf.

Chapter 7

Subjective Well-Being and Objective Measures: Insecurity and Inequality in Emerging Markets

Carol Graham and Stefano Pettinato

> Mill wrote: "Men do not desire to be *rich,* but to be richer than other men."
>
> —Pigou, *The Economics of Welfare*

Many recent studies evaluating individuals' subjective well-being—or broadly speaking, their "happiness"—suggest the need to revisit standard assumptions about the role of rational, material self-interest in determining economic behavior.[1] These studies, which focus primarily on the developed economies, find little correlation between aggregate economic growth and happiness. While they find that, on average, the wealthy are happier than the poor within individual societies, they find no evidence that happiness increases as societies grow wealthier or that happiness differs between wealthier and poorer societies (above a certain absolute minimum income).[2]

In developed economies, people's happiness depends far less on income than on other factors such as employment, health, marriage, and age. Similarly, happiness seems to depend strongly on macroeconomic variables other than income growth, such as unemployment, inflation, and volatility.

These findings by no means undercut the importance of economic growth as a necessary condition for achieving a wide range of fundamental societal objectives, including economic development, enhanced social welfare, and reduced poverty. Yet they do suggest that factors other than income growth affect individuals' assessments of their own welfare and may also influence their responses to economic incentives and policies.

Although research on happiness has so far focused on the developed economies, a better understanding of the role of relative income differences and of nonincome determinants of economic behavior could have important implications for the future direction and sustainability of market economies in developing countries as well. Our objective in this paper is to bring to bear on these questions some empirical evidence from two emerging market economies: Peru and Russia.

Economists have traditionally measured preferences by looking at behavior (revealed preferences). In this paper we use survey data on subjective well-being to capture individual preferences with respect to macroeconomic and microeconomic variables. While not without flaws, the approach can contribute to our understanding of seemingly "nonrational" economic behavior.

Individual and within-country variables, such as marital status, employment, and inflation, clearly influence happiness. Beyond this, however, we posit that several variables related to international economic integration—macroeconomic volatility, the globalization of information, increasing income mobility (both upward and downward), and inequality driven by technology-led growth—also affect how individuals perceive their well-being. The effects of these variables may be stronger in developing economies that are becoming tied into the international economy than in the advanced industrial economies, with implications for the political sustainability of market reforms and for social stability more generally.[3]

Improvement in subjective well-being and income mobility are conceptually distinct from empowerment, defined as "the expansion of assets and capabilities of poor people to participate in, negotiate with, influence, control, and hold accountable institutions that affect their lives" (Narayan 2002). Nevertheless, both are among the conditions that arguably may contribute to or result from empowerment. The complex relationship between the subjective and objective variables, moreover, parallels the relationship between subjective and objective aspects contained within the multidimensional empowerment concept. How poor people perceive movement in and out of poverty is potentially as important to understanding the potential for empowerment as are changes in poverty status measured by income data.

Globalization, as in the cases of Peru and Russia, brings changes in rewards to different cohorts and skill sets. There are many winners but also many losers as new opportunities are created for those with certain skills and those with other skills face new competition. Our data on mobility rates suggest that there is a great deal of movement up the income ladder by poor people, but also a surprising amount of movement back into poverty by people in the middle or near middle of the income distribution.

In this context, perceptions of change have particular relevance not only for revealing attitudes but also for raising questions about long-term trends. Does moving up the income ladder, at least temporarily escaping poverty, contribute to empowerment if it is not perceived as progress and is potentially ephemeral? In other words, are people really empowered by escaping poverty if they are extremely vulnerable to falling back into it?

An essential step in understanding these issues is to investigate the relationship between income mobility and perceptions of subjective well-being connected with that mobility. Our study explores three propositions related to this relationship, using panel data from Peru and Russia. The first is that relative income differences affect subjective well-being more than absolute ones do, at least above a certain absolute income. The second is that respondents' positions on the income ladder matter a great deal, with those in the middle more likely than those at the bottom to be dissatisfied with their status because they are vulnerable to downward mobility.[4] The third is that changes in status—operationalized here as income mobility—have significant effects on happiness, although not always in the expected direction.[5] Before describing our evidence, we briefly review the research on happiness.

Happiness: The Research Literature

Richard Easterlin was a pioneer of the "economics of happiness." His chief finding—that wealthy people tend to be happier than poorer ones within countries, but that no such relationship exists among countries or over time—has since been supported by numerous studies.[6] Easterlin posited that absolute income levels matter up to a certain point, after which relative income differences matter more. The importance of relative differences depends in part on social norms, which vary among societies.[7]

Psychologist Ed Diener and his colleagues found that perceptions of income differences rather than objective differences have negative effects on happiness.[8] Diener and Biswas-Diener (1999) found that while mean wealth in countries is strongly linked to mean reports of subjective well-being, economic growth in developed countries has not been accompanied by any increase in subjective well-being. Increases in individual income, moreover, do not lead to more happiness.[9]

Many studies of happiness support the proposition that relative income differences and variations in reference groups have stronger effects than absolute income differences. Merton (1957), for example, found that people's aspirations—and therefore their satisfaction or happiness—are very much determined by the reference group to which they compare themselves. Albert Hirschman (1973) has done important work on the frustration induced by relative deprivation.[10]

Several studies have also examined effects of macroeconomic and other variables on happiness. David Blanchflower and Andrew Oswald (2000), for example, found that unemployment and poor health have negative effects on happiness, while marriage and education have positive effects. Indeed, these nonincome variables have greater positive effects than does income. In another study DiTella, MacCulloch, and Oswald (1997) found that inflation has very strong negative effects on happiness.[11] Our own work on Latin America corroborates the findings of the negative effects of unemployment and inflation on happiness (Graham and Pettinato 2001). Charles Kenny (1999) explored the links between happiness and growth. Like Easterlin, he noted the importance of relative rather than absolute income differences in people's self-assessments.

A few economists have attempted to develop measures of individual welfare that capture its subjective elements. Bernard Van Praag's measure, known as the Leyden approach, captures the interaction between individual preferences and the effects of social norms and the incomes of others. It also captures the effects of changes over time, showing that individuals anticipate gains and then are often disappointed at the size or effects of the gains in retrospect (Van Praag and Frijters 1999). Individuals' happiness also depends on their stage in the life cycle.[12] Another issue in assessing subjective well-being is the direction of causality: are people happy because of their economic conditions, or do happy people assess their economic conditions more favorably?[13]

Whether and how subjective well-being affects future economic—and possibly also political—behavior are questions that require much more theoretical and empirical work. Ultimately, answers to these questions will determine the importance of the study of subjective well-being for future social science research and policy.[14]

Our paper shifts the focus from developed economies to the emerging market countries and to the effects of globalization-related trends and their interactions with demographic variables, such as age, education, and occupation.[15] We examine empirical evidence from two emerging market economies, Peru and Russia. While we focus primarily on the factors that determine subjective well-being and changes therein, we also provide some initial evidence of the effects of those patterns on future economic behavior.

Happiness and Hardship: Evidence from Peru and Russia

In both Peru and Russia, market reforms and globalization have spurred economic growth and created new opportunities for many. Yet the new ties to the global economy, along with resultant macroeconomic volatility, have subjected many others, especially those who had been securely in the middle class, to more economic risk.

Both countries could be considered "globalizers" in the 1990s, as they made major efforts to integrate into the international economy. While the transition in Russia was much more dramatic, as it entailed dismantling a command economy, both countries made major changes to the structure of the economy, with a focus on increasing the role of the private sector and shrinking the scope and role of the state. In both countries poverty had increased in the period preceding the transition. The subsequent reforms brought additional costs in terms of poverty at the same time that they generated gains for a large number of people, and very large gains for a much smaller number of very visible "big winners."

In Peru, as in much of Latin America during the 1980s and 1990s, many people escaped poverty. Yet many also fell into poverty. The workers who were most vulnerable were not the poorest workers but those most integrated into the formal economy, those whose wages were subject to shock-related fluctuations. In Russia in the 1990s, descent into poverty was the norm rather than the exception, as poverty grew at an unprecedented rate. In both nations, consumption standards rose as norms were globalized and public social insurance was scaled back.

From the mid-1980s to late 1990s, inequality increased in the former communist countries, particularly Russia. In Peru, as in other strong market reformers in Latin America, it decreased slightly (Birdsall, Graham, and Pettinato 2000). Polarization—defined as a thinning of the middle of the distribution vis-à-vis the bottom tail—decreased markedly in Peru from 1985 to 1994 and then increased slightly from 1994 to 1997. "Middle-income stress," a measure that captures the difference between the income share of the top and that of the middle, displayed similar trends.[16] In Russia, where reforms were far less complete, polarization and middle-income stress both grew.[17]

Measurement Issues

Before presenting our results, it is necessary to mention possible sources of error. Both panel data and data on perceptions present particular problems. Panel data on income mobility are rare, as obtaining such data requires following individuals over a prolonged period, a costly exercise. There are only a small number of nationally representative panels for developing countries. Even then, the data are rarely without flaws. Respondents move, leading to attrition and possible bias. Attrition tends to be greatest at the tails of the distribution, as the wealthiest respondents tend to move to better neighborhoods, and the poorest ones move in with others or return to their places of origin.[18] In addition, as respondents in the panel age, they also may become less representative of the population as a whole.

Another problem with longitudinal data is possible error in reporting income, a problem that is gravely aggravated by policy shocks such as devaluations. People who are self-employed or employed in the informal sector have difficulty estimating any sort of monthly or annual salary, in part because their income fluctuates a great deal. Therefore, expenditure data are more accurate than income data for samples with large numbers of self-employed and/or informal sector workers. It is also more difficult to underreport expenditures. Yet expenditure data miss part of the story, particularly at the upper end of the distribution, and do not capture volatility in income flows, as people tend to smooth their consumption where possible by dissaving.

Adding perceptions data to longitudinal data has benefits, but creates its own set of problems. Nevertheless, while happiness questions are not very useful in measuring the well-being of particular individuals, there is surprising consistency in the patterns of responses both within and across countries. Psychologists find that a number of well-being indicators correlate strongly with how most individuals respond to happiness or life satisfaction surveys.

The questions—for example, "How happy or satisfied are you with your life?"—are usually based on a four-point scale, with two answers above and two below neutral. The correlation coefficient between happiness and life satisfaction questions is approximately 0.50, and the microeconometric equations have almost identical forms.[19] The data are most useful in the aggregate, as how an individual answers a question on happiness, for example, can be biased by day-to-day events. Thus the same person could answer such questions quite differently from day to day or from year to year.

Accuracy in reporting is another major issue. Responses can be biased by the phrasing or the placement of questions in the survey. Another problem is bias introduced by different or changing reference norms. When we asked people in our Peru survey to compare themselves with others in their community and then with others in their country, we found much more consistency in how respondents compared themselves with those in their community than with those in their country, which is a much vaguer reference point.

Notwithstanding these difficulties in the use of longitudinal and perceptual data, the results provide valuable information that static income data alone would not. In fact, measuring trends in inequality resulting from income mobility requires panel data.[20] Although panel data, as well as sound data on perceptions, are scarce in the developing economies, both kinds of data are available for Peru and Russia, and they reveal tremendous movement up and down the income ladder. Many people in both countries—particularly those in the middle of the income distribution—have seen vast changes in their economic welfare, with consequent effects on perceptions of well-being.

Results from Panel Studies in Peru

In Peru, we collaborated with the Instituto Cuánto to reinterview a subset of households in a 1985–2000 nationally representative panel. We then compared respondents' subjective assessments of changes in their well-being with objective trends (that is, calculations of expenditure change based on their answers to questions about total household expenditures at both earlier and later times).[21] We conducted surveys in 1998, 1999, and 2000.[22] For 2000, to increase the sample size and to avoid the attrition bias that could result from such a long panel, we increased the original 152-household panel to 500 households.[23] The original panel for 1985–2000 is included, while the additional households are in a panel that begins in 1991 (table 7.1). Thus, for the 500-household sample we have objective data for 1991–2000 and subjective data for 2000.[24] Household income levels for the panel are, on average, slightly higher than those of the nationally representative sample.

The survey included questions probing perceptions of and satisfaction with changes in the household's economic welfare over the past 10–15 years; perceptions of changes in the availability and quality of public services used by the household; and respondents' assessments of their future economic prospects.

Table 7.1   Peru, 2000: Household Panel Summary Information

Variable	Frequency	Mean	Std. dev.	Minimum	Maximum
Age	500	52.95	15.29	18	93
Gender (male = 1)	500	0.53	0.50	0	1
Household expenditure (soles)[a]	500	18,892	14,544	2,790	132,202
Household members	500	4.98	2.21	1	14
Years of education	500	8.02	4.66	0	18
Area (urban = 1)	500	0.86	0.35	0	1

a. In August 2000, US$1 = S/. 3.48.

To examine perceived past mobility (PPM), we asked respondents to assess their household's economic situation today relative to their situation 10–15 years ago (possible responses: much worse, somewhat worse, same, somewhat better, much better). We also asked respondents to assess their family's job situation today relative to the situation 10–15 years ago, to compare their situation with how their parents lived, and to assess their satisfaction with their standard of living. The full questionnaire is included in the appendix.

We show trends in income mobility for different income sectors using a Markov transition matrix (table 7.2). The matrix shows great mobility, both up and down. Those in the third and fourth quintiles clearly suffered the most downward mobility. Those with the most upward mobility were in quintiles 1 and 2 (the poorest), with a significant share moving up two or even three quintiles.[25] These trends reflect the benefits for the poor of stabilizing hyperinflation and targeting public expenditures to the poorest groups, as well as changes in opportunity generated by the high post-stabilization growth.

In terms of absolute mobility, most households in the panel—58 percent—had income (expenditure) increases of 30 percent or more from 1991 to 2000.[26] Thirty percent had only marginal income changes, and 12 percent saw income fall by 30 percent or more. Despite these objective gains, however, perceptions show a negative skew. Forty-five percent of households had very negative or negative views of their economic experiences, while 24 percent were indifferent and 31 percent were positive.

The asymmetry between reported income change and perceived economic status change was even more marked in the 1998 survey, when the period over which income was measured was longer (1985–97). Fifty-eight percent of households had negative views, 28 percent were indifferent, and 12 percent were positive. We attribute this difference to recall problems, as well as to what we term a time-log effect. In other words, any given income gain will have more impact on perceptions if it occurs over a shorter time.[27]

The negative skew did not extend to self-assessments of housing improvements, as housing changes are more concrete than economic assessments over time.[28]

Table 7.2   Peru: Mobility Trends, by Expenditure Quintile (Markov Transition Matrices)

A. No Income Mobility

Quintile in T_0	Quintile in T_1					
	1	2	3	4	5	Total
1	100	0	0	0	0	100
2	0	100	0	0	0	100
3	0	0	100	0	0	100
4	0	0	0	100	0	100
5	0	0	0	0	100	100
Total	100	100	100	100	100	100

B. Perfect Income Mobility

Quintile in T_0	Quintile in T_1					
	1	2	3	4	5	Total
1	20	20	20	20	20	100
2	20	20	20	20	20	100
3	20	20	20	20	20	100
4	20	20	20	20	20	100
5	20	20	20	20	20	100
Total	100	100	100	100	100	100

C. Income (Expenditure) Mobility in Peru, 1991–2000

Quintile 1991	Quintile 2000					
	1	2	3	4	5	Total
1	45	25	19	6	5	100
2	25	25	23	14	13	100
3	16	23	22	20	19	100
4	11	18	18	32	21	100
5	3	9	18	28	42	100
Total	100	100	100	100	100	100

Those with the greatest absolute gains show a strong negative skew on perceptions of economic progress. Of the high performers in the sample (those with expenditure improvements of 30 percent or more during 1991–2000), 44 percent said they were worse off and only 30 percent said they were better off. Of the worst performers (those with declines of 30 percent or more), 55 percent stated, accurately, that they were worse off, yet 21 percent said that

Figure 7.1   Peru: Perceived Past Mobility versus 1991–2000 Income Mobility

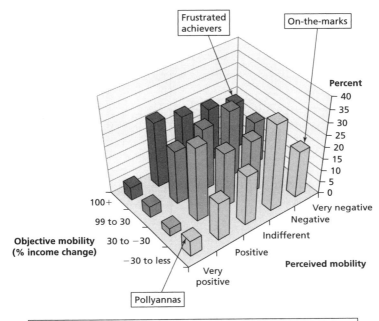

- ● **Frustrated achievers:** fared well, yet assessed their situation negatively
- ● **On-the-marks:** assessed their situation accurately
- ● **Pollyannas:** fared poorly, yet assessed their situation positively

their situation had not changed and 23 percent saw themselves as better off (figure 7.1).

Our regression analysis of the determinants of perceived past mobility found no significant effects for many of our demographic variables—gender, education, and marital status (table 7.3). Age had a significant and negative correlation with PPM, without the quadratic effect usually found on perceptions variables (see Graham and Pettinato 2001). Living in an urban area had a negative and significant correlation with PPM. Income level (as measured by log of equivalized expenditure) had a positive and significant correlation.

Income change over 1991–2000, measured by changes in log-expenditure, had no effects on PPM, but change over 1994–2000 had a positive and significant correlation, probably because of recall issues, as well as the possible "time-log" effect noted earlier. These income changes had stronger effects for those at the lower end of the income ladder.[29] Short-term *fluctuations* in income had stronger effects on the subjective assessments of the poor than on those of wealthier groups, as the poor have less margin to absorb such fluctuations.[30]

Relative income differences no doubt influence these assessments of well-being, as in the case of Easterlin's studies. Nonincome forces may also be at play. Regarding the upwardly mobile, Hirschman (1973) noted many years ago that although "the economist, with his touching simplicity, would tend to

Table 7.3   Peru, 2000: Perceived Past Mobility
(ordered logit estimations)

Independent variable	1	2	3
Age	−0.026	−0.023	−0.023
	−4.771	−4.302	−4.336
Male dummy	−0.190	−0.163	−0.185
	−1.090	−0.935	−1.062
Education	0.003	0.022	0.021
	0.178	1.204	1.154
Married	0.119	0.086	0.118
	0.694	0.506	0.686
Urban	−0.664	−0.494	−0.454
	−2.801	−2.142	−1.969
log-Expenditure	0.420		
	2.772		
Mobility '91–'00		0.789	
		0.754	
Mobility '94–'00			2.647
			2.205
N	500	500	500
Pseudo R²	0.024	0.020	0.023

Note: z-stats below coefficients.

think there was no problem: being better off than before, these people are also likely to be more content . . . social history has taught us that it is much more complicated."

Cultural differences play a part, as do higher expectations and more experience answering surveys among urban respondents. As in the earlier surveys, in 2000 urban (and more educated) respondents were more likely than rural ones to use extreme responses ("much worse" rather than "worse," for example). Among upwardly mobile respondents—those who had income gains of 30 percent or more—49 percent of urban respondents assessed their past progress negatively, as against 20 percent of rural respondents. In contrast, 51 percent of upwardly mobile rural respondents said their situation was the same, as against 21 percent of urban ones. "Frustrated achievers"—those respondents who were upwardly mobile during 1991–2000 yet reported negative PPMs—are clearly more prevalent in urban areas (table 7.4).

The negative skew in perceptions was higher for respondents in the middle quintile of the income distribution than for either poorer or richer respondents. While 51 percent of those in the middle quintile who were upwardly mobile assessed their progress as negative or very negative, 36 percent of respondents in the lowest income quintile saw their situation negatively. Meanwhile,

45 percent, 43 percent, and 45 percent of those in quintiles 2, 4, and 5 respectively held negative views.[31] Poor respondents were much more likely than wealthy ones to assess their situation as the same: 41 percent of those in the first quintile answered "same," while only 19 percent of those in the fifth quintile did so (figure 7.2). Again, poor—and particularly rural—respondents are less likely to opt for extreme responses; they also have lower reference norms.

Economic trends in Peru, as in most emerging market countries, have played out differently among different income groups. The wealthy have reaped the market's rewards for skills and education, while the poor have gained from expanded transfers and public expenditures (Graham and Kane 1998; World Bank 1999). The rewards for those in the middle have varied, depending on their skill and education levels. Because those in the middle are more likely than the poor to see the wealthy as a reference group, they

Table 7.4   Portrait of Frustrated Achievers in Peru and Russia

Peru, 2000

	Whole sample (N = 500)		Frustrated achievers (N = 128)		Nonfrustrated achievers (N = 160)		Difference between FAs and NFAs
	Mean	Std. dev.	Mean	Std. dev.	Mean	Std. dev.	
Age	52.95	15.29	55.67	15.09	49.49	14.90	**
Area (urban = 1)	0.86	0.35	0.93	0.26	0.78	0.42	**
Gender (male = 1)	0.53	0.50	0.51	0.50	0.57	0.50	
Education	8.02	4.66	8.03	4.52	8.12	4.68	
Equivalence household expenditure '00	8,922	7,314	9,885	6,144	10,809	9,957	
Coefficient of variation ('91, '94, '96, '00)	0.42	0.19	0.43	0.19	0.48	0.19	**
Economic satisfaction	2.91	0.80	2.53	0.78	3.21	0.64	**
Job satisfaction	2.58	1.16	1.88	0.90	3.15	1.03	***
Perception of economic opportunity	3.03	0.75	2.74	0.71	3.28	0.65	***
Economic Ladder Question	3.82	1.52	3.73	1.47	3.98	1.59	*
Prospect of upward mobility	3.29	1.03	3.03	1.13	3.54	0.89	**

(table continues on following page)

Table 7.4 (continued)

Russia, 1998

	Whole sample (N = 2,289)		Frustrated achievers (N = 217)		Nonfrustrated achievers (N = 90)		Difference between FAs and
	Mean	Std. dev.	Mean	Std. dev.	Mean	Std. dev.	NFAs
Age	54.47	15.40	51.58	13.97	50.37	16.09	
Gender (male = 1)	0.21	0.41	0.24	0.43	0.25	0.43	
Education	8.41	2.35	8.62	2.13	8.91	1.97	
Equivalence household income '98	2,698	2,935	4,753	5,964	6,114	5,574	***
Coefficient of variation ('95, '96, '97, '98)	0.56	0.38	0.64	0.62	0.55	0.23	**
Life satisfaction	1.91	1.00	1.82	0.88	2.45	1.25	**
Economic Ladder Question	2.93	1.48	3.00	1.56	3.72	1.52	**
Prospect of upward mobility	2.06	1.00	2.07	1.02	2.58	0.97	**
Pro-democracy attitude	0.53	0.54	0.45	0.53	0.70	0.51	***
Satisfaction with market reform process	0.74	0.55	0.65	0.59	0.96	0.57	***
Fear of unemployment	3.96	1.37	4.15	1.22	3.57	1.56	**
Restrict the rich	3.22	0.79	3.16	0.82	2.89	0.94	**

* Significant at the 0.10 level.
** Significant at the 0.05 level.
*** Significant at the 0.01 level.

can suffer frustration and stress even while enjoying upward mobility.[32] In contrast, absolute income gains among the poorest sectors have a consistent and positive impact on life satisfaction.

The mean education and expenditure levels of frustrated achievers were virtually the same as those of their nonfrustrated counterparts. Surprisingly, the frustrated achievers experienced *less* volatility in income.[33] Nevertheless, the frustrated achievers had much lower scores on virtually all of our perceptions variables. They had lower mean prospects of upward mobility (POUM) scores and much lower mean scores for economic satisfaction, for job satisfaction, and on a "prospects for improving future standard of living" question.

Figure 7.2   Peru, 2000: Perceived Mobility among Upwardly Mobile (1991–2000), by Expenditure Group

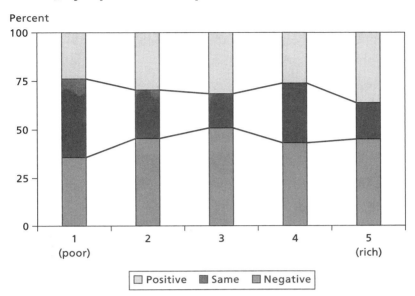

On average, the frustrated achievers were seven years older (56) than the nonfrustrated group (49)—a statistically significant difference. Age or life cycle effects may help explain the negative perceptions. Van Praag and Frijters (1999), for example, find that middle-aged respondents give greater weight to present and anticipated income than do either the young or the old, who place greater importance on past income. Middle-aged respondents are also more likely to have immediate expenditure needs because of the likelihood of having one or more dependents than are the young or the old.

Our regressions on the Peru sample as a whole found a significant and negative relationship between age and PPM, and between age and economic satisfaction (tables 7.3 and 7.5). As in the case of PPM, we did not get the usual quadratic relation with age. In larger samples, life satisfaction usually decreases with age and then begins to increase monotonically at a certain point, somewhere in the mid-40s for the advanced industrial economies and Latin America, and slightly later for Russia.[34] This discrepancy may be explained by small sample size or by the slightly different phrasing of the question in Peru, that is, "How satisfied are you with your present standard of living?" rather than the usual "How satisfied are you with your life?" The economic element in the question may dominate the usual demographic effects on life satisfaction.

In contrast, when we looked at the determinants of job satisfaction in Peru, we did get a significant and quadratic age effect, although the low point was around 70, an age at which most people have retired or greatly reduced time at work. The primary determinants of job satisfaction in Peru were log-expenditure and age. Education levels were insignificant.[35]

Table 7.5   Peru, 2000: Economic Satisfaction
(ordered logit estimation)

Independent variable	1
Age	−0.013
	−2.132
Male dummy	0.160
	0.826
Education	0.033
	1.533
Married	0.009
	0.046
Urban	−0.830
	−3.096
log-Expenditure	0.756
	4.452
N	500
Pseudo R^2	0.036

Note: z-stats below coefficients.

The negative skew was less evident in respondents' perceptions of their satisfaction with their current standard of living. Only 23 percent saw it as "bad" or "very bad," while 58 percent said it was "fair," and 19 percent said "good" or "very good." And most households (68 percent) were confident that their children would do better than they had; only 14 percent thought they would do worse. (Future expectations are especially affected by noneconomic factors such as hope and determination.) By contrast, only 21 percent of respondents thought that they had done better than their parents, while 61 percent thought that their parents had done better.

Respondents were also asked to assess their opportunity to improve their standard of living in the future, and to compare that opportunity with those of their parents and their children. Seventeen percent thought that their opportunity for improvement was bad or very bad, 61 percent thought it was fair, and 22 percent thought it was good or very good. A striking 49 percent thought that their parents had had better opportunity to enhance their standard of living; 22 percent felt the chances were the same, and 29 percent of respondents felt they had greater opportunity than their parents. Expectations for children remained higher, however: 59 percent expected their children would have greater opportunity, and only 13 percent expected they would have less.

What are the implications of these negative perceptions for future economic and political behavior? We cannot answer this definitively, but some of our results are suggestive. Using the regionwide Latinobarómetro data, we find that assessing one's present economic situation as being more positive than one's past situation (PPM), controlling for other variables, has a positive correlation with happiness, suggesting that our frustrated achievers are less happy than other respondents.[36] Similarly, for our Peru sample, having a positive PPM was correlated positively with economic satisfaction. Our analysis of data from Russia (discussed below) yields a similar correlation between PPM and happiness.[37]

Recent theoretical research on ego and identity suggests that assessing one's situation positively can lead to a bias in processing information, in which individuals reject or ignore information that could change their positive self-image. Those with negative self-images, meanwhile, are more likely to seek out new information and to take risks (Köszegi 2000). With this logic, one could posit that our frustrated achievers would continue to seek out new opportunities, despite their negative assessments of the past.

Reference Groups in Peru and Latin America

Decades ago, Duesenberry (1949) called attention to sociological research that found that people who associated with others who had more income than they did tended to be less satisfied with their income than people who associated with others who had the same income. More recent research on savings suggests that having a higher reference norm or comparison income can lead to conspicuous consumption and lower savings rates. Our frustrated achievers thus may be opting for immediate consumption rather than saving, in order to "keep up with" the reference groups to which they aspire. Their behavior could also be motivated by the new availability of imported consumer goods.

We posited that differences between the reference groups of our frustrated achievers and those of the nonfrustrated ones might yield some insights into the effects of frustration on future behavior. In the 2000 survey, we included an Economic Ladder Question (ELQ) to gauge how people compare themselves to others in their country. The question is phrased: "On a ladder of nine steps, where the poorest are on the first step and the richest are on the ninth step, where would you place yourself?" At our request, this question was also included in the 2000 regionwide Latinobarómetro survey.[38]

The Latinobarómetro results show that as people assess their position on the economic scale, they cluster, not surprisingly, around the middle, with most respondents placing themselves in the middle categories, even if they are slightly above or below them objectively. Average ELQ responses for those in the lowest income decile were 3.42, just above the third rung of the ladder, while average responses for those in the wealthiest decile were 5.33, just above the middle of the ladder (figure 7.3). In Peru mean responses for the lowest quintile are 3.0, and for the wealthiest 4.5. This regression toward the mean suggests that reference norms are at play (figure 7.4).

In Peru, we found that years of education, being married, and expenditure levels (log-expenditure) were all positively correlated with ELQ responses. Rather surprisingly, age and changes in income (regardless of whether measured using changes in logs or not) were insignificant, as was our urban

Figure 7.3   Latin America, 2000: Economic Ladder Question Averages, by Wealth Decile

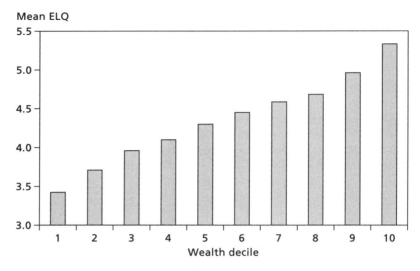

Note: Deciles were constructed using a wealth index based on household possessions and standard of living.

Figure 7.4   Peru, 2000: Economic Ladder Question Averages, by Expenditure Quintile

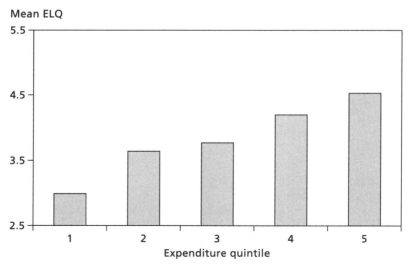

Note: Quintiles were constructed using household expenditure adjusted for economies of scale in household size using a single-parameter equivalence elasticity of 0.5.

Table 7.6 Peru, 2000: Economic Ladder Question
(ordinary least squares regression)

Independent variable	1	2
Age	0.000	0.004
	−0.101	0.863
Male dummy	−0.166	−0.147
	−1.201	−1.028
Education	0.032	0.068
	2.066	4.577
Married	0.290	0.258
	2.124	1.818
Urban	0.179	0.460
	0.900	2.264
log-Expenditure	0.748	
	6.293	
Mobility '91–'2000		1.528
		1.551
Constant	−3.291	2.604
	−3.329	8.397
N	500	500
R^2	0.142	0.078

Note: t-stats below coefficients.

dummy variable, after controlling for income levels (table 7.6). Our frustrated achievers, meanwhile, had slightly lower mean ELQ scores than did their nonfrustrated counterparts. In Latin America as a whole, we get a similar positive correlation of ELQ responses with education, wealth, and marital status. We also get a quadratic age effect.[39]

We also explored differences in how individuals evaluated their economic situation over the past 10 years vis-à-vis their community and their country. People were more optimistic when they assessed themselves in relation to their community. Only 15 percent of respondents said they had fared worse than others in their community, while 24 percent said they had fared worse than others in their country; 25 percent said they had fared better than others in their community, while only 16 percent said they had fared better than others in their country.

These results suggest that reference norms at the community level are lower than those outside the community. The frustrations of our achievers may thus be driven by national or possibly global trends, rather than by community trends, particularly as the difference between community and national assessments of upwardly mobile respondents was remarkably similar to that for the sample as a whole.[40]

Table 7.7   Peru, 2000: Frustrated Achievers and Reference Groups

Personal situation compared to . . .

. . . the rest of your local community

	Frustrated achievers	*Nonfrustrated achievers*	*Total*
Worse	23.4	8.1	14.9
Same	61.7	55.0	58.0
Better	14.8	36.9	27.1
Total	100.0	100.0	100.0

. . . the rest of your country

	Frustrated achievers	*Nonfrustrated achievers*	*Total*
Worse	33.6	13.8	22.6
Same	57.0	66.3	62.2
Better	9.4	20.0	15.3
Total	100.0	100.0	100.0

Interestingly, our frustrated achievers were much more negative in their comparisons with their respective reference groups than were the non-frustrated upwardly mobile respondents. Far fewer frustrated achievers (14.8 percent) said that they had done *better* than others in their community than did nonfrustrated achievers (36.9 percent). Similarly, a far smaller share of frustrated (9.4 percent) than nonfrustrated (20.0 percent) achievers believed that they had done better than others in their country (table 7.7).

Two additional perceptions variables suggest differences in perceptions about economic *change* and about economic *status*. The Mobility Assessment Discrepancy (MAD) is the ratio between subjective and objective income mobility.[41] When MAD is equal to 1 the respondent was accurate in his or her perception of mobility. A high MAD ratio (>1) implies that the respondent assesses his or her situation as better than it actually is; a low MAD (<1), as worse. The Perceptions Gap (PG) is the ratio between the respondent's ELQ response and his or her actual income decile. A high PG suggests overstating one's perceived income status; a low PG, understating it. Not surprisingly, the frustrated achievers have, on average, lower PG ratios.

Results from Panel Studies in Russia

For Russia, we have objective income data from a recent household survey for the years 1995 to 1999, a period of extensive macroeconomic volatility. This ongoing survey, the Russia Longitudinal Monitoring Survey (RLMS), interviews more than 10,000 individuals (or around 3,800 households) each year and reinterviews many in the following years. When we identified the households that were also asked questions about subjective well-being and

Table 7.8   Russia, 1995–98: Positional Mobility (Markov Transition Matrix)

1995 quintile	1	2	3	4	5	Total
			1998 quintile			
1	39.3	26.4	15.5	9.8	9.0	100.0
2	24.7	28.4	21.8	15.5	9.6	100.0
3	16.4	20.7	24.7	22.5	15.7	100.0
4	10.9	14.9	21.8	26.4	26.0	100.0
5	9.2	9.6	15.8	25.8	39.6	100.0
Total	100.5	100.0	99.6	100.1	99.9	

perceptions of past progress, we ended up with a panel that covers more than 2,000 households.[42]

In terms of objective mobility, as in Peru, we see extensive movements both up and down the income ladder, although downward trends were more dominant in Russia. Incomes fell an average of 10 percent for 77 percent of the household sample over the period.[43] Of those in the fourth quintile, 48 percent moved down, with 11 percent ending up in the bottom quintile and 15 percent in the second quintile (table 7.8). Of those in the top income quintile, only 40 percent remained there, while 9 percent fell to the bottom quintile.

The results on perceptions were similar to those in Peru, although the negative skew was stronger for Russia: 72 percent of those with income gains of 100 percent or more had negative assessments, and 76 percent of those with income losses accurately assessed their trajectories. In Peru, many respondents who fared poorly assessed their situation positively, but in Russia few did (figures 7.1 and 7.5).

In Russia, the "frustrated achievers" and their nonfrustrated counterparts had virtually identical education profiles.[44] Age had a quadratic effect, with the probability of being frustrated increasing until age 54, and then decreasing. In contrast to Peru, the frustrated achievers in Russia had lower mean incomes than the nonfrustrated groups and also experienced more income volatility (table 7.4).[45] In Peru the effects of age seem to dominate over those of income as plausible explanations for the frustrations of the achievers. In Russia, both age and income matter. The frustrated achievers were, on average, more concerned about unemployment, less favorable toward the market, and less positive about democracy than the nonfrustrated group.

High economic volatility in Russia affected subjective assessments. When we look at the determinants of happiness, perceived past mobility, and prospects of upward mobility, controlling for mean income levels, income volatility has negative effects on all three. Not surprisingly, our frustrated achievers experienced more volatility than their nonfrustrated counterparts in Russia. In Peru, in contrast, volatility had no significant effects on any of these three variables.[46] This difference has two related plausible explanations. Volatility was slightly higher in Russia than in Peru for the periods observed.[47]

Figure 7.5   Russia: Perceived Past Mobility versus 1995–99 Income Mobility

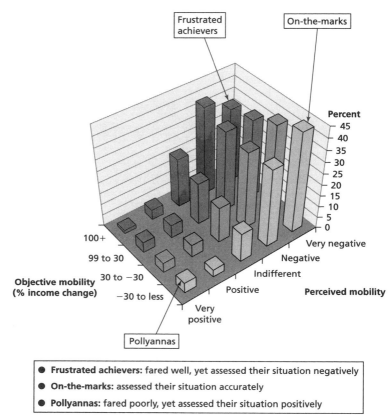

- **Frustrated achievers:** fared well, yet assessed their situation negatively
- **On-the-marks:** assessed their situation accurately
- **Pollyannas:** fared poorly, yet assessed their situation positively

And for Peru we use household expenditure as a measure rather than income, which varies more than expenditure.

Happiness—that is, satisfaction with life—in Russia had a quadratic relationship with age, falling until age 49 and then increasing. This was similar to our results for Latin America, but not for Peru. Mean happiness levels are strongly and positively correlated with income in Russia (table 7.9). Controlling for age, happiness increases with working and having been paid in the past month, but decreases for "working" in a broad sense. Being an employer had a positive effect on happiness, while being owed money by one's employer had the strongest negative effect on happiness of any variable. The owner of one's place of employment (government, foreign company, etc.) had no significant effect on happiness, while concern about losing one's job had a strong negative effect. Unemployment had a strong negative effect, as in Latin America.

When respondents were asked whether they thought the government should restrict the incomes of the rich, those who disagreed were more educated, had higher incomes, and had high assessments of their future chances of getting ahead. Again, there was a quadratic relationship with age, but in this

Table 7.9 Russia, 1998: Happiness
(ordered logit estimation)

Independent variable

Age	−0.069
	−3.579
Age^2	0.001
	3.368
Male dummy	0.365
	3.647
Education	0.048
	2.131
Married	0.001
	0.006
log-Income	0.498
	9.237
N	2,030
Pseudo R^2	0.028

case an inverted U, with middle-aged respondents more in favor of restricting the rich. Those in favor of restricting the incomes of the rich were more likely to be receiving pensions and to be employed by the government. Our frustrated achievers were also more likely to favor restricting the rich.

When respondents were asked whether market reforms should continue, support for the market had a quadratic relation with age, with support initially decreasing and then at a certain point increasing with age. Support for the market was higher for women, for those who were employed and receiving wages on time, and for those employed by a foreign firm. There was a negative correlation between support for the market and being employed by a Russian firm.

The ELQ was also included in the RLMS in 1998. Average ELQ responses are slightly higher in the bottom than in the second decile, and at the third decile begin to increase again (figure 7.6). A plausible explanation may be that those at the lowest levels are operating at a subsistence or barter level, working in enterprises that pay wages in kind if at all, which makes it difficult to accurately assess income or status.

By contrast, in Latin America and Peru average ELQ levels increase monotonically with income (figures 7.3 and 7.4). The Russia sample includes a greater share of rural respondents, who tend to have lower reference norms than their urban counterparts. In Russia, people outside modern urban areas are also more likely to be outside the market economy. Finally, as with happiness and assessments of past and future economic progress, income volatility (as opposed to income) had negative and significant effects on ELQ responses in Russia. And, as in Peru, frustrated achievers had a lower mean ELQ than did their nonfrustrated counterparts.

The dramatic rise in poverty during the transition years in Russia has shifted reference norms downward. Milanovic and Jovanovic (1999) found

Figure 7.6   Russia, 1998: Economic Ladder Question Averages, by Income Decile

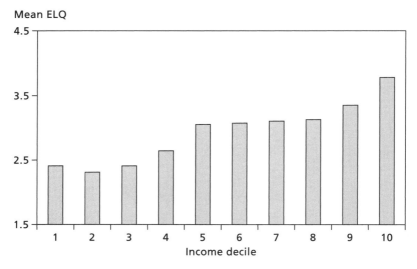

Note: Deciles were constructed using household income adjusted for economies of scale in household size using a single-parameter equivalence elasticity of 0.5.

that subjective perceptions of the minimum income needed for a family to live—the subjective poverty line—fell from 1993 to 1996, and by the end of the period closely approximated the official minimum income level, which began well below the subjective level and remained the same throughout the period.

Conclusions

At the outset, we posited that relative income differences matter more to happiness than do absolute ones; that respondents' positions on the income ladder matter; that change in status, measured by income mobility, has strong effects (although not always necessarily in the expected direction); and that age and education have effects independent of other variables.

Most studies of subjective well-being find that, above a certain absolute level of basic income, relative income differences matter more than absolute ones.[48] Our results—and in particular the negative skew in the assessments of the most upwardly mobile respondents—confirm the importance of relative income differences. Upwardly mobile individuals are most likely to look beyond their original cohort for reference groups. And in very unequal societies that have adopted international consumption standards, the reference point for the upwardly mobile may seem unattainable regardless of absolute income gains. The respondents in our sample tended to be much more critical when assessing their progress vis-à-vis their country than when assessing it vis-à-vis their community, and our frustrated achievers were far more critical than the average respondent.

These income differences are more important for those in the middle of the distribution than for either the very wealthy or the very poor. For our Peru sample, those in the middle, not the poor, were the most frustrated in spite of their absolute gains. For our Latin America sample, the effects of wealth gains on happiness were of a logarithmic nature and were stronger for the poor than for those in the middle or at the top.[49]

Income mobility also had effects on happiness, with greater objective gains often associated with increased frustration rather than increased subjective well-being. One factor here is, no doubt, reference groups. Another is that both the Peru and Russia surveys were conducted at times of high macroeconomic volatility, with related high mobility, when few income gains were guaranteed to be stable or permanent. Volatility had a clear negative effect on life satisfaction in Russia, and it increased the probability of belonging to the frustrated achiever group. And regardless of the explanation for these negative perceptions, all our data suggest that they have negative effects on happiness.

The frustrations of our achievers can be explained in several other ways, including recall problems in assessing past earnings, particularly for non-salaried workers, and the willingness of urban respondents to make extreme statements. Behavioral traits may also play a role. Although our frustrated achievers are less "happy" than our nonfrustrated respondents, the direction of causality is uncertain. To answer this question, we need new data as well as tools available to psychologists.

These are preliminary findings in a research area that is fairly new, at least for the developing economies. Despite these limitations, our analysis makes three general contributions. First, it supports the findings in research on happiness in the developed economies, which highlight the importance of variables other than absolute income gains in enhancing welfare. Second, it links the findings in the happiness literature—as well those in our own surveys—to the broader debates on the effects of increasing international economic integration on social welfare within countries.

Finally, the large and consistent gap we find between objective income trends and subjective assessments of the upwardly mobile may have implications for the future economic and political behavior of precisely the group that is critical to the sustainability of market policies.[50] Exploring the feedback effects of this perceptions gap is the next stage of this research.

Appendix: Cuánto Survey on Perceptions of Economic Progress

Good morning/good afternoon. My name is . . . and I am representing the Cuánto Institute, a company that specializes in public opinion polls and questionnaires. We're conducting interviews to understand opinion concerning aspects of the well-being of the population, particularly at the household level. For this purpose, a household is considered to be a person or group of people, related or not, who regularly reside in the same residence, living here full or part-time, and who share their food.

(Notes in italics are directed to the interviewer/response coder.)

1. CHANGES IN WELL-BEING OVER TIME

1.1 The current economic situation of your household, compared to what it was 10–15 years ago, is . . . *(show card 1)*
1 Much worse
2 Somewhat worse
3 Same
4 Somewhat better
5 Much better

1.2 The current employment situation of you and the members of your household, compared to 10–15 years ago, is . . . *(show card 1)*
1 Much worse
2 Somewhat worse
3 Same
4 Somewhat better
5 Much better

1.3 In comparison to you, your parents lived . . . *(show card 1)*
1 Much worse
2 Somewhat worse
3 Same
4 Somewhat better
5 Much better

1.4 The current access to health services for you and your household, compared to 10–15 years ago, is . . . *(show card 1)*
1 Much worse
2 Somewhat worse
3 Same
4 Somewhat better
5 Much better

1.5 The current access to educational services for you and your household, compared to 10–15 years ago, is . . . *(show card 1)*
1 Much worse
2 Somewhat worse
3 Same
4 Somewhat better
5 Much better

1.6 The current access to basic services like water, light, and sewerage for your household, compared to 10–15 years ago, is . . . *(show card 3)*
1 Worse
2 Same
3 Better

1.7 The current state of your housing, compared to 10–15 years ago, is . . . *(show card 1)*
1 Much worse
2 Somewhat worse
3 Same

    4 Somewhat better

    5 Much better

1.8 The purchasing power of your household, compared to 10–15 years ago, is . . . *(show card 2)*

    1 Less

    2 Same

    3 Greater

1.9 The current level of security in your area (with respect to violence, crime), compared to 10–15 years ago, is . . . *(show card 2)*

    1 Less

    2 Same

    3 Greater

1.10 The performance of your local government, compared to 10–15 years ago, is . . . *(show card 1)*

    1 Much worse

    2 Somewhat worse

    3 Same

    4 Somewhat better

    5 Much better

1.11 I am going to mention some services that are offered to your community. Tell me how these services have changed in the last 10–15 years. *(show card 3)*

	Worse	*Same*	*Better*	*N/A*
Schools	1	2	3	4
Sewerage	1	2	3	4
Water	1	2	3	4
Electricity	1	2	3	4
Security	1	2	3	4
Local police	1	2	3	4
Roads	1	2	3	4

2. EXPECTATIONS FOR THE FUTURE

2.1 The economic situation of your household in the future, compared to what it is now, will probably be . . . *(show card 1)*

    1 Much worse

    2 Somewhat worse

    3 Same

    4 Somewhat better

    5 Much better

2.2 The standard of living that your children will have in the future, compared to what you have now, will probably be . . . *(show card 1)*

    1 Much worse

    2 Somewhat worse

    3 Same

4 Somewhat better

5 Much better

2.3 How would you rate your opportunity to have a higher standard of living in the future? *(show card 4)*

1 Very bad

2 Bad

3 Fair

4 Good

5 Very good

2.4 In what period of time do you think you will be able to reach a satisfactory standard of living?

1 1 to 2 years

2 3 to 5 years

3 6 to 10 years

4 More than 10 years

5 Never

3. LEVEL OF CURRENT SATISFACTION AND EXPECTATIONS OF PROGRESS

3.1 In relation to your current standard of living, your level of satisfaction is . . . *(show card 4)*

1 Very bad

2 Bad

3 Fair

4 Good

5 Very good

3.2 Your current opportunity to improve your standard of living is . . . *(show card 4)*

1 Very bad

2 Bad

3 Fair

4 Good

5 Very good

3.3 Your parents' opportunity to improve their standard of living, compared to your opportunity, was . . . *(show card 2)*

1 Less

2 Same

3 Greater

3.4 Your opportunity to have a better standard of living than that of your parents has been . . . *(show card 2)*

1 Less

2 Same

3 Greater

3.5 Your children's opportunity to have a better standard of living than yours will be . . . *(show card 2)*

1 Less

2 Same
3 Greater

4. ORGANIZATIONS AND PARTICIPATION

4.1 In your community, do any of the following organizations exist? *(read all and mark in column 4.1)*

4.2 Within your community, do you or have you belonged to, had some connection to, or received some benefit from any of these organizations? *(read only those organizations mentioned in response to 4.1, and mark in column 4.2)*

4.3 What kind of benefits do you hope to gain from participating in these organizations? *(mark in column 4.3)*
1 Economic benefits
2 Emergency aid (e.g., food)
3 Recreation
4 New contacts and relationships

4.4 Outside of your community, do you or have you belonged to, had some connection to, or received some benefit from any of these organizations? *(read all and mark in column 4.4)*

	4.1		4.2		4.3	4.4	
Organization	Yes	No	Yes	No	Code	Yes	No
Parents' association	1	2	1	2		1	2
Religious community/church	1	2	1	2		1	2
Club or association	1	2	1	2		1	2
Mothers' association	1	2	1	2		1	2
Community organization	1	2	1	2		1	2
Professional association	1	2	1	2		1	2
Trade union	1	2	1	2		1	2
Political party/civic organization	1	2	1	2		1	2
Town council	1	2	1	2		1	2
Public soup kitchen	1	2	1	2		1	2
"Glass of Milk" program	1	2	1	2		1	2
Community action group	1	2	1	2		1	2
Development committee	1	2	1	2		1	2
Fraternity or brotherhood	1	2	1	2		1	2
Security association/community watch	1	2	1	2		1	2
Self-defense organization	1	2	1	2		1	2
Cooperative enterprise	1	2	1	2		1	2
Farmers' association	1	2	1	2		1	2
Indigenous people's association	1	2	1	2		1	2
Immigrants' association	1	2	1	2		1	2

1. On a ladder of nine steps, where the poorest are on the first step and the richest are on the ninth step, where would you place yourself?

1	2	3	4	5	6	7	8	9

2. Compared to the other members of your community, in the last 10 years, you have fared:
   1 Better
   2 Same
   3 Worse

3. Compared to the other people in your country, in the last 10 years, you have fared:
   1 Better
   2 Same
   3 Worse

4. Have you fulfilled the economic expectations you had 10 years ago?
   1 Yes
   2 No

5. Are you satisfied with your household income?
   1 Yes
   2 No

6. How much more would you need to be satisfied?
   Amount: _____

7. What would you spend it on?
   1 Food, clothing, shoes, home
   2 Education for your children or grandchildren
   3 Free time and entertainment
   4 Other

8. In your estimation, what monthly income would your family need to live normally?
   Amount: _____

9. In your estimation, what monthly income would your family need to be considered rich?
   Amount: _____

10. In your estimation, what monthly income would mean that your family is considered poor?
    Amount: _____

Notes

The authors acknowledge generous support for this research from the John D. and Catherine T. MacArthur Foundation and the Tinker Foundation. They also thank Alan Angell, Martha Merritt, Guy Pfeffermann, and Peyton Young for helpful comments on this paper, as well as Andrew Oswald for comments on an earlier version of this work. An earlier version of this article was published in the *Journal of Development Studies*.

1.   Most of these studies use the term "happiness" interchangeably with the more cumbersome term "subjective well-being," accepting that the former has dimensions that go well beyond the economic ones considered by this literature. For an excellent review of these definitions and the literature, see Easterlin (2000). For a review from the behavioral sciences perspective, see Diener and Biswas-Diener (1999).

2.   In the United States, real per capita income has more than doubled since World War II. The average reported level of happiness, however, is the same as it was in the late 1940s. The story is similar for Europe. Even in Japan, which had a fivefold increase in per capita income in the three decades following the 1950s, there was no change in average happiness levels. See Easterlin (2000). Blanchflower and Oswald (2000) actually find that average happiness levels decreased from the 1970s to the 1990s in the United States and the United Kingdom.

3.   For a conceptual framework and initial exploration of the possible effects of globalization on economic and social mobility, see Birdsall and Graham (2000).

4.   Distributional "stress" on the middle class, related to globalization, is discussed in Birdsall, Graham, and Pettinato (2000). In a more theoretical exploration, Robson (1992) highlights the potential stress on the middle sectors that arises when status as well as wealth is included in the utility function.

5.   The few studies that have examined the effects of social mobility on happiness were conducted several decades ago and focused on social class. When social class is assessed by asking people to rate themselves, there is a correlation with happiness of about 0.25 to 0.30 in American and European studies. The link between happiness and high social class, meanwhile, is much stronger in more unequal societies for which data exist, such as India, and lower for more equal ones, such as Australia (see Argyle 1999). Therefore it is plausible to assume that significant changes in mobility rates in such contexts could have some effects on happiness.

6.   See, for example, Diener (1984), Blanchflower and Oswald (2000), and Frey and Stutzer 1999b. Deaton and Paxson (1994) highlight the role of negative shocks, such as poor health, in determining lifetime mobility patterns. Such shocks, no doubt, also affect subjective assessments of well-being.

7   For a review of different societies' tolerance for inequality, see Esping-Andersen (1990). For an overview of trends in mobility and opportunity in the United States, see McMurrer and Sawhill (1998).

8.   They also point out the possibility that it is not that perceived discrepancies drive the unhappiness, but rather, that unhappy people are more likely to perceive differences (Diener et al. 1993).

9.   A related finding is that winning lotteries tends to cause disruption rather than increased happiness. A plausible explanation is that such large income boosts may result in people purchasing nicer homes and other luxury goods, placing them in a new reference group and among new neighbors, and in the end they do not fit in. On this point, see Argyle (1999).

10.   Hirschman uses the analogy of a traffic jam in a tunnel, where initially those in a stalled lane gain hope from movement in other lanes. Yet if their lane never moves, then that hope turns into frustration.

11.   They also found that married people are happier than single people, that couples without children are happier than those with them, and that women are happier than men. See Frey and Stutzer (1999b) and Oswald (1997). For the same issues in the transition economies, see Namazie and Sanfey (1998).

12.   Current income has the greatest time weight, and past incomes carry more weight than incomes in the future. This varies by age, however, with the young and the old

placing the greatest weight on past income, and the middle-aged bracket deriving its norm mostly from present and anticipated income (see Van Praag and Frijters 1999). Lowenstein, Prelec, and Weber (1999), meanwhile, find that people become less happy as they anticipate retiring, but then happiness levels increase shortly after retirement.

13. In a theoretical analysis, Köszegi (2000) shows that people who assess their capabilities optimistically are also likely to process information in a biased manner, that is, one that supports their optimistic assessments. In the most extreme cases they may stop seeking out information altogether.

14. Richard Thaler (2000), discussing the future of economics, cited emotion as one of three areas that the profession had to incorporate into its analysis, as material self-interest is only one determinant of behavior.

15. Diener and colleagues (1993) find that while there is a positive correlation between gross national product and subjective well-being, rapid economic growth is accompanied by less rather than more happiness.

16. In Birdsall, Graham, and Pettinato (2000), we developed a new measure that is designed to capture the difference between the top of the distribution and the middle, for which we have adopted the term "middle-income stress." The measure compares the median income of the population that generates the top 50 percent of total income to the median income of the total population. The ratio captures the income difference between the wealthy and the middle sectors. Another new measure, Wolfson's (1997) polarization index, captures the extent to which the distribution is concentrating at the tails and thinning out at the middle, with a focus on the share of the bottom half.

17. For detail on the limited nature of the reforms in Russia see Gaddy and Ickes (1998).

18. In our studies, we had a 38 percent attrition rate over a five-year period in Russia, and a 25 percent attrition rate for the three-year period covered by our perceptions survey in Peru (for the 1991–2000 living standards measurement survey, we had less attrition).

19. Blanchflower and Oswald (2000) get a correlation coefficient of 0.56 for British data for 1975–92 where both questions are available. Graham and Pettinato (2002) get a correlation coefficient of 0.50 for Latin American data for 2000–01, in which alternative phrasing was used in different years.

20. The study of mobility is an area that has been much further developed by sociologists than by economists. For a summary of new economics research in this area, see Birdsall and Graham (2000).

21. A full national sample was not possible for the panel studies in the early 1990s, because of the guerrilla movement's control of some areas of the country. The perceptions study involved the collaboration of Nancy Birdsall, Carol Graham, and Richard Webb of Cuánto S.A. and was undertaken with funds from the Inter-American Development Bank, the Brookings Center on Social and Economic Dynamics, and the MacArthur and Tinker foundations.

22. The results of the 1998 pilot survey are described in greater detail in Webb (1999), and the 1999 survey results are presented in Graham and Pettinato (1999).

23. Carter and May (2001), among others, find that attrition bias tends to be at the tails of the distribution, which is not surprising: it suggests that poor households that cannot "make it" move away, as do those who "strike it rich." By adding more than double the original number of households—with the new ones from a shorter panel—we sought to eliminate as much of this bias as possible.

24. The full panel study was repeated in 1985, 1990, 1991, 1994, 1996, 1997, and 2000. The 2000 perceptions study coincided with the full panel study, which allowed us to update the objective data.

25. A comparison of these movements with data from the United States highlights their extremity. In the United States, about half the families that start in either the top or bottom quintile of the income distribution are still there after a decade, and only 3–6 percent rise from the bottom to the top or fall from the top to the bottom (Krugman 1992).

26. This is measured on the basis of household expenditure data in Lima 2000 prices, adjusted for household size using a one-parameter equivalence scale with elasticity of 0.5. For details on the implications of using this or other equivalence methods, see Figini (1998).

27. For details on the results from earlier years, see Graham and Pettinato (1999).

28. Assessments of the state of public services were even more optimistic, reflecting substantial government efforts to make improvements in this arena.

29. There were no significant effects on PPM when we used changes in equivalence expenditure, rather than log-expenditure, for the same time period (1994–2000).

30. In an ordered logit estimation with economic satisfaction as the dependent variable, we find that mean expenditure per capita (1991–2000) has positive and significant effects on economic satisfaction, while in the same estimation, expenditure per capita for 2000 is insignificant. When we use the log of both these expenditure measures, which highlights the impact of these trends for those with less income, we find that the mean over time is insignificant, while expenditure levels for 2000 are positive and significant.

31. Our quintiles are constructed on the basis of the respondents in the panel, using household expenditure, adjusted for household size considering economies of scale (see note 26). These quintiles are not the same as national income quintiles, as the households in our panel were, on average, slightly wealthier than those in the nationally representative sample.

32. Hirschman's (1973) "tunnel effect" may also be at play here.

33. This was measured by the coefficient of variation, defined as the standard deviation for each household divided by its mean expenditure levels for the 1991–2000 period. The coefficient for Russia was significantly higher for the frustrated than for the nonfrustrated group, meanwhile. Data for Russia are income-based rather than expenditure-based, and the former varies more.

34. See Blanchflower and Oswald (2000) for the advanced industrial economies; Graham and Pettinato (2001) for Latin America.

35. On job satisfaction in Britain, see Clark and Oswald (1996). The effects of education on job satisfaction may be mixed because in many countries in transition or crisis, people may be overqualified for their jobs.

36. The phrasing of the question in the Peru survey was slightly different: "How satisfied are you with your current standard of living?" In the Latinobarómetro and in the Russia Longitudinal Monitoring Survey, the question was, "How satisfied are you with your life?"

37. Having a pro-market attitude also has a similar strong, positive, and consistent effect on happiness. We discuss this in detail in Graham and Pettinato (2001).

38. Our wealth data in Latinobarómetro are much less precise than the expenditure data for Peru.

39. The difference here may be explained by the difference in sample size: the 17,000 observations in Latinobarómetro, rather than the 500 in Peru, probably better capture whatever age effects exist.

40. The results of regression analysis to identify the determinants of these responses were disappointing and inconsistent. Years of education was the only variable that was

significant and positively correlated to responding that one had done better than one's community. Income mobility (changes in log-expenditure from 1994 to 2000) was the only significant variable (positive) for assessments vis-à-vis the country.

41. This was a ratio between PPM responses (five categories) and objective "mobility quintiles," which were defined according to percentage expenditure mobility in 1991–2000. We did not correct for standard bias.

42. The RLMS has been conducted in Russia since 1995 by the Russian Institute of Nutrition, the University of North Carolina at Chapel Hill, and the Institute of Sociology of the Russian Academy of Sciences.

43. As in the case of Peru, we have used household income adjusted for size using a 0.5 equivalence factor.

44. For Russia we also defined frustrated achievers as those with income improvements of at least 30 percent and with negative or very negative perceptions of mobility in the preceding five years.

45. They not only had a higher mean coefficient of variation, but the coefficient was significant and positive in a logit estimation with the probability of being frustrated as the dependent variable and with age, age squared, education level, and the coefficient of variation on the right side. Results are available from the authors.

46. We defined volatility as the standard deviation of household equivalized income for the 1995–98 period, and used ordered logit regressions (on economic satisfaction for Peru), and controlled for age, gender, education, and mean income levels. Results are available from the authors.

47. Peru's economy was stabilized in 1990, and while there was still quite a bit of variation in growth rates, the overall policy framework was far more stable than Russia's from 1995 to 1998. For our panels, meanwhile, the standard deviation in income or expenditure was higher in Russia than in Peru.

48. Cross-country studies conducted in the 1980s and a more recent study conducted in Switzerland find a greater importance for relative income differences, and accord little importance to absolute increases over time. See Easterlin (1974) and Frey and Stutzer (1999a).

49. Our Latin America data set only has assessments of household wealth, based on a bundle of assets ranging from running water and electricity to second cars and vacation homes. Unfortunately, it does not have income data, which would be preferable.

50. The effects of current economic outcomes on future behavior, such as saving, provides a theoretical starting point for research in this area. On saving and anticipated income, see, for example, Carroll (1994). There is also some literature that uses past mobility and perceptions of future mobility to explain voting behavior and, in particular, attitudes toward redistribution. See Benabou and Ok (1998) and Piketty (1995).

References

Argyle, Michael. 1999. "Causes and Correlates of Happiness." In *Well-Being: The Foundations of Hedonic Psychology,* ed. Daniel Kahneman, Ed Diener, and Norbert Schwarz, 353–73. New York: Russell Sage Foundation.

Benabou, Roland, and Efe Ok. 1998. "Social Mobility and the Demand for Redistribution: The POUM Hypothesis." NBER Working Paper 6795, National Bureau of Economic Research, Cambridge, MA.

Birdsall, Nancy, and Carol Graham. 2000. *New Markets, New Opportunities? Economic and Social Mobility in a Changing World.* Washington, DC: Brookings Institution and Carnegie Endowment for International Peace.

Birdsall, Nancy, Carol Graham, and Stefano Pettinato. 2000. "Stuck in the Tunnel: Have New Markets Muddled the Middle?" Center on Social and Economic Dynamics Working Paper 14, Brookings Institution, Washington, DC.

Blanchflower, David G., and Andrew J. Oswald. 2000. "Well-Being Over Time in Britain and the USA." NBER Working Paper 7487, National Bureau of Economic Research, Cambridge, MA.

Carroll, Christopher D. 1994. "How Does Future Income Affect Current Consumption?" *Quarterly Journal of Economics* 109 (1): 111–47.

Carter, Michael R., and Julian May. 2001. "One Kind of Freedom: Poverty Dynamics in Post-Apartheid South Africa." *World Development* 29 (12): 1987–2006.

Clark, Andrew E., and Andrew J. Oswald. 1996. "Satisfaction and Comparison Income." *Journal of Public Economics* 61 (3): 359–81.

Deaton, Angus, and Christina Paxson. 1994. "Intertemporal Choice and Inequality." *Journal of Political Economy* 102 (3): 437–67.

Diener, Ed. 1984. "Subjective Well-Being." *Psychological Bulletin* 95 (3): 542–75.

Diener, Ed, and Robert Biswas-Diener. 1999. "Income and Subjective Well-Being: Will Money Make Us Happy?" Department of Psychology, University of Illinois.

Diener, Ed, Ed Sandvik, Larry Siedlitz, and Marissa Diener. 1993. "The Relationship Between Income and Subjective Well-Being: Relative or Absolute?" *Social Indicators Research* 28: 195–223.

DiTella, Rafael, Robert J. MacCulloch, and Andrew J. Oswald. 1997. "The Macroeconomics of Happiness." Discussion Paper 19, Centre for Economic Performance, Oxford University, Oxford, UK.

Duesenberry, James S. 1949. *Income, Saving, and the Theory of Consumer Behavior.* Cambridge, MA: Harvard University Press.

Easterlin, Richard A. 1974. "Does Economic Growth Improve the Human Lot?" In *Nations and Households in Economic Growth,* ed. Paul A. David and Melvin W. Reder, 89–125. New York: Academic Press.

———. 2000. "Where Is Economic Growth Taking Us?" Paper presented at Mount Holyoke Conference on the World Economy in the 21st Century: Challenges and Opportunities, Mount Holyoke, MA, February 18–19.

Esping-Andersen, Gosta. 1990. *Three Worlds of Welfare Capitalism.* Princeton, NJ: Princeton University Press.

Figini, Paolo. 1998. "Inequality Measures, Equivalence Scales, and Adjustment for Household Size and Composition." Luxembourg Income Study Working Paper 185, Syracuse University, Syracuse, NY.

Frey, Bruno, and Alois Stutzer. 1999a. "Happiness, Economics, and Institutions." University of Zurich.

———. 1999b. "Measuring Preferences by Subjective Well-Being." *Journal of Institutional and Theoretical Economics* 155 (4): 755–78.

Gaddy, Clifford G., and Barry W. Ickes. 1998. "Russia's Virtual Economy." *Foreign Affairs* 77 (5): 53–67.

Graham, Carol, and Cheikh Kane. 1998. "Opportunistic Government or Sustaining Reform: Electoral Trends and Public Expenditure Patterns in Peru, 1990–95." *Latin American Research Review* 33 (1): 71–111.

Graham, Carol, and Stefano Pettinato. 1999. "Assessing Hardship and Happiness: Mobility Trends and Expectations in the New Market Economies." Center on Social and Economic Dynamics Working Paper 7, Brookings Institution, Washington, DC.

————. 2001. "Happiness, Markets, and Democracy: Latin America in Comparative Perspective." *Journal of Happiness Studies* 2: 237–68.

————. 2002. *Happiness & Hardship: Opportunity and Insecurity in New Market Economies*. Washington DC: Brookings Institution Press.

Hirschman, Albert O. 1973. "Changing Tolerance for Income Inequality in the Course of Economic Development." *Quarterly Journal of Economics* 87 (4): 544–66.

Kenny, Charles. 1999. "Does Growth Cause Happiness, or Does Happiness Cause Growth?" *Kyklos* 52 (1): 3–26.

Köszegi, Botond. 2000. "Ego, Overconfidence, and Task Choice." Department of Economics, University of California, Berkeley.

Krugman, Paul. 1992 . "The Right, the Rich, and the Facts: Deconstructing the Income Distribution Debate." *American Prospect* 3 (11): 19–31.

Lowenstein, George, Drazen Prelec, and Roberto Weber. 1999. "What, Me Worry? A Psychological Perspective on the Economics of Retirement." In *Behavioral Dimensions of Retirement,* ed. Henry J. Aaron, 215–47. Washington, DC: Brookings Institution; New York: Russell Sage Foundation.

McMurrer, Daniel, and Isabel Sawhill. 1998. *Getting Ahead: Economic and Social Mobility in America*. Washington, DC: Urban Institute Press.

Merton, Robert K. 1957. *Social Theory and Social Structure*. Rev. ed. London: Free Press of Glencoe.

Milanovic, Branko, and Branko Jovanovic. 1999. "Change in the Perceptions of the Poverty Line During the Times of Depression: Russia, 1993–1996." *World Bank Economic Review* 13 (3): 531–60.

Namazie, Ceema, and Peter Sanfey. 1998. "Happiness in Transition: The Case of Kyrgyzstan." Discussion Paper DARP 40, Distributional Analysis Research Programme, London School of Economics.

Narayan, Deepa, ed. 2002. *Empowerment and Poverty Reduction: A Sourcebook*. Washington, DC: World Bank.

Oswald, Andrew J. 1997. "Happiness and Economic Performance." *Economic Journal* 107 (445): 1815–31.

Pigou, A. C. 1920. *The Economics of Welfare*. London: Macmillan.

Piketty, Thomas. 1995. "Social Mobility and Redistributive Politics." *Quarterly Journal of Economics* 110 (3): 551–84.

Robson, Arthur J. 1992. "Status, the Distribution of Wealth, Private and Social Attitudes Towards Risk." *Econometrica* 60 (4): 837–57.

Thaler, Richard H. 2000. "From Homo Economicus to Homo Sapiens." *Journal of Economic Perspectives* 14 (1): 133–41.

Van Praag, Bernard M. S., and Paul Frijters. 1999. "The Measurement of Welfare and Well-Being: The Leyden Approach." In *Well-Being: The Foundations of Hedonic Psychology,* ed. Daniel Kahneman, Ed Diener, and Norbert Schwarz. New York: Russell Sage Foundation.

Webb, Richard. 1999. "Household Perceptions of Mobility in a New Market Economy: Peru 1998." In Birdsall and Graham 2000, 267–90.

Wolfson, Michael C. 1997. "Divergent Inequalities: Theory and Empirical Results." Research Paper Series 6, Analytical Studies Branch, Statistics Canada, Ottawa.

World Bank. 1999. *Poverty and Social Developments in Peru, 1994–1997.* Washington, DC: World Bank.

Chapter 8

Self-Rated Power and Welfare in Russia

Michael Lokshin and Martin Ravallion

> A discipline that does not have independent measures of its dependent
> variable, for example, utility, risks its standing as a scientific discipline.
>
> —Robert Lane, *The Market Experience*

It is evident that different people within a given society, with one set of laws
and institutions, have different abilities to directly influence the actions of others. In short, there is inequality of personal power, just as there is inequality of
economic welfare as often measured by income or consumption. Some policy-
oriented discussions have argued that redressing power inequality—by taking
actions that selectively empower those with little power—should be seen as
a distinct policy objective, side by side with the more traditional aims of
promoting affluence or reducing income poverty. For example, *World Development Report 2000/2001: Attacking Poverty* puts the need for "empowerment" on the same level as promoting economic "opportunity" and "security"
(World Bank 2000).

This begs the question as to whether power is assigned differently than
economic welfare within a society. The answer is far from obvious. One might
assert that command over wealth is largely a result of one's power, but this is
surely a simplistic view of how an economy allocates economic rewards. Similarly, the view that "money buys power" is surely too simple a model of how
power is allocated. Realized power presumably depends on one's effort to participate in political and other institutions. The abilities needed to acquire
power through such efforts may well be quite different from those characteristics that are rewarded by markets.

Before assessing the role that empowerment can play in public policy, it is necessary to have a deeper understanding of how power itself is assigned to people. Does lack of power in a given society go hand in hand with poverty, or is it determined by other factors? Is there a trade-off between power and wealth, such that some factors that promote affluence do not enhance individual power? Does focusing on empowerment detract from the income focus of mainstream development efforts? What additional implications does valuing empowerment hold for income redistribution policy? Does the frequent focus on gender inequalities in discussions of empowerment reflect differences in the perceptions of men and women about their power?

One possible area of investigation relevant to answering these questions is the expressed perceptions of people about their own power. This chapter provides an overview of results from an empirical investigation of such perceptions in Russia. We examine how individual perceptions of power compare with both subjective and objective indicators of individual economic welfare. We also examine how much agreement there is between subjective "power" and "welfare," and consider the influence of a variety of factors or covariates on both sets of perceptions.

Such use of subjective data has antecedents in research in several disciplines. In psychology, there is now a large literature on subjective welfare and its covariates (for a survey see Diener et al. 1999). Various types of subjective data on power have been used in the social sciences. In political science, subjective data have been used in research on "power consciousness" (Aberbach 1977), political efficacy (for example, Stewart et al. 1992), and political freedom (Gibson 1993). In sociology and social psychology, subjective questions on powerlessness have been used to study alienation (Roberts 1987) and paranoia (Mirowsky and Ross 1983). There has also been research in sociology on related aspects of self-perception, such as subjective class identification (Davis and Robinson 1988).

Economists have traditionally resisted the use of subjective survey data. However, research interest in subjective welfare data among economists is now growing, partly as a result of the inherent difficulties of inferring welfare from objective data. Easterlin (1995) and Oswald (1997), among others, have focused on the links between subjective welfare and income. Van Praag (1968), Kapteyn (1994), Pradhan and Ravallion (2000), and others have used subjective data for identifying welfare.

The relationship between power and affluence or economic welfare, however, has received little attention in the literature. In one of the few exceptions, Ross and Mirowsky (1992) find evidence for the United States that wage employment, higher earnings, and higher education are all associated positively with a greater subjectively assessed "sense of control" over one's life. Using subjective welfare data for Switzerland, Frey and Stutzer (2000, 2002) find that the people's ability to influence outcomes of the local political process raises their subjective welfare. However, we know of no previous attempts to examine the joint socioeconomic determinants of power and economic welfare, including the role played by income in particular.

The Russian Survey

Russia is of particular interest as a setting for an enquiry into the perceived relationships between power and economic welfare because of the complex changes in the years since the breakup of the Soviet Union. Under Communism, higher economic welfare tended to go hand in hand with power, given the significance of the state and party in assigning economic benefits. One suspects that the assignment of power and affluence has become more complex since 1990, as a variety of factors have probably weakened the correlation between power and welfare. Economic welfare has clearly become more unequal, and a high degree of income inequality has emerged.

Recent survey data for Russia offer an opportunity to examine the extent to which perceived power is now associated with economic welfare, and to consider the factors affecting both. We used the November–December 2000 and October 1998 rounds of the Russia Longitudinal Monitoring Survey (RLMS).[1] These included both objective background variables and subjective assessment questions, the latter based on Cantril (1965) ladders for both power and welfare. For assessing perceived power, the survey asked:

> *Please imagine a nine-step ladder where on the bottom, the first step, stand people who are completely without rights, and on the highest step, the ninth, stand those who have a lot of power. On which step are you today?*

We refer to this as the Power Ladder Question (PLQ). The corresponding welfare question is:

> *Please imagine a nine-step ladder where on the bottom, the first step, stand the poorest people, and on the highest step, the ninth, stand the rich. On which step are you today?*

We call this the Welfare Ladder Question (WLQ).

There is always a degree of fuzziness about how to interpret answers to such subjective questions (though the precision of answers to standard "objective" questions is also questionable, and a degree of subjectivity enters many survey responses). The PLQ leaves it up to the individual to decide what it means to be "without rights" or to have "a lot of power." Power has many potential dimensions: the respondent may be thinking of electoral power, power in decision making at home or at work, or power over personal or family economic issues. This points to a potentially large set of possible determinants of responses to the PLQ.

Similarly, the respondent is free to interpret the WLQ as she or he sees fit. The WLQ might be considered as reflecting a narrower concept than "welfare"; it may be better to view it as a scale of "affluence" or "poverty." However, in analyzing responses to the WLQ from earlier rounds of the same survey, Ravallion and Lokshin (2002) found that the answers could not be interpreted as solely reflecting real household income (household income deflated for differences in the cost of living and in household size and composition). There was evidence of significant individual income effects. But the ladder score was also strongly influenced by education, employment, health status, area of residence, and other characteristics, independently of income. The WLQ is clearly capturing a broader concept of welfare than income or even affluence. It appears instead to be closer to the concept of utility or welfare as used by economists.

Our hypothesis was that an exploratory study of the answers to these questions could throw useful light on the extent to which individual power and welfare are influenced by the same factors. For this purpose, it was essential that the surveys also collected a standard set of objective socioeconomic characteristics that are potential covariates of both power and welfare. Having such data allowed us to deal with a limitation of past work on subjective power, namely that those data sets contained only a few such possible covariates. For example, Gibson (1993, 959) compares perceptions of political freedom in the Soviet Union in 1990 across identified covariates and argues that "perceptions of [political] repression have evenly diffused throughout society." Since Gibson's data set contains only a few covariates, however, it is unclear to what extent his conclusion is limited to those covariates.

A further advantage of our data is that they are longitudinal, so we can look at how perceptions of power and welfare have changed over time. By choosing the period 1998–2000 we also expected to observe significant welfare gains, since the 1998 survey was done soon after the 1998 financial crisis in Russia, which adversely affected household welfare (Lokshin and Ravallion 2000).

Armed with these data, we address the following questions:

- How much do self-perceptions of current power and welfare agree? How much of this is attributable to observable covariates?
- How much does income inequality attenuate aggregate power and welfare? How important is inequality within the household versus between households?
- How do the answers to these questions differ between men and women?

Respondents' Perceptions of Power and Welfare

Our RLMS data covered a sample (in 2000) of 3,800 households (8,300 adults, 6,700 of them with data for 1998).[2] All adults in the sampled households were asked to rate their own power and economic welfare, using the PLQ and WLQ. Only a small number of respondents (less than 1 percent in each case) put themselves on rungs 8 or 9 of either ladder. In compiling the results, therefore, we decided to collapse the seventh, eighth, and ninth rungs into one. Thus, the subjective rankings are based on two seven-rung Cantril ladders.

Table 8.1 summarizes responses to the WLQ and PLQ. The row total gives the number on each power rung, while the column totals are for welfare.

Table 8.1   Contingency Table of Welfare and Power Ranks, Russia, 2000

A. Full Sample

Cramer's V = 0.336

Power rank	Welfare rank							Total
	1 (poorest)	*2*	*3*	*4*	*5*	*6*	*7 (richest)*	
1 (least powerful)	629	356	386	216	202	36	15	1,840
2	98	514	410	261	199	22	8	1,512
3	40	183	645	371	288	61	17	1,605
4	26	63	219	536	268	92	12	1,216
5	26	35	157	233	767	130	38	1,386
6	4	9	26	77	97	127	48	388
7 (most powerful)	3	8	18	30	68	91	102	320
Total	826	1,168	1,861	1,724	1,889	559	240	8,267

B. Males Only

Cramer's V = 0.331

Power rank	Welfare rank							Total
	1 (poorest)	*2*	*3*	*4*	*5*	*6*	*7 (richest)*	
1 (least powerful)	248	122	149	90	77	13	6	705
2	35	207	180	114	87	10	4	637
3	16	67	303	173	127	34	9	729
4	9	36	105	233	118	31	5	537
5	9	19	77	106	361	61	20	653
6	2	7	10	36	51	52	29	187
7 (most powerful)	1	4	8	19	37	43	45	157
Total	320	462	832	771	858	244	118	3,605

C. Females Only

Cramer's V = 0.343

Power rank	Welfare rank							Total
	1 (poorest)	*2*	*3*	*4*	*5*	*6*	*7 (richest)*	
1 (least powerful)	381	234	237	126	125	23	9	1,135
2	63	307	230	147	112	12	4	875
3	24	116	342	198	161	27	8	876
4	17	27	114	303	150	61	7	679
5	17	16	80	127	406	69	18	733
6	2	2	16	41	46	75	19	201
7 (most powerful)	2	4	10	11	31	48	57	163
Total	506	706	1,029	953	1,031	315	122	4,662

A standard measure of association for contingency tables is Cramer's V, which tests the null hypothesis of no association between the row variable and the column variable in the table (see, for example, Agresti 1984). Cramer's V takes a value between 0 (no relationship) and 1 (perfect correlation). The value for the sample as a whole implied by table 8.1 is 0.336 (with a standard error of 0.006). For males it is 0.331 (standard error of 0.009), while for females it is 0.343 (standard error of 0.009).

Thus there is a significant positive association between power ranks and welfare ranks. However, the match between the two is far from perfect. Of the

Table 8.2 Movements Up and Down the Power and Welfare Ladders, Russia, 1998–2000

A. Full Sample

Cramer's V = 0.212   *Change in welfare rank*

Change in power rank	−4	−3	−2	−1	0	+1	+2	+3	+4	Total
−4	84	19	27	44	70	32	26	15	7	324
−3	11	25	43	30	53	23	9	1	0	195
−2	11	27	74	94	130	63	18	13	7	437
−1	15	30	82	206	265	169	62	20	9	858
0	26	21	98	271	740	398	193	75	31	1,853
+1	7	17	44	148	316	370	178	69	33	1,182
+2	5	7	25	68	151	203	190	74	32	755
+3	4	2	9	34	88	82	86	81	30	416
+4	3	2	4	8	52	95	80	43	74	361
Total	166	150	406	903	1,865	1435	842	391	223	6,381

B. Males Only

Cramer's V = 0.203   *Change in welfare rank*

Change in power rank	−4	−3	−2	−1	0	+1	+2	+3	+4	Total
−4	36	8	14	21	25	14	5	8	3	134
−3	5	8	14	15	27	13	3	0	0	85
−2	4	11	35	49	53	28	12	7	5	204
−1	6	15	38	86	126	63	28	7	3	372
0	11	8	46	107	300	152	76	30	10	740
+1	4	10	22	60	143	158	77	21	16	511
+2	3	5	4	32	65	92	73	27	14	315
+3	2	1	4	16	43	38	33	35	15	187
+4	2	0	4	4	22	39	35	17	24	147
Total	73	66	181	390	804	597	342	152	90	2,695

(table continues on following page)

Table 8.2   (continued)

C. Females Only

Cramer's V = 0.223   *Change in welfare rank*

Change in power rank	−4	−3	−2	−1	0	+1	+2	+3	+4	Total
−4	48	11	13	23	45	18	21	7	4	190
−3	6	17	29	15	26	10	6	1	0	110
−2	7	16	39	45	77	35	6	6	2	233
−1	9	15	44	120	139	106	34	13	6	486
0	15	13	52	164	440	246	117	45	21	1,113
+1	3	7	22	88	173	212	101	48	17	671
+2	2	2	21	36	86	111	117	47	18	440
+3	2	1	5	18	45	44	53	46	15	229
+4	1	2	0	4	30	56	45	26	50	214
Total	93	84	225	513	1,061	838	500	239	133	3,686

Note: There were a few individuals whose welfare and/or power perceptions changed by more than four rungs between 1998 and 2000. We combined these into the top (+4) and bottom (−4) categories.

240 people who put themselves on the highest welfare rung, more than half did *not* also place themselves on the highest power rung. Of the group on the lowest welfare rung, 24 percent did not also see themselves as being the least powerful. The greater source of mismatching is in the upper off-diagonal rather than the lower one. That is, there are many people who do not think of themselves as poor but who nonetheless feel relatively powerless. This pattern holds for both men and women.

Table 8.2 shows the changes in power and welfare ranks from 1998 to 2000. Among all adults surveyed, 42.5 percent registered a higher ladder rung for their power in 2000 than in 1998, while 45.3 percent showed a similar upward movement for their perceived welfare. Movement downward was less, with 28.4 percent reporting a lower power rung, and 25.5 percent a lower welfare rung.

Table 8.2 thus shows that there were net gains in power over this period. Indeed, the number of people who moved up a given number of rungs of the power ladder exceeded the number falling the same number of rungs. As with economic welfare, the allocation of power is clearly not a zero-sum game. While it is widely recognized that it is possible for everyone's economic welfare to rise simultaneously, this is not so clear for power. To the extent that "power" means power over others, one person's gain in influence could well mean someone else's loss. Our results clearly show a case in which such a zero-sum assumption does not hold.

There are also clear correlations between changes in perceived power and changes in perceived economic welfare. Among those who felt that their power had risen by a rung or more, 63.5 percent also reported being at a higher rung of the welfare ladder, while only 14.1 percent felt that their welfare had fallen. For those who reported that their welfare had risen, 59.6 percent also said that their power was at least one rung higher, while only 16.3 percent said that it had fallen a rung or more. As measured with Cramer's V, the correlation for the sample as a whole is 0.212 (standard error of 0.007), while it is 0.203 (0.011) and 0.223 (0.009) for males and females respectively. This association in the changes over time implies that the correlation shown in table 8.1 is influenced by factors other than a common time-invariant individual effect, such as the respondent's personality.

Explaining Subjective Power and Welfare

We explored whether perceived welfare and power share common covariates. Is there any variable that influences one but not the other, or that has opposing effects? How much of the empirical association found in the last section is attributable to differences in the ways that these variables respond to observed covariates, versus other nonobserved factors?

The qualitative answers to the PLQ and WLQ can be thought of as being generated by underlying continuous variables representing perceived power and welfare.[3] These are assumed to be determined in part by individual and household per capita income as well as other observable variables. In addition, we allow for unobservable variables, grouped together into independent and identically normally distributed error terms.

While a positive income effect is expected at the individual level, there is also a widely held view that there are diminishing returns to income in raising welfare. This assumption has a long history in economics, but it has also received some support from empirical work on subjective welfare (see for example Lane 1991, chap. 26, and Frey and Stutzer 2002, chap. 4). To capture this effect empirically, we assume that the relationship between incomes and the latent continuous variables can be represented by second-degree polynomials. Assuming that the levels of the ladder rungs are comparable across persons, and that the error terms are normally distributed, we can use an ordered probit to model the responses. Our regression specifications are described in greater detail in Lokshin and Ravallion (2005). The results of the regression for selected variables, as discussed below, are shown in table 8.3.

The income variable we use is total monthly disposable income, which includes wages and salaries, social security, private transfers, and imputed income in kind and from home production. We initially assume that all income is exogenous to power, although later we relax this assumption. To convert to real values we use region-specific deflators based on the work of Popkin and colleagues (1995). We also include geographic dummy variables that can help pick up errors in the deflators due to any omitted cost-of-living differences. We use household and individual characteristics of the respondents to control for heterogeneity at given incomes. The set of other explanatory variables includes individual characteristics such as respondents' age, age squared, and dummy variables for educational attainment and marital status. Demographic characteristics include household size and household size squared, and the shares of children, adult women, and pensioners in the household.

Table 8.3 Ordered Probits for Power and Welfare Ranks

| | Full sample | | | | Males | | | | Females | | | |
| | Power rank | | Welfare rank | | Power rank | | Welfare rank | | Power rank | | Welfare rank | |
Variable	Coeff.	S. err.	Coeff.	S. err.	Coeff.	S. err.	Coeff.	S. err.	Coeff.	S. err.	Coeff.	S. err.
Income per capita	1.270	0.237	2.363	0.229	1.462	0.379	2.316	0.362	1.105	0.309	2.400	0.299
Income per capita^2	−1.019	0.296	−1.612	0.280	−1.652	0.480	−1.713	0.444	−0.656	0.388	−1.629	0.366
Individual income	1.144	0.220	1.478	0.217	0.899	0.313	1.741	0.309	1.376	0.323	1.214	0.318
Individual income^2	−1.048	0.295	−1.232	0.291	−0.813	0.399	−1.738	0.394	−1.143	0.454	−0.532	0.449
Individual characteristics												
Male	0.056	0.026	−0.014	0.026								
Female	*Reference*											
Age	−0.029	0.004	−0.040	0.004	−0.038	0.007	−0.046	0.007	−0.023	0.005	−0.035	0.005
Age^2/100	0.020	0.005	0.030	0.004	0.031	0.008	0.038	0.008	0.013	0.006	0.025	0.005
Single	*Reference*											
Married	−0.005	0.046	0.100	0.045	0.048	0.078	0.138	0.077	−0.066	0.063	0.029	0.062
Divorced	−0.069	0.064	−0.069	0.062	0.038	0.113	0.034	0.110	−0.117	0.079	−0.117	0.077
Widowed	−0.052	0.065	−0.069	0.063	0.111	0.136	−0.061	0.133	−0.094	0.079	−0.092	0.076
Unemployed	−0.183	0.045	−0.258	0.044	−0.124	0.062	−0.263	0.061	−0.238	0.066	−0.231	0.065
Russian	*Reference*											
Non-Russian	0.188	0.035	0.140	0.034	0.270	0.053	0.216	0.052	0.127	0.046	0.086	0.045

(table continues on following page)

Table 8.3 (continued)

Variable	Full sample				Males				Females			
	Power rank		Welfare rank		Power rank		Welfare rank		Power rank		Welfare rank	
	Coeff.	S. err.	Coeff.	S. err.	Coeff.	S. err.	Coeff.	S. err.	Coeff.	S. err.	Coeff.	S. err.
Education												
High school	Reference											
Technical/vocational	0.073	0.028	0.067	0.028	0.124	0.043	0.051	0.043	0.035	0.038	0.081	0.037
University	0.316	0.037	0.152	0.037	0.394	0.057	0.160	0.056	0.258	0.050	0.151	0.049
Household characteristics												
Household size	0.070	0.027	0.105	0.026	0.044	0.043	0.088	0.042	0.088	0.036	0.114	0.035
Household size^2	-0.002	0.003	-0.007	0.003	-0.001	0.004	-0.006	0.004	-0.004	0.004	-0.007	0.004
Share of children 0–6 years	0.218	0.130	0.332	0.128	0.231	0.208	0.218	0.205	0.183	0.173	0.390	0.170
Share of children 7–14 years	-0.082	0.088	0.107	0.086	-0.034	0.136	0.265	0.133	-0.169	0.126	-0.037	0.123
Share of women	0.070	0.092	0.136	0.090	0.214	0.175	0.317	0.172	-0.063	0.131	-0.005	0.128
Share of pensioners	-0.120	0.074	0.104	0.072	-0.110	0.122	0.106	0.120	-0.167	0.106	0.075	0.103
Urban	Reference											
Rural	0.040	0.029	0.047	0.028	0.057	0.044	0.040	0.044	0.027	0.038	0.051	0.036

Regional dummies

	Reference											
Moscow and St. Petersburg												
Northern and Northwest	−0.306	0.072	−0.095	0.070	−0.461	0.111	−0.130	0.108	−0.196	0.096	−0.058	0.093
Central Black-Earth	−0.126	0.061	−0.021	0.059	−0.115	0.093	0.056	0.091	−0.137	0.080	−0.070	0.079
Volga-Vaytski and Volga	−0.123	0.061	−0.052	0.060	−0.144	0.094	−0.043	0.092	−0.115	0.081	−0.055	0.080
North Caucasian	0.155	0.065	0.287	0.064	0.063	0.098	0.220	0.097	0.217	0.086	0.344	0.084
Ural	−0.082	0.063	0.105	0.061	−0.058	0.095	0.144	0.094	−0.100	0.083	0.080	0.081
Western Siberian	−0.090	0.067	0.015	0.066	−0.157	0.103	0.070	0.101	−0.046	0.089	−0.021	0.087
Eastern Siberia and Far East	0.010	0.066	0.105	0.065	−0.017	0.100	0.150	0.098	0.030	0.088	0.076	0.086

Auxiliary parameters

C1	−1.148	0.130	−1.506	0.127	−1.350	0.203	−1.532	0.200	−1.143	0.177	−1.532	0.173
C2	−0.587	0.129	−0.877	0.126	−0.789	0.202	−0.915	0.199	−0.579	0.177	−0.893	0.172
C3	−0.058	0.129	−0.205	0.126	−0.237	0.202	−0.205	0.199	−0.066	0.177	−0.245	0.172
C4	0.383	0.129	0.372	0.126	0.200	0.202	0.381	0.199	0.381	0.177	0.327	0.172
C5	1.142	0.130	1.286	0.127	0.969	0.203	1.305	0.200	1.133	0.178	1.237	0.173
C6	1.581	0.131	1.926	0.129	1.416	0.205	1.908	0.203	1.568	0.179	1.910	0.176
Aldrich-Nelson pseudo R^2	0.138		0.155		0.127		0.147		0.148		0.166	
Log likelihood	−13852.034		−13937.598		−6014.005		−5944.830		−7817.901		−7972.113	
N	8,266				3,538				4,728			

187

We also examine the effect of employment status. A number of studies have found that unemployment lowers subjective welfare (Clark and Oswald 1994; Oswald 1997; Blanchflower and Oswald 1997; Winkelmann and Winkelmann 1998). There is less evidence regarding the effect on power, and arguments could be made in both directions. For example, the Marxian literature has viewed employment for a wage as "alienating." Against this view, it can be argued that an unemployed person would feel less control over the things that matter to his or her welfare than someone with a job (for example, see Lane 1991, part 5). Ross and Mirowsky (1992) find evidence that employment has positive effects on perceived power in the United States.

We also include a dummy variable for whether the respondent is Russian or not (85 percent of the sample is Russian). Survey evidence for Western Europe and North America suggests that minorities often face discrimination and social exclusion that attenuates perceived welfare and power. For example, Ross and Mirowsky (1992) find that minority groups in the United States tend to have less "sense of control" over their lives. It is not clear, however, that the Russian setting would be similar in this respect, given that the presence of minority groups in Russia typically does not stem from a history of migration (voluntary or otherwise) to deal with labor shortages. In a sample of 1,500 Soviet adults in 1990, Gibson (1993) finds that perceptions of governmental repression and self-censorship are uncorrelated with minority status (indeed, the reported correlation coefficients are less than 0.005 in both cases).[4]

We also estimate a model adding attitudinal variables related to self-reported health status and expectations about the future, following our earlier work on subjective welfare in Russia (Ravallion and Lokshin 2002). There are obvious concerns about the endogeneity of these variables with respect to the ladder measures. However, it is still of interest to study their correlations with subjective power and welfare, and how their inclusion in the regressions affects other coefficients. These estimations are not in this chapter but can be found in Lokshin and Ravallion (2005).

Effects of Income

For the total sample, and for the samples of males and females separately, table 8.3 presents the results of the ordered probits predicting perceived welfare and power. Comparing the actual distributions of respondents across the welfare and power ladders with the models' predicted distributions shows a very good fit (results are presented in Lokshin and Ravallion 2005). Indeed, for power, the actual and predicted distributions across the ladder rungs are identical when rounded off to the nearest percentage point. This holds for males and females separately, as well as for the full sample. The fit is equally good for welfare on the full sample, although when the sample is divided into gender groups, there are a few cases in which a difference in the distribution across ladder rungs persists when rounded off to the nearest percentage point.

The coefficients on the income variables in table 8.3 show positive relationships for both per capita household income and individual income. These tend to be steeper for welfare than for power, particularly in the case of per capita household income. We also find a strong indication for both power and welfare that the function relating income to the latent continuous variable underlying the ladder responses is a concave relationship (as implied by the significant negative coefficient for the effect of the squared income terms). That is, the effect of income on perceived power and welfare decreases at higher income levels.

Effects of Income Inequality

The impacts of income inequality depend on the curvature of the relationship between income on the one hand and power and welfare on the other. If the continuous variable representing power or welfare is strictly concave with respect to income, then higher income inequality around the same mean income results in lower mean power or welfare.

To measure how much difference such inequality makes, we simulated the effect on power and welfare of equalizing incomes. We did this in two steps. First we equalized incomes within households, replacing actual individual incomes with average income within the individual's household, and then calculated the predicted distributions across welfare and power ladders. We repeated the procedure assuming full equality of income per person across households.

We find that even with complete equalization of incomes there is only a small drop in the proportion of respondents who rate themselves as being among the least powerful. Income equalization has only a slightly greater impact on perceived economic welfare. Partial equalization within households naturally has less impact, though the impact on perceived power is noticeably greater for women than for men. For women, modal power shifts up one rung with either partial or complete income equalization. Detailed results for these simulations are presented in Lokshin and Ravallion (2005).

Effects of Other Factors

A number of other significant covariates are found, resulting in different perceived levels of power and welfare for different individuals at the same income. Male respondents tend to have higher perceived power. However, there is no such gender difference in perceived welfare. Younger respondents feel that they have less power (the maximum perceived power is attained at about 75 years of age) and perceive themselves as less affluent (the maximum is at age 65). Being unemployed lowers both power and welfare, although the effect of employment status is larger in the case of welfare.

Non-Russians in the sample tend to have higher perceived power and welfare than Russians. The effect is stronger for power than for welfare, and stronger for males than for females. This is not consistent with the arguments and evidence for Western Europe and North America, which point to discrimination and social exclusion among minorities. As we have noted, the Russian setting may be rather different in this respect. It remains puzzling, however, that Russians see themselves as less powerful and with lower welfare than others in the society. Possibly we are picking up a personality or cultural trait that has little relationship to objective circumstances. Or possibly it is the Russians in the sample who have been affected most by the breakup of the Soviet Union and the transition to a market economy.

We find a strong effect of education on both perceived power and welfare. Individuals with university degrees and with technical or vocational degrees have significantly higher perceived power and welfare in comparison to respondents with only a high school diploma. The effect of education is almost twice as high for power as for welfare.

Living in larger households increases subjective perceptions of both power and welfare, as does the presence of children 0–6 years of age in the household.

Coefficients on the regional dummies indicate significant geographic effects. Geographic proximity to the seat of political power clearly matters. Respondents from almost all regions feel less powerful than respondents living in Moscow and St. Petersburg. However, the regional differences are generally less pronounced (and less significant statistically) for perceived welfare.

Comparing the results for males and females reveals that while perceived male welfare and power peak around age 60, female welfare and power are increasing functions of age over the whole range of the data. We observe a stronger effect of education on perceived power for males than for females, but this difference disappears for welfare. Being divorced has a stronger negative effect on both perceived power and welfare for women than for men, though the effects are not statistically significant. Being unemployed attenuates power and welfare for both men and women, as it did for the sample as a whole. However, the effect of unemployment on power is stronger for women than for men, while the welfare effect is similar. Living in larger households has a positive and significant impact on the subjective power and welfare of females, but for males this effect is not significant. The presence of children 0–6 years of age increases the perceived welfare of women, but does not have any significant effect on men's welfare. Having more women in the household increases perceived power and welfare of men, although the effects cannot be considered statistically significant. But this has no effect for women.

While we have noted a number of differences, broadly speaking our results suggest that the factors that determine subjective perceptions of economic welfare have similar effects on perceptions of power. We find that the predicted levels of welfare and power are strongly correlated for the total sample as well as for the samples of males and females separately. The correlation between these two indicators is stronger for females. The correlation coefficient between predicted perceptions for women is 0.940 (standard error of 0.013) as compared to 0.875 (standard error of 0.033) for men.

Elaborating the Model

One possible concern about the above results is that income may be endogenous in the regressions for power. In particular, it might be argued that higher personal power perceptions have a positive effect on income, so that correlation results in part from that effect rather than from the effect of income. There is no obvious identification strategy to deal with this possibility; any potential instrument for individual income would be a potential covariate of welfare or power. However, it is also possible to test whether our conclusions would hold under a different specification, simply by reestimating our model with the respondent's own income excluded. Thus we drop the individual's own income and replace household income with its value excluding the individual's income. This assumes that the endogeneity problem is individual-specific, that is, that it does not spill over to the incomes of other household members. We found that our main findings described above are quite robust to this change in specification (detailed results are given in Lokshin and Ravallion 2005).

In an extended specification, we added attitudinal variables on health and expectations for the future to the basic model in table 8.3 (see Lokshin and Ravallion 2005). For the WLQ the results echo earlier findings (Ravallion and Lokshin 2002), namely that perceived ill health reduces subjective welfare, as does the expectation that things will get worse in the future. When we use these as additional regressors for PLQ, we again find considerable agreement in how they affect power and welfare. Ill health attenuates perceived power, as do expectations that things will get worse in the future. Other coefficients are reasonably robust, with one notable exception. This is that the significant positive effect of being male on perceived power vanishes in the extended model, an effect attributable to the attitudinal differences. In the extended model there are again high correlations between the predicted values of perceived power and welfare. For the full sample the correlation coefficient is 0.943 (standard error of 0.010), while it is 0.906 (0.022) for males and 0.950 (0.011) for females (Lokshin and Ravallion 2005).

We explored further why the gender effect on power vanishes when we control for the attitudinal differences. Adding the expectations variables into the equation does not change the gender effect on power. However, adding the health variables effectively eliminates the gender difference in power to insignificant levels. This implies that the gender difference in perceived power is largely attributable to the fact that women tend to see themselves as less healthy than men (Lokshin and Ravallion 2005).

A further extension to our model that we explored was to consider the possibility that current perceptions of power and wealth could depend on past perceptions. To test this, we extended our main specification by including lagged power and wealth perceptions from 1995. On doing so we found that power rank in 1995 has a positive and significant effect on the current power ranking. Similarly, individuals who ranked themselves higher on the wealth ladder in 1995 had similar rankings five years later. However, the economic welfare rank in 1995 is uncorrelated with the power rank in 2000. Indeed, those who had high perceived power in 1995 report a lower current perception of economic well-being.

These findings confirm that there is "stickiness" in perceptions of power and welfare. Allowing for this does not have much effect on our conclusions about the role played by other factors. Strikingly, we find no sign of positive cross-effects. Higher lagged welfare does not raise current power, and higher lagged power actually entails lower current welfare, with other factors held constant. Thus, while power and welfare are positively correlated and both are partially self-perpetuating, it appears that the transition process in Russia may be attenuating the perceived welfare of those who previously saw themselves as powerful.

Conclusions

If "empowerment" of specific groups in society is to be seen as a distinct policy objective, in addition to more traditional goals of reducing poverty or inequality in economic well-being, then one should be able to establish that power is in fact determined by different factors. Our study addressed this question by examining self-perceptions of power as reported in an unusual data set for Russia, which combined subjective data on power and welfare with the standard objective data collected in socioeconomic surveys.

We find that the self-assessed power of adults in Russia is in fact correlated with their economic welfare, both as they perceive it themselves and by conventional objective measures such as incomes. This correlation, however, is not very strong. On each ladder, the lower two rungs together account for about a quarter of the total sample, but in large part the two groups of lowest-ranked respondents do not consist of the same people. Only about half of those who perceive themselves as poor also see themselves as powerless, and vice versa.

The main reason that this correlation is not stronger is that many people, both men and women, who do not see themselves as poor nonetheless feel that they have little power. We find that 42 percent of the sample placed themselves on a lower rung of the power ladder than of the welfare ladder. In contrast, only 18 percent—less than half as many—rated themselves more highly in power than in economic welfare. In other words, in terms of self-perceptions, the scope for empowerment in Russia is clearly not confined to the poor.

Looking at the changes over time, we also find a statistically significant correlation between power and welfare, suggesting that the cross-sectional correlation is not driven solely by latent personality traits. Perceived welfare gains or losses are likely to be associated with gains or losses in perceived power. Perceived welfare and perceived power moved in opposite directions between 1998 and 2000 for only 13 percent of respondents. Still, it was the case that 40 percent of those who felt that their welfare had risen by a rung or more did not feel that they had reached a higher rung on the power ladder. And a slightly smaller proportion of those who felt that their power had risen by a rung or more did not feel that they had risen on the welfare ladder.

These modest levels of association might be taken to suggest that there is scope for a policy agenda for empowerment that is qualitatively distinct from that for raising economic welfare. However, when we examine the factors that are responsible for both sets of subjective rankings, the policy implications are not so clear. Indeed, we are struck by the similarity in observable covariates, implying that the relevant policy interventions addressing these factors would be similar for both welfare and power.

Even differences that were found, such as the fact that gender is more important for perceived power than for perceived welfare, disappear when controlling for other factors such as differences in perceived health. To give another example, although unemployment reduces power more than it reduces welfare, it is a strong determinant of both. Looking at the results as a whole, there is strong agreement in how perceptions of power and welfare react to differences in individual and household characteristics. The predicted values show a very high correlation (around 0.9, and even higher for men and women separately). The weaker correlation between perceived power and perceived welfare thus seems to be driven by idiosyncratic factors that are not readily accountable in terms of observable characteristics in our survey. Arguably, it is the observable objective characteristics that are the ones most amenable to policy intervention. So our results suggest that the policies that enhance individual welfare are likely to be very similar to those that promote individual power.

Among the characteristics that influence perceived power and welfare, income is particularly important. However, this does not justify an exclusive or narrow focus on incomes. Consistent with past work in the literature, we find many significant covariates of welfare at given incomes, suggesting that people's perceptions of how "poor" they are can be affected by many factors other than their incomes, either individually or at the household level. What is striking about our findings is that both income and these other factors determine individuals' self-perceptions of power as well as economic welfare.

Notes

This paper draws heavily on work published recently by the authors in *Journal of Economic Behavior and Organization* (Lokshin and Ravallion 2005), which gives greater detail on the theory, methods, and results. The authors are grateful to Monica Das Gupta, Deepa Narayan, Mead Over, Vijayendra Rao, Dominique van de Walle, Bernard van Praag, Michael Woolcock, and seminar participants at the World Bank and two peer reviewers for this volume for their comments.

1.   The RLMS has been conducted in Russia since 1995 by the Russian Institute of Nutrition, the University of North Carolina at Chapel Hill, and the Institute of Sociology of the Russian Academy of Sciences. See http://www.cpc.unc.edu/projects/rlms.

2.   Data from both rounds are available on the RLMS Web site: http://www.cpc.unc.edu/projects/rlms.

3.   For a theoretical model incorporating this assumption see Lokshin and Ravallion (2005).

4. Gibson's comparisons with similar data for the United States indicate larger differences in perceived constraints on political freedom between U.S. whites and African Americans than found among Soviet citizens of different backgrounds in the 1990s. In fact, Gibson's results suggest that African Americans see themselves as absolutely less free than Soviet citizens.

References

Aberbach, Joel D. 1977. "Power Consciousness: A Comparative Analysis." *American Political Science Review* 71 (4): 1544–60.

Agresti, A. 1984. *Analysis of Ordinal Categorical Data.* New York: John Wiley.

Blanchflower, David G., and Andrew J. Oswald. 1997. "A Study of Labour Markets and Youth Unemployment in Eastern Europe." Warwick Economic Research Paper 499, Department of Economics, University of Warwick, Coventry, UK.

Cantril, Hadley. 1965. *The Pattern of Human Concerns.* New Brunswick, NJ: Rutgers University Press.

Clark, Andrew E., and Andrew J. Oswald. 1994. "Unhappiness and Unemployment." *Economic Journal* 104 (424): 648–59.

Davis, Nancy J., and Robert V. Robinson. 1988. "Class Identification of Men and Women in the 1970s and 1980s." *American Sociological Review* 53: 103–12.

Diener, Ed, Eunkook Suh, Richard E. Lucas, and Heifi L. Smith. 1999. "Subjective Well-Being: Three Decades of Progress." *Psychological Bulletin* 125 (2): 276–302.

Easterlin, Richard A. 1995. "Will Raising the Incomes of All Increase the Happiness of All?" *Journal of Economic Behavior and Organization* 27 (1): 35–47.

Frey, Bruno, and Alois Stutzer. 2000. "Happiness, Economy and Institutions." *Economic Journal* 110 (466): 918–38.

———. 2002. *Happiness and Economics: How the Economy and Institutions Affect Human Well-Being.* Princeton, NJ: Princeton University Press.

Gibson, James L. 1993. "Perceived Political Freedom in the Soviet Union." *Journal of Politics* 55 (4): 936–74.

Kapteyn, Arie. 1994. "The Measurement of Household Cost Functions: Revealed Preference Versus Subjective Measures." *Journal of Population Economics* 7: 333–50.

Lane, Robert E. 1991. *The Market Experience.* Cambridge: Cambridge University Press.

Lokshin, Michael, and Martin Ravallion. 2000. "Welfare Impacts of Russia's 1998 Financial Crisis and the Response of the Public Safety Net." *Economics of Transition* 8 (2): 269–95.

———. 2005. "Rich *and* Powerful? Subjective Power and Welfare in Russia." *Journal of Economic Behavior and Organization* 56(2): 141–72.

Mirowsky, John, and Catherine E. Ross. 1983. "Paranoia and the Structure of Powerlessness." *American Sociological Review* 48 (2): 228–39.

Oswald, Andrew J. 1997. "Happiness and Economic Performance." *Economic Journal* 107 (445): 1815–31.

Popkin, B., A. Baturin, M. Mozhina, and T. Mroz, with A. Safronova, I. Dmitrichev, E. Glinskaya, and M. Lokshin. 1995. "The Russian Federation Subsistence Level: The Development of Regional Food Basket and Other Methodological Improvements." Carolina Population Center, University of North Carolina, Chapel Hill.

Pradhan, Menno, and Martin Ravallion. 2000. "Measuring Poverty Using Qualitative Perceptions of Consumption Adequacy." *Review of Economics and Statistics* 82 (3): 462–71.

Ravallion, Martin, and Michael Lokshin. 2002. "Self-Rated Economic Welfare in Russia." *European Economic Review* 46 (8): 1453–73.

Roberts, Bruce R. 1987. "A Confirmatory Factor-Analytic Model of Alienation." *Social Psychology Quarterly* 50 (4): 346–51.

Ross, Catherine E., and John Mirowsky. 1992. "Households, Employment and the Sense of Control." *Social Psychology Quarterly* 55 (3): 217–35.

Stewart, Marianne C., Allan Kornberg, Harold D. Clarke, and Alan Acock. 1992. "Arenas and Attitudes: A Note on Political Efficacy in a Federal System." *Journal of Politics* 54 (1): 179–96.

Van Praag, Bernard M. S. 1968. *Individual Welfare Functions and Consumer Behavior*. Amsterdam: North-Holland.

Winkelmann, Liliana, and Rainer Winkelmann. 1998. "Why Are the Unemployed So Unhappy? Evidence from Panel Data." *Economica* 65: 1–15.

World Bank. 2000. *World Development Report 2000/2001: Attacking Poverty*. New York: Oxford University Press.

Chapter 9

Applying Q Methodology to Empowerment

Steven R. Brown

"I think I can, I think I can, I think I can . . ."

—Piper, *The Little Engine That Could*

A disparity exists between the conceptualization of empowerment on the one hand and its measurement on the other. Conceptually, we are challenged "to look at the world through the eyes and spirit of the poor, to start with poor people's realities" (Narayan, Patel, et al. 2000, 274), but implementation typically falls short of this worthy goal. For instance, most of the thinking about poverty reduction appears to have gone into creating empowering *opportunities*—for example, providing basic services, improving local and national governance, developing pro-poor markets, and establishing access to justice (Narayan 2002, xxi). These are no doubt necessary prerequisites: after all, it is fruitless to empower people if they are not also given opportunities to better themselves.

However, opportunities are external to the impoverished person. Although providing such opportunities may alter the person's *potential reality,* they are not empowering in and of themselves unless they enter into that person's *actual reality*. That is, external actions may "create the conditions in which poor people . . . make decisions" (Narayan 2002, xix). But objective opportunities, while necessary, are insufficient for empowerment. It is also necessary that they become a functional part of the person's perspective.

The World Bank has tried to incorporate the perspectives of those to be empowered through its Voices of the Poor project, which included 60,000 interviews with poor people in 60 countries.[1] While the project's intent is to "let the data speak" (Narayan, Patel, et al. 2000, 295), it falls somewhat short of this goal due to unnecessary methodological limitations. The categories used in the project's content analysis program, for instance, are those chosen by the investigators. For example, "humiliation" was considered an aspect of poverty because *the research team noted* that humiliation was a constant theme throughout the reports" (294, emphasis added). Had humiliation not been noticed, presumably no recording of its incidence would have taken place. As the report acknowledges, "What you measure is what you see" (274). This naturally raises the specter of topics that are unmeasured because they are undetected.[2]

If we are to take seriously the premise that we "start with poor people's realities," what is required is a method that empowers the poor to reveal their own concerns in terms that are their own and that are functionally significant for them (Brown 2002a, 2003). Q methodology, by analyzing responses to a set of statements from a diverse group of respondents from the target group, provides a convenient and precise way to allow the categories to emerge from the opinions provided by the poor themselves. While the emergent categories still are given names by the researchers, the structuring of the categories (with the possible emergence of totally unexpected categories) is derived from the respondent-supplied statements. Thus Q methodology provides the basis for a scientific approach to subjectivity that enables poor people or any other group to express themselves with minimal involvement from outsiders and minimal bias from externally imposed or ostensibly derived meanings.

Introducing Q Methodology

Q methodology was first proposed in 1935 by British physicist/psychologist William Stephenson (1953) and enjoyed popularity in American clinical and counseling psychology in the 1950s and 1960s before lapsing into disuse. It came under renewed attention in communication and political science in the 1970s and 1980s and has gained popularity since then (see, for example, Brown 1980, 1994–95, forthcoming; Donner 2001).[3] Q methodology adheres to tenets of empiricism (Brown 2002b), and its data are subject to advanced quantitative analysis, yet it shares many of the presuppositions of qualitative methods (Brown 1996).

Q methodology is now routinely employed in political science, communication, psychology, advertising, health science, public policy, and other fields. The broad applicability of Q methodology has been widely demonstrated at the levels of culture, community (in both public and private sectors), and even the individual, wherever subjectivity is at issue. It has been used in decision and policy making (Addams and Proops 2000; Gargan and Brown 1993); in the clarification of perspectives among community stakeholders (Brown et al. 2003); in the resolution of conflicts (Focht 2002); in business relations (Parris 1999; Potter 2003); in the elucidation of emergent and long-standing identities (Davis 1997; Dryzek and Holmes 2002; Robyn 2000); in journalistic practices (Bublic and Sitaraman 1998); in the examination of emergent political leadership (Tolymbek, forthcoming); and in the study of social attitudes and values from the cultural level to the level of the individual personality (Brown and Kil 2002; Salazar and Alper 2002).

It is only recently that Q methodology has drawn the attention of researchers focused on issues of empowerment and poor people (Brown 2004; see also the ongoing doctoral research of Züger Cáceres, 2003, 2004). Consequently, the illustrations below are necessarily fragmentary and hypothetical rather than definitive, and are intended to suggest Q methodology's potential based on successful applications in studies related to poverty.

Foundational to Q methodology is the concept of *concourse* (Stephenson 1978). This term refers to a set of subjective communications on any topic, for example, what it is like to live in poverty, what it means to be empowered, etc. The World Bank's Voices of the Poor project has already gathered a concourse that is more than adequate. The following statements provide a small sampling, paraphrased from the first two volumes in the *Voices* series (Narayan, Patel, et al. 2000; Narayan, Chambers, et al., 2000):

No one ever asks what I think.

It is my destiny to be poor.

We need to vote better—to monitor and demand our rights.

I depend on everyone, but no one needs me.

I can solve some of the problems myself.

I am ashamed at what I have become.

I place my hope in God, since the government is no longer involved in such matters.

The future lies in the education of our children.

Every day I am afraid of the next.

I just live hour to hour.

I don't have the strength or power to change anything.

There should be no special privileges for anyone.

The statements gathered by the Voices project number in the thousands. But merely listing the statements does not reveal how they may be organized into perspectives. What points of view are at issue in the national discussions about poverty? What limited number of discursive patterns underlie and contribute to the structure of such a concourse, which is already very large and easily expanded by additional research?

To answer questions of this kind requires a *Q sample*. Such a sample is a purposive selection of statements, such as those listed above, chosen to include a relatively comprehensive and diverse subset of the full set of statements in the concourse. Frequently, such a Q sample is structured to include statements in different categories.[4] This serves the same objective as intentionally selecting respondents so as to "ensure inclusion of minority groups, refugees, or other locally relevant unique conditions" (Narayan, Chambers, et al. 2000, 6)—that is, to ensure diversity.

Unlike the case in social science scales and even content analysis, the a priori categorizations of statements in a Q sample are not subject to tests of validity and reliability. This is because the categories are not used as a basis for analysis, but merely as a way of injecting diversity and comprehensiveness into the statement set as it is being composed. These initial categories, it should be clear, are quite distinct from the analytic categories that emerge later from the way in which the statements are actually sorted and arranged by participants. They are used to ensure inclusion of relevant aspects of the respondents' communications, not to analyze the set of responses.

Once selected, the Q-sample statements are typed on cards. They are then submitted to participants for *Q sorting,* which requires that each person rank-order the statements from most agree (+4) to most disagree (–4). It is at this point that participants with a sense of empowerment would begin to distinguish themselves instrumentally from those with a sense of powerlessness. That is, the empowered would be expected to give high scores to statements such as "I would like to join an organization that would protect our rights" and "I can solve some of the problems myself." In contrast, the unempowered would be more apt to give high scores to statements such as "I depend on everyone, but no one needs me."

Figure 9.1 shows a hypothetical Q-sort distribution of 42 statements by one respondent.

Q sorts carried out by a relatively small but diverse set of participants (typically no more than 40) provide data that can be used for *correlation* and *Q-factor analysis.* These procedures reveal the number of distinct ways in which the statements tend to be grouped, or, effectively, subgroups of people who tend to answer in similar ways. Table 9.1 shows a hypothetical case with only six poor persons. On first administration of the Q sort (time$_1$), persons 1, 3, and 4 have responded similarly; this is indicated by factor I. Persons 2 and 5 have responded similarly, revealing factor II. Both response patterns are distinct from that shown by person 6, who is alone in defining factor III. These factors emerge from the data, regardless of the names and interpretations the researcher may decide to apply to them.

Figure 9.1   Example of a Q-sort Distribution (*N* = 42)

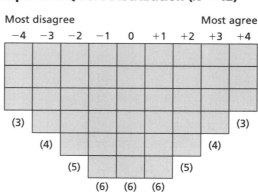

Table 9.1   Operant Factors

	Time$_1$				Time$_2$		
Person	*I*	*II*	*III*	*Person*	*I*	*II*	*III*
1	X			1	X		
2		X		2			X
3	X			3			X
4	X			4	X		
5		X		5		X	
6			X	6			X

Note: X = significant factor loadings.

The *factor scores* (that is, the scores from +4 to –4, assigned to each of the 42 statements in each of the three factors) show which statements people identified by each factor are most likely to agree with, disagree with, or be neutral toward.[5] The results available to the researcher, therefore, show a full response pattern emerging from the data, which the researcher can then relate to the conceptual and practical issues of concern. For example, factors I and II might be taken as two different patterns of response among unempowered poor people, with factor III reflecting a more empowered standpoint. Upon returning to the village and readministering the same Q sort (time$_2$), it might be discovered (again hypothetically) that persons 2 and 3 have now abandoned their previously unempowered stances on factors I and II and have experienced a "mind-set shift" (Narayan, Chambers, et al. 2000, 288) to the empowered outlook of factor III. Such a shift can be seen in table 9.1.

This hypothetical illustration shows several potential advantages in using Q methodology for the measurement of empowerment. First, Q methodology goes beyond content analysis in that it reveals the ways in which the many discrete opinions expressed by the poor are laced together into overall viewpoints. Content analysis may show the weight given to different opinions by different groups, revealing, for example, that women more frequently express a certain opinion than do men. But Q methodology allows participants, in effect, to create their own categories; that is, the participants' Q sortings are the driving force behind the categories of thought that are then documented by the Q-factor analysis. If all participants hold the same beliefs, this will register as a single Q factor. If there are two belief systems at issue, then there will be two factors, and so on. The number and character of the factors that emerge is a function of the participants themselves, not of how the investigator categorizes the statements used. Indeed, it is a common occurrence in Q-methodological studies that wholly unexpected Q factors emerge.

Second, these factors normally reveal a limited number of ways in which the impoverished are segmented subjectively. This in turn suggests that the "voices of the poor" may be subject to deconstruction into types (for example, voice I, voice II, voice III, etc.). In Q methodology, such factors are considered *operants* (Delprato and Brown 2002; Stephenson 1977); that is, they represent *functional* segmentations that have emerged from the behaviors (that is, Q sortings) of the participants themselves (Brown 2002a). Because these groupings thus reflect distinctions made by the respondents themselves, they can be considered as more likely predictors of the respondents' actions than conventional research categorizations such as men/women, middle/lower class, empowered/powerless, and so forth. Q factors are grounded in the realities people perceive. In this sense, they can be considered *indigenous* categorizations.

Third, the factors in Q methodology can be used for generalizations with respect to the subjectivity at issue, despite the small number of participants involved. Large samples in the Voices of the Poor project are required for generalizations with respect to demographic factors. Q factors, on the other hand, provide windows into the thinking of social segments. The set of statements and factor scores associated with each factor illustrate a particular style of thinking. If three factors are identified, for example, the style of thinking associated with factor III will differ in general from that associated with factors I and II. Q-methodological studies as such do not show the proportion of persons associated with each factor group, since the groups used to define the factors are not large random samples. But they do provide unequivocal evidence of the existence of the groups and reveal something about the thinking of each.

Once the groups have been delineated, procedures are used to incorporate them into questionnaires (Brown 2002c) along with other relevant variables. This additional step also allows for confirming the extent to which the same factors apply to a wider population. That Q methodology facilitates the detection of even the weakest voices has led to its adoption by groups that have a special interest in empowerment, such as feminists (Gallivan 1994; Senn 1996; Snelling 1999) and racial minorities (Hunter and Davis 1992; Smith 2002; Thomas, McCoy, and McBride 1993).

Illustrative Applications of Q Methodology

The potential for insight provided by Q methodology is illustrated by several projects currently underway involving such wide-ranging problems as poverty alleviation among Peruvian farmers, dairy herd improvement in Uruguay, health care in Serbia, and the use of cell phones in Rwanda. The first of these four studies is reported in greater detail in order to illustrate the techniques used in the methodology.

Agricultural Schooling in Peru

The Farmer Field Schools (FFS) of Peru enable farmers to return to school and eventually obtain a certificate in integrated pest management. Project planners and researchers are interested, in addition, in the potential effects of participation in these schools on empowerment of the participants. Züger Cáceres and Amani (2003) have collected statements from interviews with Peruvian farmers involved in the project. The selection was made in order to include statements representing the range of Lasswell's (1963) value categories: power, enlightenment, wealth, well-being, skill, affection, and respect, with the category of rectitude being replaced by gender relations. Within each value category, the cross-classification of indulgent (I) or deprivational (D) was applied to produce a matrix (see note 4).

Exemplary expressions include the following (translated from Spanish):

I lend money to my neighbors when the need arises. (I: wealth)

Securing resources for investment is almost impossible. (D: wealth)

It is important to be informed on politics. (I: enlightenment)

Talking in front of many people is very difficult. (D: skill)

I have come to believe that those born poor will die poor. (D: well-being)

Meetings are much more interesting when men and women participate. (I: gender)

As indicated previously (note 4), these initial categories are used as a heuristic device to help conceptualize and organize the concourse. They are not used as a basis for the subsequent analysis. That analysis instead depends solely on the ways in which participants themselves sorted the statements rather than on the ways in which the statements were conceptualized a priori.

From this concourse, 48 statements were included in a Q sort that was administered to 28 participants (primarily male), some of whom had participated in FFSs and some of whom had not. The fact that many of the farmers could not read required adjustments in the procedures used. Interviewers first read the statements aloud and asked the farmers whether they agreed, disagreed, or had no opinion about each of the statements. In follow-up questions, interviewers then asked whether their agreement or disagreement was strong or only moderate. This produced the equivalent of a Q sort ranging from +2 (most agree) to −2 (most disagree).[6]

Preliminary analysis of the Peruvian data indicates that there were four distinct attitudes expressed by the farmers, which clearly indicates the inadequacy of any simplistic division into only two categories of empowered versus unempowered farmers. The first two factors were somewhat correlated ($r = 0.44$) and can be considered representative of two distinct empowered points of view. Participants identified by both these factors, for example, tended to agree that "a good education is extremely essential for our children," that "meetings are much more interesting when men and women participate," and that "it is always interesting to experiment and try out new things at home or in the field," all statements with a progressive ring.

However, the factor scores associated with other statements indicate that the group forming factor I, which might be labeled *modern,* has more

Table 9.2   Distinguishing "Modern" and "Inhibited" Perspectives Identified by Factors I and II

Factor I (Modern)	Factor II (Inhibited)	Statement
0.21	−2.17	33. Many times I can improve my situation without having to rely on external support.
0.24	−1.65	15. When someone is ill the members of the community always offer their help.
0.74	−0.75	29. Sometimes I lose hope, but there is always a solution to the problem.
0.80	−0.36	31. There is always something left over to give someone who is in more need of it at that moment.
−1.83	0.62	22. Women do not know enough to have an opinion on important issues; they have very low self-esteem.
−1.92	0.09	48. Pride is a luxury that only the rich can permit themselves.
−0.97	1.22	38. Men have more talent for learning; they want to know more.
−0.85	0.62	04. Talking in front of many people is very difficult.
−0.27	0.99	07. I cannot confide in anyone but myself.

thoroughly internalized the values and optimism of empowerment. The group associated with factor II, which might be labeled *inhibited,* shows signs of pessimism and of adhering to more traditional values. The factor scores of different statements on factors I and II are shown in table 9.2. The left two columns contain factor scores in normalized (z-score) form for the two factors.

As the positive statement scores for factor I indicate, the "moderns" are more inclined than the "inhibiteds" toward self-reliance (statement 33), are more optimistic (29), feel a stronger and more reciprocal tie to the community (15), and are able to maintain a sense of generosity (31). They also reject any statements that are critical of women (22, 38). The inhibiteds, on the other hand, still feel a sense of dependency (33) and demonstrate less confidence in the community (15). Despite sharing the view that community meetings are more interesting with women present, the inhibiteds are less likely to express respect for women (22, 38). There is some evidence of personal insecurity among the inhibiteds, indicated by a deficit in social skills (04), an inability to confide in others (07), and a lack of pride (48).

Almost all of the moderns had been participants in the FFS. Many of the inhibiteds were also participants, however, so this does not differentiate between the two groups. Males and females were in both groups, although males were more prevalent among the moderns, as were persons with more education. In short, demographic divisions based on gender, education, or involvement in the FFS program are not sufficient to predict the factor groupings.

Table 9.3 Distinguishing the "Organizer" Perspective Identified by Factor III

Factor III (Organizers)	Factor IV (Withdrawn)	Statement
1.31	−0.65	26. I would like to exchange more ideas with people from other communities.
1.31	−0.16	39. When neighbors cooperate on ventures they can achieve wonderful things.
0.67	−1.23	47. It's much nicer to work together with neighbors than to work alone.
0.67	−0.69	17. The farmers should unite their forces so that their voices can be heard.
−2.05	−0.08	13. The situation of the poor will never change; their efforts are in vain but they are used to it.

These groupings therefore point to functional divisions, and can provide the basis for thinking about the situation in new ways tied to the viewpoints of the participants themselves.

Factors III and IV appear on first inspection to be variants of the same unempowered outlook. The persons comprising factor III seem to have no illusions for themselves. More than any of the other three groups, they accept the view that "those born poor will die poor." Similarly, those persons defining factor IV lead all other groups in assigning the most negative score to the view that "I have many plans and dreams for the future." Both such response patterns might be considered to reflect a lack of empowerment. A careful examination of the scores associated with other statements, however, shows differences, suggesting that factor III could also be considered as indicating a variant of empowerment (table 9.3).

Organizers, as persons associated with factor III might be characterized, favor the uniting of farmers (17), are anxious to exchange ideas with others (26), are optimistic about what can be accomplished through cooperation (39, 47), and reject the idea that nothing can be done to alleviate poverty (13). The organizers' perspective may be summed up as "those born poor will die poor . . . unless they do something about it."

On the other hand, those individuals associated with factor IV seem more *withdrawn,* as suggested by the response patterns shown in table 9.4. These participants do not appear to be in dire economic straits themselves (03, 19). However, they seem somewhat isolated from their neighbors (11, 12). Like the inhibiteds, the withdrawns also find social interaction personally difficult (04, 20, 34). Unlike the inhibiteds, however, they experience social distancing that compounds their social discomfort.

As already noted, this Peruvian research project is in its early stages (Züger Cáceres 2004), and the interpretations above are tentative. It is already

Table 9.4   Distinguishing the "Withdrawn" Perspective Identified by Factor IV

Factor III (Organizers)	Factor IV (Withdrawn)	Statement
–2.05	1.12	19. We can eat well here every day.
–0.99	0.63	03. I can often afford to buy a little something for my children.
0.02	1.41	04. Talking in front of many people is very difficult.
–2.05	0.42	34. The things discussed at work meetings are too difficult to understand; it is better to stick to my daily chores.
0.67	1.20	20. Participating in a group where I don't know anyone at all is uncomfortable.
0.31	–1.69	11. I lend money to my neighbors when the need arises.
–0.99	–1.98	12. Neighbors often come over to ask questions or to seek my advice.

clear, however, that the results show a greater social complexity than would be revealed by analysis constrained by categories such as age, gender, FFS enroll-ment, or similar conventional research categories. Such categories may to some extent be correlated with the subgroups revealed by Q methodology. For example, further study might reveal proportionately more males than females among the moderns compared to the inhibiteds. What is directly consequen-tial for empowerment, however, is not gender as such, but frame of mind. It may be the case that some mind-sets are found more among males than among females. With Q methodology, however, it becomes possible to identify the rel-evant mind-set and deal with it directly, rather than focus on the correlated background factors such as gender, age, or other traits that are less directly rel-evant. An advantage of Q methodology is that it reveals functional groups, operantly defined—that is, the factor groupings arise solely as a function of the ways in which the participants themselves organized the statements. This places the study of empowerment on a different footing.

Dairy Herd Improvement in Uruguay

The study by Kramer, de Hegedus, and Gravina (2003) utilizes Q methodol-ogy as a way to differentiate dairy farmers' motivations for not participating in the Instituto Nacional Mejoramiento Lechero (INML), a dairy herd genetic registry project in Uruguay. Statements were drawn from interviews with ad-ministrators, technicians, and dairy farmers. Thirty-two of these statements were then administered in a Q sort to 27 individuals, including 7 INML pro-gram personnel and 20 farmers not participating in the project.

The selection of statements was made using an initial division into those that focused on the farmers versus those that emphasized context. These were further subdivided into statements dealing with economic versus social dimensions of the problem. This gave rise to four combinations, and eight statements were chosen from each of the four cells, producing a Q sample of 32 statements. Producers selected to participate in the Q sort were chosen by a similar procedure to ensure diversity, from groups defined in terms of herd size (more versus less than 100 head) and involvement in various non-INML dairy projects (participants versus nonparticipants). The statements were sorted from +4 (most agree) to –4 (most disagree).

Factor analysis of the responses revealed four distinct perspectives. The first emphasized reliance on technical experts (for example, for help in entering data into the computer); the group associated with this factor was labeled *technicians*. These individuals dismiss the relevance of external barriers to participation, such as low milk prices, and are willing to participate if technical support can be provided. The *activists,* by contrast, are interested in enhancing efficiency. They give higher scores than other groups to statements such as "If we want the producers to participate we have to help them to become more efficient as in other parts of the world," and "The only way for producers to participate more in the project is through the improvement of the entire technological process of the industry chain, so that the producers can become more competitive." The *independents* reject technical assistance and training and demonstrate a go-it-alone mentality, as indicated by high scores on statements such as the following: "I don't like to be pressured to participate; it is my decision and no one else's," and "All of my needs are covered, so I don't see why I need to participate in the project." Finally, the *economists* are more inclined to self-interested reactions, such as "I don't believe milk prices are likely to increase, so I don't think I will participate to keep records."

Despite differences among the four types, one particularly useful finding that emerged from the study pointed to an important consensus. The statement "If we want producers to participate, the project must work with other organizations that are actually currently providing services to the producers" elicited agreement from all groups. Technicians and economists agreed most strongly, with scores of +4 and +3 respectively, but activists and independents also registered agreement with scores of +2. This consensus suggested a marketing strategy (which INML had in fact already begun implementing) aimed at working through already existing organizations in a complementary rather than competitive way.

Post-conflict Health Care in Serbia

In a study of 73 primary health care (PHC) physicians, directors, and policy makers concerning the needs and obstacles to improving Serbia's war-torn health care system (Nelson et al. 2003), the use of Q methodology showed the existence of two factors, one expected but the other unanticipated. Focus groups were used to obtain the initial concourse of communicability relative to these matters. A set of 23 statements was then administered in the form of a Q sort ranging from +3 (most agree) to –3 (most disagree).

As would have been anticipated under these conditions, the overwhelmingly large first factor highlighted scarcity and lack of material means as the source of discontent. This group strongly agreed with statements citing shortage of financial resources; low wages, leading to frustrated and poorly motivated employees; shortages of medication and medical supplies; lack of family practice physicians; and lack of a well-developed, computerized health information system.

In addition to the expected first factor, however, a second, less-expected factor highlighted issues related to organization and personnel. This was indicated by agreement with statements such as that PHC administrative personnel lack knowledge and training, that physicians simply make referrals to higher levels of care, that the health system is poorly organized, and that health care workers lack professional training and development. As in the Uruguayan study, the Serbian study also revealed elements of consensus, such as a complaint that "Patients are given too many rights in our health care system."

Thus Q methodology, used in coordination with qualitative procedures and a survey, produced actionable results based on participants' views. It showed that most PHC physicians and decision makers viewed their problems as mainly economic, including inadequate salaries, as would be expected. But it also revealed irrational budgetary allocations and personnel issues. Thus the recommendations included not only the expected requests for adequate funding and replacement of obsolete equipment, but also requests for implementation of continuing education programs and other remedial steps related to the second set of problems.

Mobile Phone Use by Rwandan Entrepreneurs

With line-connected phones scarce in developing countries, cell phones can have an empowering effect on entrepreneurs, who, as Donner (2003) points out, may be hearing a dial tone for the very first time. Donner's study examined views on mobile phone use from the standpoint of 32 owners of micro, small, and medium-sized enterprises in Rwanda, using a Q sort of 32 statements.

All participants assigned positive scores to the view that "Having a mobile phone makes me feel more connected to the world." The study, however, revealed four distinct outlooks within this positive consensus.

The *productive* entrepreneurs stress that the new technology helps them earn or produce more, as reflected in the statements to which they assigned higher scores than the other groups: "Getting a mobile phone changed the way I do business," "My mobile phone helps me find work," and "My mobile phone helps me make more money in a day." The *convenient* users saw the new technology more in terms of the way in which it facilitated doing business: "My business is easier now that I have a mobile phone," "My mobile phone lets me get more done during the day," and "My mobile phone saves me time." The *indispensable* users are hooked on the new technology: "I can't do business without my mobile phone" and "My phone gives me access to new customers." Consequently, this group, more than the others, is interested in "learning about new features or mobile phone models." The *intrinsic* users appear focused on the social rather than the business potential of mobile phones, as indicated in the following statements to which they give higher scores:

> *Having a mobile phone makes me more important.*
>
> *I share my mobile phone with my family or friends.*
>
> *I use my mobile phone to stay in touch with my friends.*
>
> *Having a mobile phone makes me happy.*
>
> *My mobile phone is stylish.*

More than the first two groups, the intrinsics and the indispensables report that "I give my mobile phone number to many people." But the "many people" to whom the indispensables refer are likely customers, whereas the intrinsics are less discriminating. The productive, convenient, and indispensable groups are three varieties of *Homo faber* and are apt to have the biggest impact on the Rwandan economy. The intrinsics can be considered *Homo ludens* (Huizinga 1949) and will likely have greater effect on the culture. Only time will tell whether work or play will have the longer-term influence. Still, Donner (2003) notes that this study shows the potential of Q methodology for uncovering different patterns and thus offsetting the tendency to regard entrepreneurs in the developing world as if they were one homogeneous group. Instead, their responses show a variety of attitudes toward the absorption of technology.

Potential Directions for Future Applications

Although the real-world applications of Q methodology summarized above were not specifically focused on priority empowerment issues, they reveal social attitudes and preferences of some relevance to empowerment. The general model, as illustrated in table 9.1, suggests a number of options for future research strategies and interventions that would apply the methodology in a more focused way to empowerment.

First, as in table 9.1 and in the Peruvian example, Q methodology can show distinctions among different varieties of unempowered participants (types I, II, etc.). This could provide the basis for development of more tailored interventions. It is quite likely that a single formula (for example, provision of particular economic opportunities) may be ineffective for helping unempowered people with certain views and attitudes but may be successful for others. Being able to distinguish a population by functional subtypes provides opportunities to modify strategies to take these differences into consideration.[7]

Second, the ability to identify individuals by operant types raises the possibility of composing groups that can serve as micromodels of the larger society (Brown 1974), and of using these micromodels for prototyping new practices.[8] In terms of the hypothetical example in table 9.1, for example, factors I and II represent unempowered subtypes that exist in the larger population. One could set up an artificial group that would include community members 1, 3, and 4 (factor I) and 2 and 5 (factor II). Then the group members could be provided with experiences hypothesized to be empowering, such as mediation training (see, for example, Maxwell 1997). Practitioners often become vague and abstract when it comes to appraising empowerment (for examples, see Fetterman 1996, 2001; Rodwell 1996), but this task becomes less ambiguous within an operant framework. In the hypothetical case in table 9.1, participants' views would be recorded at time$_2$. Changes in factor loadings compared to time$_1$ would indicate whether there had been a "mindset shift" (and by whom) in the direction of the more empowered factor III, which would be taken as an indicator of a greater "sense of hope, excitement and direction" (Rodwell 1996, 308). The factors identified as operant types are themselves operational definitions, thus substituting for separate operational definitions of dimensions defined externally.

Changes identified through these procedures can also be used to identify potential leaders. An empowering process "helps people develop skills so they can become independent problem solvers and decision makers" (Fetterman 1996, 4). Inspection of the micromodel results in table 9.1 would identify participants 2 and 3 (but not 1, 4, or 5) as leadership candidates by virtue of their mental flexibility in moving toward the empowered outlook of factor III.

In the study and implementation of empowerment among the impoverished, therefore, Q methodology has the potential to serve as a supplement to strategies that emphasize the material world outside the individual, including incentive structures and institutional arrangements. In contrast to these other strategies, it can provide a more direct measure of the way in which the world is viewed "through the eyes and spirit of the poor."

Notes

For permission to summarize their work while still in progress, the author thanks Jonathan Donner (Columbia University); Brett Kramer (Iowa State University) and Pedro de Hegedus and Virginia Gravina (Agriculture College of Uruguay); Brett D. Nelson, Lauren Beste, and Michael J. Van Rooyen (Johns Hopkins University School of Medicine) and Snežana Simić, Dejana Vuković, and Vesna Bjegović (Belgrade University School of Medicine); and Regula Züger and Anamika Amani (International Potato Center, Lima).

1.   The *Voices of the Poor* series includes three volumes: *Can Anyone Hear Us?* (Narayan, Patel, et al. 2000); *Crying Out for Change* (Narayan, Chambers, et al. 2000); and *From Many Lands* (Narayan and Petesch 2002).

2.   The tendency to reach conclusions on the basis of imposed or inferred categories is endemic to social research generally, and to content analysis in particular. Spreitzer (1995), for instance, postulates four dimensions of empowerment (meaning, competence, self-determination, impact), which are then superimposed onto participants'

responses. Zimmerman (1995, 585) expresses doubt that global measures of this kind are possible since empowerment "takes different forms for different people," but in the same breath he illustrates his point in terms of age, socioeconomic status, and sex, as if men or members of the middle class or the elderly could be counted on to adopt the same form of empowerment by virtue of their membership in a common category.

3.   There are more than 2,000 publications in which Q methodology is used. The latest developments appear in the journals *Operant Subjectivity, Journal of Human Subjectivity,* and *Q-Methodology and Theory* (the last of these in Korean), and are discussed at the annual meetings of the International Society for the Scientific Study of Subjectivity. Additional information can be found at http://www.qmethod.org.

4.   Structuring typically proceeds according to Fisherian principles of experimental design. In the case of the Voices concourse this might involve cross-classifying (a) empowering and (b) disempowering statements with considerations such as (c) personal, (d) relational, and (e) collective (Narayan 2002, 27, note 1), which gives rise to $(2)(3) = 6$ combinations. With $m = 7$ replications of each combination, a Q sample of size $N = 42$ results. It is important to note that the structuring of Q samples only serves as an expedient for comprising the statement set and does not obtrude upon or predetermine the subsequent results; that is, the meanings attributed to statements by participants are often quite different from the meanings assumed by the researcher. In the analysis of results, the former takes precedence over the latter.

5.   Factor scores are calculated by merging the Q sorts that are associated with a factor and weighting each Q sort as a function of the magnitude of its factor loading. The end product is a single Q sort (factor array) that is a composite of all the Q sorts making up that factor; the same applies to the other factors. The result, therefore, is one composite Q sort representing each of the factors. For technical details, consult Brown (1980, 239–47).

6.   When dealing with nonliterate populations, modifications of Q-sort administration such as this are sometimes necessary. In some situations, the Q sample itself can be visual rather than textual, thereby obviating the need for literacy. Castañeda de León (1983), for example, presented children aged 4–6 with a set of photographs of other children in a variety of social interactions (fighting with others, crying, playing alone, interacting with mother, etc.) and instructed them to sort the pictures to represent themselves. Fairweather and Swaffield (1996) examined land-use preferences by presenting New Zealand residents with land and water-resource scenes.

7.   An illustration is provided by Dennis and Goldberg (1996), whose use of Q methodology led to discovery of two types of obese women. The self-starters had high self-esteem and could simply be given exercise and dieting instructions and then left on their own, whereas those with low self-esteem first had to receive esteem-building counseling before weight loss was possible. Self-esteem is a prerequisite for empowerment (Rodwell 1996), for the impoverished as well as the obese, and different strategies may have to be adopted for those lacking it. Brunner (1983) likewise provides an illustration (using Q-factor analysis) of defective public policy unable to address the needs of significant subgroups that were hidden in the data for lack of context-sensitive procedures that could bring them to light.

8.   The theory of prototyping and its relationship to experimentation and intervention is outlined in Lasswell (1963, 95–122). The best known applications include empowering patients at the Yale Psychiatric Institute (Rubenstein and Lasswell 1966) and empowering the Vicosino Indians of Peru (Dobyns, Doughty, and Lasswell 1971). For a current discussion of the Vicos prototype in the context of World Bank projects, consult Brunner (2004).

References

Addams, H., and J. Proops, eds. 2000. *Social Discourse and Environmental Policy: An Application of Q Methodology*. Cheltenham, UK: Edward Elgar.

Brown, S. R. 1974. "The Composition of Microcosms." *Policy Sciences* 5 (1): 15–27.

———. 1980. *Political Subjectivity: Applications of Q Methodology in Political Science*. New Haven, CT: Yale University Press.

———. 1994–95. "Q Methodology as the Foundation for a Science of Subjectivity." *Operant Subjectivity* 18 (1/2): 1–16.

———. 1996. "Q Methodology and Qualitative Research." *Qualitative Health Research* 6 (4): 561–67.

———. 2002a. "Structural and Functional Information." *Policy Sciences* 35 (3): 285–304.

———. 2002b. "Subjective Behavior Analysis." *Operant Subjectivity* 25 (3/4): 148–63.

———. 2002c. "Q Technique and Questionnaires." *Operant Subjectivity* 25 (2): 117–26.

———. 2003. "The Indigenization of Methodology (Revisited)." *Journal of Human Subjectivity* 1 (1): 1–21.

———. 2004. "A Match Made in Heaven: A Marginalized Methodology for Studying the Marginalized." Paper presented at the International Research Seminar on Marginality and Welfare Democracy, Växjö University, Sweden, March.

———. Forthcoming. "The History and Principles of Q Methodology in Psychology and the Social Sciences." *History of the Human Sciences*.

Brown, S. R., T. Clark, M. Rutherford, K. Byrd, and D. Mattson. 2003. "Clarification of Perspective and Pursuit of the Community Interest: Carnivore Conservation in the Northern Rockies." Paper presented at the annual Policy Sciences Institute, Yale Law School, New Haven, CT, October.

Brown, S. R., and B. O. Kil. 2002. "Exploring Korean Values." *Asia Pacific: Perspectives* 2 (1): 1–8. http://www.pacificrim.usfca.edu/research/perspectives/app_v2n1.html.

Brunner, R. D. 1983. "Case-wise Policy Analysis: Another Look at the Burden of High Energy Costs." *Policy Sciences* 16 (2): 97–125.

———. 2004. "Context-Sensitive Monitoring and Evaluation for the World Bank." *Policy Sciences* 37 (2): 103–36.

Bublic, J. M., and S. Sitaraman. 1998. "Mediated Images of International Understanding: The Case of India and the United States." *Gazette* 60 (6): 477–91.

Castañeda de León, L. 1983. "Correlación entre privación temprana y conducta asocial: Methodología Q aplicada en la Clínica del Niño Sano del Hospital Roosevelt de Guatemala." Medical thesis, Universidad de San Carlos de Guatemala.

Davis, T. C. 1997. "Patterns of Identity: Basques and the Basque Nation." *Nationalism and Ethnic Politics* 3 (1): 61–88.

Delprato, D. J., and S. R. Brown. 2002. "Q Methodology and the Operant Construct." *Operant Subjectivity* 25 (3/4): 139–47.

Dennis, K. E., and A. P. Goldberg. 1996. "Weight Control Self-Efficacy Types and Transitions Affect Weight-Loss Outcomes in Obese Women." *Addictive Behaviors* 21 (1): 103–16.

Dobyns, H. F., P. L. Doughty, and H. D. Lasswell, eds. 1971. *Peasants, Power, and Applied Social Change.* Beverly Hills, CA: Sage.

Donner, J. C. 2001. "Using Q-sorts in Participatory Processes: An Introduction to the Methodology." In *Social Analysis: Selected Tools and Techniques*, ed. R. A. Krueger, M. A. Casey, J. Donner, S. Kirsch, and J. N. Maack, 24–49. Social Development Papers 36. Washington, DC: World Bank.

———. 2003. "What Mobile Phones Mean to Rwandan Entrepreneurs." Paper presented at conference on Mobile Communication: Social and Political Effects, Budapest, April.

Dryzek, J. S., and L. Holmes. 2002. *Post-communist Democratization: Political Discourses across Thirteen Countries.* Cambridge: Cambridge University Press.

Fairweather, J. R., and S. R. Swaffield. 1996. "Preferences for Scenarios of Land-Use Change in the Mackenzie/Waitaki Basin." *New Zealand Forestry* 41 (1): 17–26.

Fetterman, D. M. 1996. "Empowerment Evaluation: An Introduction to Theory and Practice." In *Empowerment Evaluation: Knowledge and Tools for Self-Assessment* and *Accountability*, ed. D. M. Fetterman, S. J. Kaftarian, and A. Wandersman, 3–46. Thousand Oaks, CA: Sage.

———. 2001. *Foundations of Empowerment Evaluation.* Thousand Oaks, CA: Sage.

Focht, W. 2002. "Assessment and Management of Policy Conflict in the Illinois River Watershed in Oklahoma: An Application of Q Methodology." *International Journal of Public Administration* 25 (11): 1311–49.

Gallivan, J. 1994. "Subjectivity and the Psychology of Gender: Q as a Feminist Methodology." In *Women, Girls, and Achievement*, ed. J. Gallivan, S. D. Crozier, and V. M. Lalande, 29–36. Toronto: Captus University Publications.

Gargan, J. J., and S. R. Brown. 1993. "'What Is to Be Done?' Anticipating the Future and Mobilizing Prudence." *Policy Sciences* 26 (4): 347–59.

Huizinga, J. 1949. *Homo Ludens: A Study of the Play-Element in Culture.* London: Routledge and Kegan Paul. (Orig. pub. 1944.)

Hunter, A. G., and J. E. Davis. 1992. "Constructing Gender: An Exploration of Afro-American Men's Conceptualization of Manhood." *Gender and Society* 6 (3): 464–79.

Kramer, B., P. de Hegedus, and V. Gravina. 2003. "Evaluating a Dairy Herd Improvement Project in Uruguay: Testing and Explaining Q Methodology." *Journal of International Agricultural and Extension Education* 10 (2): 41–50.

Lasswell, H. D. 1963. *The Future of Political Science.* New York: Atherton Press.

Maxwell, J. P. 1997. "Conflict Management and Mediation Training: A Vehicle for Community Empowerment?" *Mediation Quarterly* 15 (2): 83–96.

Narayan, D., ed. 2002. *Empowerment and Poverty Reduction: A Sourcebook.* Washington, DC: World Bank.

Narayan, D., R. Chambers, M. K. Shah, and P. Petesch, eds. 2000. *Voices of the Poor: Crying Out for Change.* New York: Oxford University Press for the World Bank.

Narayan, D., with R. Patel, K. Schafft, A. Rademacher, and S. Koch-Schulte. 2000. *Voices of the Poor: Can Anyone Hear Us?* New York: Oxford University Press for the World Bank.

Narayan, D., and P. Petesch, eds. 2002. *Voices of the Poor: From Many Lands.* New York: Oxford University Press for the World Bank.

Nelson, B. D., S. Simić, L. Beste, D. Vuković, V. Bjegović, and M. J. Van Rooyen. 2003. "Multimodal Assessment of the Primary Healthcare System of Serbia: A Model for Evaluating Post-conflict Health Systems." *Prehospital and Disaster Medicine* 18 (1): 6–13.

Parris, K. 1999. "Entrepreneurs and Citizenship in China." *Problems of Post-Communism* 46 (1): 43–61.

Piper, W. 1930. *The Little Engine That Could.* New York: Platt and Munk.

Potter, A. C. 2003. "Cross Cultural Management and Discourses of Negotiation: An Application of Q Methodology." Master's thesis, Asian Institute of Technology, Bangkok.

Robyn, R. 2000. "A Methodological Approach to National Identity in Europe." *Politique Européenne* 1 (1): 84–107.

Rodwell, C. M. 1996. "An Analysis of the Concept of Empowerment." *Journal of Advanced Nursing* 23 (2): 305–13.

Rubenstein, R., and H. D. Lasswell. 1966. *The Sharing of Power in a Psychiatric Hospital.* New Haven, CT: Yale University Press.

Salazar, D. J., and D. K. Alper. 2002. "Reconciling Environmentalism and the Left: Perspectives on Democracy and Social Justice in British Columbia's Environmental Movement." *Canadian Journal of Political Science* 35 (3): 527–66.

Senn, C. Y. 1996. "Q-Methodology as Feminist Methodology: Women's Views and Experiences of Pornography." In *Feminist Social Psychologies: International Perspectives*, ed. S. Wilkinson, 201–17. Buckingham, UK and Philadelphia: Open University Press.

Smith, J. M. 2002. "Fear as a Barrier? African American Men's Avoidance of Counseling Services." *Journal of African American Men* 6 (4): 47–60.

Snelling, S. J. 1999. "Women's Perspectives on Feminism: A Q-Methodological Study." *Psychology of Women Quarterly* 23 (2): 247–66.

Spreitzer, G. M. 1995. "An Empirical Test of a Comprehensive Model of Intrapersonal Empowerment in the Workplace." *American Journal of Community Psychology* 23 (5): 601–29.

Stephenson, W. 1953. *The Study of Behavior: Q-technique and Its Methodology.* Chicago: University of Chicago Press.

———. 1977. "Factors as Operant Subjectivity." *Operant Subjectivity* 1 (1): 3–16.

————. 1978. "Concourse Theory of Communication." *Communication* 3 (1): 21–40.

Thomas, D. B., C. McCoy, and A. McBride. 1993. "Deconstructing the Political Spectacle: Sex, Race, and Subjectivity in Public Response to the Clarence Thomas/Anita Hill 'Sexual Harassment' Hearings." *American Journal of Political Science* 37 (3): 699–720.

Tolymbek, A. Forthcoming. "Political Leadership Style in Kazakhstan." PhD diss., Kent State University, Kent, OH.

Zimmerman, M. A. 1995. "Psychological Empowerment: Issues and Illustrations." *American Journal of Community Psychology* 23 (5): 581–99.

Züger Cáceres, R. 2003. "Do Participatory Interventions Empower People?" Paper presented at meeting of the International Society for the Scientific Study of Subjectivity, Canton, OH, October.

————. 2004. "Assessing Empowerment with Q-methodology." Paper presented at meeting of the European Association for Research on Learning and Instruction, Center for Qualitative Psychology, University of Tübingen, Germany, October.

Züger Cáceres, R., and A. Amani. 2003. "Evaluación del impacto de escuelas de campo en pobreza y bienestar." Centro Internacional de la Papa, Consultative Group on International Agricultural Research, Lima.

SECTION FOUR

Community and Local Governance Levels

Chapter 10

Analytical Issues in Measuring Empowerment at the Community and Local Levels

Norman Uphoff

Devising operational measures of empowerment is made more challenging by the inherent ambiguity and elusiveness of what is to be measured—*power.* Empowerment is commonly understood as the condition of having power, and being able to exercise it and obtain the benefits thereof. We thus cannot measure empowerment properly without a valid understanding of what constitutes power.

An important reason that both terms have remained ambiguous is what the philosopher Alfred North Whitehead (1929) called "the fallacy of misplaced concreteness." This is the incorrect attribution of certain qualities to something that does not and cannot possess them. For example, it is not meaningful to say "The United States does . . ." or "The United States wants . . ." Why? Because the United States is a geographic entity that cannot literally do or want anything. Moreover, the population of the United States is seldom if ever so united and fully agreed that, as a whole, it does or wants anything in any real sense. It is more correct and meaningful to say "The government of the United States does . . ." or "The president of the United States, speaking on behalf of the country, wants . . ." These latter formulations attribute agency and intention more accurately.

Such verbal shorthand is used all the time, of course. But unfortunately, it conflates the actions and statements of certain actors with inanimate or incoherent aggregations, so that it becomes difficult to attribute either intentionality or responsibility. Especially if we want to measure something, and to promote it effectively, we need to be concerned with things that really exist. While descriptions and abstractions are necessary, they should not be confused with what is actually existing.

It will be argued here that empowerment, like power, does not exist in its own right but is rather a reflection or representation of other things that do exist. This does not mean that we cannot measure empowerment. Because the elements that go into empowerment exist and have real-world consequences, the summation that the term "empowerment" conveys has meaning and relevance. But it does require more sophistication and deeper thought than when we deal with phenomena whose ontological status is simpler.

It may seem pedantic to raise ontological questions when our purpose is to produce practical results for a very desirable outcome: empowering the poor. But we need to be clear about what it is that we aim to measure. Empowerment presents special problems because it derives from power, a concept that has long raised serious ontological issues.[1]

Even the weak criterion sometimes suggested for things as ill-defined as art or pornography—"you'll know it when you see it"—does not work with power and empowerment because these can be identified or verified only by their *results*. These results are associated, in ways that are complex and often undeterminable, with various processes that lead to these outcomes, and they are very sensitive to context. Simply suggesting that "power is what power does or accomplishes" gives no assistance for understanding the substance of power or for using power to achieve certain purposes such as improving the lives and futures of the poor.[2]

As a preface to addressing the measurement of empowerment with respect to community and local governance, I want to share some thoughts on power based on many years of wrestling with this concept, one of the most contentious in the social sciences. Empowerment is the condition of possessing and exercising whatever it is that confers "power." For almost 20 years I taught a course on power at Cornell University, taking undergraduates through the literature on this subject from Plato, Aristotle, and Machiavelli to Dahl, Blau, and Parenti. The course was, I am afraid, more successful in helping students learn to think rigorously, analytically, and critically than in informing them what power *is*, since this remains ontologically elusive. The biblical admonition "By its fruits ye shall know it" applies in this case, but this advice does not clarify what power *is*. Unless we have clear ideas about what constitutes power, the folk admonition applies: "If you don't know where you are going, any road will get you there." We can neither assess nor enhance empowerment of the poor without a rigorous and reliable comprehension of power.

Weber's Analysis of Power

The most widely cited and influential analytical treatment of this subject is still that by the German social scientist Max Weber, whose consideration of power in his comprehensive work on economic and social organization (1947) is meticulously reasoned and carefully worded.[3] Weber defined power as (a) the *probability* that (b) someone *in a social relationship* (c) will be able to achieve his or her *will,* that is, whatever is desired, (d) despite *resistance,* and (e) regardless of the *bases* upon which this probability rests. Let us consider each of these elements in turn.

Probability

The key element in Weber's definition is the equation of power with *a probability.* This means that power is never a certainty, nor is it a thing. Statements about power refer to relationships in which someone achieves (or does not achieve) what he or she wants or needs. Power is thus something different from the relationship itself. Statements about probability have an ex ante orientation, describing the likelihood or expected frequency of an occurrence, when what will actually occur is not yet definitely known. With regard to power and the poor, the term refers to the probability that someone will be able to accomplish, achieve, acquire, or maintain something that he or she wants, whether it is material or immaterial—food, shelter, wealth, job security, respect, affection, peace of mind. The converse—getting something that one does *not* want—has never been considered as a manifestation of power. Indeed, it represents the opposite of power.

Whether one will actually get what is desired can only be known ex post, when it becomes an accomplished fact. This is often spoken of in binary terms: 1.0 = successful exercise of power, 0.0 = failure to exercise power. Before an outcome is known, the probability of success can be very high, even 0.9999; but there is some possibility that what is desired will *not* be achieved, making the outcome less than absolutely certain, less than 1.0. There is always some chance, however small, that any effort to exercise "power" will be unsuccessful, as even the very powerful do not always get exactly what they want. Weber's appreciation of this fact helps keep our analyses and assessments realistic by taking account of the uncertainties of the real world, which is always probabilistic.

While power is commonly described in binary terms, stating that power exists and is possessed (or is not), it can easily be stated in terms of *degrees* of success in getting what one wants. For example, 0.75 could represent a favorable compromise; 0.50 could represent getting half of what one wants; 0.10 could reflect a near-defeat that came with a face-saving concession. Alternatively, the measurement continuum can be expanded by considering unwanted outcomes as having a *negative* value. A defeat would then be given a score like −1.0 instead of zero, with zero as a kind of midpoint between success and failure in the exercise of power, representing an indeterminate outcome or mixed result. There are many ways of conceptualizing power, all having different implications for measuring it quantitatively.

These kinds of conceptual issues need to be resolved in any systematic effort to quantify power. It makes a large difference whether power is defined in positive-sum or in zero-sum terms, for example. Both are valid but they give us quite different frameworks for analysis. Because power has so many different possible conceptualizations, it remains difficult to achieve full agreement on how to measure it. This has prompted me to focus more on results and on causes than on the abstraction of power.

These issues are difficult enough to resolve when trying to analyze power in two-person relationships. In fact, most power situations and problems involve multiple actors, formally referred to in game theory as n-person relationships. The number of dyadic power relationships increases exponentially whenever n increases. While game theory provides some interesting insights on behavioral regularities, its literature on power has been largely inconclusive, producing little meaningful quantification. N-person relationships quickly become inordinately complex, given the existence of competing and contradictory objectives as well as diverse and divergent power bases (for example, see Harsanyi 1962). Efforts at rigorous analysis quickly become too abstract to be of much use to development decision makers.

My starting point for thinking about power and empowerment, especially of the poor, is that we need to be clear about what is real. Of most relevance are the *outcomes* of power relationships: whether someone was able to achieve all or only part of what was desired, was unable to get what was desired, or indeed got what was actually *un*desired. It is also important to factor in the *costs* of achieving objectives, which is not done in most of the literature on power. Power should be assessed considering not only success, but also the costs of success, absolute or relative.[4]

Power is usually referred to as an absolute, reflecting whether an objective was achieved or not. The usual meaning of the term thus refers more to effectiveness than to efficiency. But the latter is certainly relevant. Considering *relative* power—for example, how cost-effective is the attainment of a certain goal—makes analysis more complicated. Is a person more powerful if a only few goals are sought but all are achieved, compared to many goals being sought and only some being achieved? What if more goals are achieved in absolute terms in the latter instance than in the first, but they are a smaller percentage of what was sought? What if the few goals are achieved more cheaply in terms of the resources expended to attain them? How does this compare with achieving many goals but at a high cost, in total or in cost per goal attained? Any effort at quantification of power quickly becomes arguable, given the subjectivity involved in choosing between absolute and relative manifestations of power.

Considering the costs of getting others to comply with one's wishes leads to thinking about factors like "reputation." We know that a reputation for power enables certain persons to achieve goals with little or no expenditure of effort or resources. Usually getting more results while spending less is seen as a manifestation of greater power. But reputation-based power, if it is not backed by effective resources, can collapse quickly (see the section on costs of power, below). So is power that rests purely or mostly on psychological factors as real and as effective as that which rests on more material bases? And how do we assess power that may be great in one time period but evanescent in subsequent periods?

"Power" refers in most people's implicit lexicons to ex ante probabilities that a person can and will achieve what he or she wants. For poor people, these wants typically include food security, stable income, shelter, clothing, health care, schooling for children, protection by the authorities against victimization, equitable enforcement of laws, respect—those desires expressed most often in the *Voices of the Poor* series (Narayan, Patel, et al. 2000; Narayan, Chambers, et al. 2000). Such probabilities are not themselves something real; they are only estimations based on an analytical construct. But they are associated with very real consequences: food security, personal safety, effective influence on public policy, etc. And they have real causes: literacy, job security, legal rights, etc. What is real and determining is the complex of factors, generally highly interactive and contingent, that *produce* desired outcomes. These factors, processes, and outcomes are real, but none of them are, literally, power. Power is a second-order effect of a multitude of relationships—material, psychological, cultural, legal, and so forth. Any statements just about probabilities will remain more descriptive than explanatory.

Stable Relationships

Weber restricted power to *social* relationships, that is, to associations that are ongoing and continuous, not irregular or random occurrences. This may seem too restrictive as a definition. But for our purposes, being concerned with empowerment of the poor, it is an important and acceptable qualification. We are interested not in what may happen once in a lifetime or unpredictably, but rather in what affects the outcomes of daily existence and lifetime conditions. Thus, power should be understood and assessed in terms of stable relationships, though they can be changing in favor of the more or the less empowered.

Intentionality

The crux of Weber's definition and of most understandings of power is the achievement of *desired objectives,* the satisfaction of particular needs or wants. Recent work on poverty and its reduction has focused very appropriately on what poor people themselves think, need, and want (Narayan, Patel, et al. 2000; Narayan, Chambers, et al. 2000). Weber's linking of power to the ability to achieve what is desired and intended means it is not considered a manifestation of power to get what one does *not* want. Power is something different from causation in general. As discussed below, empowerment of the poor differs from "basic needs" analysis and policies in that it has intrinsic and unavoidable subjective dimensions; an empowerment approach does not assume that outsiders can decide for poor people by some "objective" criteria what they need.

But if power is linked with people's own objectives and valuations, it is necessarily a hybrid of objective and subjective phenomena. If a person has few wants but achieves them all, he or she is not only satisfied, but also powerful according to his or her expectations (if not by others' evaluations).

Conversely, a person who has many wants but can satisfy only a few of them is not very powerful in his or her own assessment. Power is about one's reach as well as one's grasp.

Some might object that this makes power too relative and subjective. Are not persons who get more desired outcomes, even if they don't get everything they want, more powerful than persons who get only a few desired things, whether their aspirations are great or modest? This is a fair question. But such comparisons are more appropriate for assessing satisfaction of basic needs than for evaluating empowerment. If we want to make purely objective statements, we should stick to summative assessments of some predetermined set of needs, bypassing the ambiguities of the term "power." In fact, empowerment involves more than satisfying needs. It is connected to people's wants and desires, things that affect their dignity, satisfaction, and personal fulfillment. The number of goods and services received is not a measure of empowerment.

Costs of Power

The qualification that Weber introduces concerning *resistance* is important because achieving goals without cost or without effort is not really a manifestation of power. Breathing air and getting up in the morning (unless one is physically or otherwise constrained from doing so) are not matters of power or empowerment. Free goods are outside the realm of power. Including resistance within the definition of power takes account of any opposition there may be to people's getting what they want. This is particularly relevant when thinking about empowerment of the poor.

This relates to the complicated matter of rights. Having rights that are recognized and fulfilled, such as the right to health care or free speech, is certainly within the domain of empowerment. If these rights are granted without any exertion by the persons who then enjoy them, they are still surely an aspect of empowerment. Rights might appear to be free goods but they are not. Their achievement and maintenance invariably involves costs, past if not present, and they commonly require protection. So even rights are best regarded within a Weberian framework. Resistance of some sort is invariably associated with any established right, to create it and to maintain it.

Resistance is relevant in thinking about empowerment because it is always useful to ask who or what stands in the way of people, particularly poor people, achieving what they want. Weber's definition of power points out that we should think about sources and amount of resistance as part of any power assessment.

Power Resources

The last clause in Weber's definition, referring to the *bases* for having a higher probability of getting compliance with one's wishes, gives the concept its firmest ontological grounding. It directs our attention to the actual factors that enhance (or diminish) a person's chances of achieving his or her desired goals. These power bases are variously referred to as power resources or power assets, or in still other terms. As it turns out, most such references are to six general types of resources, as set forth in the next section.

A Typology of Power Resources

Weber's analysis prompted me to review the social science literature on power to identify the various *kinds* of power bases that have been proposed by political scientists, sociologists, and economists (Uphoff 1989). These bases can be summarized in terms of six categories of resources (assets) that can be accumulated and utilized to achieve objectives. These are analogous to the categories of land, labor, and capital in economic analysis. The six types of resources for achieving one's needs and wants are the following:

- *Economic* resources (power bases/assets), meaning control over land, labor, or capital, as well as the goods and services produced therefrom. This category includes wealth and assets as well as the income streams derived from them when they are used to achieve objectives. These include not just economic forms of production and consumption but also goods or services such as influence on public policies, access to higher education, or housing in a more prestigious and safer neighborhood.
- *Social* resources, that is, social status or standing based on social roles or on meeting socially valued criteria. These clearly affect one's ability to achieve one's goals. These "goods" can be consumed for personal satisfaction, producing the "services" of respect, esteem, and deference, or they can be drawn upon to achieve objectives beyond self-satisfaction, becoming power bases (assets) affecting outcomes such as getting public services, good employment, or respect from law enforcement officers.
- *Political* resources. These are primarily a consequence of the incumbency of authority roles that entitle people to claim that they are speaking in the name of the state and can employ whatever resources state institutions possess to enforce decisions.[5] Being able to influence the exercise of authority and to achieve objectives thereby, by voting or any other means, creates power within the domain of politics. This can be used to affect the domains of economic and social life, with outcomes such as health care, employment, and educational opportunity.
- *Informational* resources. Knowledge can be productive and beneficial in its own right; more important as a power resource will be knowledge that is productive or beneficial for others. Such knowledge will be desired by others, giving rise to the adage "knowledge is power." The power that comes from possession of knowledge is governed by dynamics of supply and demand, and is therefore relative rather than absolute.

- *Moral* resources, meaning the legitimacy accorded to decision makers, their roles, the decisions they make, or the system of governance that leads people to defer to and accept others' decisions as right and proper. Such legitimacy can be accorded to nonstate actors such as a Gandhi or a Martin Luther King, as well as to office holders, who will always claim legitimacy for themselves and their decisions. Like status and information, legitimacy is a "soft" resource, conferring power based upon highly subjective factors. However, it is important for empowerment because it can have very real consequences.
- *Physical* resources. These create the physical force that people may be willing and able to exert against others to compel their cooperation or compliance. This is referred to as "coercion" if it is done with a claim of legitimacy, or as "violence" if it is not accepted as legitimate.[6]

There is no need to go into more detail here on these power bases. They offer an inclusive framework for dealing with economic, social, and political relationships in a supra-disciplinary way.[7] For understanding empowerment, they help organize and make more concrete the basic factors in economic, social, and political life that determine people's ability to get what they desire. They can be regarded, literally, as the factors of power production.

Connected Domains for Analysis and Measurement of Power

Given Weber's encompassing conceptualization of power, measuring empowerment involves more than one set of factors. The two most obvious sets of real things that can be measured are

- *power resources*—assets that can be accumulated, invested, expended, transacted, and exchanged, creating potentials and possibilities for achieving objectives; and
- *power results*—whatever is achieved by the use of these resources or assets.

However, neither of these is power itself. They are, respectively, the sources of power and the fruits of power. Power itself remains different from these means and ends, eluding direct measurement. There are also a number of elements or steps in between that are part of the creation and exercise of power, notably capabilities, process, and context.

Capabilities

Possession of power resources in itself confers limited or incomplete power. While these resources increase the probability that a person will be able to achieve certain objectives, actual results depend upon the skill and effectiveness with which resources are acquired, accumulated, used, wielded, exchanged, or withheld. Being endowed with resources is only one part of empowerment.

Capabilities such as skill and confidence enable a person to use available endowments more effectively, and thus add to power by raising the probability that desired outcomes will be achieved.

Power capabilities can be either individual or collective. Personal elements such as confidence and experience complement tactical and strategic skills. For empowerment of the poor, group capabilities are particularly important, since organization, by aggregating and pooling people's assets, can enhance the results attainable from any given individual or group endowment.

This potential becomes more important for poor people because their respective individual resource endowments are so meager. Individually, they can exercise relatively little power by expending or withholding their own personal resources.[8] Active and effective efforts are needed if desired benefits are to flow from utilizing resources. Power capabilities are thus also a critical part of empowerment.[9] Measuring empowerment needs somehow to encompass this domain of capabilities because people with similar resource endowments achieve quite different results in life, depending on how well they utilize their assets.

Processes

Less delimitable than resources and capabilities, though no less real, are the processes whereby resources (power inputs) are converted, through capabilities (management skills and organizational capacities), into results (power outputs). This conversion does not occur in abstract relationships but actually through structured circumstances that involve roles, rules, rights, precedents, procedures, access, and so on.

For example, when elections are determined by a majority or plurality vote rather than by proportional representation, the votes of poor people will have less weight so long as they are a minority or a majority that is fractured by ethnic or other differences. Similarly, when the poor lack access to a country's mass media, they will have difficulty directing attention to their plight and claims. The voices of poor people will have more influence on policies and resource allocations if a country's mass media are open to communicating their situation and demands. Thus, a variety of process factors affect the ability of poor sectors to advance their interests, positively or negatively. These are distinguishable from people's resource endowments and capabilities.

Context

As other chapters in this volume show, the processes that affect poor people's power occur within larger contexts of cultural, social, economic, and political factors. These consist in turn of norms, beliefs, attitudes, traditions, and so on, that influence whether the processes that affect the lives of the poor function in benign or malign ways. They also affect the resource endowments and capabilities of the poor, such as by encouraging or discouraging the aspirations of the poor to improve their lives, a capability factor suggested by the work of Appadurai (2004).

Contexts cannot be measured in any direct or simple way because they are made up of many factors, often countervailing. Ceteris paribus assessments can be made of specific contextual factors. But what is important is whether the net effect of context and process factors is to constitute an environment that is enabling or disabling for the poor. The four domains that constitute the main factors in the power "equation" are shown in table 10.1.

Table 10.1   Analytical Framework for Measurement and Promotion of Empowerment of the Poor

Direct focuses		*Indirect focuses*	
Assets	*Capabilities*	*Processes*	*Context*
Individual/household levels		**Institutional/societal levels**	
Power resources:	*Individual traits:*	*Institutions, roles, e.g.:*	*Norms, values, e.g.:*
• Economic	• Personal skills	• Democratic	• Power distribution
• Social	• Interpersonal	institutions and	among nonpoor
• Political	skills	processes, e.g.,	actors (sources of
• Informational	• Experience	election of	resistance)
• Moral	• Confidence	representatives by	• Cultural barriers,
• Physical	• Aspiration	majority rather	e.g., patriarchy,
	• Energy and	than proportional	discrimination
	persistence	representation	• Capability of state
Group/collective levels		• Established rights, e.g., free speech	institutions, e.g., effectiveness
Power resources:	*Organizational capabilities:*	• Access to media	• Social structure, e.g., mobility,
• Economic	• For collective	• Fairness of legal	segmentation of
• Social	action, including	system, police, and	the poor
• Political	self-help	courts	• Social norms of
• Informational		• Permeability of	participation,
• Moral	*Shared skills:*	decision processes	equity, etc.
• Physical	• Experience	to claims of poor	
	• Confidence	actors, a result of	
	• Aspiration	the above factors	
		plus context	

Direct focuses are the *initial and changing conditions* of the poor, which provide the means for achieving needs and wants at individual or household levels. Indirect focuses are the *initial and changing opportunity structures* for the poor, that is, various enabling or disabling conditions that operate at institutional or societal levels.

Some Implications of This Analysis
Implications for Measurement

Power resources are conventionally measured, aggregated, and compared, across individuals or groups and over time, in most quantitative treatments of power. Some of these assets are amenable to cardinal measurement, for example, economic resources, voting power, years of education as a proxy for information or access thereto, or force of numbers. However, others lend themselves only to ordinal measurement, notably status, legitimacy, and positions of authority. Some measurement of these bases for achieving changes in the status and conditions of the poor is feasible, although aggregating these measures into a number that reflects individual or collective capability to achieve certain objectives across any and all environments, and for any and all purposes, remains beyond our current methodological knowledge.

Unfortunately, capabilities, process, and context factors present much more complex problems of measurement. Case studies where many factors are similar but there are identifiable differences in capabilities, process, or context can be written up and assessed comparatively. Alternatively, where changes are introduced in capabilities, process, or context, and where the impact of these changes on poor people's ability to achieve what they need and want can be tracked, researchers can infer causal relationships to offer some guidance for policy and institutional interventions. With the framework laid out in table 10.1, ceteris paribus conclusions can be drawn about empowerment that take explicit account of contextual or process differences and that identify ways in which processes and contexts can be changed to favor empowerment of the poor.

Attempts to measure power dynamics will always confront the fact that people's efforts to achieve their objectives are subject to both structural and stochastic influences. These include

- *systematic biases* that constrain or favor success in power exercises, as well as
- *random and chance factors* that will be unpredictably encountered in such efforts.

The first set of factors, systemic ones, can be analyzed and evaluated with some objectivity and confidence. However, random and chance factors are inherent in both processes and contexts, and they will invariably color and confound efforts to assess structural effects.

Simple causal models of power processes will always contain large margins of error. Rather than gloss over this, we need to try to factor these uncertainties into our analysis and measurement. Likewise, we should avoid attributing deterministic causation to processes and outcomes that remain always subject to chance influences and deliberate actions of individuals and groups, enhancing or diminishing the empowerment of the poor.

Implications for Promotion

This analytical understanding of power produces a number of suggestions for how each of these domains could be enhanced to promote greater empowerment of the poor. It also suggests some measurement strategies to build an effective knowledge base to guide actions on behalf of the poor. These are listed in table 10.2.

Table 10.2   Opportunities for Promoting and Measuring the Empowerment of the Poor

Interventions for promotion			
Assets	*Capabilities*	*Processes*	*Context*
Investments and policies to increase the power resource endowments of poor persons and households	*Training* for poor persons *Catalytic efforts* to strengthen or establish organization among the poor	*Policy reforms* *Institutional changes* and reforms	Actions to reinforce *positive influences* that enhance the power of poor actors Actions to counter *negative influences* that diminish the power of poor actors

Focuses for measurement			
Assets	*Capabilities*	*Processes*	*Context*
Tools for measuring the various power resources of the poor *Comparative studies of the effects of ceteris paribus changes* in the power resource endowments of the poor on their ability to achieve their objectives	*Evaluations of training strategies and methods* for empowering the poor *Evaluations of methods for enhancing organizational capacities* of the poor *Comparative studies of the effects of changes* in organizational and personal capacities of the poor on empowerment	*Case studies* with appropriate quantification of how certain policies or institutions—and changes in these—can affect the empowerment of the poor, including effects of assets, capabilities, and processes	*Case studies* to assess how significant are various contextual factors that affect the power of the poor, and what effects certain changes in these contextual factors have on assets, capabilities, and processes

This analysis, by focusing attention on assets, capabilities, processes, and context in turn, implies points of intervention and certain strategies to increase empowerment of the poor. The most fundamental is to increase the power resource endowments of the poor. Since these resources are quite varied, the steps to do this would also vary. For impact and sustainability, the steps should be made mutually reinforcing.

Capability enhancement should focus on both individuals and groups, with various sorts of participatory training provided to build psychological strength as well as personal skills. There is knowledge about how to create or strengthen organizational capacity among the poor, with evidence that this can create sustainable abilities of large numbers of poor people to achieve their most urgent needs.[10] However, too often such efforts are undertaken in a "blueprint" manner or in directed ways that do not create genuine empowerment or effectiveness.[11] There are many examples of large-scale initiatives that establish local capabilities for resource mobilization and management, in the process increasing the abilities of the poor to improve their conditions.[12]

With a coherent research program to examine the impacts of processes and context on the empowerment of the poor, it should be possible to design policy and institutional reforms that will improve the rights, access, and effectiveness of the poor and their agents. Other steps can be taken based on such knowledge to affect the cultural, normative, and other parameters that constrain or bolster the power of the poor. There is considerable knowledge already in the literature on measures that can contribute to empowering the poor, but it is not systematic, nor does it meet scientific criteria of reliability or precision.

Considerations for Community and Local Empowerment

While one can think of "empowering communities and localities" as a distinct process, our specific concern is how the empowerment of individuals and households classified as poor can be enhanced *at community and other local levels*. Thus, we are not talking about empowering communities and localities as such. While this may be desirable in the context of decentralization initiatives, it would require that we specify what communities or localities want, a difficult assignment. With our focus on poverty reduction, the unit of analysis and action is the individual or household. But this does not mean we are concerned only with this level.

Different Levels of Empowerment

Some strategies for empowering the poor focus on individuals and households directly, while other strategies with the same objective have a broader scope, with different, larger units of analysis and action. It can be argued that efforts to empower the poor that *only* consider individuals or households as separate units of analysis and action will miss opportunities to benefit the poor, because collective action is not part of the strategy, and will also have less sustainability because there is no reinforcement of the efforts made by individuals and households.

Given our concern with the poor and poverty reduction, the question is how changes in resource endowments and capabilities aggregated at the community or other local level can enhance the power of the poor. If one attempts to empower the poor only within a household context, or only by enhancing individual endowments and capabilities, opportunities are forgone, including relatively low-cost and potentially very cost-effective ones.

Much poverty reduction is a result of individuals' or households' efforts, made in response to prevailing situations, utilizing their respective endowments and capabilities. But this represents a kind of "privatization" of poverty reduction. Many of the things needed to meet the needs and wants of the poor require collective action, for example:

- Establishing and maintaining a clean village water supply
- Banding together to purchase raw materials in bulk at lower price for making handicrafts, and marketing as a group to gain access to more favorable markets and to reduce the time that must be spent when selling products individually
- Improving local sanitation to reduce diarrheal and other diseases that are unnecessarily endemic among the poor (improving hygiene can be a more individual effort)
- Deterring police, moneylenders, and other local power figures from victimizing petty vendors, day laborers, unmarried women, lower castes, and other vulnerable groups

Many of the constraints, injustices, and indignities identified as particular burdens in *Voices of the Poor* require not just individual or public sector actions but actions by the poor themselves. Empowerment of the poor thus can be promoted through some combination of (a) *directly enhancing poor people's respective assets and capabilities* so that they have a higher probability of achieving what they need and desire through their own efforts—a "private" approach to empowerment of the poor; and (b) *establishing assets and capabilities at higher levels of decision making and activity* that lead to the same or similar outcomes, that is, enhancing the abilities of the poor to get what they need and want.

The latter is a collective strategy of empowerment, important because the first can never be sufficient to meet all of the needs and wants of the poor. Also, the second approach is often needed to protect gains made through the first approach. In either case, one can seek to enable poor people to have more effect from whatever assets and capabilities they have, individually and collectively, by making the environment (process and context) more enabling than disabling.

Roles and Functions

For people to become organized and act collectively, they need to have a variety of recognized *roles,* formal or informal. They also need supporting *rules, precedents, and procedures* that will enable them to perform four basic functions that are essential for any organization and collective action:

- Decision making
- Resource mobilization and management
- Communication and coordination
- Conflict resolution (Uphoff 1986a)

Collective action of any sort, whether through legally established local government bodies, through formally constituted organizations such as cooperatives, or through informal sets of actors who have ongoing social relationships and common purposes, will require performance of these four functions.[13]

To build up capacities of the poor to utilize their limited resources more effectively to achieve goals and benefits on their own behalf, one of the basic strategies for empowerment that goes beyond individual and household units and aims will be either

- *strengthening* such roles, rules, precedents, and procedures where they already exist, or
- *establishing* them where they do not.

Organizing the poor to advance their interests and meet their needs requires more than the creation or existence of some formal organization. Agreement on common purposes and on how the costs and benefits of collective action will be shared is important in a constitutional sense. But the capacity for achieving purposes, despite resistance, depends on actual performance of these functions. The activities associated with these four functions enable people to accomplish more with their resources than they could operating as separate individuals or households.

Levels of Collective Action

There are a number of levels of decision making and activity beyond the individual and household levels. Several of these are commonly grouped under the rubric "local" (see Uphoff 1986b for analysis of this usage in the context of local institutional development). There are three such levels at which collective action is possible—and for the poor desirable: group, community, and locality.

At the *group* level, people associate according to common characteristics and interests in order to promote their shared interests, for example, as farmers or fishermen, women or men, youths, members of an ethnic or religious group, or speakers of a common language. These associations are usually fairly small, but similar organizations or branches can be federated up to higher levels of operation. The group level remains the foundation unless the organization is a mass one, without small-group base units.

The *community* level is determined by people's place of residence, so that neighbors living in some proximity join to protect and advance shared interests. This level is more heterogeneous than the group level, though bonds of kinship are likely to give greater strength to the association among community members.

The *locality* level represents a set of communities that have ongoing patterns of interaction and cooperation. It may be based on proximity, common-pool natural resources, exchange of labor, a central market, shared religion or ethnicity, or other interests. Residents within a locality may attend the same weekly market, schools, church, mosque, or temple, thus acquiring a degree of social solidarity that is absent or attenuated at higher administrative levels of organization, such as districts or subdistricts.

For empowering the poor, the first level of collective action—the group level—has many advantages because it is more homogeneous, based on members having a self-identified, shared characteristic. This could be poverty or a condition that contributes to poverty, for example, having a livelihood such as artisanal fishing, trash collection, or shoe repair. Groups formed on this basis are commonly thought of as mutual self-help groups. The homogeneous make-up of such groups offers the poor some advantages but can also constitute a weakness, since all members will be relatively poorly endowed with resources.

An interesting question is whether it is possible to enlist or establish organizations at the community and locality levels that will serve effectively to reduce poverty and enhance the power of the poor. If the poor constitute a majority at these levels, any inclusive organization should be oriented toward meeting their needs. Resources of richer persons can possibly be co-opted to improve the situation of poorly endowed persons. However, there is a long history of heterogeneous organizations serving the interests of their richer members even when their poorer members are most numerous. Contextual factors such as an ethos of egalitarianism versus an acceptance of inequality have an effect on the operation of local organizations that are heterogeneous in membership.

It is also important to ask whether community and locality organizations can be designed or given incentives so that they make net contributions to empowerment of the poor, even if they are not totally devoted to this purpose. If so, resources besides those of the poor will be mobilized to improve the livelihoods and help attain the needs and wants of poor people. This may not always be feasible, but as an empowerment strategy, it deserves consideration.

How can the poor persuade community and locality organizations to take seriously the problems created by poverty and to redress these imbalances through their decision making, resource mobilization, communication, and conflict resolution? Allies from higher levels, whether units of government or external institutions such as nongovernmental organizations (NGOs), can help encourage such efforts, but they cannot dictate the internal dynamics of community or locality organizations (Ostrom 1990).

In some cases the poor may represent an important (swing) voting block, so that organizational leadership from the richer majority will need to attend to problems of poorer members. But if voting power does not count for much, the poor can be easily ignored. While ballots can be a source of empowerment, this is only so if electoral processes confer a real share of authority. The most reliable means to give the poor some leverage, even if they are a minority, is to have activities where the better-off benefit from the participation of the poor, or incur some costs from their nonparticipation.

A concrete case of such interdependence is management of the hill irrigation systems in Nepal studied by Martin and Yoder (1987). They examined the conditions under which tail-enders, invariably poorer than head-enders because the latter have more abundant and assured water supplies, had some influence on the decisions and operations of water user associations. The longer the irrigation canal bringing water from a perennial or seasonal source, and the more labor needed to maintain the canal and respond to emergency situations (threats of canal breach), the more equitable was the distribution of water. Where canals were short and less labor was needed, head-enders could ignore or marginalize tail-enders with less cost to themselves.[14]

We are faced with an unfortunate trade-off. Organizations of and for the poor that are smaller and more homogeneous can be more easily and more reliably used by the poor to advance their interests. However, these organizations will also have fewer economic, social, and political resources. Larger organizations with a more robust and diversified asset base will be less amenable to influence or control by the poor, but they can potentially have more impact on efforts that benefit the poor, such as creating infrastructure, improving public health, or influencing central decision makers to invest more in rural development.

Organizational Leadership and Vulnerability

When thinking about local organizations to empower the poor, we are also faced with what Michels (1915) called "the iron law of oligarchy." With good empirical evidence he asserted that the larger and more established an organization becomes, the more likely it is to be dominated by a minority, whether these leaders are richer members or the formerly poor now ascendant over their brethren. While strong leadership can make an organization more powerful and more effective, it also increases the likelihood that the organization will serve the interests of a minority rather than those of the majority of members. Indeed, Michels showed that this tendency is stronger in organizations whose members are less well-endowed with power resources, that is, economically poorer and having less education and lower social status.[15]

Lipset and colleagues, in their classic trade union case study (1962), showed that leaders can in fact be kept accountable to members through internal electoral competition. But in this case, the members (typographers) were somewhat better educated and more economically secure than most union members in America at the time. It is more than coincidence that the trade unions in the United States that have the most autocratic histories, such as longshoremen and teamsters, have also had memberships relatively lower in personal power assets of income, social status, and education.

Historically, the performance of organizations involved in rural development with poverty reduction as a goal has not been as dismal as Michels's analysis predicted. Takeover by the rich and domination of the poor in organizations is not inevitable (Esman and Uphoff 1984; Krishna, Uphoff, and Esman 1997). However, the "iron law" is not easily alloyed and remains a warning for everyone. The odds favor eventual oligarchic rule and an eclipse of internal democracy. Procedures and structures for internal democracy, accountability, and transparency are thus more important in organizations of, by, and for the poor than in organizations whose members are better endowed.

For example, "vigilance committees" that oversee and balance executive leadership are increasingly found in Latin American organizations at the grassroots. However, such measures should not hamstring or immobilize leadership, since initiative and even boldness are needed for effectiveness in seeking the interests of the poor. Building and maintaining consensus behind the purposes and strategies of an organization is compatible with, indeed a prerequisite for, strong leadership.

Solidarity is an important factor in enhancing the power of the poor because it allows all available resources to be concerted toward common objectives rather than being dissipated or negated by conflict. Leadership of course can play a key role in forging and maintaining solidarity, while division and factionalism is usually a reflection of competition between leadership elements. It is often thought that social heterogeneity makes conflicts more likely, diminishing group power. However, as Krishna (2002) has shown from studies of Indian villages in the state of Rajasthan, heterogeneous communities can achieve effective collective action, with "social entrepreneurs" who catalyze cooperation among subgroups having diverse characteristics. Conversely, in basically homogeneous communities factionalism can be evoked by ambitious leadership mobilizing support on personal, familial, or other bases. Esman and Uphoff (1984) also show that social heterogeneity or homogeneity is not a good predictor of the effectiveness of rural development through local organizations. Leadership factors and the contextual influences of values and ethos play a larger role than do socioeconomic characteristics per se.

The Role of Cognitive Factors

In analyzing organizational potentials and processes for benefiting the poor by enhancing their ability to achieve their needs and wants, it is easier to focus on "objective" factors—roles, rules, precedents, and procedures. These can be observed and changed through decisions and actions, and thus are more amenable to intervention or purposeful construction. Moreover, they are very important for the poor themselves.

However, it would be a mistake to overlook the more subjective dimensions of organizational performance, loosely characterized as norms, values, attitudes, and beliefs. In my own experience of introducing local organizations for improving irrigation management, working with farmers considered to be among the poorest in Sri Lanka and Nepal, I have found that one needs to look beyond *structural* elements of social organization to appreciate the effects of *cognitive* elements, even if these are harder to identify or affect (Uphoff 1996). The next section of the chapter describes experiences that illustrate the analysis offered here.

This appreciation of cognitive factors, stemming from practical engagement in poverty reduction efforts, has informed my thinking about social capital (Uphoff 1999; Uphoff and Wijayaratna 2000; Krishna and Uphoff 2002). This distinction between cognitive and structural elements can, I think, be usefully integrated into all social science analysis because it makes explicit the complementary sources of human activity that occur in groups of any scale: (a) incentives and patterns that arise from *individual* consciousness and intentions, and (b) second-order realities that are constructed from *shared* ideas and aspirations.

In social science, what are ostensibly structural factors, because they are grounded in collectively validated and maintained patterns of thinking that affect evaluations and behaviors, are in fact basically subjective; that is, they are a matter of ideas, values, expectations, and beliefs. Their being shared gives them a degree of objectivity, stability, and measurability. While social structures are not physical like buildings or infrastructure, they become visible parts of social reality by virtue of widespread cognitive understanding and support.

Taking these factors into account represents an advance upon earlier concerns with "basic needs." It is not that these concerns were not worthy and beneficial, but they remained essentially paternalistic and did not address human needs and potential in their fullest sense. Meeting basic needs provides a foundation for improving the prospects of the poor, but we need to venture into less material and less tangible realms if efforts by the World Bank and others are to be mobilized for realizing the broader objectives of human development.

An Example of Large-Scale Empowerment, from the Bottom Up

How does all of this work in practice? There is no single formula or strategy for empowerment. The following example, however, shows how the framework developed above can be applied to a particular case in which resources, capabilities, processes, and contexts were used to enhance empowerment, on a sustainable basis, for several tens of thousands of poor farm households, and eventually several hundred thousand, in Sri Lanka.

The strategy in this case was not initially to increase the power resources of the poor but rather to enhance their ability to utilize these resources through farmer organization. This enhanced their resource endowments at the same time that changes were made in both processes and context. The various changes were positively reinforcing, with positive-sum results as gainers greatly outnumbered any losers. Initial resistance to the changes from engineers and richer farmers who had gained from the disorganized situation was overcome because the new system was so evidently more productive and legitimate, increasing water productivity and agricultural production and also reducing conflicts as farmer solidarity became established and appreciated from all sides. Opponents were co-opted as an effective cohort of leadership emerged from within the farming community (for detailed documentation, see Uphoff 1996).

The Project Setting

In 1980 the U.S. Agency for International Development (USAID) started implementing a water management improvement project in Sri Lanka, focused on the Left Bank of the Gal Oya irrigation scheme, the largest and most inefficient system in the country. The initial plan was to institute a more rigid management regime that would require farmers to follow schedules for channel maintenance and water distribution, both activities best described as chaotic at the time of project inception. Examples of water theft and conflict over water were legion—80 percent of control structures were broken or inoperative in 1980, and water was reliably measured and controlled at only seven locations in a 25,000-hectare area. These problems reflected the unpredictable and unresponsive main system management, which put water users in a vulnerable and deprived situation, eliciting conflict and uncooperative behavior.

The initial project design made no provision for water user associations, assuming that the imposition of "discipline" would make best use of the scarce water supply. The lower third of the Left Bank never received water deliveries during the dry season; the middle third had only erratic and inadequate deliveries; and even farmers in the top third experienced shortages at the end of long distribution (secondary) canals where head-enders hoarded available water. The formation of an association was added just before the project design was finalized so that water users could be mobilized to provide free labor for rehabilitating field channels (tertiary canals).

This decision looked at first like another imposition upon the poor. The average landholding size in Gal Oya Left Bank was about 1.7 acres, and the level of poverty was one reason why USAID decided to invest in this system. As it turned out, because the project design made no provision for payment to have tertiary rehabilitation done, unless farmers cooperated in carrying out this work on a voluntary basis there would be few if any productive benefits from primary- and secondary-level improvements in canal infrastructure. Water would still not reach the fields as intended and raise agricultural productivity.

The Intervention

The introduction of water user associations created, in a bottom-up way, roles among farmers for decision making, resource mobilization and management, communication and coordination, and conflict resolution. Association members established their own rules, precedents, and procedures. Farmers drew upon indigenous norms and customs of voluntary group labor for community benefit, a tradition known as *shramadana,* to improve the run-down channel systems within their control. Meanwhile, engineers and consultants rehabilitated the higher-level canals that delivered water to field channels. Eventually, and faster than expected, a four-tier structure of farmer organization came into operation, coordinating farmer decisions with those of engineers and vice versa, and also linking farmers to extension, credit, and other services needed.

Ironically, by making engineers and project managers dependent upon farmers for the effective implementation of the project, the project design "empowered" water users. Engineers had to be more solicitous toward and cooperative with the farmer organizations, seeking their ideas and inputs to redesign the system, not just ordering them to carry out plans set from above, because the restoration and operation of field channels had to be done on a voluntary basis.

Once more respectful relations were established with government technicians and officials, the farmers undertook impressive demonstrations of self-help. Young organizers (catalysts) began facilitating bottom-up, channel-based, informal organizations. Within six weeks, 90 percent of the farmers in a more than 2,000-hectare pilot area were doing some combination of (a) channel cleaning—some channels had not been maintained for 10, 15, or even 20 years, so were quite silted up; (b) distribution of water, rotating deliveries so that head-end, middle, and tail-end farmers got equitable shares of whatever water was available in that water-short season;[16] and (c) saving of water, reducing offtakes upstream to be able to donate any excess water deliveries downstream to farmers more in need of them.

The engineers' attitudes toward farmers had previously been decidedly negative. Many of the settlers had not relocated to Gal Oya entirely voluntarily, some being designated by village headmen to move to Gal Oya, and others being former prisoners given early release to resettle there. Settlers were seen by outsiders, and saw themselves, as "rejects" from the rest of society. However, once the engineers saw constructive, responsible behavior among farmers, including preventive maintenance, something not seen before, their attitudes and working relations with the farmers became more positive.

Once field channels were cleaned and water was being rotated and even saved, the irrigation system operated more efficiently, even before the planned main-system improvements had been completed. Water efficiency quickly doubled, so twice as much area could be irrigated as before. This gave positive economic benefits to farmers, particularly to the poorest among them, namely the tail-enders who seldom had received water for a dry-season crop before. Such successes reinforced cooperation among farmers at the same time that it enhanced their status in the eyes of engineers. The authority of farmer-representatives was only de facto, based on consensus among users to regulate tertiary-level operations. However, the representatives became part of more formal decision-making bodies at secondary and primary levels. Such grants of authority empowered farmers collectively in ways that had not been dreamed of only a year before.

The economic, social, and political resources of farmers were thus all enhanced, but so was their information. The farmer-organizers carried out training programs, and the system of farmer organization reaching from the field channel level up to the project level facilitated the flow of information both upward and downward, where before there was an information vacuum. Social sanctions made the use of force obsolete,[17] and the whole effort acquired a legitimacy in the eyes of farmers, engineers, local officials, and politicians that was remarkable to observe.

Along with the increase in farmers' endowments of resources, there were enhancements of capabilities. The farmer-representatives chosen by consensus, and rotated according to farmers' wishes, quickly gained both experience and confidence, bolstered by formal training.

With this, we saw changes in a number of processes. Farmer-representatives now sat on the district agricultural committee presided over by the district minister, and were able to speak directly to him. Engineers could deal with organized groups of farmers rather than with thousands of scattered individuals; they began meeting regularly (and in the field) with water users to identify problems and find solutions. Farmers' explicit efforts to exclude partisan influences on water distribution (including requiring any farmer chosen as a representative to resign any party office held) meant that politicians could no longer play divide-and-control games. These and other changes meant that the operational context in which decisions were made and resources were allocated at higher levels was modified to be more open to farmer ideas and interests. What resources they had to draw on could be wielded more effectively.

Beyond this, the cultural and ideational context was affected in farmers' favor. Norms of participatory management were introduced; these were consistent with the espoused democratic ideology of the country, but were not previously manifested because of long-standing feudal relationships and presumptions of bureaucratic and technocratic superiority. The ideals of equitable opportunities for livelihood, well established in the traditional culture, were publicly articulated, so that tail-enders could legitimately claim an equal share of water vis-à-vis head-enders. The very visible and much-appreciated efforts of young women organizers legitimated an active role for women farmers in water management. Empowerment was thus a process that operated in these four different ways, or at the four different "levels" indicated in tables 10.1 and 10.2.[18]

Results

The farmer organizations established in Gal Oya between 1981 and 1985 became a model for the whole country, with the Cabinet revising national policy in 1988 to feature participatory irrigation management. Over 500,000 farmers today are members of such participatory management systems throughout Sri Lanka, working with the Irrigation Management Department or the

Mahaweli Economic Authority. Some of these organizations are less effective than those created in Gal Oya because much less effort was invested in their formation, but such investments in "social capital" (Uphoff and Wijayaratna 2000) can be well justified in economic terms.

There is evidence that these creations have been sustainable, not just productive. In 1997, a dozen years after external assistance was withdrawn precipitously, the Left Bank farmer organizations were told that the reservoir's supply at the start of the dry season was too low to provide a full season of water issues. The farmers were advised that there would be no cultivation that year and that they should not waste their seeds and labor. Farmers were understandably upset about this situation, which threatened to deprive them of income they needed to survive through the year. One farmer did some research and figured out that the engineers had forgotten to consider probable inflow to the reservoir during the dry season, even without additional rain, from the water table in the watershed. The organizations lobbied for the Irrigation Department to give them whatever water would be available and to let them utilize it as best they could.

The department calculated that it could give them 60,000 acre-feet of water, but it advised them (a) to use this on only the upper 15,000 acres, not the full 65,000 acres of the Left Bank, applying the standard water duty of 4 feet/acre-foot, so as to use the water most efficiently, avoiding seepage and conveyance losses; (b) not to grow rice, because this is a "thirsty" crop; and (c) not to blame the engineers if the crop failed, because they had been warned that planting was not feasible.

The farmer organizations nonetheless made the decision to share the available water equally, among head-end, middle, and tail-end reaches of the Left Bank, not wanting to favor one area over another. They decided that farmers could plant whatever crop they wanted to, but at their own risk. They were correct in gambling that there would be more water supply, and the department was able to issue a total of 98,000 acre-feet during the season. But this was only about one-third of the usually expected water duty.

What was the result? According to records of the Departments of Irrigation and Agriculture, farmers planted rice on almost all 65,000 acres of the Left Bank and obtained average yields of 85–95 bushels per acre, which matched or even exceeded their usual yields, despite the small amount of water. (It is now established that rice should not be grown as an aquatic plant, and that keeping the soil just moist, and well aerated, gives superior yields; see Uphoff 2003.) Farmers through their organizations were able to demonstrate superior technical capabilities, raising the water-use efficiency several fold. An evaluation post-project had concluded that in normal years the farmer organizations at least doubled water-use efficiency and quadrupled water productivity.

Even more impressive, it should be noted that in the Left Bank, the upper and middle reaches are cultivated by Sinhalese farmers, mostly resettled into the scheme from all over the island during the 1950s, while the lower reaches are inhabited by Tamil farmers, who moved there from coastal communities at about the same time. This means that the Sinhalese majority had agreed to share water equally with the Tamil downstream minority, at a time when armed conflict was going on elsewhere in the country between Sinhalese government forces and Tamil secessionists. Thus the empowerment of Gal Oya farmers was accompanied by an unprecedented level of interethnic solidarity (Uphoff 2001).

Conclusions

The Gal Oya case study has been reported, very briefly, to show that the concepts of empowerment discussed in the rest of this chapter are operational and have ontological validity. While there are many more examples of failed efforts than of successful ones to introduce and institutionalize new relationships among poorer and marginalized populations in interaction with government, NGOs, or other outside organizations, experience shows that empowerment is possible and beneficial, not just for the poor but on regional and national bases.

Measuring the effects of empowerment is easier than measuring empowerment itself. In the Gal Oya case, about US$20 million value-added of rice was grown in 1997 alone, when nothing would have been produced if engineers' rather than farmers' wishes and interests had prevailed. This amount was more than USAID's project cost. However, most of the elements that contributed to this empowerment can be identified and documented, with rough if not always very exact measures. Ordinal measurement is more feasible than cardinal measurement for many of these elements, and summation into single numbers is not possible within any presently meaningful methodology. But for practical purposes of promoting empowerment among the poor, such precision and cumulation are not necessary.

Most public policy actions in this area will have to be initiatives based on ceteris paribus logic, and none will be complete or perfect a priori. Empowerment will have to be an iterative process, working in a "learning process" mode (Korten 1980). Particular training, legislation, or community organization can be introduced with some degree of confidence, assessing the incremental benefits for empowerment as experience accumulates, making "course corrections" as needed. Beyond the effects of specific interventions, we should start building up knowledge of what combinations and sequences of action can be most effective, and cost-effective, for these purposes. Measurement advances will be helpful for evaluating such knowledge. However, very refined and detailed measurements are not needed to pursue this opportunity for advancing an applied social science that promotes successful poverty reduction through mobilization of the capabilities and aspirations of the poor themselves.

Notes

1.   Ontology is a branch of philosophy that considers the nature of "reality." It tries to make explicit, coherent, and defensible the assumptions being made about what

exists, about what *is.* Such assumptions shape and subtly predetermine what is consequently observed, measured, manipulated, and so forth.

2.   References made here to "the poor" are the same kind of verbal shorthand that creates trouble when talking about "power." But there is no opportunity to sort out that complication here. References to "the poor" should not be read as implying that this category is homogeneous. A bigger problem with such terminology is that classifying persons only or primarily in terms of their poverty emphasizes what they *lack* rather than what they *have.* This is a mistake in much of the antipoverty literature and most programs. Such aggregation obscures, rather than highlights, individual differences in capabilities as well as in aspirations. For increasing people's empowerment, it is important to pay attention to and build upon these differences, since capabilities and aspirations are major factors that can contribute to power.

3.   The translation of this work cited here, by A. M. Henderson and Talcott Parsons, is the one most widely known and most often cited. However, it includes only the first volume of Weber's monumental writings on social and economic organization, the one that contains Weber's analysis of power as a factor in social and economic life. Weber's analysis of authority, contained in a second volume, elaborates on his analytical thinking about power, but this was published in English many years later in a translation by Guenther Roth and Claus Wittich titled *Economy and Society* (Berkeley: University of California Press, 1968). Weber's analysis of authority unfortunately is not as well known among non-German social scientists as is his discussion of power.

4.   Weber brought consideration of costs into his analysis of power when he stipulated the variable of "resistance."

5.   This accords with Weber's definition of the modern state. His definition of authority as "a special case of power" started me thinking about what would be the other, parallel kinds of power (Uphoff 1989).

6.   Weber defines the modern state as able to uphold a claim to a monopoly on the legitimate use of force, a very precise and important insight into the nature of political systems. Revolutionaries who do not accept the state's claim of legitimacy refer to the state's use of force as violence, and their own use of it as a legitimate exercise of coercive power to achieve objectives they consider right and proper.

7.   This was the conclusion of Kenneth Boulding when he reviewed the first presentation of this analytical framework (Ilchman and Uphoff 1969) in *The American Political Science Review* in June 1970. The book was republished by Transaction Books in 1998 as a social science classic.

8.   This idea was introduced into the social science literature by Michels (1915) when he declared: "Organization is the weapon of the weak in their struggle with the strong."

9.   This analytical (and practical) argument parallels the one that Krishna (2002) makes regarding the importance of "agency" for understanding and benefiting from "social capital."

10.   The last section of this chapter discusses a case of such empowerment under difficult circumstances. The strategy and practices employed are documented and discussed by Uphoff (1996) and Uphoff and Wijayaratna (2000).

11.   An analysis of 150 rural local organizations showed that the average performance score for those initiated by government agencies was only 16, compared with 153 and 138 for those initiated by community members themselves or by local leaders. Fortunately, local organizations initiated in a "catalyzing" manner by outside agencies, governmental or nongovernmental, had a respectable score of 114 (Esman and Uphoff 1984, 164).

12.   See the set of 18 cases presented by Krishna, Uphoff, and Esman (1997) and the analysis of how and why these cases succeeded (Uphoff, Esman, and Krishna 1998).

The analysis and suggestions in this chapter are grounded in personal involvement with as well as academic study of empowerment processes.

13. Without subscribing to the structural-functional school of sociology, one can acknowledge that these four functions correspond to those that Talcott Parsons (1951) ascribed to all social organization: goal attainment, adaptation, integration, and pattern maintenance. The terminology used here is less abstract than that of Parsons.

14. This is consistent with Wade's analysis (1968) of Indian irrigation systems. Headenders, as upstream water users, get first opportunity to withdraw water from the source; tail-enders are downstream and have to depend on what water remains flowing through the system. Wade found less collective action in larger command areas, but these were public sector systems in which an irrigation bureaucracy would ensure water at least to the head of a canal. Richer, more "powerful" head-end farmers could benefit from nonmaintenance of the canal and ensuing maldistribution of water. In Nepal, head-enders needed the cooperation and assistance of tail-enders to make sure that water from the source reached the command area. Interdependence thus conferred power on the poorer members.

15. Michels, who wrote at the beginning of the twentieth century, did not reach this conclusion happily, having spent much of his life participating in or observing European socialist parties and trade unions. Unfortunately, he often gets bracketed as an "elitist" with Pareto and Mosca, contemporary social scientists who were more satisfied than Michels with their conclusions about the probability of elite domination.

16. Project implementation started in a year when the reservoir was only 25 percent full. The reservoir normally was low (having filled only twice in the previous 30 years), but this was an unusually water-short season. Our program considered canceling the farmer organization effort because such scarcity would normally lead to a higher level of conflict, making the establishment of cooperation among farmers more difficult. In fact, the opposite dynamic prevailed: the crisis situation made farmers more willing to change behaviors and seek cooperative solutions.

17. One farmer-representative at the start of the program's second year proudly told me: "We used to have murders over water; now we don't even have any conflicts." When I looked skeptical he defended his statement, saying that I could go inspect the local police station records to verify this if I doubted him.

18. A much longer chapter could be written about how this process worked. A similarly instructive chapter could be written on another outstanding example, the Federation of Community Forestry Users (FECOFUN), formed in Nepal during the 1990s. Started from the bottom up, it has a membership today of 5 million, representing 60 percent of the rural population. As explained by Britt (1998, 2003), it was created despite (and maybe facilitated by) national political turmoil during that decade. Legal rights were conferred, altering the context for forest management, but there were also cultural redefinitions of concepts such as *hamro ban* (our forest) that legitimated collective action, supported by professionals and some politicians in addition to millions of mostly poor rural people.

Local organizations put up some of their own economic resources, which were increased through better forest management, which in turn enhanced local power. The forest user groups became in many places paralocal government bodies, compensating for weaknesses in the official institutional infrastructure. Legislation providing for decentralization, consistent with national policy directions, was important but not a sufficient basis for local empowerment. External aid, as in the case of Gal Oya, was also important, but was actually not a very large amount. One could delineate in detail how changes in various resources, capabilities, processes, and context all contributed to creation of one of the most promising examples of empowerment for the poor that I know. The point here is that analytical and real factors in empowering poor people can mesh.

References

Appadurai, Arjun. 2004. "The Capacity to Aspire: Culture and the Terms of Recognition." In *Culture and Public Action*, ed. Vijayendra Rao and Michael Walton. Stanford, CA: Stanford University Press.

Britt, Charla. 1998. "Community Forestry Comes of Age: Forest-User Networking and Federation-Building Experiences from Nepal." Paper presented at Crossing Boundaries, seventh annual conference of the International Association for the Study of Common Property, Vancouver, Canada, June 10–14. http://dlc.dlib.indiana.edu/archive/00000023/.

———. 2003. "Power, Politics, and Policy Formulations: Third-Generation Issues Facing Community Forestry in Nepal." Paper presented at regional conference of the International Association for the Study of Common Property, Chiang Mai, Thailand, July.

Esman, Milton J., and Norman Uphoff. 1984. *Local Organizations: Intermediaries in Rural Development*. Ithaca, NY: Cornell University Press.

Harsanyi, John. 1962. "Measurement of Social Power, Opportunity Costs and the Theory of Two-Person Bargaining Games, and Measurement of Social Power in N-Person Reciprocal Power Situations." *Behavioral Science* 7 (1): 67–80, 81–92.

Ilchman, Warren F., and Norman Uphoff. 1969. *The Political Economy of Change*. Berkeley: University of California Press. Reprint, New Brunswick, NJ: Transaction, 1998.

Korten, David C. 1980. "Community Organization and Rural Development: A Learning Process Approach." *Public Administration Review* 40 (5): 480–511.

Krishna, Anirudh. 2002. *Active Social Capital: Tracing the Roots of Democracy and Development*. New York: Columbia University Press.

Krishna, Anirudh, and Norman Uphoff. 2002. "Mapping and Measuring Social Capital through Assessment of Collective Action to Conserve and Develop Watersheds in Rajasthan, India." In *The Role of Social Capital in Development: An Empirical Assessment*, ed. C. Grootaert and T. van Bastelaer, 85–124. Cambridge: Cambridge University Press.

Krishna, Anirudh, Norman Uphoff, and Milton J. Esman, eds. 1997. *Reasons for Hope: Instructive Experiences in Rural Development*. West Hartford, CT: Kumarian Press.

Lipset, Seymour Martin, James Coleman, and Martin Trow. 1962. *Union Democracy*. Garden City, NY: Doubleday.

Martin, Edward, and Robert Yoder. 1987. "Institutions for Irrigation Management in Farmer-Managed Systems: Examples from the Hills of Nepal." IIMI Research Paper 5, International Irrigation Management Institute, Kandy, Sri Lanka.

Michels, Robert. 1915. *Political Parties: A Sociological Study of the Oligarchical Tendencies of Modern Democracy.* Reprint, Glencoe, IL: Free Press, 1959.

Narayan, Deepa, Robert Chambers, Meera K. Shah, and Patti Petesch. 2000. *Voices of the Poor: Crying Out for Change.* New York: Oxford University Press for the World Bank.

Narayan, Deepa, with Raj Patel, Kai Schafft, Anne Rademacher, and Sarah Koch-Schulte. 2000. *Voices of the Poor: Can Anyone Hear Us?* New York: Oxford University Press for the World Bank.

Ostrom, Elinor. 1990. *Governing the Commons: The Evolution of Institutions for Collective Action.* Cambridge: Cambridge University Press.

Parsons, Talcott. 1951. *The Social System.* Glencoe, IL: Free Press.

Uphoff, Norman. 1986a. *Improving International Irrigation Management with Farmer Participation: Getting the Process Right.* Boulder, CO: Westview.

———. 1986b. *Local Institutional Development: An Analytical Sourcebook with Cases.* West Hartford, CT: Kumarian Press.

———. 1989. "Distinguishing Power, Authority and Legitimacy: Taking Max Weber at His Word Using Resource-Exchange Analysis." *Polity* 22 (2): 295–322.

———. 1996. *Learning from Gal Oya: Possibilities for Participatory Development and Post-Newtonian Social Science.* London: Intermediate Technology Publications.

———. 1999. "Understanding Social Capital: Learning from Analysis and Experience of Participation." In *Social Capital: A Multifaceted Perspective,* ed. Partha Dasgupta and Ismail Serageldin. New York: Oxford University Press for the World Bank

———. 2001. "Ethnic Cooperation in Sri Lanka: Through the Keyhole of a USAID Project." In *Carrots, Sticks and Ethnic Conflict: Rethinking Development Assistance,* ed. M. J. Esman and R. J. Herring, 113–39. Ann Arbor: University of Michigan Press.

———. 2003. "Higher Yields with Fewer External Inputs: The System of Rice Intensification and Potential Contributions to Agricultural Sustainability." *International Journal of Agricultural Sustainability* 1 (1): 38–50.

Uphoff, Norman, Milton J. Esman, and Anirudh Krishna. 1998. *Reasons for Success: Learning from Instructive Experiences in Rural Development.* West Hartford, CT: Kumarian Press.

Uphoff, Norman, and C. M. Wijayaratna. 2000. "Demonstrated Benefits from Social Capital: The Productivity of Farmer Organizations in Gal Oya, Sri Lanka." *World Development* 28 (11): 1875–90.

Wade, Robert. 1968. *Village Republics: Economic Conditions for Collective Action in South India.* Cambridge: Cambridge University Press.

Weber, Max. 1947. *The Theory of Social and Economic Organization.* Trans. A. M. Henderson and Talcott Parsons. New York: Oxford University Press.

Whitehead, Alfred North. 1929. *Process and Reality.* New York: Macmillan.

Chapter 11

Peace, Conflict, and Empowerment: The Colombian Case

Caroline Moser

The linkage between empowerment and development effectiveness was convincingly argued in *World Development Report 2000/2001: Attacking Poverty* (World Bank 2000) and is now well established. The linkage between peace and development is not yet as widely known or understood. Nevertheless, there is emerging evidence that peace building is an integral component of development, and that participation in such efforts by individuals, organizations, and communities can contribute to their empowerment. Experiences with measuring participation in peace processes, therefore, can offer insights into possible approaches to the measurement of empowerment.

This chapter examines community perceptions of participation in ongoing peace processes in Colombia, particularly those aspects that can also be seen as constituting aspects of empowerment. It is based on empirical data provided by participatory evaluations of two peace-building projects recently undertaken in Colombia. Both were national initiatives but were implemented through project interventions at the local level. The objectives of these projects were not explicitly to "empower" local communities, organizations, or individuals, but rather to support peace building in Colombia by strengthening the capacity of local social actors to participate in peace processes. In participatory evaluations undertaken at the project completion stage, in 2001–02, project participants assessed changes in levels of their participation in peace processes that had occurred as a result of their involvement in the project.

The Colombian experience can help shed light on three analytical debates relevant to the question of measuring empowerment:

- The relationship between peace, development, and empowerment

- The use of participatory methodologies to measure empowerment through participation in peace processes
- The identification of some potential indicators for measuring empowerment through participation in peace processes

Peace, Development, and Empowerment

The World Bank's *Empowerment and Poverty Reduction: A Sourcebook* posits three analytical linkages between empowerment and development effectiveness. Empowerment enhances development by encouraging good governance and growth, by helping growth to be pro-poor, and by influencing the outcomes of development projects. In addition, empowerment contributes to quality of life and human dignity (Narayan 2002, 2–8).

The important linkages between peace and development effectiveness stem from the devastating impacts that conflict and violence and their associated fear and insecurity impose on development outcomes. War and conflict have long been accepted as critical development issues (Collier et al. 2003; Stewart and FitzGerald 2001). Indeed, open conflict affects at least 35 of the poorest countries in the world. In the past decade, violent crime and the resulting insecurity have also begun to be recognized as significant development constraints that contribute to keeping millions of people in poverty (Ayres 1998; Findlay 1994; Moser 1998). Peace and security in many contexts are essential preconditions to the achievement of the most basic development outcomes.

There are also clear linkages between empowerment and peace. Macroeconomic research on conflict and crime has shown close association with power structures characterized by corruption, greed, and inequality (Collier and Hoeffler 2000; Fajnzylber, Lederman, and Loayza 2002). At the same time, micro-level studies have illustrated how crime and violence serve to disempower the poor through their impact on individual, household, and community capabilities, assets, and institutions (Moser and McIlwaine 2004).

As has been amply demonstrated in post-conflict contexts, sustainable peace requires not only the signing of formal peace accords but also the participation of citizens in reconstruction and peace-building interventions at the local level (Colletta and Cullen 2000). Empowered citizens can participate more effectively in such processes. This suggests an important analytical link between empowerment and development to be added to those listed above: empowerment contributes not only to good governance and quality of life but also to achieving peace and security, which in turn creates conditions for development.

The connections between peace and empowerment go both ways. By raising people's self-confidence, building organizational capacity, and fostering alliances toward common objectives, participation in peace processes can itself be empowering. This is reflected in the Colombian experiences described below.

The Contribution of Participatory Methodologies

Within this broader analytical debate concerning the relationships between peace, empowerment, and development, this chapter focuses on the contribution that participatory methodologies can make to the measurement of empowerment associated with participation in peace processes. There is an extensive debate underway concerning the advantages and limitations of quantitative as against qualitative poverty-focused research, and within this the particular contribution of participatory appraisal and evaluation tools and techniques (see Brock and McGee 2002; Booth et al. 1998; Chambers 1994; Kanbur 2002; Hentschel 1999; Norton et al. 2001). The examples provided by the evaluations discussed here help to illustrate the viability and robustness of participatory methodologies as a useful tool or technique with which to measure participation in peace processes, and by extension, empowerment of the participants in these processes.

Background: Local Peace-Building Projects in Colombia

Colombia, a middle-income Latin American country, is in the midst of a civil war in which guerrilla groups, paramilitaries, and government military forces are all involved in a violent militarized conflict across the country.[1] The war is particularly intense in resource-rich areas, such as petroleum and coca-growing areas. More recently, insurgency activities have also moved into the capital, Bogotá, and other big cities including Medellín and Cali. Local civilian populations are severely affected by the conflict, particularly in poor rural and urban communities.

The inability of the government to end the civil war by political or military means at the national level has resulted in a proliferation of small-scale initiatives that seek to build peace and *convivencia*—harmonious coexistence—at the local community level.[2] As a social anthropologist with knowledge of Colombia (see, for instance, Moser et al. 2000; Moser and McIlwaine 2004), I was invited to undertake evaluations of two such projects. This provided the opportunity to introduce the participatory methodology described in this chapter.

The first of these projects was the Local Initiatives for Peace in Colombia project, which sought to support the peace process by strengthening partnerships or alliances between local communities, municipalities, civil society organizations, and private sector institutions. This was achieved through financial support to partnership activities as well as through highly participatory consultations, training, and dissemination of best practices at the regional and national levels. The project's four components were a partnership for peace convocation, a local seedcorn fund to support peace initiatives (referred to in this chapter as the Local Fund), a study tour in which project participants visited peace-building initiatives in Northern Ireland, and a number of synthesis workshops. The project was a co-financed initiative with support from the Corona Foundation in Bogotá and the U.K. Department for International Development, and was managed through the World Bank's Trust Fund Facility. It was also intended to help the World Bank identify and support best practices in local peace building, consistent with the overall country assistance strategy goal for Colombia of creating conditions for durable peace and sustainable development (see Moser et al. 2000).

The second project was known as the "Sida Seedcorn Fund: Capacity Building Initiatives to Strengthen Women's Participation in the Peace Process in Colombia." By funding small initiatives, it seeks to strengthen the coordination between women's organizations to promote their participation in the peace process in Colombia. The project responded to critical constraints affecting women's participation in peace efforts, notably disunity within the women's movement in Colombia and the lack of voice and capacity of excluded women. Toward this end, the fund targeted women's NGOs involved with women in situations of social exclusion and economic vulnerability, particularly Afro-Colombian, indigenous, and rural women, ex-combatant women, and displaced women. It also supported women's networks or groups seeking to be political actors in the country's peace process and to bring a gender perspective to that process.

This project was funded by Sida (the Swedish International Development Cooperation Agency) and also managed through the World Bank's Trust Fund Facility. With a budget of US$90,000 it was able to support 11 initiatives out of 85 proposals submitted. Those supported included the following (see Moser and Clark 2001, 2002):

- Establishment of the first network of women ex-combatants
- Efforts by an indigenous women's group in the Sierra Nevada de Santa Marta to design a code of conduct for external actors (guerrilla, paramilitary, or army) entering their communities
- Financial assistance to enable a woman from one of the groups supported to participate as a representative of civil society in negotiations with the FARC at Caguan, held under the auspices of the Colombian National Peace Council
- The development of a pacifist political agenda by a pacifist women's group that included e-mail contact with women combatants in one of the guerrilla groups around gender issues

The Participatory Evaluation Tools

Both the Colombian project evaluations used quantitative methods as well as qualitative participatory "evaluation" techniques.[3] Quantitative descriptive information, obtained from written documentation and interview sources, provided useful knowledge about project inputs and outputs. However, the qualitative participatory evaluation was an essential complement for both methodological and logistical reasons. It provided a number of useful tools to measure people's own perceptions of changes in the levels of their participation as a result of the projects, insights available only from the participants themselves. Furthermore, evaluations were undertaken in a context of civil war, where travel to most of the project locations was not possible for security reasons. Therefore, a participatory evaluation workshop was an essential alternative to site visits, particularly in the case of the Local Initiatives for Peace project.

Table 11.1 lists some of the participatory evaluation tools used in the evaluation workshop of the Local Initiatives for Peace project. Similar tools were used in the other project evaluation. While some of these relate to the success or failure of the project itself, others focus more specifically on empowering aspects of the project. Table 11.1 therefore also includes the composition of the focus group that used it.

Potential Key Indicators

In both the Colombian projects, attempts were made to qualitatively measure empowerment by assessing whether or not there were any changes in people's capacity to participate in the peace process. As with all indicators, the development of empowerment indicators faces considerable definitional and measurement challenges. At the same time, there are analytical and methodological problems that are specific to the measurement of peace as a component of empowerment. Some of these issues are briefly discussed below.

Defining Key Concepts

In the participatory evaluation workshops, project members were asked to define the meanings of two foundational concepts underlying the project objectives: "*convivencia*" and "strengthening an alliance." Perceptions of meanings attached to these terms varied depending on the context and the social actors defining them. Since indicators relate to object definitions, this in itself suggests that a variety of indicators may be relevant. The 27 project members who participated in the Local Initiatives for Peace evaluation workshop identified three slightly different interpretations of *convivencia*. Interestingly enough, these related more to long-term peaceful coexistence than to short-term resolution of conflict. Perceptions of "strengthening an alliance" also varied, with "commitment" as the most important characteristic, closely followed by "capacity and participation" and "effort" (table 11.2).

Constructing Composite Indicators

The fact that empowerment is such a "soft" concept means that it may rely far more on composite indicators than do more "hard-edged" development areas such as water or education. This is illustrated by the evaluation of the Sida Seedcorn Fund, in which different project members themselves identified the indicators they considered important for measuring changes in their level of empowerment through participation in peace projects.[4] Table 11.3 summarizes some of the indicators identified most frequently. These were at three

Table 11.1   Participatory Evaluation Tools Used in the Local Initiatives for Peace Project Evaluation Workshop

Participatory tool	Objective of participatory tool	Composition of group
ZOPP[a] with prioritization by voting	Definition of critical concepts: *convivencia* and strengthening of an alliance	Entire group
Listings and rankings	Indicators of strengthening alliances based on the projects being executed	Focus groups comprising participants from the different projects
Project timeline relative to timelines of intensity of conflict at local and national level	External political and conflict variables that influence project implementation	Project members from same region of the country
Causal flow diagrams	General inputs and outputs of different types of projects, focused either indirectly or directly on peace and *convivencia*	Project members by types of projects (education, production, local development, peace, and *convivencia*)
Matrix and associated causal flow diagrams	Indicators of project outcomes: inputs, outputs, and outcomes of individual projects	Members of same project
Institutional maps	Indicators of strengthening alliances: Number of institutions in each alliance and their relative importance Relationship between alliance members and most important institutions in area focused on *convivencia*	Members of same project
Timeline of the project implementation process	Obstacles and opportunities in project implementation: identification of potential changes and improvements in the project planning process	Mixed groups
Brainstorming	Future strategies and directions for the next phase of the Local Fund	Entire group

Source: Moser, Clark, and Olaya 2002.

a. ZOPP stands for Zielorientierte Projektplanung, or Objective-Oriented Project Planning. It was developed by the German donor agency GTZ.

Table 11.2   Perceptions of the Meanings of "*Convivencia*" and "Strengthening an Alliance" in the Local Initiatives for Peace in Colombia Project Evaluation Workshop

Concept	Meanings	Prioritization by votes
Convivencia	Tolerance and respect for difference	10
	Capacity to relate and live together and alongside each other	9
	Process of participation, negotiation, and a peaceful approach to the resolution of conflicts	8
Strengthening an alliance	Commitment	9
	Capacity and participation	6
	Effort	6
	Processes	4
	Trust	2

Source: Moser, Clark, and Olaya 2002.

Note: Prioritization was a four-stage process. First, each participant wrote on a card his or her definition of *convivencia* and of strengthening an alliance. Next, these were placed on the wall for all to read, and cards expressing a similar meaning were grouped together by two participants under a "mother card." Finally, each participant had one vote to prioritize the most appropriate meaning as identified in the mother cards. The score assigned to each meaning represents the number of participants who chose it as the best one.

levels—individual, organizational, and inter-institutional—with the different indicators within each level providing composite, qualitative measures.

Individual Indicators

At the individual level, changes in self-esteem were identified as a particularly important indicator of women's reduced level of fear and increased capacity to participate in the peace process. Indeed, changes at the individual level were considered a critical precondition for changes at other levels. In some cases low self-esteem was symptomatic of women's position in society, and it was more apparent among excluded groups, such as indigenous women, than among professional women. The expression *Sí puedo* (Yes I can) came up repeatedly in all groups as an expression of women's increasing confidence in themselves and in their role in the peace process.

Also at the individual level, two sets of attitude changes were identified as critical to measuring the success of the projects. One related to gender identity and discrimination. The other related to peace, in terms of what it means and one's potential role in achieving it. Many women involved in the projects had

Table 11.3 Descriptive Indicators of Changes in Capacity to Participate in the Peace Process Identified by Sida Seedcorn Fund Project Members

Level	Indicators of change	Examples from projects supported by the Sida Seedcorn Fund
Individual	Self-esteem, measured through: • Increased ability to speak in public • Letting go of trauma of past • Recognizing one's own agency and capability and overcoming sense of victimhood	Particularly important in indigenous projects such as Comunarwa and ACIN[a] and achieved through capacity-building workshops Corporación Colombiana de Teatro: Using drama to process the pains and losses of displaced women and turn them from victims into actors National Network of Women Ex-combatants: Using life histories and testimonies to "construct a new identity without denying one's past" and to affirm a new type of "agency" of ex-combatant women for peace
	Attitude toward relative importance of gender identity	National Network of Women Ex-combatants: Reconstructing their identity as women and accepting their history as shaped by gender
	Attitude toward peace	Sí Mujer: Dialogue with active women combatants Oye Mujer: Businesswomen developing the attitude that peace is an issue and a process of concern to them
	Level of participation in meetings	Sí Mujer: Those not in agreement with the contact with armed groups leaving the organization
	Time allocated by women to working in activities related to conflict and peace	Oye Mujer: Businesswomen dedicating more time than before to the issue of peace and conflict
Organizational	Internal cohesion, measured through: • Ability to accomplish an activity • Ability to reach internal consensus in the group • Change in outside perception and profile of the group	National Network of Women Ex-combatants: Organization of work plan and division of activities created friction between the women over pressure to complete tasks Asamblea de Mujeres por la Paz: Production of book as common project was identified as indicator of intra-organizational strength Mujeres Jóvenes Popular: Asked to represent youth in local municipality planning and attend national-level dialogues for peace
Inter-institutional	Contact with other organizations Coordination with other organizations	Humanizar: Through project able to gain access to the civil society dialogue process at Caguan involving representatives of the armed groups, such as the FARC, and the government High Commission for Peace

Source: Moser and Clark 2001.

begun with divergent attitudes toward conflict, the meaning of peace building, and their role both as ordinary people and as women in the process. The main alternatives consisted of either speaking out against conflict and violence or staying silent from fear or lack of understanding. Participants pointed to attitude changes leading to an increase in the number of women who opted to speak out instead of staying silent. This change was closely related to changes in self-esteem and to acknowledgment of the potential role each individual could play in the peace process. Finally, changes in time allocated by women to working in activities related to conflict and peace were the simplest indicator of individual-level change.

Organizational Indicators

Key changes at the organizational level had to do with strengthening groups' capacity to manage their projects. Local organizational capacity is identified in the World Bank's empowerment sourcebook as a key element of empowerment (Narayan 2002, 21). A number of proxy indicators were identified, all of which related broadly to better internal cohesion within the project group. Many groups identified project outputs as a useful proxy. These included numbers of events, activities, or other specific products generated by the project, based on the assumption that without internal cohesion groups would not have had sufficient consensus to carry out activities. Others identified internal cohesion in terms of ability to reach consensus on how to approach a particular issue or problem.

Inter-institutional Indicators

Finally, a set of inter-institutional indicators were developed that focused on increasing collaboration between groups participating in the peace process. Two key indicators were identified to assess how far groups had been able to consolidate strategic alliances or establish new ones. First was the establishment of new contacts with institutions already important in helping groups reach their objective, and second was the development of new collaborative initiatives with other institutions. The second proved most difficult to evaluate, partly because few of the groups were working at the inter-institutional level (itself an indicator of lack of empowerment). Moreover, it was often difficult for groups to identify the extent to which successes in collaborative work were specifically the consequence of the Seedcorn Fund rather than the result of long-term processes.

One Group's Experience: Ex-combatant Women

The evaluation carried out with ex-combatant women in the Sida Seedcorn Fund project provides an interesting example of insights gained through the participatory exercise. Probably the most crucial of the indicators these women identified was the rebuilding of lost self-esteem through the reconstruction of identity and agency. For members of the National Network of

Women Ex-combatants, life histories and testimonies were part of a process of social rehabilitation and reintegration. They spoke of the importance of recovering one's history (*recuperar su historia*) and rediscovering oneself (*reconocerse*) and of constructing a new identity without denying one's past (*construir una nueva identidad sin negar el pasado*). The very ability to write about themselves and their experiences was a huge step forward for many of them. Many women, during their involvement in armed groups, had been actively discouraged from writing anything down for fear of discovery by the enemy or of leaving behind a paper trail. To put to paper previously unspoken thoughts, feelings, and experiences was a difficult task but one that the ex-combatants found both challenging and liberating. It was described in terms of reclaiming one's voice (*recuperar la palabra*).

In their evaluation, the ex-combatant women listed and ranked indicators of changes they perceived in their capacity to participate in the peace process (table 11.4). Changes were ranked on a scale of 1 to 3, with 1 representing minimum change and 3 representing maximum change. The group also chose to change the titles of the working levels from "organizational" and "interinstitutional" to "project groups" and "network," as they felt the latter terms reflected more accurately the levels at which they were working. As table 11.4 shows, there is still a considerable way to go in terms of developing trust at the network level, with the majority of ex-combatant women still very reluctant to use written documents.

Table 11.4   Rankings of Indicators of Changes in Capacity to Participate in the Peace Process by Women Ex-combatants in the Sida Seedcorn Fund Project

Individual level		Project group level		Network level	
Indicator	Score	Indicator	Score	Indicator	Score
Time spent on project	2–3	Level of interaction between women of different demobilized groups	3	Regional recognition and acceptance	1.5
Self-confidence/ ability to talk in public about women, conflict, and peace	3				
Value accorded one's own history	2	Number of activities completed	3	Number of written replies to written invitations to contact ex-combatants in different parts of Colombia	1
Ability to write about one's experience	2				
Trust in others	2–3				

Source: Moser and Clark 2001, 2002.

The Quantification of Qualitative Data

One of the most important constraints on the use of qualitative data is the tendency to dismiss it as "apt illustration" or "anecdotal evidence" (Moser 2002). For this reason it is critically important, where sufficient data exist, to further develop the methodology so as to provide quantified data. This section describes two modest efforts to quantify the results of qualitative data. Both are based on participatory methodologies, in the first case institutional mapping, and in the second, listings and rankings of indicators of change.[5]

Institutional Mapping

At the inter-institutional level, institutional mapping using Venn diagrams provided an essential, if qualitative, participatory tool that enabled groups to identify those institutions perceived as most important in the peace process. It also provided recommendations as to which institutional linkages needed strengthening. In mapping, each project team drew its own project as the central point, then surrounded it with different institutions they considered important in reaching their objectives. They located these institutions either inside or outside the parameter of their working environment, with circles of different sizes denoting relative importance. They then identified whether their relationship with each institution was negative or positive in terms of helping them reach their objectives.

Figure 11.1, drawn by a women's group in western Colombia, identifies the regional government (*gobernación departamental*) and the National Women's Network (Red Nacional de Mujeres) as the most important institutional linkages in helping the group achieve its objectives. The relationship with these two is positive and productive. The Colombian government's Social Solidarity Network (Red de Solidaridad Social) was also perceived as a relatively important institution, mainly in relation to the project component dealing with displaced women. However, this relationship was identified as both positive and negative.

A similar institutional mapping exercise was carried out with six of the initiatives supported by the Sida Seedcorn Fund project. The quantification of the maps drawn by these six groups identified the relative importance of different institutions in the peace process.

Of a total of 59 institutions listed, only seven were listed by more than one group (table 11.5). This important finding highlights the fact that in Colombia a large number of organizations and institutions are engaged in the peace processes, but with very little overlap between them. There is also very limited engagement with state institutions. The result is shallow inter-institutional networks and low levels of collaboration—or social capital—between organizations. This helps to explain the weak capacity to build common agendas and proposals that has been identified as one of the main obstacles to building a cohesive civil society movement for peace in the country.

Figure 11.1   Institutional Map Drawn by Members of a Women's Organization in Western Colombia

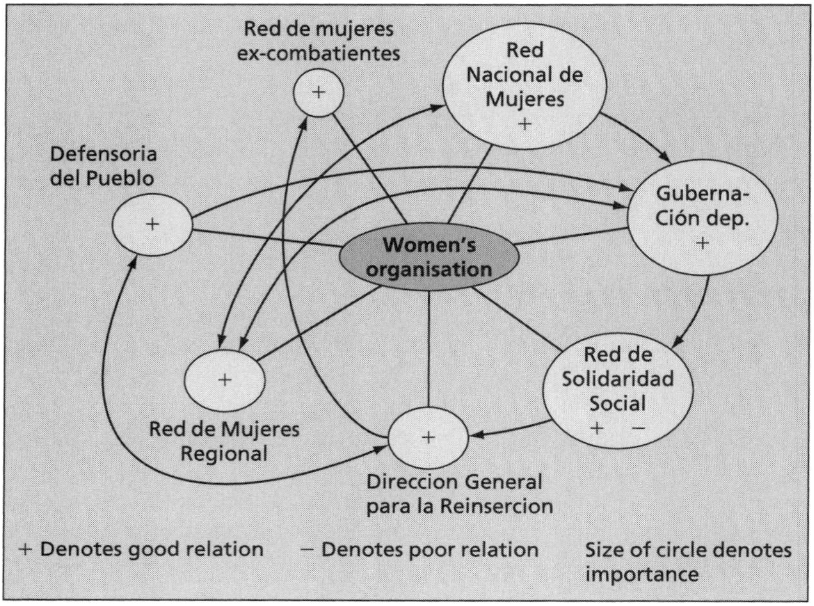

Note: The labels in the drawing are reproduced as written by the participants. Red Nacional de Mujeres = National Women's Network; gobernación departamental = regional government; Red de Solidaridad Social = Social Solidarity Network; Dirección General para la Reinserción = National Reconciliation Office (under the Interior Ministry); Red de Mujeres Regional = Regional Women's Network; Defensoría del Pueblo = Human Rights Ombudsman's Office; Red de Mujeres Ex-combatientes = Network of Women Ex-combatants.

In the Local Initiatives for Peace project, institutional maps were used to measure the range and diversity of institutional alliances, as well as changes in the number of alliance members between the signing of the project agreement and the participatory evaluation (table 11.6). As the table shows, in several cases there were increases in the number of alliances during the course of the project. The Escuela de Liderazgo, Paisajoven in Medellín, for example, increased the number of collaborating institutions from seven to 10. Such success in attracting other institutions to the alliance while implementing the project was identified as an important indicator of increasing inter-institutional collaboration.

Quantitative Measurement of Indicators

Although neither of the participatory evaluations was sufficiently sophisticated to quantitatively measure different indicators across the entire project universe, this was undertaken at the level of individual projects. It was more successful in the Sida Seedcorn project than in the Local Initiatives for Peace

Table 11.5 Results of Institutional Mapping: Seven Most Important Social Institutions Identified by Six Sida Seedcorn–Funded Projects

Institution	Sí Mujer	ACIN	RNME	Project Mujeres Jóvenes Popular	Humanizar	Oye Mujer	No. of listings	Total ranking
Red Nacional de Mujeres	2 (+)		2 (+)		2 (+)	3 (+)	4	9
Asamblea Nacional Permanente de la Sociedad Civil por la Paz	1 (+)		1 (+)	1 (−)			3	3
FARC	1 (+/−)		2 (−)		1 (−)		3	4
ELN	1 (−)		2 (−)		1 (−)		3	4
Defensoría del Pueblo	3 (+)	2 (+)				1 (+)	3	6
Other women's organizations	3 (+)				1 (+)		2	4
Dirección General para la Reinserción			1 (−)			1 (+)	2	2

Source: Moser and Clark 2001, 2002.

ACIN: Asociación de Cabildos Indígenas del Norte del Cauca (Association of Indigenous Councils of the Northern Cauca)
RNME: Red Nacional de Mujeres Ex-combatientes (National Network of Women Ex-combatants)
FARC: Fuerzas Armadas Revolucionarios de Colombia
ELN: Ejército de Liberación Nacional de Colombia

project, because in the former, participatory focus group evaluation exercises could be undertaken with participants in individual projects.[6] Table 11.7 shows results of a listing and ranking exercise carried out by the project committee of Oye Mujer, which participated in the Sida Seedcorn project. Oye Mujer's objective was to build and strengthen the networks between four very diverse groups of women in the Department of Tolima: displaced women, ex-combatants, businesswomen, and grassroots organizers.

For each of these target groups, the project committee listed and ranked changes in the capacity or willingness to participate in the project in terms of individual, organizational, and inter-institutional indicators. Each indicator was measured on a scale of 1 to 3 with 1 a minimum level and 3 a maximum level of change. The results revealed differences between the different indicators, as well as between the four target groups. As table 11.7 shows, the greatest progress in changing perceptions was made with businesswomen, followed by displaced women. This does not mean that other groups were not successful in terms of their participation, only that the change in

Table 11.6   Results of Institutional Mapping: Changes in Alliances under the Local Initiatives for Peace Project

Project objective	Project name	Number of institutions signing agreement	Number of institutions identified in the participatory evaluation
Strengthening of alliances	Catatumbo	6	5
	Escuela de Liderazgo	7	10
	AGROACTUAR	4	8
	SEPAS	5	3
	ASOHECO	—	14
Training and management	Red de Convivencia Escolar	13	12
	COASOBIEN	3	3
	Corporación para el Desarrollo de Versalles	1	15
Consolidation	Borromeo	4	4
	ALCONPAZ	6	6
	Paz y Bien	—	12
Replication	Federación Nacional de Cafeteras	6	—
	Olimpiadas Culturales	9	12
	UNIBAN (GESTA)	7	4

Source: Moser, Clark, and Olaya 2002.
— No information.

participation by businesswomen—traditionally a group disinclined to consider that the armed conflict has anything to do with them—was greatest. Of particular significance was the change in inter-institutional indicators, suggesting the important networking role that businesswomen's groups could play in peace-building processes. Finally, the results also show that, overall, the greatest changes were made at the individual level in terms of time commitment; the least change was perceived in individual self-confidence.

Future Challenges: Outcome Indicators of Empowerment?

Empowerment as much as peace is the outcome of a lengthy and complex process. One of the biggest outstanding challenges, therefore, is the development of robust indicators that are able to measure the outcome of empowerment through participation in peace processes.

Table 11.7   Rankings of Indicators of Changes in Capacity to Participate in the Peace Process, by Different Target Groups in the Oye Mujer Project

		Target group				
Level	Indicator	Displaced women	Ex-combatant women	Business-women	Women's grassroots organizations	Total (average)
Individual	Time commitment to project	3	2	3	—	8 (2.6)
	Self-confidence	2	1	2	—	5 (1.6)
Organizational	Organizational capacity	2	2	2	1	7 (1.7)
Inter-institutional	Contacts made	1	2	3	2	8 (2.0)
	Total (average)	8 (2)	8 (2)	10 (2.5)	3 (1.5)	

— Not available.

Outcome indicators are notoriously difficult to measure, not only because they occur a long way downstream but also because they may not take the form anticipated, with the issue of attribution particularly problematic. Nevertheless, the Local Initiatives for Peace project evaluation made an effort to grapple with this issue. Four mixed small groups started by identifying indicators to measure the strengthening of an alliance. This resulted in a range of issues, some of them difficult to measure numerically (table 11.8).

Finally, small groups, divided by the sector in which their projects were located, sought to identify long-term impact indicators. These included the following:

- Improvement in coexistence relationships
- Local education policies with strategic lines relating to the theme of *convivencia*
- Affirmation of a social pact between youth gangs
- Strengthened social capital
- Consolidation of networks and alliances in different sectors

This exercise illustrated some of the challenges associated with conceptualizing indicators, as well as the context-specific nature of such indicators. Both of these results provide useful lessons for those seeking to develop indicators of empowerment at a more general level.

In sum, the development of indicators of empowerment relating to participation in peace processes is still in its infancy. Despite the limitations identified, however, participatory methodologies have provided powerful tools for practice as well as for research and are increasingly used by those who are

Table 11.8   Indicators of Strengthened Alliance Identified by Four Focus Groups in the Local Initiatives for Peace Project Evaluation Workshop

Group	Indicator of strengthened alliance
1	Ownership of the process
	Change of attitude toward teamwork
	Greater representation in management and leadership
2	Strengthened collaboration between partners in the alliance as shown by:
	• Common objective defined
	• Projects and processes designed in the short, medium, and long term
	• Projects implemented
	• Resources of all types mobilized jointly
	Levels of ownership pertaining to the objectives of the alliance:
	• Common objectives defined
	• A common discourse constructed and publicly expressed
	• Resources of all types mobilized jointly
	Capacity built in area of:
	• Management
	• Theoretical and practical methodologies for conflict resolution
3	Capacity of management, operation, and administration of the alliance
	Commitment of the partners in the alliance
	Levels of communication between the actors
4	The partners contribute according to their strengths and assume risks
	The partners demonstrate that the alliance helps them to fulfill and complete their mission and that they have incorporated the alliance as a form of organization and cooperation in their institutional culture
	The partners fulfill the tasks necessary to achieve their objectives

Source: Moser, Clark, and Olaya 2002.

working within peace processes. Thus, the participatory methodologies in Colombia that started with research (Moser and McIlwaine 2004), and were then applied to evaluation (as described in this chapter), are now providing the methodological framework for a national initiative to strengthen the capacity of women's organizations to build consensus and work collaboratively on Colombian peace initiatives.

The objective of the Colombian Women's Initiative for Peace project is to assist in forming a women's peace movement in the country by strengthening the capacity of women from 22 civil society and trade union organizations. These organizations represent grassroots women, including peasants, trade unionists, Afro-Colombians, youth, and indigenous women, along with academics (IMP 2003). The project's origins lie in a collaborative initiative supported by the Swedish trade union movement with donor support from Sida. The initiative began in 2002 and is expected to continue until 2006.

Under the project's auspices over the last three years, an extensive range of participatory techniques have been incorporated into consensus-building processes undertaken in bimonthly national committee meetings, regional and sector workshops throughout the country, and a national-level constituent assembly (*constituyente*) involving 300 women. Most recently, dissemination, validation, and peace negotiation processes are being rolled out at the local level across the country. At all stages participants use participatory methodologies to plan, implement, and assess their progress. The associated indicators they are developing will undoubtedly inform the next stages of more analytical work on the measurement of empowerment through participation in peace processes.

Notes

1.   The main guerrilla groups are the FARC (Fuerzas Armadas Revolucionarios de Colombia) and the ELN (Ejército de Liberación Nacional de Colombia). The main paramilitary group is the AUC (Autodefensas Unidas de Colombia).
2.   *Convivencia* derives from the Spanish *convivir,* meaning to live together, especially in harmony. It has no exact equivalent in English. The nearest would be "coexistence," but the meaning is not exactly the same, so the Spanish term is used throughout this chapter.
3.   These were developed by adopting and adapting participatory urban appraisal techniques first used in research on community perceptions of urban violence in Jamaica (Moser and Holland 1997) and in Colombia and Guatemala (Moser and McIlwaine 1999, 2004).
4.   This was done through a process of iterative triangulation with focus groups from the 11 projects until consensus was reached.
5.   For a further explanation of the quantification of qualitative data see Moser and McIlwaine (2004).
6.   As mentioned above, for security reasons it was not possible to make field visits in the Local Initiatives for Peace project evaluation. Instead, that evaluation was carried out during a two-day workshop in Bogotá, with each project generally represented by two project members. The small number of participants from each project was not considered sufficiently representative to carry out a ranking and listing exercise in focus groups.

References

Ayres, R. L. 1998. *Crime and Violence as Development Issues in Latin America and the Caribbean.* Washington, DC: World Bank.

Booth, D., J. Holland, J. Hentschel, P. Lanjauw, and A. Herbert. 1998. *Participation and Combined Methods in African Poverty Assessments: Reviewing the Agenda.* London: Social Development Division, UK Department for International Development.

Brock, K, and R. McGee, eds. 2002. *Knowing Poverty: Critical Reflections on Participatory Research and Policy.* London: Earthscan.

Chambers, R. 1994. "The Origins and Practice of Participatory Rural Appraisal." *World Development* 22 (7): 953–69.

Colletta, N. J., and M. L. Cullen. 2000. *Violent Conflict and Transformation of Social Capital: Lessons from Cambodia, Rwanda, Guatemala, and Somalia.* Washington, DC: World Bank.

Collier, P., L. Elliot, H. Hegre, A. Hoeffler, M. Reynal-Querol, and N. Sambanis. 2003. *Breaking the Conflict Trap: Civil War and Development Policy.* Washington, DC: World Bank; New York: Oxford University Press.

Collier, P., and A. Hoeffler. 2000. "Greed and Grievance in Civil War." Policy Research Working Paper 2355, World Bank, Washington, DC.

Fajnzylber, P., D. Lederman, and N. Loayza. 2002. "Inequality and Violent Crime." *Journal of Law and Economics* 45 (1): 1–40.

Findlay, M. 1994. "Crime, Economy and Social Development." Background paper prepared for the 1995 World Summit for Social Development. United Nations Research Institute for Social Development, Geneva.

Hentschel, J. 1999. "Contextuality and Data Collection Methods: A Framework and Application to Health Service Utilization." *Journal of Development Studies* 35 (4): 64–94.

IMP (Iniciativa de Mujeres Colombianas por la Paz). 2003. "Agenda de las Mujeres por la Paz." Bogotá.

Kanbur, R., ed. 2002. *Qual-Quant: Qualitative and Quantitative Methods of Poverty Appraisal.* Delhi: Permanent Black.

Moser, C. 1998. "The Asset Vulnerability Framework: Reassessing Urban Poverty Reduction Strategies." *World Development* 26 (1): 1–19.

———. 2002. "'Apt Illustration' or 'Anecdotal Information': Can Qualitative Data be Representative or Robust?" In Kanbur 2002. Delhi: Permanent Black.

Moser, C., and F. Clark. 2001. "Sida Seedcorn Fund: Capacity Building Initiatives to Strengthen Women's Participation in the Peace Process in Colombia." Evaluation report for Swedish International Development Cooperation Agency (Sida) and the World Bank Trust Fund. Available on Overseas Development Institute Web site (http://www.odi.org.uk).

———. 2002. "¿Como evaluamos las iniciativas de Mujeres por la Paz en Colombia?" Swedish International Development Cooperation Agency (Sida) and World Bank, Bogotá.

Moser, C., with F. Clark and E. Olaya. 2002. "The Local Initiatives for Peace Project—Colombia." Final evaluation report for UK Department for International Development and the World Bank Trust Fund. Available on Overseas Development Institute Web site (http://www.odi.org.uk).

Moser, C., and J. Holland. 1997. *Urban Poverty and Violence in Jamaica.* Washington, DC: World Bank.

Moser, C., S. Lister, C. McIlwaine, E. Shrader, and A. Tornqvist. 2000. "Violence in Colombia: Building Sustainable Peace and Social Capital." Environmentally and

Socially Sustainable Development Sector Management Unit Report 18652-CO, World Bank, Washington, DC.

Moser, C., and C. McIlwaine. 1999. "Participatory Urban Appraisal and Its Application for Research on Violence." *Environment and Urbanization* 11 (2): 203–26.

————. 2004. *Encounters with Violence in Latin America: Urban Poor Perspectives from Colombia and Guatemala.* New York: Routledge.

Narayan, Deepa, ed. 2002. *Empowerment and Poverty Reduction: A Sourcebook.* Washington, DC: World Bank.

Norton, A., with B. Bird, K. Brock, M. Kakande, and C. Turk. 2001. *A Rough Guide to PPAs: Participatory Poverty Assessment: An Introduction to Theory and Practice.* London: Overseas Development Institute.

Stewart, F., and V. FitzGerald, eds. 2001. *War and Underdevelopment.* 2 vols. Oxford: Oxford University Press.

World Bank. 2000. *World Development Report 2000/2001: Attacking Poverty.* New York: Oxford University Press.

Chapter 12

Measuring Empowerment at the Community Level: An Economist's Perspective

Asim Ijaz Khwaja

Experiences over the past few decades suggest a shortcoming of top-down approaches to development. Since the 1980s, the new watchwords have been "participatory" or "community-led" development (Mansuri and Rao 2004; Uphoff 1996) and, more recently, "empowerment." The World Bank's *Empowerment and Poverty Reduction: A Sourcebook* defines empowerment as "the expansion of assets and capabilities of poor people to participate in, negotiate with, influence, control, and hold accountable institutions that affect their lives" (Narayan 2002, 14). Before empowerment can be integrated into development policy, however, it must be clearly conceptualized, and reliable measures must be developed. This is particularly important given that such measures of empowerment are likely to become project goals for development agencies.

This chapter offers an economist's perspective on how one would begin to construct measures of empowerment and the issues involved in doing so. I do not propose to offer a laundry list of potential measures applicable in all circumstances; such an exercise is almost certainly futile, as good measures are likely to be context-dependent. A more promising approach is to develop a general framework for conceptualizing empowerment, which can then be employed by researchers and practitioners to develop measures appropriate to a particular context and goals. While the chapter puts forward a theoretical framework, it also draws heavily on my own empirical work (Khwaja 2001, 2004) in order to demonstrate how this framework can be applied in the field and to provide empirical support for it.

Even before developing a general framework, it is imperative to make some basic distinctions among alternative understandings of empowerment. In particular, the researcher/practitioner needs to clarify whether empowerment is construed as an *end in itself* or as a *means to an end,* or both. The chapter accordingly begins with a section on the importance of making this distinction.

The second section develops a particular theory of empowerment and explains how this theory allows us to construct context-specific measures of empowerment. In order to illustrate both the theory and such measures, this chapter considers a specific case based on an empirical study conducted by the author, namely, the collective maintenance of community infrastructure projects in Baltistan, northern Pakistan. The study uses data from a primary survey I conducted of 99 rural communities in the region. In addition to community- and household-based surveys, the study also included technical surveys of all externally initiated infrastructure projects in these communities. The primary purpose was to examine the determinants of a community's collective success in maintaining these public infrastructure projects. Since maintenance of these projects was solely the responsibility of the community, their upkeep also provided a measure of the community's collective potential (for detailed empirical results of the study see Khwaja 2001).

The third section of the chapter describes an important and difficult empirical issue that arises if empowerment is to be viewed as a means to an end: establishing that there is a causal relationship between a particular measure of empowerment and the outcome or end of interest. This section also draws on my previous work to illustrate how one can investigate such causal inferences. More generally, this section cautions that while theory can suggest empowerment measures, causal channels should be subjected to rigorous empirical analysis. This is necessary in order to show that the measures affect outcomes of interest and are consequently useful for policy.

Empowerment: An End or a Means to an End?

The literature on empowerment shows two understandings of the concept. Empowerment is sometimes understood as a means to a specific end, such as increased welfare of the empowered agent. It is also often conceived as an end valuable for its own sake. It is hardly surprising that a concept as broad as empowerment can be understood in more than one way. However, if one is to develop and then use measures of empowerment in policy initiatives, it is essential to be explicit about which understanding is being used. The theoretical framework and measures constructed, as well as the process of establishing whether the measures have a causal impact, will be quite different in the two cases.

For an illustration of these issues, consider one aspect of empowerment as defined in the World Bank's empowerment sourcebook (Narayan 2002):

expanding poor people's capabilities. This is undoubtedly an important goal. Before attempting to develop measures, however, it must be clarified whether the researcher is asserting that such capabilities are important *only* because they lead to an increase in the welfare or well-being of the poor, as measured by standard socioeconomic indicators, or whether an expansion in these capabilities has value even if they do not influence any other aspect of welfare. In either case, the assumption is that empowerment is valuable because it affects an agent's overall welfare. The distinction here is whether this effect is true by definition, that is, empowerment is *defined* as a component of an agent's welfare or utility (empowerment as an end), or whether it is true by causation, that is, empowerment *influences a component* of welfare such as the agent's income or health status (empowerment as a means to an end).

Expressed mathematically, one is trying to posit whether the relationship between a particular aspect of empowerment is given by equation (1) below or by the systems of equations (2), where U_i is an agent i's measure of welfare, E_i is a measure of how empowered she is, X_i is a list of other factors that directly affect her welfare, and $f(.)$ and $g(.)$ are functions. The triple equal sign indicates that the relationship is posited to be definitionally true and must therefore be defended as such. These equations are illustrated in figure 12.1.

(1) Empowerment as an end: $U_i \equiv f(E_i, X_i)$

(2) Empowerment as a means: $U_i \equiv f(X_i)$ and $X_i^j = g(E_i)$ for one or more factors j

Now consider the process of laying out a theoretical framework and constructing measures using the second understanding of empowerment— empowerment as a means to achieve a specific end. If, for example, we view "expanding poor people's capabilities" as a means to achieve greater income of the poor, then we first need to articulate how such expanded capabilities can lead to an increase in income, that is, the nature of function $g(.)$ above. The definition of empowerment used in the sourcebook suggests one potential channel: expanded capabilities allow the poor to "*influence* . . . institutions that affect their lives" (Narayan 2002, 14, emphasis added). That influence, it may be hypothesized, can in turn affect their income.

To take an example from my work on public infrastructure projects, the Baltistan study mentioned above, consider delivery of a local public project to a community. Suppose that the poor in the community would benefit from an irrigation channel. However, the better-off minority in the community prefer an alternative project, such as electricity generation. In the absence of influence by the poor, the latter project will be chosen. If the capabilities of the poor are sufficiently expanded, however, they can exert their influence in favor of the project that provides most benefit to them. Such a theoretical framework would suggest that measures of empowerment should reflect capabilities related to such potential influence. One measure could be whether the poor were given an equal vote in project selection, for example, by the project provider going to all community households and asking them which project

FIGURE 12.1   Empowerment as an End or as a Means to an End

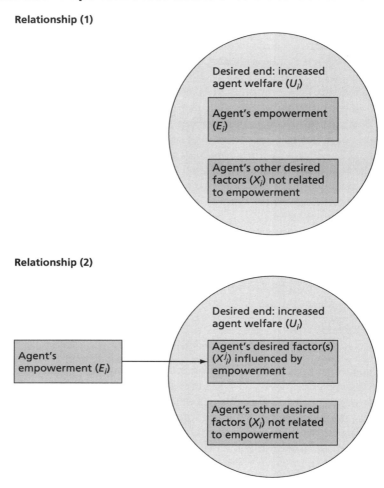

Relationship (1)

Desired end: increased agent welfare (U_i)

Agent's empowerment (E_i)

Agent's other desired factors (X_i) not related to empowerment

Relationship (2)

Desired end: increased agent welfare (U_i)

Agent's empowerment (E_i)

Agent's desired factor(s) (X^j_i) influenced by empowerment

Agent's other desired factors (X_i) not related to empowerment

they prefer. In another context we may arrive at a different measure, based on another possible causal relationship. The point is that specifying the relevant goal makes it possible to evaluate potential measures as ones that can be plausibly argued to have an effect on it. Whether or not that is the case can then be subject to empirical investigation.

In contrast, consider the same aspect of empowerment, expanding the capabilities of the poor, but now suppose that it is viewed as an end in itself. Such a view is suggested in the *same* definition of empowerment, which also refers to the expansion of capabilities of poor people to "*participate* in . . . institutions that affect their lives" (Narayan 2002, 14, emphasis added). One could presumably argue that such participation has direct value—that it is itself a component of the welfare of the poor. As before, a theoretical framework, such as that illustrated in function $f(.)$ in equation (1), would provide the basis for constructing particular measures. Using the same example of public projects, one could postulate that increased capabilities are directly provided in the form of activities that allow the poor greater participation. One such measure of participation, and hence of empowerment, in a development project could be whether the poor take part in all the planning meetings. Note that this measure is different from the one we came up with when viewing empowerment as a means to an end. Specifically, we no longer require that this measure result in poor people "influencing" the project decisions. If one assumes that attendance of poor people at meetings is important because we care about participation in its own right, it does not matter whether the participation leads to real influence. Nevertheless, in this case it is still important to establish that the particular measure used can be plausibly argued and subsequently shown to be an indicator of participation in the project decisions.

The above examples highlight the different consequences for theories and measures of viewing empowerment as a means to an end or as an end in itself. They also suggest a trade-off between these two approaches. When empowerment is regarded as a means to achieve an outcome, the most difficult tasks are likely to be laying out a theoretical framework showing how empowerment affects the outcome that is desired (such as changes in wealth, income, or other socioeconomic indicators) and then empirically showing that the measures chosen indeed causally affect this outcome. When empowerment is viewed as an end in itself, the theory and measures are often not that difficult to develop. In the example above, the "participation in planning meetings" measure is plausibly connected to empowerment understood as increased capabilities of the poor to participate in institutions that affect their lives. In this case, however, what is more difficult to establish is that the aspect of empowerment identified has *direct* welfare value. The more specific the measure chosen—such as participation in a set of meetings—the harder it is to establish that this measure is broad enough to have direct value, or alternatively, that it *causally* affects a broader notion of empowerment that is plausibly a part of agent welfare.

The point here is not to suggest that empowerment should only be viewed in one way—either as an end or as a means to an end. In fact, it is likely that both interpretations are correct. However, it is important to make the distinction and to be explicit about which is being used in a particular study, since they imply distinct theoretical frameworks and measures and require addressing different sets of issues. In this chapter, the primary focus is on viewing empowerment as a means to an end and illustrating how theory can be used to construct potential measures and defend them empirically. While much of what follows could also be applied if empowerment were viewed as an end in itself, economic methodology has fewer tools to establish whether empowerment has direct welfare value. That alternative is accordingly less developed in the following discussion.

From Theoretical Framework to Empirical Measures

In order to establish causality from empowerment measures to an outcome of direct value—whether an aspect of empowerment itself or a socioeconomic welfare outcome—one has to start with a theoretical framework for such effects, that is, what factors to include in equations (1) and (2) and what form the functions $f(.)$ and $g(.)$ take. Such a theoretical framework both lays out the hypothesized causal relationships and suggests measures to construct. Once such a framework has been developed and related measures constructed, we can subject them to empirical investigation. If we can establish that causal relationships do exist, the measures can appropriately be used as policy instruments.

The best way of illustrating this is to offer a potential theory of empowerment and then show how it translates into measures of empowerment for an actual case.

If empowerment is viewed as an end in itself, then the theory should start by defining empowerment concretely and in a manner that justifies why it can be viewed as an end. The more precise this definition, the easier it will be to construct measures that capture empowerment. For example, one could claim that (part of) empowerment is the granting of "voice" to the empowered agent and that voice is an inalienable right included in an individual's overall welfare. The theory would then explain what it means for an agent to have voice. This would require suggesting both measures of empowerment in terms of voice, and factors that, while not directly measures of voice, influence voice.

If empowerment is viewed as a means to an end, on the other hand, then this theory must start by indicating the particular end of interest and then describe the processes through which empowerment affects this end. This is the process followed in this chapter, which lays out a specific theory that views empowerment as a means to achieve increased economic welfare of the agent. This theory is then applied to data collected in the Baltistan study, showing how to generate measures of empowerment and empirically test them.

The goal is not to convince the reader of the particular theory of empowerment presented, or to present such a theory in a comprehensive way, but rather to illustrate a general process that may be used for other theories as well. In other words, the intent is to show how constructing measures of empowerment should begin with a theory of empowerment, which then provides the basis for development of measures.

Theory Development

The empowerment sourcebook identifies four key elements of empowerment: (a) access to information, (b) inclusion/participation, (c) accountability, and (d) local organizational capacity (Narayan 2002, 18). These elements can be used to develop a theory of empowerment that explains how empowerment of the agent (an individual, community, group, etc.) brings about desirable outcomes such as an increase in the agent's economic welfare or, more specifically, provision of basic services, access to justice, and improved governance.

The exercise starts by hypothesizing that the two underlying theoretical components in empowerment are information and influence, and then seeks to formalize these two concepts. Each is considered in only the most simple form, with two types of actors: an agent from the beneficiary community and an external agent. Further elaboration of such a model with inclusion of additional factors, such as who controls information and how its flow can be constrained by power brokers, falls outside the scope of this illustrative exposition.

Information

Information as a component of empowerment is conceptualized as both *provision of* information and *access to* information by the empowered agent, to and from the external agent or organization respectively. When poor people or communities are empowered, they are both able to provide information about their own preferences and gain information from outside that may in turn enhance their capacity to make optimal choices. Both types of information are likely to lead to increased welfare of the empowered agent.

Greater *provision of* information is expected to benefit the agent, as the final outcome is more likely to match the agent's needs. For example, when a decision must be made about which public project to build in a community, if an empowered community can express its preferences to the local government and make sure that the project is chosen accordingly, the project is more likely to succeed. The development literature abounds with instances of failed projects built without any local consultation (Tendler 1997), such as drinking water schemes that failed because people preferred walking to the local well (the value of time saved by an in-house tap being outweighed by the value of having a regular social space away from home).

Access to information, the result of information flows from external institutions to the agent, can also help by allowing the agent to make more informed decisions. For example, in the Baltistan study, it was surprising how often a community asked an external agency to construct a particular type of project based on inadequate information. Because communities incorrectly assumed that the external agency only provided certain types of projects and that asking for anything else would result in their not receiving a project at all, they often excluded projects that reflected their most pressing needs. Such errors might have been avoided had the community been empowered to obtain information at will from the external agency.[1]

In addition to being a separate component, information is also an aspect of the other three key elements of empowerment listed above. Participation can be partly thought of as a means of providing and gaining information. Similarly, such transfer of information is essential to social accountability and also helps foster local organizational capacity. It is important to note that the concept of information as used here is broader then simply the pro forma act of "asking and telling." Information exchange as a component of empowerment also implies that both parties are willing to supply information that is relevant to achieving goals. Unless the agent or community is empowered in other respects as well, there is no assurance that such information exchange can effectively take place. Unempowered agents may be unwilling or unable to express their preferences fully—unwilling because they may correctly perceive that there is little chance of these preferences being met, or unable because they lack enough information to choose the best option without more direct participation in the decision-making process.

Influence

While information, as formalized above, is necessary, it is by no means sufficient to produce the desired outcome. The second component, influence or "bargaining power," is also required. Agents may be able to share information perfectly. But unless they have the ability to influence the decision and, moreover, *know* that they have this ability, they will have little incentive to either provide or gain the requisite information. Even if they do so, they have no assurance that this information exchange will actually affect how the decision is made.

Formally, this chapter defines the influence component of empowerment as the agent's "relative ownership" of a particular decision. This is based on extending the property rights concept in economics, which defines ownership of a physical asset in terms of "residual control rights" over the asset (Grossman and Hart 1986; Hart and Moore 1990), to also include less tangible "assets" such as decisions. This extension to the property rights theory suggests that ownership of such assets should be given to agents whose effort or investment is more important in influencing the return for that particular decision. The idea behind this is intuitive: by giving greater influence in a decision to the agent whose investment matters most for the decision, we are ensuring that this agent will have a high incentive to make the investment. This leads to higher overall benefits from that decision for all parties involved.

A detailed model was developed to examine the role of community participation in decision making in the context of the Baltistan study (Khwaja 2004). In the study, a local community's influence in externally initiated public projects is measured by the community's nominal participation in decisions that affect the sustainability of the project and hence the benefits accruing from it. The community's participation in a project decision is viewed as a means of empowerment to the extent that such participation brings a greater likelihood of influencing the outcome of the decision. The property rights theory can be used to evaluate which of the two agents involved, the community or the external organization, should be more empowered to make the decision. Specifically, this theory suggests that this choice should depend on the nature of the decision. For a particular decision, the agent with the more important investment in the outcome should have greater influence.

It is hypothesized that a community's influence, as measured by its participation in a decision, may be desirable in some cases but not in others. This idea stands in contrast to much of the literature, which often views community participation as an unqualified good (Narayan 1995; Isham, Narayan, and

Pritchett 1995; World Bank 1996). Deciding usage rules for a community project is an example of a decision that the community is best suited to make. Hence, empowering the community by increasing its participation would be preferred. The data in the Baltistan study confirm that greater community participation in this decision is indeed associated with better project performance. Regression analysis shows that a 10 percentage points increase in community participation in nontechnical decisions (see table 12.1) is associated with a 5.5 percentage points increase in quality of project upkeep (measured on a 0–100 scale). This result is not surprising, as there are numerous examples of development projects that failed because external agencies ignored community preferences in favor of standard blueprints or other externally imposed rules.

The theoretical framework, however, also suggests that in some cases external agencies may be better placed to decide than communities. The implication is that decisions in such instances should be *less* influenced by the local agents. An example is deciding the appropriate scale of a project, such as its physical dimensions or planned productive capacity. Such decisions may require engineering knowledge; in the context of the Baltistan study, this would imply greater investment on the part of the external organization. This prediction is indeed confirmed by the data: regression analysis shows that a 10 percentage points increase in community participation in *technical* decisions (see table 12.1) is associated with a 3.8 percentage points decrease in quality of project upkeep (Khwaja 2001, 2004). This result is robust, even when community- and project-level controls are taken into account. Thus, as predicted by the theoretical framework, empowering the community by increasing its participation in these decisions is actually associated with *lower* project performance, presumably because this community role lessens the influence of the external agency whose judgment is needed for technical decisions.

This theory and these examples are not presented as generally applicable. Rather, they are intended to illustrate how defining a theoretical framework with hypothesized causal connections facilitates the construction of appropriate measures.[2] The theory provides a structure that restricts the search for potential measures of empowerment to those that capture the information and/or influence aspects of empowerment. Moreover, while the general theory may apply to cases beyond the particular study, appropriate measures may vary from one context to another. A variable that is a useful measure of empowerment in one environment, where it captures the information an agent provides, may not be most appropriate in another environment or at a different time in the same environment, where the nature of the information transfer is different. The benefit of laying out a theory is that it provides general rules yet allows for development of context-sensitive measures, as illustrated in the following section.

Potential Measures

Taking the summary theory presented above as a starting point, the next logical step is to search for and explore causal relations between potential

Table 12.1 Participation Levels in Project Actions and Decisions: Summary Statistics

Action/decision	Observations (N)	Mean (%)	Standard deviation
Nontechnical			
Selecting project	132	80	29
Deciding level and distribution of community labor contribution in project construction	132	36	33
Deciding level and distribution of community nonlabor (cash) contribution in project construction	132	24	30
Deciding wage to be paid for community labor used in project construction	132	36	35
Deciding on any compensation paid for nonlabor community resources used in project construction (e.g., land given up)	119	13	25
Labor work for project construction	132	85	24
Monetary contribution for project construction	132	36	41
Deciding project usage/access rules (e.g., who gets to use the project when)	132	13	23
Deciding sanction measures for project misuse (e.g., amount and nature of fines levied)	132	14	21
Raising internal (to community) funds for project construction and maintenance	132	9	19
Deciding on distribution of project benefits (e.g., allocation of water, electricity across households)	129	19	32
Deciding on maintenance system, policies, and rules	132	20	29
Deciding on level and distribution of community monetary contribution in project maintenance	132	17	28
Deciding on level and distribution of community labor work toward project maintenance	132	28	34
Deciding on nature, level, and extent of any sanctions imposed for not participating in project maintenance	132	22	29
Overall participation in nontechnical decisions	132	30	19
Technical			
Deciding project site	132	23	31
Deciding project scale (length, capacity)	132	18	27
Deciding design of project	132	11	21
Deciding time frame for project construction	132	10	19
Raising external (to community) funds for project construction and maintenance	132	22	34
Overall participation in technical decisions	132	17	18

Note: Participation is measured in percentage terms. Thus 80 percent mean participation in the first decision (selecting the project) implies that of all respondents surveyed in all 132 projects, 80 percent said they had directly participated in the decision. In contrast, only 23 percent of the respondents had directly participated in deciding the site of the project.

measures and desirable outcomes. The following examples, in the areas of information and influence, illustrate the point.

First consider measures related to information, in the context of the Baltistan study. Suppose that knowledge available about the society and field-work both suggest that the traditional and effective way to elicit information from the villagers is to hold a public meeting where everyone can express his or her views openly. The implication is that a possible measure of empower-ment is the extent to which all villagers have access to such public meetings. Similarly, one may judge that it is better to hold such a meeting at a traditional public gathering point rather than in an individual's home. Once such a mea-sure has been implemented in the context of a particular project, it becomes possible to test whether such an information exchange actually has the expected effect on project outcomes.

A different context might imply a different measure of information ex-change. In a more hierarchical setting, for example, information might be harder to elicit through public meetings. In such a case, the relevant question to ask is whether each villager is able to express his or her opinions individually and pri-vately. This is better done by speaking with villagers individually in their homes rather than in a central place open to public observation. In such a context empowerment would be measured not by access to public meetings but rather by the degree to which individuals had opportunities to offer their opinions pri-vately. Yet a third context might require setting up local coordination mecha-nisms so that each person is assured that others will also be willing to report. This might be the case if no one wants to "snitch" on a fellow community mem-ber, even if that member is taking undue advantage or misusing a public good.

Before suggesting potential measures for influence, it is necessary to detail the elements needed to define influence in a particular context. Influence takes its meaning in reference to a particular activity or event: one talks about in-fluence *in* a society, electoral campaign, or project. In the Baltistan study the issue is influence in public projects.

In turn, one can subdivide such an activity into attributes, and then con-sider influence with respect to each one. Relevant attributes for an irrigation channel project might include the project design and length, duration and method of construction, maintenance system, and so on. Table 12.1 lists various actions and decisions that were considered in the Baltistan study as important attributes of a public project.

Once an activity is characterized by such a set of attributes, an individual's influence on a particular attribute can be defined as his or her control right over this attribute. The following example illustrates how such a consideration can help refine the measure. A meeting is held to decide which project will be built in a village. All the villagers show up at the meeting and a decision is reached after some negotiations. This may be considered empowering since all the villagers attended the meeting. Bringing rights into the picture allows a more precise perspective. One may consider both (a) attending the meeting and (b) voting in the meeting. While all villagers had the right to attend, and did in fact show up, there is no reason to presume that all had the right to vote on decisions. If the decision was in fact made by the village head, then the influence of other villagers might have been quite low. What measure to use to capture this control right will thus depend on the context. In the context of the Baltistan study, asking whether an individual participated in a certain decision was considered an effective way to measure such rights, because the society was not too hierarchical and therefore nominal participation was believed to result in real influence.

Finally, influence measured for individual units (persons, groups, or countries) can subsequently be aggregated, with a group's influence on an activity considered to be a function of the individual members' influence. In the Baltistan study, the procedure was to conduct individual interviews and ask community members whether they or their household members had participated (either directly or through a proxy) in various decisions about the project. Empowerment at the community level was then estimated by averaging these responses. Table 12.1 gives the average participation levels for each of these decisions in all the projects surveyed. These participation levels then serve as measures of influence and hence empowerment of the community.[3]

In sum, the process proceeds in a series of steps. First one identifies the relevant attributes that define an activity. Table 12.1, for example, lists some of the decisions that affect a public project, ranging from the selection and conceptualization of the project to its implementation, usage, and maintenance. For each attribute, one then considers the control rights over the attribute and how individuals have access to those rights. In the Baltistan study, this was done by aggregating the nominal participation of a representative group of project beneficiaries in the community. Such a simple technique illustrates the approach, and can be elaborated as desired. For example, one could also introduce individuals' relative power in the group, indicated by wealth or socioeconomic status (see note 2), or consider the role actors outside or inside the group play in affecting the relative influence of group members. In this regard, mixed-methods approaches, relying on techniques other than survey questions, can be extremely useful in shedding additional light on information flows and relative influence structures.

The main benefit of the approach suggested here is to provide a structure for measuring influence without making the concept overly rigid. The researcher or practitioner must ask what influence means, whose influence is referred to, and how an activity is best described. In order to operationalize control rights, it is also necessary to consider the underlying power structure in the particular context. The approach allows flexibility. It does not presume, for example, that increasing an agent's influence is necessarily beneficial to the agent's welfare. What control rights are considered optimal depends on which agent has the most to offer to the outcome, although such judgments may be particularly difficult if the resulting reallocation of rights leads to undesirable equity outcomes.

While the discussion above examines empowerment as a means rather than an end, similar considerations of constructing measures according to a theoretical framework and specific context would apply if empowerment were viewed as an end. In either case, however, the next step of subjecting measures to empirical tests is particularly challenging. For example, if we view empowerment as a means to an end, then we need to establish that the empowerment measures are indeed causally related to the end. Moreover, even if empowerment is viewed as an end, it is likely that the measures that one arrives at are not obviously indicative of empowerment. It may then be necessary to strengthen the conceptual case by establishing a causal link between such measures and other acknowledged indicators of empowerment. The next section of this chapter addresses potential issues in establishing such causal links.

Establishing Causality

While coming up with the appropriate theoretically based instruments is a crucial step toward formulating an empowerment-based development framework, there is another essential step. That is to *empirically* establish causality from a measure to the desired outcome (be it empowerment or a socioeconomic end). It is not possible to infer the direction of causation simply from correlations, since the measure being taken as a cause may itself be influenced by other factors affecting the outcome or by the outcome itself. Such "endogeneity" problems must be addressed in order to confirm that the observed relationship between the proposed measure and the desired outcome is in fact a causal one.

The estimate of the relationship between the measure of interest and the outcome may be incorrect because the measure is correlated to the part of the outcome that remains unexplained (that is, the measure is endogenous). There are a variety of reasons why such endogeneity problems may arise, as illustrated in figure 12.2. The figure shows both the causal relationship from empowerment to welfare factor that we are trying to establish and problems that may make establishing such a relationship difficult.

One classic problem, illustrated in figure 12.2 in the bottom-right box, is that of an "omitted" variable. This is a variable that affects both the outcome

Figure 12.2   Empowerment as a Means: The Problem of Causality

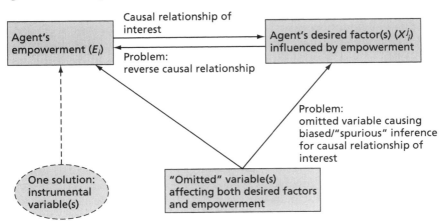

(the factor affecting the agent's welfare) and the empowerment measure. If this is not taken into account, one may erroneously assume a causal relationship between empowerment and the outcome when in fact the correlation is instead explained by a third factor—the omitted variable. In the context of the Baltistan study, suppose participation in project decisions is taken as a measure of empowerment. Our outcome of interest is project performance since it is expected that better-performing projects raise agent welfare. However, even if there is a positive relation between participation and the project performance, it may be incorrect to assume a causal relationship. Both project participation and performance may be influenced by a third factor, such as the level of organization of the community. In this case, the effect of the level of organization of the community might be mistakenly identified as the effect of participation. In an extreme case, participation may have no effect on performance at all; the relationship may be entirely spurious, that is, entirely due to the factor(s) not specified in the model. While this problem can be corrected by simply including this omitted factor, such variables are often hard or even impossible to measure even when they are identified.

Alternatively, as also illustrated in figure 12.2, the actual relationship may be fully or partly the reverse of what we imagine, that is, the empowerment measure may itself be affected by the outcome of interest. Continuing with the earlier example, it could be that if a project is doing well, then participation in the project increases. In this case, the causal relationship is not that participation of the community *causes* a project to perform well but rather that a well-performing project *attracts* community members and increases their participation. This problem can partly be addressed by collecting information on participation in decisions that took place prior to a project's performance being revealed. However, as such information is often collected by using recall data, one may still get reverse causation through "halo" effects; that is, a respondent may tend to report greater prior participation for projects that are currently doing well. One possible solution, used in the Baltistan study, was to show that such halo effects are unlikely by demonstrating that respondents who declared higher project participation were not more likely to report that the project was in a better state. Such solutions may not be possible in many cases, and instead more general empirical techniques will be required.

There is a wide array of empirical methods intended to address such concerns, ranging from careful experimental design to the use of instrumental variables and fixed-effect estimations. Each tries to solve the above problems by establishing or creating exogeneity of the causal factor of interest. In other words, one tries to construct situations where it is clear that the factor in question is not correlated with the unexplained part of the outcome—that is, it is "exogenous."

In randomized or experimental design techniques (prevalent in the medical sciences) one creates such exogeneity by randomly assigning a "treatment" (the factor of interest) to some groups but not others. In the Baltistan study this would have involved selecting some projects at random and introducing community participation in them but not in others. However, carrying out such experimental studies is often not feasible for practical reasons or is undesirable on ethical or fairness grounds.

The instrumental variables approach relies on identifying a measure or instrument associated with the causal factor of interest—the measure of empowerment—that is known or assumed not to be causally linked to the outcome. For example, for the participation measure, it could be the case that among two projects implemented by the same external agency, one took place before a change in the agency's policies in the direction of greater participation. This change in the agency could then be used as an instrumental variable for participation. However, one also has to argue that this instrument only affects the outcome through the particular measure of empowerment and not directly or through any other unobserved factor. These conditions are relatively stringent, and it is often difficult to find suitable instruments.

Finally, a "fixed effects" approach tries to get around these problems by forcing a comparison *only* across projects for which there is unlikely to be an endogeneity problem. This approach was used in the Baltistan study. Consider again the relationship between participation (the empowerment measure) and project performance. To respond to the concern that more "organized" communities have both higher participation and better performance, one could only compare projects within the same community. Since the omitted community-level variable would be the same for all projects in a community, it could not be responsible for any observed differences. Such an approach, however, would of course not compensate for possible omitted variables at the project level.

The point here is not to recommend these particular techniques or others that could be added. It is rather to stress that causality is an essential issue to address in evaluating measures of empowerment. A plausible relationship between an empowerment measure and a particular outcome is not adequately verified by observing a correlation between the two. Such a correlation is simply an *association* and *not necessarily a causal relation*. One can advance toward establishing causality by considering other possible reasons that the measure of empowerment may be related to the outcome. Often some concerns can be allayed by a careful examination of the context or by drawing on other quantitative or qualitative sources. Remaining concerns may be addressed, to whatever extent possible, by use of the empirical techniques outlined above. The degree to which all concerns can be addressed will, of course, vary. However, any researcher or practitioner must at least acknowledge and discuss these concerns and evaluate how serious are those that are not fully addressed.

Conclusions

In sum, in order to develop an empowerment framework for development that can be implemented, it is necessary first to distinguish between aspects of empowerment that are considered of direct value, that is, as ends in themselves, and those that are means to an end. If one takes the first view, then there needs to be a justification that a particular aspect of empowerment is itself valuable, in sufficient detail to allow for specifying measures of empowerment and then empirically establishing that they indeed causally affect empowerment.

If empowerment is instead viewed as a means to specific ends, such as commonly valued socioeconomic outcomes, then a theory is required specifying how empowerment is hypothesized to affect these outcomes, followed by procedures to establish empirically that the empowerment measures are causally related to such outcomes. In this chapter, the second alternative was illustrated by developing an outline of a theory of empowerment in terms of information and influence affecting project performance outcomes. The theory was then combined with context-dependent knowledge to develop measures.

The chapter made use of an economist's perspective and focused on survey-based measures in particular. However, the framework developed should also prove amenable to the use of other methods. The critical point is that any measures developed, whether survey-based or otherwise, must not only be based on theory and specified plausibly, but must also be tested by methods that attempt to establish causality. Such a process, moving from theory to measures to empirical tests, may seem overly exacting. But it is essential if empowerment is to avoid the fate of previous development slogans that have been misunderstood, misapplied, and eventually discarded.

Figure 12.1 illustrates the two possible relationships between empowerment and the desired outcome, increased welfare of the agent. These correspond to equations (1) and (2) mentioned above. In relationship (1), empowerment is directly included in agent welfare, along with other factors. Since this relationship is definitionally true—empowerment is defined to be part of agent welfare—it is represented by a circle. However, even in this formulation, whether a particular *measure* affects empowerment is unlikely to be definitionally true and would need to be causally established (this can be illustrated by a directed arrow from the measure to agent empowerment but has not been included in the figure to keep it simple). Relationship (2) shows empowerment (or any of its measures) as affecting factors that are components of agent welfare. Since this is a hypothesized causal relationship, it is indicated by a directed arrow.

Figure 12.2 highlights the problem of causality where one is trying to infer that a particular measure of empowerment causes an increase in a factor that affects agent welfare (such as agent wealth). The figure illustrates the causal relationship of interest but also shows two problems, reverse causality and omitted variables, that may lead to difficulties in establishing the correlation between the empowerment measure and the welfare factor as causal. It also illustrates one possible solution of using instrumental variables (that only affect the empowerment measure but do not directly affect the welfare factor or the other omitted variables).

Notes

1.   For 9 percent of all projects surveyed, community members said that they had chosen the project from a list of projects they "knew" the external agency provided or had suggested. This proportion is quite large given that the external agencies we

examined were, if anything, far more careful than is typical about using participatory tools to elicit community preferences. Interestingly, another 10 percent of projects were chosen either because they were perceived as having been suggested by the external agency or because they had been chosen by a neighboring village.

2.   Community heterogeneity has a detrimental effect on overall project upkeep while inequality across community members has a U-shaped relationship, with initial increases lowering project upkeep (Khwaja 2001). The theory outlined here did not explore empowerment *within* a community (i.e., empowering one community member relative to another). However, one can envisage a framework in which community heterogeneity and inequality would affect a member's influence and hence degree of empowerment *within* the community. This may in turn affect how well a collective task, such as upkeep of a public project, is performed.

3.   In fact, the participation measures can also be thought of as measures that capture the informational aspect of empowerment, since it is likely that greater participation of the community also means that it is providing and receiving more information. These measures are divided into those relating to nontechnical decisions and those relating to technical decisions. This is because the theory suggests that decisions that benefit more from local information (nontechnical decisions) are best decided primarily by the community, while decisions requiring technical inputs are best left to those who can offer such technical advice. In the context of this study, the latter implied participation by an external agency's engineers. The study confirmed the validity of making such a distinction: while community participation in nontechnical decisions increased sustainability of the local public good, community participation in technical decisions actually decreased sustainability. Without the theory, we would have aggregated community participation in all types of decisions, thereby missing the two opposite effects. Thus the theory was essential not only in arriving at each measure, but also in telling us how they should be grouped.

References

Grossman, Sandy J., and Oliver D. Hart. 1986. "The Costs and Benefits of Ownership: A Theory of Vertical and Lateral Integration." *Journal of Political Economy* 94 (4): 691–719.

Hart, Oliver, and John Moore. 1990. "Property Rights and the Nature of the Firm." *Journal of Political Economy* 98 (6): 1119–58.

Isham, Jonathan, Deepa Narayan, and Lant Pritchett. 1995. "Does Participation Improve Performance? Establishing Causality with Subjective Data." *World Bank Economic Review* 9 (2): 175–200.

Khwaja, Asim Ijaz. 2001. "Can Good Projects Succeed in Bad Communities? Collective Action in the Himalayas." Faculty Research Working Paper RWP01–043, Kennedy School of Government, Harvard University, Cambridge, MA.

———. 2004. "Is Increasing Community Participation Always a Good Thing?" *Journal of the European Economic Association* 2 (2–3): 427–36.

Mansuri, Ghazala, and Vijayendra Rao. 2004. "Community-Based and -Driven Development: A Critical Review." Policy Research Working Paper 3209, World Bank, Washington, DC.

Narayan, Deepa. 1995. "The Contribution of People's Participation: Evidence from 121 Rural Water Supply Projects." ESD Occasional Paper Series 1, World Bank, Washington, DC.

———, ed. 2002. *Empowerment and Poverty Reduction: A Sourcebook*. Washington, DC: World Bank.

Tendler, Judith. 1997. *Good Government in the Tropics*. Baltimore: Johns Hopkins University Press.

Uphoff, Norman. 1996. *Learning from Gal Oya: Possibilities for Participatory Development and Post-Newtonian Social Science*. London: Intermediate Technology Publications.

World Bank. 1996. *The World Bank Participation Sourcebook*. Washington, DC: World Bank.

Chapter 13

Mixing Qualitative and Econometric Methods: Community-Level Applications

Vijayendra Rao and Michael Woolcock

Integrating qualitative and quantitative approaches in the measurement of empowerment can help yield insights that neither approach would produce on its own. In assessing the impact of programs and policies designed to empower the poor, researchers should recognize that both quantitative and qualitative methods have some important limitations when used in isolation, and that some of these can be overcome by incorporating complementary approaches. This chapter examines the strengths and weaknesses of orthodox stand-alone quantitative and qualitative approaches and proposes a basic framework for integrating them. It illustrates this with practical examples of using "mixed-methods" approaches in the measurement of empowerment at the community level in diverse settings.

Assessing the Merits of Quantitative and Qualitative Approaches

The advantages of quantitative methods for measuring program effectiveness in general, and empowerment in particular, are well known. Used properly, they permit generalizations to be made about large populations on the basis of much smaller (representative) samples. Given a set of identifying conditions, they can help establish the causality of the impact of given variables on project outcomes. In principle, they also allow other researchers to validate the original findings by independently replicating the analysis. Quantitative researchers argue that by remaining several steps removed from the people from whom data have been obtained, and by collecting and analyzing the data in numerical form, they are upholding research standards that are at once empirically rigorous, impartial, objective, and (potentially) reproducible.

In social science research, however, these same strengths can also be a weakness. Many of the most important issues in empowering the poor—their identities, perceptions, aspirations, and beliefs, for example—cannot be meaningfully reduced to numbers or adequately understood without reference to the immediate context in which they live. Most surveys are designed far from the places where they will be administered and for this reason tend to reflect the preconceptions and biases of the researchers; there is little opportunity to be "surprised" by new discoveries or unexpected findings. Although good surveys undergo several rounds of rigorous pretesting, the questions themselves are not usually developed using systematically collected insights from the field. Thus, while pretesting can identify and correct questions that are clearly ill-suited to the task, these problems can be considerably mitigated by the judicious use of qualitative methods in the process of developing the questionnaire.

Qualitative methods can also help in circumstances where a quantitative survey may be difficult to administer. Certain marginalized communities, for example, are relatively small in number (the disabled, widows) or difficult for outsiders to access (sex workers, victims of domestic abuse), rendering them unlikely subjects for study through a large representative survey. In many developing country settings, even central governments—let alone local nongovernmental organizations or public service providers—lack the skills and especially the resources needed to conduct a thorough quantitative analysis. Moreover, external researchers who have little or no familiarity with the local area or even the country in question often draw on data from context-specific household surveys to make broad "policy recommendations," yet rarely provide useful results to local program officials or the poor themselves. Scholars working from qualitative research traditions in development studies contend that their approaches rectify some of these problems by providing more detailed attention to context, reaching out to members of minority groups, working with available information and resources, and engaging the poor as partners in the collection, analysis, and interpretation of data in many forms.[1]

Furthermore, quantitative methods are best suited to measuring levels and changes in impacts and to drawing inferences from observed statistical relations between those impacts and other covariates. They are less effective in understanding *process*—that is, the mechanisms by which a particular outcome is instigated by a series of events that ultimately result in the observed impact. These process issues are central to understanding empowerment. For example, consider a community-driven development (CDD) project that sets up a committee in a village and provides it with funds to build a primary school. Even if a perfect quantitative impact evaluation were conducted, it would typically measure quantitative outcomes such as the causal impact of the CDD funds on increasing school enrollment or whether benefits were well targeted to the poor. With carefully constructed questions, one could perhaps get at some more subtle issues, such as the heterogeneity in levels of participation in decision making across different groups, or even more subjective outcomes such as changes in levels of intergroup trust in the village. Nevertheless, the quantitative analysis would not be very effective in describing the local politics in the village that led to the formation of the committee or the details pertaining to deliberations within it. How were certain groups included and others excluded? How did some individuals come to dominate the process? These and other process issues can be crucial to *understanding* impact, as opposed to simply *measuring* it. Qualitative methods are particularly effective in delving deep into issues of process; a judicious mix of qualitative and quantitative methods can therefore help provide a more comprehensive evaluation of an intervention.

Qualitative approaches on their own, of course, also suffer from a number of important drawbacks. First, the individuals or groups being studied are usually small in number or have not been randomly selected, making it highly problematic though not impossible to draw generalizations about the wider population. Second, groups are often selected idiosyncratically (for example, on the basis of a judgment call by the lead investigator) or on the recommendation of other participants (as with "snowball" sampling procedures, in which one informant—say, a corrupt public official—agrees to provide access to the next one). This makes it difficult to replicate, and thus independently verify, the results. Third, the analysis of qualitative data often involves interpretative judgments on the part of the researcher, and two researchers looking at the same data may arrive at different conclusions. Quantitative methods are less prone to such subjectivities in interpretation, though not entirely free of them. Fourth, because of an inability to "control" for other mitigating factors or to establish the counterfactual (that is, what would have happened in the absence of the intervention), it is hard, though again not impossible, to make compelling claims regarding causality.[2]

It should be apparent that the strengths of one approach potentially complement the weaknesses of the other, and vice versa. Unfortunately, however, research in development studies generally, and the measurement of empowerment in particular, tends to be heavily polarized along quantitative and qualitative methodological lines. That is largely because researchers are selected, trained, socialized, evaluated, and rewarded by single disciplines (and their peers and superiors within them) with clear preferences for one research tradition over the other. This practice ensures intellectual coherence and "quality control," but discourages innovation and forfeits any potential gains that could be derived from integrating different approaches. We are hardly the first to recognize the limitations of different approaches or to call for more methodological pluralism in development research—indeed, notable individuals at least since Epstein (1962) have made path-breaking empirical contributions by working across methodological lines.[3] What we are trying to do, however, is to take the strengths and weaknesses of each approach seriously and discern practical (if no less difficult) strategies for combining them on a more regular basis as part of attempts to better understand issues such as empowerment (see also Kanbur 2003; Rao 2002; White 2002).[4] What might this entail?

Distinguishing between Data and Methods in the Measurement of Empowerment

A possible point of departure for thinking more systematically about mixed-methods approaches to measuring empowerment is to distinguish between forms of data and the methods used to collect data (see Hentschel 1999). This distinction posits that data can be either quantitative (numbers) or qualitative (text), just as the methods used to collect those data can also be quantitative (for example, large representative surveys) or qualitative (such as interviews or observation). This gives rise to a simple 2 × 2 matrix (figure 13.1). Most development research and program evaluation strategies call upon quantitative data and methods or qualitative data and methods (that is, the upper right or lower left quadrants). It is instructive to note, however, that qualitative methods can also be used to collect quantitative data—see for example the detailed household data from a single village in India over several decades, reported in Bliss and Stern (1982) and Lanjouw and Stern (1998). Similarly, quantitative methods can be used to collect qualitative data, as when open-ended or "subjective" response questions are included in large surveys (for example, Ravallion and Pradhan 2000), or when quantitative measures are derived from a large number of qualitative responses (for example, Isham, Narayan, and Pritchett 1995). Other examples from development that fall into this latter category include comparative case study research, where the number of cases is necessarily small, but the units of analysis are large—such as the impact of the East Asian financial crisis on Korea, Thailand, and Indonesia.

Figure 13.1   Types of Data and Methods

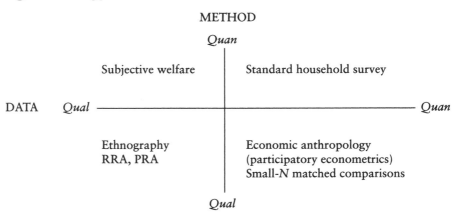

Source: Adapted from Hentschel (1999).
Note: RRA = rapid rural appraisal; PRA = participatory rural appraisal.

Having made this distinction, we will consider in more detail the nature of some of the qualitative methods that are available to development researchers, before exploring some of the ways in which these methods could be usefully incorporated into a more comprehensive mixed-methods strategy for evaluating empowerment programs and projects. Three approaches are identified: participation, ethnography, and textual analysis. The particular focus of this chapter is on the use of qualitative methods to generate more and better quantitative data and to understand the process by which an empowerment intervention works, in addition to ascertaining its overall final impact.[5]

The first category of qualitative methods can be referred to as participatory approaches (Mikkelsen 1995; Narayan 1995; Robb 2002). Introduced to scholars and practitioners largely through the work of Robert Chambers (see, most recently, Kumar and Chambers 2002), participatory techniques such as rapid rural appraisal (RRA) and participatory poverty assessment (PPA) help outsiders learn about poverty and project impacts in cost-effective ways that reflect experience on the ground. Since the rapid rural appraisal is usually conducted with respondents who are illiterate, RRA researchers seek to learn about the lives of the poor using simple techniques such as wealth rankings, oral histories, role playing, games, small group discussions, and village map drawings. These techniques permit respondents who are not trained in quantitative reasoning, or who are illiterate, to provide meaningful graphic representations of their lives in a manner that can give outside researchers a quick snapshot of an aspect of their living conditions. RRA can be said to deploy *instrumental* participation research, in which novel techniques are being used to help the researcher better understand her or his subjects. A related approach is to use *transformative* participation techniques, such as participatory rural appraisal (PRA). In this case the goal is to facilitate a dialogue, rather than extract information, to help the poor learn about themselves and thereby gain new insights that can lead to social change ("empowerment").[6] In PRA exercises, a skilled facilitator helps villagers or slum dwellers draw visual diagrams of the processes that lead to deprivation and illness, of the strategies that they use in times of crisis, and of the fluctuation of resource availability and prices across different seasons. Eliciting information in this format helps the poor conceive of potentially more effective ways to respond, in ways that were not previously obvious, to the economic, political, and social challenges in their lives.

A crucial aspect of participatory methods is that they are typically conducted in groups. Therefore, it is essential that recruitment of participants be conducted so that representatives from each of the major subcommunities in the village are included. The idea is that if the group reaches a consensus on a particular issue after some discussion, then this consensus will be representative of views in the village because outlying views would have been set aside in the process of debate. For this technique to work, however, the discussion has to be extremely well moderated. The moderator must be dynamic enough to steer the discussion in a meaningful direction, deftly navigating his or her way around potential conflicts and, by the end, establishing a consensus. The moderator's role is therefore key to ensuring that high-quality data are gathered in a group discussion; indeed, an inept or inexperienced moderator can affect the quality of the data much more acutely than an equivalently inept interviewer working with a structured quantitative questionnaire. Alternatively, with particularly vulnerable groups such as widows, it is usually best to conduct participatory exercises with homogeneous groups, both to give members a sense of support as they speak (often about quite painful subjects) and to ensure that more dominant groups or individuals do not, intentionally or otherwise, drive the discussion.

Other oft-used qualitative techniques face similar constraints. Focus group discussions, for example, in which small, intentionally diverse or homogeneous groups discuss a particular issue, are also guided by a moderator, whose task is to discern consensus on key issues. Focus groups are thus similarly dependent on the quality of the moderator for the quality of the insights they yield. A focus group differs from a PRA in that it is primarily instrumental in purpose and typically does not use the mapping and diagramming techniques that are characteristic of a PRA or RRA. Here, however, it should be noted that divergence from the consensus can also provide interesting insights, just as outliers in a regression can sometimes be very revealing. Another important qualitative technique that uses interview methods is the key-informant interview, which is an extended one-on-one exchange with someone who is a leader or unique in some way that is relevant to the study. Finally, the qualitative investigator can undertake varying degrees of "participant observation," in which the researcher engages a community at a particular distance—as an actual member (for example, someone who writes a memoir of growing up in a slum), as a perceived actual member (a spy or police informant in a drug cartel, for example), as an invited long-term guest (such as an anthropologist), or as a more distant and detached short-term observer.[7]

A fifth qualitative approach is textual analysis. Historians, archeologists, linguists, and scholars in cultural studies use such techniques to analyze various forms of media, ranging from archived legal documents, newspapers, artifacts, and government records to contemporary photographs, films, music, and television reports. (An example below shows the use of textual analysis in supplementing quantitative surveys in an evaluation of democratic decentralization in India.) Participatory, ethnographic, and textual research methods are too often seen as antithetical to or a poor substitute for quantitative approaches. In the examples that follow, we show how qualitative and quantitative methods have been usefully combined in development research and the measurement of empowerment, providing in combination what neither could ever do alone.

Mixed-Methods Research and Empowerment: Pitfalls, Principles, and Examples

Having briefly outlined the *types* of qualitative methods available to researchers and evaluators, we now sketch the different *methods of integrating* qualitative and quantitative techniques. The examples presented below are drawn from attempts to combine different methodological traditions in empowerment research, but we stress from the outset that there are several good (as well as bad) reasons why mixed methods are not adopted more frequently. First, integrating different perspectives necessarily requires recruiting individuals with different skill sets, which makes such projects costly in terms of time, talent, and resources. Second, coordinating the large teams of people with diverse backgrounds that are often required for serious mixed-methods projects generates coordination challenges above and beyond those normally associated with program evaluation. Third, these challenges, combined with institutional imperatives for quick turnaround and for "straightforward" policy recommendations, mean that mixed-methods research is often poorly done. Fourth, we simply lack an extensive body of evidence regarding the ways that different methods can best be combined under particular circumstances; more research experience is needed to help answer these questions and guide future efforts.

These concerns notwithstanding, it is nonetheless possible to discern a number of core principles and strategies for successfully mixing methods in project evaluation. The most important of these is to begin with an important, interesting, and researchable question and then to identify the most appropriate method (or combination of methods) that is likely to yield fruitful answers (Mills 1959). If taken seriously, this principle is actually remarkably difficult to live up to, since it is rare to find a good question that maps neatly and exclusively onto a single method. Three fields in which faithful efforts have been made, however, are comparative politics, anthropological demography, and anthropological economics. The first concerns itself primarily with questions that give rise to small sample sizes and large units of analysis—most commonly case studies of countries or large organizations studied historically—and is not discussed in detail here.[8] The second and third, however, are better suited to large sample sizes and small units of analysis, and thus lessons from them are especially relevant to efforts to mix methods in research and evaluation pertaining to the measurement of empowerment.[9]

Methods of Integration

Qualitative and quantitative methods can be integrated in three different ways, which for convenience we call *parallel, sequential,* and *iterative.* In parallel approaches, the quantitative and qualitative research teams work separately but compare and combine findings during the analysis phase. This approach is best suited to very large projects, such as national-level poverty assessments, where closer forms of integration are precluded by logistical and administrative realities. In the Guatemala poverty assessment (World Bank 2003), for example, two separate teams were responsible for collecting the qualitative and quantitative data. Previous survey material was used to help identify the appropriate sites for the qualitative work (five pairs of villages representing five major ethnic groups in Guatemala). But the findings themselves were treated as an independent source of data and were integrated with the quantitative material only in the write-up phase of both the various background papers and the final report. That is, while useful in their own right, the qualitative data did not inform the design or construction of the quantitative survey, which was done separately. These different data sources were especially helpful in providing a more accurate map of the spatial and demographic diversity of the poor, as well as, crucially, a sense of the immediate context within which different ethnic groups experienced poverty, details of the local mechanisms that excluded them from participation in mainstream economic and civic activities, and the nature of the barriers they encountered in their efforts to advance their interests and aspirations. The final report also benefited from a concerted effort to place both the qualitative and quantitative findings in their broader historical and political context, a first for a World Bank country poverty study.

Sequential and iterative approaches—which we call more specifically *participatory econometrics*—seek varying degrees of dialogue between the qualitative and quantitative traditions at all phases of the research cycle and are best suited to projects of more modest scale and scope.[10] Though the most technically complex and time consuming, these approaches are where the greatest gains are to be found from mixing methods in project and policy evaluation. Participatory econometrics works on the following premises:

- The researcher should begin a project with some general hypotheses and questions, but should keep an open mind regarding the results and even the possibility that the hypotheses and questions themselves may be in need of major revision.
- The researcher should both collect and analyze data.
- A mix of qualitative and quantitative data is typically used to create an understanding of both measured impact and the processes that resulted in the impact.
- Respondents should be actively involved in the analysis and interpretation of findings.
- It is desirable (especially for policy purposes) to be able to make broad generalizations and discern the nature of causality; consequently, relatively large sample sizes and quantitative data amenable to econometric analysis are likely to be needed.

This approach characterizes recent research on survival and mobility strategies in the slums of Delhi, in which extensive qualitative investigation in four different slum communities preceded the design of a survey that was then administered to 800 randomly selected households from all officially listed Delhi slums (Jha, Rao, and Woolcock, forthcoming). The qualitative material not only made it possible to design a better survey, it also provided useful information about governance structures, migration histories, the nature and extent of property rights, and mechanisms underpinning the procurement of housing, employment, and public services.

The classical, or sequential, approach to participatory econometrics entails three main steps. First, researchers use PRA-type techniques, focus group discussions, in-depth interviews, or all three, to obtain a grounded understanding of the primary issues. Second, they construct a survey instrument that integrates understandings from the field. Third, the researchers derive hypotheses from qualitative work and test them with survey data. An intermediate step of constructing theoretical models to generate hypotheses may also be added (Rao 1997).

An example of the use of sequential mixed methods in measuring empowerment is a study of the impact of social investment funds in Jamaica (Rao and Ibáñez, forthcoming). The research team compiled case study evidence from five matched pairs of communities in Kingston. In each pair, one community had received funds from the Jamaica Social Investment Fund (JSIF) while the other had not; the nonfunded community was selected to match the funded community as closely as possible in terms of social and economic characteristics. The qualitative data revealed that the JSIF process was elite-driven, with decision-making processes dominated by a small group of motivated individuals, but that by the end of the project there was nonetheless broad-based satisfaction with the outcome. The quantitative data from 500 households mirrored these findings. These data showed that, initially, the social fund did not address the expressed needs of the majority of individuals in the majority of communities. By the end of the JSIF cycle, however, during which new facilities were constructed, 80 percent of the community expressed satisfaction with the outcome. A quantitative analysis of the determinants of participation demonstrated that individuals who had higher levels of education and more extensive networks dominated the process. Propensity-score analysis revealed that the JSIF had a causal impact on improvements in trust and the capacity for collective action, but that these gains were greater for elites within the community. This evidence suggests that both JSIF and non-JSIF communities are now more likely to make decisions that affect their lives—a positive finding indicative of widespread efforts to promote participatory development in the country—but that JSIF communities do not show higher levels of community-driven decisions than non-JSIF communities. A particular strength of this analysis is that here a development project that is both "qualitative" (participatory decision making) and "quantitative" (allocating funds to build physical infrastructure) *by design* has been evaluated using corresponding mixed methods.

An iterative approach to participatory econometrics is similar to the sequential approach, but it involves regularly returning to the field to clarify questions and resolve apparent anomalies. Here, qualitative findings can be regarded as an initial source of information, but one that must be updated with quantitative investigation. One example comes from a study conducted among potters in rural Karnataka, India. Research on marriage markets in this population led to work on domestic violence (Rao 1998; Bloch and Rao 2002), on unit price differentials in everyday goods, that is, why poor people pay more than rich people for the same goods (Rao 2000), and on public festivals (Rao 2001a, 2001b). The initial interest in marriage markets thus evolved in several different but unanticipated directions, uncovering understudied phenomena that were of signal importance in the lives of the people being studied. Moreover, the subjects of the research, with their participation in PRAs and PPAs, focus group discussions, and in-depth interviews, played a significant role in shaping how research questions were defined. This made an important contribution to the analysis and informed the subsequent econometric work, which tested the generalizability of the qualitative findings, measuring the magnitude of the effects and their causal determinants.

Iterative mixed-methods approaches to empowerment research are most likely to be useful in projects that have a diverse range of possible impacts, some of which may be unknown or unintended, and where some form of "participation" has been a central component of project design and implementation. Two evaluations of participatory (community-driven development) projects currently under way in Indonesia demonstrate the benefits of using iterative mixed-methods approaches. The first is concerned with designing a methodology for identifying the extent of a range of impacts associated with a project emphasizing the empowerment of the urban poor (known as the Urban Poverty Project 2, or UPP2). The second deals with assessing whether and how a similar project already operating for three years in rural areas (the Kecamatan Development Program, or KDP) helps to mediate local conflict.

UPP2 is a CDD project that provides money directly to communities to fund infrastructure projects and microcredit. To do this, the project organizes an elected committee called the BKM. In addition to poverty alleviation and improvements in service delivery, one of UPP2's goals is to create an accountable system of governance in poor urban communities. Here again, both outcomes and process are of interest, and therefore the evaluation is a prime candidate for a mixed-methods approach. The evaluation follows a difference-in-difference approach, in which a baseline survey is conducted in a random sample of communities that will benefit from the intervention. These communities have been matched using a poverty score employed by the government to target UPP2 to poor communities. The "control" communities are those with low poverty scores in relatively rich districts, whereas the "experimental" communities are those with high scores in relatively poor districts.

In the UPP2, two rounds of fieldwork were conducted by an interdisciplinary team of economists, urban planners, and social anthropologists.[11] In the first round, two to three days of field visits were conducted in each of eight communities that had benefited from a similar project known as UPP1. The aim of this initial round of fieldwork was to understand the UPP2 process, decide on a data collection methodology, and identify "surprises," or unforeseen issues, that could affect the survey. Some of these issues included the key role that facilitators played in the success or failure of a project at the local level, the inherent competition between BKMs and existing mechanisms for governance (such as the municipal officer, or *pak lurah*), and the crucial role that custom, tradition, and local religious institutions played in facilitating collective action. A quantitative survey methodology was developed that would give an in-depth structured questionnaire to key informants such as the head of the BKM, the *pak lurah,* the community activist, and the local facilitator. In addition, a random sample of households within each community would receive a household questionnaire. When microcredit groups were formed in the experimental communities, they too would be given a household questionnaire.

To supplement this material, a qualitative baseline was also designed. The sample size of this baseline was limited by the high cost of conducting in-depth qualitative work in many communities. Therefore, it was decided to do a case-based comparative analysis. In each province researchers chose two "experimental communities" (one with a high degree of urbanization and the other with a low degree of urbanization) and two "control communities" (matched to the experimental communities using the poverty score). Since UPP2 is working in three provinces (Java, Kalimantan, and Sulawesi), this made for a total sample of 12 communities. A team of field investigators spent one week in each community conducting a series of focus group discussions, in-depth interviews, and key-informant interviews in two groups. One group snowballed[12] from the municipal office, focusing on the network of people around the formal government, while another group of investigators snowballed from the local mosque, church, or activist group to understand the role of informal networks and associations in the community. The idea is that the qualitative work provides in-depth insights into processes of decision making, the role of custom (*adat*) and tradition in collective action, and the propensity for elite capture in the community. Hypotheses generated from the qualitative data were then tested for their generalizability with the quantitative data.

Finally, the whole process will be repeated three years after the initiation of the project to collect follow-up data. The follow-up will provide a difference across control and experimental groups, and a second difference across time to isolate the causal impact of UPP2 on the community and to examine the process by which communities changed because of the UPP2 intervention.

The Kecamatan Development Program in Indonesia—the model on which the UPP2 program is based—is one of the world's largest social development projects, and Indonesia itself is a country experiencing wrenching conflict in the aftermath of the Suharto era and the East Asian financial crisis. Although primarily intended as a more efficient and effective mechanism for getting targeted small-scale development assistance to poor rural communities, KDP requires villagers to submit proposals for funding to a committee of their peers, thereby establishing a new (and, by design, inclusive) community forum for decision making on key issues (Guggenheim, forthcoming). Given the salience of conflict as a political and development issue in Indonesia, the question is whether these forums are able to complement existing local-level institutions for conflict resolution and in the process help villagers acquire a more diverse, peaceful, and effective set of civic skills for mediating local conflict. Such a question does not lend itself to an orthodox stand-alone quantitative or qualitative evaluation, but rather to an innovative mixed-methods approach (Barron, Smith, and Woolcock 2004).

In this instance, the team decided to begin with qualitative work, since there was surprisingly little quantitative data on conflict in Indonesia and even less on the mechanisms (or local processes) by which conflict is initiated, intensified, or resolved.[13] Selecting a small number of appropriate sites from across Indonesia's 13,500 islands and 350 language groups was not an easy task. However, the team decided that work should be done in two provinces that were very different demographically, in regions within those provinces that (according to local experts) demonstrated both a high and low capacity for conflict resolution, and in villages within those regions that were otherwise comparable as determined by propensity-score matching methods but that either did or did not participate in KDP. Such a design enables researchers to be confident that any common themes emerging across either the program or nonprogram sites are not wholly a product of idiosyncratic regional or institutional capacity factors. Thus quantitative methods were used to help select the appropriate sites for qualitative investigation, resulting in eight selected subdistricts (two demographically different regions by two high/low capacity provinces by two program/nonprogram subdistricts). Three months of intensive fieldwork was undertaken in each of these eight sites. The results from the qualitative work—useful in themselves for understanding process issues and the mechanisms by which local conflicts are created and addressed—will also feed into the design of a new quantitative survey instrument. This will be administered to a large sample of households from the two provinces and used to test the generality of the hypotheses and propositions emerging from the qualitative work.

A recent project evaluating the impact of *panchayat* (village government) reform in rural India also combines qualitative and quantitative data with a "natural experiment" design.[14] In 1994 the Indian government passed the 73rd amendment to the Indian constitution to give more power to democratically elected village governments by mandating that more funds be transferred to their control and that regular elections be held. One-third of the seats in the village council are reserved for women and another third for scheduled castes and tribes, groups that have traditionally been discriminated against.

The four southern Indian states of Karnataka, Kerala, Andhra Pradesh, and Tamil Nadu have implemented the 73rd amendment in different ways. Karnataka immediately began implementing the democratic reforms, Kerala emphasized greater financial autonomy, Tamil Nadu delayed elections by several years, and Andhra Pradesh emphasized alternative methods of village governance outside the *panchayat* system. Thus, contrasting the experiences of the four states could provide a nice test of the impact of decentralization on the quality of governance. The problem, of course, is that any differences across the four states could be attributed to differences between their cultures and histories (for instance, Kerala's outcomes might reflect the noted "Kerala model"). Culture and history are difficult to observe, so the evaluation design exploited a natural experiment.

The four states were created in 1955 in a manner that made them linguistically homogeneous. Before 1955, however, significant portions of the four states belonged to the same political entity and were either ruled directly by the British or placed within a semi-autonomous "princely state." When the states were reorganized, "mistakes" were made along the border regions. As a result, certain villages that originally belonged to the same political entity and shared the same culture and language found themselves placed in different states. Such villages along borders can be matched and compared to construct a "first difference," which controls for the effects of historical path dependency and culture. Data on levels of economic development and other covariates that could affect differences across states are also being collected, as are data on several quantitative outcomes, such as objective measures of the level and quality of public services in the village and perceptions of public service delivery at the village level.

One challenge is to study the extent of participation in public village meetings (*gram sabhas*) in which villagers and members of the governing committee are supposed to discuss problems facing the community. Increases in the quality of this form of village democracy would be a successful indicator of improvements in participation and accountability. Quantitative data, however, are very difficult to collect here because of the unreliability of people's memories about what may have transpired at a meeting they attended. To address this issue, the team decided to directly record and transcribe village meetings. This tactic provides textual information that can be analyzed to directly observe changes in participation.

Another challenge was in collecting information on inequality at the village level. Some recent work has found that sample-based measures of inequality typically have standard errors that are too high to provide reliable estimates. PRAs were therefore held with one or two groups in the village to obtain measures of land distribution within the village. This approach was able to generate excellent measures of land inequality, and since these are primarily agrarian economies, measures of land inequality should be highly correlated with income inequality. Similar methods were used to collect data on the social heterogeneity of the village. All this PRA information has been quantitatively coded, thus demonstrating that qualitative tools can be used to collect quantitative data. In this example the fundamental impact assessment design was kept intact, and qualitative and quantitative data were combined to provide insights into different aspects of interest in the evaluation of the intervention.

Use of Mixed Methods in Time- and Resource-Constrained Settings

Some final examples demonstrating the utility of mixed-methods approaches come from settings where formal data (such as a census) are limited or unavailable and where there are few skilled or experienced staff and very limited resources or time. Such situations are common throughout the developing world, where every day many small (and even not so small) organizations undertake good-faith efforts in desperate circumstances to make a difference in the lives of the poor. Are they having a positive impact? How might their efforts and finite resources be best expended? How might apparent failures be learned from and successes be appropriately documented and used to leverage additional resources from governments or donors? In these circumstances, calls for or requirements of extensive technical project evaluation may completely overwhelm existing budgets and personnel, multiplying already strong disincentives to engage in *any* form of evaluation (Pritchett 2002). The absence of formal data, skilled personnel, and long time horizons, however, does not mean that managers of such programs should ignore evaluation entirely. If nothing else, managers and their staff have detailed contextual knowledge of the settings in which they themselves do and do not work, as do those people they are attempting to assist. From a basic commitment to "think quantitatively but act qualitatively" and to "start and work with what one has," local program staff have been able to design and implement a rudimentary evaluation procedure that is not a substitute for but—we hope—a precursor to a more thorough and comprehensive package (Woolcock 2001).

In St. Lucia, for example, the task manager preparing a social analysis had a budget to collect qualitative data from only 12 communities out of a sample of 469 (Woolcock 2001). He wanted to ensure that those selected were as diverse as possible on eight key variables: employment structure, poverty level, impact of a recent hurricane, access to basic services, proximity to roads, geography (seeking regional variance, but with no two communities contiguous to one another), and exposure to the St. Lucia Social Development Program. How could one choose 12 communities so that they satisfied these criteria, with only a 10-year-old census to work from?

The team decided to use the census data to make the first cuts in the selection process, using income data to identify the 200 poorest communities (on the assumption that, over a 10-year period, the ordinal ranking of the income levels of the communities would not have changed significantly). The census also contained data on the number of households in each community receiving particular forms of water delivery and sewerage (public or private pipe, well, and so forth). This enabled the team to construct a "quality of basic services" index, scored on a 1 (low) to 7 (high) scale, and to rank the 200 poorest communities according to their quality of basic services. Finally, using geographic data, it was possible to measure the distance of all 200 communities from the main ring road that encircles St. Lucia. Dividing the sample in half on the basis of their distance measures, those closer to the road were labeled "urban" and those farther from the road "rural." The team was thus able to construct a simple 2×2 matrix, with high/low quality of basic services on one axis and rural/urban location on the other. St. Lucia's 200 poorest communities now fell neatly onto these axes, with 50 communities in each cell.

This procedure was followed up the next day in a four-hour session with field staff—all St. Lucian nationals—which narrowed the field down to 16 communities. Twenty field staff gathered for this meeting, and after a brief presentation on the task at hand and the steps already taken with the census data, they were divided into four groups. Each group was given the names of 50 poor communities from one of the 2×2 cells above and was then asked to select five communities from this list that varied according to exposure to the recent hurricane, major forms of employment, and whether or not they had participated in the initial round of the St. Lucia Social Development Program.

After two hours, the four groups reconvened with the names of their five communities, and over the final hour all field staff worked together to whittle the list of 20 names down to 16 to ensure that regional coverage was adequate and that no two communities were contiguous across regional boundaries. After an additional round of negotiation with senior program staff, the list was reduced to the final 12 communities, a group that maximized the variance according to the eight different criteria required by the task manager.

Reliance on quantitative or qualitative methods alone could never have achieved this result. Formal data were limited and dated, but nonetheless still useful. At the same time, it would have been unrealistic and invalid to rely exclusively on local experts, although their input was key. Combining the best aspects of both methods, however, enabled the team to generate a sample with maximum diversity, validity, *and*—importantly—full local ownership.

What Do Qualitative Methods Add to Quantitative Approaches?

There is clearly a large and important role for approaches to measuring empowerment that are grounded exclusively in sophisticated quantitative methods. This chapter has endeavored to show that these approaches nonetheless have many limitations, and that considerable value can be added by systematically and strategically including more qualitative approaches. By making a distinction between data and the methods used to collect them, we have shown that a range of innovative development research is currently under way in which qualitative data are examined using (or as part of) quantitative methods. The focus of this chapter, however, has been on the use of qualitative methods to improve, complement, and supplement quantitative data. By way of summary and conclusion, we outline six particular means by which qualitative methods demonstrate their usefulness in program evaluation.

(1) By generating hypotheses grounded in the reality of the poor

As the above examples demonstrate, when respondents are allowed to participate directly in the research process, the econometrician's work can avoid stereotypical depictions of their reality. The result may be unexpected findings that prove important. Thus the primary value of participatory econometrics is that hypotheses are generated from systematic fieldwork, rather than from secondary literature or flights of fancy. More specifically, the use of PRAs and PPAs, focus groups, and other methods allows respondents to inform researchers of their own understandings of poverty, which are then tested for their generalizability by constructing appropriate survey instruments and administering them to representative samples of the population of interest.

(2) By helping researchers understand the direction of causality, locating identifying instruments, and exploiting natural experiments

Participatory econometrics can be of great value in improving econometrics beyond its obvious utility in generating new hypotheses. It can be very helpful in understanding the direction of causality, in locating identifying restrictions, and in exploiting natural experiments (Ravallion 2001). For instance, in a recent study, researchers discovered that sex workers in Calcutta suffer economically when they use condoms because of a client bias against condom use (Rao et al. 2003). The econometric problem here is that identifying such compensating differentials is very difficult, because they tend to be plagued by problems of unobserved heterogeneity and endogeneity. Qualitative work in this case helped solve the problem by locating an instrument to correct for the problem. It turned out that an HIV-AIDS intervention that instructed sex workers on the dangers of unsafe sex was administered in a manner uncorrelated with income or wages, yet had a great influence on the sex workers' propensity to use condoms. Using exposure to the intervention as an exclusion restriction in simultaneously estimating equations for condom use and wages enabled the researchers to demonstrate that sex workers suffered a 44 percent loss in wages by using condoms.

(3) By helping to explain the nature of bias and measurement error

In a study of domestic violence in rural Karnataka, India, for example, a question in the survey instrument asked female respondents whether their husbands had ever beaten them in the course of their marriage (Rao 1998). Only 22 percent of the women responded positively—an improbably low rate of domestic violence, in fact much lower than studies in Britain and the United States had shown for those countries. In probing the issue with in-depth interviews, researchers discovered that the women had interpreted the word *beating* to mean *extremely severe* beating—that is, when they had lost consciousness or were bleeding profusely and needed to be taken to the hospital. Hair pulling and ear twisting, which were thought to be everyday occurrences, did not qualify as beating. (Responses to a broader version of the abuse question, comparable to the questions asked in the U.S. and U.K. surveys, elicited a 70 percent positive response.) Having tea with an outlier can be very effective in understanding *why* she is an outlier.

(4) By facilitating cross-checking and replication

In participatory econometrics, the researcher has two sources of data, qualitative and quantitative, generated from the same population. That allows for immediate cross-checking and replication of results. If the qualitative and quantitative findings differ substantially, it could be indicative of methodological or data quality problems in one or the other. In the Delhi slums project (Jha, Rao, and Woolcock, forthcoming), the focus group discussions revealed several narratives of mobility, that is, of people leaving the slums, but this mobility was not reflected in the quantitative data because the sample did not include households who live outside slums. This finding indicates an important sample selection problem in the quantitative data that limits their value in studying questions of mobility. At the same time, the qualitative data gave the impression that religious institutions were an important source of credit and social support for the urban poor. That this finding was not visible in the quantitative data suggests that it is not generalizable to all the residents of Delhi slums but is particular to the families participating in focus group discussions and in-depth interviews.

(5) By providing context that helps researchers interpret quantitative findings, while using quantitative data to establish the generalizability of qualitative findings

Participatory econometrics allows the researcher to interpret the quantitative findings in context. The more narrative, personalized information provided by open-ended focus group discussions and in-depth interviews, the better the researcher can understand and interpret a quantitative result. In the work on domestic violence in India, for instance, a strong positive correlation was found between female sterilization and risk of violence. This finding would have been very difficult to explain without the qualitative data, which revealed that women who were sterilized tended to lose interest in sex with their husbands. At the same time, their husbands developed (unjustified) fears that their wives would be unfaithful now that they were able to have sex without getting pregnant. These circumstances together caused sterilized women to be at much greater risk for violent conflicts within the home. The strong correlation between sterilization and abuse observed in the quantitative data did not necessarily "prove" that the qualitative finding was generalizable. But by demonstrating that the average sterilized woman in the population was in a more conflictual relationship, the quantitative findings were consistent with the qualitative.

(6) By identifying externalities to an intervention, improving the measurement of outcomes, and finding ways to measure "unobservables"

In recent work looking at the relationship between prices and poverty in rural southern India, qualitative work found that the poor were paying much higher unit prices for the same goods because the rich were able to obtain quantity discounts (Rao 2000). This finding led to the collection of a household-level consumer price index that corrected for the purchasing power of households affected by the variation in household-specific prices. The improved "real" income measures of inequality were found to be 17–23 percent higher than conventional inequality measures.

In the UPP2 evaluation in Indonesia, qualitative work helped emphasize the crucial role that project facilitators played in the effectiveness of CDD projects at the community level. This recognition led to a special quantitative questionnaire being administered to facilitators that would allow the team to examine the role of street-level workers in project effectiveness. "Unobservables" can also be made observable through field investigations. In the Indian *panchayat* project, focus group discussions proved to be very effective at uncovering villages that were oligarchic and ruled by a small group of intermarrying families. This ability to see unobservables can be potentially very important in determining the effectiveness of democratic decentralization initiatives at the village level.

Conclusion

Assessing the impact of any development project or policy is a difficult methodological and political task. These challenges are compounded for projects designed to empower the poor, primarily because the typical interventions in this domain—unlike more "standardized" programs such as tax credits, textbooks, or immunizations—are highly context-specific and entail numerous exchanges between providers and clients. They are thus, by design, highly heterogeneous (Whiteside, Woolcock, and Briggs 2005), and researchers are likely to require an innovative combination of qualitative and quantitative methods in order to understand whether and how such interventions are having the desired impact. As this chapter has endeavored to show, there are numerous—but largely underexplored—opportunities in development research and evaluation to combine different methods in complementary ways to get a better understanding of project processes, contexts, and impacts. Generating a more informed evidence base for designing, implementing, and assessing empowerment initiatives requires these methodological innovations along with new spaces for exploring how such innovations might be achieved.

Notes

This essay is an adapted version of "Integrating Qualitative and Quantitative Approaches in Program Evaluation," in *Evaluating the Poverty and Distributional Impact of Economic Policies*, ed. François J. Bourguignon and Luiz Pereira da Silva (Washington, DC: World Bank; New York: Oxford University Press, 2003).

1.   On the specific role of qualitative methods in program evaluation, see Patton (1987).

2.   On the variety of approaches to establishing "causality," see Salmon (1997), Mahoney (2000), and Gerring (2001).

3.   See, for example, Tashakkori and Teddlie (1998), Bamberger (2000), and Gacitua-Mario and Wodon (2001).

4.   King, Keohane, and Verba (1994) and Collier and Adcock (2001) provide a more academic treatment of potential commonalities among quantitative and qualitative approaches.

5.   For an extended discussion of the rationale for social analysis in policy, see World Bank (2002a). More details on the use of qualitative tools and techniques in assessing project impact are available in World Bank (2002b).

6.   The Self-Employed Women's Association (SEWA) in India has used a related approach with great success, helping poor slum dwellers compile basic data on themselves that they can then present to municipal governments for the purpose of obtaining resources to which they are legally entitled. On the potential abuse of participatory approaches, however, see Cooke and Kothari (2001) and Brock and McGee (2002).

7.   See, for example, the exemplary anthropological research of Berry (1993) and Singerman (1996).

8.   For a more extensive treatment of methodological issues in comparative politics, see Ragin (1987) and the collection of articles in Ragin and Becker (1992).

9. For more on methodological issues in anthropological demography, see Obermeyer et al. (1997).
10. See Rao (2002) for more on what participatory econometrics entails. Econometrics per se refers to a particular strand of statistical procedures concerned with testing economic theories and models. Central to these procedures, for our purposes, is the task of ascertaining the nature and direction of causality, primarily using regression techniques.
11. One of the authors of this chapter, Vijayendra Rao, is a member of the evaluation team.
12. This refers to a snowball sample, where new respondents are contacted on the basis of information collected from previous respondents. This method of sampling is useful in studying network interactions.
13. Author Michael Woolcock is a member of this evaluation team.
14. This project is a collaboration among Tim Besley, Rohini Pande, and Vijayendra Rao.

References

Bamberger, Michael. 2000. *Integrating Qualitative and Quantitative Research in Development Projects*. Washington, DC: World Bank.

Barron, Patrick, Claire Smith, and Michael Woolcock. 2004. "Do Participatory Development Projects Help Mediate Local Conflicts? A Mixed Methods Framework for Assessing the Kecamatan Development Project, Indonesia." Working Paper 9 (revised version), Conflict Prevention and Reconstruction Unit, Social Development Department, World Bank, Washington, DC.

Berry, Sara. 1993. *No Condition Is Permanent: The Social Dynamics of Agrarian Change in Sub-Saharan Africa*. Madison: University of Wisconsin Press.

Bliss, Christopher, and Nicholas Stern. 1982. *Palanpur: The Economy of an Indian Village*. New York: Oxford University Press.

Bloch, Francis, and Vijayendra Rao. 2002. "Terror as a Bargaining Instrument: A Case Study of Dowry Violence in Rural India." *American Economic Review* 92 (4): 1029–43.

Brock, Karen, and Rosemary McGee, eds. 2002. *Knowing Poverty: Critical Reflections on Participatory Research and Policy*. London: Earthscan.

Collier, David, and Robert Adcock. 2001. "Measurement Validity: A Shared Standard for Qualitative and Quantitative Research." *American Political Science Review* 95 (3): 529–46.

Cooke, Bill, and Uma Kothari. 2001. *Participation: The New Tyranny?* London: Zed.

Epstein, Scarlet. 1962. *Economic Development and Social Change in South India*. Manchester, UK: University of Manchester Press.

Gacitua-Mario, Estanislao, and Quentin Wodon, eds. 2001. "Measurement and Meaning: Combining Quantitative and Qualitative Methods for the Analysis of Poverty and Social Exclusion in Latin America." Technical Paper 518, World Bank, Washington, DC.

Gerring, John. 2001. *Social Science Methodology: A Criterial Framework.* New York: Cambridge University Press.

Guggenheim, Scott. Forthcoming. "Local Institutions and Local Development in Indonesia." In *The Search for Empowerment: Social Capital as Idea and Practice at the World Bank,* ed. Anthony Bebbington, Michael Woolcock, Scott Guggenheim, and Elizabeth Olson. Bloomfield, CT: Kumarian Press.

Hentschel, Jesko. 1999. "Contextuality and Data Collection Methods: A Framework and Application to Health Service Utilization." *Journal of Development Studies* 35 (4): 64–94.

Isham, Jonathan, Deepa Narayan, and Lant Pritchett. 1995. "Does Participation Improve Performance? Establishing Causality with Subjective Data." *World Bank Economic Review* 9 (2): 175–200.

Jha, Saumitra, Vijayendra Rao, and Michael Woolcock. Forthcoming. "Governance in the Gullies: Democratic Responsiveness and Community Leadership in Delhi's Slums." *World Development.* Working paper available at http://www.cultureandpublicaction.org/bijupdf/GovernanceintheGullies.pdf.

Kanbur, Ravi, ed. 2003. *Qualitative and Quantitative Poverty Appraisal: Complementarities, Tensions, and Way Forward.* New Delhi: Permanent Black.

King, Gary, Robert O. Keohane, and Sidney Verba. 1994. *Designing Social Inquiry: Scientific Inference in Qualitative Research.* Princeton, NJ: Princeton University Press.

Kumar, Somesh, and Robert Chambers. 2002. *Methods for Community Participation.* London: Intermediate Technology Publications.

Lanjouw, Peter, and Nicholas Stern. 1998. *Economic Development in Palanpur over Five Decades.* New York: Oxford University Press.

Mahoney, James. 2000. "Strategies of Causal Inference in Small-N Analysis." *Sociological Methods and Research* 28 (4): 387–424.

Mikkelsen, Britha. 1995. *Methods for Development Work and Research: A Guide for Practitioners.* New Delhi: Sage.

Mills, C. Wright. 1959. *The Sociological Imagination.* New York: Oxford University Press.

Narayan, Deepa. 1995. *Toward Participatory Research.* Washington, DC: World Bank.

Obermeyer, Carla Makhlouf, Susan Greenhalgh, Tom Fricke, Vijayendra Rao, David I. Kertzer, and John Knodel. 1997. "Qualitative Methods in Population Studies: A Symposium." *Population and Development Review* 23 (4): 813–53.

Patton, Michael. 1987. *How to Use Qualitative Methods in Evaluation.* Newbury Park, CA: Sage.

Pritchett, Lant. 2002. "It Pays to Be Ignorant: A Simple Political Economy of Rigorous Program Evaluation." *Journal of Policy Reform* 5 (4): 251–69.

Ragin, Charles. 1987. *The Comparative Method: Moving beyond Qualitative and Quantitative Strategies.* Berkeley: University of California Press.

Ragin, Charles, and Howard Becker, eds. 1992. *What Is a Case? Exploring the Foundations of Social Inquiry.* Cambridge: Cambridge University Press.

Rao, Vijayendra. 1997. "Can Economics Mediate the Link between Anthropology and Demography?" *Population and Development Review* 23 (4): 833–38.

———. 1998. "Wife-Abuse, Its Causes and Its Impact on Intra-Household Resource Allocation in Rural Karnataka: A 'Participatory' Econometric Analysis." In *Gender, Population, and Development,* ed. Maithreyi Krishnaraj, Ratna M. Sudarshan, and Abusaleh Sharif, 94–121. New York: Oxford University Press.

———. 2000. "Price Heterogeneity and Real Inequality: A Case-Study of Poverty and Prices in Rural South India." *Review of Income and Wealth* 46 (2): 201–12.

———. 2001a. "Poverty and Public Celebrations in Rural India." *Annals of the American Academy of Political and Social Science* 573: 85–104.

———. 2001b. "Celebrations as Social Investments: Festival Expenditures, Unit Price Variation and Social Status in Rural India." *Journal of Development Studies* 37 (1): 71–97.

———. 2002. "Experiments in 'Participatory Econometrics': Improving the Connection between Economic Analysis and the Real World." *Economic and Political Weekly* (May 18): 1887–91.

Rao, Vijayendra, Indrani Gupta, Michael Lokshin, and Smarajit Jana. 2003. "Sex Workers and the Cost of Safe Sex: The Compensating Differential for Condom Use in Calcutta." *Journal of Development Economics* 71 (2): 585–603.

Rao, Vijayendra, and Ana María Ibáñez. Forthcoming. "The Social Impact of Social Funds in Jamaica: A 'Participatory Econometric' Analysis of Participation, Targeting and Collective Action in Community-Driven Development." *Journal of Development Studies.* Working paper available at http://econ.worldbank.org/files/24159_wps2970.pdf.

Ravallion, Martin. 2001. "The Mystery of the Vanishing Benefits: An Introduction to Evaluation." *World Bank Economic Review* 15 (1): 115–40.

Ravallion, Martin, and Menno Pradhan. 2000. "Measuring Poverty Using Qualitative Perceptions of Consumption Adequacy." *Review of Economics and Statistics* 82 (3): 462–71.

Robb, Caroline. 2002. *Can the Poor Influence Policy? Participatory Poverty Assessments in the Developing World.* Rev. ed. Washington, DC: International Monetary Fund.

Salmon, Wesley. 1997. *Causality and Explanation.* New York: Oxford University Press.

Singerman, Diane. 1996. *Avenues of Participation.* Princeton, NJ: Princeton University Press.

Tashakkori, Abbas, and Charles Teddlie. 1998. *Mixed Methodology: Combining Qualitative and Quantitative Approaches.* Thousand Oaks, CA: Sage.

White, Howard. 2002. "Combining Quantitative and Qualitative Approaches in Poverty Analysis." *World Development* 30 (3): 511–22.

Whiteside, Katherine, Michael Woolcock, and Xavier Briggs. 2005. "Assessing Social Development Projects: Integrating the Art of Practice and the Science of Evaluation." Development Research Group, World Bank, Washington, DC.

Woolcock, Michael. 2001. "Social Assessments and Program Evaluation with Limited Formal Data: Thinking Quantitatively, Acting Qualitatively." Social Development Briefing Note 68, Social Development Department, World Bank, Washington, DC.

World Bank. 2002a. "Social Analysis Sourcebook: Incorporating Social Dimensions into Bank-Supported Projects." Social Development Department, World Bank, Washington, DC. http://www.worldbank.org/socialanalysissourcebook/Social%20AnalysisSourcebookAug6.pdf.

———. 2002b. "User's Guide to Poverty and Social Impact Analysis of Policy Reform." Poverty Reduction Group and Social Development Department, World Bank, Washington, DC. http://www.worldbank.org/poverty/psia/draftguide.pdf.

———. 2003. Poverty in Guatemala. Poverty Reduction and Economic Management Unit, Human Development Sector Management Unit, Latin America and the Caribbean Region, World Bank, Washington, DC.

SECTION FIVE

National Level

Chapter 14

Assessing Empowerment at the National Level in Eastern Europe and Central Asia

Christiaan Grootaert

Over the past two decades, the concept of poverty has gradually been broadened from a narrow income or expenditure focus to include health, education, and social and political participation. *World Development Report 2000/2001: Attacking Poverty* brought this enhanced concept firmly into the policy sphere by proposing a poverty reduction strategy based on promoting opportunity, facilitating empowerment, and enhancing security (World Bank 2000c). The implications of this strategy for World Bank operations were discussed by the institution's Board of Executive Directors in June 2001 (World Bank 2002b). The tools to facilitate empowerment in practice were further explored in the Bank's *Empowerment and Poverty Reduction: A Sourcebook* (Narayan 2002).

One aspect that has hindered the integration of the empowerment notion in poverty analysis is the difficulty of measuring empowerment and progress in enhancing it. The purpose of this chapter is to suggest a number of indicators that can be used to quantify empowerment and to illustrate this in the case of nine countries in the Eastern Europe and Central Asia (ECA) region. The selected countries are those that participate in the World Bank's Poverty Reduction Strategy Paper (PRSP) process and are thus among the poorest in the region: Albania, Armenia, Azerbaijan, Georgia, Kyrgyz Republic, the former Yugoslav Republic of Macedonia, Moldova, Tajikistan, and Uzbekistan. For comparative purposes, corresponding indicators are given for five other countries in the ECA region and for three countries in the Organisation for Economic Cooperation and Development (OECD). The proposed indicators cover both the micro and macro levels, since empowerment requires action at the levels of the household, the community, and the state. Data are not yet available for all proposed indicators, but the hope is that agreement on a suitable set of indicators will lead to their inclusion in countries' data collection efforts.

This chapter presents empirical results for only a set of priority indicators, which were ultimately aggregated to give a summary picture of empowerment at the country level. The original study on which this chapter is based (Grootaert 2002) contains empirical results for all proposed indicators for which data are available. The full set of indicators are listed in the tables in the appendix to this chapter.

The Meaning of Empowerment

Empowerment is defined here in the context of its role in a poverty reduction strategy. Interestingly, *World Development Report 2000/2001* (*WDR*) does not provide a definition of empowerment. One has to derive the meaning of the term from the actions proposed by the report under the heading of "facilitating empowerment." These actions fall in three categories:

- Making state institutions more responsive to poor people
- Removing social barriers
- Building social institutions and social capital

The empowerment sourcebook does provide a specific definition: "Empowerment is the expansion of assets and capabilities of poor people to participate in, negotiate with, influence, control, and hold accountable institutions that affect their lives" (Narayan 2002, 14). This definition is clearly more narrow and specific than what could be understood from the common-parlance use of the term "power." Most notably, it associates empowerment with poor people (implying that nonpoor people have adequate power and do not need to be empowered[1]) and limits the range of actions to those that involve an interaction with institutions. Indeed, the sourcebook clarifies that "empowering poor men and women requires the removal of formal and informal institutional barriers" (xix).

The formal institutions in question include the state, markets, civil society, and international agencies.[2] Informal institutions include norms of social exclusion, exploitative relations, and corruption. This relatively narrow focus of the empowerment concept is helpful from the point of view of quantification because it immediately provides a range of topics for the selection of indicators.

WDR 2000/01 and the empowerment sourcebook both put the primary focus on state reform. Empowerment is thus not necessarily a grassroots or bottom-up activity, but one in which the state is a key actor. This top-down aspect will have to be reflected in indicators, which will need to capture functions and behaviors of the state related to the sharing of its power, its responsiveness to its constituency, and the transparency of its actions.

A focus on state reform indicators is especially important for ECA countries because the success of the transition from socialism has been determined to a large degree by the institutional structures that countries inherited from the socialist period. Countries with better institutional checks and balances in the form of more mature political democracies, stronger civil societies, and better legal frameworks were more successful in establishing political and economic accountability, enacting pro-poor reforms, and thus empowering their citizens (World Bank 2000b).

A focus on state reform does not imply that empowerment at the community level is not important. Grassroots initiatives, often fueled by local groups and organizations, have led to the empowerment of communities. In some instances, the success of local empowerment efforts have even created pressure for reform at the regional and national levels. In practice, empowerment will of course be most successful where interaction and coordination occurs between efforts at the different levels. The role of the community is brought to the fore in the second and third set of actions proposed in the *WDR*'s framework, namely removing social barriers and building social capital.

WDR 2000/01 and the empowerment sourcebook both discuss aspects of social exclusion and discrimination as barriers to empowerment. A series of indicators of social stratification and inequality in economic, social, and political outcomes will attempt to capture this aspect.

The third element of the *WDR*'s strategy for facilitating empowerment, the building of social institutions and social capital, is not an explicit part of the sourcebook's definition of empowerment but is implicit in the strategies it recommends, which all aim to promote institutional reform at large. This institutional reform must be based on four key elements of empowerment: (a) access to information, (b) inclusion and participation, (c) accountability, and (d) local organizational capacity.

Box 14.1 summarizes the approaches to empowerment followed in *WDR 2000/01* and the empowerment sourcebook and provides guidance for tackling the measurement question.

The following sections discuss the three pillars of empowerment set forth by *WDR 2000/01*, namely, reforming the state, removing social barriers, and building social capital.

Making State Institutions More Responsive to Poor People

The reform of the state to make its actions more beneficial to poor people is a wide-ranging task that requires changes in all three branches of government: executive, legislative, and judiciary. *WDR 2000/01* groups these changes in four categories: reforming public administrations, reforming the legal system, decentralizing power, and promoting democratic politics.

Reforming Public Administrations

In many developing countries, poor people are not well served by the public administration. This can happen because the public administration does not provide the services that the poor need or because the poor are not informed about the services that are available, or both. Often interaction with various levels of the public administration is characterized by corruption, the burden of which falls disproportionately on poor people. Changing the situation to

Box 14.1   Understanding Empowerment

World Development Report 2000/2001: Attacking Poverty

Key elements:

- Making state institutions more responsive to poor people
- Removing social barriers
- Building social institutions and social capital

Empowerment and Poverty Reduction: A Sourcebook

"Empowerment is the expansion of assets and capabilities of poor people to participate in, negotiate with, influence, control, and hold accountable institutions that affect their lives."

Key elements:

- Access to information
- Inclusion and participation
- Accountability
- Local organizational capacity

Sources: World Bank 2000c; Narayan 2002.

empower poor people will in the first place require reform of the public administration.

The starting point is the need for the public sector to pursue activities that are socially justified and that contribute to reducing poverty. This can be monitored on the basis of public expenditure reviews and impact studies that determine the types of expenditures that primarily benefit the poor, such as primary and secondary education, preventive health care, the construction of local roads, and so on. Once agreement has been reached on such a list (which is likely to be country-specific), the share of the government's budget devoted to such activities becomes a monitorable indicator.

Even with the right mix of activities, efficient delivery of services will require a well-functioning public administration. While improving the functioning of the public sector is a highly complex task, a number of basic ingredients contribute to this outcome, such as merit-based recruitment and compensation. Empirical evidence indicates that merit-based recruitment is associated with less corruption and less bureaucratic delay. Compensation of public servants that is severely below the pay scale in the private sector is also likely to create a drain on performance. The World Bank's Governance Research Indicators Dataset includes a broad measure of government effectiveness, reflecting quality of both inputs (bureaucracy, civil servants) and outputs

Table 14.1   Government Effectiveness

Country	Percentile rank		Point estimate		Standard deviation	
	2000/01	1997/98	2000/01	1997/98	2000/01	1997/98
Albania	20.6	22.3	−0.89	−0.65	0.25	0.29
Armenia	15.0	22.3	−1.03	−0.65	0.27	0.29
Azerbaijan	18.1	16.6	−0.95	−0.83	0.21	0.24
Georgia	28.1	31.2	−0.72	−0.51	0.27	0.30
Kyrgyz Republic	31.9	27.4	−0.61	−0.58	0.31	0.30
Macedonia, FYR	30.6	27.4	−0.63	−0.58	0.28	0.27
Moldova	12.5	35.0	−1.10	−0.46	0.21	0.24
Tajikistan	7.5	3.8	−1.31	−1.42	0.28	0.34
Uzbekistan	21.3	7.0	−0.86	−1.30	0.22	0.25
ECA comparators						
Czech Republic	70.6	75.8	0.58	0.59	0.18	0.21
Hungary	72.5	76.4	0.60	0.61	0.17	0.21
Latvia	59.4	61.8	0.22	0.07	0.21	0.24
Poland	62.5	80.3	0.27	0.67	0.17	0.21
Russia	33.1	25.5	−0.57	−0.59	0.17	0.21
OECD comparators						
Germany	95.0	91.1	1.67	1.41	0.19	0.23
Sweden	91.3	93.6	1.51	1.57	0.19	0.25
United States	93.1	90.4	1.58	1.37	0.19	0.23
Regional averages[a]						
Eastern Europe	51.0	48.6	−0.03	−0.13	—	—
Former Soviet Union	21.0	19.1	−0.89	−0.83	—	—
OECD	90.4	90.5	1.42	1.38	—	—

Source: World Bank Governance Research Indicators Dataset, http://info.worldbank.org/governance/.
a. In the governance database, Albania, Czech Republic, Hungary, Latvia, FYR Macedonia, and Poland are in Eastern Europe; Armenia, Azerbaijan, Georgia, Kyrgyz Republic, Moldova, Russia, Tajikistan, and Uzbekistan are in the former Soviet Union; Germany, Sweden, and the United States are OECD countries.

(public services). Table 14.1 shows that in the nine ECA countries in this study, the level of government effectiveness is low: all the countries have large negative scores and find themselves in the bottom third globally. The situation is especially bad in Tajikistan, Moldova, and Armenia. The ECA comparator countries do much better (except for the Russian Federation) and three of them are situated among the 25 percent best-performing countries globally. Effectiveness in the delivery of government services is clearly an aspect of empowerment that has improved greatly with the transition process undertaken in Eastern and Central Europe. The results of this table are confirmed by measures of bureaucratic quality provided by the International Country Risk Guide (ICRG).

A major indicator of the extent to which the state is responsive to the poor is the absence of corruption. Corruption is a regressive tax that hurts the poor and small businesses the most. There has been a notable increase in data collection about corruption in countries across the world, and for many countries corruption indicators are available at the national, subnational, and agency levels. The main difficulty is that the data collection is rarely consistent across countries so that different databases usually need to be combined to establish globally comparable indicators. Of special interest for the ECA region are the World Business Environment Survey (WBES) and the Business Environment and Enterprise Performance Surveys (BEEPS), which both contain a large number of questions on corruption. Corruption in the ECA region is generally perceived to be at very high levels (World Bank 2000a).

There are two available composite indexes that measure the absence of corruption: the "control of corruption" indicator in the World Bank governance database, and Transparency International's Corruption Perceptions Index (CPI). Table 14.2 indicates that both measures are broadly consistent in the way they rank countries (which is not surprising since they use some of the same original sources). Both measures give the highest scores (less corruption) to Hungary, Poland, and the Czech Republic. The lowest scores (more corruption) are for Tajikistan, Russia, and Azerbaijan. All nine PRSP countries considered here have solidly negative scores on the control of corruption measure, but seven of the nine have maintained or improved their relative position between 1997/98 and 2000/01. Severe deterioration occurred in Moldova and Russia.[3]

Corruption manifests itself in many different forms, but it can usefully be disaggregated along two dimensions: administrative corruption and state capture. Administrative corruption refers to bribes and other illicit payments to public officials in order to obtain an advantageous implementation of existing laws, rules, and regulations. State capture refers to actions by individuals, groups, or firms to influence the formation of laws, rules, regulations, and policies to their advantage (World Bank 2000a).

At the level of firms, administrative corruption can be measured by the frequency with which firms have to make irregular payments to get things done. Table 14.3 shows that in many of the countries reviewed here, this frequency is quite high. In Azerbaijan, 50 percent of firms report that they "always" or "mostly" have to make "additional payments" to get things done. In five other countries, the figure ranges between 23 percent and 31 percent. These figures refer only to the most pervasive forms of corruption. If the standard is relaxed to include cases where firms have to make payments "frequently" or "sometimes," the figures exceed 50 percent in all nine PRSP countries reviewed.[4]

Table 14.2 Control of Corruption

| | World Bank Governance Research Indicators Dataset[a] | | | | | | | | Transparency Inter-national CPI 2001[b] | |
| | Percentile rank | | Point estimate | | Standard deviation | | | | | |
Country	2000/01	1997/98	2000/01	1997/98	2000/01	1997/98			Score	Standard deviation
Albania	32.9	9.0	−0.60	−0.99	0.20	0.23			—	—
Armenia	24.2	21.2	−0.80	−0.80	0.23	0.23			—	—
Azerbaijan	10.6	7.7	−1.00	−1.05	0.18	0.19			2.0	0.2
Georgia	28.6	25.0	−0.69	−0.74	0.20	0.24			—	—
Kyrgyz Republic	20.5	24.4	−0.85	−0.76	0.23	0.24			—	—
Macedonia, FYR	36.0	33.3	−0.51	−0.52	0.25	0.20			—	—
Moldova	23.0	40.4	−0.83	−0.39	0.18	0.19			3.1	0.9
Tajikistan	9.3	1.9	−1.08	−1.32	0.24	0.26			—	—
Uzbekistan	29.2	10.3	−0.66	−0.96	0.20	0.19			2.7	1.1
ECA comparators										
Czech Republic	66.5	71.2	0.31	0.38	0.16	0.16			3.9	0.9
Hungary	75.8	78.2	0.65	0.61	0.15	0.16			5.3	0.8
Latvia	55.9	49.4	−0.03	−0.26	0.19	0.18			3.4	1.2
Poland	69.6	73.1	0.43	0.49	0.15	0.16			4.1	0.9
Russia	12.4	27.6	−1.01	−0.62	0.15	0.16			2.3	1.2

(table continues on following page)

Table 14.2 (Continued)

Country	World Bank Governance Research Indicators Dataset[a]						Transparency International CPI 2001[b]	
	Percentile rank		Point estimate		Standard deviation		Score	Standard deviation
	2000/01	1997/98	2000/01	1997/98	2000/01	1997/98		
OECD comparators								
Germany	89.4	91.7	1.38	1.62	0.19	0.19	7.4	0.8
Sweden	99.4	99.4	2.21	2.09	0.19	0.20	9.0	0.5
United States	91.3	89.1	1.45	1.41	0.19	0.20	7.6	0.7
Regional averages								
Eastern Europe	54.0	50.2	−0.01	−0.11	—	—	—	—
Former Soviet Union	21.7	17.9	−0.82	−0.86	—	—	—	—
OECD	90.1	90.8	1.53	1.52	—	—	—	—

Sources: World Bank Governance Research Indicators Dataset, http://info.worldbank.org/governance/. Transparency International Corruption Perceptions Index, http://www.transparency.org.

— Not available.

a. In the governance database, Albania, Czech Republic, Hungary, Latvia, FYR Macedonia, and Poland are in Eastern Europe; Armenia, Azerbaijan, Georgia, Kyrgyz Republic, Moldova, Russia, Tajikistan, and Uzbekistan are in the former Soviet Union; Germany, Sweden, and the United States are OECD countries.
b. The Corruption Perceptions Index (CPI) of Transparency International ranges from 0 to 10, with 10 indicating the lowest level of corruption and 0 the highest.

Table 14.3   Corruption from Businesspeople's Perspective

Country	Percentage of firms saying that they "always" or "mostly" pay bribes to get things done
Albania	25.7
Armenia	29.4
Azerbaijan	50.0
Georgia	22.8
Kyrgyz Republic	13.4
Macedonia, FYR	—
Moldova	24.5
Tajikistan	—
Uzbekistan	31.0
ECA comparators	
Czech Republic	16.1
Hungary	12.5
Latvia	—
Poland	13.4
Russia	17.1
OECD comparators	
Germany	5.8
Sweden	0.0
United States	6.5

Sources: World Business Environment Survey, 2000 (http//info.worldbank.org/governance/wbes/); Hellman, Jones, and Kaufmann 2000.
— Not available.

Making the Legal System More Responsive to Poor People

The rule of law refers to a country's formal rules that are upheld through the judicial system. For the rule of law to be a mechanism of empowerment, two conditions must be met: (a) the rules have to apply equally to all citizens, and (b) the state must be subject to the rules. Legal reform is part of a growing number of World Bank projects, and a frequent priority is to simplify and clarify existing laws. Excessive complexity increases the cost of using the legal system and constitutes a bias against the poor. Simplification of the rules is especially important in areas of the law that touch poor people's lives frequently, such as labor disputes, land titling, human rights abuses, and police violence.

Implementation of the rule of law is captured by one of the indicators in the World Bank's governance database, which considers aspects such as effectiveness and predictability of the judiciary, enforceability of contracts, and absence of crime. Table 14.4 indicates that eight of the nine PRSP countries reviewed here have mildly negative scores, and are situated in a fairly

Table 14.4   Rule of Law

Country	Percentile rank 2000/01	Percentile rank 1997/98	Point estimate 2000/01	Point estimate 1997/98	Standard deviation 2000/01	Standard deviation 1997/98
Albania	27.6	16.2	−0.71	−0.92	0.20	0.20
Armenia	45.3	49.1	−0.35	−0.15	0.21	0.20
Azerbaijan	21.8	32.3	−0.78	−0.56	0.19	0.18
Georgia	39.4	34.7	−0.43	−0.49	0.21	0.21
Kyrgyz Republic	26.5	36.5	−0.72	−0.47	0.22	0.21
Macedonia, FYR	45.9	44.3	−0.33	−0.26	0.27	0.20
Moldova	40.0	53.3	−0.42	−0.02	0.19	0.18
Tajikistan	4.7	4.8	−1.25	−1.33	0.22	0.22
Uzbekistan	27.6	19.2	−0.71	−0.87	0.20	0.19
ECA comparators						
Czech Republic	72.9	70.7	0.64	0.54	0.16	0.16
Hungary	77.1	74.9	0.76	0.71	0.15	0.16
Latvia	65.9	59.9	0.36	0.15	0.18	0.18
Poland	70.6	70.7	0.55	0.54	0.15	0.16
Russia	17.1	26.9	−0.87	−0.72	0.15	0.16
OECD comparators						
Germany	90.6	92.2	1.57	1.48	0.18	0.21
Sweden	95.3	95.2	1.70	1.62	0.18	0.22
United States	91.2	88.0	1.58	1.25	0.18	0.21
Regional averages[a]						
Eastern Europe	57.0	53.3	0.13	0.02	—	—
Former Soviet Union	26.5	29.0	−0.72	−0.65	—	—
OECD	90.4	89.8	1.46	1.39	—	—

Source: World Bank Governance Research Indicators Dataset, http://info.worldbank.org/governance/.

a. In the governance database, Albania, Czech Republic, Hungary, Latvia, FYR Macedonia, and Poland are in Eastern Europe; Armenia, Azerbaijan, Georgia, Kyrgyz Republic, Moldova, Russia, Tajikistan, and Uzbekistan are in the former Soviet Union; Germany, Sweden, and the United States are OECD countries.

— Not available.

narrow range internationally from the 22nd percentile to the 46th percentile. The exception is Tajikistan, which is in the bottom 5 percent. There is no clear trend over time, with some countries having improved their position and others having worsened it.

Regulatory quality also has an empowering dimension, as it affects many aspects of personal and business life. Overall regulatory quality is quite low in the nine PRSP countries considered here (scores between −0.14 and −1.46), but the trend is favorable: all but one country improved their relative positions vis-à-vis the rest of the world between 1997/98 and 2000/01 (table 14.5). The exception is Moldova, where the indicator dropped from −0.28 to −1.11. This parallels the drop in government effectiveness in that country noted earlier (see table 14.1). Except for Hungary, the ECA comparators all showed declines in regulatory quality. The most notable change was in Russia, from −0.30 to −1.40, which dropped the country's rank from the 30th to the 6th percentile.

Pro-poor Decentralization

Decentralization is generally seen as an important means for steering development in a direction that takes the needs of local communities more into account. Decentralization is defined as the formal devolution of power to local decision makers. The transfer of tasks from the central to the local level has to be matched by a genuine transfer of fiscal and enforcement power to the local level. There are a number of dimensions to this process: fiscal, administrative, and political decentralization (Shariari 2001).

Effective decentralization requires that these three aspects be implemented in a simultaneous and coordinated fashion. Only then will decentralization have the potential to be an empowering process. A number of concerns have been raised in the ECA region about the extent to which decentralization can be a pro-poor process given the region's institutional legacy. Much fiscal decentralization has occurred not as a result of grassroots desires, but in direct response to fiscal crises at the level of the central government. Governments responded by transferring administrative responsibility for public service delivery to local authorities, but at the same time they withdrew financial support, thus creating serious problems with unfunded mandates. In fact, central governments retained much decision-making power. In a number of cases, this has led to inefficiencies and conflicts between different layers of bureaucracies. Personal contacts and initiatives, rather than strong institutions, became the prime forces for gaining more local access to resources and effective local service delivery. Often the process has been characterized by limited participation of local communities and civil society. In such a situation it is not clear that decentralization will have favorable equity effects. Capture by local elites is a distinct risk when decentralization takes place in a situation where local power structures are highly unequal (see Shariari 2001 for a study of these issues in Bulgaria).

Table 14.5 Regulatory Quality

Country	Percentile rank 2000/01	Percentile rank 1997/98	Point estimate 2000/01	Point estimate 1997/98	Standard deviation 2000/01	Standard deviation 1997/98
Albania	35.5	21.6	−0.21	−0.70	0.35	0.26
Armenia	23.1	22.8	−0.53	−0.57	0.35	0.26
Azerbaijan	39.1	13.8	−0.14	−1.00	0.35	0.26
Georgia	17.8	18.0	−0.75	−0.85	0.37	0.27
Kyrgyz Republic	20.7	19.2	−0.63	−0.76	0.37	0.27
Macedonia, FYR	34.9	29.3	−0.23	−0.31	0.72	0.33
Moldova	12.4	30.5	−1.11	−0.28	0.35	0.26
Tajikistan	5.9	4.8	−1.46	−1.52	0.38	0.27
Uzbekistan	11.2	7.2	−1.17	−1.40	0.37	0.27
ECA comparators						
Czech Republic	72.2	73.1	0.54	0.57	0.26	0.19
Hungary	85.2	85.0	0.88	0.85	0.26	0.19
Latvia	62.7	68.3	0.30	0.51	0.32	0.26
Poland	67.5	71.3	0.41	0.56	0.26	0.19
Russia	6.5	29.9	−1.40	−0.30	0.26	0.19
OECD comparators						
Germany	91.1	89.2	1.08	0.89	0.29	0.23
Sweden	91.1	85.0	1.08	0.85	0.29	0.23
United States	95.3	96.4	1.19	1.14	0.27	0.23
Regional averages[a]						
Eastern Europe	53.9	53.7	0.13	0.11	—	—
Former Soviet Union	14.9	16.7	−1.06	−0.93	—	—
OECD	88.0	86.8	1.01	0.88	—	—

Source: World Bank Governance Research Indicators Dataset, http://info.worldbank.org/governance/.

a. In the governance database, Albania, Czech Republic, Hungary, Latvia, FYR Macedonia, and Poland are in Eastern Europe; Armenia, Azerbaijan, Georgia, Kyrgyz Republic, Moldova, Russia, Tajikistan, and Uzbekistan are in the former Soviet Union; Germany, Sweden, and the United States are OECD countries.

— Not available.

The share of the budget transferred from the central state to local authorities is a priority indicator of fiscal decentralization, but there are no comparable databases available to tabulate this measure. This purely fiscal indicator would need to be supplemented with indicators that measure the extent of effective control over these resources, that is, the extent of administrative decentralization. Political decentralization can be monitored through the existence of regular elections for local government, and the fraction of the population that votes in them. Popular participation in the decision-making process will often be helped greatly when people can form associations and organizations to lobby for common demands for service and participation and to exercise control (for example, through "vigilance" or oversight committees). A count of such organizations and their membership is thus another useful indicator of the extent of participation at the local level.

Promoting Democratic Politics

The democratic political process promotes empowerment by virtue of the emphasis it places on human freedom. This is manifested in the granting of political rights and civil liberties to citizens. Civil and political freedoms are among the oldest and best-established political indicators; some well-known examples are the Gastil and Freedom House indicators of freedoms. Six of the nine PRSP countries reviewed here are rated "partly free" in 2000/01 by Freedom House (table 14.6). The Kyrgyz Republic, Tajikistan, and Uzbekistan are rated as "not free." Four countries changed status over the course of the last decade (that is, compared to the situation just after the breakup of the Soviet Union): Georgia improved from not free to partly free, and the Kyrgyz Republic, Tajikistan, and Uzbekistan deteriorated from partly free to not free. On political rights, Moldova gets the highest score and Uzbekistan the lowest. On civil liberties, FYR Macedonia is rated best, and Tajikistan and Uzbekistan worst. The ECA comparator countries, except Russia, all receive the highest possible score on political rights, and the second-highest rating on civil liberties.

An important element of civil liberties, worth looking at separately, is the independence of the media. A recent publication by Freedom House (Karatnycky, Motyl, and Schnetzer 2001) rated this element for all transition countries and found that the media in the nine PRSP countries are far from free, with the most government control occurring in Uzbekistan and Azerbaijan. Only Georgia and FYR Macedonia score better than the overall average for transition countries.

In addition to empowering its citizens with civil and political freedoms, democracy promotes political stability and orderly transitions of power without the use of violence. The World Bank's governance database includes a composite indicator of this political process. Table 14.7 indicates that political stability and the absence of political violence are still distant goals in the ECA region. All nine PRSP countries have solidly negative scores, and five of them (Armenia, Georgia, FYR Macedonia, Tajikistan, and Uzbekistan) are in the bottom quintile globally. The trend is also alarming: seven of the nine countries have worse indicators in 2000/01 than in 1997/98.[5] And one of the two "improvements" is Tajikistan, which still has the worst indicator (-1.77) in the sample.

Table 14.6   Country Ratings of Political Rights, Civil Liberties, and Freedom Status by Freedom House

Country	Political rights[a] 2000/01	1991/92	Civil liberties[a] 2000/01	1991/92	Freedom status[b] 2000/01	1991/92
Albania	4	4	5	4	PF	PF
Armenia	4	5	4	5	PF	PF
Azerbaijan	6	5	5	5	PF	PF
Georgia	4	6	4	5	PF	NF
Kyrgyz Republic	6	5	5	4	NF	PF
Macedonia, FYR[c]	4	3	3	4	PF	PF
Moldova	2	5	4	4	PF	PF
Tajikistan	6	3	6	3	NF	PF
Uzbekistan	7	6	6	5	NF	PF
ECA comparators						
Czech Republic[d]	1	2	2	2	F	F
Hungary	1	2	2	2	F	F
Latvia	1	2	2	3	F	F
Poland	1	2	2	2	F	F
Russia	5	3	5	3	PF	PF
OECD comparators						
Germany	1	1	2	2	F	F
Sweden	1	1	1	1	F	F
United States	1	1	1	1	F	F

Source: Freedom House, http://www.freedomhouse.org.
a. Measured on a scale of 1 to 7, with 1 representing the highest degree of freedom and 7 the lowest.
b. F = free; PF = partly free; NF = not free.
c. FYR Macedonia data are for 2000/01 and 1992/93.
d. 1991/92 figures are for Czechoslovakia.

A key element for achieving democratic accountability is the undertaking of free and fair elections. Freedom House has rated the most recent parliamentary and presidential elections in the ECA countries (Karatnycky, Motyl, and Schnetzer 2001). Only one PRSP country, Moldova, was considered to have had free and fair parliamentary elections.

Finally, strong civil society organizations can promote the political empowerment of poor people by bringing pressure on the state to better serve poor people's interests. Freedom House has recently provided an overall assessment of the strength of civil society in transition countries, based on the presence of nongovernmental organizations (NGOs), their capacity and sustainability,

Table 14.7 Political Stability and Absence of Political Violence

Country	Percentile rank 2000/01	Percentile rank 1997/98	Point estimate 2000/01	Point estimate 1997/98	Standard deviation 2000/01	Standard deviation 1997/98
Albania	25.9	14.7	−0.60	−1.00	0.37	0.25
Armenia	17.9	31.4	−0.84	−0.45	0.41	0.25
Azerbaijan	22.2	34.6	−0.70	−0.36	0.27	0.23
Georgia	14.8	21.8	−1.00	−0.76	0.41	0.31
Kyrgyz Republic	39.5	62.2	−0.32	0.32	0.48	0.31
Macedonia, FYR	6.8	33.3	−1.45	−0.40	0.37	0.31
Moldova	40.1	42.9	−0.29	−0.20	0.27	0.23
Tajikistan	3.1	2.6	−1.77	−1.86	0.42	0.33
Uzbekistan	13.0	37.2	−1.17	−0.33	0.29	0.27
ECA comparators						
Czech Republic	75.9	78.8	0.74	0.81	0.23	0.22
Hungary	76.5	89.7	0.75	1.25	0.22	0.22
Latvia	67.9	68.6	0.50	0.46	0.28	0.23
Poland	72.8	80.8	0.69	0.84	0.22	0.22
Russia	33.3	24.4	−0.41	−0.69	0.22	0.22
OECD comparators						
Germany	90.7	92.3	1.21	1.32	0.22	0.25
Sweden	95.1	96.8	1.38	1.41	0.22	0.26
United States	88.9	85.9	1.18	1.10	0.23	0.25
Regional averages[a]						
Eastern Europe	54.7	55.7	0.15	0.14	—	—
Former Soviet Union	31.0	36.7	−0.55	−0.39	—	—
OECD	90.0	88.2	1.21	1.16	—	—

Source: World Bank Governance Research Indicators Dataset, http://info.worldbank.org/governance/.

a. In the governance database, Albania, Czech Republic, Hungary, Latvia, FYR Macedonia, and Poland are in Eastern Europe; Armenia, Azerbaijan, Georgia, Kyrgyz Republic, Moldova, Russia, Tajikistan, and Uzbekistan are in the former Soviet Union; Germany, Sweden, and the United States are OECD countries.

— Not available.

the legal and political environment in which they function, the existence of free trade unions, and the participation of interest groups in the policy-making process. Table 14.8 indicates that in most PRSP countries in the ECA region, the strength of civil society is rated average. The exceptions are Uzbekistan and Tajikistan, where civil society is very weak. In contrast, the ECA comparator countries have a strong civil society, except Russia.

Table 14.8   The Strength of Civil Society

Country	Rating
Albania	4.00
Armenia	3.50
Azerbaijan	4.50
Georgia	4.00
Kyrgyz Republic	4.50
Macedonia, FYR	3.75
Moldova	3.75
Tajikistan	5.00
Uzbekistan	6.50
ECA comparators	
Czech Republic	1.50
Hungary	1.25
Latvia	2.00
Poland	1.25
Russia	4.00
OECD comparators	
Germany	—
Sweden	—
United States	—

Source: Freedom House (Karatnycky, Motyl, and Schnetzer 2001).
Note: Ratings are on a scale of 1 to 7, where 1 is the highest level of strength of civil society and 7 is the lowest.
— Not available.

Removing Social Barriers

The second major pillar in the *WDR*'s approach to empowerment is the removal of social barriers. Social barriers and discrimination on the basis of ethnicity, race, gender, religion, or social status can prevent people from taking advantage of opportunities for economic and social advancement and can lock them in poverty traps. Social institutions can reinforce existing inequalities or they can serve as a vehicle to overcome them. While local action, especially on the part of the community, is unquestionably critical in both the removal of social barriers and the building of social institutions, it will generally require an effort at the level of the central state as well.

Social stratification and inequality are manifested not only in terms of income differentials, but also, and even more significantly, in terms of unequal access to resources such as land and credit. Standard economic statistics on average income levels, average land holdings, or ownership of other assets across socioeconomic groups can help to illustrate the extent of this inequality. They can be supplemented by statistics on access to education, health, and other public services, disaggregated over the relevant socioeconomic groups. Unfortunately, there are no internationally comparable databases that contain such statistics, although this type of disaggregated analysis is commonly done in country-specific economic and sector studies and poverty assessments.

In the context of the ECA region, social stratification and inequality on the basis of ethnicity and gender deserve specific attention. Ethnic minorities are present in many countries of the region. In Central and Eastern Europe, the Roma population constitutes the largest ethnic minority.[6] Between 7 and 9 million Roma live throughout Europe, and in Bulgaria, FYR Macedonia, Romania, and the Slovak Republic they make up between 9 percent and 11 percent of the population. Roma are an extremely diverse minority, consisting of many subgroups based on linguistic, historical, and occupational distinctions. In their entirety, though, they are characterized by very high poverty, often 5 to 10 times the national average, and a lack of participation and empowerment. The children of Roma households have school enrollment rates far below children in non-Roma households, and the heads of Roma households have unemployment rates far above the heads of other households. Low education levels and overrepresentation in low-skilled jobs gave Roma households an unfavorable starting point at the outset of transition. Past and present discrimination and exclusion further lower their ability to escape poverty. The monitoring of the living conditions and welfare of the Roma population is an important element of measuring social stratification in the countries where Roma live. This is best done in the context of country-specific poverty assessments or similar analyses, or through cross-country studies focused on the ethnic dimension (such as those in Ringold 2000 and Revenga, Ringold, and Tracy 2002).

Measures of income inequality such as the Gini coefficient can be seen as (weak) proxies for the overall state of economic stratification and inequality in society. Such indicators, however, have to be interpreted very cautiously in the case of ECA countries, because the socialist system often led to artificially low indicators of inequality. Market reforms will often lead to increases in inequality, and not all such increases should be deemed socially undesirable. Based on income statistics, Albania, FYR Macedonia, and Uzbekistan still show low or medium levels of inequality, but the other PRSP countries and Russia have Gini coefficients exceeding 0.4 (table 14.9). Armenia shows by far the highest income inequality.

Gender discrimination and resulting inequality by gender in economic and social outcomes is a fact of life in many countries. This has political, legal, social, and economic ramifications. On the political side, women almost always hold a much smaller share of elected offices and political power than men do. This can be the result of both formal legal systems and informal customs. The extent of gender inequality in the political sphere can be observed by calculating the percentage of political offices, both elected and nonelected, occupied by women.

Table 14.9   Income Inequality

Country	Gini coefficient	Period
Albania	0.27[a]	1996–99
Armenia	0.59	1996–99
Azerbaijan	—	
Georgia	0.43	1996–99
Kyrgyz Republic	0.47	1996–99
Macedonia, FYR	0.37	1996–99
Moldova	0.42	1996–99
Tajikistan	0.47	1996–99
Uzbekistan	0.33	1993
ECA comparators		
Czech Republic	0.25	1996
Hungary	0.31	1996
Latvia	0.32	1998
Poland	0.33	1996
Russia	0.49	1998
OECD comparators		
Germany	0.30	1994
Sweden	0.25	1992
United States	0.41	1997

Sources: World Bank 2000b for PRSP countries, except Uzbekistan; World Bank 2000c for Uzbekistan and other countries.
a. Measures inequality of consumption.
— Not available.

In the legal sphere, laws may restrict women's rights in situations of divorce, inheritance, and the establishment of ownership of land and productive resources. An examination of relevant laws can lead to the establishment of an indicator of the extent to which women have or do not have equal rights.

As part of its work on the Human Development Index, the United Nations Development Programme (UNDP) has calculated two composite measures of gender differentiation in economic, social, and political status. The Gender-related Development Index (GDI) captures the same set of indicators as the Human Development Index—life expectancy, educational attainment, and income—but adjust the results for gender inequality.[7] The Gender Empowerment Measure (GEM) captures gender inequality in key areas of economic and political participation and decision making by looking at women's share of parliamentary seats and senior positions in the private and public sectors, and income differentials between men and women (UNDP 2002).

Table 14.10 shows that the GDI values are fairly high in the PRSP countries for which data are available, and only slightly below the GDI values for the ECA comparator countries. The GEM is not available for the PRSP countries, but the figures indicate a wider gap between the ECA comparator countries and the OECD countries than is the case for the GDI. This suggests that women in the ECA region have achieved greater equality with men in the spheres of income, education, and health than in the sphere of political participation. This is confirmed by the last three columns of table 14.10, which show the share of women in parliamentary seats, ministerial-level posts, and subministerial-level posts. In all but a few cases the figures are below 10 percent. The situation is only slightly better in the ECA comparator countries (and not better at all in Russia). Even the OECD countries are far away from gender parity in political office.

Building Social Institutions and Social Capital

The third and final pillar in the process of empowerment is the building of social institutions and social capital. Social capital refers to the organizations and networks, and the underlying norms and values, that govern the interactions among people in society. Social capital plays an important role in enhancing the productivity of other assets available to the poor, in protecting their basic needs, and in managing risk. Social capital in the form of solidarity and innovation networks can help household-based enterprises obtain information about trading partners and gain access to technology and marketing information in order to increase profits. Linking or vertical social capital is especially important as a vehicle to improve access to resources from beyond the household's immediate social and economic environment.

As is the case with other types of empowerment, the formation of local organizations will often play a key role, and strengthening the capacity of such local organizations helps empower their members. Community-driven development programs, which in recent years have proved their value in many sectors, rely on local social capital for their success. The role of social capital for empowerment in ECA countries is especially important in light of the legacy of the strongly centralized, authoritarian socialist regimes, which had a devastating impact on local community and society (World Bank 2000b). Local networks are now often critical for survival and access to essential services in situations where the state fails to provide an effective social safety net and equal access to services (Kuehnast and Dudwick 2002; Rose 1999). The challenge is to transform these networks from mere survival mechanisms into inclusive community-based institutions.

Table 14.10 Measures of Gender Inequality

Country	Gender-related Development Index (0–1) (2002)	Gender Empowerment Measure (0–1) (2002)	Seats in parliament held by women (%) (2000)	Women at ministerial level (%) (1998)	Women at subministerial level (%) (1998)
Albania	0.708	—	5.2	10.5	12.5
Armenia	0.718	—	3.1	0.0	4.9
Azerbaijan	—	—	12.0	10.0	4.7
Georgia	—	—	7.2	3.8	5.9
Kyrgyz Republic	—	—	—	4.3	2.8
Macedonia, FYR	—	—	7.5	8.7	23.9
Moldova	0.697	—	8.9	0.0	15.3
Tajikistan	0.659	—	—	6.5	6.1
Uzbekistan	0.683	—	6.8	3.3	12.5
ECA comparators					
Czech Republic	0.841	0.537	13.9	16.7	13.5
Hungary	0.813	0.487	8.3	5.3	12.1
Latvia	0.770	0.540	17.0	6.7	27.3
Poland	0.811	0.512	12.7	17.2	9.1
Russia	0.769	0.426	5.7	7.5	4.3
OECD comparators					
Germany	0.905	0.756	33.6	8.3	4.7
Sweden	0.923	0.794	42.7	43.5	24.3
United States	0.927	0.707	12.5	26.3	33.4

Source: UNDP 2002.
— Not available.

Three types of indicators have been developed to measure the strength of local social institutions and social capital. Structural social capital is measured by the density of networks and associations, the extent of their democratic functioning, the diversity of membership, and the linkages between different associations. Cognitive social capital is captured by indicators of trust and adherence to local norms and values. Finally, indicators of collective action measure the extent to which the community can get together to address problems of common benefit, such as the management of common resources.

No internationally comparable databases exist that contain these measures of social capital, even though the number of country studies collecting data on social capital is increasing rapidly.[8] In the ECA region, an extensive study on social capital was done for Bosnia and Herzegovina (World Bank 2002a). The study used a series of indicators of structural and cognitive social capital at the household and village levels and found that in the postwar period, social capital had declined as manifested in lower levels of interpersonal trust, sociability, and mutual help. Table 14.11 shows a low level of membership in voluntary organizations (structural social capital), especially among women, the poor, people with low education, and those living in Serb majority areas. Sociability—the practice of social interaction with others in the community, an indicator of cognitive social capital—was found to be lower with new than with old neighbors, and higher with people of the same nationality than with those of different nationality (table 14.12). Results on mutual help showed the same pattern. All this reflects increased social cleavages following the war.

Table 14.11   Membership in Voluntary Associations in Bosnia and Herzegovina

Population	Level of membership (%)
Men	37.1
Women	22.3
Urban residents	27.5
Rural residents	31.3
Low education	21.1
High education	39.0
Low income	22.2
High income	51.8
Bosniac majority area	32.6
Croat majority area	35.2
Serb majority area	20.2

Source: World Bank 2002b.

Table 14.12   Sociability in Bosnia and Herzegovina

	Number of times invited in a 3-month period		
Guests	Never (%)	1–3 times (%)	More (%)
Relatives	22.2	40.6	36.9
Closest friends	25.9	41.6	32.1
Work colleagues	59.3	24.4	10.7
Old neighbors—same nationality	52.1	28.7	16.3
Old neighbors—different nationality	67.4	14.8	7.4
New neighbors—same nationality	64.4	18.7	9.2
New neighbors—different nationality	76.0	7.2	4.2

Source: World Bank 2002b.
Note: Respondents were asked: "In the past three months, how many times did you invite the following people in your home for lunch, dinner, or similar occasion?" Percentages may not add to 100 due to "don't know/didn't answer" category.

Overview of Indicators and Recommendations for Data Collection

In total, approximately 50 indicators can be used to measure and monitor empowerment. Roughly half of those are currently available in easily accessible and internationally comparable databases. The appendix includes summary tables of the indicators for each type of empowerment action discussed in this chapter.

This chapter presented detailed empirical results for a dozen priority indicators selected from the full set. The selection was largely subjective, but preference was given to indicators that are easily obtainable from existing databases, that are available on an annual basis, and that already enjoy wide recognition and acceptance. A minimum of one indicator was selected for each major type of empowerment action, even if it did not meet the preference criteria. Table 14.13 gives an overview of the priority indicators. Since each indicator uses a different scale, we standardized the presentation by reverse-scoring indicators if needed, so that higher values correspond with higher empowerment in all cases, and by normalizing scores on a 0–100 scale.[9] Table 14.14 shows the resulting standardized indicators, as well as their numerical average, which we labeled "empowerment score." The use of a simple arithmetic average to calculate an aggregate score is of course a mere convenience device, and has no theoretical foundation.[10] Alternative weighting schemes could easily be applied to the data in table 14.14.

The results indicate that the ECA countries considered here broadly fall into four clusters. Tajikistan has the least empowered citizenry, with an average score of only 23.2 (out of 100). The country scores poorly on every indicator for which data are available.

Table 14.13   Priority Empowerment Indicators

Empowerment action	Indicator	Data source
Reform of public administration	Government effectiveness in service delivery (scale)	World Bank governance database
	Corruption Perceptions Index (scale)	Transparency International
	Incidence of illicit payments (%)	WBES/BEEPS
Reform of legal system	Rule of law indicator (scale)	World Bank governance database
	Regulatory quality (scale)	World Bank governance database
Decentralization	Share of central budget transferred to local authorities (%)	—
Democracy	Indicator of civil liberties and political rights (scale)	Freedom House
	Voice and accountability indicator (scale)	World Bank governance database
	Civil society strength indicator (scale)	Freedom House
Removal of social barriers	Share of women in political office (%)	UNDP
	Measure of income inequality (Gini coefficient)	World Development Indicators
Building of social capital	Density of networks and associations	—

— Not available.

Next are Uzbekistan and Azerbaijan, with average empowerment scores in the low 30s. These two countries do well on one or two indicators. For example, Azerbaijan has good regulatory quality and Uzbekistan has fairly low income inequality.

The third cluster consists of the other six PRSP countries, which all have empowerment scores in the 40–45 range. Given the nature of the data underlying the component indicators, differences of 5 points or less in overall scores are probably not meaningful. One could add Russia to this group, with a score of 38.2.

The four remaining ECA comparator countries do much better. Latvia has an empowerment score of 58.6, and the Czech Republic, Hungary, and Poland all fall in the narrow range of 64 to 68. The economic benefits brought to these countries by the transition process can in part be attributed to the increased empowerment of their citizens (World Bank 2000b). Two of the OECD comparators, Germany and the United States, score only about 5 points higher,

Table 14.14 Normalized Priority Indicators and Summary Measure

Country	Government effectiveness	Corruption perceptions	Illicit payments	Rule of law	Regulatory quality	Civil liberties and political freedoms	Voice and accountability	Civil society	Women in political office	Income inequality	Average: empowerment score
Albania	32.2	—	74.3	35.8	45.8	41.7	50.2	50.0	9.4	—	42.4
Armenia	29.4	—	70.6	43.0	39.4	50.0	45.6	58.3	2.7	—	42.4
Azerbaijan	31.0	20.0	50.0	34.4	47.2	25.0	36.0	41.7	8.1	—	32.6
Georgia	35.6	—	77.2	41.4	35.0	50.0	48.6	50.0	5.6	—	42.9
Kyrgyz Republic	37.8	—	86.6	35.6	37.4	25.0	38.6	41.7	3.6	60.0	40.7
Macedonia, FYR	37.4	—	—	43.4	45.4	58.3	50.6	54.2	13.4	—	43.2
Moldova	28.0	31.0	75.5	41.6	27.8	66.7	52.4	54.2	8.1	66.0	45.1
Tajikistan	23.8	—	—	25.0	20.8	16.7	36.2	33.3	6.3	—	23.2
Uzbekistan	32.8	27.0	69.0	35.8	26.6	8.3	26.4	8.3	7.5	67.0	30.9
ECA comparators											
Czech Republic	61.6	39.0	83.9	62.8	60.8	91.7	70.8	91.7	14.7	75.0	65.2
Hungary	62.0	53.0	87.5	65.2	67.6	91.7	73.8	95.8	8.6	69.0	67.4
Latvia	54.4	34.0	—	57.2	56.0	91.7	66.2	83.3	17.0	68.0	58.6
Poland	55.4	41.0	86.6	61.0	58.2	91.7	74.2	95.8	13.0	67.0	64.4
Russia	38.6	23.0	82.9	32.6	22.0	33.3	43.0	50.0	5.8	51.0	38.2
OECD comparators											
Germany	83.4	74.0	94.2	81.4	71.6	91.7	78.4	—	15.5	70.0	73.4
Sweden	80.2	90.0	100.0	84.0	71.6	100.0	83.0	—	36.8	75.0	80.1
United States	81.6	76.0	93.5	81.6	73.8	100.0	74.8	—	24.1	59.0	73.8

Note: Each normalized indicator ranges from 0 to 100, with 100 reflecting the most favorable situation. See text for details on the normalization procedure.

which underlines the extent of the achievement in the empowerment area in the Czech Republic, Hungary, and Poland. Finally, of the comparator countries included in this study, Sweden achieves the highest empowerment score of 80.1.

Future Data Collection

Existing international databases are sufficiently rich to provide a useful set of indicators to assess the status of empowerment, as this chapter has demonstrated. The main shortcoming in the current situation is that the available indicators are concentrated in certain aspects of empowerment, such as corruption, the rule of law, civil liberties, and political rights, while other dimensions are covered barely or not at all, such as decentralization and building of social capital.

The indicators drawn from sources outside the World Bank, such as Freedom House, Transparency International, ICRG, and so forth, have been in existence for many years and in all likelihood will continue to be available on an annual basis. Four of the 12 priority empowerment indicators proposed in this chapter come from these external sources.

The main World Bank data sources are the Governance Indicators database and WBES/BEEPS. The governance database consists of two rounds of data collection, in 1997/98 and 2000/01, and has six very useful indicators for monitoring empowerment. Four of these were included in the priority indicators. The main strength of this database is the comprehensiveness of its sources and the econometric aggregation procedure.

In order to complete the assessment of empowerment by means of the 12 priority indicators, the two top priorities for data collection are decentralization and social capital.

In addition, the empirical assessment of empowerment would benefit from data collection on the following five issues:

- Extent to which government spending benefits the poor
- Extent of merit-based recruitment and compensation in the public sector
- Extent of oversight of the executive branch by the legislative branch
- Availability of government information to the public
- Differences by gender, ethnic group, or other socioeconomic category in economic outcomes and access to services

These recommendations add up to an ambitious agenda for strengthening future data collection. Efforts will be needed to enhance the collection of empowerment indicators at the national, community, and household levels.

At the *national level,* the priority is to improve the collection of administrative data. Attention should focus on the government accounts, which need to be made more transparent in showing financial inflows and outflows.

Data at the *community level* are essential for monitoring multiple aspects of empowerment such as decentralization, participation in local elections and local decision making, and functioning of local associations and NGOs.

Lastly, while *household surveys* have been the prime source of data on poverty and well-being, they have so far played only a small part in monitoring empowerment. This role can be enhanced significantly, especially in the area of social capital. The best approach here is to design specific modules to be added to living standards surveys or household income and expenditure surveys. An example is the Social Capital Integrated Questionnaire, which contains modules on structural and cognitive social capital, collective action, information and communication, social cohesion, and empowerment (Grootaert et al. 2004).

Appendix: Summary Tables of Indicators

Summary Table 14.15   Indicators of Reform of Public Administration

Empowerment action	Indicator	Data source
Focus on social priorities	Share of government budget for poverty-reducing activities (%)	Public expenditure reviews; government budget
	Government effectiveness in service delivery (scale)	World Bank governance database
Merit-based recruitment and compensation	Quality of bureaucracy (scale)	ICRG
	Incidence of merit-based recruitment (scale)	—
	Incidence of merit-based compensation (scale)	—
	Ratio of average salary in public over private sector	Labor force surveys
Oversight by legislative branch	Incidence of legislative review of government budgets (scale)	—
Disseminating information	Availability of government information to public (scale)	—
Curbing corruption	Control of corruption indicator (scale)	World Bank governance database
	Corruption Perceptions Index (scale)	Transparency International
	Incidence of illicit payments (%)	WBES/BEEPS
	Share of firm revenue paid in illicit payments (%)	WBES/BEEPS
	Perception of corruption as business obstacle (scale)	WBES/BEEPS
	Share of firms affected by state capture actions (%)	BEEPS

— Not available.

Summary Table 14.16   Reforming the Legal System

Empowerment action	Indicator	Data source
Equal application of the rule of law	Rule of law indicator (scale)	World Bank governance database
	Quality of judiciary (scale)	WBES
	Protection of property rights (scale)	WBES
	Impact of crime on business (scale)	WBES
	Incidence of personal violent crime (%)	UNDP
Simplification of laws and regulations	Regulatory quality indicator (scale)	World Bank governance database
	Impact of regulations on business, by type of regulation (scale)	WBES

Summary Table 14.17   Decentralizing Power

Empowerment action	Indicator	Data source
Fiscal decentralization	Share of central budget transferred to local authorities (%)	—
Administrative decentralization	Extent to which local authorities hold mandates for provision of public services (scale)	—
Political decentralization	Existence of regular and free local elections (scale)	—
	Share of population voting in local elections (%)	—
	Citizen participation in local government meetings (%)	—
Facilitating local associations	Number of local associations (N)	—
	Share of population that is member of local associations (%)	—

— Not available.

Summary Table 14.18   Promoting Democratic Politics

Empowerment action	Indicator	Data source
Promoting civil liberties and political rights	Freedom House indicator of civil liberties and political rights (scale)	Freedom House
	Independence of the media (scale)	Freedom House
Ensuring democratic transitions of power	Political stability indicator (scale)	World Bank governance database
	Democratic accountability (scale)	ICRG
	Free elections (scale)	Freedom House
	Voter turnout (%)	Freedom House
Access to information	Availability of government budget information to public (scale)	—
	Access to information about laws and regulations (scale)	WBES
Strengthening civil society	Number of civil society associations (N)	—
	Share of population that is member of associations (%)	—
	Strength of civil society (scale)	Freedom House
Enhancing citizens' voice and politicians' accountability	Voice and accountability indicator (scale)	World Bank governance database

— Not available.

Summary Table 14.19   Removing Social Barriers

Empowerment action	Indicator	Data source
Reducing social stratification	Measure of income inequality (e.g., Gini coefficient)	World Development Indicators
	Asset ownership by socioeconomic category (%)	—
	Access to education and health by socioeconomic category (%)	—
Eliminating gender discrimination	Gender-related Development Index (GDI) (scale)	UNDP
	Gender Empowerment Measure (GEM) (scale)	UNDP
	Share of women in political office (parliamentary seats, ministerial and subministerial positions) (%)	UNDP
	Equal rights in law (scale)	—
Reducing conflict	Share of population affected by ethnic conflict (%)	—

— Not available.

Summary Table 14.20   Building Social Capital

Empowerment action	Indicator	Data source
Strengthening local organizations and networks	Density of networks and associations (N)	—
	Extent and diversity of membership (scale)	—
	Measures of trust and adherence to norms (scale)	—
	Extent of local collective action (scale)	—
Creating linking social capital	Linkages between associations (scale)	—
Promoting community-based development	Incidence of community-driven development programs (scale)	—

— Not available.

Notes

This chapter is a summary of a longer paper, "Assessing Empowerment in the ECA Region," written for and funded by the World Bank's study on the Non-Income Dimensions of Poverty (carried out by the Europe and Central Asia Region under task team leaders Christine Jones and Ana Revenga). The author would like to thank Carine Clert, Nora Dudwick, Christine Jones, Ana Revenga, Dena Ringold, two peer reviewers, and the editor of this volume for many helpful comments and suggestions, and Kalpana Mehra for assistance with the data collection and processing.

1.   This implication was partially refuted in a recent empirical study of Russia, which found that many people who do not see themselves as poor nevertheless feel that they have little power. Forty-two percent of the sample placed themselves lower on the power ladder than on the welfare ladder (Lokshin and Ravallion 2002).

2.   There is growing consensus that understanding and measuring empowerment requires looking at the interactions between the state, civil society, and markets. For example, a recent paper by Walton (2002) uses this framework for discussing empowerment in Latin America and the Caribbean.

3.   The decline in the relative position of Moldova between 1997/98 and 2000/01, portrayed by the control of corruption indicator, is partially contradicted by the CPI, which shows an improvement for Moldova from 2.6 in 2000 to 3.1 in 2001.

4.   The range of possible answers offered to respondents was: always, mostly, frequently, sometimes, seldom, never.

5.   As a reminder, this does not signal an absolute deterioration but a downward shift in the position of these ECA countries relative to the other countries in the database.

6.   This discussion of the Roma population is based on Ringold 2000 and Revenga, Ringold, and Tracy 2002.

7.   A technical note on the adjustment procedure can be found in UNDP (2002).

8.   Indicators of the type suggested have been constructed in recent years for Argentina, Bangladesh, Bolivia, Burkina Faso, India, Indonesia, Kenya, Madagascar, and panama. For a review, see Grootaert (2001) and Grootaert and van Bastelaer (2001), (2002).

9.   The normalization was done using the theoretical minimum and maximum of each indicator. This has the advantage of showing more clearly where each country is situated in the feasible range of each indicator. The drawback is that there is implicit under- and overweighting of low- and high-scoring indicators. The alternative is to normalize using the actual minimum and maximum occurring in the sample. The drawback of this approach is that it introduces arbitrariness, depending upon which countries are included in the sample. Specifically, the presence of one "outlier" can seriously affect the normalized value of the indicator for all countries included. For that reason this procedure is usually reserved for indexes based on large samples. For example, it is used in UNDP's Human Development Index constructed for almost all countries in the world.

10.   The same convenience device underlies some well-known indexes such as the Human Development Index (UNDP 2002).

References

Grootaert, C. 2001. "Does Social Capital Help the Poor? A Synthesis of Findings from the Local Level Institutions Studies in Bolivia, Burkina Faso, and Indonesia." Local Level Institutions Working Paper 10, Social Development Department, World Bank, Washington, DC.

———. 2002. "Assessing Empowerment in the ECA Region." Social Development Division, Environmentally and Socially Sustainable Development Network, Europe and Central Asia Region, World Bank, Washington, DC.

Grootaert, C., D. Narayan, V. Nyhan-Jones, and M. Woolcock. 2004. "Measuring Social Capital: An Integrated Questionnaire." World Bank Working Paper 18, World Bank, Washington, DC.

Grootaert, C., and T. van Bastelaer. 2001. "Understanding and Measuring Social Capital: A Synthesis of Findings and Recommendations from the Social Capital Initiative." Social Capital Initiative Working Paper 24, Social Development Department, World Bank, Washington, DC.

———, eds. 2002. *Understanding and Measuring Social Capital: A Multidisciplinary Tool for Practitioners.* Washington, DC: World Bank.

Hellman, J., G. Jones, and D. Kaufmann. 2000. "Seize the State, Seize the Day: State Capture, Corruption, and Influence in Transition." Policy Research Working Paper 2444, World Bank, Washington, DC.

Karatnycky, A., A. Motyl, and A. Schnetzer, eds. 2001. *Nations in Transit 2001.* Washington, DC: Freedom House.

Kuehnast, K., and N. Dudwick. 2002. "Better a Hundred Friends than a Hundred Rubles? Social Networks in Transition—The Kyrgyz Republic." Social Development Division, Environmentally and Socially Sustainable Development Network, Europe and Central Asia Region, World Bank, Washington, DC.

Lokshin, M., and M. Ravallion. 2002. "Rich *and* Powerful? Subjective Power and Welfare in Russia." Policy Research Working Paper 2854, World Bank, Washington, DC.

Narayan, D., ed. 2002. *Empowerment and Poverty Reduction: A Sourcebook.* Washington, DC: World Bank.

Revenga, A., D. Ringold, and W. M. Tracy. 2002. *Poverty and Ethnicity: A Cross-Country Study of Roma Poverty in Central Europe.* World Bank Technical Paper 531, World Bank, Washington, DC.

Ringold, D. 2000. *Roma and the Transition in Central and Eastern Europe: Trends and Challenges.* Washington, DC: World Bank.

Rose, R. 1999. "What Does Social Capital Add to Individual Welfare? An Empirical Analysis of Russia." Social Capital Initiative Working Paper 15, Social Development Department, World Bank, Washington, DC.

Shariari, H. 2001. "Delivery and Intergovernmental Relationships as a Result of New Institutional Arrangements." Social Development Division, Environmentally and Socially Sustainable Development Network, Europe and Central Asia Region, World Bank, Washington, DC.

UNDP (United Nations Development Programme). 2002. *Human Development Report 2002: Deepening Democracy in a Fragmented World.* New York: Oxford University Press.

Walton, M. 2002. "Citizens, the State and Markets in Latin America and the Caribbean." Latin America and the Caribbean Region, World Bank, Washington, DC.

World Bank. 2000a. *Anticorruption in Transition: A Contribution to the Policy Debate.* Washington, DC: World Bank.

———. 2000b. *Making Transition Work for Everyone: Poverty and Inequality in Europe and Central Asia.* Washington, DC: World Bank.

———. 2000c. *World Development Report 2000/2001: Attacking Poverty.* New York: Oxford University Press.

———. 2002a. "Bosnia and Herzegovina: Local Level Institutions and Social Capital Study." Social Development Division, Environmentally and Socially Sustainable Development Network, Europe and Central Asia Region, World Bank, Washington, DC.

———. 2002b. *Poverty Reduction and the World Bank: Progress in Operationalizing the World Development Report 2000/2001.* Washington, DC: World Bank.

Chapter 15

The CIVICUS Civil Society Index

Carmen Malena and Volkhart Finn Heinrich

Other chapters of this volume explore how empowerment can be measured at the individual, household, community, and local levels. This chapter presents the CIVICUS Civil Society Index project (CSI) as an example of an effort to measure empowerment at the national level in a way that allows international comparison.[1]

The chapter begins by exploring the concepts of *empowerment* and *civil society* and clarifying links between them. It then introduces the CSI and examines the features that distinguish it from other efforts to assess civil society, in particular from an empowerment perspective. The chapter next describes in greater detail the content of the CSI (that is, exactly what it seeks to measure) and explains the participatory research and scoring methodology, emphasizing the importance of the CSI as an empowerment process in its own right as well as a measurement tool. Although the CSI is still in its implementation phase and country findings are not yet available, the chapter concludes with some preliminary observations and a review of key operational challenges for the future.

The Concepts of Empowerment and Civil Society

To "empower" simply means to "enable" or "give power to." In order to give operational meaning to the concept, one must specify the empowerment *of whom* to do *what*. The World Bank's *Empowerment and Poverty Reduction: A Sourcebook* specifies that it is concerned with the empowerment "of poor people to participate in, negotiate with, influence, control, and hold accountable institutions that affect their lives" (Narayan 2002, 14).

"Civil society" is broadly defined as the space in society where collective citizen action takes place (Knight, Chigudu, and Tandon 2002; Bratton 1994). In other words, it is the space where individual members of society voluntarily come together, in formal or informal gatherings, groups, associations, or organizations, to participate in public life. Here, individual citizens can express their views, affirm their collective identity, and negotiate their interests. They can also seek to collectively interact with, influence, and hold accountable actors and institutions, related to both the state and the market, that affect their lives.

While the notion of civil society covers *all* members of society, this research initiative follows many analysts and researchers in focusing particular attention on the role of traditionally marginalized groups, such as poor people, women, and minorities, and the extent to which civil society serves the interests of these groups. In this sense, civil society can be understood as the principal societal space where the empowerment of citizens is developed and practiced (especially poor people and other marginalized groups), that is, where citizens may participate in, negotiate with, influence, control, and hold accountable institutions that affect their lives. Viewed from this perspective, the concept of civil society is very closely related to that of empowerment as defined in the World Bank's empowerment sourcebook (Narayan 2002). A strong civil society can thus be associated with a high level of citizen empowerment and a weak civil society with a less empowered citizenry.

Addressing issues of empowerment necessitates an understanding of the concepts of *power* and *power relations*. Power relations come into play in virtually every social relationship. They are played out between individuals and between groups of people every day and at every level of human interaction—within the household, in the workplace, in the community, and at national and international levels. There are different types of power (for example, personal, political, economic, social, intellectual) and different sources of power (including knowledge, rights, political authority, money and other assets, gender, and social status).

Issues of power and power relations are central to the concept of civil society. For some political theorists, the civil society concept implies the goal of building a healthy society by establishing an appropriate balance of power among citizens, the state, and market institutions (Uphoff and Krishna 2004; CIVICUS 1997). Other scholars and practitioners emphasize the importance of analyzing and understanding power relations within civil society, as the principal sphere where the values and interests of diverse (and often conflicting) societal groups are debated and negotiated (Howell and Pearce 2002; Chandhoke 2001). Finally, civil society is also understood as an arena where individual citizens are empowered and where crucial skills related to democratic power sharing, negotiation, and collective action are developed (Diamond 1994).

The CIVICUS Civil Society Index: An Introduction

The CSI is an action-research project to assess the state of civil society in countries around the world. Its immediate objectives are (a) to generate and share useful and relevant knowledge on the state of civil society and its role in society at large, and (b) to increase the capacity and commitment of civil society stakeholders to strengthen civil society. The ultimate aims of the CSI are to enhance the strength and sustainability of civil society and to strengthen civil society's contribution to positive social change.

During its pilot phase in 2000–01, the CSI was implemented in 13 countries and territories (Heinrich and Naidoo 2001).[2] Drawing on lessons learned from the pilot phase, aspects of the CSI conceptual framework and research methodology were redesigned (Batliwala 2002). The newly revamped CSI is currently being implemented in more than 60 countries, states, and territories across the globe, as listed in box 15.1. Preliminary findings by country are expected to be available beginning in mid-2005.[3]

The CSI is designed to assess four different dimensions of civil society: (a) the *structure* of civil society, (b) the external *environment* in which civil society exists and functions, (c) the *values* held and advocated in the civil society arena, and (d) the *impact* of activities pursued by civil society actors. Each dimension is made up of several subdimensions, which in turn are composed of several indicators. In measuring the state of civil society, the CSI adopts a multidisciplinary approach. It integrates political, economic, social, and cultural factors and uses quantitative as well as qualitative methods and measures.

The CSI is initiated and implemented by and for civil society organizations. It is based on the principle that efforts to measure empowerment should themselves serve to empower. The CSI therefore employs a range of participatory research and consultation methods aimed at promoting multistakeholder learning, dialogue, and action. It actively involves a broad range of stakeholders, including governments, academics, donor organizations, and the public at large, and makes its findings available to them.

The following sections outline the conceptual framework, research methodology, and empowering characteristics of the CSI in greater detail.

Conceptualizing Civil Society from an Empowerment Perspective

With its diverse historical roots, ranging from Scottish Enlightenment thinkers and de Tocqueville to Marx and Gramsci, and its usage by different strands of modern political philosophy and development theory, the civil society concept is probably one of the social science concepts most difficult to define. As German sociologist Ulrich Beck puts it, "The most precise

**Box 15.1   Countries, States, and Territories Participating
in the Civil Society Index, 2003–05**

Argentina	Jamaica
Armenia	Jordan
Australia	Korea, Republic of
Azerbaijan	Lebanon
Bangladesh	Macedonia, FYR
Bolivia	Malawi
Bosnia and Herzegovina	Mauritius
Botswana	Mexico
Brazil	Mongolia
Bulgaria	Mozambique
Burkina Faso	Nepal
China	Nigeria
Colombia	Northern Ireland (United Kingdom)
Congo, Democratic Republic of	Orissa (India)
Congo, Republic of	Palestine
Costa Rica	Poland
Croatia	Puerto Rico
Czech Republic	Romania
Ecuador	Russian Federation
Egypt, Arab Republic of	Scotland (United Kingdom)
England	Serbia and Montenegro
Ethiopia	Sierra Leone
Fiji	Slovenia
Gambia, The	South Carolina (United States)
Germany	Timor-Leste
Ghana	Turkey
Guatemala	Uganda
Honduras	Ukraine
Hong Kong (China)	Uruguay
Indonesia	Uzbekistan
Italy	Wales (United Kingdom)

statement one can make about civil society is that it is an extraordinarily vague idea" (2001, 15; translation mine).

Because civil society is such a complex notion, the CSI's task of defining and operationalizing the concept, identifying its essential features, and designing a strategy to assess the state of civil society was also a complex and potentially controversial process.

While this process drew on conceptual tools from other fields and disciplines, this was the first time an attempt had been made to develop a comprehensive conceptual framework to assess the state of civil society cross-nationally. The CSI's dual objectives of generating an assessment of civil society and initiating an action-oriented exercise among civil society stakeholders guided the development of the conceptual framework. The following guidelines were adopted as conceptual building blocks consonant with these objectives.

Design a framework that is globally relevant and applicable. Both the concept and the reality of civil society vary greatly around the world. Given the global nature of the CSI, the conceptual framework seeks to accommodate cultural variations in understandings of civil society and the diverse forms and functions of civil society in different countries. In particular, the CSI seeks to avoid a "Western" bias in defining key concepts and choosing indicators. While recognizing the debate among civil society scholars as to whether the civil society concept is even applicable to non-Western contexts (Kasfir 1998; Blaney and Pasha 1993; Lewis 2002; Hann and Dunn 1996), the project contends that collective citizen action is a feature common to all societies. The concept of civil society is therefore useful in describing this universal reality irrespective of its philosophical roots.

Balance contextual validity and cross-country comparability. The CSI seeks to generate information about civil society that can be compared across countries. There is a tension, however, between seeking "standardized" information that can be compared across national boundaries and maintaining adequate flexibility to ensure that country-specific factors can be taken into account. The CSI is specifically designed to achieve an appropriate balance between these two opposing demands by generating a range of different products, from a context-rich country report to internationally comparable numeric scores.

To balance context specificity and cross-country comparability, the set of proposed indicators represents only a "core" of universally applicable indicators. In many countries, additional country-specific indicators (such as civil society's role in peace building or emergency relief) can be added by the country team, so that the indicator set exhaustively covers all main features of civil society. Added indicators are not judged to jeopardize cross-country comparability *as long as* they are valid indicators for the respective (sub)dimension. Recognizing the immense variety of social, cultural, and political contexts in which civil society functions around the world, the CSI is striving for broadly *equivalent* rather than identical assessments (van Deth 1998; Przeworski and Teune 1966/67). Thus, the existence of different indicator sets in different countries can, if each is adapted appropriately, actually be a sign of valid (that is, contextual) assessments.

Be as inclusive as possible. Debates on how to operationalize and measure civil society and how to strengthen real civil societies are still in their infancy. Given the current lack of consensus around the concept of civil society, the CSI framework seeks to accommodate a variety of theoretical perspectives by identifying and generating knowledge about a range of different features and dimensions of civil society. The CSI has therefore adopted an inclusive and multidisciplinary approach in terms of the civil society definition, indicators, actors, and processes. It makes use of the development-oriented literature as well as approaches situating civil society in relation to democracy and governance. This eases the task of conceptualization and data collection and also facilitates engagement within the field of research on civil society and related themes, such as democracy, governance, and development.

Reflect the reality of civil society. There is much debate concerning civil society's normative content. Some argue that to belong to civil society, actors must be democratic (Diamond 1994), seek the public good (Knight and Hartnell 2001), or at least adhere to basic civil manners (Shils 1991; Merkel and Lauth 1998). While such normative definitions and concepts are useful in defining civil society as an ideal, they are less useful in seeking to understand and assess the reality of civil society across the globe. The CSI seeks to assess the state of civil society. Such an assessment would obviously be predetermined to yield a more positive result if, from the outset, any undesirable or "uncivil" elements were excluded from the investigation by definition. The CSI, therefore, adopts a realistic view. It acknowledges that civil society is composed of positive and negative elements, peaceful and violent forces, and actors that may advance or obstruct social progress. It also acknowledges that civil society is not a homogeneous entity, but rather a complex arena where diverse values and interests interact and power struggles occur (Fowler 1996, 18).

Take a normative stance. In selecting certain indicators and scaling them from "most negative" to "most positive," the CSI had to make normative judgments as to what the defining features of civil society are, what functions civil society should serve, what values it should embrace, and so on. To tackle this issue, the CSI took guidance from universal standards (such as the United Nations Declaration of Human Rights) from CIVICUS's own values (see http://www.civicus.org) and from the literature by scholars and civil society actors on civil society's characteristics, roles, and enabling factors.

Ensure an action orientation. The CSI, unlike academically focused research initiatives, aims to generate practical information for civil society practitioners and other primary stakeholders. It therefore seeks to identify aspects of civil society that can be changed and to generate information and knowledge relevant to action-oriented goals. This action orientation informs the choice of indicators, particularly in the structure, values, and impact dimensions (discussed below).

The CSI defines civil society as "the arena between family, government, and market where people voluntarily associate to advance common interests." In conceptualizing civil society as an arena, the project emphasizes the importance of civil society's role in providing a public space where diverse societal values and interests interact. While acknowledging theoretical boundaries between civil society and the spheres of state and market, we understand these boundaries to be "fuzzy." The three realms are conceived in functionalist terms. That is, individual actors can traverse and even cohabit these realms, depending on the nature of their action rather than on their sector of origin or organizational form. The framework thus deemphasizes organizational forms and allows for a broader focus on the functions and roles of informal associations, movements, and instances of collective citizen action.

Reflecting its practical interest in strengthening civil society, the CSI conceptualizes civil society as a *political* phenomenon, rather than defining it in *economic* terms as a synonym for the nonprofit sector. This is because the CSI is interested in collective public action in the broader context of governance and development and not primarily in the economic role of nonprofit organizations in society. This political perspective on civil society leads the CSI to pay attention to issues of *power* and *power relations,* within the civil society arena as well as between civil society actors and institutions of the state and the private sector.

Dimensions of the CSI

To assess civil society in a given country holistically, the CSI seeks to measure four key dimensions of the state of civil society. The choice of these four dimensions was guided by the rich body of theoretical work on civil society, particularly that dealing with civil society's defining features and essential roles, and by the accumulated practical knowledge of civil practitioners from around the world who have documented their experiences and identified key "real world" influencing factors and challenges. The selection also reflects the core principles of CIVICUS, which served to establish the CSI's normative stance and its concern with issues of equity, empowerment, tolerance, and nonviolence.

The first dimension of the CSI, *structure,* refers to the structural characteristics of the civil society arena and its actors. The second dimension focuses on the external *environment* in which civil society exists and functions and the extent to which various aspects of that environment are enabling or disabling. The third dimension assesses the *values* held and advocated in the civil society arena and the extent to which these values serve the common good. The fourth dimension has to do with the *impact* of activities pursued by civil society actors, in particular with regard to governance and development.

Each dimension is made up of several subdimensions, which in turn are composed of a number of indicators. The CSI uses a total of 25 subdimensions and 74 indicators to analyze the state of civil society. The dimensions and subdimensions of the CSI are described below.

Dimension 1: Structure

The importance of understanding civil society's structure and composition is well established in the literature (Salamon et al. 1999; Welzel 1999; Bratton 1994, 2). This dimension of the CSI explores the overall size, importance, level of organization, and resources of the civil society arena in a given country. It also seeks to assess the main characteristics of civil society actors and the relationships among them. The dimension of structure is composed of the following six subdimensions, with a total of 21 indicators:

1. *Breadth of citizen participation.* This subdimension, reflecting civil society's overall size and strength, shows the proportion of citizens who are involved in some way in civil society. Indicators include the percentages of citizens who undertake nonpartisan political actions, donate to charity, belong to a civil society organization (CSO), do volunteer work, or participate in community activities.

2. *Depth of citizen participation.* In assessing the strength of civil society, it is also important to know how frequently and extensively people engage in civil society activities. This subdimension looks at how *much* people give to charity, how *much* volunteer work they do, and how *many* different CSOs they belong to.

3. *Diversity within civil society.* Since the CSI regards civil society as an arena where conflicting interests and power relations are played out, the equitable representation of different social groups within civil society, especially traditionally marginalized groups, is considered an important feature. This subdimension looks at the participation of women, minorities, and other social groups in CSO leadership and membership. It also assesses the geographic representation of CSOs in order to determine whether rural populations or specific regions of the country are underrepresented.

4. *Level of organization.* This subdimension looks at features of the infrastructure for civil society, indicating its stability and maturity, as well as its capacity for collective action. Indicators relate to the existence and effectiveness of CSO umbrella bodies, efforts to self-regulate, the level of civil society support infrastructure, and international linkages.

5. *Interrelations.* An important determinant of the strength of civil society is the extent to which diverse actors share information and cooperate with one another. This subdimension explores examples of communication and cross-sectoral alliance building to assess the extent of linkages and productive relations among civil society actors.

6. *Resources.* This subdimension looks at the capacity of civil society in terms of the level of resources available to it. It assesses the extent to which CSOs have adequate financial, human, and technological resources to achieve their goals.

Dimension 2: Environment

Although not part of civil society itself, the environment for action by civil society is nonetheless crucial in assessing civil society's status and devising potential initiatives for strengthening its capabilities. The root causes of potential problems may well lie in the environment rather than within civil society itself. This dimension is divided into seven subdimensions with a total of 23 indicators intended to show how enabling the external environment is for civil society and citizen empowerment. The aspects included go beyond the traditional focus on legal factors (CIVICUS 1997; ICNL 1998; Salamon and

Toepler 2000) to include assessments of political, constitutional, social, economic, and cultural factors, as well as the attitudes and behavior of state and private sector actors toward civil society. The subdimensions include:

1. *Political context*. The political context in any given country defines the overall backdrop and establishes important parameters for civil society's activities. Component indicators include citizens' political rights, the extent of political party competition, the rule of law, corruption, state effectiveness, and decentralization.

2. *Basic freedoms and rights*. This subdimension includes those constitutional rights that directly relate to the functioning of civil society, namely basic civil liberties (such as freedoms of expression, assembly, and association), information rights, and press freedom. Indicators under this subdimension measure the extent to which these freedoms and rights are ensured by law and in practice.

3. *Socioeconomic context*. This subdimension includes the socioeconomic situation in the country and its impact on civil society. Indicators measure the presence in the country of a range of conditions considered seriously disabling to civil society—for example, widespread poverty, civil war, severe ethnic or religious conflict, severe economic or social crisis, severe socioeconomic inequity, or pervasive adult illiteracy.

4. *Sociocultural context*. While civic norms such as trust are often regarded as a key component of social capital (Putnam 1993) and sometimes as a component of civil society (Bratton 1994, 2), the CSI considers these norms as an important *social resource* for civil society to draw on. As such, they are part of civil society's external environment. This subdimension includes levels of trust, tolerance, and public-spiritedness among members of society as indicators showing to what extent sociocultural norms and attitudes are conducive to civil society.

5. *Legal environment*. This subdimension provides an assessment of the extent to which the existing legal environment is enabling or disabling to civil society. The specific indicators for this subdimension draw upon the substantial body of existing work in this area.[4] They include an assessment of CSO registration procedures, legal constraints on CSO advocacy activities, CSO tax exemptions, and tax benefits to promote philanthropy.

6. *State–civil society relations*. The crucial importance of relations between the state and civil society is well established in the literature (Boris and Steuerle 1999; Greenstein, Heinrich, and Naidoo 1998; Rosenblum and Post 2002; Kuhnle and Selle 1992). This subdimension focuses on the nature and quality of state–civil society relations, including issues of CSO autonomy, state–civil society dialogue, and relationships of cooperation and support between the state and civil society.

7. *Private sector–civil society relations*. The impact of relations between the private sector and civil society has traditionally received less attention in the literature, but it is an area of growing concern (see, for example, CIVICUS 1999; Serrano 2001; Covey and Brown 2001; Yablonski 2001; Social Venture Network 1999). This subdimension encompasses private sector attitudes

toward civil society as well as levels of corporate social responsibility and corporate philanthropy.

Dimension 3: Values

A focus on the principles and values adhered to, practiced by, and promoted by civil society is an innovative feature of the CSI. This aspect of civil society has traditionally received scant attention in the literature, in part because civil society's values are often considered to be positive, progressive, or democratic by definition. The CSI project, in contrast, considers that assessing the ratio of tolerant versus intolerant, progressive versus fundamentalist, pro-poor versus anti-poor civil society actors in a country is crucial for judging its overall state. The prevalence of values such as democracy and transparency is also a critical measure of civil society's normative foundation. The seven subdimensions and 14 indicators for this dimension reflect a set of universally accepted social and political norms, drawn from sources such as the Universal Declaration of Human Rights as well as from CIVICUS's own values. Indicators cover both how these values are practiced within civil society and civil society's efforts to promote the values in society at large.

1. *Democracy.* This subdimension assesses the extent to which civil society organizations practice internal democracy (as in selecting leaders and making decisions) and how actively they are involved in promoting democracy within society at large.

2. *Transparency.* This subdimension focuses on corruption and financial transparency within civil society, as well as on civil society's actions to promote transparency at the societal level.

3. *Tolerance.* This subdimension includes the balance between tolerant and intolerant forces within civil society as well as the extent to which civil society is engaged in promoting tolerance within society at large.

4. *Nonviolence.* While civil society can play an important role in denouncing violence, resolving conflicts, and building peace, it is also at times an arena where groups use violent means to express their interests. This subdimension assesses the presence of violent forces within civil society as well as civil society's efforts to promote nonviolence at the individual, household, and societal levels.

5. *Gender equity.* This subdimension assesses gender-equitable practices within CSOs as well as civil society's actions to promote gender equity at the societal level.

6. *Poverty eradication.* This subdimension examines the extent to which civil society actors are engaged in addressing poverty issues and promoting pro-poor policies, which are considered important indicators of civil society's values.[5]

7. *Environmental sustainability.* This subdimension assesses the extent to which civil society is actively engaged in promoting environmental sustainability—that is, protecting the environment and promoting sustainable forms of development that meet the needs of both current and future generations.

Dimension 4: Impact

A final important measure of the state of civil society is the impact civil society actors have on people's lives and on society as a whole. The types of roles that civil society can and should play in the areas of governance and development, and the desired impact of those roles, have been discussed extensively in the literature (Smith 1983; Salamon, Hems, and Chinnock 2000; Fowler 1999; Kendall and Knapp 2000; Edwards 2004). Drawing on the existing literature, this dimension encompasses five subdimensions, each representing an essential "core function" of civil society. These five subdimensions, with 16 indicators, assess how *active* and how *successful* civil society has been in fulfilling each defined role. This dimension, therefore, implies a broad notion of impact, referring not only to the end result (how much influence civil society has had in a particular area), but also to the process (how actively civil society has engaged in that area).

1. *Influencing public policy.* The first subdimension focuses on how active and successful civil society is in influencing public policy. The impact is considered in three specific issue areas: (a) the national budget process, (b) one priority human rights issue identified by in-country stakeholders, and (c) one priority social policy issue identified by in-country stakeholders.

2. *Holding the state and private corporations accountable.* The importance of civil society's role as "watchdog," holding state entities and private corporations accountable for their decisions and actions, is broadly acknowledged by both scholars and practitioners (Lanegran 1995; Diamond 1994; Hyden 1995). This subdimension assesses the extent to which civil society is active and successful in monitoring and holding to account both state and private sector actors.

3. *Responding to social interests.* The extent to which civil society's positions and actions mirror the priority concerns of the population at large is considered an important indicator of civil society's impact. Civil societies vary—from those that are elitist and out of touch with ordinary citizens to those that are responsive and effectively take up and voice societal concerns. This subdimension analyzes civil society's function as a representative or articulator of societal interests. Investigating this subdimension requires looking both at how effectively civil society responds to priority social concerns and at the level of public trust in civil society, since the latter is considered a proxy indicator for civil society's responsiveness.

4. *Meeting societal needs.* Another widely recognized function of civil society is to contribute to meeting pressing societal needs, especially those of poor people and other marginalized groups. This subdimension looks at civil society's performance both in meeting those needs directly (for example, by promoting self-help initiatives or delivering services) and in lobbying the state for improved service provision. The subdimension also looks specifically at civil society's relative effectiveness in meeting the needs of marginalized groups.

5. *Empowering citizens.* A final core function of civil society is its role in contributing to the empowerment of citizens. For the purposes of the CSI,

empowering citizens is defined as *contributing to a process whereby citizens have more choice and are able to take more control over decisions that affect their lives* (CIVICUS 2003). The five indicators of this subdimension aim to capture various essential elements of empowerment as both a means and an end. These include civil society's impact on (a) informing and educating citizens on issues of public interest, (b) building capacity for collective action (that is, supporting individuals and groups in their efforts to organize, mobilize resources, and work together to solve common problems), and (c) building social capital (by promoting trust, tolerance, and public-spiritedness). Additional indicators look specifically at how actively and successfully civil society empowerment efforts target (d) women and (e) poor people.

CSI Research and Scoring Methodology

The CSI measures each of the 74 indicators of the state of civil society, assigning a score from 0 (most negative) to 3 (most positive).[6] Indicator scores are then aggregated (by simple averaging) into a score for each subdimension and, finally, into an overall score for each of the four dimensions of civil society.

Such summary indicators are clearly only as valuable as the knowledge base about civil society on which they draw and the process by which the scores are determined. The unique contribution of the CSI project is to involve a wide range of civil society actors themselves in a participatory research process to produce the index. The CSI research and scoring methodology was developed according to the following principles:

Draw on a wide variety of data sources. Given the lack of secondary data on civil society in many countries, the project attempts to make use of all forms of existing relevant information from reliable sources and also undertakes its own primary (quantitative and qualitative) research as necessary.

Participatory methods of research. The CSI is not just an information-gathering exercise but an action-research project with the ultimate goal of contributing to the strengthening of civil society. The in-country research process is largely controlled and implemented by civil society actors. While the project draws on all available sources of information, a core source of knowledge about civil society is civil society stakeholders themselves. The project uses participatory methods of research to consult with a large number of stakeholders, soliciting both individual and group responses to a mix of closed and open-ended questions.

Stakeholder learning and action. The research methodology is explicitly designed to promote learning and, ultimately, action on the part of participants. In addition to the organization of a final national-level workshop, processes of data collection are intended to contribute to participant learning. This is done, for example, through group-based approaches that challenge participants to see themselves as a part of a "bigger picture," to think beyond their own organizational or sectoral context, to reflect strategically about

relations within civil society and between civil society and other parts of society, to identify key strengths and weaknesses of their country's civil society,
and to assess collective needs.

The implementation of the CSI project at the country level is coordinated
by a *national index team,* made up of a national coordinating organization
(most often a civil society support organization, think tank, or umbrella organization), a participatory researcher, and a civil society expert. The national
index team is assisted by a 12-person *national advisory group,* made up of a diverse set of civil society and non–civil society stakeholders. The national index
team, assisted by its national advisory group, begins by reviewing the CSI conceptual framework and research methodology as proposed by CIVICUS and
adapting this as necessary to its country context. The national advisory group
conducts an initial *social forces analysis* (an analysis of key actors and power
relations in society at large to help situate civil society) and prepares a *map of
civil society* in the country (charting key forces and actors within civil society
and relations between them).

The national index team then coordinates secondary and primary research on each of the four identified dimensions of civil society. This research
involves the following elements:

Secondary data review. A thorough review of all existing data on civil society (related to the four identified dimensions) is conducted, and findings are
summarized in an initial overview report. This report represents the basis for
a first draft country report. It serves to identify data gaps and determine the
extent and nature of primary research needs.

Media review. A review is undertaken of principal written (and, in some
cases, broadcast) media over the preceding year to gather information on issues related to the four dimensions of civil society. This review serves both to
gather information on civil society activities and to provide insights into how
the media perceive and portray civil society.

Fact-finding studies. This research includes seeking out existing but unpublished data on civil society, interviewing key informants, and conducting
two specific studies designed to gauge the extent of corporate social responsibility and civil society's policy impact in selected policy areas.

Regional stakeholder consultations. A core aspect of the CSI research
methodology is the organization of consultative workshops with civil society
stakeholders in different parts of the country. In each case, a diverse group of
15–20 stakeholders is asked to respond to individual questionnaires (covering
issues related to each of the four dimensions of civil society) and subsequently
to participate in a daylong group consultation. The participants discuss the
results from the questionnaire, specifically those issues that generated disagreement or particular interest.[7] The group consultation is intended to scrutinize and validate individual responses, generate collective reflection, build
consensus, and clarify issues of disagreement.

Community surveys. This research, carried out in several locations
throughout the country, gathers views from the grassroots to complement the
other research methods that rely on civil society stakeholders, experts, and the

media. A total of approximately 300 ordinary citizens are asked about their attitudes toward and participation in civil society.

Once the various forms of research have been carried out and the data analyzed and written up, findings are presented to the national advisory group. On the basis of this evidence, this diverse group of 12 stakeholders acts as a jury and collectively attributes a score of 0 to 3 to each of the 74 indicators. Members of the jury are provided with scoring guidelines that provide a qualitative description of each possible score (0, 1, 2, or 3) for each indicator. These descriptions are based upon real-life scenarios and are designed to accommodate country-level particularities while at the same time establishing common benchmarks that allow for cross-country comparison.

Box 15.2 provides an example of score descriptions for one sample indicator: the "autonomy" indicator in the state–civil society relations subdimension of the environment dimension.[8]

Jury members discuss each indicator based on the available data and then decide by majority vote which score description best reflects the current country situation. Indicator scores are then aggregated into subdimension scores and, finally, into dimension scores. The results of the scoring exercise can be summarized graphically in the form of a diamond by plotting the scores along four axes (figure 15.1).[9]

Box 15.2   Example of Indicator Scoring

Dimension: Environment

Subdimension: State–civil society relations

Indicator: Autonomy

Description: To what extent can civil society exist and function independently of the state? To what extent are CSOs free to operate without excessive government interference? Is government oversight reasonably designed and limited to protect legitimate public interests?

Score descriptions:

Score 0: The state controls civil society.

Score 1: CSOs are subject to frequent unwarranted interference in their operations.

Score 2: The state accepts the existence of an independent civil society but CSOs are subject to occasional unwarranted government interference.

Score 3: CSOs operate freely. They are subject only to reasonable oversight linked to clear and legitimate public interests.

Figure 15.1   Civil Society Diamond

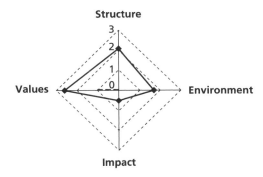

In a final phase, research findings and scores are presented and validated at a national workshop attended by a broad range of stakeholders. The workshop also discusses strategies for prioritizing and addressing identified weaknesses in civil society. Ideally, an action plan for initiatives to strengthen civil society is drafted. A final country report, including (a) a full description and analysis of research findings; (b) indicator, subdimension, and dimension scores; and (c) the outcomes and recommendations of the national workshop, is published for national and international readership and action.

The CSI as Measure and Process of Empowerment

A unique feature of the CSI is its focus on empowerment as both a *measure* and a *process*. In other words, the CSI aims both to measure various dimensions and aspects of empowerment and to serve as an empowering process in and of itself.

As described above, the CSI project conceptualizes civil society in political terms. By measuring civil society's structure, environment, values, and impact, the CSI assesses and analyzes a variety of factors that determine both the level of citizen empowerment in a given country and the underlying societal factors and power structures that enable or disable the empowerment of citizens.

The CSI examines power relations at several different levels. The initial social forces analysis aims to identify key forces at the *societal level* and to analyze the nature of relations between them. It includes a basic assessment of the balance of power among the arenas of state, market, and civil society. The CSI is also designed to examine power relations *within civil society,* assessing the relative levels of empowerment among different key sectors and groups. The CSI includes a number of indicators that explore the nature of power relations *within organizations of civil society* (such as power relations between individual members on the basis of organizational hierarchy, gender, economic or social status, etc.). Other indicators measure the impact of civil society in *empowering citizens*, in particular, *traditionally marginalized societal groups* (such as women and poor people). At each of these levels, the aim of the CSI is to accurately assess the current situation and promote more equitable power relations.

With regard to process, the CSI shares some crucial features with academic research exercises on civil society and related themes, such as the Johns Hopkins Comparative Nonprofit Sector Project, the Civil Society and Governance Programme at the Institute of Development Studies at the University of Sussex, and the European Science Foundation Network on Citizenship, Involvement, and Democracy. These common characteristics include the use of specific research tools, such as population surveys, desk studies, and focus groups, as well as the rigorous conceptualization of the subject through an elaborate framework of indicators.

The CSI, however, aims not only to produce knowledge but also to promote social change. As a result, it employs a carefully designed participatory process of *action research* designed not only to study or question but also to empower the subjects of its research. Thus civil society stakeholders are actively involved in all stages of the CSI process, from the initial design to the implementation, deliberation, and dissemination stages. The CSI combines the above-mentioned social science standards and tools with approaches and processes rooted in participatory action research (Fals-Borda and Rahman 1991; Chambers 1997; Knight, Chigudu, and Tandon 2002, 33–36) and civil society–strengthening frameworks and strategies (for example, Fox and Woodward 1997; Fowler 1996). The CSI employs a combination of empirical data gathering and normative assessment. The engagement of researchers, practitioners, and civil society activists throughout the project helps to break down barriers and contributes to the development of a mutually empowering relationship. It is this rare mix of actors, tools, processes, and frameworks, attempting to bridge academic research canons with actor-oriented empowerment approaches, that distinguishes the CSI from other projects in the field.

However, participation is not seen as a panacea (Cooke and Kothari 2001). Nor is it applied indiscriminately throughout the project cycle. On the contrary, each project stage seeks to employ an appropriate type of participation by the relevant group of actors (table 15.1).

At the heart of the CSI's knowledge-action link is the national CSI workshop, which brings together a variety of civil society stakeholders. Many of them have been actively involved in the CSI research process, as national advisory group members, participants in the regional stakeholder consultations, and key informants for specific research questions. The national workshop has two goals. First, it aims to engage stakeholders in critical discussion and reflection on the results of the CSI initiative in the country, in order to arrive at a common understanding of the current state of civil society and major challenges. This is a prerequisite for the second goal, namely for participants to use the findings as a basis for identifying specific strengths and weaknesses in civil society as well as potential areas of improvement. If deemed appropriate, the national workshop can culminate in the development of a specific

Table 15.1   Participation in the CSI Project Cycle

Stage	Type of participation	Lead actor	Actors involved
Design	Consultation	CIVICUS	Pilot-phase partners, experts, NGOs
Country-level adaptation	Consultation; decision making	National index team	National advisory group
Research	Input; consultation	Participatory researcher	Regional stakeholders, experts, citizens in communities
Data aggregation (scoring)	Decision making	National advisory group	National index team
Reflection (national workshop)	Input; discussion; decision making	National index team	National workshop participants
Action planning	Input; discussion; decision making	National index team	National workshop participants and other stakeholders

Figure 15.2   The CSI Project Cycle

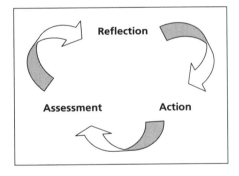

action agenda to be carried out by the stakeholders. This cycle of assessment, reflection, and action (figure 15.2), coupled with the generally participatory nature of the project, forms the core of CSI's attempt to successfully link research with action.

One way in which this process empowers civil society actors is by building their self-awareness and their sense that they are part of something larger, namely civil society itself. Reflecting on and engaging with broad civil society issues that go beyond the narrower concerns of their respective organizations can help CSO representatives expand their horizons. These generic civil society issues, on which there is presumably more commonality than difference among civil society actors, are central to the CSI process. A strong collective self-awareness among civil society actors can also be a catalyst for joint advocacy activities to defend civic space when under threat or to advance the common interests of civil society in relation to external forces.

In many instances, of course, civil society actors and other stakeholders will not be able to find common ground because of irreconcilable differences in values, interests, or strategies. Even then, however, the impact of dialogue, constructive engagement, and "agreeing to disagree" should not be underestimated (Edwards 2004, 100). This is especially important in the many places where civil society is beset by internal fragmentation, parochialism, and conflict within the sector as well as with government.

There are many ways to strengthen the cohesiveness and long-term sustainability of civil society. The CSI's unique approach is to combine a *scientific assessment* with a *participatory approach* to convene, engage, and mobilize civil society's diverse actors and external stakeholders.

Preliminary Observations and Key Challenges

The CSI project, making use of the analytical framework and operational processes described above, brings together diverse tools with the common aim of empowering civil society stakeholders through a scientific, participatory, and broad-based assessment and action planning exercise. While the project implementation has not progressed far enough to identify concrete results and definite lessons learned, some initial reflections on the progress made thus far can be shared. Because the project is in an early stage, these reflections necessarily focus on the CSI as a process rather than on the results of the research.

Civil Society: A Divided Sector?

As the first major project activity, the national advisory groups in a number of countries have held their first meetings. This meeting serves as a "reality check" in which national civil society stakeholders can consider the project's proposed methodology and approach. In most countries the advisory groups adopted the CSI approach without major changes, but in some cases interesting discussions, particularly around the definition of civil society, ensued. It became clear that the value-free definition of civil society, including, for example, undemocratic or intolerant CSOs, challenged existing civil society concepts, particularly in Central and Eastern Europe. In this region it also proved difficult to bring trade unions to the table as advisory group members or as participants in regional stakeholder consultations. These trade union representatives apparently do not consider themselves part of civil society; this is most likely a consequence of the particular role of unions during Communist rule, when they were essentially a part of the state apparatus.

In other regions of the world, some national advisory group members were skeptical that the concept of civil society adds much value to existing working concepts, such as the voluntary sector or NGO sector. In Scotland, for example, the national coordinating organization decided to use the CSI project to put the idea of civil society—so far foreign to Scotland—to an empirical test.

Across countries, a primary purpose of the CSI is to explore whether religious organizations, professional associations, trade unions, and voluntary organizations benefit from engaging in dialogue and exploring common concerns.

As noted above, a specific task of the first national advisory group meeting is to conduct a "social forces analysis" in which group members work together to identify and map the key social actors in society. Global training workshops conducted by CIVICUS for national coordinating organizations have already revealed their vastly different comfort levels with regard to the social forces analysis, which borrows heavily from participatory action-research tools such as Venn diagrams. Whereas participants from Asia and Africa apparently had no difficulty including the social forces analysis in their research repertoire, some participants from European countries and post-Soviet states suggested that such a tool lacked methodological rigor and validity, referring to it as "a game."

Interestingly, however, in most advisory group meetings the social forces analysis was conducted and participants subsequently evaluated it as useful in drawing a picture of the roles of civil society actors amid other forces in the larger society. The general pattern found was that civil society organizations are rarely among the more prominent and powerful actors—with the exception, in some cases, of trade unions and religious organizations. This finding is supported by the initial results of the media reviews, which examined the representation of civil society issues and actors in the national media. These also suggested a higher public profile for trade unions and faith-based organizations. In Germany, for example, trade unions and to a lesser extent churches receive far more media coverage than other types of CSOs such as foundations and associations, which garnered only scant attention in the three national newspapers monitored by the German coordinating organization.

On the other hand, the other research outputs produced by the national coordinating organizations do not provide much data on trade unions or religious bodies. The overview reports, which summarize secondary data on civil society along the four CSI dimensions, rely heavily on data gathered for NGOs or voluntary organizations. Additionally, information provided by regional stakeholders through questionnaires or in stakeholder consultations focuses mainly on examples from the NGO sector.

Thus, a first observation emerging from the CSI's preliminary research is an apparent division within civil society. On the one hand are membership-based entities such as unions and faith-based organizations, which tend to enjoy more public recognition and more influence than other CSOs. On the other hand are the advocacy NGOs, foundations, and other public-interest organizations that are often conceived as the core of civil society. It will be interesting to see whether other research tools, such as community surveys and key informant interviews, support this emerging division within civil society. Also, findings from regions such as Latin America and Africa, where unions, churches, and NGOs tend to have much stronger links with each other and more common interests than in Central and Eastern Europe, might well show another, more coherent, pattern of intra–civil society relationships.

Challenges Going Forward

Project experience to date has shown that the adoption of a participatory approach, aimed at promoting stakeholder learning and empowerment, is essential to the success of the CSI. In practice this is extremely difficult to achieve. The first challenge is to find national partner organizations that truly believe in and will commit themselves to an empowering process. This commitment entails giving up ownership of and, consequently, credit for the project to the national advisory group and other stakeholders. It also implies adopting an inclusive and consultative approach, that is, cooperating with other groups that might historically have been competitors or even adversaries. In times of scarce resources and fierce competition among CSOs, commitment to such an approach cannot be taken for granted.

A second challenge is resource mobilization. With civil society stakeholders at country level taking on full ownership of the process, the national coordinating organization also assumes the task of raising the necessary resources for project implementation. There have been many obstacles to obtaining these resources, including inappropriate and politically driven donor agendas, lack of recognition of the relevance of knowledge-based multistakeholder processes for civil society, and scarce donor assets.

Another external challenge has been specific political environments in countries where civil society is under threat from, or in outspoken opposition to, government. As the CSI relies upon an inclusive consultative approach, political oppression of civil society and a generally hostile government attitude toward civil society can stifle the project process. In Bangladesh, for example, the project is effectively on hold due to deep government–civil society tensions. In other countries, establishment of the national advisory group has been postponed in order to keep a low project profile and avoid provoking the scrutiny of an authoritarian regime.

Additionally, the CSI project is continually challenged to take its participatory and empowering nature seriously, that is, to go beyond the "usual suspects" (typically well-connected CSOs in the major urban centers) and involve marginalized groups and poor people who do not usually feature on the national agenda. This requires consistent outreach efforts and a considerable investment of time, energy, and resources.

Finally, the CSI project seeks to put into practice the saying that "knowledge is power" by ensuring that knowledge generated by the project is broadly shared, debated, and acted upon. This is a significant challenge, given the weaknesses among civil society organizations already discussed.

In sum, the CSI project is an ambitious experiment in action research that seeks to both measure and promote citizen empowerment. Innovative and distinctive aspects of the CSI include its efforts to define and operationalize the concept of civil society in a holistic and multidimensional manner, to offer a framework that allows for comparison between countries, and to combine academic research with participatory approaches in a way that empowers civil society stakeholders at the local through international levels. The CSI has faced and continues to face enormous challenges in its efforts to achieve its goals. Nonetheless, the enthusiasm and commitment of the hundreds of civil society stakeholders currently involved in the project can be taken as a tentative sign that such an initiative is worth the effort.

Notes

1.   CIVICUS: World Alliance for Citizen Participation is an international civil society network based in Johannesburg, South Africa.
2.   Participating in the pilot phase were Belarus, Canada, Croatia, Estonia, Indonesia, Mexico, New Zealand, Pakistan, Romania, South Africa, Ukraine, Uruguay, and Wales.
3.   For more information regarding the CIVICUS Civil Society Index, please visit the CIVICUS Web site at http://www.civicus.org or contact the CSI team at index@civicus. org.
4.   We would like to acknowledge the invaluable assistance of the International Center for Not-for-Profit Law in developing these indicators.
5.   Although the notion of poverty eradication is usually applied to the poor countries of the global South and, to a lesser extent, to post-communist countries, the CSI project strongly believes that it is relevant in Northern countries as well. Efforts to address poverty issues in these countries often focus on a specific social group, such as single-parent households or the elderly.
6.   A complete list of the 74 CSI indicators can be accessed at http://www.civicus.org.
7.   This approach draws on the "Delphi method," which proposes several iterative stages through which research participants arrive at a commonly agreed-to assessment regarding complex social questions.
8.   Score descriptions for all 74 indicators are available at http://www.civicus.org.
9.   This simple visual representation, developed for CIVICUS by Helmut Anheier (2004), has proved useful in presenting results in a user-friendly manner to a broad public. It also facilitates the comparison of results from different countries or in the same country over time. It should be noted, however, that the civil society diamond is simply one aspect of a more in-depth country report that describes and analyzes findings in much greater detail.

References

Anheier, Helmut K. 2004. *Civil Society: Measurement, Evaluation, Policy.* London: Earthscan.

Batliwala, Srilatha. 2002. "Evaluation of the Pilot Phase of the CIVICUS Index Project." CIVICUS: World Alliance for Citizen Participation, Washington, DC.

Beck, Ulrich. 2001. "Zivilgesellschaft light?" *Süddeutsche Zeitung,* June 23–24, 15.

Blaney, David L., and Mustapha Kamal Pasha. 1993. "Civil Society and Democracy in the Third World: Ambiguities and Historical Possibilities." *Studies in Comparative International Development* 28 (1): 3–24.

Boris, Elizabeth T., and Eugene C. Steuerle. 1999. *Nonprofits and Government: Collaboration and Conflict.* Washington, DC: Urban Institute Press.

Bratton, Michael. 1994. "Civil Society and Political Transition in Africa." *IDR Reports* 11 (6). Institute for Development Research, Boston.

Chambers, Robert. 1997. *Whose Reality Counts? Putting the First Last.* London: Intermediate Technology Publications.

Chandhoke, Neera. 2001. "The 'Civil' and the 'Political' in Civil Society." *Democratization* 8 (2): 1–24.

CIVICUS. 1997. "Beyond Philanthropy: Corporate Citizenship and Civil Society." *CIVICUS World Newsletter,* January–February, 1.

———. 1999. "Promoting Corporate Citizenship: Opportunities for Business and Civil Society Engagement." CIVICUS, Washington, DC.

———. 2003. *Assessing the State of Civil Society: A Toolkit for Implementing the CIVICUS Civil Society Index.* Johannesburg: CIVICUS.

Cooke, Bill, and Uma Kothari. 2001. *Participation: The New Tyranny?* London: Zed.

Covey, Jane, and L. David Brown. 2001. "Critical Cooperation: An Alternative Form of Civil Society-Business Engagement." *IDR Reports* 17 (1). Institute for Development Research, Boston.

Diamond, Larry. 1994. "Rethinking Civil Society: Towards Democratic Consolidation." *Journal of Democracy* 5 (3): 4–17.

Edwards, Michael. 2004. *Civil Society.* London: Polity.

Fals-Borda, Orlando, and Muhammad Anisur Rahman. 1991. *Action and Knowledge: Breaking the Monopoly with Participatory Action-Research.* New York: Apex.

Fowler, Alan. 1996. "Strengthening Civil Society in Transition Economies, from Concept to Strategy: Mapping an Exit in a Maze of Mirrors." In *NGOs, Civil Society, and the State: Building Democracy in Transitional Societies,* ed. Andrew Clayton, 12–33. Oxford: INTRAC.

———. 1999. "Advocacy and Third Sector Organizations: A Composite Perspective." In *International Perspectives on Voluntary Action: Reshaping the Third Sector,* ed. David Lewis, 242–57. London: Earthscan.

Fox, Leslie, and Mark Woodward. 1997. "Building the Capacity of Civil Society in Africa: A Strategy and Framework." Capacity Building Technical Group, Africa Region, World Bank, Washington, DC.

Greenstein, Ran, Volkhart Heinrich, and Kumi Naidoo. 1998. *The State of Civil Society in South Africa: Past Legacies, Present Realities, and Future Prospects.* Johannesburg: CASE.

Hann, Chris, and Elizabeth Dunn, eds. 1996. *Civil Society: Challenging Western Models.* New York: Routledge.

Heinrich, Volkhart Finn, and Kumi Naidoo. 2001. "From Impossibility to Reality: A Reflection and Position Paper on the CIVICUS Index on Civil Society Project 1999–2001." CIVICUS, Washington, DC.

Howell, Jude, and Jenny Pearce. 2002. *Civil Society and Development: A Critical Exploration.* Boulder, CO: Lynne Rienner.

Hyden, Goran. 1995. "Assisting the Growth of Civil Society: How Might It Be Improved?" Uppsala Studies in Democracy 10, Department of Government, Uppsala University, Uppsala, Sweden.

ICNL (International Center for Not-for-Profit Law). 1998. "Legal Assessment Questionnaire." ICNL, Washington, DC.

Kasfir, Nelson. 1998. "The Conventional Notion of Civil Society: A Critique." *Journal of Commonwealth and Comparative Politics* 36 (2): 1–20.

Kendall, Jeremy, and Martin Knapp. 2000. "Measuring the Performance of Voluntary Organizations." *Public Management* 2 (1): 105–32.

Knight, Barry, and Caroline Hartnell. 2001. "Civil Society—Is It Anything More than a Metaphor for Hope for a Better World?" *Alliance* 6.

Knight, Barry, Hope Chigudu, and Rajesh Tandon. 2002. *Reviving Democracy: Citizens at the Heart of Governance.* London: Earthscan.

Kuhnle, Stein, and Per Selle. 1992. "Government and Voluntary Organizations: A Relational Perspective." In *Government and Voluntary Organizations: A Relational Perspective,* ed. Stein Kuhnle and Per Selle, 1–33. Aldershot, UK: Ashgate.

Lanegran, Kimberly. 1995. "South Africa's Civic Association Movement: ANC's Ally or Society's 'Watchdog'? Shifting Social Movement–Political Party Relations." *African Studies Review* 38 (2): 101–26.

Lewis, David. 2002. "Civil Society in African Contexts: Reflections on the Usefulness of a Concept." *Development and Change* 33 (4): 569–86.

Merkel, Wolfgang, and Hans-Joachim Lauth. 1998. "Systemwechsel und Zivilgesellschaft: Welche Zivilgesellschaft braucht die Demokratie?" *Aus Politik und Zeitgeschichte* B6–7: 3–12.

Narayan, Deepa, ed. 2002. *Empowerment and Poverty Reduction: A Sourcebook.* Washington, DC: World Bank.

Przeworski, Adam, and Henry Teune. 1966/67. "Equivalence in Cross-National Research." *Public Opinion Quarterly* 30 (4): 551–68.

Putnam, Robert D. 1993. *Making Democracy Work: Civic Traditions in Modern Italy.* Princeton, NJ: Princeton University Press.

Rosenblum, Nancy L., and Robert C. Post, eds. 2002. *Civil Society and Government.* Princeton, NJ: Princeton University Press.

Salamon, Lester, Helmut K. Anheier, Regina List, Stefan Toepler, S. Wojciech Sokolowski, and Associates. 1999. *Global Civil Society: Dimensions of the Nonprofit Sector.* Baltimore: Johns Hopkins University, Center for Civil Society Studies.

Salamon, Lester M., Leslie C. Hems, and Kathryn Chinnock. 2000. "The Nonprofit Sector: For What and for Whom?" Johns Hopkins Comparative Nonprofit Sector Project Working Paper 37, Johns Hopkins University, Baltimore.

Salamon, Lester, and Stefan Toepler. 2000. "The Influence of the Legal Environment on the Development of the Nonprofit Sector." Center for Civil Society Studies Working Paper 17, Center for Civil Society Studies, Johns Hopkins University, Baltimore.

Serrano, Gani. 2001. "Cross-Sectoral Collaboration for Sustainable Change." Background paper for the Fourth CIVICUS World Assembly, Vancouver, Canada, August 19–23.

Shils, Edward. 1991. "The Virtue of Civil Society." *Government and Opposition* 26 (1): 3–20.

Smith, David Horten. 1983. "The Impact of the Volunteer Sector on Society." In *America's Voluntary Spirit: A Book of Readings,* ed. Brian O'Connell, 331–44. New York: Foundation Center.

Social Venture Network. 1999. *Standards of Corporate Social Responsibility.* San Francisco: Social Venture Network.

Uphoff, Norman, and Anirudh Krishna. 2004. "Civil Society and Public Sector Institutions: More than a Zero-Sum Relationship." *Public Administration and Development* 24 (4): 357–62.

van Deth, Jan W. 1998. "Equivalence in Comparative Political Research." In *Comparative Politics: The Problem of Equivalence,* ed. Jan W. van Deth, 1–19. New York: Routledge.

Welzel, Christian. 1999. "Humanentwicklung und der Phasenwechsel der Zivilgesellschaft: Ziviles Engagement in 50 Nationen." In *Im Schatten demokratischer Legitimität: informelle Institutionen und politische Partizipation im interkulturellen Demokratievergleich,* ed. Hans-Joachim Lauth and Ulrike Liebert, 207–36. Opladen.

Yablonski, Christopher. 2001. "Patterns of Corporate Philanthropy: Mandate for Reform." Capital Research Center, Washington, DC.

Chapter 16

Empowerment as a Positive-Sum Game

Stephen Knack

If policies for empowerment of the poor are conceived as increasing the proportion of power in society held by the poor, then obstacles posed by political resistance to such policy changes are likely to be very substantial. Such an understanding often implies a "zero-sum" approach. That is, the total amount of power available is assumed to be fixed, so that if the poor get more, the nonpoor will have their power reduced by the same amount.

This chapter focuses on an alternative approach, that is, on identifying options for economic and political change that can benefit the poor without necessitating a comparable decline in benefits to the nonpoor. Taking such an approach, and relying on concepts familiar to economists, the chapter identifies a significant range of policy options for empowerment that are potentially beneficial to both poor and nonpoor.

After an initial section elaborating the concepts used, the chapter explores positive-sum approaches to both economic and political policy changes that may promote empowerment. It also suggests ways in which such changes may be measured, particularly by cross-national surveys.

Efficiency, Redistribution, and Empowerment

The central concept of economic theory is *efficiency*. Policies and behaviors are evaluated in terms of whether they add more value than they subtract. A "Pareto efficient" change is one that makes at least some people better off, without making anyone else worse off. Pareto efficiency is a very demanding criterion, and its use would lead to an extreme status quo bias toward maintaining existing policies. In practice, economists typically assess policies and actions in terms of "potential Pareto efficiency": by this criterion, a policy change is efficient if the sum of the gains to those benefiting exceeds the sum of the losses to those made worse off from the change. In either case, economists emphasize positive-sum games: identifying and advocating policies that add more value to society than they subtract.

Other social sciences, including political science and sociology, place a much greater emphasis on the concept of *power*. In contrast to an efficiency orientation, an emphasis on power leads inevitably to zero-sum analyses of social policy and behavior. If women's decision-making power within households increases, men's decreases. If poor people's representation in political life increases, the representation of the nonpoor declines. If one nation's military power increases, its rivals' ability to conquer it or to defend themselves decreases.

A zero-sum approach to empowering the poor envisions making the poor better off by moving from one point on a social welfare function to another, such as from A to B in figure 16.1, in which the poor's utility—the benefits to the poor—increases at the expense of the nonpoor. A positive-sum approach is represented by a move from A to C, from one social welfare function to a higher one, in which the utility of the poor increases while that of the nonpoor is also increased or at worst remains unchanged.

The term "empowerment" can have various meanings. The definition adopted here is from the World Bank's *Empowerment and Poverty Reduction: A Sourcebook* (Narayan 2002). Empowerment is "the expansion of assets and capabilities of poor people to participate in, negotiate with, influence, control, and hold accountable institutions that affect their lives." Empowerment increases "one's authority and control over the resources and decisions that affect one's life." This definition is useful, because it does not conflate hypothesized causes with their effects. In other words, empowering the poor does not

Figure 16.1   Zero-Sum versus Positive-Sum "Empowerment"

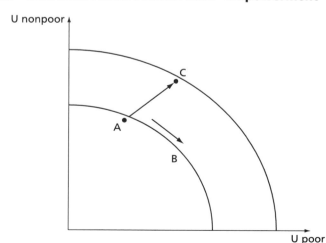

necessarily make them better off, it simply implies that their capacity to make themselves better off is enhanced.

In most cases, strengthening the political voice of poor people is likely to make them better off. Macroeconomic policy is one area, however, in which greater political voice for the poor is sometimes thought to have perverse effects on their welfare. Political parties and other forces claiming to represent the poor often advocate looser control of the money supply, as inflation erodes the value of debt. However, studies have shown that the poor are disproportionately harmed by high inflation (Easterly and Fischer 2001), in part because the financial assets of the wealthy are more likely to be indexed to inflation. Limited understanding of macroeconomic processes can make voters vulnerable to manipulation by politicians, inducing them to support policies that often make them worse off. This possibility is one justification for establishing independent central banks and giving technocrats who are relatively immune to political pressures responsibility for macroeconomic and fiscal policy. Such solutions are not likely to be sustainable in the long run, however, without disseminating information about the effects of different policies to the poor and their representatives. Building popular support for reform through education and by identifying and developing compensatory mechanisms where appropriate will often be required to achieve the social consensus needed to carry through difficult reforms, such as reducing spending in the face of fiscal crises (Narayan 2002, 6, 43).

Enfranchisement of the poor was opposed by most leading nineteenth-century political philosophers on grounds that it would produce economically ruinous "leveling." However, the poor were eventually enfranchised, in large part because elites began to realize that predictable levels of redistribution resulting from universal suffrage were less damaging than the prospect of unpredictable redistribution associated with political and social instability (Acemoglu and Robinson 2000).

Several different policy outcomes are possible. Empowerment of the poor not only may sometimes make the poor worse off, particularly where poor information can be exploited by opportunistic leaders; it sometimes can make the nonpoor better off. Where empowering poor people makes them worse off, it is inefficient, that is, a negative-sum game. In other cases, it is a zero-sum game, as the poor can benefit only at the expense of someone else. But in many cases, it can be positive-sum, and these opportunities should be identified and pursued by reformers. Attempts by donor organizations and nongovernmental organizations to empower the poor should focus on means by which the poor are likely to be made better off without making others worse off. Not only is this approach consistent with efficiency, it will also often be the only politically feasible way to empower the poor. If the nonpoor currently have all of the power, then their cooperation will be necessary to implement economic, political, and social reforms that empower the poor—just as in nineteenth-century Great Britain.

Within the two broad categories of economic rights and political rights, the remainder of this chapter identifies specific areas in which the poor can be

Table 16.1　Rights and Positive-Sum versus Zero-Sum Approaches

Type of rights	Positive-sum approach	Zero-sum approach
Economic rights	Improve security of property rights	Alter distribution of rights that disadvantages the poor
Political rights	Broaden accountability relationships	Increase participation of poor relative to nonpoor

empowered without disempowering a substantial number of the nonpoor. Existing inefficient sets of rights will almost always have some constituency that will suffer when rights are expanded or redistributed, so reform will not be Pareto efficient in the sense of making no one worse off. But often the "losers" from such reforms constitute only a small, well-organized group, such as a repressive governing regime or dominant minority clan or ethnic group, so that reform can easily pass the criterion of potential Pareto efficiency.

Table 16.1 illustrates the argument in brief. A zero-sum approach to empowering the poor by increasing their economic rights might focus on the distribution of assets or rights between the rich (or middle class) and the poor. An effective positive-sum approach, which is shown by the evidence to improve the well-being of all economic classes in most instances, is to improve the security of property rights and contract enforceability. This issue is addressed in the second section of this chapter.

A zero-sum approach to political rights might focus on increasing the political representation of the poor relative to that of the rich. For example, voting turnout rates for the poor could be increased, potentially electing more representatives who reflect poor people's interests rather than the interests of the nonpoor.[1] To the extent that money can influence election outcomes, campaign finance reform and the secret ballot are two means of preventing the nonpoor from dominating political processes. Public financing of parties and campaigns might reduce the ability of the well-off to influence poor voters to vote for candidates who do not represent their interests. The secret ballot prevents vote buying by moneyed interests, since it undermines the credibility of voters' promises to vote for a particular candidate in exchange for a bribe.

In contrast, a positive-sum approach to political reform would focus on changing the nature of political participation and the types of demands and expectations voters have of political candidates and public officials. In particular, where voters' exercise of political voice tends to focus on private goods—patronage, in effect—rather than on broad public policies, outcomes tend to be far less efficient. Efficient and responsive government requires that citizens overcome a large collective problem, namely that individual voters face insufficient incentives to articulate their preferences for public goods and to monitor the performance of public officials and exercise voice (through voting and other means) when needed to hold them accountable to broad public interests. This point is developed empirically in the third section.

Empowerment through Property and Contract Rights

Does effective protection of property rights benefit primarily the rich? It is now widely accepted that nations with more secure property rights and effective contract enforcement tend to exhibit stronger economic performance (see, for example, North 1990; Knack and Keefer 1995). What remains less clear to many, however, is whether secure property rights and effective contract enforcement empower the poor. Neo-Marxist and other radical traditions view them as benefiting the rich at the expense of the poor. This perception is based on the assumption that the poor have little property to protect, unlike rich landowners or capitalists. Similarly, contractual agreements can be perceived as being the product of unequal bargaining power, with rich creditors, landowners, or capitalists enforcing contract provisions against poor borrowers, tenants, employees, or consumers. If wealthy elites write the laws and commercial codes and select the judges, legal systems may mostly protect the interests of the well-off, often at poor people's expense. Privatization of communal lands without sufficient compensation has in some instances disempowered rural poor people in Africa and Latin America.

Most donor agencies, however, have recently come around to the view that enforcement of property and contract rights is more often pro-poor, not only by encouraging growth in per capita incomes that are typically accompanied by reductions in poverty (Squire 1993), but also by contributing to favorable shifts in the distribution of income. This view holds that institutions for promoting secure property rights and enforcement of contracts can have powerful egalitarian effects, enabling individuals with little property and no political connections to invest in human capital and in small enterprises. Fair and transparent procedures for property, contracts, and government regulation of business facilitate the entry of informal sector entrepreneurs and workers—most of whom are low- or middle-income—into the formal sector, and promote the accumulation of physical and human capital, raising profits and wages (de Soto 1989).[2]

Predictability of rights and policies—even those seemingly biased toward the rich—carries enormous advantages relative to less secure economic environments. Strong and predictable property and contract rights are necessary for the emergence of well-developed financial markets, which are at least as important for poor and middle-income borrowers as for the well-off, who can more easily arrange alternative sources of credit.[3] Unlike the rich, the poor may depend on credit for acquiring secondary-level education, because of the income foregone in the short term when children of poor families attend school instead of working.

Unpredictability of public policy and of property rights enforcement tends to be associated with government corruption, as both result from insufficient constraints on executive power. There is some evidence that government expenditures are diverted away from services that benefit the poor in more corrupt nations (Mauro 1998). Capital-intensive projects tend to offer more opportunities for kickbacks than health and education spending.

To the extent that government incompetence and corruption undermine public service delivery, the poor may be disproportionately affected, because they are more dependent on publicly provided health services and education. Similarly, the poor are less able to purchase private substitutes (security guards, alarm systems, etc.) for police services.

If bribe seekers can price-discriminate, corruption may not disproportionately tax the poor. Kaufmann, Zoido-Lobatón, and Lee (2000) present survey evidence from Ecuador that bribe payments to government officials constitute a larger share of firm revenues for small than for large firms. However, this is not a general finding from these firm surveys, according to one of the authors of the Ecuador study. For example, large and small firms pay about the same share of revenues in the form of bribes in Cambodia. On the other hand, household surveys consistently indicate that poorer families pay a larger share of their incomes as bribes in exchange for public services[4]—indicating that price discrimination is more difficult with households than with firms, and/or that poorer households are more dependent than richer households on public services.

Cross-country evidence can be useful in examining whether corruption and uncertain protection of property and contract rights disproportionately harm the poor. One way to address the question is by breaking it into two parts and noting, for example, that property rights are significantly related to growth (see, for example, Knack and Keefer 1995), and that growth is associated with reductions in poverty rates (for example, Squire 1993). Thus, one might conclude, secure property rights must make the poor better off. However, it is conceivable that the source of growth matters: most episodes of growth are accompanied by reductions in poverty, but the exceptions could be those in which, for example, growth is generated by secure and stable property and contract rights rather than by public investments in primary or secondary education, health, or infrastructure. It is therefore worth presenting more direct evidence.

For this purpose, Knack (2002a) obtained data on income share by quintile from the "high quality" subset of the Deininger and Squire (1996) time-series compilation in inequality. Average annual growth in per capita income was computed for each of the five income quintiles for the same period, using the purchasing power–adjusted income data from Summers and Heston (1991). Barro-type (1991) growth regressions were run for each of the five quintiles, using the property rights indexes constructed by Knack and Keefer (1995) from International Country Risk Guide and Business Environmental Risk Intelligence data.

Depending on the period examined, and on which property rights index was used, the impact of property rights on growth was at worst neutral across the five quintiles, and at best double the impact for the bottom quintile as for the top quintile (Knack 2002a). These findings strongly indicate that more secure property and contract rights improve incomes for all groups, not merely for those who have the most property in need of protection.

Evidence showing that corruption reduces incomes for all income classes, and particularly for the poor, implies that empowering people in ways that reduce corruption are positive-sum policies. One example is increased representation of women in politics and public office, which is usually advocated on grounds that it will make women and children better off by reallocating resources toward public programs that tend to benefit them instead of men. However, a side benefit of increasing women's share of parliamentary seats and high ministerial positions is that it is associated with significant reductions in corruption (Swamy et al. 2001). Because reducing corruption in turn is linked to growth, enhancing women's representation can improve well-being for both women and men—even though men's share of high-level government positions declines.

Mancur Olson (1994) has argued that much of the poverty in the developing world is the product of institutions chosen by politically connected individuals and groups, who tend to be well off, in their own interests. Olson claims that the legal and other governmental institutions that best ensure property rights and contract enforceability are the very same set of institutions that best improve the welfare of the poor. Results described in this section support Olson's view—and the consensus but largely untested view of the major donor institutions—that good governance not only reduces poverty rates but also improves (or at least does not worsen) income inequality. Improving the quality of governance is not the only way, and may or may not be the most effective way, of empowering the poor or of reducing poverty. However, there is no evidence that an efficiency/equity trade-off predominates in strengthening property and contract rights in developing countries. To the contrary, the enormous gains in material welfare resulting from institutional reform appear to benefit the poor at least as much as they benefit other classes.

Citizen Voice and Clientelistic versus Programmatic Politics

Putnam (1993, 101) found that in the more civic regions of Italy, citizen-initiated contacts with government officials tend to concern public issues, while in the less civic regions, such contacts "overwhelmingly involve requests for jobs and patronage." In the more civic regions, citizens view government as a provider of necessary public goods from which everyone benefits, while citizens of less civic regions view government as a source of private goods.

Banfield (1958) provides a fascinating case study of one of the less civic towns of southern Italy, in which collective action failures on the part of the citizenry resulted in an indifferent and corrupt government. Collective action in the public interest could not be organized because it depended on unselfish inducements and a degree of interpersonal trust and organizational loyalty that did not exist in the town, where many villagers found "the idea of public-spiritedness unintelligible" (18). Despite widespread dissatisfaction with the lack of a local hospital or public transportation to a middle school in a nearby town, there was "no organized effort to bring pressure to bear on the government" (31). The only voluntary association in the town, consisting of 25 upper-class men, engaged solely in social activities for the members and did not involve itself in community affairs. There were few checks on public officials, because it was not in the narrow self-interest of citizens to get involved: "For a private citizen to take a serious interest in a public problem" was "regarded as abnormal and even improper." On the other hand, it was considered normal to lobby officials to provide personal favors (87). Voter choices were not based on class, ideology, or the public interest, but simply rewarded the party providing jobs or other particularistic favors.[5]

Empowering individual poor people, therefore, by making it easier for them to vote or to contact public officials, will not necessarily make them collectively better off if they use this new-found voice to more effectively demand patronage. Even nominally pro-poor programs that take the form of targeted redistribution—such as free food or temporary employment in public works—may have less impact on welfare than cheaper and more broadly based programs to improve basic health and education services (Keefer and Khemani 2003). Efficient choice of public policies and effective provision of public goods—for most of the poor and nonpoor alike—require changes in information, electoral rules, or social norms that alter incentives of voters and politicians to indulge in patronage practices.

Cross-country evidence on this problem is provided by several questions included in a Gallup International survey administered to more than 30,000 respondents in 45 countries in August 2002.[6] Only 13.9 percent of respondents said that they had contacted a public official, local or national, in the past year to provide their opinion on a broad public issue ("programmatic" or "public-interested" contacting). More respondents, 22.4 percent, replied that they had contacted a public official for help with a problem affecting them or their family (this is termed "clientelistic" or "particularized" contacting in the political science literature; see Verba and Nie 1972). There is enormous variation across countries; for example, only 6 percent of Japanese respondents contacted public officials about personal problems, compared to 64 percent of Cameroonians. Only 5 percent of respondents in Argentina, compared to 36 percent in the United States, contacted public officials to provide an opinion on broad public issues. The share of all contacts that are programmatic rather than clientelistic varies from a low of 17 percent for Russia to a high of 57 percent for the United States and 59 percent for Croatia. Figure 16.2 plots in two dimensions the percentage of respondents for each country who report each type of contact.

Figure 16.2   Contacting Officials on Public and Personal Problems

Proportion of contacts on public issues

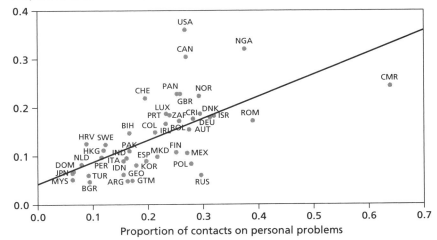

Note: See country key following figure 16.6.

Figure 16.3   Control of Corruption and Contacting Officials

Control of corruption

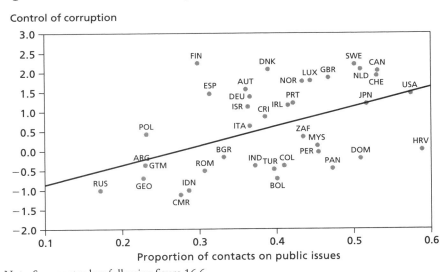

Note: See country key following figure 16.6.

These cross-country differences appear to have enormous consequences for the quality of governance. Figure 16.3 plots on the horizontal axis the percentage of all contacts that are of the programmatic sort. The vertical axis plots countries' scores on a "control of corruption" index from Kaufmann, Kraay, and Zoido-Lobatón (1999). Countries in which contacts tend to be public-interested have significantly higher scores on the control of corruption index—that is, less corruption (correlation = 0.43, significant at 0.004). The relationship is similar for another index from Kaufmann and his colleagues on "government effectiveness" (correlation = 0.38, significant at 0.01).

The Kaufmann indexes are based primarily on perceptions of experts and investors. Results are similar, however, using measures of government performance in the Gallup survey. Respondents were asked whether their country—and their local community, in a similar question—was run "by a few big interests looking out for themselves" or "for the benefit of all the people." In countries where contacts tend to be of the public-interested type, fewer respondents replied that their country was run by a few big interests (correlation = −0.37, significant at 0.01). The relationship with respondents' perceptions of capture by a few big interests at the local level was even stronger (correlation = −0.47, significant at 0.001; see figure 16.4).

The nature of citizens' interactions with elected and appointed officials may be deeply entrenched and difficult to alter. However, there is some potential for donor-assisted change. First, improved information about policies, the behavior of officials, and their relation to outcomes can change incentives facing both voters and politicians (Besley and Burgess 2002; Keefer and Khemani 2003; Strömberg 2004). Voters can observe for themselves the private or narrowly targeted public goods (such as local school buildings, and jobs to construct and staff them) that they receive from officials, and reward them at the polls. Much more information, and the ability to process it, is often required to credit or blame officials appropriately for their role in providing or failing to provide quality public services. Greater literacy, access to free and independent media, and enhanced transparency of government decision making can help improve

Figure 16.4   Local Capture and Contacting Officials

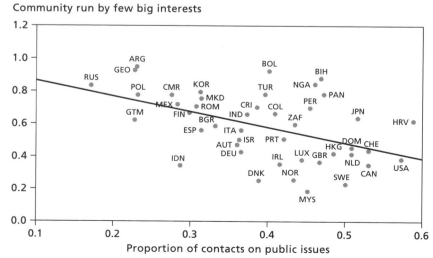

Note: See country key following figure 16.6.

Figure 16.5   Age of Democracy and Contacting Officials

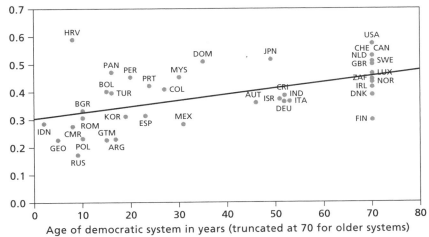

Proportion of contacts on public issues

Age of democratic system in years (truncated at 70 for older systems)

Note: See country key following figure 16.6.

citizens' ability to demand improved policies and services with respect to broad public goods, and to monitor and sanction poor performance.

Political institutions also matter. Keefer (2002) argues that the age of a democracy is important. In relatively new democracies, parties have had less time to build policy reputations, and candidates are unlikely to be able to make credible promises to all voters. Candidates therefore cannot win votes effectively by promising to provide broad public goods, such as higher-quality health and education services. Instead, they rely on targeted promises to specific individuals or groups to whom they can make credible promises (because of past dealings or ethnic loyalties). Figure 16.5 shows that the percentage of contacts with public officials that are public-interested rises in more established democracies, where reputation effects make promises more credible, allowing candidates to compete on (and voters to reward them for) providing broad public goods. Contacting of both types is significantly lower in countries with closed-list proportional representation systems, where voters are in effect selecting only parties, not individual candidates.

Interestingly, in some countries where clientelism prevailed in some regions, ideologically based parties effectively competed in other regions, with positive effects on provision of public services. Examples include Communist parties in Emilia-Romagna (Italy) and in Kerala (India).

Social capital, namely of the "bridging" sort, also contributes to better provision of broad-based and effective public services benefiting the poor. Where citizens trust each other to cooperate for the common good, they are more likely to make public-interested contacts but are no more likely to engage in particularized contacting. Figure 16.6 depicts the cross-country relationship

Figure 16.6   Interpersonal Trust and Contacting Officials

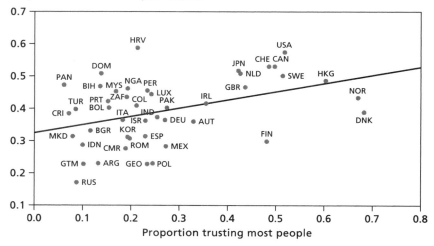

Key to figures 16.2–16.6

ARG	Argentina	ISR	Israel
AUT	Austria	ITA	Italy
BGR	Bulgaria	JPN	Japan
BIH	Bosnia and Herzegovina	KOR	Korea, Rep. of
BOL	Bolivia	LUX	Luxembourg
CAN	Canada	MEX	Mexico
CHE	Switzerland	MKD	Macedonia, FYR
CMR	Cameroon	MYS	Malaysia
COL	Colombia	NGA	Nigeria
CRI	Costa Rica	NLD	Netherlands
DEU	Germany	NOR	Norway
DNK	Denmark	PAK	Pakistan
DOM	Dominican Republic	PAN	Panama
ESP	Spain	PER	Peru
FIN	Finland	POL	Poland
GBR	United Kingdom	PRT	Portugal
GEO	Georgia	ROM	Romania
GTM	Guatemala	RUS	Russia
HKG	Hong Kong	SWE	Sweden
HRV	Croatia	TUR	Turkey
IDN	Indonesia	USA	United States
IND	India	ZAF	South Africa
IRL	Ireland		

between the percentage of Gallup survey respondents who agree that "most people can be trusted" and the public-interested share of all contacts with officials. Building social capital is an enormous challenge, but improving education, communications, and transportation potentially can broaden the perspective of citizens and facilitate experience, understanding, and compromise across regions, ethnic groups, and even income classes. This in turn encourages the growth of broad-based movements and organizations that monitor the efficiency and integrity of government. Donors must be careful, however, not to distort the functioning, membership, and goals of individual civil society organizations by flooding them with resources (Gugerty and Kremer 2002).

Implications for Measuring Empowerment

E mpowerment of the poor and other disadvantaged groups—the less educated, rural, women, and members of certain ethnic groups—can be measured in part through data collected by government and donor agencies, on literacy and relative schooling for example. Some aspects of empowerment, such as sense of political efficacy, different forms of political participation, and information regarding politics and public issues, are not captured very well in the standard data. Nationally representative surveys conducted by cross-country networks, such as Gallup International, Afrobarometer, Latinobarómetro, or the World Values Surveys, are potentially useful means of collecting such data. Of these networks, Gallup's annual Voice of the People survey is unique in allowing organizations to purchase space for questions. The August 2002 Gallup survey results used in this chapter suggest that such surveys produce reasonably valid and useful data. Demographic variables included in the surveys would readily permit comparison between the poor and nonpoor on such issues as, for example, level of political information, efficacy, participation rates, and satisfaction with various public services, were questions on those topics to be added to the survey.[7] Further thought is needed regarding questions on information that would be applicable to respondents in countries with differing political systems and salient public issues.

Appendix: Survey Measures of Empowerment

Included in August 2002 Gallup International "Voice of the People" survey:

1. Generally speaking, would you say that most people can be trusted or that you can't be too careful in dealing with people? (Gallup International, 2002; World Values Surveys, 1995)
    Most people can be trusted
    Can't be too careful
    Don't know
    It depends (volunteered)

2. Generally speaking, would you say that this country is run by a few big interests looking out for themselves, or that it is run for the benefit of all the people? (Gallup International, 2002; World Values Surveys, 1995)

    Run by a few big interests

    Run for all the people

    Don't know

3. Generally speaking, would you say that your local government is run by a few big interests looking out for themselves, or that it is run for the benefit of all the people? (Gallup International, 2002)

    Run by a few big interests

    Run for all the people

    Don't know

4. Have you contacted any public officials (either local or national) in the last year, either for help with a problem affecting you and your family, or to provide your opinion on a broader public issue? (Gallup International, 2002) (Mark all that apply)

    For help with a problem

    To provide my opinion on a public issue

    Yes (on something else—volunteered)

    No

Not included in August 2002 Gallup International "Voice of the People" survey:

5. I'm going to read out some forms of political action that people can take, and I'd like you to tell me, for each one, whether you have actually done any of these things, whether you might do it or would never, under any circumstances, do it. (World Values Surveys, 1995)

    Signing a petition

    Joining in boycotts

    Attending lawful demonstrations

    Joining unofficial strikes

    Occupying buildings or factories

6. How would you rank the importance of the following activities as part of the job of members of the national legislature:

    Helping people in their districts who request favors or help with personal problems

    Making sure their districts get their fair share of government money and projects

    Working on issues affecting the nation as a whole

7. How would you rank the importance of the following reasons for preferring one political party over another?

    The policies that the parties advocate affecting the nation as a whole

    The share of government money and projects going to the part of the country in which you live

    The help you or your family may get if you need a favor or help with a personal problem

8. Which statement do you feel is closer to the way things really are: with enough effort we can wipe out political corruption OR it is difficult for people to have much control over the things politicians do in office.
9. How much do political parties help make the government pay attention to what the people think: a good deal, some, or not much?
10. How much do elections make government pay attention to what the people think: a good deal, some, or not much?
11. How much does having interest groups make government pay attention to what the people think: a good deal, some, or not much?
12. Do you think that the parties pretty much keep their campaign promises or do they usually do what they want after the election is over?
13. Have you encountered any of these problems with your local public schools during the past 12 months? (Mark all that apply)
    No textbooks or other supplies
    Poor teaching
    Frequent and unjustified absence of teachers
    Overcrowded classrooms
    Facilities in poor condition
    Illegal payments required
    No experience with public schools in last 12 months
    None of the above
14. Have you encountered any of these problems with your local public clinic or hospital during the past 12 months? (Mark all that apply)
    Frequent and unjustified absence of doctors
    Treated disrespectfully by staff
    No drugs available
    Long waiting times
    Facilities not clean
    Illegal payments required
    No experience with public clinic/hospital in last 12 months
    None of the above

Notes

1.   Hill and Leighley (1992) find that in the United States, states in which the poor are better represented at the polls offer more generous means-tested social assistance.
2.   According to *World Development Report 2000/2001*, "in Ghana in 1993 an investor had to obtain 24 administrative approvals for 24 services before starting any activity—around two years of procedural approval, with an uncertain outcome" (World Bank 2000).
3.   Feder and colleagues (1988) found that formal title to land (controlling for other factors) improved farmers' access to credit.
4.   This information was provided in personal correspondence from Young Lee.
5.   See Knack (2002b) and Boix and Posner (1998) for additional arguments and evidence on the relationship between "social capital" and government performance.
6.   See appendix, questions 1–4.
7.   See appendix, questions 5–14, for possible ways of asking about these issues.

References

Acemoglu, Daron, and James A. Robinson. 2000. "Why Did the West Extend the Franchise?" *Quarterly Journal of Economics* 115 (4): 1167–99.

Banfield, Edward C. 1958. *The Moral Basis of a Backward Society.* Chicago: Free Press.

Barro, Robert. 1991. "Economic Growth in a Cross Section of Countries." *Quarterly Journal of Economics* 106 (2): 407–33.

Besley, Tim, and Robin Burgess. 2002. "The Political Economy of Government Responsiveness: Theory and Evidence from India." *Quarterly Journal of Economics* 117 (4): 1415–52.

Boix, Carles, and Daniel N. Posner. 1998. "Social Capital: Explaining Its Origins and Effects on Government Behavior." *British Journal of Political Science* 28 (4): 686–93.

Deininger, Klaus, and Lyn Squire. 1996. "A New Data Set: Measuring Income Inequality." *World Bank Economic Review* 10 (3): 565–92.

de Soto, Hernando. 1989. *The Other Path: The Invisible Revolution in the Third World.* New York: Harper and Row.

Easterly, William, and Stanley Fischer. 2001. "Inflation and the Poor." *Journal of Money, Credit and Banking* 33 (2): 160–78.

Feder, Gershon, Tongroj Onchan, Yongyuth Chalamwong, and Chira Hongladarom. 1988. *Land Policies and Farm Productivity in Thailand.* Baltimore: Johns Hopkins University Press.

Gugerty, Mary Kay, and Michael Kremer. 2002. "The Impact of Development Assistance on Social Capital: Evidence from Kenya." In *The Role of Social Capital in Development: An Empirical Assessment,* ed. C. Grootaert and T. van Bastelaer, 213–33. Cambridge: Cambridge University Press.

Hill, Kim Quaile, and Jan E. Leighley. 1992. "The Policy Consequences of Class Bias in State Electorates." *American Journal of Political Science* 36 (2): 351–65.

Kaufmann, Daniel, Aart Kraay, and Pablo Zoido-Lobatón. 1999. "Aggregating Governance Indicators." Policy Research Working Paper 2196, World Bank, Washington, DC.

Kaufmann, Daniel, Pablo Zoido-Lobatón, and Young Lee. 2000. "Governance and Anticorruption Diagnostic Study for Ecuador." World Bank Institute, Washington, DC.

Keefer, Philip. 2002. "Clientelism, Credibility and Democracy." Development Research Group, World Bank, Washington, DC.

Keefer, Philip, and Stuti Khemani. 2003. "Democracy, Public Expenditures, and the Poor." Originally prepared as background paper for *World Development Report 2004: Making Services Work for Poor People.* Policy Research Working Paper 3164, World Bank, Washington, DC.

Knack, Stephen. 2002a. "Social Capital, Growth, and Poverty." In *The Role of Social Capital in Development: An Empirical Assessment*, ed. C. Grootaert and T. van Bastelaer, 42–82. Cambridge: Cambridge University Press.

———. 2002b. "Social Capital and the Quality of Government: Evidence from the U.S. States." *American Journal of Political Science* 46 (4): 772–85.

Knack, Stephen, and Philip Keefer. 1995. "Institutions and Economic Performance: Cross-Country Tests Using Alternative Institutional Measures." *Economics and Politics* 7 (3): 207–27.

Mauro, Paolo. 1998. "Corruption and the Composition of Government Expenditure." *Journal of Public Economics* 69: 263–79.

Narayan, Deepa, ed. 2002. *Empowerment and Poverty Reduction: A Sourcebook.* Washington, DC: World Bank.

North, Douglass C. 1990. *Institutions, Institutional Change and Economic Performance.* Cambridge: Cambridge University Press.

Olson, Mancur. 1994. "Who Gains from Policies that Increase Poverty?" IRIS Center Working Paper 137, Center for Institutional Reform and the Informal Sector, University of Maryland, College Park.

Putnam, Robert. 1993. *Making Democracy Work: Civic Traditions in Modern Italy.* Princeton: Princeton University Press.

Squire, Lyn. 1993. "Fighting Poverty." *American Economic Review Papers and Proceedings* 83 (2): 377–82.

Strömberg, David. 2004. "Radio's Impact on Public Spending." *Quarterly Journal of Economics* 119 (1): 189–221.

Summers, Robert, and Alan Heston. 1991. "The Penn World Tables (Mark V): An Extended Set of International Comparisons, 1950–88." *Quarterly Journal of Economics* 106 (2): 327–68.

Swamy, Anand, Stephen Knack, Young Lee, and Omar Azfar. 2001. "Gender and Corruption." *Journal of Development Economics* 64 (1): 25–55.

Verba, Sidney, and Norman H. Nie. 1972. *Participation in America: Political Democracy and Social Equality.* Chicago: University of Chicago Press.

World Bank. 2000. *World Development Report 2000/2001: Attacking Poverty.* New York: Oxford University Press.

Chapter 17

Democracy and Poverty

Ashutosh Varshney

Two embarrassments mark the record of development since World War II: one pertaining to the market forces, another concerning democracy. In the mid-1980s, and especially in the decade of the 1990s, more and more countries embraced the logic of market-oriented economics. The argument for a freer acceptance of market-based economic strategies stemmed partly from the failure of *dirigisme,* the erstwhile dominant economic strategy, and partly from the assumption that the economic growth generated by market forces would lead to mass well-being and was a surer way of conquering poverty.

One can debate whether poverty has declined or not, and by how many percentage points. Even if one agrees that poverty has indeed come down in the era of globalization—which I happen to believe—the fact remains that global poverty is still extensive. As much as a third of the world, perhaps slightly less, could still be below the $1 a day poverty line set by the World Bank.[1] Those who made a fervent case for the embrace of market forces might still say in their defense that the situation would have been better if governments had been more resolute in their embrace of neoliberalism. But it can't be denied that markets have been much freer in the past 20 years than at any time since World War II (Sachs and Warner 1995). And if a third, or even a fourth, of the world is still below the poverty line, one can only call it an embarrassment for those who thought markets would deliver the masses out of poverty (Stiglitz 2002). Markets may well be necessary for poverty reduction, but they are patently not sufficient, at least in the short to medium run. We need to make them work better for poor people. After the experiences of the 1990s, we need a humble admission of this basic point.

This chapter, however, is not about the "market embarrassment." It is primarily about the embarrassment of democratic development. What is the nature of this latter embarrassment?

Poverty Reduction in Democracies: A Mediocre Record

In the most meticulous and comprehensive statistical examination yet of the relationship between democracy and development, Przeworski and colleagues provide compelling evidence for a hunch long held by observers of development. "The lists of miracles and disasters," they argue, "are populated almost exclusively by dictatorships . . . The [economic] tigers may be dictatorships, but [all] dictatorships are no[t] tigers" (2000, 178).

Indeed, Przeworski and his team could explicitly have taken another analytic step, a step that can be logically derived as a syllogism from what they say. Moving beyond a bimodal distribution—miracles and disasters—they could have also constructed a third, in-between category. They would have found that democracies tend to fall almost exclusively in the unspectacular but undisastrous middle. No long-lasting democracy in the developing world has seen the developmental horrors of Mobutu's Zaire, but none has scaled the heights of a Taiwan, Republic of Korea, or Singapore.

Can this argument be extended from economic growth, which is Przeworski's focus, to the poverty-eradicating record of democracies in the developing world? Would it be true to say that while no democracy has attacked poverty as successfully as Singapore, Korea, or Taiwan, none has made economic life as awful for its poor people as Haiti, Chad, Zambia, or Niger, among the worst performers on poverty alleviation in the developing world (World Bank 2000, 282–83)?

Surprising as it may seem, not enough is known about the relationship between democracy and poverty. Instead, a great deal of literature is available on the relationship between democracy and economic growth. Unless it is incorrectly assumed that what is good for economic growth is necessarily good for poverty reduction, the implications of the theoretical literature on economic growth are not straightforward. Inferences can only be drawn with appropriate caution.

I argue below that the poverty-eradicating record of democracies in the developing world is, indeed, neither extraordinary nor abysmal. Democracies have succeeded in preempting the worst-case scenarios, such as famines (Sen 1989), and have avoided a consistent or dramatic deterioration in the welfare of the poor, but they have not achieved the best results, namely, eradication of mass poverty. The performance of dictatorships, by comparison, covers the whole range of outcomes: the best, the worst, and the middling. Some dictatorial regimes have successfully eradicated poverty. In others the problem has worsened, or no significant change in mass poverty is observable. In still others, the progress has been slow but steady, much as it has been in many democracies. The promise of democracy was greater in the eyes of liberals. Hence the embarrassment of democratic development.

Why should we have expected poor democracies to do better at poverty alleviation? One reason is sheer numbers. In the United States and Europe a very small proportion of the population, typically less than 5 percent of the total, lives in abject poverty. Poor people in these richer economies, their numbers being so small, can hardly leverage themselves into a great electoral or political force in order to push governments to do more for them. But poor democracies possess, by definition, many poor people. In the developing world the poor constitute a large plurality of the population, sometimes even a majority. At least in principle, poor people in poor democracies, if not in poor dictatorships, *ought to experience over time some degree of empowerment by virtue of their numbers alone.* They should therefore be able to exercise pressure on the government to address poverty effectively through public policy. If the poor have the right to vote, then a 30 percent voting bloc can often be decisive, especially in a first-past-the-post electoral system, in which elections are often decided on the basis of a plurality of the popular vote. Election victories in a Westminster-style democratic system often do not require majorities, especially if the electoral contestation is between more than two political parties, as is often the case. Most stable democracies in the developing world, listed later on in this chapter, have a Westminster-style system. Yet mass poverty remains extensive in them.

Of course, it can be argued that the validity of this theoretical reasoning and expectation depends on whether the poor actually do vote, or vote as much as the richer classes do. If the poor do not vote, or are not allowed to vote because of manipulation or coercion by the local elite, or they vote according to the wishes of the local elite because the elite are the patrons and the poor their dependent clients, then we should expect poor people to remain as powerless as always, and thus incapable of exerting pressure on even a democratic government. What do we know about whether, and how freely, the poor vote in the developing world? Disaggregated statistics along the rich-poor divisions are not available for most poor democracies. For India, however, turnout rates have been systematically disaggregated, and it is clear that over the past 15–20 years the poor have tended to vote much more than the middle and upper classes (Yadav 2000, 2004). We also know that in this period, the patron-client relationships between the upper or dominant castes on one hand and the lower and generally poorer castes on the other have been considerably undermined across much of India (Varshney 2000a; Weiner 2001). Yet poverty alleviation in India has continued to be quite slow.

Voting, however, is not the only mechanism of influence available to poor people in a democratic polity. The poor can also, at least in theory, be politically mobilized into, let us say, a poor people's movement, and can thereby exercise their weight and push the government to adopt pro-poor policies.[2] Both mobilization and voting are available as options and can be viewed as two forms of *pressure from below.* These mechanisms are not present in the same way in authoritarian systems, for given the absence of political freedoms, opportunities for the mobilization of the poor are significantly fewer, and voting is either perfunctory or nonexistent. Of course, in theory, authoritarian polities can feel a significant amount of *pressure from above*—stemming from a commitment of the political elite to reducing poverty, or from international pressures—and may therefore make a significant attempt to eliminate poverty.

But dictatorships do not feel a systematic pressure from below, whereas democratic systems can be subjected to both kinds of pressure.

In short, as many political theorists have argued since the nineteenth century, universal-franchise democracies ought to significantly empower the poor. By extension, there should be a great deal of pressure on poor democracies to eliminate poverty. However, defying this theoretical expectation, poor countries that are viewed as having had long-lasting periods of democratic rule— India, Costa Rica, Venezuela, Colombia, Botswana, Jamaica, Trinidad and Tobago, and Sri Lanka, among others—still on the whole have a substantial proportion of their populations stuck below the poverty line.

This experience raises some questions. Do poor democracies really feel enough pressure from below to remove poverty? If they do not, then why not? If they do, then what causes actual outcomes to fall short? Do these governments follow economic policies that best tackle the problem of mass poverty? If not, why not?

In response to these questions, I make two arguments. First, if we draw a standard distinction between direct and indirect methods of poverty alleviation, it is possible to show that in the developing world, democracies find it politically easier to subscribe to the direct methods of poverty alleviation, despite the by-now widely recognized economic inferiority of such methods. Indirect methods have little political appeal in democracies, even though their greater long-term effectiveness is clear in economic thinking. Direct methods consist of public provision of income (for example, food-for-work programs, and credit and producer subsidies for small farmers) or a transfer of assets to the poor (for example, through land reforms). Indirect methods are essentially mediated by growth—not any kind of growth, but one that aims at enhancing *opportunities* for the poor to increase their incomes. Over the past two decades, the conventional wisdom in economics has moved toward the superiority of indirect methods, suggesting that they are more productive in use of resources and also more sustainable in the long run (in terms of how long the provision of public resources can be financed, without impairing the capacity to provide them further). The political logic, however, goes in the opposite direction in democracies. Because of electoral and mass pressures, democracies tend to have an elective affinity for direct methods of poverty alleviation. Not given to electoral renewal of mandates, authoritarian polities avoid this problem. If indirect methods are better at eradicating poverty, it follows that authoritarian countries—*some, not all,* as argued later—would have greater success with poverty eradication.

My second argument has to do with the distinction between class and ethnicity. At its core, class is an economic category, but ethnicity is defined in terms of a birth-based (ascriptive) group identity, imagined or real. Ethnic politics of subaltern groups is typically not couched in terms of poverty. Rather, it uses the language of *dignity and social justice,* in which poverty is typically only a component, incorporated in a larger theme emphasizing self-respect, equality of treatment, and an end to everyday humiliation. If the poor, irrespective of the ethnic group they come from, were to vote or mobilize strictly on economic grounds, they would also press the decision makers to attack poverty a great deal more forcefully. However, at least in multiethnic democracies, not only is it easier to mobilize the poor as members of ethnic communities, but that is also how they often vote—along lines of ethnicity, not class. Poverty and denial of dignity together constitute a more serious force in democratic politics than poverty alone.

That being so, *even with direct methods,* a democratic polity is better able to attack poverty if (a) ethnicity and class roughly coincide for the poor, rather than clash, and (b) the subaltern ethnic group is relatively large. If the poor belong to very different ethnic groups (defined by caste, language, race, or religion), and no ethnic group is large enough to constitute a significant voting bloc, the pressure on the political elite to ease poverty decreases significantly.

In short, my argument is that no democracy in the developing world has successfully eliminated poverty because, on one hand, direct methods of poverty alleviation have greater political salience in democracies, and on the other hand, the poor are typically not from the same ethnic group. The former hurts the poor because it can be shown that some indirect, market-based methods of poverty alleviation—not all market-based methods, but those that generate employment for the poor and give them greater capabilities to pursue their interests and withstand shocks and crises—are more effective than direct methods in attacking poverty. And the latter goes against them because a split between ethnicity and class militates against the mobilization and voting of the poor as a class and dilutes the exertion of pro-poor political pressure on governments.

Conceptual Considerations

The term "poverty" today is used in three ways. The conventional usage is linked to consumption and hence income, focusing primarily though not exclusively on a caloric floor that the human body, on average, needs to function normally. In this narrow sense, hunger and endemic malnutrition more or less define poverty. In the richer parts of the world, we typically try to reduce the number of calories our bodies consume every day. In the developing world, the first challenge is not to reduce caloric intake but to provide a minimally adequate number of calories daily to millions of people. The $1 a day yardstick used by the World Bank primarily conforms to this hunger-based definition of poverty, sometimes called *income poverty.*

The term "poverty" is also used more broadly, however, to encompass other fundamental dimensions of human life and development beyond income and consumption—for instance, deprivation with respect to education and health. This is sometimes called *human poverty.* Sen (1999) broadens this concept even more by adding to education and health other factors such as freedom, thus introducing the notion of *capability poverty.* I will not use the term poverty in these latter two senses. It is not that education, health, and freedom are not valuable; they certainly are. It is simply that I am clearer about the relationship between democracy and income poverty than about democracy and the broader concepts of poverty.

In his seminal works on democratic theory, Dahl (1971, 1989) defines democracy in terms of two basic criteria: contestation and participation. The first criterion has to do with how freely the political opposition contests the rulers. The second asks whether all groups, irrespective of social and economic status, or only some groups participate in politics and determine who the rulers should be. The first principle is also called political liberalization, and the second political inclusiveness.

Democracy may have an identifiable impact on poverty, but it should be noted that poverty itself does not enter into the definition of democracy. The best we can say is that if poverty, despite the presence of democratic institutions, obstructs the free expression of political preferences, it makes a polity *less* democratic, but it does not make it *un*democratic. So long as contestation and participation obtain, democracy is a continuous variable, not a discrete or dichotomous variable. Dichotomies need to be distinguished from variations in degree. As Dahl famously put it, before the civil rights movement of the 1960s the United States was less democratic than it is today, and America's future can be even more democratic if there is greater reduction in economic inequalities (1971, 29).[3] In the presence of contestation and participation, an absence of poverty certainly makes a polity more democratic, but elimination of poverty by itself does not constitute democracy. There is no democracy without elections.

Another important conceptual issue should be clarified. In the advanced industrial countries, democracy is a stock variable, but in the developing world, it is a flow variable. In the poorer countries, a military coup or a wanton suspension of the legislature by the executive can dramatically alter the democratic score of a country, as it were. That is to say, on a 0–1 scale, the values of democracy in poorer countries can easily fluctuate between 1 and 0, but richer countries typically don't have coups and their governments don't normally suspend legislatures.

This difference in the institutionalization of political structures has serious implications for how we go about measuring the impact of democracy on poverty. For analytical tractability, it is necessary, first, to identify which countries have been relatively stable democracies—that is, democracies for a long enough period—in the developing world. An exercise like this is not necessary in the developed world, where democratic stability can be assumed. It is difficult, though not impossible, to analyze the impact of democracy on poverty if democracy itself is not stable.

If we construe "long enough" to mean *three-fourths of the period since 1950 or since independence,* then countries that would meet the criterion of democratic longevity are few and far between.[4] They include India, Botswana, Costa Rica, Venezuela, Papua New Guinea, Sri Lanka (between 1950 and 1983), and the Philippines (between 1950 and 1969, and since 1986). Also included are the former British colonies in the Caribbean (principally Jamaica, Trinidad and Tobago, Barbados, and the Bahamas), along with some other very small states[5] (Huntington 1983; Weiner 1989). Some would add Malaysia to this list as well, but it should be noted that Malaysia is by now seen as a long-lasting, consociational-type democracy, where participation may be high but contestation between political parties is limited by consensus, and political competition, by agreement, is designed around ethnic groups rather than individuals (Lijphart 1977).[6] Malaysia, in other words, is a particular kind of democracy, not one in the standard sense.[7] For our purposes here, we can count it as a democracy, given that universal-franchise elections are regularly held, so long as we remember the specific nature of electoral competition and consider its economic implications.

In short, it is the countries above that are critical for analyzing the relationship between democracy and poverty. Democracy has come to many more countries than ever before in the so-called "third wave" that began in the 1970s (Huntington 1991), but if we enlarge the canvas to include the entire post-1950 period, it will be hard to add many more countries to the small list above. By contrast, the number of countries that remained authoritarian for long periods after 1945 is very large. This asymmetry means that we have only a small number of observations about long-lasting democracies. If the N were larger, we could have a robust statistical analysis of their economic consequences for the poor. Until the new democracies of the third wave have established their longevity and thus produced many more democratic observations for inclusion, rigorous qualitative reasoning may well be our best analytic option (King, Keohane, and Verba 1994).[8]

Poverty Eradication: The Broad Picture

Whether democratic systems have reduced poverty, it should be clear, is not a cross-sectional question. We need at least two sufficiently distanced periods for analysis, if not an entire time series. Such data on an intercountry basis do not exist. Global figures for poverty were first calculated for 1985 based on an international poverty line of $1 a day (World Bank 2000). Though doubts remain as to the authenticity of such large-N, intercountry statistics, the World Bank's figures are now customarily used for discussion of world poverty.[9] Note, however, that even if we agree with the World Bank, all we can say is that even of late, about 30 percent of the world population has remained more or less below the $1 a day poverty line.

We simply do not know the numbers of the poor, either globally or in individual countries, for the 1950s or 1960s in any systematic sense. If, to gather such statistics, we rely on the reports available for each country, we find that the criteria used by different countries to define and measure poverty do not match, and often the criteria have not been consistently used even within the same country. A methodologically tight time series on poverty for the entire developing world is not available, nor is it easy to create figures for the pre-1985 period.

Luckily, some broad conclusions can nonetheless be presented, for they do not depend on statistical accuracy but on statistical reasonableness. Complete data sets would be necessary if we were to make finer judgments—for example, if we were asked to rank-order all developing countries on poverty eradication, just as the United Nations Development Programme's human development reports rank all countries on a so-called human development index. But since all we need is categorical judgments, rather than a comprehensive rank-ordering, the available statistics, despite being incomplete, do permit some fairly robust conclusions.

On poverty alleviation, there is a huge variation in the record of authoritarian countries. Spectacular authoritarian successes at attacking poverty (Republic of Korea, Taiwan, and Singapore) coexist with miserable failures (in much of Sub-Saharan Africa and Latin America). And many countries also fall in the middle between the two extremes. According to *World Development Report 2005,* the following developing countries still had more than 40 percent of their populations below the international poverty line of $1 a day in the late 1990s (or later): Burkina Faso, Burundi, Central African Republic, Ghana, Madagascar, Malawi, Mali, Nicaragua, Niger, Nigeria, Sierra Leone, and Zambia (World Bank 2004, 258–59).[10] It is noteworthy that these countries *have all been mostly authoritarian over the past four or five decades* (Przeworski et al. 2000, 59–69).

By comparison, long-lasting democracies—India, Jamaica, Botswana, Venezuela, the Philippines, Sri Lanka, Costa Rica, and Trinidad and Tobago—are neither the biggest successes nor the greatest failures. In the early 1960s, Korea, Taiwan, and Singapore were roughly as poor, or poorer, than these countries (Adelman and Morris 1973), but by now they have wiped out mass poverty. Indeed, economically speaking (though not politically), Singapore today is a developed country, nearly as rich as the United Kingdom and without the obvious signs of poverty one sees in parts of Britain.[11]

In short, the violent authoritarian fluctuations contrast sharply with a certain middling democratic consistency. Democracies may not necessarily be pro-poor, but authoritarian systems can be viciously anti-poor. Democratic attacks on poverty have simply been slow but steady—unspectacular but undisastrous, as it were. Why?

As noted above, there are two main reasons: the political preference in poor democracies for direct rather than indirect methods of reducing poverty, and the salience of ethnicity rather than class in multiethnic democratic politics. These factors are examined in detail below.

Direct versus Indirect Measures

As is often noted in the economic literature, direct methods of poverty alleviation represent income transfers to the poor (producer and credit subsidies, or targeted employment programs), and at a more radical level, asset transfers (land reforms). The indirect methods are growth-mediated. Economic growth, according to mainstream economic wisdom today, is best achieved through trade liberalization and a generally more market-oriented economic strategy than was typically adopted in developing countries until the late 1970s. Thus these trade- and market-oriented policies have also, by implication, become the indirect methods of poverty eradication in economic thinking.[12]

Two clarifications, however, must be added. First, the emphasis on a growth-mediated strategy does not imply that all growth strategies are good for poverty alleviation. A labor-intensive growth strategy is better than one that is capital-intensive. Stated another way, there is a difference between Korea and Brazil. Both relied heavily on high growth, but the former went primarily for a labor-absorbing export-oriented strategy in the late 1960s and the 1970s, whereas the latter concentrated mostly on a capital-intensive import substitution strategy between the 1950s and 1970s. Korea has more or less eradicated mass poverty; Brazil has not.

Second, a growth-based strategy of poverty alleviation does not entail a full-blown external liberalization of the economy, nor does it imply a complete absence of reliance on direct methods. Many consider trade liberalization to be infinitely superior to the liberalization of capital markets (Bhagwati 1998; Sachs, Varshney, and Bajpai 1999; Stiglitz 2002), and there are a great many arguments about the ambiguous effects of dramatic privatization as well (Stiglitz 2002). Market-based methods may on the whole be better, but not all of them work. What is clear is that so long as growth is generating enough resources, it may even be possible for public authorities to allocate more for direct measures, such as food-for-work programs. Therefore, even the sustenance of some direct methods, if not all, relies heavily on growth-generating policies. *Direct measures can often be more effectively implemented in the long run in the framework of growth-enhancing, trade-oriented policies.*

In democratic politics, however, these arguments have a very different meaning. Whether their impact on poverty is lasting or not, direct methods have clearly comprehensible and demonstrable short-run linkages with the well-being of the poor.[13] The impact of indirect methods—exchange rate devaluations, tariff reductions, privatization of public enterprises and, generally, a market-oriented economic strategy—on poverty is not so clear-cut, immediate, and intuitively obvious. Long-run and indirect links do not work well in democratic politics: the effect has to be simple, intuitively graspable, clearly visible, and capable of arousing mass action (Varshney 1999).

Direct evidence on how the masses look at market-oriented economic reforms is also available. In a large survey of mass political attitudes in India conducted in 1996, about five years after reforms were initiated there, it was found that only 12 percent of the rural electorate had heard of the reforms, although 32 percent of the urban voters knew of them (Yadav and Singh 1997). This was so even though a change in the trade regime implied that the protection offered to manufacturing relative to agriculture had gone down significantly and that agriculture's terms of trade had improved. Furthermore, only 7 percent of poor Indians, who are mostly illiterate, were aware of the dramatic changes in economic policy, compared to nearly 66 percent of college graduates. Thus, India's economic reforms, toasted enthusiastically in the domestic and international economic community since 1991, had barely made an impression on the rural folk and the poor even five years after their inauguration. An equally dramatic direct attack on poverty, however economically unsound, would almost certainly have registered more prominently. Even as late as 2004, reforms did not figure prominently in India's election and mass politics; other issues were more important (Suri 2004).

An affinity between electoral democracy and direct methods has on the whole—and so far—limited the ability of democracies to eradicate poverty. A better alignment of the political and the economic may be possible in authoritarian countries, where politicians do not have to carry the masses with them in election campaigns and where the long-run and indirect methods of poverty removal can simply be implemented by decree (if a political elite is committed to the poor, which it may or may not be).

Class versus Ethnicity

The argument above emphasizes that direct methods of poverty alleviation, even though politically attractive in poor democracies, are not well suited to end mass poverty. The argument does not imply that direct methods will have no impact. To repeat, both approaches can make a dent in poverty; one is simply more productive and sustainable in the long run.

Within the parameters of direct action, however, the best results are obtained in societies where class and ethnicity coincide for the poor, not in those where class and ethnicity clash. The former are called ranked ethnic systems in the literature, and the latter unranked ethnic systems (Horowitz 1985). If ranked ethnic systems are also democratic, the poor can exert more effective pressure on governments, and the effect on poverty is greater than is normally possible in unranked ethnic systems. Why should this be so? And what kind of evidence do we have to support the claim?

In generating collective action, the greater power of ethnicity vis-à-vis class can be explained in three ways. Two of them treat all kinds of ethnic mobilization together, contrasting them with class mobilization. The third separates ethnic mobilization of the dominant groups from that of the subaltern. All three are relevant, the third especially so.

First, developments in collective action theory seek to show why ethnicity solves the collective action problem better than class does. Class action is bedeviled by free-riding (or, what would be analogous, by problems encountered in a prisoner's dilemma). But the main strategic problem in ethnic collective action is one of *coordination,* not free-riding (Hardin 1995). In prisoner's dilemma games, it is rational for individuals to not cooperate with others. Coordination games are different from the prisoner's dilemma game. Instead of privileging individual defection from cooperation, coordination games rely on "focal points" to facilitate convergence of individual expectations; hence they show how collective mobilization becomes possible.[14] Ethnicity can serve as a focal point; class cannot, at least not easily.

The idea of focal points comes from Schelling's seminal treatment of the coordination problem in bargaining. In the famous Schelling example:

> When a man loses his wife in a department store without any prior understanding on where to meet if they get separated, the chances are good that they will find each other. It is likely that each will think of some obvious place to meet, so obvious that each will be sure that the other is sure that it is obvious to both of them. (1963, 54)

A focal point is distinguished by its "prominence" or "uniqueness": it has the instrumental power of facilitating the "formation of mutually consistent expectations" (84). Ethnicity can be viewed as one such focal point for mobilization. There is no equivalent in class action.

The second line of reasoning, not deployed in the political economy literature as the reasoning above typically is, has emerged from the theories of ethnicity and nation building. Compared to class, the shared identities of caste, ethnicity, and religion are more likely to form historically enduring bonds and provide common histories, heroes, and villains (Anderson 1983). Moreover, the poor as a class rarely have leaders from their own ranks. In contrast, a poor ethnic community can give rise to a small middle class, and thereby generate its own leaders. An example from India is worth noting. The people formerly known as untouchables, far and away India's poorest caste historically, were offered affirmative action in the public sector and civil service in 1950. As a result, a civil service–based middle class emerged by the 1980s and was able to organize the group in several parts of India in the form of a political party, the Bahujan Samaj Party (BSP).[15] The BSP has been in power three times in the biggest state of India, Uttar Pradesh.

A third explanation also comes from the field of ethnicity and nationalism, focusing especially on the distinction between the ethnic politics of exclusion, which typically expresses the interests of dominant groups, and the ethnic politics of resistance, which reflects the interests of the subaltern (Varshney 2003). In subaltern ethnic politics, economic issues dealing with the poverty of the group are typically part of a larger template emphasizing equality of treatment and an end to quotidian insults and humiliation in public spaces—in schools, fields, and places of work and worship, and on roads and public transport. In contemporary times, the political equality of democracy clashes with a historically inherited world where group-based hierarchy, humiliation, and degradation continue to exist (Taylor 1992). The denial of basic human dignity and the practice of discrimination on grounds of one's birth, *when added to poverty*, constitute a much more powerful font of resistance than poverty alone.

Clearly, such a distinction between ethnicity and class may not be present everywhere. It will certainly not mark the politics of monoethnic societies such as Korea, Japan, and Taiwan, or societies where the subaltern ethnic group is not only poor but also small and has yet to develop a middle class.[16] For all of these reasons, in the literature on ethnicity, East Asia (Horowitz 1985) and

Latin America (Dominguez 1994) have traditionally been considered outliers, though with the rise of indigenous people's movements, that may have begun to change for Latin America. On the whole, East Asia and Latin America have seen a lot of class politics but not enough ethnic politics, at least not yet. In comparison, in South and Southeast Asia, Sub-Saharan Africa, and Eastern and Central Europe, ethnicity has often trumped class.

Ranked Ethnic Systems and Poverty: The Malaysian and Indian Examples

Let me now turn from theoretical reasoning to the empirical world. What examples can be cited for the claim that unless poverty is linked to ethnic identity, it does not necessarily become a great force in democratic politics?

While we know a great deal about the ethnic profiles of most poor democracies, intercountry comparisons on poverty, as already stated, are rendered difficult by the absence of a time series and by lack of consistency in measurement criteria. Still, from what we know, of all poor democracies—consociational or adversarial—Malaysia has shown by far the best results on poverty reduction. The proportion of population below the poverty line has declined in Malaysia from 49.3 percent in 1970 to less than 2.0 percent in 1997 (World Bank 2004, 259). We must, however, note two special features of the Malaysian political economy.

First, when democracy was instituted, the majority ethnic group, the Malays, was vastly more rural and poor than the largest minority group, the Chinese. Once inaugurated, democratic politics became ethnically structured, and the Malay acquired constitutionally mandated political hegemony through quotas in the political and bureaucratic structures. Once the majority ethnic group, led by its small upper and middle class, came to power, the political elite undertook a large number of direct measures, in both the countryside and the cities, to increase the incomes of their ethnic group, including allocation of private equity for Malay companies after 1970 (Jomo 1990).

Second, the direct measures were undertaken *within the larger framework of a trade-oriented economic policy*. Since 1963, Malaysia has been an open economy, reducing its average tariff to less than 40 percent, not allowing non-tariff barriers to cover more than 40 percent of trade, and not letting its currency become overvalued by more than 20 percent (Sachs and Warner 1995, 21). By comparison, it may be noted that Sri Lanka, often compared to Malaysia in both size and potential (and, one might add, considerably more literate and peaceful than Malaysia in the 1950s and 1960s), used direct poverty alleviation measures only. It was able to alleviate poverty significantly, but not as much, or as successfully, as Malaysia. Unlike Malaysia, open since 1963, Sri Lanka remained a closed economy until 1978.[17] By the late 1970s, the fiscal ability of Sri Lanka to run its direct antipoverty programs was clearly in doubt (Bruton et al. 1992).

Though indicative, these *inter*country comparisons may not be as methodologically tight as *intra*country comparisons, where a great many factors other than ethnicity can be controlled for and the effect of ethnicity on poverty can be identified with greater certitude.[18] In India, detailed and disaggregated statistics on poverty are available for individual states going back to the 1960s. Patterns of state politics and policy can thus be clearly linked to the outcomes for poverty.

The states of Punjab and Kerala have shown the best results.[19] In Punjab, the green revolution, an indirect and growth-based method, has been key to poverty alleviation. In Kerala, the method was direct. Land reforms and extensive job reservations in government employment were the twin strategies.

Was the emphasis on direct methods in Kerala a result of the poor organizing themselves as a class? On the face of it, this would appear to be the case, primarily because a Communist party, repeatedly elected to power after 1957, led the campaign for land reforms and social justice. Its rhetoric was based on class.

However, both social history and electoral data make clear that there was a remarkable merging of caste and class in Kerala, the former defined ethnically, the latter economically. At the center of this coincidence is the Ezhava caste, estimated to constitute a little over 20 percent of the state's population. The Ezhavas traditionally engaged in "toddy tapping" (production of fermented liquor) and were therefore considered "polluting" by the upper castes. The catalogue of everyday humiliations for the Ezhavas was painfully long:

> They were not allowed to walk on public roads; . . . They were Hindus, but they could not enter temples. While their pigs and cattle could frequent the premises of the temple, they were not allowed to go even there. Ezhavas could not use public wells or public places. . . .

> An Ezhava should keep himself at least thirty-six feet away from a Namboodiri (Brahmin); . . . He must address a caste Hindu man as Thampuran (My Lord) and woman as Thampurati (My Lady); . . . He should never dress himself up like a caste Hindu; never construct a house on the upper caste model; . . . the women folk of the community . . . were required, young and old, to appear before caste Hindus, always topless. (Rajendran 1974, 23–24)

At the turn of the century, experiencing some mobility and developing a small middle class, the Ezhavas rebelled against the indignities of the Hindu social order and started fighting for their civil rights. Led by a famous Ezhava saint, Sri Narain Guru, sometimes called the Gandhi of Kerala, their protest movement aimed at self-respect and education. Self-respect entailed withdrawal from toddy tapping, a movement into modern trades and professions, and a nonviolent attack on the symbolic order. Since they were denied entry to temples and were only allowed to worship "lower gods and spirits," the Ezhavas, the Guru said, would have their own temples, in which they would worship "higher gods" to whom they would offer flowers and sweets, not animals and liquor reserved for the lower gods. Meanwhile, to improve their economic and social status, they would educate themselves. And to facilitate all of these activities, they would set up an organization. "Strengthen through organization, liberate by education" was the motto.[20]

These issues, all caste-based, decisively restructured the politics of Kerala in the 1930s. Entry into temples, an attack on the social deference system concerning dress, access to public roads, and more equal access to education drove the civil rights campaign. It was only subsequently that tenancy rights and land reforms spurred the mobilization for economic rights, and it was not until 1940 that the Communist Party of Kerala was born.[21]

If the fit between the Ezhava caste and the rural poor had not been so good in the 1930s and 1940s, class mobilization would have made little headway. Class politics was inserted into the campaign for caste-based social justice.[22] To this day, the Ezhava caste continues to be the principal base of the Communist Party Marxist (CPM). Historically, people of similar class positions, if Nair, have gone on the whole with the Congress Party; if Christian, with the Kerala Congress; if Muslim, with the Muslim League (Nossiter 1982, 345–75).

Concluding Observations

Democracies in poor countries have neither attacked poverty as successfully as some dictatorships in the past five decades, nor failed as monstrously as many authoritarian countries have. Dictatorships fall in all categories of performance: some have abolished mass poverty; many have allowed poverty to worsen; and still others, like democracies, have made some progress but have not eliminated mass poverty. By comparison, democracies have avoided the worst-case scenarios on poverty alleviation, but they have not achieved the best-case scenarios. They have simply been locked in the middle category: slow but not spectacular. Malaysia is about the only exception to this generalization, but there is consensus among scholars of democracy that it is at best a half democracy, never achieving the status of a fully competitive democracy since independence in 1957.

So why have democracies not done better? My argument is twofold. First, democracies have been more inclined toward the direct approach to alleviating poverty. Generally speaking, direct methods are not as effective as some (though not all) indirect growth-based methods, nor are they as fiscally sustainable. When direct attacks on poverty are made in the framework of growth-based strategies, they work much better. Until the era of trade- and market-oriented economic policies began in the 1980s, democracies tended not to embrace indirect methods, for while there were clear economic arguments in favor of growth-based methods, their political appeal in democracies was limited. The politics and economics of market-based approaches to eliminating poverty were not in agreement.

Second, the poor have not been a political force in poor democracies because they are often split among ethnic groups. Poor people are more easily mobilized as members of ethnic, identity-based communities than as an economic class. As a result, despite their large numbers, they are rarely, if ever, empowered as an economic class and are unable to pressure democracies as a united force. Only when the poor as a class and the poor as an ethnic group coincide, and this class/ethnic group is also numerically large, has this obstacle typically been overcome—partially or wholly. Such coincidence, however, is not common. More often than not, ethnicity and class tend to cross-cut each other.

Whether the first equation above has changed with the worldwide rise of market-oriented economic policies is still to be investigated definitively. From what we know, market-driven growth processes may have reduced poverty to some extent, but substantial mass poverty still exists in the developing world (Houtzager and Moore 2003). It would appear that the key question continues to be how to make markets—domestic and global—work for the poor. At the very least, we need some detailed empirical studies of the process through which, since the late 1980s, some of the previously poor have crossed the poverty line and some of those above that line have fallen below. As years of fieldwork in developing countries have made clear (Narayan et al. 2000), we need to understand the world of the poor not through our own assumptions, but through careful empirical analyses of what matters in their world, and how, and why.

Notes

For their comments on earlier versions of this chapter, I am grateful to Jagdish Bhagwati, Amitava Dutt, Raghav Gaiha, Ronald Herring, Peter Houtzager, Phil Keefer, Atul Kohli, and two anonymous reviewers. I should note that some of these scholars continue to have differences with my arguments. Research assistance by Bikas Joshi and Xavier Marquez is also greatly appreciated. Some of the arguments made here are presented in a different form in Varshney (2000b).

1.   The World Bank's calculation of the poverty line at $1 a day is based on its assessment of a minimal consumption bundle that a human being needs in order to survive physically; this is converted into dollars and adjusted for the purchasing power in a given case. Food, sufficient to provide a minimum number of calories required by the human body, typically constitutes the largest proportion of this consumption bundle.

2.   It can be argued following Olson (1965) and Bates (1981) that large numbers of the poor would in fact impede, rather than facilitate, collective action. But this is truer in authoritarian countries than in democratic ones (see Varshney 1995, 193–200).

3.   Similarly, by allowing a great deal of contestation but restricting participation according to class (and also gender), England in the nineteenth century was less democratic than it is today, but it was democratic nonetheless, certainly by nineteenth-century standards.

4.   The year 1950 is a convenient starting point, for beyond Latin America, independent since the early nineteenth century, decolonization of nonwhite colonies began with Indian independence in 1947, and more and more developing countries became independent after that.

5.   For example, Mauritius, the Solomon Islands, and Vanuatu all have populations of less than a million. For a fuller listing, see Przeworski et al. (2000, 59–76).

6.   Political parties in India and Sri Lanka may also seek to represent specific ethnic groups, but there has been no constitutional pact, or political requirement, that they

must do so. Parties are free to build cross-ethnic alliances if that aids their political fortunes.

7.   According to Przeworski et al. (2000), Malaysia has never been a democracy. They do not recognize countries with consociational democracy as democracies, hence their categorization. I use Malaysia as an example of limited democracy in this chapter.

8.   The analytic implication of such a small-N world, one might add, is very different from the one we encounter when we examine the impact of democracy on economic growth *globally*. Inclusion of both developed and developing countries makes the number of democracies sufficiently large, allowing for sophisticated statistical analysis (Barro 1997). However, Przeworski et al. (2000, ch. 1) offer a proposal about how this problem might be overcome for statistical analysis.

9.   For example, see Reddy and Pogge (forthcoming).

10.   With the exception of the Central African Republic (1993), Mali (1994), and Sierra Leone, poverty data in these countries were collected after 1995.

11.   In 2003, Singapore's per capita income was $24,180, compared to $27,650 for the United Kingdom.

12.   For a fuller elaboration, see Varshney (2000b).

13.   On land reforms, my argument is slightly more complicated. Precisely because the direct linkages are so attractive, all democracies have had land reforms on the policy agenda, which is not true of all authoritarian countries. But few democracies or dictatorships have implemented land reforms. If land reforms are implemented, argue some scholars, they can successfully attack poverty (Herring 1983; Kohli 1987). For why this may be true only under very specific conditions, not generally, see Varshney (1995, ch. 1; 2000b, 733–35). It should also be noted that land reforms are typically implemented at the time of, or soon after, revolutions, or by foreign occupiers. Neither democracies nor authoritarian systems seem to have the political capacity to implement them.

14.   Coordination games proceed according to the following logic. So long as others in the group are cooperating, it is rational for me to cooperate—for if all cooperate, the likelihood of the group gaining power (or realizing group objectives) goes up tremendously. Hardin (1995, 36–37) observes that "power based in coordination is superadditive, it adds up to more than the sum of individual contributions to it." He notes that all one needs to keep the coordination game going is a "charismatic leader," a "focus," and a mechanism through which information about others cooperating is provided to each individual. "Coordination power is . . . a function of reinforcing expectations about the behavior of others."

15.   On the emergence of the BSP, see Chandra (2004).

16.   Or, as sociologists have often reminded us, societies where the hegemony of the privileged groups is yet to be broken.

17.   With the exception of two brief periods, 1950–56 and 1977–83 (Sachs and Warner 1995, 23).

18.   With respect to Sri Lanka, for example, it has been argued that compared to other countries, it had fewer inequalities at the time of independence. Thus, Sri Lanka's good, though not spectacular, performance is not simply a function of the policies pursued after independence. The performance was path-dependent. See Bhalla and Glewwe (1986).

19.   For a quick overview of all states, see Ravallion and Datt (1996).

20.   For a detailed analysis, see Rao (1979).

21.   In a disarmingly candid statement (1994), E. M. S. Namboodiripad, a Kerala-based politician who was the greatest Communist mobilizer of twentieth-century

India, admitted before his death that the inability of the decades-long class mobilization in Kerala to overwhelm the religious divisions of the state might be rather more rooted in historical realities than Marxists had expected.

22. For a compelling argument that this merger facilitated the emergence of a Communist movement, see Menon (1994). While talking about the peasants and workers, the Communists could repeatedly use caste issues, which had great resonance in Kerala.

References

Adelman, Irma, and Cynthia Morris. 1973. *Economic Growth and Social Equity in Developing Countries*. Stanford, CA: Stanford University Press.

Anderson, Benedict. 1983. *Imagined Communities*. London: Verso.

Barro, Robert. 1997. *Determinants of Economic Growth: A Cross-Country Empirical Study*. Cambridge, MA: MIT Press.

Bates, Robert. 1981. *Markets and States in Tropical Africa*. Berkeley: University of California Press.

Bhagwati, Jagdish. 1998. "The Capital Myth." *Foreign Affairs* 77 (3): 7–12.

Bhalla, Surjit S., and Paul Glewwe. 1986. "Growth and Equity in Developing Countries: A Reinterpretation of the Sri Lankan Experience." *World Bank Economic Review* 1 (1): 35–63.

Bruton, Henry, with Gamini Abeysekera, Nimal Sanderatne, and Zainal Aznam Yusof. 1992. *The Political Economy of Poverty, Equity and Growth: Sri Lanka and Malaysia*. New York: Oxford University Press for the World Bank.

Chandra, Kanchan. 2004. *Why Ethnic Parties Succeed*. Cambridge: Cambridge University Press.

Dahl, Robert A. 1971. *Polyarchy*. New Haven, CT: Yale University Press.

———. 1989. *Democracy and Its Critics*. New Haven, CT: Yale University Press.

Dominguez, Jorge, ed. 1994. *Race and Ethnicity in Latin America*. New York: Garland.

Hardin, Russell. 1995. *One for All: The Logic of Group Conflict*. Princeton, NJ: Princeton University Press.

Herring, Ronald. 1983. *Land to the Tiller*. New Haven, CT: Yale University Press.

Horowitz, Donald. 1985. *Ethnic Groups in Conflict*. Berkeley: University of California Press.

Houtzager, Peter, and Mick Moore, eds. 2003. *Changing Paths*. Ann Arbor: University of Michigan Press.

Huntington, Samuel P. 1983. "Will More Countries Become Democratic?" *Political Science Quarterly* 99 (2): 193–218.

———. 1991. *The Third Wave: Democratization in the Late Twentieth Century*. Norman: University of Oklahoma Press.

400 Measuring Empowerment

Jomo, K. S. 1990. *Growth and Structural Change in the Malaysian Economy*. London: Macmillan.

King, Gary, Robert O. Keohane, and Sidney Verba. 1994. *Designing Social Inquiry: Scientific Inference in Qualitative Research*. Princeton, NJ: Princeton University Press.

Kohli, Atul. 1987. *The State and Poverty*. Cambridge: Cambridge University Press.

Lijphart, Arend. 1977. *Democracy and Plural Societies: A Comparative Exploration*. New Haven, CT: Yale University Press.

Menon, Dilip. 1994. *Caste, Nationalism and Communism: Malabar, 1900–1948*. Cambridge: Cambridge University Press.

Namboodiripad, E. M. S. 1994. "Presidential Address." Presented at the First International Congress of Kerala Studies, August 27–29. In *Proceedings of the International Congress on Kerala Studies,* vol. 1, *Addresses and Abstracts*. Thiruvananthapuram, India: AKG Centre for Research and Studies.

Narayan, Deepa, with Raj Patel, Kai Schafft, Anne Rademacher, and Sarah Koch-Schulte. 2000. *Voices of the Poor: Can Anyone Hear Us?* New York: Oxford University Press for the World Bank.

Nossiter, T. J. 1982. *Communism in Kerala*. Berkeley: University of California Press.

Olson, Mancur. 1965. *The Logic of Collective Action*. Cambridge, MA: Harvard University Press.

Przeworski, Adam, Michael E. Alvarez, Jose Antonio Cheibub, and Fernando Limongi. 2000. *Democracy and Development: Political Institutions and Well-Being in the World, 1950–90*. Cambridge: Cambridge University Press.

Rajendran, G. 1974. *The Ezhava Community and Kerala Politics*. Trivandrum, India: Kerala Academy of Political Science.

Rao, M. S. A. 1979. *Social Movements and Social Transformation: A Study of Two Backward Classes Movements in India*. Delhi: Macmillan.

Ravallion, Martin, and Gaurav Datt. 1996. "India's Checkered History in the Fight Against Poverty: Are There Lessons for the Future?" *Economic and Political Weekly* 31 (September, special issue): 2479–86.

Reddy, Sanjay G., and Thomas W. Pogge. Forthcoming. "How *Not* to Count the Poor." In *Measuring Global Poverty*, ed. Sudhir Anand and Joesph Stiglitz. New York: Oxford University Press. http://www.socialanalysis.org/.

Sachs, Jeffrey, Ashutosh Varshney, and Nirupam Bajpai. 1999. Introduction to *India in the Era of Economic Reforms,* ed. Jeffrey Sachs, Ashutosh Varshney, and Nirupam Bajpai. New York: Oxford University Press.

Sachs, Jeffrey, and Andrew Warner. 1995. "Economic Reform and the Process of Global Integration." *Brookings Papers on Economic Activity* 1995 (1): 1–118.

Schelling, Thomas. 1963. *The Strategy of Conflict*. New York: Oxford University Press.

Sen, Amartya. 1989. "Food and Freedom." *World Development* 17 (6): 769–81.

———. 1999. *Development as Freedom*. New York: Knopf.

Stiglitz, Joseph. 2002. *Globalization and Its Discontents*. New York: W. W. Norton.

Suri, K. C. 2004. "Democracy, Economic Reforms and Election Results in India." *Economic and Political Weekly* 39 (51): 5404–11.

Taylor, Charles. 1992. *Multiculturalism and the Politics of Recognition*. Princeton, NJ: Princeton University Press.

Varshney, Ashutosh. 1995. *Democracy, Development and the Countryside*. Cambridge: Cambridge University Press.

———. 1999. "Mass Politics or Elite Politics? India's Economic Reform in Comparative Perspective." In *India in the Era of Economic Reforms*, ed. Jeffrey Sachs, Ashutosh Varshney, and Nirupam Bajpai. New York: Oxford University Press. Previously published in *Journal of Policy Reform*, December 1998.

———. 2000a. "Is India Becoming More Democratic?" *Journal of Asian Studies* 59 (1): 3–25.

———. 2000b. "Why Have Poor Democracies Not Eliminated Poverty? A Suggestion." *Asian Survey* 40 (5): 718–36.

———. 2003. "Nationalism, Ethnic Conflict, and Rationality." *Perspectives on Politics* 1 (1): 85–99.

Weiner, Myron. 1989. "Institution Building in India." In *The India Paradox: Essays in Indian Politics*, 77–95. New Delhi: Sage.

———. 2001. "The Struggle for Equality: Caste in Indian Politics." In *The Success of India's Democracy*, ed. Atul Kohli, 193–225. Cambridge: Cambridge University Press.

World Bank. 2000. *World Development Report 2000/2001: Attacking Poverty*. New York: Oxford University Press.

———. 2004. *World Development Report 2005: A Better Investment Climate for Everyone*. New York: Oxford University Press.

Yadav, Yogendra. 2000. "Understanding the Second Democratic Upsurge: Trends of Bahujan Participation in Electoral Politics in the 1990s." In *Transforming India*, ed. Francine Frankel, Zoya Hasan, Rajeev Bhargava, and Balveer Arora, 120–45. Delhi: Oxford University Press.

———. 2004. "The Elusive Mandate of 2004." *Economic and Political Weekly* 39 (51): 5383–98.

Yadav, Yogendra, and V. B. Singh. 1997. "The Maturing of a Democracy." *India Today*, August 31.

Chapter 18

Empowering the Poor: What Does Democracy Have to Do with It?

Larry Diamond

Morally and analytically, there is no more vexing phenomenon than the persistence of mass poverty. Over the past half century, remarkable gains have been made in reducing infant mortality, extending life expectancy, raising levels of income and education, and reducing the incidence of severe diseases (USAID 2003). Huge investments of analytical work, empirical research, and development assistance have been made in the quest to eliminate, or at least dramatically reduce, absolute poverty, which leaves an individual to survive on less than $2 or even $1 per day. Yet absolute poverty persists on a mass scale throughout much of what has been termed, rather euphemistically, the "developing" world. Why?

The perspective adopted here is that the obstacles to the elimination of poverty are heavily, if not fundamentally, political. This is not to deny that poverty is, by definition, an economic phenomenon, resulting from inadequate income with which to live a minimally dignified and decent life and inadequate assets (human, financial, and infrastructural) with which to generate such incomes. Neither is it to neglect the many ways in which social norms and relations structure and reproduce poverty. It is merely to acknowledge that transforming these economic and social realities requires, in large measure, policy responses by the state to empower the poor.

Empowerment implies providing the poor with assets—education, health care, credit, potable water, electricity, roads—that enable them to be productive. It also requires an enabling environment for poverty reduction, including a transparent and efficient state bureaucracy, a fair and accessible justice system, and protection for their property rights (Narayan 2002). When the poor are able to nourish themselves and protect their health, raise their skills, educate their children, finance their productive activities, transport their crops and goods to markets, register their property and enterprises, and protect their rights without discrimination, they are well capable of producing their way out of poverty.

However, in every nation where much of the population remains trapped in absolute poverty, circumstances conspire to prevent the poor from doing these things. These circumstances are invariably political, in that they involve powerful actors at various levels of society and the political system who benefit from a "disabling environment" for poverty reduction and use their power to perpetuate it. This privileged and quite often predatory elite is typically a tiny minority. Logically, one would expect that democracy—a political system that includes regular, free, and fair elections in which the people choose their rulers—should empower the poor majority to constrain these powerful elites by choosing leaders, parties, and policies that favor poverty reduction.

Yet, as many analyses have shown (see, for example, Varshney 2000), many democracies do a lackluster or only mediocre job of reducing poverty. Of course, sustainable poverty reduction requires overall economic growth, and to the extent that a poor economy suffers international trade reverses or other shocks, it may experience a recession through no real fault of its own. But shocks are by definition temporary. The long-term persistence of high levels of absolute poverty in a given society is logically attributable to systemic conditions. And these conditions, I would argue, emanate to some considerable extent from bad governance.

The first section of this chapter offers a theory of failed development—which is to say, persistent poverty—based on the nature of governance. The second section explores the ambiguous relationship between democracy and development, explaining why democracy *in principle* should help empower the poor and promote development, then briefly reviewing the cross-national empirical evidence on this question. It explains why democracy often does not help development much, and why the enduring reduction of poverty requires a broader context of good governance beyond the narrow electoral arena. The third section discusses two priorities for achieving democracy at the national level: free and fair elections, and democratization of political parties. The fourth section explores three key dimensions of democracy and good governance and suggests some indicators to measure these dimensions. The final section offers concluding reflections.

The Political Roots of Development Failure

The deepest root cause of persistent mass poverty is not a lack of resources or international isolation. Rather, it is a lack of good governance—the inability or unwillingness of those in power to apply public resources effectively to generate public goods.[1] Both good and bad governance have striking effects on a country's ability to empower the poor and move out of poverty.

Good Governance and Development

Good governance has several dimensions. One is the *capacity* of the state to function in the service of the public good. Effective functioning requires knowledge of the policies and rules that best serve the public good, and hence training of state officials to that end. It requires a professional civil service with a set of norms and structures that promote fidelity to public rules and duties, in part by rewarding those who perform well in their roles. This relates intimately to the second dimension of good governance, *commitment to the public good*. Where does this commitment come from? It may be generated by dedicated and charismatic leadership. Or it may derive from a cultural ethic that appreciates—and a structure of institutional incentives that rewards—disciplined service to the nation or the general community over the use of office for private benefit. Or it may, in part, be induced by the structure of political incentives (domestic and international) that leaders confront. In every modern society, however, this commitment must, at a minimum, be reinforced by institutions that punish betrayals of the public trust.

A third dimension of good governance is *transparency*, the openness of state conduct to the scrutiny of other state actors and of the public. Transparency is closely related to *accountability*. Governing agents are more likely to be responsible when they must answer for their conduct to the society in general and to other specific institutions that monitor their behavior and can impose sanctions upon them. Effective oversight requires open flows of information, and hence transparency, so that monitors can discover facts and mobilize evidence. This requires a system of government in which different institutions hold one another accountable, compelling them to justify their actions. Power is thus constrained, bound not only "by legal constraints but also by the logic of public reasoning" (Schedler 1999, 15).

Transparency and accountability are bound up with a fourth dimension of good governance, the *rule of law*. Governance can only be good and effective when it is restrained by the law, when the law is applied equally to the mighty and the meek, and when there are professional independent authorities to enforce the law in a neutral, predictable fashion.

A fifth dimension of good governance consists of mechanisms of *participation* and dialogue that enable the public to provide input to the policy process, to correct mistakes in policy design and implementation, and to promote social inclusion. Policies will be more likely to be stable and sustainable when they enjoy popular understanding and support. This requires some means for distinct organized interests—and for historically marginalized groups such as women and minorities—to have input into governmental decisions, and some means by which they can protest policies and actions that harm their interests.

Finally, when good governance functions in the above five ways, it also breeds *social capital,* in the form of networks and associations that draw people together in relations of trust, reciprocity, and voluntary cooperation for common ends. Social capital not only fosters the expansion of investment and commerce, embedded in relations of trust and predictability, it also breeds the civic spirit, participation, and respect for law that are crucial foundations of political development and good governance. In other words, it generates a political culture of responsible citizenship.

In many respects, then, good governance constitutes a "virtuous cycle" in which several elements reinforce one another to advance the public good (Putnam 1993, 167–76). Conceptualized in this way, good governance promotes broad-based development, and thus poverty reduction. By generating and defending broad commitment to the public welfare, it increases the likelihood that public resources will be used to generate public goods that raise the general quality of life. When government itself is transparent and disciplined in its commitment to the public good, it provides credible signals to the rest of society about what types of behaviors are expected. In providing a fair means for the resolution of disputes, the rule of law generates an enabling environment for economic growth and some means for attenuating inequality. In incorporating groups that historically have been confined to the margins of society, good governance mitigates social conflict and harnesses the full range of talent and resources in the society. In fostering the accumulation of social capital, good governance cultivates trust (in individuals and in government), cooperation, compliance with the law, and confidence in the future.

Bad Governance and the Persistence of Poverty

Countries that have failed to realize their development potential in the past half century have invariably suffered yawning deficits of good governance. Why is bad governance such a pervasive and profound obstacle to development? Just as good governance promotes the accumulation of financial, physical, social, and political capital, bad governance inhibits or drains away that accumulation.

Consider the archetypical badly governed country. Corruption is endemic throughout the system of government at every level. Public infrastructure decays or is never built because the resources for it are diverted to private ends. Decisions on public expenditures are tilted toward unproductive investments—sophisticated weapons, white-elephant construction projects—that can deliver large kickbacks to the civilian officials and military officers who award them. Schools are not built or maintained, clinics are not stocked and staffed, roads are not repaired because the funds for these are squandered or stolen. Businesses cannot get licenses to operate and small producers cannot get title to their land because it would take half a year and a small fortune to navigate the shoals of a bloated, corrupt state bureaucracy. Every interaction with the state—to obtain a building permit, register a marriage or a death, report a crime, or receive a vaccination—exacts its petty, unofficial price.

In such a context of rotten governance, individuals seek governmental positions in order to collect rents and accumulate personal wealth—to convert public resources into private goods. Governmental decisions and transactions are deliberately opaque in order to hide their corrupt nature, but exposure of corrupt deeds typically brings little more than embarrassment because the rule of law does not function to constrain or punish the behavior of public officials. Power is heavily centralized and institutions of scrutiny and accountability function only on paper, or episodically, to punish the more marginal miscreants or the rivals of the truly powerful. Corruption is also rife at the bottom of the governance system because that is the climate that is set at the top, and because government workers cannot live on the salaries they are paid.

Institutions of political participation may or may not exist in this venal environment, but if they do, the government is not responsive to them. Instead, political participation cleaves society vertically, typically along ethnic lines, into competing chains of patron-client relations that all mobilize for one purpose: to get control of public resources so that they can convert them into private goods. In such a society, violent conflict is also rife, or never far from the surface, because ordinary people are exploited and desperate, rights are routinely abused, and communities are mutually resentful of any perceived advantage of the other in a zero-sum game. The only way to generate truly sustainable development in this context is to bring about a fundamental transformation in the nature and quality of governance. Granted, the ways people think and behave must change. But individual behavior is not the largest or quickest point of leverage. Such changes can only be effective if the social environment of incentives and expectations is transformed. That in turn requires a shift toward more responsible, professional, open, and accountable governance. In particular, it requires specific and well-functioning institutions of democracy, horizontal accountability, and the rule of law.

The Relationship between Democracy and Development

The relationship between democracy and economic development has been the focus of intensive research and theorizing for decades. For a time, particularly during the 1970s and 1980s, the fashionable argument was that economic growth in lower-income countries might be better served by a period of "developmental dictatorship" (Huntington and Nelson 1976). However, the weight of theory and evidence is now swinging behind the benefits of empowerment, and thus of democracy, for development in general, and for lifting up the poor in particular. To achieve this, however, democracy must extend beyond occasional elections to provide real accountability and access to power.

The Empowering Benefits of Democracy

Poverty is not just a lack of resources. It is also a lack of voice and political power that would enable the poor to articulate and defend their interests. Because they are poor, ill-clothed, and "backward," they are treated in an abrupt, contemptuous, and even humiliating manner by public officials (including the police), who identify psychologically with the upper strata and/or sell their services and decisions to those who can pay for them. Because they are poor, illiterate, and unorganized, poor people lack access to justice, and thus cannot demand transparency or challenge abuses in the courts. All of this renders them utterly vulnerable to exploitation by the powerful (for evidence, see Narayan et al. 2000).

In principle, democracy should provide a corrective, empowering the poor in the following ways. First, when competitive elections are truly free and fair, they serve as an instrument to remove corrupt, unresponsive, or ineffectual leaders. They thus provide an incentive for leaders to govern more effectively in the public interest and to attend to the needs and concerns of the poor majority. Second, democracy provides nonelectoral means for the poor to articulate and defend their interests, and to participate in the making of public policy—through nongovernmental organizations (NGOs), informal associations, community-based organizations, interest groups, social movements, and the mass media. Third, democracy enables all these actors in civil society, as well as elected representatives at various levels of government, to monitor the conduct of public officials and to seek redress in the courts and administrative forums. With such participation and debate, the poor are more likely to feel some sense of ownership of the resulting policies, which they perceive can help them craft their way out of poverty. However, all of this depends not just on democracy, but also on freedom.

Does Democracy Promote Development?

The empirical evidence about the relationship between democracy and development is ambiguous. We do know that there is a much higher incidence of stable democracy among higher-income countries, and that globally democracy is highly correlated with development. This is at least in part because rich countries are much more likely to sustain democracies than poor ones (Przeworski et al. 2000). Going back to Lipset (1959), and before him to Aristotle, it has been a basic tenet of political science that democracy is more viable in relatively prosperous, middle-class societies. But do democracies grow more rapidly—and eliminate poverty more effectively—than authoritarian regimes?

This question is more difficult to answer, and the statistical evidence is contradictory and ambiguous. Overall, two reviews of the literature in the early 1990s, by Inkeles and Sirowy (1991) and Przeworski and Limongi (1993), concluded that there was no clear and consistent relationship. For Inkeles and Sirowy, the evidence seemed to suggest that "political democracy does not widely and directly facilitate rapid economic growth, net of other factors" (149). Recently, however, Roll and Talbott (2003), using cross-sectional data from 1995 through 1999, found that 80 percent of the variance in per capita national income could be explained by nine separate influences that heavily involved factors of governance, such as political rights, civil liberties, and property rights. Moreover, with a highly innovative time-series design, they also found that following political regime changes, democracies clearly did perform better in terms of economic growth than dictatorships.

To understand the relationship, we need to disaggregate countries and time periods. One reason that democracy often does not appear in statistical analyses to have a clear positive relationship to economic growth may be the strong growth performance of the "East Asian tigers"—the Republic of Korea, Taiwan, Singapore, and Hong Kong—under authoritarian rule, particularly in the 1960s and 1970s. More recently, Thailand has begun rapid economic growth under authoritarian, or semi-authoritarian, rule, and Malaysia has grown rapidly under semi-authoritarian rule. China started the process of economic reform and opening earlier than India and has outstripped it in growth performance, though India has improved markedly in recent years.

Before deriving policy conclusions, one needs to ask: How replicable is the East Asian historical experience, or was it somewhat unique to place and time? A case can be made that the "tigers" were able to impose a strong sense of self-restraint and discipline—to limit predatory corruption—both for cultural reasons and because they faced an existential threat from the spread of communism and the growing power of China. They realized that in order to survive, they had to deliver development. Moreover, they had or they crafted a degree of national solidarity that was conducive to viewing the development process as a collective national enterprise for the public good. In the cases of Korea, Taiwan, and Thailand, huge amounts of U.S. aid early on also made a difference.

In Africa and Central Asia, there is no such pressure for good governance to ensure regime survival that ruling elites readily recognize. Societies are deeply divided along ethnic, clan, religious, and regional lines, leading each group to see the state as something to be captured for its own group benefit rather than for the overall "national" good. Thus, authoritarian rule in these circumstances is unlikely to generate economic development, and certainly not with the broad distribution that reduces poverty. Rather, it facilitates the domination of one group or coalition over others and fosters an extractive, predatory attitude toward governance. In these circumstances, a benevolent, development-oriented leader or ruling party is unlikely to emerge. And if, as in Uganda, such a leadership does emerge, its commitment to good governance will eventually fray if it is not disciplined by the instruments of vertical and horizontal accountability that democracy provides.

Authoritarian rule, particularly of a prolonged or indefinite nature, therefore offers poor prospects for sustained poverty reduction in the countries that still suffer from mass poverty. However, democracy does not provide any guarantee of better performance. Much depends on the type and degree of democracy.

The Limits of (Purely) Electoral Democracy

There are several reasons why democracy often fails to do much to empower the poor. These derive not from the intrinsic limitations of democracy as a political system, but rather from the fact that democracy often functions in a limited, shallow, illiberal fashion. Of course, many regimes that claim to be democracies are instead "pseudo-democracies" or "electoral authoritarian regimes" (Diamond 1999, 2002; Schedler 2002). These regimes have many of the superficial features of democracy, in particular, regular electoral competition between different political parties. In some of them, elections may even be fairly competitive and may lead to opposition parties winning control of some subnational governments and some significant share of seats in parliament (as in Kenya, Malaysia, and Mexico before the reforms of the late 1990s). But their elections are not completely free and fair, and therefore it is not possible to defeat the ruling party through normal electoral means. To the extent that the ruling party knows it can rig itself back into power, a key mechanism of vertical accountability and democratic responsiveness breaks down.

Where elections are free and fair, the poor stand a better chance of effecting poverty-reducing changes in budget priorities, policies, and institutions—but even then, the chance is not always that much better. Electoral democracy, which we are defining as a system that has free and fair electoral competition for the principal positions of power in the country,[2] may be diminished in several respects that impede its potential for poverty alleviation and empowerment. First, the arena of electoral competition may be distorted by corruption, so that while the polling is not grossly rigged on voting day, parties and candidates obtain the resources to compete through the sale of political decisions and influence. Such corruption in party and campaign finance diminishes the need of political competitors, particularly incumbents, to be responsive to the majority of their constituents and gives them a shortcut to electoral victory.

Related to this are two characteristic problems with political parties, having to do with the lack of internal democracy and transparency. Where parties are opaque, autocratic, and hierarchical, dominated by a single leader or small circle, they are less effective at representing a broad range of interests and may wind up imposing candidates on constituencies. Second, such parties tend to be extremely vertically organized, not only inside the party leadership structure but also at every level in a cascading pyramid of patron-client relations. They seek to "represent" impoverished constituencies by mobilizing them along ethnic, religious, or other cultural lines, by distributing state jobs to loyal followers, and by distributing a dollop of cheap goods around election time in place of any real policy response to poverty. In the narrow sense, such a system may be democratic, but it may lead either to individual political machines entrenching themselves in different districts, towns, and states, or to a succession of largely corrupt and exploitative governments.

Democracy should provide alternative, nonelectoral means to check and reverse bad governance. These come through the activities of civil society and of institutions of horizontal accountability—the courts, parliamentary oversight, audit and counter-corruption agencies, ombudsmen, human rights commissions, and so on. But when democracy is illiberal and hollow, these institutions also fail to function effectively. Some democracies allow for true electoral competition but nevertheless have very weak rule of law, with extensive abuse of citizen rights by the police and government officials. Civil society organizations may not be free to organize, and the press may not be free to report, investigate, and criticize. Or civil society may be dominated by NGOs that are externally funded and driven, led by the educated middle class, and only faintly sensitive (at best) to the frustrations and needs of the poor (Ottaway and Carothers 2000).

These deficiencies of democracy do not only stem from abusive or "delegative" democracy at the national level (O'Donnell 1994). Just as often, they stem from the weakness of the state—its inability to break local power monopolies, discipline local police forces, protect the weak and vulnerable, and enforce accountability and the rule of law at all levels of public life. In large federal democracies such as India, Brazil, and Nigeria, it is in fact the state and local governments, and the local political bosses, who are responsible for the worst abuses of human rights, which invariably harm mainly the poor. A growing body of evidence suggests that one of the chief problems for development is that the state is lacking in capacity and authority (Joseph 2003). In important respects it can be said that rural people, and poor people generally, are "undergoverned" (Osmani 2000, 4).

Reforming Governance at the National Level

There is a good reason why development assistance still focuses largely on nations and national state structures. True, some states have collapsed, and we are seeing alternatives to the classic Westphalian state structure in such places as Somalia. But for the most part, national states persist as the framework for governance and as indispensable facilitators of economic growth and poverty reduction. If we are going to witness large reductions in poverty, it will only be because states themselves become more capable, effective, open, accountable, responsive, honest, and just. Clearly, the improvement of governance cannot happen only at the center, and indeed cannot involve only formal state structures at any level. But improving the quality of governance at the national level is a *fundamental condition* for reducing poverty "from the bottom up."

Although the rigid divide between donor activities for economic development and those for democracy assistance is beginning to soften, it persists. There is still a tendency to view donor assistance for economic development—and particularly poverty reduction—as social, economic, and technical, in other words, as nonpolitical. This may be the biggest mistake in efforts to relieve poverty. After a half century of international development assistance, the persistence of poverty is not for want of effort, resources, and international goodwill, though we could use more of all of these. It is not primarily a failing of technical understanding, though we can always do with more of that, too. It is certainly not a consequence of fate. Poverty persists because of power disparities. At every level of organized life, the powerful attempt to prey on the weak and disorganized (and not only in low-income countries). Two principal forces contain this predation: open and competitive markets, and resourceful and authoritative states, the latter preventing and correcting market distortions through democracy and the rule of law. Unless these forces are brought to bear to level accumulated power disparities, poverty will be reproduced from generation to generation.

In designing democratic and other governance institutions, the social, economic, and historical context is important to bear in mind. However, certain broad, generic features of governance will work to promote development, empowerment, social justice, and poverty alleviation. One obvious priority is to strengthen the overall training, capacity, and professionalism of state bureaucrats, including their technical understanding of economic policies that promote development. With specific respect to the elements of democratic good governance, two priorities are elaborated in more detail below: free and fair elections, and democratic political parties.

Free and Fair Elections

If elections are to be an instrument for registering citizen preferences and holding public officials accountable, they must be free and fair—and thus neutrally and professionally administered. Like other aspects of governance, elections will be subverted by those who seek shortcuts to power and privilege unless there are strong rules and institutions to prevent it. Electoral administration consists of a daunting range of tasks, any of which may be compromised by fraud or ineptitude. These include registering voters; publishing and distributing voter lists; registering and qualifying parties and candidates; establishing and enforcing rules on campaigning and campaign finance; ensuring the security of campaigners, voters, and the polling stations; administering the polls during voting; counting the ballots; reporting, collating, and announcing the results; investigating and adjudicating complaints; and certifying the results (Pastor 1999, 77–78). This set of tasks requires a professional and permanent administration that is able to administer competently and regulate impartially, an administration that is not subject to direction or manipulation by incumbent officials or the ruling party.

Democratic Political Parties

Where governance is bad in democracies and quasi-democracies, political parties are invariably a major part of the problem. Quite often they are corrupt, insular, internally undemocratic, detached from societal interests, and ineffective in addressing the country's problems.

Yet in a modern society, democracy cannot function without political parties. They structure electoral competition, organize government, and recruit leaders. And even if parties are only one among many vehicles for stimulating political participation and representing interests, they remain essential to the overall functioning of democracy (Diamond and Gunther 2001, 7–9; USAID 1999, 7–8).

Development assistance must meet the challenge of helping democratic political parties to become more capable and mature as organizations, more internally competitive and transparent, and more externally responsive and accountable. Toward this end, party assistance programs should focus on three traditional objectives:

1. *Organizational development:* Helping parties to research issues, assess public opinion, develop policies and platforms, craft long-term strategies, build professional staffs, recruit members, raise funds, and manage resources.
2. *Electoral mobilization:* Helping parties to select and train candidates, craft campaign messages, manage campaign organizations, improve communication skills, contact voters, identify and mobilize supporters, and activate women and youth.
3. *Governance:* Helping parties to function effectively as a legislative caucus, constitute a government or opposition (including at the regional and local levels), forge coalitions, reform electoral laws, and monitor elections through poll-watching.

In addition, two innovative arenas merit more emphasis in the coming years:

1. *Internal democratization:* Helping parties to develop more democratic and transparent means of selecting candidates (such as through primaries and caucuses), choosing leaders, making decisions, formulating policies, and eliciting member participation.[3]
2. *Reforming party and campaign finance:* Helping party, legislative, governmental, and civil society actors to identify alternative rules and systems for reporting and monitoring financial donations to parties and campaigns, auditing party accounts, providing public funding to parties and campaigns, and widening the access of all political parties to the electronic mass media. Also, helping parties to promote higher standards of ethical conduct among their leaders, candidates, and members, and helping civil society actors and electoral administrations to develop better technical means to monitor party and campaign finance.

Political parties will not be strengthened by party assistance alone. Interest groups and NGOs can be supported in efforts to forge channels of communication and working relations with political parties. Civil society activists can be given training if they opt to enter the arena of party and electoral politics. One of the crucial challenges of improving party politics is recruiting better-educated and more public-spirited actors into the process.

Conceptual and Methodological Issues for Future Research

We still have a long way to go to clearly establish how, how much, and under what circumstances democracy may foster development and empowerment. Better empirical specification of the relationship between political regimes and development must clearly address three conceptual and methodological issues: (a) how to define democracy, (b) how to measure democracy, and (c) how, more broadly, to categorize the world's different political systems.

Conceptualizing Democracy

The preceding discussion has defined democracy as a system of government in which the principal positions of government power are filled through regular, free, fair, and competitive (and therefore multiparty) elections. There must be some degree of freedom of movement, speech, organization, and assembly if elections are to be sufficiently free and fair to qualify as democratic. Yet, as stressed earlier, political systems can be democratic in relation to electoral competition and nevertheless quite corrupt, abusive, unresponsive, and unaccountable in the way they govern between elections.

Democracy in the larger sense can be seen as having three dimensions: electoral/political democracy, civil liberties (human rights), and responsible/accountable government.[4] Each of these depends in different ways on the rule of law.

Electoral Democracy

A primary dimension of democracy is the right to participate and compete in political life, and to have that participation and competition be consequential for governance. In this respect, a system is democratic to the extent that it offers extensive political rights, as articulated in the Freedom House checklist of political rights.[5] In such a system, the head of government and members of parliament are elected through competitive elections that are free, in the sense that alternative parties representing popular interests and preferences can organize and campaign; fair, in that they are neutrally administered, with honest tabulation of the votes; and meaningful, in the sense that the voters are able to endow their freely elected representatives with real power. The latter criterion implies that there are not significant "reserved domains of power" in which electorally unaccountable actors—the military, religious leaders, local oligarchs, foreign powers, and so on—exercise hidden power. Also, political rights to vote, organize, and contest must include virtually all adults (with exceptions for a few categories such as the mentally incapacitated). To the extent that women or any ethnic, religious, or other minority group are denied full rights of political participation, the system is less than democratic.

If the political rights of all citizens to participate and contest are to be secure, they must be protected and upheld by independent institutions that are not under the control of the ruling authorities. One such institution is an independent electoral administration. But the ultimate protection against electoral fraud and the abuse of political rights is an independent judiciary, which ensures that the laws are respected and abuses are redressed (including, if necessary, through the disqualification of some candidates and the ordering of new elections). Whether this function is performed in part by special electoral tribunals or by the regular courts is less important than that it reside in authorities that are politically neutral and independent.

A common mistake in classifying political systems is to score a country as "democratic" because it has multiparty elections that are at least somewhat competitive. Unless these elections are *truly* free and fair, they do not produce a democracy. A number of regimes in the world today—such as Nigeria, Tanzania, Russia, and Ukraine—are at least ambiguous in this regard, and by a demanding standard fail the test. Others, like Iran, Malaysia, Ethiopia, and Gabon, are sometimes classified as democracies when they manifestly are not, because elections are not fully free, fair, open, and competitive.

Civil Liberties

The second dimension of democracy concerns individual and associational freedom. There must be some degree of freedom if the electoral element of democracy is to be authentic. But democracy is deeper, more liberal and democratic, when there is full freedom of expression and belief (including freedom of political thought and of religious belief and practice, and freedom of speech and the press); when there is freedom for groups (including economic interest groups such as trade unions and peasant organizations) to organize, assemble, demonstrate, and petition peacefully; when individuals are free from political terror, unjustified imprisonment, torture, or other abuse by the police and other state or nonstate authorities; when citizens have the right to due process and to equal treatment before the law; and when these rights are protected and upheld by an independent, professional, nondiscriminatory judiciary.

Several practical indicators of quality of democracy on the civil liberties dimension suggest themselves:

- Fear is absent as a factor in civic life.
- All military and police agencies are subjected to the control and scrutiny of democratically elected officials, and the military is barred from domestic intelligence and security functions.
- There are no political prisoners and torture is not used against detainees.
- A vigorous press (including print and broadcast media) is pluralistic in its ownership and sources of control, and thus independent of political control.
- A vibrant civil society exists in which a multiplicity of interest groups, professional associations, NGOs, informal networks, social movements, and community-based organizations are freely able to express the diversity of interests in society and mobilize for policy alternatives and social change.

- Ethnic, religious, and other cultural groups are able to use (and reproduce) their language and culture and practice their faith without fear or discrimination, so long as they do not impinge on the rights of others.

Responsible and Accountable Government

A third dimension of democracy is what is sometimes referred to as "good governance," though the latter is really a broader term that encompasses the first two dimensions of democracy as well. Government must be transparent, honest, professional, and dedicated to its explicit purpose, which is serving the collective public good. The most important aspect here is the effective control (one can never speak of elimination) of corruption. But responsible and accountable government also entails restraint of abuse of power, so that government power at all levels is exercised in conformity with the constitution and laws of the country, and in the service of the public good. It also entails the recognition and protection of private property rights—their violation being one of the most common ways in which state power is abused. This includes the right to establish private enterprises and to gain for them legal recognition and protection without undue delay or illegal exaction.

Responsible government requires effective mechanisms of horizontal accountability, by which various agencies of government scrutinize and check each other, and in particular, check the executive and administrative arms of the state. Although the judiciary is typically considered the most important such check, it is only one of many, as noted above. Some indicators of this dimension, then, are the following:

- Government officials carry out their responsibilities honestly and transparently, free of corruption and bribery.
- Political parties and election campaigns are financed transparently, according to the law, and free of bribery (in the sense of exchanging past or future government decisions for political contributions).
- Private individuals and enterprises have formal protection for their property rights, and freedom to conduct legitimate commerce.
- The judiciary is neutral, professional, honest, and independent of partisan or executive control.
- There exist other agencies of horizontal accountability that are independent and effective, such as counter-corruption commissions, supreme audit agencies, ombudsmen, human rights commissions, economic regulatory agencies, and parliamentary oversight committees.
- Government transactions and operations are transparent and open to scrutiny, and citizens have the effective legal right to obtain information on the functions and decisions of government.

Note that I do not propose here to include measures of overall government effectiveness or capacity. We should not presume that a government that is democratically elected, liberal, responsible, and accountable is *necessarily* effective in utilizing government resources for development and empowerment of the poor. That is a matter of theoretical argument and must be assessed through empirical investigation.

Internal Variation within Countries

Beyond the expected variation between countries, there is significant internal variation within countries. Large developing democracies, such as Brazil, India, and Pakistan (when it was democratic, which it is not today), show considerable variations in the character and quality of governance between different jurisdictions. This is the case even in many medium-sized countries. Some states, districts, and cities may enjoy real democracy, good protection for individual and group rights, and even decent governance, while others have so much electoral fraud and violence, human rights abuse, corruption, and distortion of the rule of law that they represent authoritarian enclaves within a system that is nationally democratic. Such internal variation cannot be captured with a single national "score," because people do not just live in a nation. They live in a rural district or town or city that is part of a national governance system, but that also is part of a state or province within the nation. We cannot understand whether and why development happens—and people move out of poverty—at different rates in different parts of a country, unless we can conceptualize and measure these differences in the character of governance across different jurisdictions.

It is likely that the three dimensions of governance are strongly correlated across governance jurisdictions within countries, at least as much as they are across countries. Where a national political system is generally rotten and oppressive, or in very small systems, there will not be much internal variation on any of the dimensions. But in relatively large countries whose democracies (or near democracies) are not fully liberal, consolidated, and institutionalized, there is likely to be significant variation in the quality of governance. When that is the case, one can hypothesize that those subnational jurisdictions that score better on electoral democratic rights will also tend to score better on civil liberties and accountability. As a result, they are likely to perform demonstrably better in empowering the poor and reducing poverty.

Measuring Democracy

A first task in measuring democracy is to determine how the three dimensions or scales—electoral/political democracy, civil liberties (human rights), and responsible/accountable government—are to be weighted relative to one another. I do not see any compelling reason not to weight them equally. Whatever weighting scheme is used, it will be important not only to assess the impact of liberal, democratic, accountable government on development and poverty reduction, but also to assess the individual impact of each dimension measured separately, to the extent that they vary independently of one another.

Defining the Scales

As to how each scale is calibrated, one could assign a certain score for each item within a dimension or scale of democracy, based on how well the political jurisdiction appeared to be meeting the test. For the most part, assessments on these different questions will necessarily be subjective. Therefore, it is important that a scale not pretend to greater precision than it is capable of. For example, a subjective assessment of the overall state of judicial independence can probably distinguish reasonably well (in terms of intersubjective coder reliability) about five points on a scale of judicial integrity:

1. *No integrity:* The judiciary is completely compliant politically and/or totally corrupt and ineffectual.
2. *Very little integrity:* The judiciary may rule honestly in small cases, but is always subject to political instruction, is extensively corrupt, and almost never defends citizen rights against the state.
3. *Moderate integrity:* The judiciary operates with some honesty and professionalism in ordinary criminal and civil cases, but suffers from significant corruption and is politically biased and pliant in important cases.
4. *Substantial integrity:* Some judges and prosecutors are corrupt and politically partisan, but most courts enforce and interpret the law in a neutral, impartial, and predictable manner.
5. *Very high integrity:* The courts are completely independent of political control; they decide the law and enforce accountability in a neutral, impartial, and predictable manner, holding everyone equal before the law; and corruption in the judiciary is rare and vigorously punished.

Note here that this hypothetical scale of judicial integrity combines assessments of judicial probity and judicial independence. In fact, these are two somewhat different dimensions; they could be separately assessed and then the scores averaged into a summary judgment of judicial integrity.

Two principles are suggested for a subjective coding scheme on governance. First, a numerical score must be tied to some specific depiction of empirical reality, as in the above illustrative framework, or different coders can easily impute different meanings to different raw point scores. And second, the coder must be able to distinguish between the different points on the scale. In general, with more than five or six of these points, it becomes very difficult for subjective coders to make reliable distinctions. A workable approach might be, for most items, to have a scoring scheme of four to six points, while enabling a coder to place a jurisdiction midway between two scores in a difficult or ambiguous situation. The scores could then be standardized to 100 and averaged with the other items if each is to be weighted equally, or weighted in a variety of ways. Each component scale—electoral, liberal, accountable—could be scored from 0 to 100, and the overall score could be summarized with the average of these three scales.

What NOT to Count

Measuring democracy entails subjective assessment that can be informed but not mechanically generated by objective indicators. On the accountability dimension, there may be a few objective components that can be utilized (such as the number of days it takes to register a business). In general, however, objective measures are not very useful.

One objective indicator that has been used in some quantitative measures of democracy, the voter turnout rate, is deeply flawed and misleading. Some authoritarian states have, or at least report, very high turnout rates, near 100 percent. Some democracies have low and declining rates of voting. In part, variation is affected by whether voting is compulsory or not. It is possible to argue that not voting is also a democratic right and that compulsion is a diminution of liberal democracy. More importantly, apathy as reflected in high rates of voter abstention may signal alienation from the democratic process, or serious substantive problems in the functioning of democracy. But those problems must be directly assessed, rather than inferred from voter turnout rates that can have many possible explanations.

Similarly, we should not *mechanically* take the degree of electoral support for opposition candidates as a measure of the extent of democracy. There is no way, in principle, to argue that a political system in which the ruling party gets only 37 percent of the presidential vote is intrinsically more democratic than one in which the ruling party gets 55 percent of the presidential vote. Nor can we say that a political system in which the ruling party has only a bare legislative majority is necessarily more democratic than one in which the ruling party has 60 percent or more. All of these are possible indications of the competitiveness of the political system, but they must be placed in context. If the ruling party wins only a weak plurality of the presidential vote but does so by means of electoral fraud and intimidation (as in Kenya in 1997), that is not democracy. Conversely, if a ruling party wins two-thirds of the seats in parliament in rigorously free and fair elections, which are fully open to challenging parties but in which most voters simply do not prefer the challengers (as in South Africa in 2004), the mere fact of that electoral dominance cannot be taken as a negation of democracy. Certainly at the national level, but also to some extent at the local level, the absence of a significant opposition vote and presence in the legislature can be taken as *prima facie* evidence of an obstruction of democracy. But that obstruction must then be subjectively investigated and assessed.

For the same reason, we cannot declare a political system a nondemocracy simply because the ruling party has not been defeated in a national election (as for example in Botswana).[6] We have to examine whether elections are truly free, fair, and open, whether opposition parties have power at other levels of authority (as they have had from time to time in Botswana), and whether electoral dominance is perpetuated by effective governance and politicking or by undemocratic means.

Categorizing Political Systems

We can categorize "a country" as to the level or nature of democracy, but it is important to keep in mind that we are really categorizing a political system. This in turn is composed of political subsystems (again, particularly in large countries) that may vary in their levels and forms of democracy. That said, we can distinguish eight broad categories of national political systems in relation to the three dimensions of democracy outlined above:

1. *Liberal, accountable democracies* score high on all three dimensions. Elections are competitive, open, free, and fair and are not marred by fraud or intimidation at any level. Civil liberties and the rule of law are upheld by a neutral, professional, and independent judicial system. With rare exceptions, all citizens, no matter their color, ethnicity, gender, or social status, are equal before the law. Governance is transparent, and corruption and abuse of power are contained and punished by autonomous agencies of horizontal accountability.

2. *Liberal, (partially) irresponsible democracies* have more or less clean, democratic elections and good protections for civil liberties but suffer significant problems of political corruption.

3. *Semi-liberal democracies* have more or less clean, democratic elections but suffer significant problems in protecting citizen rights, particularly in terms of abuses by the police and some local and state governments. Government is less than transparent and honest, as many public officials are corrupt and corruption is not reliably probed and punished.

4. *Illiberal democracies* have elections that are democratic, though not entirely free of fraud and coercion in some localities. But they suffer extensive violations of citizen rights and a weak rule of law in which the judiciary is politically pliant and/or corrupt and ineffectual. As a result, corruption also extends deeply into political and civic life.

5. *Electoral authoritarian regimes (pseudo-democracies)* have regular elections between competing political parties, but these elections are not free and fair. Although opposition parties may win a significant share of the vote and hold up to a third (or even more) of the seats in parliament, they are not able to win national power in a free and fair contest. Neither are they able to effectively constrain the ruling party. Parliament may be an arena for some scrutiny, representation, and debate, and the courts may from time to time rule independently, and there may be some real space for civil society to organize, criticize, and challenge within limits, but the executive dominates other branches and is not accountable vertically or horizontally. With very rare exceptions (most notably Singapore), these "hybrid" regimes are therefore at best semi-democratic, semi-liberal, and only partially accountable. At the lower end of this category, multiparty elections take place in a context of predatory corruption and pervasive, sometimes brutal,

violations of human rights, in which opposition political forces and strongholds are especially victimized.

6. *Authoritarian regimes* either do not allow competitive multiparty elections or do so in extremely repressive, essentially ritualistic and meaningless conditions. These regimes are typically dominated by one of four types of authority: the military (a declining category), a single ruling party, an absolute monarchy, or a (nonhereditary) personal autocrat. These regimes do not protect civil liberties or the rule of law. They may commit extensive human rights violations, and it is not possible for citizens to hold state officials accountable for their abuses. Corruption may be moderate or extreme. There may be some space for independent organizations and media but only so long as they do not directly criticize or challenge the regime. Those who do criticize are at serious risk of arbitrary punishment, and may be killed, imprisoned, tortured, or otherwise victimized. The rule of law is generally weak in these systems, as the courts are subject to the dictates of ruling authorities.

7. *Totalitarian regimes* allow no civil freedom or independent organization of any kind. There is no political opposition, no civil society, no rule of law, and no organization of any kind that is not controlled by the state or ruling party. These regimes (generally driven and justified by some ideology, such as communism or fascism) commit the worst violations of human rights, and have been responsible for the largest instances of mass murder by the state (Rummel 1995, 1997).

8. *Collapsed or failed states* have no coherent central state authority of any kind. It is not clear that they can or should be included in studies of the relationship between poverty and democracy. Violent conflict and state collapse have rather obvious implications for the generation of poverty and humanitarian crisis.

Based on the above schema, the chapter appendix presents an illustrative list of countries, characterizing their national political systems at their average level over the past decade.

One way of roughly locating these regimes empirically is with reference to the Freedom House scales of political rights and civil liberties. Each year Freedom House rates each country on a scale of 1 (most free) to 7 (least free) on each of these two dimensions. Liberal democracies are those that obtain a 1 or 2 on each dimension (the Freedom House survey does not separately and effectively measure accountability). Semi-liberal democracies have a 3 on civil liberties and usually a 2 or 3 on political rights (very rarely a 1). Illiberal democracies range from 3 to 4 on political rights and 4 to 5 on civil liberties.[7] But many political systems (on close inspection, probably most) that score a 4 on political rights are better classified as electoral authoritarian regimes.

Electoral authoritarian regimes encompass wide variation. At the upper end, elections are sufficiently competitive and the political system pluralistic enough that many observers mistake them for democracies. In these systems, human rights abuses are generally less severe. These regimes tend to score a 4 or 5 on each dimension of political rights and civil liberties. At the lower end of more extensive domination and abuse, electoral authoritarian regimes score a 5 or 6 on each dimension.

Authoritarian regimes also vary in their degree of repressiveness. While none allow any kind of real multiparty electoral competition, and thus score a 6 or 7 on political rights, they vary on the civil liberties dimension from 5 to 7. Totalitarian regimes, such as the Democratic People's Republic of Korea, always score a 7 on each dimension, but not all countries that are 7 and 7 (for example, Syria, Saudi Arabia, Sudan) can be said to be totalitarian. In many cases, the absence of civil and political rights does not translate into the degree of terror and the totality of control that uniquely characterize totalitarian regimes. In this sense, totalitarian regimes are truly "off the charts" of the Freedom House coding framework, which is not fully sensitive at either end of either scale.

Concluding Reflection

There is growing evidence, including from within the World Bank itself, that governance matters. And there is growing recognition in development assistance circles that poverty reduction and empowerment of the poor require broad improvements in governance. Yet policy and practice lag well behind understanding. International donors remain reluctant to violate too blatantly international norms of sovereignty, and there is a powerful tendency for political conditionality to give way to gestures of compliance. Yet if poverty is, to a considerable degree, a political phenomenon, then a *serious* effort to reduce, once and for all, the structural conditions of mass poverty is also a political action. There is no getting around it. Is the world ready for the scope of *political* intervention that will be needed to build democracy, promote freedom, increase accountability, empower the poor, and thereby truly reduce poverty?

Appendix: Illustrative Classification of Countries Based on Their Political Systems

The following table gives examples of countries whose national political systems over the past decade could be characterized as falling into one of the categories described above. The two types of liberal democracy have been combined into a single category, and the category of electoral authoritarian regimes has been divided into two, corresponding to the upper and lower ends of this range. The table excludes totalitarian regimes, of which very few are left in the world today, and collapsed or failed states. Categorization is based substantially on the Freedom House scores for 2003, a year that saw some countries meet the minimum empirical conditions of liberal democracy (see above) for the first time.

Table 18.1 Illustrative Classification of Countries Based on Their Political Systems

Type of regime	Examples
Liberal democracy	Argentina, Benin, Botswana, Bulgaria, Chile, Costa Rica, Czech Republic, Estonia, Ghana, Hungary, Latvia, Lithuania, Mali, Mauritius, Mexico, Poland, Romania, South Africa, Uruguay
Semi-liberal democracy	Albania, Bolivia, Brazil, Ecuador, El Salvador, Ghana, Honduras, India, FYR Macedonia, Madagascar, Namibia, Nicaragua, Papua New Guinea, Peru, the Philippines, Senegal, Thailand, Serbia and Montenegro
Illiberal democracy	Armenia, Bangladesh, Colombia, Georgia, Guatemala, Indonesia, Malawi, Moldova, Mozambique, Niger, Nigeria, Sri Lanka, Turkey, Venezuela
Competitive electoral authoritarian regime	Ethiopia, Gabon, Gambia, Malaysia, Morocco, Pakistan, Russia, Tanzania, Togo, Ukraine, Zambia
Other electoral authoritarian regime	Algeria, Angola, Azerbaijan, Belarus, Cambodia, Cameroon, Egypt, Iran, Jordan, Kazakhstan, Kyrgyz Republic, Tunisia, Uganda, Zimbabwe
Authoritarian regime	Burma, China, Eritrea, Sudan, Swaziland, Syria, Uzbekistan, Vietnam

Source: Based on country scores in Freedom House (2003).

Notes

1.   Public goods benefit the entire community. They are nonrival and nonexcludable in consumption: in other words, the consumption of such goods by one person does not reduce the amount available to others, and they are available to all (even those who do not pay). An example of a pure public good is national security, which is available to all citizens of a country simultaneously. There are also some quasi-public goods, access to which may not necessarily be nonexcludable. Examples include physical infrastructure (sanitation, potable water, electric power, telecommunications, public transport), and social, economic, and political infrastructure (schools, clinics, markets, courts, a neutral and capable state bureaucracy). Ultimately, development enables individuals to enjoy private goods, but it requires that public resources be used to advance the public welfare.

2.   For the criteria of electoral freedom and fairness that distinguish democracies, in this most minimal sense, from nondemocracies, see Diamond (2002).

3.   While most political parties in emerging democracies need to become more internally democratic, there is a trade-off between internal democracy and party

coherence. For example, if there is no role for the central party leadership in candidate selection, a party may lack unity of purpose, programmatic or ideological coherence, and organizational discipline. See the report of the workshop on Democratization of Political Parties in East Asia held in Seoul, Korea, in 2000 (Democracy Forum for East Asia 2000).

4.   These correspond to Guillermo O'Donnell's (1999) democratic, liberal, and republican dimensions of governance.

5.   See the methodological discussion in the annual Freedom House survey of the world (2003) or on the organization's Web site (http://www.freedomhouse.org).

6.   See Przeworski et al. (2000) for an example of such simplistic reasoning.

7.   Occasionally, Freedom House has scored a country, such as Turkey a few years ago, a 5 on political rights and nevertheless classified it as a democracy. This is a contradiction in terms. Once a country descends to a 5 on political rights, electoral contestation and party competition are so constrained that the system cannot be termed democratic.

References

Democracy Forum for East Asia. 2000. "Democratization of Political Parties in East Asia." Report of the conference on Democratization of Political Parties in East Asia, Seoul, March 21–22. http://www.ned.org/forum/asia/march00/introduction.html.

Diamond, Larry. 1999. *Developing Democracy: Toward Consolidation*. Baltimore: Johns Hopkins University Press.

———. 2002. "Elections Without Democracy: Thinking about Hybrid Regimes." *Journal of Democracy* 13 (2): 21–35.

Diamond, Larry, and Richard Gunther, eds. 2001. *Political Parties and Democracy*. Baltimore: Johns Hopkins University Press.

Freedom House. 2003. *Freedom in the World 2003: The Annual Survey of Political Rights and Civil Liberties*. New York: Freedom House.

Huntington, Samuel P., and Joan Nelson. 1976. *No Easy Choice*. Cambridge, MA: Harvard University Press.

Inkeles, Alex, and Larry Sirowy. 1991. "The Effects of Democracy on Economic Growth and Inequality: A Review." In *On Measuring Democracy: Its Consequences and Concomitants*, ed. Alex Inkeles, 125–56. New Brunswick, NJ: Transaction.

Joseph, Richard. 2003. "Africa: States in Crisis." *Journal of Democracy* 14 (July): 159–70.

Lipset, Seymour Martin. 1959. "Some Social Requisites of Democracy." *American Political Science Review* 53 (March): 69–105.

Narayan, Deepa, ed. 2002. *Empowerment and Poverty Reduction: A Sourcebook*. Washington, DC: World Bank.

Narayan, Deepa, with Raj Patel, Kai Schafft, Anne Rademacher, and Sarah Koch-Schulte. 2000. *Voices of the Poor: Can Anyone Hear Us?* New York: Oxford University Press for the World Bank.

O'Donnell, Guillermo. 1994. "Delegative Democracy." *Journal of Democracy* 5 (January): 55–69.

———. 1999. "Horizontal Accountability in New Democracies." In *The Self-Restraining State: Power and Accountability in New Democracies,* ed. Andreas Schedler, Larry Diamond, and Marc F. Plattner, 29–51. Boulder, CO: Lynne Rienner.

Osmani, S. R. 2000. "Participatory Governance, People's Empowerment and Poverty Reduction." UNDP/SEPED Conference Paper Series 7, United Nations Development Program, Social Development and Poverty Elimination Division, New York.

Ottaway, Marina, and Thomas Carothers. 2000. "Toward Civil Society Realism." In *Funding Virtue: Civil Society Aid and Democracy Promotion,* ed. Marina Ottaway and Thomas Carothers, 293–310. Washington, DC: Carnegie Endowment for International Peace.

Pastor, Robert A. 1999. "A Brief History of Electoral Commissions." In *The Self-Restraining State: Power and Accountability in New Democracies,* ed. Andreas Schedler, Larry Diamond, and Marc F. Plattner, 75–81. Boulder, CO: Lynne Rienner.

Przeworski, Adam, and Fernando Limongi. 1993. "Political Regimes and Economic Growth." *Journal of Economic Perspectives* 7 (3): 51–70.

Przeworski, Adam, Michael E. Alvarez, Jose Antonio Cheibub, and Fernando Limongi. 2000. *Democracy and Development: Political Institutions and Well-Being in the World, 1950–90.* Cambridge: Cambridge University Press.

Putnam, Robert D. 1993. *Making Democracy Work: Civic Traditions in Modern Italy.* Princeton, NJ: Princeton University Press.

Roll, Richard, and John R. Talbott. 2003. "Political Freedom, Economic Liberty, and Prosperity." *Journal of Democracy* 14 (July): 75–89.

Rummel, Rudolph J. 1995. "Democracies ARE Less Warlike than Other Regimes." *European Journal of International Relations* 1 (4): 457–79.

———. 1997. *Power Kills: Democracy as a Method of Nonviolence.* New Brunswick, NJ: Transaction.

Schedler, Andreas. 1999. "Conceptualizing Accountability." In *The Self-Restraining State: Power and Accountability in New Democracies,* ed. Andreas Schedler, Larry Diamond, and Marc F. Plattner, 13–28. Boulder, CO: Lynne Rienner.

———. 2002. "Elections Without Democracy: The Menu of Manipulation." *Journal of Democracy* 13 (April): 36–50.

USAID (United States Agency for International Development). 1999. *USAID Political Party Development Assistance.* Technical Publication Series PN-ACR-216. Washington, DC: USAID Office of Democracy and Governance.

———. 2003. *Foreign Aid in the National Interest.* Washington DC: USAID. http://www.usaid.gov/fani.

Varshney, Ashutosh. 2000. "Why Have Poor Democracies Not Eliminated Poverty? A Suggestion." *Asian Survey* 40 (5): 718–36.

Chapter 19

Measuring Democratic Governance: Central Tasks and Basic Problems

Gerardo L. Munck

National states have long had an interest in producing data on their resources and populations. The generation of statistics on a wide range of economic, military, demographic, and social issues coincided with the development and consolidation of state bureaucracies; indeed, "statistics" literally means the "science of the state." The body of state-produced data has grown steadily over the years as states have sought to track a growing number of issues and as more states have developed the capability to generate data. Moreover, as a result of the efforts of intergovernmental organizations such as the International Monetary Fund, the World Bank, and the United Nations' multiple programs and agencies, data gathered by governments throughout the world have been brought together and used to build cross-national databases. Prominent examples, such as the World Bank's World Development Indicators and the data published in the United Nations Development Programme's *Human Development Report,* are the results of a lengthy collective effort whereby procedures to generate data have been tested, fine-tuned, and increasingly standardized.

The production of data on explicitly political matters and on the political process in particular has been a different story. The generation of data, in particular comparable data, on politics has persistently lagged behind that on other aspects of society (Rokkan 1970, 169–80; Heath and Martin 1997). Some noteworthy efforts have been made by sources independent of states, university researchers in particular, since roughly the 1960s. But it has only been quite recently, with the spread of democracy throughout the globe and the events of 1989 in the communist world, that interest in data on politics has become widespread.

The current period is without doubt unprecedented in terms of the production of data on what, for the sake of succinctness, could be labeled as democratic governance. Academic work has been given a new impulse. National development agencies, intergovernmental organizations (IGOs), multilateral development banks, and a large number of nongovernmental organizations (NGOs) have launched various initiatives (Santiso 2002). The generation of comparable cross-national data on democratic governance has become a growth industry and, very rapidly, a huge number of data sets have become available.[1]

Another important change in recent years involves the uses of data on politics. Nowadays, statistical analyses on the causes and consequences of democratic governance are regularly invoked by a variety of actors to justify their support of, or opposition to, different policies. NGOs use data for purposes of advocacy and to keep government accountable. In turn, governments, IGOs, and the multilateral banks are increasingly putting emphasis on governance-related conditionalities and making decisions informed by data on democratic governance.[2] What used to be primarily an academic quest has become deeply enmeshed with politics, as data on politics have become part of the political process itself.

These developments reflect an appreciation of politics as a central aspect of society and are largely salutary. Most significantly, they offer the promise of increased knowledge about politics and the use of this knowledge to improve policy making and accountability. But they also raise some concerns. Producers of data on democratic governance usually present their data as scientific products. Even when they do not, the reception of data by the public, and to a large extent by public officials, is influenced by the special status associated with information presented in quantitative, statistical terms. Indeed, one of the selling points of data on democratic governance is that they draw on the power of an association with science. Yet this claimed or assumed scientific status verges on being a misrepresentation of the current state of knowledge regarding the measurement of democratic governance.

The fact is that we still do not have measuring instruments that have been sufficiently tested and refined, and that garner a broad consensus. Many current instruments are open to serious methodological critique and also differ, sometimes quite considerably, with regard to fundamental features (Munck and Verkuilen 2002). Data generated on supposedly the same concepts can lead to significant divergences in the way the world is described and the causes seen to affect outcomes of interest (Casper and Tufis 2002). Despite recent advances, we are still at an early, relatively exploratory phase in the measurement of democratic governance.

This chapter focuses on one key implication of this assessment of the state of knowledge: the need to develop instruments to measure democratic governance in a highly valid and reliable manner. It does not propose new instruments and does not even consider any of the available instruments in depth. Rather, it considers current attempts at measurement as a whole and discusses, first, some central tasks to be tackled in the development of measuring instruments, and second, some basic problems with measuring instruments that should be avoided. The overall aim is to take stock of where we stand and to offer suggestions as to how future work might be oriented.

An appendix to the chapter presents a select list of data sets on democratic governance. This list shows that currently available data sets constitute a considerable resource. Recent efforts have resulted in data sets on a range of aspects of the electoral process, on governmental institutions and the decision-making process, on the rule of law, and so on. Yet the discussion of the continuing challenges regarding the construction of measuring instruments suggests the need to use these existing data sets with caution. Until measuring instruments that address the tasks and resolve the problems discussed in this chapter have been developed, the data generated with existing instruments should be used with deliberate care and prudence.

Central Tasks in the Development of Measuring Instruments

Measuring instruments are not ends in themselves but rather tools used to generate data. Thus, once established measuring instruments are available, they recede into the background and attention focuses on the data produced with these instruments. However, because we still lack instruments that can be used to measure democratic governance in a sufficiently valid and reliable manner, a focus on instruments is justified. Though existing work offers important clues as to how a suitable measuring instrument could be developed, some key issues remain to be resolved. These issues concern four central tasks in the development of measuring instruments:

1. The formulation of a systematic, logically organized definition of the *concepts* being measured
2. The identification of the *indicators* used to measure the concept
3. The construction of *scales* used to measure variation
4. The specification of the *aggregation rule* used to combine multiple measures when a composite measure or index is sought[3]

Concepts

An initial task in the process of measurement is the explicit formulation of the concepts to be measured. This involves identifying attributes that constitute the concept under consideration, and delineating the manner in which these multiple attributes relate to each other in a logical fashion and also distinguish the concept from other closely related ones. This is a task to which political philosophers, and political and social theorists, have made invaluable contributions, and certain books are such obligatory points of reference that they might be considered classics.[4] But there continues to be a lack of broad-based consensus and clarity regarding basic conceptual matters. Different authors routinely invoke different attributes in defining the same concept, specify the connection among the same attributes in various ways, and use a number of concepts that are hard to distinguish from each other with clarity. Indeed, it is striking that the field of democratic governance includes so many idiosyncratically and vaguely defined, and unclearly differentiated, concepts: democracy, democratic consolidation, democratic quality, liberal democracy, rule of law, democratic governability, good governance, as well as democratic governance itself, the label used here to refer to the field as a whole.[5]

The stakes associated with these conceptual issues are high. Efforts at measurement take definitions of concepts as their point of departure, and much depends on whether the concept to be measured is formulated clearly and thus provides a good anchor for the data generation process. The validity of any measures will inescapably be affected by these conceptual choices. The ability to generate discriminating measures hinges on such conceptual matters,[6] as does the possibility of cumulative work by different researchers. Thus, greater attention needs to be given to the challenge of systematizing the concepts to be measured, building on insights that have been developed and refined over the years and that are likely to enjoy a substantial degree of consensus.

One promising strategy is to begin with the political regime, which concerns the mode of access to government offices, and to distinguish the regime from other aspects of the broader conceptual map encompassed by the term "democratic governance." The regime is, after all, the classic locus of democratic theory and an aspect of the broader problematic of democratic governance on which much work has been done and on which a fairly important degree of consensus has developed.[7] Beyond the regime, it is useful to introduce a broad distinction between the process whereby states make and implement legally binding decisions, which might be labeled as the governance dimension, and the outcomes and content of state decisions from the perspective of all citizens, including those that occupy a position within the state, which might be labeled as the rule of law dimension (table 19.1).

This proposal, to be sure, is tentative. Yet it drives home a key and somewhat unappreciated point: especially when the concepts of interest are broad in scope, concepts must be logically disaggregated. Indeed, unless the boundaries among closely related concepts are specified, the problem of conceptual conflation undercuts the possibility of advancing an analytic approach. Moreover, this proposal also provides a basis for beginning a focused discussion of the linkages among the central concepts used by distinct communities of scholars and practitioners who use different concepts yet are clearly grappling with the same underlying issues. Such linkages have been discussed in the context of the concepts of democracy, human rights, and human development.[8]

A conceptual linkage of particular interest in the context of measurement issues is that between democratic governance and empowerment. Empowerment has been understood as referring to "the expansion of assets and capabilities of poor people to participate in, negotiate with, influence, control, and hold accountable institutions that affect their lives" (Narayan 2002, 14). It is seen as entailing four core elements: access to information, inclusion and participation, accountability, and local organizational capacity (18–22). Clearly,

Table 19.1 The Concepts of Political Regime, Governance, and Rule of Law

Concept	Aspect of the political process	Some central elements
Political regime	Access to government offices	Elections and their competitiveness, inclusiveness, fairness, etc.
		Candidate selection process
		Electoral system
Governance	Decision making within the state	Executive-legislative relations
		Judiciary
		Federalism
		Bureaucracy
		Mechanisms of direct democracy
Rule of law	State treatment of citizens	Corruption
		Civil and human rights
		Property rights
		Press freedom

multiple points of overlap exist with the concepts used in the literature on democratic governance. Empowerment and democratic governance share a concern with citizens' ability to exercise control over state power, an issue seen as multidimensional. More pointedly, information, inclusion, accountability, and organization are all central to the ways in which analysts of democratic governance evaluate citizens' access to government offices and their continued involvement in decision making between elections. There are, therefore, fruitful points of convergence between the concepts that deserve to be further explored. But there are also differences, such as the greater emphasis within the empowerment framework on the ways in which material resources affect citizens' ability to effectively exercise their rights, and the attention within the democratic governance framework to the ways governments are constituted and decisions are made within the state. These differences suggest that one key challenge is to coherently weave together frameworks that have been developed with similar motivations in mind, that is, to offer an encompassing approach to the study of societies.

Indicators

A second task to be tackled in developing a measuring instrument concerns the choice of indicators, that is, the observables used to operationalize various concepts. This task has been addressed quite rigorously in discussions by academics about the measurement of democracy, democratic institutions, and human rights.[9] Other important contributions include various manuals and handbooks prepared by NGOs, IGOs, and development agencies on broad topics such as democracy and democratic governance (USAID 1998, 2000a; Beetham et al. 2001), as well as on more specific topics such as electoral observation (NDI 1995; OSCE/ODIHR 1997), corruption (USAID 1999; see also Heidenheimer and Johnston 2002), and gender equality (OECD/ DAC 1998; ECLAC 1999; UNECE 2001; see also Apodaca 1998). Finally, this task has been addressed by a large number of conferences and many working groups that bring together academics and practitioners with representatives of various NGOs, IGOs, and development agencies (United Nations 2000).[10]

The work on indicators in recent years has produced important advances. As a result, current knowledge is considerably more sophisticated than it was some two decades ago. Nonetheless, existing indicators suffer from some problems, a central one being the failure to ensure that indicators fully tap into the meaning of the concepts being measured. In this regard, it should be noted that the common strategy of focusing on formal institutions is problematic. At the very least, the measurement of democratic governance must consider whether actors act according to the rules of formal institutions. And if actors do not channel their actions through formal rules, the behavior of these actors has to be registered in some other way. Thus it is clearly the case that such institutions are only part of what needs to be measured and that measurement cannot be reduced to a matter of formal rules. Yet overcoming this shortcoming is anything but easy, for it is quite difficult to identify indicators beyond formal institutions that capture the actual political process and are also firmly rooted in observables. Put in more technical terms, a lingering problem that affects many efforts at defining indicators is their inability to measure concepts both fully, so as to ensure content validity, and on the basis of observables, so as to guarantee replicability.

Scales

A third task to be undertaken in developing a measuring instrument is the construction of scales that spell out the level of measurement selected to measure variation. This task has direct implications for the potential use of data, whether for performing academic analysis or—as is increasingly the case—for monitoring collectively determined goals. Yet relatively little work has focused on how to think about variation in the attributes of democratic governance. Moreover, the debate that has taken place, on the choice between dichotomous and continuous measures of democracy, has generated little agreement (Collier and Adcock 1999).

The gaps in our knowledge regarding this task are indeed quite large. We need to devise ways to construct scales that capture the rich variety of intermediary possibilities in a systematic way and hence to identify multiple thresholds, to link each threshold with concrete situations or events with clear normative content, and to explicitly address the relationship among thresholds. These are all basic issues that affect the possibility of constructing meaningful scales to measure the attributes of democratic governance and should be the focus of more research.[11]

Aggregation Rule

Finally, a fourth task that is frequently relevant in constructing a measuring instrument concerns the specification of the aggregation rule used to combine multiple measures. This is not a necessary step in generating data. But there is a clear benefit to combining data on the various attributes of a concept: the creation of a summary score that synthesizes a sometimes quite large amount of data. This advantage partly explains why data generation has commonly included, as one goal, the creation of indexes. However, a satisfactory way to address this task still has not been found. Some useful guidance concerning an aggregation rule can be drawn from existing theory and indexes, but various problems persist. Most critically, attention to theory has been relatively absent. This is the case with data-driven methods, but even ostensibly theory-driven methods are presented in quite an ad hoc manner, with little justification, or they simply rely on default options. Moreover, there is little consensus concerning how disaggregate data should be aggregated into an index.[12]

More work is thus needed on the following issues. First, it is necessary to address the relationship between indicators and the concept being measured and to specify whether indicators are considered "cause" or "effect" indicators of the concept (Bollen and Lennox 1991).[13] Second, if the indicators are considered to be cause indicators, it is necessary to explicitly theorize the status of each indicator and the relationship among all indicators and to justify whether indicators should be treated as necessary conditions or whether substitutability and compensation among indicators might be envisioned (Verkuilen 2002, ch. 4). Third, more needs to be done to integrate theory and testing in the determination of an aggregation rule. These are central issues that have nonetheless rarely been addressed in a systematic manner in current efforts to develop measuring instruments.

Basic Problems with Measuring Instruments

The development of suitable measuring instruments also requires, more urgently, the avoidance of some basic problems. Such problems are not only common but also highly consequential, being found in various proposals that link data to policy choices and political conditionalities. Indeed, if the generation of data on democratic governance and the use of these data as an input in the policy process are to gain legitimacy, it will probably depend more than anything else on the concerted effort to understand and overcome these shortcomings. Thus, even though these problems are associated with the tasks discussed above, a separate discussion of five basic problems is merited.

Incomplete Measuring Instruments

Various initiatives that purport to use measures of democratic governance to monitor compliance with certain standards offer vague enunciations of principles (for example, the European Union's accession democracy clause) or a list of items or questions (for example, the African Peer Review Mechanism of the New Partnership for Africa's Development).[14] These enunciations or lists provide some sense of which concepts are to be measured. But they are not measuring instruments, because they are silent on a broad range of issues that are required to construct a measuring instrument. And the incomplete specification of a measuring instrument opens the door to the generation of data in an ad hoc way that is susceptible to political manipulation. If data are to be used in making political decisions, it is imperative to recognize that a list of items or questions provides, at best, a point of departure, and to fully assume the responsibility of developing a measuring instrument.

Denying Methodological Choices

A standard approach to preventing the political manipulation of data is to emphasize the need for objective data, the idea being that such data are not subject to politicking. But the commonly invoked distinction between objective and subjective data (see, for example, UNDP 2002, 36–37) is frequently associated with a simplistic view of the data generation process that can actually hide significant biases. The human element cannot be removed from the measurement process, since a broad range of methodological choices necessarily go into the construction of a measuring instrument. Thus, the best that can be done is to be up-front and explicit about these methodological choices, to justify them theoretically and subject them to empirical testing, and to allow independent observers to scrutinize and contest these choices by making the entire process of measurement transparent. This is the most effective way to generate good data and to guard against the real danger: not subjective data but rather arbitrary measures that rest on claims to authority.[15]

Delinking Methodological Choices from the Concept Being Measured

If choices and hence subjectivity are an intrinsic aspect of measurement, it is critical to ensure that the multiple choices involved in the construction of measures are always made in light of the ultimate goal of the measurement exercise: the measurement of a certain concept. This is so obvious that it might appear an unnecessary warning. Yet the delinking of methodology from the concept being measured is a mistake made by such significant initiatives as the Millennium Challenge Account (MCA) of the U.S. government. Indeed, while the MCA supposedly uses data as a means to identify countries that are democratic—the guiding idea being that democracies make better use of development aid and should thus be targeted—the methodology used to generate a list of target countries does not capture the concept of democracy and does not guarantee that democracies will be identified.[16] When it comes to constructing measuring instruments, and especially when methodological choices might be presented as technical in nature, it is essential to constantly link these choices explicitly and carefully back to the concept being measured.

Presenting Measurement as a Perfect Science

The results of the measurement process—quantitative data—tend to be taken, and sometimes presented, as flawless measures. But such interpretations overlook one of the central points in measurement theory: that error is an inescapable part of any attempt at measurement. This is not merely a technical issue that might be sidestepped at little cost. Nor is it a fatal flaw that implies that the resulting measures should be distrusted and, at an extreme, rejected. Rather, all this point implies is that measurement is a precise but not a perfect science, and that measurement error should be factored into an estimate of the degree of confidence that is attached to data. Yet this critical point is frequently overlooked and data are presented as though they were error-free, something that can lead to mistaken results. A prominent example of such a problem is, again, the MCA.[17] But it is not an isolated example. Therefore, efforts to construct measuring instruments and to interpret data must be forthcoming about the unavoidable nature of measurement error and must factor such error into any conclusions derived from the analysis of data.

Overcomplexification

Finally, it is not a bad thing to consider displays of technical virtuosity in measurement exercises with a degree of suspicion. To be sure, measurement involves a range of sometimes quite complex issues and these should all be given the attention they deserve. But it is also useful to emphasize that good data are readily interpretable and to warn against overcomplexification. Indeed, there are grounds to suspect that a measuring instrument that is hard to grasp reduces the accessibility and interpretability of data without necessarily adding to their validity. Numerous examples of such overcomplexification exist in the field of democratic governance and a sign of this is the real difficulty even experts face in conveying the meaning of many indexes in ways that make real, tangible sense. Thus, a good rule of thumb in constructing measuring instruments is to keep things as simple as possible.

Conclusions

The distance between science and politics has been greatly reduced as data about politics, and the analyses of those data, are increasingly used in politics and are becoming a part of the political process itself. We live in an age in which data, especially quantitative data, are widely recognized as tools for scientific analysis and social reform but are also closely intertwined with the language of power. Thus, it is only proper that social scientists assume the responsibilities associated with the new salience of data on politics by contributing to the generation of good data and by exercising scrutiny over the ways in which data, and analyses of data, on democratic governance are put to political uses.

The construction of adequate measuring instruments remains an important challenge. In this regard, it is essential to acknowledge that currently available instruments are contributions to a fairly new and still unfolding debate about how to generate data on politics. We can only hope that this debate, which should address the tasks discussed in this chapter, will generate significant advances that will lead to broadly accepted instruments.

In the meantime, it is sensible to highlight the need for caution concerning claims about data on politics. This means, most vitally, that the basic problems with measuring instruments discussed above must be avoided. These problems could undermine the legitimacy of using data for policy purposes and solidify opposition to initiatives seeking to build bridges between science and politics. In addition, this means that currently available data sets on democratic governance, such as those included in this chapter's appendix, must be used with care. After all, inasmuch as measuring instruments remain a matter of debate, the data generated with those instruments must be considered as quite tentative and subject to revision. The exercise of caution might run against the tendency of some advocates to play up achievements in the measurement of democratic governance. But a conservative strategy, which puts a premium on avoiding the dangers of "numerological nonsense" (Rokkan 1970, 288), is the strategy most likely to ensure the continuation and maturation of current interest in data on democratic governance.

Appendix: Select List of Data Sets on Democratic Governance

The following list of data sets gives a sense of the resources that are currently available.[18] The presentation is organized in terms of the conceptual distinction between the political regime, governance, and rule of law introduced in table 19.1, distinguishing also between indexes, that is, aggregate data, and indicators, that is, disaggregate data. All these data sets take the nation-state as their unit of analysis. A final table presents some resources on subnational units.

The measurement of the concept of political regime has been a concern within academia for some time, and the generation of indexes in particular has been the subject of a fair amount of analysis (table 19.2). These indexes have tended to be minimalist, in the sense that they do not include important components such as participation. Moreover, though they tend to correlate quite highly, there is evidence that there are significant differences among them. Nonetheless, most of these indexes are firmly rooted in democratic theory and, with some important exceptions (especially the Freedom House Political Rights Index), offer disaggregate measures as well as an aggregate measure. Beyond these indexes, in recent times much effort has gone into generating measures of important elements of the democratic regime (table 19.3). In comparative terms, the measurement of the democratic regime and its various elements is more advanced than the measurement of other aspects of the political process.

The measurement of the concept of governance reveals some bright spots and some problems (tables 19.4 and 19.5). At the disaggregate level, important progress has been made and the Database on Political Institutions in particular is a valuable resource in this regard. However, we still lack a good

Table 19.2 Political Regime Indexes

Name	Components	Scope	Source
Freedom House's Political Rights Index	Free and fair elections for the chief executive Free and fair elections for the legislature Fair electoral process Effective power of elected officials Right to form political parties Power of opposition parties Freedom from domination by power groups (e.g., the military, foreign powers, religious hierarchies, economic oligarchies) Autonomy and self-government for cultural, ethnic, religious, or other minority group	172 countries, 1972–present	Freedom House, http://www.freedomhouse.org.
Governance Research Indicators Dataset (2002): Voice and Accountability Index	Government repression Orderly change in government Vested interests Accountability of public officials Human rights Freedom of association Civil liberties Political liberties Freedom of the press Travel restrictions Freedom of political participation Imprisonment	199 countries, 1996–2002	Daniel Kaufmann, Aart Kraay, and Massimo Mastruzzi, http://www.worldbank.org/wbi/governance/govdata2002/index.html.

(table continues on following page)

437

Table 19.2 Political Regime Indexes (continued)

Name	Components	Scope	Source
	Government censorship Military role in politics Responsiveness of the government Democratic accountability Institutional permanence		Mark J. Gasiorowski, "An Overview of the Political Regime Change Dataset," *Comparative Political Studies* 29, no. 4 (1996): 469–83; and Gary Reich, "Categorizing Political Regimes: New Data for Old Problems," *Democratization* 9, no. 4 (2003): 1–24.
Political Regime Change Dataset	Competitiveness Inclusiveness Civil and political liberties	147 countries, independence–1998	
Political Regime Index	Contestation Offices/election executive Offices/election legislature	141 countries, 1950–2002	Adam Przeworski, Michael E. Alvarez, José Antonio Cheibub, and Fernando Limongi, *Democracy and Development: Political Institutions and Well-Being in the World, 1950–1990* (New York: Cambridge University Press, 2000),

Index	Components	Country coverage	Source
			ch. 1, and pantheon.yale.edu/~jac236/Research.htm. Update by José Antonio Cheibub and Jennifer Gandhi upon request from Cheibub (jose.cheibub@yale.edu).
Political Regime Index	Free and competitive legislative elections Executive accountability to citizens Enfranchisement	All sovereign countries, 1800–1994	Carles Boix, *Democracy and Redistribution* (New York: Cambridge University Press, 2003), 98–109.
Polity IV: Democracy and Autocracy Indexes	Competitiveness of participation Regulation of participation Competitiveness of executive recruitment Openness of executive recruitment Constraints on executive	161 countries, 1800–2001	http://www.cidcm.umd.edu/inscr/polity/.
Polyarchy Dataset	Competition Participation	187 countries, 1810–2002	Tatu Vanhanen, http://www.fsd.uta.fi/english/data/catalogue/FSD1289.

Table 19.3   Political Regime Indicators

Name of data set	Indicators	Scope	Source
Cross-National Indicators of Liberal Democracy, 1950–1990	Over 800 variables	Most of the world's independent countries, 1950–90	Kenneth A. Bollen, Cross-National Indicators of Liberal Democracy, 1950–1990 (computer file). 2nd ICPSR version, produced by University of North Carolina at Chapel Hill, 1998. Distributed by Inter-university Consortium for Political and Social Research, Ann Arbor, MI, 2001.
Cross-National Time-Series Data Archive	Type of regime (civil, military, etc.) Type of executive Executive selection (elected or not) Parliamentary responsibility Legislative selection (elected or not) Competitiveness of nominating process for legislature Party legitimacy (party formation)	The world, 1815–1999	Arthur Banks, http://www.databanks.sitehosting.net/index.htm.
Data on Campaign Finance	Direct public financing Disclosure laws Access to free TV time Limits on spending on TV	114–43 countries, c. 2001	Michael Pinto-Duschinsky, "Financing Politics: A Global View," *Journal of Democracy* 13, no. 4 (2002): 69–86.
Database on Electoral Institutions	Elections under dictatorship and democracy Electoral system	199 countries, 1946 (or independence)–2000	Matt Golder, http://homepages.nyu.edu/%7Emrg217/elections.html.
Database of Electoral Systems	Type of electoral system	Entire world, present	International IDEA (Institute for Democracy and Electoral Assistance), http://www.idea.int/esd/data.cfm.

Database of the EPIC Project	Electoral systems Legislative framework Electoral management Boundary delimitation Voter education Voter registration Voting operations Parties and candidates Vote counting	56 countries, present	Election Process Information Collection, http://www.epicproject.org/.
Database on Political Institutions	Use of legislative election Use of executive election Method of candidate selection Fraud and intimidation in voting process Threshold required for representation Mean district magnitude Type of electoral law (proportional representation, plurality) Legislative index of political competitiveness Executive index of political competitiveness	177 countries, 1975–95	Thorsten Beck, George Clarke, Alberto Groff, Philip Keefer, and Patrick Walsh, "New Tools in Comparative Political Economy: The Database of Political Institutions," *World Bank Economic Review* 15, no. 1 (September 2001): 165–76; and http://www.worldbank.org/research/bios/pkeefer.htm.
Dataset of Suffrage	Right of suffrage	196 countries, 1950–2000	Pamela Paxton, Kenneth A. Bollen, Deborah M. Lee, and Hyojoung Kim, "A Half-Century of Suffrage: New Data and a Comparative Analysis," *Studies in Comparative International Development* 38, no. 1 (2003): 93–122; and http://www.unc.edu/~bollen/.

(table continues on following page)

Table 19.3 Political Regime Indicators (continued)

Name of data set	Indicators	Scope	Source
Electoral Systems Data Set	Party control over candidate nomination and order of election Pooling of votes Number and specificity of citizen votes District magnitude	158 countries, 1978–2001	Jessica S. Wallack, Alejandro Gaviria, Ugo Panizza, and Ernesto Stein, "Electoral Systems Data Set," 2003, http://www.stanford .edu/~jseddon/.
Global Database of Quotas for Women	Constitutional quota for national parliament Election law quota or regulation for national parliament Political party quota for electoral candidates Constitutional or legislative quota for subnational government	Entire world, 2003	International IDEA, http://www.idea.int/quota/index.cfm.
Global Survey of Voter Turnout	Voter turnout	171 countries, 1945–present	International IDEA, http://www.idea.int/vt/index.cfm.
Index of Malapportionment	Malapportionment	78 countries, c. 1997	David J. Samuels and Richard Snyder, "The Value of a Vote: Malapportionment in Comparative Perspective," *British Journal of Political Science* 31, no. 4 (October 2001): 651–71; and upon request from David Samuels (dsamuels@polisci.umn.edu).
Women in National Parliaments Statistical Archive	Number and percentage of seats held by women in national parliaments	181 countries, 1945–present	Inter-Parliamentary Union, Women in Parliaments 1945–1995: A World Statistical Survey (Geneva: IPU, 1995); and http://www.ipu.org/wmn-e/classif-arc.htm.

Table 19.4 Governance Indexes

Name	Components	Scope	Source
Governance Research Indicators Dataset (2002): Political Stability Index	Decline in central authority Political protest Ethno-cultural and religious conflict External military intervention Military coup risk Political assassination Civil war Urban riot Armed conflict Violent demonstration Social unrest International tension Disappearances, torture Terrorism	199 countries, 1996–2002	Daniel Kaufmann, Aart Kraay, and Massimo Mastruzzi, http://www.worldbank.org/wbi/governance/govdata2002/index.html.
Governance Research Indicators Dataset (2002): Government Effectiveness Index	Skills of civil service Efficiency of national and local bureaucracies Coordination between central and local government Formulation and implementation of policies Tax collection Timely national budget Monitoring of activities within borders National infrastructure Response to domestic economic pressures	199 countries, 1996–2002	Daniel Kaufmann, Aart Kraay, and Massimo Mastruzzi, http://www.worldbank.org/wbi/governance/govdata2002/index.html.

(table continues on following page)

443

Table 19.4 Governance Indexes (continued)

Name	Components	Scope	Source
	Response to natural disasters Personnel turnover Quality of bureaucracy Red tape Policy continuity		
The Political Constraint Index (POLCON) Dataset	Number of independent branches of government Veto power over policy change Party composition of the executive and legislative branches Preference heterogeneity within each legislative branch	234 countries, variable dates–2001	Witold J. Henisz, http://www-management.wharton.upenn.edu/henisz/.
Public Integrity Index	Civil society, public information and media Electoral and political processes Branches of government Civil service and administration Oversight and regulatory mechanisms Anti-corruption and rule of law	25 countries, 2003	Center for Public Integrity, http://www.publicintegrity.org/ga/default.aspx.
State Failure Problem Set	Ethnic wars Revolutionary wars Genocides and politicides Adverse regime changes	96 countries, 1955–2002	State Failure Task Force, http://www.cidcm.umd.edu/inscr/stfail/sfdata.htm.
Weberian State Scale	Agencies generating economic policy Meritocratic hiring Internal promotion and career stability Salary and prestige	35 countries, 1993–96	Peter Evans and James Rauch, http://weber.ucsd.edu/~jrauch/webstate/.

Table 19.5 Governance Indicators

Name of data set	Indicators	Scope	Source
Country Risk Service	War Social unrest Orderly political transfers Politically motivated violence Institutional effectiveness Bureaucracy	100 countries, 1997–present	Economic Intelligence Unit, http://www.eiu.com/.
Cross-National Time-Series Data Archive	Legislative effectiveness vis-à-vis the executive Number of seats in legislature held by largest party Party fractionalization index	The world, 1815–1999	Arthur Banks, http://www.databanks.sitehosting.net/index.htm.
Database on Political Institutions	System (presidential, assembly-elected president, parliamentary) Presidential control of congress Herfindhal index of government and opposition Party fractionalization Position on right-left scale; rural, regional, nationalist, or religious basis Index of political cohesion Number of veto players Change in veto players Polarization	177 countries, 1975–95	Thorsten Beck, George Clarke, Alberto Groff, Philip Keefer, and Patrick Walsh, "New Tools in Comparative Political Economy: The Database of Political Institutions," *World Bank Economic Review* 15, no. 1 (September 2001): 165–76; and http://www.worldbank.org/research/bios/pkeefer.htm.
Executive Opinion Survey of the *Global Competitiveness Report*	Judicial independence	102 countries, 2003	World Economic Forum, http://www.weforum.org.

Table 19.6 Rule of Law Indexes

Name	Components	Scope	Source
Fraser Institute, Economic Freedom of the World Index	Size of government Legal structure and security of property rights Access to sound money Freedom to exchange with foreigners Regulation of credit, labor, and business	123 countries, 1970–present (every 5 years)	The Fraser Institute, http://www.freetheworld.com/download.html.
Freedom House's Civil Liberties Index	Free and independent media Free religious institutions Freedom of assembly, demonstration, and public discussion Freedom to form political parties Freedom to form organizations Independent judiciary Rule of law Protection from terror, torture, war, and insurgencies Freedom from government indifference and corruption Open and free private discussion Freedom from state control of travel, residence, employment, indoctrination Rights of private business Personal freedoms (gender equality, etc.) Equality of opportunity	172 countries, 1972–present	Freedom House, http://www.freedomhouse.org.

Index	Description	Coverage	Source
Freedom House's *Religious Freedom in the World* Survey	...	... 2000	... Paul Marshall, ed., *Religious Freedom in the World: A Global Survey of Freedom and Persecution* (Nashville: Broadman & Holman, 2000); and Freedom House, http://www. freedomhouse.org/religion/ publications/rfiw/index.htm.
Freedom House's Press Freedom Survey	Influence on the content of the news media of laws and administrative decisions Political influence over the content of news systems, including intimidation of journalists Economic influences on news content exerted by the government or private entrepreneurs	186 countries, 1993–present	Freedom House, http://www. freedomhouse.org/research/pressurvey.htm.
Governance Research Indicators Dataset (2002): Control of Corruption Index	Severity of corruption within the state Losses and costs of corruption Indirect diversion of funds	199 countries, 1996–2002	Daniel Kaufmann, Aart Kraay, and Massimo Mastruzzi, http://www. worldbank.org/wbi/governance/ govdata2002/index.html.
Governance Research Indicators Dataset (2002): Regulatory Quality Index	Export and import regulations Burden on business of regulations Unfair competitive prices Price control Discriminatory tariffs Excessive protections Government intervention in economy Regulation of foreign investment Regulation of banking Investment profile Tax effectiveness Legal framework for business	199 countries, 1996–2002	Daniel Kaufmann, Aart Kraay, and Massimo Mastruzzi, http://www. worldbank.org/wbi/governance/ govdata2002/index.html.

(table continues on following page)

Table 19.6 Rule of Law Indexes (continued)

Name	Components	Scope	Source
Governance Research Indicators Dataset (2002): Rule of Law Index	Legitimacy of state Adherence to rule of law Losses and costs of crime Kidnapping of foreigners Enforceability of government contracts Enforceability of private contracts Violent crime Organized crime Fairness of judicial process Speediness of judicial process Black market Property rights Independence of judiciary Law and order tradition	199 countries, 1996–2002	Daniel Kaufmann, Aart Kraay, and Massimo Mastruzzi, http://www.worldbank.org/wbi/governance/govdata2002/index.html.

Table 19.7 Rule of Law Indicators

Name of data set	Indicators	Scope	Source
CIRI Human Rights Data Set	Physical integrity rights Civil liberties Workers' rights Women's rights	161 countries, 1981–present	David L. Cingranelli and David L. Richards, http://www.humanrightsdata.com.
Corruption Perceptions Index	Corruption	133 countries, 1995–present	Transparency International, http://www.transparency.org/surveys/index.html.
Country Risk Service	Government pro-business orientation Transparency/fairness (of the legal system) Corruption Crime	100 countries, 1997–present	Economic Intelligence Unit, http://www.eiu.com/.
Dataset of Labor Rights Violations	Labor rights to organize, bargain collectively, and strike	200 countries, 1981–2000	Layna Mosley and Saika Uno, "Dataset of Labor Rights Violations, 1981–2000," University of Notre Dame, Notre Dame, IN, 2002.
Executive Opinion Survey of the *Global Competitiveness Report*	Corruption	102 countries, 2003	World Economic Forum, http://www.weforum.org.
Journalists killed statistics	Violence against journalists	Entire world, 1992–present	Committee to Protect Journalists, http://www.cpj.org/killed/Ten_Year_Killed/Intro.html.

(table continues on following page)

Table 19.7 Rule of Law Indicators (continued)

Name of data set	Indicators	Scope	Source
Minorities at Risk	Ethno-cultural distinctiveness Group's spatial concentration Length of group's residence in country Group's presence in adjoining country Group's loss of autonomy Strength of group's cultural identity Cultural differentials Political differentials Economic differentials Demographic stress Political discrimination Economic disadvantage Cultural discrimination Identity cohesion Organizational cohesion Administrative autonomy Mobilization Orientation to conventional vs. militant strategies of action Autonomy grievances Political (non-autonomy) grievances Economic grievances Cultural grievances	267 communal groups, 1945–present	Minorities at Risk Project, http://www.cidcm.umd.edu/inscr/mar/.

	Intra-group factional conflict		
	Intra-communal antagonists		
	Severity of intra-group conflict		
	Group protest activities		
	Anti-regime rebellion		
	Government repression of group		
	International contagion and diffusion		
	Transnational support for communal groups		
	Advantaged minorities		
Political Terror Scale	Right to life and personal integrity	153 countries, 1976–present	Political Terror Scale, http://www.unca.edu/politicalscience/faculty-staff/gibney.html.
United Nations Surveys of Crime Trends and Operations of Criminal Justice Systems	Total recorded crime incidents Criminal justice system	82 countries, 1970–2000	United Nations Criminal Justice Information Network, http://www.uncjin.org/Statistics/WCTS/wcts.html.
World Prison Brief	Prison population Pre-trial detainees/remand prisoners Occupancy level	214 countries, c. 2002	International Centre for Prison Studies, http://www.kcl.ac.uk/depsta/rel/icps/.

Table 19.8 Subnational-Level Indicators

Name of data set	Indicators	Scope	Source
—	Federal structure of the state	The world, 2002	Ann L. Griffiths and Karl Nerenberg, eds., *Handbook of Federal Countries: 2002* (Montreal and Kingston: McGill-Queen's University Press, 2002).
Database on Political Institutions	Appointed or elected state/province and municipal executives Appointed or elected legislatures Autonomous or self-governing regions, areas, or districts State or provincial authority over taxing, spending, or legislating	177 countries, 1975–95	Thorsten Beck, George Clarke, Alberto Groff, Philip Keefer, and Patrick Walsh, "New Tools in Comparative Political Economy: The Database of Political Institutions," *World Bank Economic Review* 15, no. 1 (September 2001): 165–76; and http://www.worldbank.org/research/bios/pkeefer.htm.
IMF's Government Finance Statistics	Number of tiers or units of administration (state/province/region/department; municipality, city/town) Number of jurisdictions	The world, 2001	International Monetary Fund, *Government Finance Statistics Manual 2001* (Washington, DC: IMF, 2001).
World Bank Database of Fiscal Decentralization Indicators	Subnational expenditure share of national expenditures Subnational revenue share of national revenues Intergovernmental transfers as a share of subnational expenditures	149 countries, 1972–2000	World Bank, Public Sector Governance, Decentralization and Subnational Regional Economics, http://www1.worldbank.org/publicsector/decentralization/data.htm.

index. Some indexes, such as the Weberian State Scale, focus on only one element of democratic governance and their scope is quite limited. Others, such as the Political Constraint Index, do not touch upon the implementation aspect although they address the policy-making process in fairly broad terms. Finally, those indexes that do address policy implementation tend to combine such a large number of indicators, which tap into a range of very diverse phenomena, that they are hard to interpret.

Significant advances and lingering problems can be identified with regard to the measurement of the concept of rule of law (tables 19.6 and 19.7). We have indicators on corruption (though they are based on the perceptions of a small group of people), human rights, labor rights, and other civil rights. Moreover, various indexes have been proposed. But many of these indexes either fail to offer disaggregate data (the problem with the Freedom House Civil Rights Index), combine components of a diverse set of concepts, or focus overwhelmingly on business and property rights to the exclusion of other groups and rights.

Finally, it is necessary to identify a significant gap in most data sets. The majority of available data sets have focused squarely on the national state as the unit of analysis and have overlooked subnational levels of government. This gap is gradually being filled by recent work on decentralization and local government (table 19.8). Nonetheless, further work is needed to develop adequate data on local and community levels of government.

Notes

In preparing this chapter, I have benefited from comments by Marianne Camerer, Deepa Narayan, Saika Uno, Jay Verkuilen, and two anonymous reviewers.

1. Recent efforts to survey the field of data on democratic governance include Foweraker and Krznaric (2000), Knack and Manning (2000), Malik (2002), Munck and Verkuilen (2002), Berg-Schlosser (2003), Besançon (2003), Landman and Häusermann (2003), and Lauth (2003).
2. For a discussion of governance-related conditionalities, see Kapur and Webb (2000), Kapur (2001), Santiso (2001), Crawford (2003).
3. For an expanded discussion of these and other tasks that must be addressed in developing a measuring instrument, see Munck and Verkuilen (2002).
4. Examples include Schumpeter (1942), Marshall (1965), Dahl (1971, 1989), and Sartori (1976, 1987).
5. On the problems with current uses of the terms "democracy," "democratic consolidation," and "democratic quality," see Munck (2001, 123–30).
6. It may not be feasible to develop indicators that are uniquely linked with one concept or one attribute of a concept, a fact that complicates the effort at measurement. But in all instances the process of measurement should begin with clearly differentiated concepts (Bollen 2001, 7283, 7285).
7. O'Donnell (2001, 2004) has emphasized the value of this strategy. For an analysis of the concept of political regime, see Munck (1996). On the emerging consensus regarding the core aspects of a democratic regime, due in large part to the influence of Dahl, see Munck and Verkuilen (2002, 9–12).

8.   On the links between democracy, human development, and human rights, see Sen (1999), Sano (2000), Fukuda-Parr and Kumar (2002), Langlois (2003), and O'Donnell (2004).

9.   On democracy and democratic institutions, see Lijphart (1984, 1999), Inkeles (1991), Shugart and Carey (1992), Beetham (1994), Collier and Levitsky (1997), and Munck and Verkuilen (2002). On human rights, see Nanda, Scarritt, and Shepherd (1981), Jabine and Claude (1992), Cingranelli (1998), Green (2001), and Landman (2004).

10.   Though most of the discussion has focused on the national level, there are also some noteworthy attempts to identify potential indicators at the subnational level. See USAID (2000b), Sisk (2001), Soós (2001), and Treisman (2002).

11.   Munck and Verkuilen (2003) present some thoughts on this issue.

12.   For examples of different aggregation rules, see Munck and Verkuilen (2002, 10, 25–27).

13.   A cause indicator is seen as influencing the concept being measured; an effect indicator is one in which the concept being measured is seen as driving or generating the indicators. Of course, a third possibility is that indicators are both a cause and an effect of the concept being measured.

14.   The European Union (EU) formally stipulated its political conditions for accession in two separate texts: the "political criteria" established by the European Council in Copenhagen in 1993, and Article 49 of the Treaty on European Union of November 1993. These documents refer to the need to guarantee "democracy, the rule of law, human rights and respect for and protection of minorities," but do not offer definitions of these broad concepts, let alone the indicators that would be used to measure these concepts and the level of fulfillment of each indicator. The political conditionality of the EU acquired substance in a series of annual reports published after 1997 evaluating the progress of countries that were candidates for accession to the EU. Yet it was done in a way that denied candidate countries a clear sense of the standards to be met and presented these countries with a moving target. On the African Peer Review Mechanism's list of indicators and the process for evaluating countries it envisions, see NEPAD (2003a, 2003b).

15.   A more complex question concerns the possibility that political actors that are being monitored may themselves take actions to alter the measures of interest. On data and strategic behavior, see Herrera and Kapur (2002).

16.   One problem is that the MCA's rule of aggregation consists of a relative rather than an absolute criterion. Specifically, countries are assessed in terms of the number of indicators on which they rank above the median in relation to a delimited universe of cases (Millennium Challenge Corporation 2004). Thus, during periods when more than half the world has authoritarian regimes—a pattern that has dominated world history until very recently—this rule would lead to the identification of authoritarian countries as targets of aid.

17.   Even though the creators of data sets used by the MCA to identify countries that are to receive development aid have provided estimates of measurement error and emphasized their importance (Kaufmann, Kraay, and Mastruzzi 2003, 23–27), this program does not incorporate estimates of measurement error in its methodology and thus potentially misclassifies countries.

18.   The list is a partial one and includes neither regional data sets nor public opinion surveys such as the regional barometers (see http://www.globalbarometer.org). For a discussion of survey-based data, see Landman and Häusermann (2003). For a useful Web site that offers links to many of the data sets listed below and that is frequently

updated, consult the World Bank Institute's "Governance Data: Web-Interactive Inventory of Datasets and Empirical Tools," at http://www.worldbank.org/wbi/governance/govdatasets/index.html.

References

Apodaca, Clair. 1998. "Measuring Women's Economic and Social Rights Achievements." *Human Rights Quarterly* 20 (1): 139–72.

Beetham, David, ed. 1994. *Defining and Measuring Democracy.* London: Sage.

Beetham, David, Sarah Bracking, Iain Kearton, and Stuart Weir, eds. 2001. *International IDEA Handbook on Democracy Assessment.* The Hague: Kluge Academic Publishers.

Besançon, Marie. 2003. *Good Governance Rankings: The Art of Measurement.* World Peace Foundation Report 36. Cambridge, MA: World Peace Foundation.

Berg-Schlosser, Dirk. 2003. "Indicators of Democratization and Good Governance as Measures of the Quality of Democracy: A Critical Appraisal." Paper presented at international conference on Reassessing Democracy, Bremen, Germany, June 20–22.

Bollen, Kenneth A. 2001. "Indicator: Methodology." In *International Encyclopedia of the Social and Behavioral Sciences,* ed. Neil J. Smelser and Paul B. Baltes, 7282–87. Oxford: Elsevier Science.

Bollen, Kenneth, and Richard Lennox. 1991. "Conventional Wisdom on Measurement: A Structural Equation Perspective." *Psychological Bulletin* 110 (2): 305–14.

Casper, Gretchen, and Claudiu D. Tufis. 2002. "Correlation versus Interchangeability: The Limited Robustness of Empirical Findings on Democracy using Highly Correlated Datasets." *Political Analysis* 11 (2): 196–203.

Cingranelli, David L., ed. 1998. *Human Rights: Theory and Measurement.* New York: St. Martin's Press.

Collier, David, and Robert N. Adcock. 1999. "Democracy and Dichotomies: A Pragmatic Approach to Choices about Concepts." *Annual Review of Political Science* 2: 537–65.

Collier, David, and Steven Levitsky. 1997. "Democracy with Adjectives: Conceptual Innovation in Comparative Research." *World Politics* 49 (3): 430–51.

Crawford, Gordon. 2003. "Promoting Democracy from Without: Learning from Within." Pts. 1 and 2. *Democratization* 10 (1): 77–98; 10 (2): 1–20.

Dahl, Robert A. 1971. *Polyarchy.* New Haven, CT: Yale University Press.

———. 1989. *Democracy and Its Critics.* New Haven, CT: Yale University Press.

ECLAC (Economic Commission for Latin America and the Caribbean). 1999. "Indicadores de Género para el Seguimiento y la Evaluación del Programa de Acción Regional para las Mujeres de América Latina y el Caribe, 1995–2001, y la Plataforma de Acción de Beijing." LC/L.1186. Santiago, Chile.

Foweraker, Joe, and Roman Krznaric. 2000. "Measuring Liberal Democratic Performance: An Empirical and Conceptual Critique." *Political Studies* 48 (4): 759–87.

Fukuda-Parr, Sakiko, and A. K. Shiva Kumar, eds. 2002. *Human Development: Concepts and Measures: Essential Readings.* New York: Oxford University Press.

Green, Maria. 2001. "What We Talk About When We Talk About Indicators: Current Approaches to Human Rights Measurement." *Human Rights Quarterly* 23 (4): 1062–97.

Heath, Anthony, and Jean Martin. 1997. "Why Are There So Few Formal Measuring Instruments in Social and Political Research?" In *Survey Measurement and Process Quality,* ed. Lars E. Lyberg, Paul Biemer, Martin Collins, Edith De Leeuw, Cathryn Dippo, Norbert Schwarz, and Dennis Trewin, 71–86. New York: Wiley.

Heidenheimer, Arnold J., and Michael Johnston, eds. 2002. *Political Corruption: Concepts and Contexts.* New Brunswick, NJ: Transaction.

Herrera, Yoshiko M., and Devesh Kapur. 2002. "Infectious Credulity: Strategic Behavior in the Manufacture and Use of Data." Paper presented at annual meeting of the American Political Science Association, Boston, August 29–September 1.

Inkeles, Alex, ed. 1991. *On Measuring Democracy: Its Consequences and Concomitants.* New Brunswick, NJ: Transaction.

Jabine, Thomas B., and Richard P. Claude, eds. 1992. *Human Rights and Statistics: Getting the Record Straight.* Philadelphia: University of Pennsylvania Press.

Kapur, Devesh. 2001. "Expansive Agendas and Weak Instruments: Governance Related Conditionalities of International Financial Institutions." *Journal of Policy Reform* 4 (3): 207–41.

Kapur, Devesh, and Richard Webb. 2000. "Governance-Related Conditionalities of the International Financial Institutions." G-24 Discussion Paper Series 6, United Nations Conference on Trade and Development, New York.

Kaufmann, Daniel, Aart Kraay, and Massimo Mastruzzi. 2003. "Governance Matters III: Governance Indicators for 1996–2002." Policy Research Working Paper 3106, World Bank, Washington, DC.

Knack, Stephen, and Nick Manning. 2000. "Towards Consensus on Governance Indicators: Selecting Public Management and Broader Governance Indicators." World Bank, Washington, DC.

Landman, Todd. 2004. "Measuring Human Rights: Principle, Practice, and Policy." *Human Rights Quarterly* 26 (4).

Landman, Todd, and Julia Häusermann. 2003. "Map-Making and Analysis of the Main International Initiatives on Developing Indicators on Democracy and Good Governance." Report prepared for the Statistical Office of the Commission of the European Communities (EUROSTAT). Human Rights Centre, University of Essex, Colchester, UK.

Langlois, Anthony J. 2003. "Human Rights Without Democracy? A Critique of the Separationist Thesis." *Human Rights Quarterly* 25 (4): 990–1019.

Lauth, Hans-Joachim. 2003. "Democracy: Limits and Problems of Existing Measurements and Some Annotations upon Further Research." Paper presented at international conference on Reassessing Democracy, Bremen, Germany, June 20–22.

Lijphart, Arend. 1984. *Democracies: Patterns of Majoritarian and Consensus Government in Twenty-one Countries.* New Haven, CT: Yale University Press.

———. 1999. *Patterns of Democracy: Government Forms and Performance in Thirty-six Countries.* New Haven, CT: Yale University Press.

Malik, Adeel. 2002. "State of the Art in Governance Indicators." Human Development Report Office Occasional Paper 2002/07, United Nations Development Programme, New York.

Marshall, T. H. 1965. "Citizenship and Social Class." In *Class, Citizenship, and Social Development,* 71–134. Garden City, NY: Doubleday.

Millennium Challenge Corporation. 2004. *Report on the Criteria and Methodology for Determining the Eligibility of Candidate Countries for Millennium Challenge Account Assistance in FY 2004.* http://www.mca.gov/countries/selection/index.shtml.

Munck, Gerardo L. 1996. "Disaggregating Political Regime: Conceptual Issues in the Study of Democratization." Working Paper 228, Helen Kellogg Institute for International Studies, University of Notre Dame, Notre Dame, IN.

———. 2001. "The Regime Question: Theory Building in Democracy Studies." *World Politics* 54 (1): 119–44.

Munck, Gerardo L., and Jay Verkuilen. 2002. "Conceptualizing and Measuring Democracy: Evaluating Alternative Indexes." *Comparative Political Studies* 35 (1): 5–34.

———. 2003. "Bringing Measurement Back In: Methodological Foundations of the Electoral Democracy Index." Paper presented at annual meeting of the American Political Science Association, Philadelphia, August 28–31.

Nanda, Ved P., James R. Scarritt, and George W. Shepherd Jr., eds. 1981. *Global Human Rights: Public Policies, Comparative Measures, and NGO Strategies.* Boulder, CO: Westview.

Narayan, Deepa, ed. 2002. *Empowerment and Poverty Reduction: A Sourcebook.* Washington, DC: World Bank.

NDI (National Democratic Institute for International Affairs). 1995. *NDI Handbook: How Domestic Organizations Monitor Elections: An A to Z Guide.* Washington, DC: NDI.

NEPAD (New Partnership for Africa's Development). 2003a. *Objectives, Standards, Criteria and Indicators for the African Peer Review Mechanism ("The APRM").* Midrand, South Africa: NEPAD Secretariat.

———. 2003b. *African Peer Review Mechanism: Organisation and Processes.* Midrand, South Africa: NEPAD Secretariat.

O'Donnell, Guillermo. 2001. "Democracy, Law, and Comparative Politics." *Studies in Comparative International Development* 36 (1): 7–36.

———. 2004. "On the Quality of Democracy and Its Links with Human Development and Human Rights." In *The Quality of Democracy: Theory and Practice,* ed. Guillermo O'Donnell, Osvaldo Iazzetta, and Jorge Vargas Cullell. Notre Dame, IN: University of Notre Dame Press.

OECD/DAC (Organisation for Economic Co-operation and Development, Development Assistance Committee). 1998. *DAC Source Book on Concepts and Approaches Linked to Gender Equality.* Paris: OECD.

OSCE/ODIHR (Organisation for Security and Co-operation in Europe, Office for Democratic Institutions and Human Rights). 1997. *The OSCE/ODIHR Election Observation Handbook.* 2nd ed. Warsaw: ODIHR Election Unit.

Rokkan, Stein. 1970. *Citizens, Elections, and Parties: Approaches to the Comparative Study of the Processes of Development.* New York: David McKay.

Sano, Hans-Otto. 2000. "Development and Human Rights: The Necessary, but Partial Integration of Human Rights and Development." *Human Rights Quarterly* 22 (3): 734–52.

Santiso, Carlos. 2001. "International Co-operation for Democracy and Good Governance: Moving Towards a Second Generation?" *European Journal of Development Research* 13 (1): 154–80.

———. 2002. "Education for Democratic Governance: Review of Learning Programmes." Discussion Paper 62, United Nations Educational, Scientific, and Cultural Organization, Paris.

Sartori, Giovanni. 1976. *Parties and Party Systems: A Framework for Analysis.* Cambridge: Cambridge University Press.

———. 1987. *The Theory of Democracy Revisited.* 2 vols. Chatham, NJ: Chatham House.

Schumpeter, Joseph. 1942. *Capitalism, Socialism, and Democracy.* New York: Harper.

Sen, Amartya. 1999. *Development as Freedom.* New York: Knopf.

Shugart, Matthew, and John M. Carey. 1992. *Presidents and Assemblies: Constitutional Design and Electoral Dynamics.* Cambridge: Cambridge University Press.

Sisk, Timothy D., ed. 2001. *Democracy at the Local Level: The International IDEA Handbook on Participation, Representation, Conflict Management and Governance.* Stockholm: International IDEA.

Soós, Gábor. 2001. *The Indicators of Local Democratic Governance Project: Concepts and Hypotheses.* Budapest: Open Society Institute and Local Government and Public Service Reform Initiative.

Treisman, Daniel. 2002. "Defining and Measuring Decentralization: A Global Perspective." Department of Political Science, University of California at Los Angeles. http://www.polisci.ucla.edu/faculty/treisman/.

United Nations. 2000. "International Human Rights Instruments. Twelfth Meeting of Chairpersons of the Human Rights Treaty Bodies, Geneva, 5–8 June 2000." HRI/MC/2000/3. New York.

UNECE (United Nations Economic Commission for Europe). 2001. "Final Report. ECE/UNDP Task Force Meeting on a Regional Gender Web-site." Statistical Division, UNECE, Geneva.

UNDP (United Nations Development Programme). 2002. *Human Development Report 2002: Deepening Democracy in a Fragmented World.* New York: Oxford University Press.

USAID (United States Agency for International Development). 1998. *Handbook of Democracy and Governance Program Indicators.* Technical Publication Series PN-ACC-390. Washington, DC: USAID Office of Democracy and Governance.

———. 1999. *A Handbook on Fighting Corruption.* Technical Publication Series PN-ACE-070. Washington, DC: USAID Office of Democracy and Governance.

———. 2000a. *Conducting a DG Assessment: A Framework for Strategy Development.* Technical Publication Series PN-ACH-305. Washington, DC: USAID Office of Democracy and Governance.

———. 2000b. *Decentralization and Democratic Local Governance Programming Handbook.* Technical Publication Series PN-ACH-300. Washington, DC: USAID Office of Democracy and Governance.

Verkuilen, Jay. 2002. *Methodological Problems in Comparative and Cross-National Analysis: Applications of Fuzzy Set Theory.* PhD diss., University of Illinois, Urbana-Champaign.

Index

Boxes, figures, notes, and tables are indicated by b, f, n, and t.

461